FIVE TO RULE THEM ALL

DAVID L. BOSCO

FIVE TO RULE THEM ALL

THE UN SECURITY COUNCIL
AND THE MAKING OF THE
MODERN WORLD

OXFORD
UNIVERSITY PRESS

2009

OXFORD
UNIVERSITY PRESS

Oxford University Press, Inc., publishes works that further
Oxford University's objective of excellence
in research, scholarship, and education.

Oxford New York
Auckland Cape Town Dar es Salaam Hong Kong Karachi
Kuala Lumpur Madrid Melbourne Mexico City Nairobi
New Delhi Shanghai Taipei Toronto

With offices in
Argentina Austria Brazil Chile Czech Republic France Greece
Guatemala Hungary Italy Japan Poland Portugal Singapore
South Korea Switzerland Thailand Turkey Ukraine Vietnam

Published by Oxford University Press, Inc.
198 Madison Avenue, New York, New York 10016

www.oup.com

Oxford is a registered trademark of Oxford University Press

Library of Congress Cataloging-in-Publication Data
Bosco, David L.
Five to rule them all : the UN Security Council and the making of the
modern world / David L. Bosco.
p. cm.
Includes bibliographical references and index.
ISBN 978-0-19-532876-9
1. United Nations. Security Council–History. I. Title.
JZ5006.7.B67 2009
341.23'23–dc22   2009008670

Photo credits: 1.1 © CORBIS; 1.2 AP Photo; 1.3 AP Photo; 2.1 UN Photo/Marcel Bolomey;
2.2 AP Photo/Tom Fitzsimmons; 2.3 © The New York Collection 1950 Sydney Hoff from
cartoonbank.com. All Rights Reserved; 2.4 UN Photo/MB; 2.5 UN Photo/Marvin Bolotsky;
2.6 AP Photo/John Lindsay; 3.1 UN Photo/BZ; 3.2 AP Photo; 3.4 UN Photo/MH; 4.1 UN
Photo/Teddy Chen; 4.2 AP Photo; 4.3 UN Photo/Milton Grant; 5.1 UN Photo/Milton
Grant; 5.2 AP Photo/Marcy Nighswandar; 5.3 AP Photo/J. Scott Applewhite; 6.1 UN
Photo/Milton Grant; 6.2, UN Photo/C Dufka; 6.4 AP Photo/Ng Han Guan; 6.5 UN Photo/
Evan Schneider; 7.1 UN Photo/Mark Garten; 7.2 © Eric Draper/White House/Handout/
CNP/Corbis; 7.3 UN Photo/Eskinder Debebe; 7.4 UN Photo/Eskinder Debebe

1 3 5 7 9 8 6 4 2

Printed in the United States of America
on acid-free paper

FOR MY PARENTS, JOSEPH AND CAROL

CONTENTS

ACKNOWLEDGMENTS

M OISÉS NAÍM, editor of *Foreign Policy*, encouraged and guided me when this project was in the formative stages. Dean Louis Goodman, Maria Green Cowles, and Tamar Gutner at the American University School of International Service generously offered me, first, a place to write and then the opportunity to teach that institution's remarkable students. My agent, Raphael Sagalyn, worked with me patiently as I turned a vague idea into a proposal. Susan Ferber at Oxford University Press believed in the project at the outset and expertly guided me at every stage.

I benefited from the patience and insight of several people at the United Nations. Norma Chan, an institution in her own right, shared her expertise and experience and arranged a trip with the Security Council to Africa. Yves Sorokobi was generous and graceful in accommodating myriad requests during that trip. Liam Murphy at the UN Information Center in Washington was unfailingly efficient in responding to a blizzard of requests to visit the archives and for assistance in locating documents.

My research assistant at the School of International Service, Margaret Olsen, tracked down council debates, unraveled obscure points, and provided thoughtful comments throughout the drafting process. Svetlana Savranskaya at George Washington University and Alexandra Kapitanskaya, a master's candidate at the School of International Service, assisted me with several Russian sources. Sam Daws helped to arrange a productive research trip to London and reviewed an early manuscript. Ed Luck at Columbia University encouraged me and directed me to several interesting sources as I began my research. Katharine Thomson at Churchill College, Cambridge, arranged access to the diaries of several British diplomats and helped me review oral history interviews with many more. Thomas

Weiss at the City University of New York offered guidance at the early stages and introduced me to the remarkable UN oral history collection he has developed. I am grateful to David Brady and Mandy MaCalla at the Hoover Institution for a very productive week on Stanford University's campus. Mike Boyer at Humanity United arranged a seminar on the book with several of his colleagues, whose questions and insights led me in new directions.

A diverse and talented group read all or part of the manuscript and offered commentary: the entire Bosco family, Ben Auspitz, Emma Chanlett-Avery, Conor Dugan, James Forsyth, Bryan Garsten, John Norris, Peter Ogden, Thomas Pickering, Eric Rosand, Dustin Sharp, Melanie Sisson, Adam Vandervoort, and Brandon Wallace. I am also grateful to two anonymous reviewers for insightful comments and suggestions. The Garstens, the Vandervoorts, and Mary Graham generously provided shelter at various points when I was in New York.

My wife, Shana Wallace, saw this project from beginning to end, read several versions of every chapter, corrected footnotes, selected photos, and provided affirmation and criticism in just the right doses. As in everything else, she was my partner in this project.

INTRODUCTION

IN JUNE 2008, a convoy of jeeps and pick-up trucks arrived at the airport in
Goma. The lakeside town in eastern Congo has been the epicenter of regional
conflict since the Rwandan genocide in 1994, when nearly a million Rwandans
sought shelter there from ethnic violence. As the world struggled to react to the
mass exodus, more than 50,000 died from cholera and other diseases. Since then,
Goma has been plagued by persistent violence between competing militia
groups, which Congo's weak central government has been unable to control.
Bands of armed men roam the countryside, occasionally attacking refugee camps
and harassing travelers.

Flanked by soldiers in blue helmets, a group of mainly middle-aged men
hailing from a dozen countries disembarked from the convoy and disappeared
inside the airport terminal. The tired and sweaty contingent represented the
United Nations' Security Council, the world's most elite and powerful diplomatic body. The diplomats had spent the day touring a refugee camp on the
outskirts of town. Sometimes stumbling over the rocky ground, they peered into
makeshift huts covered with plastic sheeting, toured medical facilities, and listened attentively to singing children. The atmosphere was almost festive as the
guardians of international peace and security checked on some of the world's
most vulnerable people. Several diplomats appeared to be moved. France's ambassador grabbed a bullhorn and promised a crowd of refugees that the Security
Council would get them home.

The delegation had arrived in Africa a week earlier to see for itself the complex crises in Sudan, Chad, and the Democratic Republic of Congo. Accustomed
to working together in the blue-and-gold chamber where the council makes its
formal decisions, the diplomats had become traveling companions. They spent

long hours together on a UN plane jetting between conflict zones. They shared meals, swapped jokes, and snapped photos of each other. The French, Belgian, and Russian diplomats stole frequent cigarette breaks. The Chinese and American ambassadors often walked side by side through the refugee camps.

Behind the collegial atmosphere, however, were significant differences in opinion about policy, particularly the question of how to handle Sudan. The council's permanent Western members—Britain, France, and the United States—were eager to pressure Sudan's government to accept more international peacekeepers and to hand over war crimes suspects to an international court. Russia and China were much more hesitant. They had lucrative energy and weapons deals with Khartoum and believed that the West was too eager to interfere in the internal affairs of a sovereign state. In council deliberations, they had delayed sanctions resolutions and softened language critical of Sudan's government.

On the third day of the trip, the council flew to the tormented Sudanese region of Darfur. Hundreds of refugees lined up to see the envoys, who arrived surrounded by guards toting automatic weapons. The sweltering ambassadors sat in a hut as camp residents told them about the crimes of the notorious *janjaweed* militias and rampant insecurity. "If we die today," one man lectured them, "you will be responsible." That night, in Khartoum, the Security Council met the man most observers blame for the suffering in Darfur: Sudan's president, Omar al-Bashir. The fifteen diplomats listened politely as Bashir denounced what he described as an international campaign to vilify his government. Pressed by several council members on the issue of war crimes, the Sudanese president insisted that he would never turn over his citizens to an international court.

Back in Goma, the delegation began preparing for its return to UN headquarters. Only a day of meetings in relatively calm western Africa stood between the council and the flight back to New York. The ambassadors, their aides, and the UN security personnel boarded the delegation's small jet. Suddenly, a shot rang out. The peacekeepers on the tarmac scurried. After a few confused moments, the pilot announced that a shot had been fired at the plane and the flight was canceled.

Then, word filtered through the cabin that the shooting had been an accident. A UN guard stowing his weapon for the flight had accidentally fired it, puncturing the plane's floor. The delegation wearily disembarked and assembled again in the airport's lounge while UN administrators rushed to find alternate transportation for their high-level charges. An hour passed, and then another. Night fell on Goma, and a few diplomats dozed. Seemingly from nowhere, the Russian envoy produced a bottle of vodka. He portioned out its contents to several colleagues, and the group stood outside, sipping from paper cups. The council members often do not share world views, but on this occasion, they could at least share a drink.

The Security Council is like no other body in history. Its five permanent members—China, France, Russia, the United Kingdom, and the United States—account for nearly 30 percent of the world's population and more than 40 percent of global economic output. In military affairs, their dominance is even more overwhelming. They control more than 26,000 nuclear warheads, 99 percent of all those in existence. They have a combined 5.5 million men and women in arms. When the Council is united, its members can wage war, impose blockades, unseat governments, and levy sanctions, all in the name of the international community. There are almost no limits to the body's authority.

The council usually meets in the UN headquarters complex on New York's East River, but it has greater power and authority than the rest of the sprawling organization. The council is a creature of great-power politics, not international bureaucracy. It is built on the assumption that five of the strongest nations have the right and duty to safeguard the globe. Most of the UN structure insists that member states are equal; the council, by contrast, grants the most powerful countries special rights and responsibilities.

The idea that the great powers should chaperone the world is not new. Coalitions of powerful nations—including the Congress of Vienna and the Holy Alliance in the eighteenth and nineteenth centuries—have tried before. The Geneva-based League of Nations, inaugurated in 1920, was the world's answer to the horror of the First World War. It constituted the first fully developed world political organization, and it had a council of major powers charged with preserving the peace. The league and its council died prematurely when they failed to prevent an even more devastating war, but the idea of a world organization endured.

During its almost seven decades of operation, the UN Security Council has launched a broad range of diplomatic, legal, and even military initiatives to provide order. Since the late-1980s, its activities have increased dramatically. The council has blessed armed interventions in places like Bosnia, Somalia, Haiti, and Kuwait. It has imposed sanctions on the regimes in Serbia, Libya, and Sudan; launched war crimes courts to try sitting heads of state; and targeted terrorist finances. During the Cold War, the United States usually felt comfortable exercising its military power without the council's permission. No longer. Even the George W. Bush administration—with its deep skepticism of the United Nations—worked to get the council's approval for its policies. For many, the 2003 U.S.-led invasion of Iraq demonstrated the perils of operating without the council's blessing, and the body has emerged from that imbroglio active and relevant. In 2007, the council authorized peacekeeping missions that involved more than 100,000 troops from dozens of nations. From nuclear proliferation to the global war against terrorism to genocide in Africa, the council is often the cockpit of global politics.

Yet even the council's vigorous post–Cold War activity has fallen well short of effective global governance. Atrocities and crimes against humanity still plague many parts of the globe. Entire countries have collapsed, and in so doing they have exported refugees, drugs, and radicalism. Since the 1980s, Pakistan, India, and North Korea have tested nuclear weapons while the council watched. These shortcomings have led to frequent and angry charges that it is feckless, impotent, and unprincipled. More than a few commentators have charged that the United Nations and its council are an impediment rather than an aid to world order.

The council's new activism has stirred hopes that it will assure world order, stop atrocities, and counter global threats like terrorism and weapons proliferation. Yet it exists in a world of realpolitik. Its members are, above all, powerful states with their own diverging interests. Time and again, the council's performance has dashed hopes that its members would somehow rise above their narrow interests and work together to establish a more peaceful and just world.

This book surveys sixty years of international crises and conflicts from the vantage point of the body created to manage them. It focuses closely on the five permanent members, who by virtue of their constant presence and veto power have often shaped the council's agenda. It traces the political currents that have determined the council's activities and the rhetoric that has provided its most dramatic moments. It explains the varied and evolving roles the institution has played. Whenever possible, it opens the closed door behind which the council often operates. And it introduces many of the remarkable personalities who have labored—and sometimes clashed—in the council chamber.

In describing the council's life and work, this book defends the Security Council's utility. Doing so requires understanding our expectations for the body, and that is not a simple task. From the council's beginning, there have been two distinct, and sometimes competing, visions of its proper role. The UN Charter gives the council the responsibility to "maintain international peace and security." This vague phrase is the key. To maintain peace and security, the council is expected to actively suppress the insecurity that besets much of the globe by resisting aggression, defusing local conflicts, stabilizing unstable states, preventing the proliferation of dangerous weapons, punishing war criminals, and enforcing international sanctions. In a rudimentary sense, the council is expected to *govern*.

Alongside this expansive vision, there has always been a more spare conception of the council's purpose: to help prevent conflict between the great powers. This vision is less often discussed; its modest reach does not suit speeches or declarations. The closest historical analogy is the Concert of Europe, the loose system of great-power relations that managed to preserve relative peace on the troubled continent for almost fifty years after the Napoleonic wars. This *concert* vision focuses less on how the Security Council interacts with the rest of the world and more on its role as a mechanism for producing consensus among the major powers.[1]

A concert perspective generates a distinct set of tests for the body's effectiveness. Instead of asking whether the council has stamped out regional conflicts, alleviated suffering, and prevented arms proliferation, one asks whether it has helped great-power relations. Has it allowed the most powerful states to compromise on contentious issues? Has it offered them face-saving ways out of crises? Has it expanded and deepened the networks of diplomatic contacts that link the leading powers? From this point of view, if the council can help to keep the great powers from each other's throats, then it has served a fundamental purpose. The security and well-being of the rest of the world are desirable, but not essential.[2]

It is possible to argue that these two concepts—governance and concert—are inextricably linked, that peace among the great powers cannot be preserved when parts of the world are in flames. The doctrine of collective security, which has influenced generations of diplomats, insists that international security is indivisible: a breach of the peace anywhere threatens the peace everywhere. After all, it was a clash in the Balkans that produced the First World War and the invasion of Poland that sparked the Second.

However compelling this may be as a moral principle, the last sixty years offer the doctrine little support. Small and large regional conflicts have started and ended without drawing the major powers into direct conflict with each other. For better or worse, the great powers are isolated from bloodshed and suffering in many parts of the world. It makes sense, then, to distinguish between the council's concert and governance functions.

When the council's effectiveness is assessed, however, it is the more ambitious governance vision that sets the bar, and the results are usually unsatisfactory. The council's members often do not agree on how conflicts should be resolved and crises should be managed. As the ongoing violence in Darfur has demonstrated, the end of the Cold War did not eliminate sharp ideological differences over sovereignty, values, and the proper limits of international action. Even when the council's members do agree, they are often incapable of charting a consistent course toward their goal. The council has shown itself to be erratic and sometimes simply incompetent at managing and overseeing peacekeeping operations, sanctions regimes, war crimes trials, and the sundry other activities it has authorized. Just a few months after the Security Council delegation visited refugees in eastern Congo, that region experienced another bout of violence that the council and the peacekeeping force it had authorized were unable to quell. New refugees crowded into the camp the ambassadors had toured.

Too often, the conversation about the council ends with a rueful acknowledgment of its limitations. For all of its shortcomings, however, the council has been a qualified success as a loose concert of the most powerful states. It has created a space and process through which the world's great powers struggle to contain conflicts and achieve compromise. This is no small feat, particularly when placed in the context of the twentieth century's bloody great-power wars. Centrifuges in Iran, massacres in the Balkans, and chaos in Iraq are security problems and human tragedies; conflicts among the world's great powers in the nuclear age would be cataclysms.

In the council's more than sixty years of existence, there has never been a sustained military clash between permanent council members. In the 1950s, China and the United States collided in Korea, but Communist China was excluded from the council at the time. Soviet and Chinese forces tangled briefly in the late 1960s, a few years before mainland China finally won a place in the council chamber. The Soviet Union and the United States reached the precipice of conflict on several occasions but always managed to pull back in time. It would be too ambitious to claim that the stretch of great-power peace the world has enjoyed is a direct product of Security Council consultation, but there are strong reasons to believe that the council has contributed to it.

The habits of consultation and negotiation that the council has cultivated influence, often in subtle ways, the course of crises. These habits can prevent miscalculation, and they can permit powerful states to save face. A quiet conversation in the council's anteroom helped to ease the dangerous Berlin blockade in the early days of the Cold War. When the Middle East descended into war in 1967 and 1973, the council served as a ready vehicle for negotiating ceasefires, dispatching peacekeepers, and avoiding superpower entanglement. In the late 1980s, the combined pressure of the council members ended the long struggle between Iran and Iraq, a conflict that was spilling over into the Persian Gulf and threatening international commerce. Even when the council "fails," it may serve a useful purpose. During the Cuban missile crisis, the Soviet veto prevented formal council action, but the dramatic debate may have helped to slow the pace of the crisis and to shape world public opinion.

At times, the council generates among its members, and particularly among the permanent members, the sense of identity and belonging that exclusive clubs usually offer. Over the course of the council's history, this identity has manifested itself most powerfully when outsiders have attempted to gain entry. At the San Francisco conference in 1945, the great powers worked together to fend off attempts by the smaller states to weaken the council's prerogatives. During the Cold War, they shared a strong reluctance to admit new members. And, as the Cold War ended, the council's permanent members agreed to protect the diplomatic prerogatives of the Soviet Union even as it rapidly shed power and territory. Russia might have lost its status as a superpower, but it was still a member of the club.

The council has also helped to train generations of leading diplomats from the major powers in the art of multilateral diplomacy. Countries send their diplomatic stars to represent them on the council, and those diplomats often go on to serve as foreign ministers, secretaries of state, national security advisors, and even presidents and prime ministers. Many observers have attributed George H. W. Bush's coalition-building prowess during the first Gulf War to his time as UN ambassador. In the mid-1990s, the U.S. ambassador to the United Nations, Madeleine Albright, and her Russian counterpart, Sergei Lavrov, spent countless hours debating policy positions in the cramped conference room that the council uses for private meetings. A few months later, Albright became the American secretary of state, and a decade after that, Lavrov was named Russian foreign minister. They carried with them their experiences on the council.

These modest but critical contributions will not satisfy those who insist that the council must do more, that it must somehow solve the problems of an ungoverned world. It has not done that, but the council has shown remarkable durability and even some capacity for change. It has evolved in important ways since its creation, expanding to give greater voice to states emerging from colonial rule and fashioning new tools to exercise its authority. It has experienced periods of intense activism, fallow times, and new bouts of energy. In certain moments, it has all but disappeared from public view, only to reappear later as the currents of world politics shifted. It does not offer simple answers to crises and conflicts, but it is a valuable tool for the world's powers as they pick their way through the clutter of daily events.

As it describes key moments in the council's history, this book will trace several persistent tensions that the institution has encountered. The first and most obvious dilemma is, which states should have council seats? The United Nations' principal architects believed that only a small council could be effective. A larger and more representative body would be incapable of reacting speedily and decisively to security crises. This judgment has been questioned ever since. What good is an effective council that does not fairly represent the world? The overall size and composition of the council are perpetual topics for discussion. Should the fifteen-member council take on new members? And, if so, how many of them should have permanent seats?

The tension between representativeness and effectiveness has manifested itself in other, less obvious ways. For years, the United Nations' members debated which Chinese government (Beijing or Taipei) should represent that country in the organization. Supporters of Communist China's claim argued that a United Nations and a Security Council without mainland China would exclude a quarter of humanity from any representation in the organization. Taiwan's advocates responded that the Communist regime was irresponsible and illegitimate and might cripple the body. A similar dispute developed over whether and how Palestine should have a voice in the council chamber. The United States and Israel maintained for many years that the Palestine Liberation Organization had no place at the council table while its supporters insisted that debates on the conflict would be meaningless without the PLO's participation.

A second, though less discussed, tension centers on how the council operates rather than who are its members. International organizations have usually been infused with a belief—almost a faith—that open diplomacy is an unalloyed good. In the 1920s, the conventional wisdom in Europe held that secret treaties and hidden diplomacy had plunged the continent into the First World War, and the League of Nations was designed in part to expose diplomacy to the light of day. The Second World War's lessons were more complex, but the insistence on open diplomacy still animated many early supporters of the United Nations. The public, the argument went, should be able to see and hear the leading powers debating issues of war and peace. It is an expectation that fits well with the governance view of the council. A legitimate governing body should not hide its deliberations. There has always been a crosscurrent of thought, however, which recognizes that quiet and confidential deliberations between powerful states are indispensable. The council has struggled with this dual understanding, and it has oscillated between a preference for loud, open deliberation and closed-door conversations. This debate has played out not only in foreign ministries and on blue-ribbon panels but also in the design and use of the physical space that the council inhabits.

Finally, there is an almost philosophical debate about whether the Security Council should be viewed primarily as a political body or a legal instrument. In many respects, it is both. Many of its resolutions are legally binding, and since the end of the Cold War, it has deployed the instruments of international law— courts, tribunals, and commissions of inquiry—in new and innovative ways. And yet the council does not make its decisions remotely like a court does. Its key choices are political compromises between different constituencies, not attempts at impartial judgment. The council's dual nature often confuses discussions about its effectiveness and potential.

It would be comforting to believe that the Security Council is simply evolving into its post–Cold War political flexibility and that, after enduring the inevitable growing pains, it will shift from the modest concert role it has often played to the broader governance function so many hope it will embrace. It may eventually do so, or it may never reach that point. In either case, the council will likely fail as often as it succeeds. As it does, there is a danger that its often hidden value as a conduit and a buffer between the great powers will be overlooked. The United Nations' greatest secretary-general, Dag Hammarskjöld, once said that the organization was designed "not to bring humanity to heaven, but to save it from hell."[3] Since 1946, the council has helped the world to avoid the lowest level of hell: conflict between nuclear-armed great powers. As the international community debates the role that the council should play in the future, it would do well not to forget the service it has offered in the past.

CHAPTER I

THE COUNCIL CREATED

IN JUNE 1940, the radios were almost always on in Geneva's grand Palais des Nations, the imposing headquarters of the League of Nations, situated on the banks of Lake Geneva. A month earlier, Nazi Germany had invaded France. German tank units drove around and then through the vaunted Maginot line. Stunned French forces were in full retreat, but for a few weeks hope persisted that the great power would resist the Nazi onslaught. Then, just past noon on the afternoon of June 17, the voice of France's Philippe Pétain crackled over the airwaves. "It is with a heavy heart that I tell you today that we must stop fighting."[1] France, he said, would seek an armistice with the Nazis. Marshal Pétain, a hero of the First World War, became the head of a rump French state based in the resort town of Vichy. Europe's fate appeared to be sealed; brute force had won out, and the dictators ruled the continent.

On bookshelves in the palace were carefully preserved copies of the speeches celebrating the league's birth in 1920. Statesmen then had insisted that a new era of international relations was dawning and that the ten million lives consumed in the First World War were not lost in vain. "They sacrificed themselves for their countries, but they laid down their lives for humanity also," said Swiss president Giuseppe Motta at the league's opening. "They had before them a vision of a great human family from which force should be banished, and where justice should reign by sovereign right."[2] Statesman after statesman pledged that they would never allow such a disaster to happen again.

The league's architects were not dreamers. They knew that the organization could not function if its ideals were not tethered to power. So they placed at the center of the organization an executive council with permanent seats for the most powerful states of the time—Britain, France, Italy, and Japan. In 1926, Germany emerged from diplomatic exile and joined the ranks of these permanent members. The Soviet Union initially scoffed at the league as a clubhouse for capitalists, but it finally joined in 1934. Only the United States, so instrumental in creating the league, never took the seat offered to it.

The league had a quorum of the great powers, but their participation, it soon became clear, did not imply commitment. Discussion and compromise—not confrontation—were the organization's preferred methods. Many of the league's architects pinned their hopes on the power of public condemnation to restrain wayward or aggressive states. "[T]he most powerful weapon at the command of the League of Nations is not the economic or the military weapon or any other weapon of material force," a British diplomat said in 1923. "The strongest weapon we have is the weapon of public opinion."[3] The covenant that created the league emphasized lengthy arbitration proceedings and judicial rulings to resolve disputes. Its provisions for enforcement were vague.

In a gentler political climate, the league might well have endured. During the relatively calm 1920s, the league helped to resolve several disputes, including the status of the Saarland, a mainly German region seized by the Allies after the war. But arbitration and open debate were no match for the insistent revisionism of Germany, Italy, and Japan. In 1931, Japan's seizure of Manchuria rudely exposed the league's shortcomings. As the Japanese tightened their grip on the region, the league dispatched a commission of inquiry that painstakingly reviewed the facts of the case and drafted a report. When the league finally did condemn the annexation, Japan simply withdrew from the organization. Germany followed suit a few months later, convinced that the league posed no obstacle to its ambitions. Italy staged its own confrontation with the league in October 1935 when it invaded Ethiopia. Haile Selassie, Ethiopia's emperor, pleaded for assistance. This new challenge occasioned passionate rhetoric, but no sustained action. The council imposed a trade embargo, but it did not have the will to sustain it for long. The league, wrote British prime minister Neville Chamberlain, "is beaten."[4]

Rather, it defeated itself. Addressing the House of Commons as it debated the situation in Manchuria in February 1933, British foreign secretary John Simon explained succinctly why the league was powerless. "I think I am myself enough of a pacifist to take the view that, however we handle this matter, I do not intend my own country to get in trouble about it." Britain's policy would be to avoid confrontation at almost all costs. "There is one great difference between 1914 and now and it is this: in no circumstances will this Government authorise this country to be party to this struggle."[5] It was a policy that the British and French followed assiduously all the way to humiliation at Munich.

In the weeks after the French capitulation to the Nazis, the league briefly descended from political failure into disgrace. Its secretary-general, the French diplomat Joseph Avenol, described Hitler and Mussolini as "great men" and curried favor with Europe's new masters by firing most of the league's remaining British staff. Only Vichy France's reluctance to have a Frenchman remain as secretary-general saved the league's last shreds of honor. In July 1940, Avenol's deputy, an Irish politician named Sean Lester, became the league's last secretary-general. As violence engulfed Europe, Lester took charge of the demoralized and diminished staff, which had abandoned most of the palace's offices and worked from the library. The Swiss government, fearful of offending the Nazis, barely tolerated the league's continued presence. On one occasion, municipal authorities threatened to cut off heating oil from the palace. Mail arrived late or not at all. Most member countries stopped paying their dues. Still, Lester and his staff persevered. They cataloged records, drafted reports, and responded to correspondence. Meaningful wartime diplomacy was impossible, but as the great powers fought all around them, the small band of officials sheltered the embers of international organization.[6]

By August 1944, the once unprepared Allied powers had become military juggernauts. The Soviet Union fielded an army of almost 12 million men. In 1944 alone, its factories produced 29,000 tanks.[7] The United States, which entered the fight late, at last turned its mammoth industrial power to the war effort. Bombers rolled off assembly lines in Detroit, Tulsa, and San Diego at a breakneck clip. In 1945, the United States manufactured nearly 50,000 aircraft.[8] Even Britain managed to construct a formidable military, including an air force that was raining tons of ordnance on German cities.

The powerful alliance was inexorably grinding away at the German military. On June 6, 1944, the D-Day invasion finally opened the second front in Europe. Men and matériel flooded into France, and Allied forces advanced inland. Even more important was Soviet progress in Eastern and Central Europe. Across a broad front, Soviet divisions advanced steadily westward. In May, the Germans abandoned the resource-rich Crimea region. In mid-August, the Soviets wrenched Romania from German control, and all of Poland was in the Red Army's sights.

The Allied leaders were not in as robust condition as their war machines. Of the Big Three, only Soviet premier Josef Stalin could plausibly claim to be more vigorous in the summer of 1944 than when the war had begun. The dictator had been in shock and confined to his quarters in June 1941 as German armies swept into his country, smashing the pact between the Soviets and the Nazis. Stalin waited two weeks to speak to the Soviet people, and when he finally did manage a radio address, his words were flat and his breathing labored.[9] Four years later, Stalin emerged from the crucible of Stalingrad as a confident wartime leader who was bearing the bulk of the Allied war effort. Franklin Roosevelt and Winston Churchill were on different trajectories. Roosevelt's Day of Infamy speech after the attack on Pearl Harbor galvanized the nation, but during the course of the war his health declined precipitously. Churchill had been beset by pneumonia and was prone to increasingly frequent mood swings. The Churchill whose defiance had braced his country as it faced the threat of invasion in 1940 now indulged in spasms of melancholy and frustrated his aides with windy and often irrelevant speeches.

Still, by dint of their conquering armies, the three tired but tested leaders had won a chance to reshape the world's security architecture. Since the disaster of the First World War, the once fanciful idea that the world needed a formal security structure had become widely accepted. This second awful war, just two decades after the first, reinforced the belief in most quarters that effective international organization was a matter of survival. The American politician Wendell Willkie, who ran against Roosevelt in 1940 on a platform of nonintervention, was by 1943 a committed internationalist. After a world tour in 1942, he wrote, "[U]nless Britons and Canadians and Russians and Chinese and Americans and all our fighting allies, in the common co-operation of war, find the instrumentalities and the methods of cooperative effort after the war, we, the people, have failed our time and our generation."[10] Isolationists and skeptics of international organization still existed, but the war had put them on the defensive.

The seeds of a new organization had been sown early in the war. In the summer of 1941, Churchill and Roosevelt drafted the Atlantic Charter, a wartime statement of purpose which included a pledge to create a "wider and permanent system of general security." The term "United Nations" appeared first in December 1941 as the title for the broad-based alliance against the Axis powers. Britain, Russia, China, and the United States signed the Declaration by United Nations on January 1, 1942, and twenty-two smaller countries followed suit the next day.[11] This first iteration of the United Nations was a wartime military alliance, not a plan for a postwar organization. For much of the war, the Allied leaders were too consumed with military matters to spend more than fleeting moments planning for the postwar world. During the Moscow meeting in October 1943, the Allied powers vaguely committed to establishing "a general international organization, based on the principle of the sovereign equality of all peace-loving states." At the level of official policy, that was as far as the allies were willing to go. Behind the scenes, however, plans were afoot.

Three Visions

Roosevelt had probably devoted more concentrated thought to a new world organization than had either Churchill or Stalin. America's distance from the concrete issues of territory and political control in Europe gave it the luxury to concentrate on what it deemed the higher questions of international law and morality. America's failure to join the League of Nations and its broader embrace of isolationism weighed heavily on Roosevelt. He was convinced that America's withdrawal from the world had permitted the calamitous rise of Nazi Germany and imperial Japan, and he was determined that American power would be deployed to stop renewed aggression. Still, it was clear to Roosevelt—and to almost everyone else—that a new postwar organization could not simply be a revived League of Nations. It had to have the means to resist and repel aggression.

With Roosevelt's blessing, the State Department began sketching plans for a new organization even before the United States formally entered the war. Sumner Welles, the brilliant and energetic deputy secretary of state, pushed Roosevelt to quickly announce plans for a new world structure that would be organized by region and that might begin operating even before the war ended. But Welles was moving too far, too fast for his immediate boss. Cordell Hull, the aging but still potent secretary of state, engineered Welles's dismissal in 1943.[12]

Hull's protégé, Leo Pasvolsky, a Russian-born academic, became the leading thinker on postwar organization in the State Department. The plans he drew up bore a remarkable likeness to the League of Nations, though with attempts to modify several of its notable defects. Hull and Pasvolsky argued strongly against a regional approach to postwar security; the new organization should be global in scope and should discourage regional alliances, which they thought smacked of cynical and discredited balance-of-power politics.[13] In a 1943 address to Congress, Hull promised extravagantly that once a new organization was created, "there will no longer be need for spheres of influence, for alliances, for balance of power, or any other of the special arrangements through which, in the unhappy past, the nations strove to safeguard their security or to promote their interests."[14]

The president himself had flirted with the idea of regional committees to keep the peace, but he soon adopted the State Department's approach of a centralized structure with global responsibility. Most important, from Roosevelt's perspective, was the dominance of the great powers. In 1942, the president had proposed that the great powers act as "policemen" to manage world affairs, cracking down on violence and aggression wherever they emerged. In his speech to the nation on Christmas Eve 1943, Roosevelt explained his vision. "Britain, Russia,

China and the United States and their allies represent more than three-quarters of the total population of the earth. As long as these four nations with great military power stick together in determination to keep the peace there will be no possibility of an aggressor nation arising to start another war."[15]

Roosevelt's ambitions sometimes turned grandiose. Over dinner at the White House in March 1943, he suggested to British foreign minister Anthony Eden that the great powers disarm all other countries and place garrisons across the globe to maintain order.[16] The small powers, the president said, "should have nothing more dangerous than rifles."[17] The real decisions "should be made by the United States, Great Britain, Russia, and China, who would be the powers for many years to come that would have to police the world."[18] An assembly of all states could meet once a year, he told the British, so that the smaller powers could "blow off steam."[19] In these moments, Roosevelt was envisioning nothing less than great-power dominion over the world. Together, the powers would actively root out the kindling, including arms stocks and territorial disputes, that might feed a new conflagration. The doctrine of collective security—the view that peace is indivisible and that all states must unite against states that breach the peace—was central to Roosevelt's thinking. His assumption that local conflicts would inevitably spread led naturally to the conclusion that the firefighters must be vigilant and assertive.

At other moments, Roosevelt displayed a more egalitarian streak and imagined an organization that could promote economic development and human rights. The president's Four Freedoms speech in January 1940 suggested a world view that incorporated social and economic justice. That theme of broad global responsibility appeared repeatedly in Roosevelt's final years. "We have learned to be citizens of the world, members of the human community," the president said in his last inaugural speech. "We have learned the simple truth, as Emerson said, that 'the only way to have a friend is to be one.'"[20] The president knew that the great powers would have to form the core of any postwar organization, but he worried that the smaller countries would resent them and he wanted to offer them more than just the rule of the strong. In fanciful moments, he thought that a Council of Great Powers could meet on an island—perhaps Hawaii or the Azores—to help assure the world of its impartiality.[21]

A politician to his core, Roosevelt sought to please as many constituencies as he could, not least his domestic political opposition. As plans for a postwar organization began to circulate, the president included Republican senators and party leaders in deliberations and ensured that his administration responded quickly to their concerns. When the Republican presidential nominee in 1944, New York governor Thomas Dewey, expressed misgivings about the direction of U.S. planning, Cordell Hull extended an invitation to meet and included one of Dewey's foreign policy aides, John Foster Dulles, in subsequent planning. The specter of an isolationist backlash haunted the president, and at several points he assured his political opponents that he did not envision a "superstate" or a global police force.[22]

For his part, Winston Churchill was less concerned about domestic political opposition than he was with Britain's newly precarious place in the world. As Soviet and American military and industrial strength grew during the war, the prime minister had become increasingly aware that Britain's influence in the postwar world would be limited. At the Tehran meeting in 1943, Britain's diminished stature became obvious to the prime minister. "There I sat with the great Russian bear on one side of me, with paws outstretched," he wrote, "and on the other side the great American buffalo, and between the two sat the poor little English donkey, who was the only one . . . who knew the right way home."[23]

In this new and unnerving world of continental superpowers, Churchill wanted to find a structure that would preserve British security—and the vast but fragile British empire. "I did not become the King's first minister," Churchill declared, "to preside over the liquidation of the British Empire." His zeal for protecting Britain's imperial holdings led to tension with Roosevelt, who sometimes lectured the prime minister on the coming end of empire. "Winston," the president said during one meeting, "you have four hundred years of acquisitive instinct in your blood and you just don't understand how a country might not want to acquire land somewhere if they can get it. A new period has opened in the world's history and you will have to adjust yourself to it."[24]

Perhaps because of his determination to preserve the empire and maximize British influence, Churchill alighted on the idea of regional councils as the basis for postwar security. He envisioned a European council, an Asian council, and one for the Americas—a "three-legged stool," he termed it.[25] Overseeing them all would be a council of the great powers, but its mandate would be limited to the most egregious breaches of the peace. That central council, Churchill wrote, "is not to rule the nations. It is only to prevent them tearing each other in pieces."[26] Here, concisely put, was a minimalist vision of a great power council. Most matters would be handled through regional organizations and conferences, and the central great power council would content itself with managing the most serious disputes between its members. This council had little in common with the roving, assertive body that Roosevelt imagined.

Churchill's emphasis on devolving authority to regional structures found little support in his own Foreign Office. The experts there, including permanent undersecretary Alexander Cadogan, career diplomat Gladwyn Jebb, and noted historian Charles K. Webster, leaned toward the American approach of a strong, centralized organization. Churchill's notion was, said Jebb later, a "slightly dotty" construct. "He hadn't thought it out. He was concentrating on winning the war and these were just the vague ideas of a chap with no particular meaning."[27] It took months of Foreign Office effort to convince the harried prime minister that a centralized organization made more sense.

At times, Churchill became almost petulant when he was asked to concentrate on the details. At a cabinet meeting in the summer of 1944, Cadogan tried to get the prime minister to review the Foreign Office's rough plans for a new organization. After a few minutes of listless debate, Churchill had had enough. "There now," he said, "in 25 [minutes] we have settled the future of the World. Who can say that we aren't efficient?"[28] Churchill's lack of attention and the Foreign Office's stretched resources combined to prevent the British from generating drafts as comprehensive as those the U.S. State Department was producing.

Still, there was strong support in Britain for international organization in some form. During its brief existence, the League of Nations had developed a cadre of influential backers in Britain who valued the attempt to create a legal and political structure to manage world security. Churchill wasn't alone in recognizing that Britain would not be strong enough after the war to provide security by itself. The continued involvement of the United States in European affairs was essential, and Britain was willing to compromise on many things to ensure it. Churchill worried about the anticolonialist instinct of the Americans, but it is not clear that his British constituents shared that concern. Exhausted Britons seemed to care little about preserving far-flung holdings.[29]

As Britain reconciled itself to the disappearance of empire, Soviet leaders were busy acquiring one. The fruits of victory, in the form of territory under the Red Army's control, were multiplying. As they did, Stalin's opinion of what the Soviet Union needed in the postwar world began to change. The postwar organization that Roosevelt and the Americans thought was essential looked less so from a Soviet perspective. But however enlarged, the Soviet Union was still exhausted and devastated. It needed a period of peace to digest its territorial acquisitions and recover its strength. The result of these competing currents was an often ambivalent Soviet attitude toward postwar organization. Stalin was happy to have the great-power alliance continue in some form, as long as Soviet interests were safeguarded through an absolute veto over its activities.

Stalin's ambivalence had historical and ideological roots as well. The Soviet government, upon which the Western allies relied so heavily to defeat Germany, had been treated as a pariah from its birth in 1917. During the civil war that followed the Bolshevik revolution, American and British troops briefly intervened on behalf of the non-Communist forces, and Churchill spoke of the need to strangle the "Bolshevik baby."[30] To the Western democracies, the Soviet Union was a frightening outsider. It claimed to be a historical movement, not merely a nation-state. Worse, it had active confederates in Western countries. For much of the interwar period, British elites had viewed the Soviet Union as a more fundamental threat than Germany, a judgment that solidified their determination to appease Hitler.[31]

The West's hostility during the 1920s was more than reciprocated, and Soviet suspicion extended to the League of Nations. A "Holy Alliance of the bourgeoisie for the suppression of the proletarian revolution" and, more succinctly, a "robbers' league" were some of the terms Soviet propagandists used for the organization.[32] Soviet derision lasted until it became clear that Nazi Germany posed a serious threat. Only then did the Soviets join the league, and it was not a happy experience. The organization could not offer an increasingly desperate Soviet Union any security from the building Nazi menace. Finally, the Soviets threw their lot in with Hitler, and the infamous 1939 Molotov-Ribbentrop pact freed the Soviets to snap up territory of their own. When the Red Army invaded Finland later that year, the league voted to expel the Soviets, the first and only time the organization removed a member state.

The Soviets therefore were ideologically inclined to view a new international organization as the creation of Western capitalism, and their recent history with the league deepened that skepticism. Accordingly, when Stalin did discuss the postwar situation, he focused much more closely on territory and borders than on rules and legal structures. When British foreign minister Anthony Eden visited Moscow in December 1941, Stalin pushed him to quickly recognize Soviet rights to part of Poland. Eden was surprised at the naked territorial ambition. "Stalin began to show his claws," he wrote at the time.[33]

On the more lofty (and, to Stalin's mind, often impractical) questions of postwar law and organization, Soviet views often did not seem to extend far beyond the judgment that a continued military alliance of the Allies was desirable and that Germany must at all costs be kept down. During Eden's 1941 visit, Stalin ruminated about a council of great powers to maintain European peace.[34] When Roosevelt spoke privately with Stalin in December 1943, the Soviet leader expressed some sympathy for Churchill's notion of regional councils, though he later backed away from this idea.[35] Stalin's own advisors were recommending a small great-power council on which the Soviets would be able to prevent any decision contrary to their interests. Whatever its precise form, the Soviets wanted a postwar organization to focus narrowly on security. The economic, development, and human rights agendas that sometimes appealed to Western politicians and activists did not interest Stalin. He saw the organization first and foremost as an instrument for securing the Soviet Union's borders.

While there was considerable uncertainty regarding the Soviet vision of a postwar organization, Churchill and Roosevelt still harbored hopes that Stalin would cooperate. During the war, a fragile but real camaraderie had developed among the three leaders. Churchill and Roosevelt regularly exchanged candid letters and cables, and when the three leaders met in Tehran in November 1943, Roosevelt was determined to extend the sphere of good feeling to Stalin. The president was convinced that he had a unique power to influence Stalin. In March 1942, Roosevelt wrote to Churchill, "I know you will not mind my being brutally frank when I tell you that I think I can personally handle Stalin better than either your Foreign Office or my State Department."[36]

During the Tehran conference, the president stayed in the Soviet embassy compound and met privately with Stalin several times, much to Churchill's chagrin. When the three leaders sat down together, Roosevelt welcomed the Soviets as "new members of the family circle."[37] Churchill, too, had warmed a bit to the Soviet dictator (now routinely referred to as "Uncle Joe"), who knew how to get a rise out of Churchill. During one of the lavish dinners at the conference, Churchill ended up drinking to the health of the proletarian masses and Stalin to the British Conservative Party.[38] Teary-eyed, Churchill presented Stalin with a sword to commemorate the victory in Stalingrad. "By the end of the war," two Russian historians have written, "the Big Three behaved almost as a private club, with shared memories and jokes that only they could understand."[39]

After the successful D-Day invasion in June 1944, Stalin's customary reserve gave way to ebullience. "Military history does not know a similar enterprise so broadly conceived, on so huge a scale, so masterfully executed," he gushed. He sent signed and dedicated photographs to Churchill and to Roosevelt to commemorate the achievement.[40] The time was right to apply the fragile great-power unity to the complex task of building a postwar organization. The three leaders agreed that a conference of experts should meet to consider the matter in August 1944. The U.S. State Department had compiled the most complete draft of a new organization and had exchanged views with the British Foreign Office and, more cursorily, with the Soviets. Roosevelt—eager to put an American stamp on the new organization—wanted the Allies to discuss the details in Washington.

A Talk in the Woods

It was the height of the capital's sweltering summer, and the State Department officials tasked with planning the conference were struggling to find a suitable location. Edward R. Stettinius, a former business executive recently appointed as American undersecretary of state, led the effort. As he and his staff hurriedly prepared, air conditioning was the immediate crisis. Only a handful of government buildings offered it, and they were all occupied. Finally, a junior State Department diplomat named Alger Hiss suggested the Dumbarton Oaks mansion.[41] Until recently the home of an American diplomat, it had been bequeathed to Harvard University in 1940. Sitting on the edge of the city's leafy Rock Creek Park, the mansion was cool, secluded, and available.

The British delegation—led by Alexander Cadogan and his deputy Gladwyn Jebb—arrived a full week before the Soviets, allowing the Western allies a few days to settle small differences and construct what Jebb termed an "Anglo-American front."[42] The Americans took the British delegation to meet Secretary of State Hull, who gave what Cadogan described as "a rambling speech about democracy and the future of the world."[43] At the Pentagon, General George C. Marshall was more succinct. He informed the British team that Allied forces were now only a dozen miles from Paris. The news gave the conference an added sense of urgency. The "postwar" was no longer sometime in the hazy future.

On August 20, the Soviets, headed by the young diplomat Andrei Gromyko, arrived in Washington, DC. Western diplomats had been impressed by Gromyko in previous meetings. Next to Viacheslav Molotov, Stalin's stony foreign minister, Gromyko seemed quite human. Molotov had supported the decision to send his own wife to the Gulag and rarely showed any hint of emotion. Gromyko, by contrast, shed tears while showing to a group of Americans the location on a map where his family was living under Nazi occupation.[44] Still, the young diplomat had little room to maneuver. Molotov and Stalin had brutally purged the Soviet diplomatic ranks during the late 1930s, and Soviet diplomats interacting with foreigners operated with explicit instructions and under constant surveillance. Gromyko almost did not make it to Dumbarton Oaks. To avoid Western Europe's still perilous airspace, his delegation flew east over Siberia. Bad weather forced their aircraft to land in a tiny village on Russia's isolated periphery. As diplomats in Washington waited nervously, the Soviet negotiating team huddled with the villagers in the town's cinema and watched a newsreel celebrating Red Army victories. Finally, the weather cleared, and the Soviets continued on their way.[45]

At the mansion, security agents and military police staked out positions at the gates to control access and keep out the press. Precautions were taken inside as well. A portrait of a famous Polish patriot was removed to avoid offending the Soviets, who were feuding with a Polish government-in-exile about who should run the country after liberation.[46] After the obligatory welcoming festivities and speeches, the delegates sat down to work, and they quickly agreed on the basic architecture of the organization.

FIGURE 1.1. A chat at Dumbarton Oaks. *From left, seated*: Gladwyn Jebb, Alexander Cadogan, Edward Stettinius, and Andrei Gromyko.

A council of the leading powers would have sole responsibility for maintaining peace and security. The delegates agreed that they "were entitled to special position[s] on the Council by virtue of their exceptional responsibility for world security."[47] At the suggestion of the Soviets, this council was dubbed the Security Council, and there was no doubt that it was where the power would lie.[48] The draft produced during the conference stated, "Members of the Organization should by the Charter confer on the Security Council primary responsibility for the maintenance of international peace and security."[49] They envisioned two separate roles for the council. When a dispute broke out between states, the council could act to facilitate negotiations and encourage mediation between the feuding parties. The council's advice in this capacity would be nonbinding but, it was hoped, influential. If the council determined that there was a threat to the peace or that an act of aggression had occurred, however, it could quickly assume the role of enforcer of the peace. And, as peace enforcer, the council's powers would be vast: it could take "any measures necessary" to restore security when it found a threat, including severing diplomatic and economic relations, imposing blockades, and deploying air, naval, and ground forces.

The council's terms of reference were designed to provide all the authority it would need to preserve peace around the globe. The language agreed to at Dumbarton Oaks conveyed energy and purpose, and it made clear that the council should have an expansive role. This was Roosevelt's influence. But Churchill's skepticism and Stalin's suspicion had their places as well. Nothing in the Dumbarton Oaks agreement *required* the council to do anything. All of the weighty phrases that would trigger forceful council action—a "threat to the peace," a "breach of the peace," an "act of aggression"—were to be defined by the council itself. The text clearly suggested that the council should play a global governance role, but it left open the possibility that it could retreat to the less ambitious function of encouraging consultations among the great powers.

It was telling that the three major Allied powers met alone, without the dozens of other states in the loose alliance against the Axis. The major powers envisioned a universal organization, but they drafted what would become its charter as an elite club. And they designed the Security Council to institutionalize that difference of status, although with a few concessions to the rest of the world. Much as some of the Allied diplomats might have preferred to keep other states off the council entirely, they knew that the body had to have at least a handful of members other than the three major powers. They determined that these outsiders should lack two of the advantages that the great powers possessed. First, their seats on the council would not be permanent. Second, they would not have the power to veto any council decisions. After some debate about the specifics, the delegates settled on a total of six nonpermanent seats for two-year terms.

An assembly of states—to become the General Assembly—would offer a voice and a vote to all members of the organization. It could take up security matters that the council was not handling, but its role was secondary. Unexpectedly, it was the assembly and not the great-power council that posed the most direct threat to the unity of the Dumbarton Oaks conference. In late August, Gromyko asserted that the Soviet Union should have a full sixteen seats in the assembly—one for each of its constituent republics. The proposal's audacity floored the American and British delegates. "My God," Roosevelt exclaimed upon hearing the news.[50] He instructed the State Department to make clear it was a deal breaker. Meanwhile, American diplomats scrambled to prevent the news from spreading, fearing it would sour Congress and the public on the planned organization. Internally, the issue was referred to in hushed tones as the "X-Matter."[51] In subsequent meetings, the United States and Britain prevailed upon Gromyko to postpone discussion of the idea until later.

To break the tension of the negotiations, the Americans planned several elaborate excursions for the delegations. A few days before the Soviet bombshell on assembly seats, the delegates (absent Gromyko, who declined the invitation) flew by military aircraft to New York and were put up at the Waldorf Astoria. That evening, the multinational group forayed out to Billy Rose's Diamond Horseshoe nightclub, then a New York City favorite. The next evening, the diplomats took in another floor show and met the Rockettes backstage. In what must have been one of the oddest briefing sessions in diplomatic history, U.S. undersecretary of state Edward Stettinius asked the senior diplomat from each delegation to say a few words to the dancers, who were wearing "scarcely anything at all." Cadogan, the lead British delegate, was apparently quite shy and said little. But the Soviet general standing in for Gromyko poured forth with stories of his wartime exploits and ended by roundly praising democracy.[52]

In early September, Stettinius organized a more wholesome field trip. He led a collection of British and Soviet delegates on a whirlwind tour through Virginia's Shenandoah Valley for a picnic lunch, on to Monticello and Charlottesville, and finally to the Stettinius country residence for a home-cooked dinner. An African-American spiritual group serenaded the diplomats while they ate. "What a day!" Cadogan told his wife. The Americans, he said, were "kind to an unimaginable degree, in some ways rather like ourselves but (as you see) so utterly different."[53]

The combination of camaraderie-building excursions and artful evasion of the X-Matter kept the conference on the rails. By the time the talks ended in early October, a draft was ready. Only a few thorny issues remained unresolved. The first was the question of what military forces would exercise the council's vast authority. Roosevelt had ruminated about great-power garrisons stationed around the world to stop aggression and enforce disarmament. At other moments, he expressed hope that an international air force and navy by itself could keep the peace. But as the discussions moved forward, the notion of assigning military forces to the Security Council on a permanent basis seemed increasingly far-fetched. The American delegation worried that many members of Congress would balk at a permanent commitment of forces abroad. Ironically, given Stalin's general skepticism, the Soviets briefly emerged as the strongest advocates of arming the council, though they emphasized an international air force that could bomb aggressors into submission. Unable to reach agreement on the point, the delegates suggested that member states put forces at the disposal of the council later through special agreements.[54]

The delegates also stumbled over the issue of the council's voting procedures. The Soviets were adamant that unanimity be the rule; otherwise, they feared, the Western powers could turn the new international machinery against them. The Soviet Union keenly felt its isolation and during a meeting with Roosevelt, Gromyko made clear that, without a unanimity requirement, "there would simply be no United Nations."[55] The Americans also favored a great-power veto on most matters, although they at least were willing to have the council consider and debate issues involving one of the great powers. The British were most resistant to a veto, in part because their diplomats met regularly with the smaller states that made up the British Commonwealth. These states—notably, New Zealand and Canada—had made clear their hostility to the idea that the great powers could essentially run the world through the council and yet immunize themselves by using the veto. The double standard was too much. Recognizing that the issue of voting procedures could not be resolved without further discussion, the delegates decided to table it.

Great Powers in Waiting

While the Americans, British, and Soviets picnicked and politicked, another delegation of diplomats watched nervously. At Roosevelt's insistence, China was invited to the conference and offered a seat on the planned council. Almost since the beginning of the war, the president had insisted that China be treated as a great power. Roosevelt always envisioned four global policemen, not three, and his championing of China's cause struck a chord with the public. Hundreds of American missionaries had traveled to and lived in China, and their accounts had helped to foster an American fascination with the country.

After Japan's attack on Pearl Harbor, those sympathies acquired a strategic dimension; bolstering a weak Chinese government was an important part of America's strategy against Japan. Wartime China was personified by Chiang Kai-shek, the ascetic general who had emerged in the 1920s as the successor to Sun Yat-Sen, the founder of China's modern nationalist movement. For all his fame, Chiang's position was precarious. He faced enemies on multiple fronts and never controlled more than a portion of China's territory; he battled Mao's Communists even as Japanese troops occupied vast portions of eastern China. Still, Chiang appeared to be China's best hope, and the United States poured money into the coffers of his Kuomintang movement. An American general became Chiang's chief of staff.

Chiang also benefited from the admiration of American media heavyweights like Henry Luce, the owner of *Time* magazine, who put the general on the cover a half dozen times. It didn't hurt Chiang's cause in the United States that he was a practicing Christian with a photogenic and charismatic wife, Meiling, who had been educated in the United States. In 1943, she made a whirlwind tour of the country to raise money for the Chinese cause. She spoke to a joint session of Congress and addressed crowds of 20,000 at Madison Square Garden and 30,000 at the Hollywood Bowl. Film stars came out to support her cause, and the inhabitants of small towns lined the railroad tracks to watch her train pass.[56]

Top American leaders were not starstruck. They knew how tenuous Chiang's hold on power was, and they worried that the millions in aid flowing to him were being squandered. Some cynical American observers even dubbed Chiang "Cash My Check." At several moments, Roosevelt mulled over the possibility of deposing Chiang and replacing him with a more capable leader. But American doubts were aired behind closed doors; in public and to its allies, the United States presented China as a trustworthy ally that deserved a seat at the great-power table.

British and Soviet diplomats grumbled that the Americans had conveniently found for themselves a "great power" that could be counted on to support American positions. They saw in China a state that could barely govern itself, let alone contribute to world security. The Soviets refused even to participate in talks with the Chinese; Stalin was determined to remain neutral in the Far Eastern war and feared that sitting down with the Chinese would compromise that position. The British were just as puzzled by Roosevelt's fixation on China. "We in the Foreign Office generally, I think, never thought that China had any chance of being a real world power for a very long time," said Gladwyn Jebb, "but we had to imagine that it was a world power in order to please President Roosevelt."[57]

The Soviet refusal to play along created some awkward moments during wartime meetings of the Allies. At Dumbarton Oaks, the solution was to have two conferences: the first with the Americans, the British, and the Soviets at the table, and the second with the Chinese instead of the Soviets. The Americans insisted that this second conference include an opening ceremony and formal negotiations, even though most major issues had already been resolved. The Chinese knew it was a charade, but Wellington Koo, the urbane, Columbia-educated diplomat leading the Chinese delegation, played his weak hand as best he could. In his years of diplomatic service, Koo had become accustomed to absorbing the indignities that accompanied interactions with many Westerners. Serving in France as China's ambassador in the 1930s, Koo was introduced to a woman who mistook him for the Japanese ambassador. "Japan is a big power, becoming more powerful by the day," she assured him politely. "You will surely be able to swallow up China."[58]

No such gaffes marred Koo's time at Dumbarton Oaks, but China's influence on the draft was marginal. Stettinius and Jebb even kept from the Chinese the X-Matter, although Roosevelt let slip the Soviet demand during a meeting with the Chinese delegation at the White House. Awkwardly for Koo and the Chinese team, relations between Chiang and the United States were tense during the Dumbarton Oaks talks, as the Chinese leader feuded with his American chief of staff, General Joseph Stilwell. During a White House meeting, Roosevelt advisor Harry Hopkins told Koo that "China was not doing her best" in the war against Japan and warned him that American support for China might not last forever.[59]

China was not the only power on the fringes of the negotiations. France, especially France's future president, was also watching with interest, although from a distance. Charles de Gaulle had appeared dramatically on the international scene in June 1940, as France crumbled. The stubborn general, long viewed with suspicion by the French military establishment, rejected the armistice his superiors had made with the Germans and made his way to London. With Churchill's blessing, de Gaulle spoke on the BBC. "Whatever might happen, the flame of French resistance must not be extinguished," he declared. "It shall not be extinguished!"[60] He instantly became the public face of French resistance, and he founded the Committee on National Liberation, which positioned itself as the government of France in exile. While the meetings at Dumbarton Oaks proceeded, de Gaulle paraded triumphantly through the center of newly liberated Paris.

Just as China had a sponsor in the United States, de Gaulle had the firm support of the British, who were eager to see France resume its customary place at the great-power table. Beyond the solicitousness of one European colonial power for another lay basic strategy. Britain could not maintain an army in Europe to keep the peace indefinitely, and France's revival would provide an essential counterweight to a possibly recidivist Germany and an encroaching Russia. "[T]he prospect of no strong country on the map between England and Russia was not attractive," wrote Churchill.[61]

It was the Americans' turn to be skeptical about expanding the ranks of the inner circle. Tension between de Gaulle's committee and the Americans emerged early in the war. In 1941, a handful of Free French naval vessels "liberated" the tiny islands of Saint-Pierre and Miquelon off the coast of Newfoundland. De Gaulle approved the mission without alerting or seeking the permission of the United States, which still had diplomatic relations with Vichy France. Cordell Hull publicly denounced the seizure and threatened to resign when Roosevelt chose to play down the incident.[62]

Roosevelt and de Gaulle did not meet until January 1943 in Casablanca. Aware of the tension, the Secret Service reportedly kept their tommy guns discreetly trained on de Gaulle throughout the session.[63] Personal animosity exacerbated the policy differences. In private correspondence, Roosevelt ridiculed de Gaulle as a "prima donna" with delusions of grandeur. "He thought he was Joan of Arc," the president wrote after one frustrating meeting.[64] Hull, for his part, described de Gaulle as "desperately temperamental" and reportedly would lapse into angry incoherence when discussing the Frenchman.[65]

De Gaulle had his own list of grievances against the United States, topped by its reluctance to recognize his committee as the government-in-exile and the American determination to maintain diplomatic links with Vichy. In a letter to

Roosevelt in October 1942, de Gaulle pleaded with the president to sever all relations with the Vichy authorities. "Notwithstanding the capitulation and the Armistice," he wrote, "France still represents a power in the world which must not be ignored. We must find a way for her to return as a participant in the war along with the United Nations."[66]

De Gaulle managed to test British patience as well. When Churchill invited de Gaulle to visit the bases in southern England on the eve of D-Day, the general arrived in an obstreperous mood. He demanded the right to modify General Dwight D. Eisenhower's statement to the French people, which did not acknowledge de Gaulle or his committee. He also refused to broadcast a statement to the French people after General Eisenhower. By doing so, he insisted, "I would appear to sanction what he said—of which I disapprove—and assume an unsuitable rank in the series of speeches."[67] De Gaulle withdrew the French liaison officers scheduled to depart with the Allied troop ships because, he argued, their duties were not clear. Churchill was apoplectic. As Allied paratroopers descended on France, Churchill ordered that de Gaulle be removed from England immediately—forcibly if necessary. Only the intervention of Foreign Minister Anthony Eden smoothed the waters. At the last minute, de Gaulle made a broadcast supporting the invasion.

Stories of that dustup quickly made their way to Washington, where they reinforced the Roosevelt administration's deep distrust of de Gaulle. The frustration came to a head just a few weeks before the conference at Dumbarton Oaks. On board the U.S. government yacht *Sequoia*, Stettinius and several other top U.S. officials lectured one of de Gaulle's representatives in Washington, Jean Monnet. "If the American public knew the truth about the deplorable manner in which de Gaulle and the committee had handled affairs," they lectured Monnet, "there would be a definite breach between this country and France that would take a generation to get over."[68]

Stalin's views toward de Gaulle were not much warmer, and he too resisted including France in the great-power council. France's ruling class, Stalin said, was rotten and corrupt.[69] After the war, France would be "charming but weak." But dogged British advocacy wore down Soviet and American doubts, and at Dumbarton Oaks, the Allies agreed to reserve a permanent seat at the council table for France, although it would not be formally offered until the French had an established government.

One more power was considered for the council's inner circle: Roosevelt insisted that the U.S. team propose Brazil. The South American behemoth was one of the few countries in Latin America with troops in action against the Axis, and its size and economic potential made it a credible candidate. But even Roosevelt's advisors thought the idea was far-fetched, and the

American negotiating team quickly yielded to British and Soviet objections. The British assumed that Brazil—like China—would be a mere proxy vote for the Americans. Already concerned about America's anticolonial instincts, Churchill did not want the balance tilted even further in that direction. Nor would the Soviets stand for yet another pro-Western vote on the council. With Brazil's brief candidacy rejected, the permanent membership of the new Security Council was all but final: the Big Three had decided to become the Permanent Five.

In early October, the delegates left Dumbarton Oaks in good spirits. They had made huge strides toward agreement on a new world organization, with the Security Council at its core. The reaction outside the mansion was enthusiastic. Thomas Connally, chair of the Senate Foreign Relations Committee, called for unified political support. The plan, he said, "meets the world demand for permanent peace machinery."[70] The *New York Times* expressed "high hope that out of this beginning there will come a new union capable of enforcing law and order."[71]

From a few quarters came words of warning. Just as the conference ended, the noted theologian and political philosopher Reinhold Niebuhr published a slim volume titled *The Children of Light and the Children of Darkness*. He did not deny that a newly globalized and technologically proficient world needed some kind of governance, but he had little patience for those "children of light" who thought it could be achieved by the mere drafting of charters. These idealists "think that we lack an international government only because no one has conceived a proper blueprint of it. Therefore they produce such blueprints in great profusion. These pure constitutionalists have a touching faith in the power of a formula over the raw stuff of human history."[72]

Events in Eastern Europe during the conference were particularly raw. Soviet forces advancing into Poland stood by as German troops massacred resisters in the Warsaw ghetto, leading to speculation that the Soviets were content to see a potential rival force extinguished. It was, said Churchill, "strange and sinister behavior."[73] The implications of the massive Soviet advance were dawning on the British and the Americans, and they began to worry almost as much about the new occupiers of Eastern Europe as they did about the Germans.

The imminent surrender of Germany—and the unresolved questions about the United Nations—meant that the remaining decisions had to be taken quickly and at the highest level. "The only hope for the world is the agreement of the Great Powers," wrote Churchill. "If they quarrel, our children are undone."[74] Roosevelt agreed: a face-to-face meeting was essential to preserve the alliance and ensure the creation of a new world organization.

Crimean Vacation

Early on the morning of February 3, 1945, a small Allied air armada approached the snowy Crimean peninsula. On board the British and American planes were Churchill, Roosevelt, and their closest political and military advisors. Negotiations to determine a venue for the critical meeting, the first among the three leaders since late 1943, had been difficult. Stalin insisted on remaining close to his capital so that he could supervise the rapid Soviet advance into Germany. The ailing Roosevelt was reluctant to travel so far from home, but he finally yielded to Stalin's request. Molotov and a coterie of high Soviet officials waited at the airstrip. They ushered the dignitaries off the planes and into tents, where they plied them with caviar, smoked salmon, and boiled eggs before showing them to their limousines.[75] For the next five hours, the British and American delegations bounced along rutted and bomb-scarred roads toward the tsarist palaces of Yalta. Soviet soldiers lined the roads and snapped salutes as the Allied leaders passed in their cars.[76]

Bringing the Big Three together in what had just been a war zone required minor logistical miracles. The U.S. Army ran communications lines from Yalta to an American ship in Sebastopol so that Roosevelt could stay in touch with Washington. The British military rushed pouches of classified material to Churchill every night. The Soviets did what they could to make the palaces comfortable for the visiting dignitaries. The food was sumptuous and the alcohol flowed freely. Still, Churchill had grounds for complaint. After hearing that his staff had encountered bedbugs during the first night at the old palace, the prime minister had his chambers fumigated by a squad of American specialists.[77]

The future of Germany was the first order of business when the three leaders convened. With surrender possible at any moment, the Allies had to determine how to divide and rule that country. Just as Britain had pushed for France to have a seat on the Security Council at Dumbarton Oaks, it now advocated that France be given a zone of occupation to manage in Germany. Stalin yielded on that point. He also agreed to enter the war against Japan no later than three months after the surrender of Germany, a major American goal for the conference. The festering problem of Poland consumed hours of discussion, as Stalin and Churchill wrangled over how to settle the competing claims of the Soviet-backed government and the London exiles. In the end, the leaders fashioned a vague and ultimately unenforceable promise that the Soviets would hold free elections in Eastern Europe. Referring to the agreement, Stalin reportedly told Molotov, "It's nothing. Go back to work. We can fulfill it in our own way later."[78]

These were critical questions, but Roosevelt had limited patience for long debates on occupation zones and Polish elections while his cherished world organization hung in the balance. The Soviets did not share his sense of urgency;

FIGURE 1.2. Winston Churchill, Franklin Roosevelt, and Josef Stalin during the Yalta conference.

as always, Stalin cared much more about facts on the ground than agreements on paper. Several of Roosevelt's advisors were angered to learn that Stalin hadn't even read a proposal that Washington had sent two months before on Security Council voting procedures.[79]

When the Soviets did finally turn their attention to the council, they proved surprisingly flexible. After some brief wrangling, the leaders reached a compromise—the so-called Yalta formula—which allowed permanent members to veto decisions on "substantive" matters but not on procedural questions. Permanent members could not, for example, squelch the mere discussion of a controversy or dispute in the council. The Big Three insisted that the council was not reverting fully to the stifling unanimity that had hampered the League of Nations' Executive Council. "The formula proposed for the taking of action in the Security Council by a majority of seven would make the operation of the Council less subject to obstruction than was the case under the League of Nations rule of complete unanimity," read the agreement.[80] Because the nonpermanent members would not have a veto, the Yalta agreement preserved, just barely, the notion that the Security Council was a step forward for international organization, and not a repetition of past mistakes.

It was not acknowledged at the time, but the Yalta agreement was a major blow to the vision of an activist council, which Roosevelt had most enthusiastically promoted. How assertive could the council be when all of its substantive decisions would require unanimous great-power approval? Even in the absence of profound ideological or strategic differences, council decision making would tend away from activism and toward the lowest common denominator. The veto power cemented at Yalta tilted the body dramatically toward being a concert of great powers rather than a global governing body.

This was a complication for another day. At the time, the Americans were delighted by the breakthrough, which they saw as a major concession from the Soviets. Roosevelt and Stalin also managed to neutralize the X-Matter that had threatened the Dumbarton Oaks meeting. The Soviet Union agreed to accept a mere three seats in the General Assembly, one each for Ukraine and Belarus in addition to the principal U.S.S.R. seat. Roosevelt did extract a promise from Stalin that, if Congress gave him trouble on the point, Stalin would not object to three seats for the United States.[81] Once again, the Western delegations parted with a sense that great things were possible and that a spirit of cooperation might endure. Alger Hiss, part of the American delegation, found the political environment at Yalta "extraordinarily congenial."[82]

Observers less sympathetic to the Soviets than Hiss also left the conference in an almost giddy mood. "We really believed in our hearts that this was the dawn of the new day we had all been praying for and talking about for so many years," remembered Harry Hopkins. "The Russians had proved that they could be reasonable and farseeing and there wasn't any doubt in the mind of the President or any of us that we could live with them and get along with them peacefully for as far into the future as any of us could imagine."[83] In a letter sent as the conference ended, British diplomat Pierson Dixon expressed a combination of awe and hope.

> I suppose it was one of the most remarkable meetings that has ever been held and the concentration of power was tremendous. Between them the three protagonists can decide the future of the world. Never before have the Three agreed so closely on great matters. The problem will be to keep them together, though the auguries are good.[84]

Roosevelt, eager to capitalize on the goodwill, pushed Churchill and Stalin to set an early date for the conference that would formally launch the United Nations. The Big Three agreed that the United States was the right venue for the meeting, not least because it would help to ensure American participation. As Eden put it, "perhaps if the constitution of the League of Nations had been debated and decided in New York or California, that body would have had a better chance of survival."[85] San Francisco would be the place.

Roosevelt planned to attend the opening and closing of the San Francisco conference, and he brushed aside the worries of some advisors that he would be politically vulnerable if the conference failed. "All those people from all over the world are paying this country a great honor by coming here and I want to tell them how much we appreciate it," the president told a White House visitor in March.[86] On April 12, 1945, Roosevelt was in Warm Springs, Georgia, working on the draft of his speech to the conference when he collapsed and died.

Responsibility for hosting the conference fell to Harry Truman. The Missouri politician was well suited to the task. He had been a keen advocate of international organization since he fought in World War I, and he lamented America's failure to join the league. "We did not accept our responsibility as a world power," he said.[87] Truman even carried in his wallet a copy of a Tennyson poem bemoaning humanity's inability to govern itself.

> Till the war-drum throbb'd no longer, and the battle-flags were furl'd,
> In the Parliament of man, the Federation of the world.

> There the common sense of most shall hold a fretful realm in awe,
> And the kindly earth shall slumber, lapt in universal law.[88]

An hour after taking the oath of office, Truman declared that the San Francisco conference should proceed on schedule. And when he addressed Congress a day after Roosevelt's funeral, Truman made a plea for the United Nations the centerpiece of his speech. "Machinery for the just settlement of international differences must be found," he said. "Without such machinery, the entire world will have to remain an armed camp." The great powers, the president insisted, "have a special responsibility to enforce the peace." But that responsibility "is to serve and not dominate the peoples of the world."[89] It was a theme the great powers had no choice but to emphasize as they prepared to meet the rest of the world at San Francisco. Somehow, they had to convince the lesser powers that only a select few would have the authority to determine critical questions of peace and security.

The invitations to the conference had gone out in March 1945. In all, forty-five nations were asked to attend, including nineteen from the Americas and the Caribbean, seven from Asia and the Middle East, and ten from Europe. Most of Africa was still colonized, and only three representatives from that continent attended. In addition to the main Axis powers, a few countries were still deemed to be outcasts. Argentina, which had collaborated with the Germans, at first did not receive an invitation, although it eventually did participate. Italy, parts of which were still occupied by German troops, was not asked to attend. In some

FIGURE 1.3. The opening of the San Francisco conference in April 1945.

cases, it was not clear to whom an invitation should be sent. Poland, for example, still lacked an internationally recognized government.

As the conference approached, the American government spared no expense to ensure its success. The U.S. military flew several Asian delegations to the conference. Legions of typists, translators, and diplomats and tons of office equipment traversed the country by rail. The government snapped up hundreds of hotel rooms in the city for the visiting delegations, and a master chef was recruited to feed them suitable meals. Other preparations were less obvious. The U.S. Army's Signal Security Agency, forerunner of the National Security Agency, prepared to provide American diplomats with daily reports on what other delegations were saying. The Americans were not the only ones in the snooping business. American intelligence intercepts indicated that Soviet agents were arriving in San Francisco. Off the coast, a large Soviet ship was anchored to allow diplomats to communicate with the Kremlin.[90]

Meanwhile, the State Department finalized plans for the actual debate and drafting that would take place at the conference. The Dumbarton Oaks draft, by now in wide circulation among diplomats and the public, would be the common starting point. Four commissions and twelve technical committees would work with the draft, amending it and redrafting as they saw fit. One group, formally designated Committee 1 of Commission III, devoted itself to the sections of the charter that dealt with the Security Council. The great powers watched carefully over the process of debate and amendment.

The conference's script was written, but some of the key actors were proving reluctant. For several weeks, it was not clear that Soviet foreign minister Molotov would attend. A few weeks after the Yalta conference, as tensions over Poland again escalated, Stalin announced that Molotov would not come to San Francisco; instead, Andrei Gromyko would lead the delegation. This was a sharp blow to the Americans and British, who took it as a sign that the Soviets were prepared to let the conference fail. A worried Churchill wrote to Roosevelt: "Does it mean that the Russians are going to run out, or are they trying to blackmail us?"[91] Urgent messages from Washington and London seeking assurances that Molotov would attend received no response. In the end, Roosevelt's death may have persuaded Stalin to relent. British foreign minister Anthony Eden concluded that Stalin sent Molotov as a gesture of respect to the late president.[92]

Molotov headed for the United States, stopping first in Washington to visit the new American president. Truman, by all accounts, lectured the Soviet diplomat. As Truman's aides waited outside the Oval Office, the president bluntly chronicled what he saw as Soviet intransigence and broken promises. "I have never been talked to like [this] in my life," Molotov said. "Carry out your agreements and you won't get talked to like that," Truman responded.[93] In San Francisco, Molotov got a chance for payback. In the weeks before the conference, sixteen Polish leaders in exile who had traveled to Moscow for talks had mysteriously disappeared, and American and British diplomats feared the worst. Stettinius brought the matter up with Molotov, who promised to find out what had happened. When the two met at a reception a short while later, according to an American eyewitness, Molotov shook hands with the U.S. secretary of state. "Oh, by the way, Mr. Stettinius," he said, "about those sixteen Poles; they have all been arrested by the Red Army." He then turned around abruptly to greet another guest. Stettinius could only stand there shocked.[94]

The Soviets were not the only delegation to arrive at San Francisco in a resentful mood. In the weeks before the conference, Paris and Washington had clashed over the French desire to have their own draft circulated at the conference. De Gaulle declined the role of conference sponsor, which was offered to each of the proposed permanent council members. In its proposed amendments to the Dumbarton Oaks draft, France attempted to champion the cause of the midsized states at the conference. It suggested narrowing the veto power, allowing the smaller states more input into council military operations, and expanding the powers of the General Assembly.[95]

The spirit of *egalité* extended only so far, and France's sensitivity about its role became apparent at the opening ceremony. It had been decided that the official languages of the conference would be English, French, Russian, Chinese, and

Spanish. But for the sake of convenience, the American planners had decided not to translate the opening speeches.[96] As Stettinius opened his speech to the assembly, however, a voice in the audience began translating his comments into French. Bewildered, Stettinius paused and turned to conference president Alger Hiss for guidance. Hiss shrugged. "We've just been outsmarted." The speech went ahead, translated loudly into French.[97]

As France was defending its language rights in San Francisco, it was reasserting its colonial rights in Syria. In late May, French forces in Damascus fired on protestors demanding independence. In all, a thousand people may have died in the violence. Churchill interceded with de Gaulle and eventually told British forces in the area to demand that French forces stand down. The United States urged the French to treat Syria and Lebanon "as fully sovereign and independent members of the family of nations."[98] De Gaulle eventually yielded, but he made clear that his withdrawal was only tactical. "We are not, I admit, in a position to open hostilities against you at the present time," he told a senior British diplomat. "But you have insulted France and betrayed the West. This cannot be forgotten."[99] Reports of the confrontation reverberated around the meeting rooms in San Francisco. "The incident has inflamed the Arabs," recalled a Canadian delegate. "It has driven the U.S. and the U.K. closer together and moved France away from the Atlantic hemisphere to the Soviet hemisphere."[100]

Tension among the great powers was considerable, but the dynamic at San Francisco also created a crosscurrent of solidarity, as the would-be permanent council members defended their privileges to dozens of nations only now being consulted. The great powers "felt that it was desirable for cosmetic reasons at least, to have some appearance that the views of the smaller states were being seriously taken into account," remembered one participant.[101] The five powers met before the conference formally convened to anticipate objections and coordinate their strategies, and they consulted frequently throughout the session. Russian-speaking Leo Pasvolsky, the star of the American team, met frequently with Soviet diplomat Arkady Sobolev to review amendments and fend off challenges from the smaller states. Cadogan teamed up with Texas senator Tom Connally, an American delegate to the conference, to put down a small-state objection. "I tell [Connally] he's our heavy artillery and I am the sniper," wrote Cadogan in his diary. "It works quite well and we wiped the floor with a Mexican last night: I think we must have shut him up for a week or so."[102]

The Five could not silence all of the critics, however, and many delegations worried less about the council's extraordinary powers than the possibility that it would be politically impotent. When the Five were united, there were almost no limits to what they could do. But if one of the Five dissented, it appeared that the council could be paralyzed. "When can one of the permanent Powers arbitrarily dissent from and prevent any action?" the delegate from New Zealand wanted to know.[103]

The Australian foreign minister, Herbert Evatt, was particularly determined to pick at the ambiguities of the Yalta agreement. The proposed council, he wrote later, "had grave defects and showed obvious signs of having been drawn up in the exclusive interests of major powers, preoccupied with problems of military security, and inclined to ensure for themselves special privileges to which they deemed themselves entitled by reason of their contribution to victory in World War II."[104] Evatt's stubborn advocacy earned him the disdain of the Five. An annoyed Alexander Cadogan called the Australian "the most frightful man in the world."[105]

Evatt proposed more than a dozen amendments to the veto rules, including getting rid of the veto entirely for disputes that did not involve armed force. As the scholar Stephen Schlesinger describes, it appeared for a few days that a full-scale revolt over the council's prerogatives was brewing.[106] Senator Arthur Vandenberg, another American delegate, scribbled in his diary, "This veto bizness is making it very difficult to maintain any semblance of a fiction of 'sovereign equality' among the nations here at Frisco."[107] Evatt helped to convince a number of already skeptical Latin American states to question the veto power, and they compiled a list of twenty-three questions about how the veto would work in practice. Unnerved, the Five summoned Evatt for a chat. The atmospherics of the meeting accentuated the power disparity. Evatt was ushered into a private elevator and "shot upwards" to the luxurious penthouse suite in the Fairmont Hotel where the great powers worked.[108]

In the end, the great powers fended off the challenge in the only way they could: by making clear that, without the veto, there would be no United Nations. Senator Connally delivered that message most theatrically. "You may go home from San Francisco if you wish and report that you have defeated the veto," he lectured the delegates in his committee as he brandished a copy of the draft charter. "Yes, you can say you defeated the veto, but you can also say, 'We tore up the Charter!'" The senator then ripped up his copy, threw the scraps on the table, and "stared belligerently at one face after another."[109]

For a brief moment, it appeared that the Yalta agreement on the veto might be unraveling from within the great-power circle as well. On June 2, Gromyko declared that the Soviets no longer accepted the idea that the council could debate any issue brought before it; the Five would have to agree before an issue could even be considered. His announcement sent shock waves through the conference and prompted emergency meetings in Washington and London. Stettinius cabled Harry Hopkins, who was already in Moscow at Truman's request to try to restore cooperation with Stalin. The crisis passed as quickly as it had appeared.

Without so much as an argument, Stalin said the disagreement was "insignificant" and saved the Yalta formula.[110]

Their internal cohesion restored, at least for the moment, the Five continued their effort to preserve the council's prerogatives. Perhaps unnerved by the near collapse of the conference, some of the states that had opposed the veto wavered. A Canadian diplomat cabled Ottawa suggesting that the issue be dropped. "Our view is that it is better to take the Organization that we can get and, having come to that decision, to refrain from further efforts to pry apart the difficult unity which the Great Powers have attained. This means forgoing the luxury of making any more perfectionist speeches."[111]

Amid the arm twisting, there was some actual give-and-take between the great powers and the rest of the nations. Indeed, one of the UN Charter's most important provisions grew out of small-country objections. The draft charter given to the delegates did not explicitly mention the right of countries to use force to defend themselves. It was an omission that made small states nervous. What if the Security Council could not or would not come to their aid because it was divided or simply slow? Did the charter actually mean that their security was wholly dependent on the vigilance of the council? Most states wanted the great powers to operate together effectively, but they were not willing to stake their survival on the Five's ability to do so. The oversight was corrected by inserting what became Article 51 of the charter. "Nothing in the present Charter," it read, "shall impair the inherent right of individual or collective self-defense if an armed attack occurs against a Member of the United Nations, until the Security Council has taken the measures necessary to maintain international peace and security."[112]

On the whole, the Security Council's enormous powers and privileges survived the conference undiminished. As a Canadian magazine concluded, "the little nations all had their say and the big powers got their way."[113] Most countries, wrote the New York Times, "reluctantly accepted the idea of virtual world dictatorship by the great powers."[114] The council's role in promoting the settlement of disputes emerged as chapter VI of the new charter. The council's "teeth" appeared in chapter VII, which endowed the council with the authority to use military force, economic sanctions, and any other means it deemed necessary to enforce the peace. The question of whether the council should have a permanent force at its disposal—which had not been resolved during the Dumbarton Oaks negotiations—remained essentially unresolved. Article 43 of the charter asked all member states to conclude "special agreements" with the council that would designate certain forces and equipment for its use, but there was no deadline for the completion of these agreements.

The charter was signed on June 26, 1945, but some final business remained. Ten months later in Geneva, the League of Nations, whose legal existence had continued even after the war ended, met for the last time. Sean Lester presided as the league disbanded and bequeathed its remaining assets, including the Geneva headquarters, to the United Nations. "The League is dead," declared the British elder statesman Lord Cecil. "Long live the United Nations."[115] A new group of great powers was getting a chance to run the world. They had gone to San Francisco as bickering nations struggling to protect their postwar interests; they left as the duly authorized custodians of the world's security.

CHAPTER 2

FITS AND STARTS (1946–1956)

A T 5:00 IN the morning on May 19, 1945, a restless Joseph Grew got out of bed, sat at his desk, and began to write. While Edward Stettinius managed the San Francisco conference, Grew, a long-time diplomat, was running the State Department back in Washington. The course of events in San Francisco and in Europe worried him. Because of the veto agreement reached at Yalta, he wrote, the Security Council "will be rendered powerless to act against the one certain future enemy, Soviet Russia." War with Russia, he continued, "is as certain as anything in this world can be certain.... As soon as the San Francisco Conference is over, our policy toward Soviet Russia should immediately stiffen, all along the line."[1]

Grew's disquiet was shared by a number of senior American and British officials. George Kennan, an American diplomat then stationed in Moscow, wrote during the Yalta conference that "an international organization for the preservation of peace and security cannot take the place of a well-conceived and realistic foreign policy." He worried that American leaders were allowing fantasies about the United Nations "to be an excuse for failing to occupy ourselves seriously and minutely with the sheer power relationships of the European peoples."[2]

In London, Britain's new foreign secretary, the blunt-spoken former trade union leader Ernest Bevin, also warned against placing too much faith in the new organization. "If the Great Powers cannot be reasonably true to the promises which they have made," he told the House of Commons, "no promise to inflict sanctions upon each other will save the world."[3] Even as the UN Charter was being signed, a sense of gloom about relations with the Soviet Union—and an awareness of how that animosity would hobble the Security Council—was spreading in Western capitals. That despair soon mingled with shock after the

United States dropped two atomic bombs on Japan in August 1945. Everyone felt that the world had changed, though no one was certain just how.[4]

But the worsening superpower rivalry and the atomic bomb did not still the machinery created in San Francisco. In late 1945, a commission of diplomats in London met to lay the groundwork for the Security Council's first meeting. Many of the key players at San Francisco returned, including Stettinius, Wellington Koo, Andrei Gromyko, and British professor Charles Webster. They met in London's Church House, where workers were still removing bomb-blast protection from the windows and cleaning up the detritus of war.

On a few issues, the tension that had arisen in San Francisco between the small states and the Five reappeared. Several countries objected to a proposed rule of procedure that would allow the council to hold closed meetings and release only a short summary of the proceedings. The Egyptian representative reminded the commission that the council "would be called upon to take extremely important decisions involving sacrifices on the part of Members of the United Nations not represented on it," and Cuba's delegate declared that the United Nations should have no "secret documents." The Five insisted that the concern was misplaced and that the rule did not imply "any idea of secret diplomacy." Even if it did, several other states argued, forcing the council to publish the proceedings of closed meetings would simply lead it to hold informal meetings with even less transparency. Amendments that would have allowed all UN members access to the private meeting records were rejected, and the provision passed as drafted.[5]

More often, the commission split down the emerging Cold War lines, with Gromyko alleging that the Western members were violating the new charter. Some delegates wondered whether the Soviets wanted the council to convene at all. "An uneasy feeling began to grow within me," remembered one diplomat, "that he was under orders from Moscow to accumulate a list of so-called violations of the Charter which could be used by the Soviet government as justification for a decision by the Soviet Union not to ratify the Charter."[6] That dark premonition proved to be unfounded. The Soviet Union ratified the United Nations Charter; for better or worse, it would be part of the system.

Not only did they choose to participate, but the Soviets signaled that they were willing to endorse the United States as the permanent seat of the new organization, a gesture that surprised many Western diplomats. To this day, the Soviet reasoning remains murky, although some observers have speculated that the Soviets wanted the organization physically distant from its own growing European sphere of influence. Within the United States, the New York area emerged as the favorite. As the seat of the U.S. government, Washington, DC, was out of the question, and the British counseled against a West Coast site, which they thought would be too distant. New York had the advantage of already being an international city in many respects. Still, more than a dozen other cities and towns offered choice land and other incentives to lure the organization. Atlantic City, New Jersey; Cape Cod, Massachusetts; and Bar Harbor, Maine, all pleaded their case. Diminutive Rhode Island suggested that the United Nations consider its entire territory in its deliberations.[7]

"We Cannot Afford to Fail"

With its final home still uncertain, the United Nations opened its temporary quarters in London. On January 17, 1946, the Security Council met for the first time. "In accordance with the Articles of the Charter, representatives having been appointed to serve on the Security Council and a meeting having been correctly convened," intoned Australian minister Norman Makin, "I declare the Security Council duly constituted and in session."[8] The representatives of the five great powers and the six countries elected by the General Assembly as nonpermanent members—Australia, Brazil, Egypt, Mexico, the Netherlands, and Poland—made brief statements. "The Security Council today begins its history. It will be a history momentous in its consequences for the human race," said Stettinius. "This time we cannot afford to fail." Several of the countries on the council had been occupied by the Nazis, and the League of Nations' failure to stop aggression hung over the room. The Dutch minister reminded the council that, less than a year ago, his people "were still under the heel of the oppressor."

> I remember very well that, in the dark days of the war, that great leader of the country which is giving us the very generous hospitality we are enjoying here—I mean Winston Spencer Churchill—talked to us of the dark valley through which we had to make a long pilgrimage in order to emerge one day into these sunlit regions where peace and liberty would reign once more. We have now emerged into those regions; and I think that this assembly of the Security Council marks a most auspicious beginning.

"Let us hope from now on the trouble-maker will be stopped," said Brazil's representative. The meeting lasted just over an hour and ended without a hint of animosity.[9]

It was not long in coming. As the war ended, the great powers had troops scattered around the globe, and in an atmosphere of mounting East-West tension, these forces became frequent points of contention. Military personnel who

FIGURE 2.1. The Security Council during its first meeting on January 17, 1946, in London.

had been engaged in the common fight against the Axis were potential kingmakers in dozens of small countries. At the council's second meeting, the council president reported that he had received a complaint that Soviet forces had not left Iranian territory as promised. Soviet troops, Iran's government charged, were preventing Iranian authorities from exercising control in the north of the country. A few days later, the Soviets complained that British troops were interfering in the internal affairs of Greece.

Gromyko shared his council duties with another Soviet diplomat, Andrei Vishinsky, who had a reputation as a ruthless and skilled debater. The knowledge that he had been the prosecutor in many of Stalin's show trials only added to the malignant aura about him.[10] A Soviet diplomat described Vishinsky's rhetorical style as "an unusual mix of solemn, sonorous Latin, a cascade of Russian proverbs, and primitive, vulgar invective."[11] In a lengthy intervention at one of the council's early meetings, Vishinsky accused British troops of aiding fascist elements in Greece. "What happens today in Greece, the horrors perpetrated through the white terror, are now widely known to everyone. I think it hardly necessary to bring proof here." Ernest Bevin, serving as Britain's representative on the council, rose to defend British conduct. By all means, he fumed, investigate the British role in Greece. "I am so tired of these charges made by the Government of the Union of Soviet Socialist Republics in private assembly," he said, "that no one will be happier than I shall be to see that the British Government has a chance to clear its conduct in connexion with this country."[12] Bevin demanded that the council make a clear determination of whether British conduct was acceptable.

Bevin, it soon became clear, had little capacity to absorb Soviet barbs with equanimity. "[Vishinsky's] calculated lunges maddened him," remembered Trygve Lie, the Norwegian diplomat who was appointed as the United Nations' first secretary-general. "[Bevin] was like a bull charging furiously at the red banner all over the field of debate."[13] Vishinsky was not the only Soviet diplomat who could incite Bevin. Molotov, the Soviet foreign minister, gravely provoked him during a conference in 1947. "I've 'ad about enough of this, I 'ave," the stocky Bevin said in his West Country accent after absorbing yet another Soviet rhetorical broadside. He rose, clenched his fists, and advanced toward Molotov. "For one glorious moment," recalled an eyewitness, "it looked as if the Foreign Minister of Great Britain and the Foreign Minister of the Soviet Union were about to come to blows."[14]

The council managed to complete its short stay in London without physical violence, but it could not avoid a procedural blow. On February 16, 1946—a few days before the council moved to New York—the Soviet Union exercised the first great-power veto. For several weeks, the council had been crafting a resolution on the withdrawal of British and French forces that were stationed in Syria and Lebanon. The text had been amended several times to accommodate Soviet objections. Then, at the last minute, Vishinsky announced his intention to vote against it; the final wording was not to his liking. That the veto was being used so early—and on a relatively minor matter—"astounded" many observers.[15] The veto had been designed as a safety valve for the defense of fundamental national interests, not as an instrument to achieve ideal resolutions.

An atmosphere of foreboding traveled with the council as it crossed the Atlantic to its new home. The move from London began a peripatetic several years for the council. Real estate, particularly on the scale needed for the United Nations, was not easy to come by in postwar New York. The council landed first in the gymnasium of Hunter College in the Bronx. A few months later, it was on to the Henry Hudson Hotel. After a few weeks of hotel life, the band of diplomats moved to a converted gyroscope factory at Long Island's Lake Success, where the council would remain until 1952.

It was an imperfect fit. Delegates living in the city had to endure long rides from there to the factory. The council chamber itself seemed designed more for the ease of photographers than for the comfort of the delegates. The members sat at a long table that exposed them to the flashbulbs from the press gallery. "The

Security Council representatives may not be shy or retiring men, but none of them can be at heart so much like an Atlantic Beach beauty contestant as the designers of the Chamber have made them out to be," remembered one diplomat. "Every influence in the place hinders concentration."[16] Some modest help arrived in the form of a new meeting table. Shaped like a horseshoe, it was fashioned from mahogany. "The shape of the new table," reported the *New York Times*, "will have the psychological effect of making the delegates feel they are conferring among themselves rather than addressing an audience."[17]

The interpreters assigned to the council situated themselves in the middle of the horseshoe, where they scribbled the shorthand notes that would allow them to quickly translate comments into French and English, the two working languages at that time. Simultaneous interpretation was still a new technique, and the council relied on consecutive interpretation for its first several years. Speeches were translated laboriously into the official council languages, one after the other. The heavy demands of interpreting hours of meetings created ample potential for embarrassment, particularly when delegates lapsed into colloquialisms or storytelling. Soviet diplomats were particularly fond of folktales, and the translators often struggled to render them into French and English. The BBC correspondent in the council's early days recalled one notable attempt. The immediate interpretation of the Soviet ambassador's comment was: "In Russia we have a proverb that the flaming head portrays the murderer." The next version was better: "In Russia we have a proverb that the red face betrays the criminal." But the story took an odd turn when translated into French: "In Russia we have a proverb that he whose nose is running should wipe it."[18]

The council's arrival in New York occasioned keen curiosity. At early meetings at Hunter College and the Hudson Hotel, autograph seekers stalked the delegates, and the press clamored for the right to televise all council meetings. Two women who worked in the council's coat check gathered signatures to sell outside. Security Council delegates were frequently invited to New York society's poshest gatherings and besieged with speaking requests. The attention being paid to the council was, in the eyes of some observers, reason enough to celebrate. "The Security Council has achieved an immense amount in an incredibly short space of time," wrote one journalist. "It has collected about itself a quite remarkable aura of international authority and prestige."[19]

That aura could not alter the stubborn problem of Soviet troops in Iran. As soon as the council was settled, the Iranian government (now with American support) again sought to place its complaint on the agenda. The Soviets resisted, and for two days the council debated whether to even consider the Iranian complaint. When it finally voted to debate the matter, the Soviet veto was useless. Including an item on the agenda was a procedural matter, to which the veto did

FIGURE 2.2. Tourists in New York City watch a live Security Council debate.

not apply. But the veto was not the only means of protest. After the vote was taken, Andrei Gromyko announced that he could no longer participate in the meeting. He slowly gathered his papers and walked out of the chamber. Iran was on the agenda, but the Soviet Union was not in the chamber to debate it.[20]

The Soviets had plenty of opportunities to hone their expressions of outrage. During the council's first several months, the Soviets found themselves isolated on issues including civil strife in Greece, how to treat the Franco regime in Spain, and the admission of new members to the United Nations. They reacted by throwing up whatever roadblocks they could. Soviet vetoes became commonplace. By the summer of 1948, the Soviet Union had exercised the veto seventeen times, driving some Western diplomats to distraction. One correspondent recalled U.S. ambassador Warren Austin stalking out of a council meeting after yet another Soviet veto. "I'm so mad I don't know what to do," he sputtered.[21] France was the only other member to use the veto, and it did so only twice.[22] The profligate Soviet use of the veto inspired harsh commentary in the West, where the practice was seen as entirely out of keeping with the spirit of cooperation behind the organization. Veteran journalist James Reston wrote in 1946, "[T]here is no doubt that in the view of the vast majority of those who have observed the United Nations since its inception, the Soviet Union has violated both the Roosevelt principle and the Big Five promise which make up the basic assumption about the veto."[23]

The criticism extended beyond the Soviets' policies and ideology; it was a rejection of their procedural tactics and reflected a particular view of how nations on the Security Council should act. Whatever the Soviet Union's narrow political interests, Western critics seemed to be saying, a council member—and particularly a permanent member—must be more than simply a self-interested state. As two leading American political scientists argued in 1952, it was not at all surprising that this call to a higher purpose found little favor in Moscow.[24] The Soviets had insisted on the veto precisely because they expected to be in the minority on the Western-dominated council. "The veto, they say, has been applied 50 times!" thundered Vishinsky in 1950. "[I]t may well be applied 150 times in such conditions, because it is a means of self-defence against the pressure, the dictation which the states that believe themselves to be strongest and mightiest ... are trying to exercise against other states in international affairs."[25]

It is possible to see in the early arguments about the use of the veto competing visions for what the council should be, visions that had been discussed and debated at Dumbarton Oaks and San Francisco but had to be tested in a real world environment. The Soviet view was minimalist, practical, and unsentimental: the council should be a place where the great powers meet to discuss issues, protected by the principle of unanimity. A state on the council has no obligation to do anything other than assert and defend its national interests; if discussion on the council helped to foster agreement, that was well and good. Against this minimalist vision was the one common among Western idealists—and enshrined in the text of the charter— that council members had a positive duty to work as agents of international peace and security and to make sacrifices that other states might not have to.

U.S. officials believed that their country was acting in that spirit, and they often pointed to the short-lived plan to place atomic weapons and technology in the hands of the international community. At the president's behest, Undersecretary of State Dean Acheson and several advisors drew up a plan in March 1946 that called for an international Atomic Development Authority to monitor and control the new technology. Truman then assigned the aging financier Bernard Baruch to sell the idea to the world. Baruch's approach was clumsy, however, and he alarmed the Soviets by calling for enforcement mechanisms that would not be subject to the council veto. The plan died quietly at the end of 1946 after yet another Soviet veto in the council. The Soviets had fought hard for an expansive veto power and were not prepared to let it erode, certainly not on something as critical as atomic energy.[26]

The frequent early use of the veto by the Soviets was a rude shock to enthusiasts for international organization, and a few months into the council's life some were already calling for a renegotiation of the charter and a radical restructuring of the council. The president of the United World Federalists, an advocacy group, proposed that the council be stripped of the veto and placed under the ultimate authority of the General Assembly.[27] Many supporters of international organization became convinced that the charter had not gone far enough; it had placed too much authority in the hands of a great-power council that appeared to be paralyzed. The reality was sinking in that the council was nothing like an effective world government; it was a fraying collection of the great powers that had been given the power to govern. A *New Yorker* correspondent, attending one of the council's first sessions, wrote, "[T]here is no compromise, really, between government and non-government. No safe middle ground.... We are in mid-passage today, a tricky moment in time."[28]

Even as the hopes for substantive great-power cooperation dimmed, the Five worked to defend the prerogatives of the council and to make it a more comfortable place to work. In January 1947, the council established an interim administration for the disputed Adriatic city of Trieste. By council order, the city became the Free State of Trieste. The issue was little more than a footnote to great-power relations—and the arrangement ultimately broke down—but the council's move was nonetheless breathtaking. With a stroke of the pen, it created an international entity, endowed it with a constitution, and offered it physical protection. It was all too much for the Australian delegate to the council. Where, he demanded, did the council get the power to essentially administer a territory and provide it with a security guarantee, particularly when there was no breach of the peace?

It was a good question, but a hopeless battle. The Soviets and the Americans had reached a compromise on Trieste, and Australia's legalistic concerns were not going to get in the way. Rebuffing the Australian challenge, a U.S. diplomat offered an expansive interpretation of the council's reach. "Any spot on the surface of the earth where, for whatever reason, conflicts may break out and men may be at each other's throats is a spot of legitimate concern to the Security Council."[29] If the council wanted to take on additional powers, nothing could stop it. "The interpretation of the functions and powers of the Security Council," wrote a member of the Australian delegation resignedly, "was largely in the hands of the Council itself."[30]

The great powers also accorded themselves plenty of space in voting procedures. The UN Charter provided that valid resolutions required the "concurring" votes of the permanent members. During the San Francisco conference, several delegations asked whether the great powers could simply abstain from a vote if they chose. At the time, the Five demurred; they intended that the Five would have to vote for or against a resolution. But once the council began operating, it became evident that the right to abstain without vetoing could be quite useful. A few years into the council's operation, the right of abstention became accepted, although the practice was never codified.[31] The small states' criticism that abstaining allowed the Five to dodge their responsibilities could not compete with the great powers' desire for maximum flexibility.

Abdication in Palestine

On one critical issue, the status of Palestine, the council was united in its determination to evade responsibility. After the First World War, the British received a mandate from the League of Nations to administer the region, which was largely Arab but had a growing population of Jewish immigrants. As the holder of the mandate, Britain was squarely in the middle of competing Arab and Jewish claims to land and authority. The British made promises to both sides and, by the end of World War II, found themselves mediating an increasingly violent dispute with limited resources and political will. Jewish extremists targeted British forces, most dramatically by blowing up Jerusalem's King David Hotel in July 1946. Finally, in September 1947, Alexander Cadogan announced, "[W]e have tried for years to solve the problem of Palestine. Having failed so far, we now bring the Palestine question to the United Nations, in the hope that it can succeed where we have not."[32]

The Five wanted nothing to do with the crisis. They were not sharply divided on the issue, but they were distracted and wary of the costs that involvement would entail. The United States supported Jewish statehood but had no desire to police the conflict and few forces to spare as it rapidly downsized its military. The Soviet Union, which had leaned toward the Arabs for many years, reversed position in 1947 and signaled support for a Jewish state. The Soviet stance appears to have been based on the hope that partition would expedite the withdrawal of British forces, which was its overriding concern. Israel's generally socialist orientation may also have given Moscow hope that the new state would be ideologically friendly. But the Soviets had little desire to intervene, not that the West would have allowed that in any case. For its part, France was embroiled in domestic political turmoil. De Gaulle had resigned as president in 1946, and a succession of new leaders was struggling to compose a coherent foreign policy. France's suspicion of Arab nationalism, however, inclined it toward a sympathetic view of the Zionist claim. Chiang Kai-shek's government in China, busy combating Mao's surging Communist movement, was the least equipped for a strenuous peacemaking effort in the Middle East.

So the council shunted the dispute to the General Assembly, which in turn appointed a high-level commission composed of representatives from small and medium-sized countries. Palestine was the crisis that nobody wanted to touch. The organization's first secretary-general, Norwegian politician Trygve Lie, struggled to goad the council into a more activist stance. "You have a right to assume," he told the panel members, likely with more hope than confidence, that "the Security Council will not fail to exercise to the fullest, and without exception, every necessary power entrusted to it by the Charter in order to assist you in fulfilling your mission."[33]

In private meetings of the Five, the British refused even to opine on whether the dispute qualified as a "threat to the peace," the charter's key threshold for council action. "I wasn't hatched yesterday, and refused to answer," Cadogan wrote in his diary. "I'll give them all the information, and they must use their own judgment." When the Americans remonstrated with him two months later about the British abandonment of the dispute, he replied with a simple question: is the council ready to dispatch troops to police the dispute? "There you have me beat—we aren't," Warren Austin conceded.[34] And so the great powers continued their dance around the issue. In August 1947, after dozens of meetings in Palestine and months of deliberation, a divided committee proposed partitioning Palestine into separate Arab and Jewish states. The Jewish representatives quickly accepted the proposal, but the Arab states unanimously rejected it. On November 29, the General Assembly as a whole endorsed the partition resolution by a vote of 33–13.

Large-scale fighting and rioting broke out almost immediately in Palestine, and in March 1948 the council finally stirred from its lethargy and called weakly for an end to the fighting. The next month, it warned of the "heavy responsibility" that any party not observing a truce would bear, but it also insisted that the General Assembly still had responsibility for the crisis. It created a truce commission to travel to the region and report back to the council. But the pace of events was by now well beyond the United Nations' control. The Jewish authorities in Palestine declared independence on May 15. Without consulting the council or even close allies, President Truman quickly recognized the new state of Israel. Even the U.S. delegation at the United Nations was blindsided by the announcement, which set off pandemonium in the General Assembly.

Soviet policy on Palestine at this point began to diverge from the West's, and it abstained from most resolutions relating to the work of the ceasefire observers. The United Nations' designated mediator, the Swedish statesman Count Folke Bernadotte, found himself with little support or guidance from the council. "The United Nations showed itself from the worst side," he said in frustration. "Even the most trivial decisions with regard to measures designed to lend force to its words were dependent on the political calculations of the Great Powers."[35] On September 17, Bernadotte was assassinated in Jerusalem by Jewish extremists. His successor, the American Ralph Bunche, managed to patch together a cease-fire, but the underlying dispute was left unresolved. Bernadotte and Bunche were the first of many generations of mediators who would try their hand at the crisis.

The young council failed miserably on Palestine. It shied away from the hard diplomatic work needed to prevent conflict, instead delegating the task to a committee of weak states. When fighting did break out, the council proved to be unable to impose its will. The 1948 war ended because Israel defeated its enemies, not because of the council's pleas for peace. For the United Nations' many devoted supporters, the council's evasion of its responsibilities was the latest sign that the major powers—including the United States—were crippling what might have been a powerful international organization. Leading American supporters of the United Nations had watched with mixed feelings in 1947 and early 1948 as the Truman administration announced huge aid packages to Greece and Turkey, which were battling Communist uprisings, and launched the Marshall Plan to aid Western Europe, all without consulting the Security Council or the General Assembly.

After the Palestine failure, the leaders of the American Association for the United Nations, an influential advocacy group, penned an angry letter accusing the Truman administration of treating the United Nations as "an instrument of policy—indeed, an instrument of power politics—to be used when convenient, and to be ignored or misused when convenient."[36] Eleanor Roosevelt, who was serving as an American delegate to the United Nations on human rights issues, complained to Secretary of State George C. Marshall that "in every possible way the United States is acting to hurt the United Nations and to act on a unilateral basis."[37] The Mideast crisis was particularly dispiriting for UN enthusiasts because the organization's failure appeared to be the result not of Cold War acrimony so much as diplomatic negligence and lack of political will. If this was how the council operated when it was not split along ideological lines, what possible use could it be in a crisis that might pit the two sides of the Cold War directly against each other?

Blockades and Openings

On June 2, 1948, Harry Franklin was shopping in the Soviet-administered zone of Berlin. An American serving with the Allied occupation authorities, Franklin was looking for a store that could repair a small motion-picture projector he owned. Suddenly, he found himself surrounded by armed Soviet soldiers, who demanded to see his identification documents. Not satisfied by the papers he produced, they hustled him off to a detention center, where he remained for sixteen hours. The news of his seizure rippled through the city, which was quickly turning into the world's most dangerous Cold War flashpoint.

Berlin sat more than a hundred miles inside the Soviet occupation zone. As the German capital, however, it had a special status; each Allied power had its own occupation zone in the city. Geography alone ensured that Berlin would be a sensitive barometer of East-West tension. For months, efforts by the Allies to coordinate the occupation of Germany had been stumbling badly. The Soviets had rejected Western efforts to unite their occupation zones economically and to introduce a new currency. By the summer of 1948, those issues were coming to a head. A meeting of the Allied occupation officials to hash out their differences ended in acrimony on June 16. Then, in the early morning hours of June 24, the lines carrying electricity from power plants in East Berlin to the West went dead. Dozens of extra Soviet border guards appeared at checkpoints leading into and out of the Western zone. Soviet soldiers demanded the right to stop and inspect trains heading toward Berlin from the West. West Berlin and its more than 2 million inhabitants could not last long without outside supplies. American and British generals hastily crafted a solution: they would supply the city with food by air for as long as they could. Meanwhile, General Lucius Clay, the American commander in Berlin, began preparing plans for an armed convoy to force through supplies by land.

Throughout the tense summer, the Western powers debated whether to bring the Berlin issue to the Security Council. Doing so, they realized, would destroy the last vestiges of the wartime alliance; it would also signal a complete failure of the mechanisms set up for administering Germany jointly. The British were hesitant. Bevin, in particular, wondered what good could come of putting the crisis on the council's agenda.[38] But he eventually yielded to the American desire for a dramatic public gesture. In late September, the United States, Britain, and France jointly accused the Soviets of threatening the Berlin population with "starvation, disease, and economic ruin."[39] The blockade, they said, was a breach of the peace and properly within the council's domain.

By the time the crisis came before the council, the body had moved to France for an agreed-upon temporary session. The United Nations' sojourn to Paris dramatized the country's recovery from occupation and its return to great-power status. It also had the effect, as the *New York Times* noted, of placing the council "nearer the center of the world's heightening tension."[40] On October 4, 1948, the council met to debate whether it could consider the Berlin crisis. The Soviet position was firm: the Berlin crisis should be handled through direct negotiations between the occupying powers; the council itself had no role. Andrei Vishinsky was in fine form for the debate. His long speech was punctuated by arm waving and laced with sarcasm. "Gentlemen," he said at one point, "you have come to the wrong address. If you do not mind, please address your complaint to the legal organ which was established under the agreement which you honored with your own signature." The speech was crafted well in advance, but improvisation was not beyond Vishinsky's power. At one point, he noticed that the Syrian delegate had fallen asleep. "I wish the distinguished delegate of Syria the best of health, if he could hear me. I beg his pardon for disturbing him, but I cannot do otherwise." With a nudge, the French ambassador roused the slumbering diplomat.[41]

Responsibility for responding to Vishinsky's barbs fell to Philip Jessup, a Columbia University law professor who was then serving as Warren Austin's deputy. The council's Berlin debate was his most public performance. The question, said Jessup, is whether "the only existing general international machinery for the preservation of peace can be used to remove a threat to the peace, or whether the Government of the USSR contends that the world be thrown back upon an unorganized international community with all that that implies."[42] Finally, after long and angry filibustering by Vishinsky, the council voted 9-2 to put Berlin on the agenda. The Western powers had made their point: the Berlin crisis was a threat to international peace, and the Security Council was the right place to debate it. The vote was a propaganda victory for the West, but it did nothing to alter Berlin's plight. The Soviets were convinced that the city would fold, and they were willing to endure public opprobrium for what appeared to be a certain victory.

To the astonishment of the Soviets—and many in the West—the airlift grew into an unprecedented operation that managed to bring in not only food but also almost everything else the city needed. By winter, planes were landing or taking off every ninety seconds in Berlin, ferrying more than 4,500 tons of vital supplies a day. Everything that could fit in the hold of a cargo plane was sent, from electrical generators to coal stuffed into canvas duffel bags. The danger of open confrontation with the Soviets was always high. Soviet fighter planes sometimes crossed through Berlin's airspace, perilously close to transports. Western pilots buzzed Soviet bases on more than a few occasions. But what had appeared to be an inevitable defeat for the West was now becoming a debacle for the Soviet Union. The blockade was simultaneously demonstrating Soviet political ruthlessness and Western military prowess. It was enough to convince undecided governments and populations in Europe to side with the West.

The persistent danger of confrontation and the daily humiliation of the Soviets pushed Stalin to seek a way out. The opening came in January 1949, when he responded to questions by the Associated Press and did not mention the issue that had ostensibly begun the crisis—the Western plan to unite the currencies in their zones of occupation. The Sovietologists in the State Department brought the interview to the attention of U.S. secretary of state Dean Acheson. After conferring with Truman, Acheson decided that Jessup should sound out his new Soviet counterpart on the Security Council, a young diplomat named Yakov Malik. Acheson saw the informality of an interaction in New York as a significant advantage.

> We concluded that a highly secret, casual approach to the Russians could better be made by Jessup at the United Nations than through the embassy in Moscow or by the [State] Department to the Russian Embassy. Fewer persons would be involved and those who were—Philip Jessup and Soviet ambassador to the United Nations [Yakov] Malik—could act [in] purely unofficial and personal capacities.[43]

On February 15, Philip Jessup loitered near the entrance to the Security Council chamber until he spotted Malik. After some talk about the weather, the American casually asked whether Stalin's failure to mention the currency issue was intentional. Malik said he had no idea. If the Soviet did find out, Jessup suggested, he would be most interested in knowing.[44] Malik called a month later and asked Jessup to meet. The next day, the American slipped into the house on the corner of Park Avenue and Sixty-eighth Street that held the Soviet mission to the United Nations. The two diplomats sat at a small table with an interpreter between them. Stalin's omission, Malik reported, was not accidental. It was the signal Jessup needed. After the meeting, he and a small State Department team began crafting a strategy for exploiting the opening. A week later, Jessup briefed the British and French UN representatives, Alexander Cadogan and Jean Chauvel, on the negotiations. For the next six weeks, Jessup and his Security Council counterparts were at the center of complicated secret diplomacy to end the crisis.

Finally, at one minute after midnight on May 12, guards on the autobahn leading into Berlin swung open a gate that had been closed for more than 300 days. Within hours, trains began arriving in the city, and electricity started flowing from the East to West Berlin again. The blockade had ended. The council—or at least the diplomatic space around it—had allowed the superpowers to creep back from the edge of conflict. "The electric tension that the Berlin Blockade generated between two non-negotiating worlds was very great," Trygve Lie reflected later. "Had there been no United Nations, it might have been so great that the electricity would have shot across the gap, setting both sides afire."[45]

Anyone who had hoped that the end of the blockade would signal a new modus vivendi was quickly disappointed. After the Berlin crisis, relations on the council became even stormier. The Soviets staged another prolonged walkout, this time over the issue of who should hold the Chinese seat. In the two years after the charter was signed, the resurgent Chinese Communists had forced Chiang Kai-shek's nationalists into a shrinking swathe of the mainland. For several months, the nationalists held out in Chungking, but that city fell in December 1949. Chiang fled the mainland by aircraft and landed on the island of Taiwan, where his supporters had prepared for a government-in-exile. There, he began hatching increasingly desperate plans to retake the mainland.

The United States insisted that the Kuomintang authorities on Taiwan remained China's legitimate representatives. The mainland might have been lost, but the seat at the Security Council still belonged to Chiang. It was a position that grew more strained as Communist control solidified. The United States might not like Communist China, but what purpose was there in denying its existence? "It was *China*, not Chiang Kai-shek, that belonged to the United Nations," wrote Trygve Lie in frustration.[46] For the Soviets, Taiwan's hold on the Chinese seat signaled that the West was hijacking the council. On January 10, 1950, Malik informed the council that unless the Communist authorities in Beijing took over the seat, the Soviets would boycott the council. The Soviet challenge produced a direct confrontation between Malik and T. F. Tsiang, the Chinese nationalist representative serving as president of the council in January. When Tsiang tried to rule on a Soviet motion, Malik quickly fired back. "I object to any ruling given by a person who does not represent anyone here."[47] A few moments later, Malik left the chamber.

The Soviets made clear that they would consider any decisions taken without them as illegitimate and any meeting without Soviet representation as "a parody of a meeting."[48] From the perspective of formal council precedent, it was not a strong case. The Soviets had already agreed that abstentions by the permanent members should not constitute vetoes. Why should a voluntary absence be any different? But those who remembered the travails of the League of Nations must have sensed that history was repeating itself. Great powers then had deserted the league's council when they found themselves outnumbered or criticized. As the weeks passed, the Soviets appeared to be on the brink of making their boycott permanent. Moscow even established an organization, the World Peace Council, which seemed designed to compete with the United Nations. For Stalin, "the risk of the Soviets' absence was less than the strategic advantages of stressing the Sino-Soviet alliance and unmasking the United Nations as a 'voting machine' obedient to America."[49] Yakov Malik was spotted around New York, but he never entered the council chamber. As spring turned to summer, the Soviet seat at the table remained empty.

The Council Goes to War

John Hickerson, a U.S. assistant secretary of state, took a phone call at home on the night of June 24, 1950. Accustomed to late night summonses, he instinctively grabbed his car keys as he answered. It was the State Department's East Asia desk officer. "There's a development and I think that you would want to come in right away," he said. "I can't discuss it on the telephone." As Hickerson sped through Rock Creek Park on his way to the State Department, he tried to guess what had happened. He and his colleagues had been speculating for months about where the Soviets would make their next move; there were plenty of places around the periphery of the new Soviet sphere that they might seek to test. Given that the call had come from an Asian-desk officer, he concluded that Communist China must have invaded Taiwan.[50]

When he arrived at the department, he instead heard fragmentary but alarming reports about a full-scale North Korean push into South Korea. At about 4:00 in the morning, northern mortars had opened fire on the South Korean defenses near the Thirty-eighth Parallel, which divided the Communist North from the pro-Western South. Some reports said that planes had bombed sites near Seoul, the capital of South Korea. It was clear that the southern forces were in full retreat. The rapidly assembling team at the State Department that night got word to Secretary of State Dean Acheson, who in turn called Truman at his family home in Missouri. Acheson and his team had one immediate recommendation for the president: call a meeting of the council. The attack was a clear case of aggression; it was the very scenario the council had been designed to confront. Truman endorsed the plan without hesitation.

Hickerson and his team worked the phones most of the night. They tracked down Ernest Gross, the experienced U.S. point man on the council, and instructed him to prepare for a meeting the next day. By early Sunday afternoon, the U.S. team was ready with a resolution that condemned the invasion, called for North Korean forces to retreat immediately, and requested that all UN member states support the organization in its effort to resolve the crisis. One question remained: would the Soviets show up at the meeting to veto the draft resolution?[51]

The council's president gaveled the meeting to order that Sunday afternoon. No Soviet representative appeared. Secretary-General Trygve Lie spoke first. "The present situation is a threat to international peace," he said. "I consider it the clear duty of the Security Council to deal with it." Gross followed him. "Such an attack," he said, "strikes at the fundamental purposes of the United Nations Charter." South Korea's ambassador made a direct plea to the council members. "We owe our existence to the United Nations," he said. "I trust that the Security

Council, which is charged with the primary responsibility for the maintenance of peace, will not fail in this imperative duty."[52]

The other council members endorsed that view, although the Egyptian representative could not help but draw an invidious parallel.

It is exhilarating to note the energetic attitude which the Security Council appears to be taking, and which is in contrast to previous laxities and delays in relation to several earlier cases, including, most conspicuously, that of the savage and premeditated attack of world political Zionism against the still bleeding lawful people of Palestine.[53]

With little further delay, the council adopted a resolution calling for an immediate ceasefire. Only Yugoslavia abstained; its ambassador could not be found and his deputy feared voting one way or the other.

Why did the Soviets stay away? Many U.S. officials believed that the Soviet team in New York—like all Soviet diplomats, they were utterly dependent on precise orders from Moscow—was simply unable to react quickly enough.[54] The Soviets may have been caught off guard by the vigorous American response, particularly in light of U.S. willingness to let Chiang Kai-shek's forces in China collapse without intervening. Why would the United States now fight so ferociously for a weak South Korean government? The Soviets had expected the United States to cut its losses; instead, the Americans had upped the ante.[55] By boycotting the council, Stalin had hoped to delegitimize an institution that the Soviets found consistently hostile to their interests. Instead, he freed the council to act and in so doing bolstered flagging Western confidence in the body.

Whatever the calculations that kept Malik out of his seat, the course was set for the Security Council's first war against aggression. Without the Soviets, the council passed a series of resolutions setting up a military command to support the South Koreans. General Douglas MacArthur, already in Japan managing the occupation, was designated as the American commander. The first American troops landed in Korea on July 1 and engaged the oncoming North Korean tanks a few days later.[56] The British and French, relieved that American isolationism had yielded fully to its desire to contain Communism, were determined to support their powerful ally. Chiang Kai-shek's Chinese delegation, meanwhile, was overjoyed. They saw an Asian war against Communism as their best hope of retaking the mainland.

For several critical weeks, the Western powers had the run of the council. The Five had become four, and they were working together to repel an act of aggression. The Soviets, for their part, maintained an unusual silence. Ernest Gross encountered Malik at a luncheon just two days after the invasion. When pressed about the Korean situation, he maintained that the South had actually provoked the conflict. He gave no indication that he would return to the council, and he told American officials that he planned to leave for the Soviet Union in early July.[57]

One of the few hints of discord in the war's early days was between Britain and the United States over whether to try to lure Communist China into the council's deliberations on the crisis. In early July 1950, Dean Acheson and Ernest Bevin exchanged a series of messages on whether it was advisable to negotiate China's seating on the council and the Soviet Union's return. The British believed that having the Communist giants at the table might prevent a wider conflict, even if it complicated the council's immediate deliberations. Worse, continued ostracizing might push Beijing further into Moscow's camp. "If China continues to be excluded from the United Nations," wrote Bevin, "and if the attitude of the West continues to be coldly hostile, must she not come to the conclusion, even when the moment arrives when she would like to move [a]way from Moscow, that she has no other course but to maintain her association?" To Acheson, the idea smacked of appeasement.[58] He drafted a sharp reply to Bevin that made clear that the United States was not willing to discuss China's UN status in the midst of a fight against Communist aggression in Korea.

The Americans saw the council as a powerful tool for legitimizing an essential fight; the British and others wanted to preserve its utility as a diplomatic space, and they were willing to risk its unanimity to do so. It was a notable example of a recurring tension for the council between preserving the ability to act and keeping all of the great powers together in the room. The British had made their point, but the American view prevailed. The Communist Chinese government had no representative at the United Nations during the war.

Sir Gladwyn to the Rescue

On the afternoon of August 1, 1950, the council chamber was buzzing with anticipation. A few days earlier, the Soviet Union had informed UN officials that it intended to take its seat again in August, just as it was scheduled to begin its month as council president. The media anticipated an epic clash between the Soviet representative and his Western counterparts. When word broke that the Soviets would return, callers flooded the United Nations' admission office for tickets.[59] Malik faced an angry and unified council, most of whose members believed that the Soviets had at least tacitly approved the North Korean invasion. Gaveling the session to order in front of a packed gallery, Malik began on the offense. "Before we proceed to the consideration of the agenda, I wish, as President, to make a ruling that the representative of the Kuomintang group seated in the Security Council does not represent China and cannot therefore take part in the meetings of the Security Council."[60] The three Western ambassadors objected that the decision on China's representative was one for the council as a whole, not the president.

Still, Malik continued his assault, and he quickly melded the China question into an attack on the United Nations' war in Korea. "The Soviet Union is consistently pursuing a policy of peace and regards the United Nations as an instrument of peace and not as a weapon of war, into which the new pretenders to world domination—the governing circles of the United States—are trying to transform this international organization."[61] When the time came to vote on the motion, Malik was easily overruled, 8–3. The Soviet conceded defeat, but not without a sly parting shot. "The results of the voting are as follows: seven against the President's ruling and three in favor of the ruling. I am not counting the vote of the representative of the Kuomintang group."[62]

Throughout the meeting, the Soviet issued a dizzying array of jibes and outlandish provocations. The Korean War, he charged, was not a war of self-defense but an act of aggression by the United States. "It is appropriate to ask the representative of the United States who is to blame for the tragic fate of many thousands of Korean mothers, children and old people, who have lost their nearest and dearest. The culprits are the ruling circles of the United States."[63] When Warren Austin or Gladwyn Jebb responded, the council gallery sometimes broke into cheers, and Malik ordered silence.[64] The British ambassador mocked the Soviet attempt to portray the conflict as a case of American aggression. "We really do seem to be living in a rather nightmarish *Alice in Wonderland* world."[65]

As Jebb tangled with Malik over the next several weeks, the British diplomat, who was accustomed to working behind the scenes, became a bona fide American celebrity. During the early days of the war, council meetings were carried live on television and radio in much of the United States, and Jebb's skewering of Malik, often in direct defense of the United States, made a vivid impression. "Imperialist powers, good gracious me!" he exclaimed at one point.

> Are we really to believe that the boys from Iowa or Colorado who are now sitting in foxholes near Chingju doing their best to defend democracy as they know it, and longing for the day when they will get back to Denver or Sioux City, are we really to believe that these people are out, like Genghis Khan, to enslave the world? If the President [Malik] will show me any one of these United States soldiers who would rather reign in Outer Mongolia than go back to Seattle, I shall gladly concede his point about "imperialist America." Until then, no: I prefer to rely not on Marx, but on the judgment of my own eyes and ears.[66]

"Point of order, Sir Gladwyn. Dinner's ready."

FIGURE 2.3. A *New Yorker* cartoon from 1950 referring to Gladwyn Jebb's rhetoric in the council.

Fan mail poured into the British delegation's offices. Admirers stopped Jebb on the street and in restaurants. He was even the subject of a flattering cartoon in the *New Yorker* that depicted a man glued to the televised council debate. "Point of order, Sir Gladwyn," his wife calls from the kitchen. "It's time for dinner."[67] The rumor circulated within the Foreign Office that Jebb regularly checked his ratings on American television and became grumpy when they slipped.[68]

Privately, the British diplomat was not above complaining about the inability of America's aging ambassador, Warren Austin, to pull his weight. After watching Austin lose his temper with a Norwegian diplomat over an inconsequential detail, an alarmed Jebb cabled London.

I really have not had enough experience to know whether all this simply means that the old fellow is losing his grip or whether there is anything sinister in his antics. The point of this letter, however, is to ask you in confidence whether you have any indication that there is any feeling in Washington that he is past his job and whether it is conceivable that we may be able to get some American representative who is not quite so ludicrous in the future?[69]

However formidable Jebb's debating skills, they could not undo the council's deadlock. With Malik wielding the veto, the body could not pass new resolutions nor effectively manage the conduct of the military effort it had launched. In military terms, the council's paralysis mattered little. MacArthur's Korean command did not need further instructions from New York (indeed, the supremely confident MacArthur seemed not even to require orders from Washington). But at a political level, the council's descent into bitter paralysis was problematic. If this was a war by and for the United Nations, the organization had to be able to express its continued support for the effort.

The solution, hit upon by the U.S. State Department, was to bypass the paralyzed council and resort to the General Assembly. There was no veto in the assembly, and its larger membership was solidly on the side of South Korea and the United States. The Americans were effectively proposing to do what the rebels at the San Francisco conference had failed to do: curb the power of the council and give the assembly a meaningful role in international security. Creative lawyers at the State Department went to work and came up with the Uniting for Peace resolution, which would grant the assembly the power to take up a threat to the peace when the veto prevented the council from doing so.[70] Acheson formally proposed the idea to the General Assembly in late September.

It was a risky strategy. Not only was the maneuver a dubious reading of the charter, but handing the General Assembly a major role in security issues could easily backfire. The British interceded with the Americans to try to prevent them from formally bypassing the council, but the United States was determined to seize the advantage that its strong majority in the assembly offered. As Dean Acheson wrote later, "[P]resent difficulties outweighed possible future ones."[71]

The Uniting for Peace resolution was a stunning rejection of the principle of great-power unanimity. "If the Security Council, because of lack of unanimity of the permanent members, fails to exercise its primary responsibility for the maintenance of international peace and security," the resolution read, "the General Assembly shall consider the matter immediately."[72] For almost three years, as war raged on the Korean peninsula, the General Assembly rather than the Security Council was the war's international nerve center.[73]

At first, the detour around the council worked well for the Americans. The General Assembly condemned North Korea and threw its support behind the American-led response. It established a committee to coordinate the offers of assistance from member states. In the end, fifteen countries, including Britain, Australia, the Philippines, and France, committed combat troops, and many more provided other types of material assistance to the war effort. On the battlefield, too, the United Nations' first war showed dramatic progress. On September 15, MacArthur staged his daring landing at Inchon, well north of the frontlines. Within days, North Korean forces were in full retreat, and it appeared that a dramatic victory for the UN forces was imminent. In early October, the General Assembly endorsed the advance of UN troops into North Korean territory and called for UN forces to achieve stability "throughout Korea."[74] Soviet diplomats at the United Nations signaled to their American colleagues that they were interested in direct talks, perhaps a reprise of the Jessup-Malik talks that had ended the Berlin blockade.[75]

As MacArthur pushed north, however, his troops began to encounter units of Chinese soldiers engaged in active combat. A few diplomatic sources reported that Communist China was alarmed at the rapid collapse of North Korea and was considering even more aggressive intervention. Still, the UN forces under MacArthur plunged ahead. In late November, thousands of Chinese troops poured across the Yalu River and into North Korea. The troops—"volunteers," the Chinese authorities called them—were often ill equipped and poorly trained, but their numbers were overwhelming. A decisive UN victory against aggression was turning into an unpredictable war that was pitting Chinese forces—with Soviet support—directly against the Americans.

The General Assembly, which had been so supportive of American leadership, began to show signs of doubt. MacArthur's abrasive style and unwillingness to compromise had already irritated smaller states at the United Nations, several of which had troops serving in Korea. As bad news filtered in from the battlefield, irritation turned to anger and alarm. India, a leading independent power, became especially suspicious of American leadership and determined to chart an independent course.[76] American diplomats came to dread interactions with Krishna Menon, India's top man in New York. The United States never lost its majority in the assembly, but it had lost some of its diplomatic self-assurance. Increasing criticism of U.S. policy brought angry reactions. Some conservative critics of the Truman administration wondered aloud whether keeping the war within the UN framework made sense any longer. With Americans and South Koreans doing most of the fighting and dying, why exactly should the United States listen to the likes of India? Diplomacy in the General Assembly was messier than the Americans had anticipated.

The assembly sessions allowed dozens of small states to debate Korea policy. Indeed, the one country that had almost no say in New York was Communist China. Not until November 1950 were its representatives even invited to address the council. Even that limited gesture occasioned a diplomatic battle. After a week of maneuvering, the United States and Taiwan lost their fight against extending the invitation. Britain, France, and several nonpermanent members parted ways with the Americans. The result outraged Taiwan's ambassador, who insisted that his veto power applied to the question. That argument was a step too far for the United States, which wanted to preserve its record of never having exercised the veto, a feat that could be used to bludgeon the Soviets. That calculation put the American representative, Ernest Gross, in the odd position of arguing in favor of being outvoted. The U.S. willingness to accept a tactical defeat won plaudits from Gladwyn Jebb. "The spectacle of a great power willingly subscribing to a ruling of the [council] president on a matter concerning the veto, even though by so doing it is…going against its own immediate interests, is at once heartening and inspiring."[77]

The Chinese accepted the invitation, and a nine-member delegation arrived in New York in late November.[78] It was a critical opportunity for dialogue. Shortly after the delegation arrived, General MacArthur cabled the Joint Chiefs of Staff with the alarming news of large-scale Chinese troop movements. "We face an entirely new war," he wrote.[79] But the Chinese visit appeared to be an act of protest rather than an exercise in diplomacy. The formal Chinese speech to the council gave no hint of accommodation. "I am here in the name of the 475 million people of China," Wu Hsui-chuan began, "to accuse the United States government of the unlawful and criminal act of aggression." He quickly moved to attack the nationalist Chinese. "I once more demand that the United Nations expel the so-called delegates of the Kuomintang reactionary remnant clique and admit the lawful delegates of the People's Republic of China."[80] The harsh speech did little to help the PRC's cause and nothing to advance compromise on the Korean conflict. Informal approaches to the Chinese had little success. British and Indian diplomats reported that the Chinese delegation was closely watched by Eastern European "bodyguards" and that access to them was restricted.[81] When the secretary-general and other diplomats did manage to speak with the Chinese, they found them resistant to any compromise. "[I]f the People's Republic had deliberately set out to antagonise the United Nations as a whole it could not have done any better than it did," a UN correspondent recalled.[82]

Would the course of the Korean War have been different if China had easier access to—or even a place inside—the council's charmed circle? Precisely what triggered China's intervention is still a matter of debate, but there is substantial evidence that miscommunication played a role. MacArthur and the U.S. leadership did not understand that their advance up the peninsula was alarming the Chinese, who may have thought that UN forces had designs on Chinese territory or that UN forces were preparing to unseat the Chinese regime altogether. In the weeks before their intervention, the Chinese attempted several backchannel communications to warn the United Nations of their willingness to intervene, but they were downplayed or disregarded.[83] China's limited access to the building made the kind of quiet diplomacy that Malik and Jessup had conducted during the Berlin crisis nearly impossible.

Instead, the conflict ended when both sides realized that total victory would cost too much. After months of bloody defensive fighting, the UN forces managed to stop the Chinese and North Korean advance in early 1951. American warplanes pounded Chinese supply lines, and cold weather took its toll on the ill-equipped Chinese. The UN forces again began to crawl their way back up the peninsula, and by the spring of 1951 they had reached the Thirty-eighth Parallel again. It was a logical point for the exhausted adversaries to cease their fire, and after nearly two years of costly but inconclusive battles, they finally did. The council's first war had reversed North Korean aggression, but it had also badly strained the institution and frayed relations not only within the council but also within the broad American-led coalition.

"A Theater or a Room?"

The latter half of the Korean War was accompanied by significant changes in the setting in which the council operated. In mid-May 1951, the United Nations began moving from its temporary quarters at Lake Success to its brand-new midtown Manhattan headquarters on the East River. It had not been a given that the United Nations would find a home in the heart of the city. For much of 1946, the United Nations' search committee had focused on suburban spots in Westchester or Fairfield counties, where land was plentiful and the organization would not have to battle city life. Philadelphia and San Francisco were still in the running, although their candidacies were fading.

In late 1946, real estate developer William Zeckendorf realized that land he had bought during the war along the East River might be just the spot the United Nations needed. The land, running from Forty-second Street to Forty-seventh Street, was occupied mainly by loud and smelly slaughterhouses, but Zeckendorf had grand plans for a condominium project. When he read a news story detailing the United Nations' struggles to find a permanent home, however, he impulsively offered the organization the land at the low rate of $8.5 million. Even that price was too steep, however, and the prospect of a Manhattan home might have slipped away but for the intervention of one of America's most powerful families. The Rockefellers hurriedly took out an option on the land and then donated $8.5 million to the United Nations for it to buy the riverside plot.

With the site at last chosen, the task became designing the headquarters, and a multinational team of architects was assembled. Led by Wallace K. Harrison, the team worked intensively for several months out of temporary offices in Rockefeller Plaza, a building Harrison had designed. The American architect Louis Skidmore, who had designed several major housing projects during the war, joined Harrison's team. From France came the opinionated and mercurial Charles-Edouard Le Corbusier. A young Brazilian architect, Oscar Niemeyer—a former student of Le Corbusier—arrived with limited English but plenty of innovative ideas. The Soviet Union dispatched Nikolai Bassov, who had achieved fame in Russia by relocating whole factories eastward during the war. From the United Kingdom came Sir Howard Robertson. Other architects arrived from Belgium, China, Uruguay, and Sweden.

Harrison instilled a sense of urgency in the group. "The sooner [the] UN settles down for good, the more people will be willing to believe in it," he said. "An international organization is like everybody else. It won't feel secure until it has a roof over its head."[84] A basic plan soon emerged. The centerpiece of the headquarters would be a modern forty-story tower for the organization's permanent Secretariat. A low-slung building connected to the Secretariat tower would house the Security Council, the Trusteeship Council, the Economic and Social Council, and a series of conference rooms. Most plans envisioned another separate wing for the General Assembly. But little else was clear, and as they sketched designs the architects encountered delicate political questions. "Is the Security Council the head or is the General Assembly?" Harrison asked at one meeting.[85] In search of advice, the team traveled to Lake Success for meetings with UN officials. "In practical terms, the Security Council is undoubtedly the most important," they were told. "It meets constantly, with two or three hundred in attendance and full press coverage. However, while the Assembly meets only twice a year, it is symbolically the most important organ."[86]

The final design reflected that judgment. The General Assembly's chamber dominated the view from First Avenue and was the first thing that visitors encountered when they entered the complex from the main Forty-eighth Street portal. The wing that housed the council chamber was barely visible, except from the East River itself. The assembly was the organization's public face, the council its inner sanctum. Designing the interior of the council chamber produced its own dilemmas, which the architects debated.

HARRISON: Should the public be in the same room with the members, seated at the table, or should there be glass separating them? Seats for the Public can be anywhere around the Council, but they shouldn't surround it; that would give it the air of a theater. It wouldn't be dignified enough. All their action would seem to be on a lower level.

LE CORBUSIER: But in the Security Council decisions must be made before
                public opinion!
HARRISON: The [council ambassadors] are the important ones, not the
                public that's watching them—a sort of audience in their
                Council room.
ROBERTSON: A glass wall between them would reduce the theatrical
                impression....
LE CORBUSIER: But the U.N. may want public opinion represented....
SKIDMORE: It's bad to separate the Public from the Council.
BASSOV: It would be unpleasant for the Delegates to have the Public
                behind glass. Could you have invisible glass?
HARRISON: Is it a theater or a room? It would be better to have the
                Delegates work with the Public on each side.[87]

At another point, the architects debated whether the council table should be surrounded by observers—a design referred to as the "bear pit"—or whether one wall of the chamber should be left empty, perhaps with windows opening onto the East River. Bassov, the Russian, hated the idea of the bear pit. "[It] reminds me too much of a circus," he exclaimed. "See the animals! See the people! The table is the ring!"[88]

In the end, the team decided against a glass partition and against the bear pit. They settled on a chamber 24 feet high, 135 feet long, and 72 feet wide. The main floor of the chamber featured the council's horseshoe table, with a sunken area in the center of the table for stenographers and secretaries. A ring of seats for delegates and a few advisors circled the table. More seats along both sides of the chamber were for diplomats not serving on the council. Rising along the north and south walls were glass-enclosed booths for simultaneous translators and the media. An elevated public gallery looked down on the chamber and out toward the East River, which would be visible through two large windows.

As construction proceeded, most UN members offered some contribution to the new building in the form of furnishings or artwork, and competition sometimes became intense. British civil servants worried about the quality of the wood paneling that the United Kingdom was considering installing in one of the headquarters' many conference rooms. "Quite a lot of other countries are planning to undertake paneling as their contribution to the new building," a Foreign Office memorandum warned, "and if our contribution is going to be paneling too, I think, from a prestige point of view, it is important that the paneling should not be less in extent nor inferior in quality and workmanship, to that given by countries such as Norway, Sweden, Australia and New Zealand."[89]

FIGURE 2.4. Workers rest during the construction of the Security Council chamber.

FIGURE 2.5. The completed council chamber during a session in April 1954.

Norway, home to Secretary-General Trygve Lie, sought and won the honor of decorating the council's chamber. The Norwegian government commissioned noted architect Arnstein Arneberg to design and furnish the interior of the chamber. For acoustic reasons, the team covered portions of the walls in material woven with pure Norwegian wool, dyed blue and gold. They covered the walls in the public gallery overlooking the chamber with a special straw material from the town of Biri. Blue-and-yellow drapes were fashioned for the large windows that looked out on the East River. Between those windows was room for a huge mural that had been commissioned.

The first meeting in the new chamber was on April 4, 1952, and a complaint against France for its behavior in Tunisia was on the agenda. The packed crowd paid almost as much attention to the room as it did to the proceedings.[90] In September, the sixteen- by twenty-six-foot mural for the east wall of the chamber arrived. The work of Norwegian artist Per Krohg, it featured scenes of humanity pulling itself out of war and misery and climbing toward productive harmony. An image of a rising phoenix was the centerpiece. It received mixed reviews. The *Los Angeles Times* called it "imaginative."[91] A BBC correspondent was less charitable, describing it as "the world's worst mural, at which I have sat and gazed for many bewildering hours."[92]

The organization's political atmosphere changed dramatically during the Korean War as well. In November 1952, Trygve Lie reluctantly departed. Soviet outrage over the secretary-general's support for the UN response in Korea had rendered his position almost untenable. So even as they exchanged bitter accusations in the council, the Five sat down to select a new leader for the organization. The representatives met for hours in a conference room. Votes were scribbled on pieces of paper, which were then burned.[93] Most names, including that of Canada's Lester Pearson, went up in smoke. Finally, the council settled on Dag Hammarskjöld, a respected Swedish diplomat almost unknown outside diplomatic circles. His low profile—and Sweden's neutrality—made him politically palatable.

As important as the change in UN leadership was the death of Josef Stalin, just two months before the Korean armistice. The troika of Soviet leaders who took his place—Nikita Khrushchev, Georgi Malenkov, and Molotov—soon moderated the tone of Soviet diplomacy. More charm and less bluster were the order of the day. Vishinsky died in 1954 and was replaced by Arkady Sobolev, the same diplomat who had teamed up with Leo Pasvolsky so effectively at the San Francisco conference. Sobolev was comfortable speaking English, knew the United Nations well, and generally eschewed the fireworks that Vishinsky had favored. The State Department, which had been drafting a no-holds-barred speech decrying Soviet tactics at the United Nations, decided to hold its fire.[94]

More was at work in the Soviet shift than a desire to improve the atmosphere. By the mid-1950s, the Soviets realized that rapid decolonization was about to produce a slew of new member states from Africa and Asia, many of which harbored deep suspicions of the West. In 1955, Khrushchev and Nikolai Bulganin, who had replaced Malenkov, made a whirlwind tour of India, Afghanistan, and Burma, showering the region with Soviet largesse and anticolonial rhetoric. If states like these could be lured away from the West, Soviet leaders realized, the United Nations might actually be turned into an asset.

Friends and Enemies

The U.S. Central Intelligence Agency's machinations in Guatemala provided an early opportunity for the Soviets to test the council's utility as a forum for condemning what it saw as American neocolonialism. In 1953, a shadowy and, it later became clear, U.S.-trained and -funded exile group emerged and began military and propaganda operations against the government of Jacobo Arbenz Guzmán. The leftist tilt of the Arbenz government worried the Eisenhower administration, which authorized a covert campaign to force it from power. In June 1954, Guatemala requested an emergency meeting of the council. The Guatemalan ambassador laid out the charges: U.S.-made planes had bombed several sites and armed infiltrators had sought to sow chaos. The ambassador suggested, without directly stating, that the U.S. government was behind the attacks.

The American strategy on the council was to deploy its many Latin American allies as a shield, and the new American ambassador, Henry Cabot Lodge, served as the field general. Lodge had arrived at the United Nations in 1952, shortly after he lost his Senate seat to John F. Kennedy. The son of a powerful senator and the scion of an influential family, Lodge had a national profile and was popular with his Security Council colleagues. He spoke good French and could parry the Soviets without losing his cool. In televised debates, his easy manner came across well, and he had a quick wit. Chairing the council on one occasion, he slipped from UN-speak into the idiom of the Senate. "For what purpose does the gentleman seek recognition," Lodge inquired when the Soviet representative raised his hand. "I am not a gentleman," said the Soviet representative. "I am the representative of the Soviet Union." Lodge replied quickly, "I had thought that the two were not mutually exclusive."[95]

After the Guatemalan ambassador finished his litany of complaints, the ambassadors from Brazil, Colombia, and Honduras in quick succession called for

FIGURE 2.6. American ambassador Henry Cabot Lodge and British ambassador Gladwyn Jebb during a speech by Soviet ambassador Andrei Vishinsky.

the dispute to be handled by the Organization of American States (OAS), the regional political organization established at the same time as the United Nations. It was a savvy, if disingenuous, maneuver. The UN Charter explicitly recognized the importance of regional organizations and called on member states to use them to settle disputes whenever possible. But, as Lodge well knew, the charter was expressly designed to help small states fend off attacks from the more powerful. In the case of a country under attack, the council, and not regional organizations, had the primary responsibility. Only the council had the legal and political tools to repel aggression.

The Soviets were having none of it. They quickly accused the United States of being behind the insurgent attacks. Guatemala's only sin, the Soviet ambassador alleged, "was to limit the appetite of the United Fruit Company." Determined to keep the United States on the hot seat for as long as possible, the Soviets rejected the attempt to shuffle the issue to the OAS. "When the forces of aggression have already been unleashed on the country, the Council cannot refuse to accept this responsibility, and no other body can take its place." The rhetoric had some support in the packed gallery; several observers stood up to shout slogans about American imperialism and were swiftly removed from the chamber.

After the Soviets made clear that they would veto a resolution referring the dispute to the OAS, an irritated Lodge took the floor to respond, and he decided to bare his teeth, warning the Soviets that they were no longer in their backyard.

> Why does the representative of the Soviet Union, whose country is thousands and thousands of miles away from here, undertake to veto a move like that? What is his interest in it? How can this action of his possibly fail to make unbiased observers throughout the world come to the conclusion that the Soviet Union has got designs on the American Hemisphere. I say to you, representative of the Soviet Union, stay out of this hemisphere and do not try to start your plans and your conspiracies over here.[96]

In the end, the council settled on a bland resolution calling on all parties to avoid the use of force.[97] Meanwhile, the coup in Guatemala proceeded apace. The Arbenz government lasted only a few days longer than the council debate. On June 27, Arbenz resigned and sought refuge in the Mexican embassy. Colonel Castillo Armas took control and began what would eventually become a brutal, decades-long campaign against the country's leftists. The council sessions had been an annoyance, but not a serious obstacle. In a White House meeting, the CIA reported to President Eisenhower that the Guatemala operation was an unblemished success.[98]

American diplomats were considerably less pleased by the performance of their Western allies on the council. While supporting the American effort to use the OAS, the French in particular had bridled at American efforts to cut out the United Nations altogether. U.S. Secretary of State John Foster Dulles instructed the American ambassador to see the French foreign minister immediately and "express our grave concern at [French] tactics in the UN Security Council meeting."[99] The French had been "hasty and reckless" and had damaged America's diplomatic efforts. In New York, Lodge also relayed a message to the wayward allies. "If Great Britain and France felt that they must take an independent line backing the present government of Guatemala," Lodge warned, "we would feel free to take an equally independent line concerning such matters as Egypt and North Africa in which we had hitherto tried to exercise the greatest forbearance."[100] In Cold War Security Council politics, the Americans usually saw friends and enemies, with little room in between.

The End of Empire

On November 3, 1954, Egypt's UN ambassador, Dr. Mahmoud Azmi, was in the midst of an impassioned speech to the council. The sixty-five-year-old diplomat was rebutting charges that Egypt was obstructing Israeli shipping in the Suez Canal. Earlier in the meeting, Israel's representative, Abba Eban, had expressed outrage at the seizure of an Israeli ship and crew. By the early 1950s, the waterway had emerged as one of the world's most sensitive points. More than 60 percent of Western Europe's oil passed through the canal, which was administered by a British- and French-dominated conglomerate named the Suez Canal Company. Britain and France both considered the waterway to be critical to their economic and political interests in the region. Israel saw it as a lifeline. And for Egypt, it was a prized national possession.

As clocks in the council chamber ticked past 4:00, Azmi delved into the details of a shipping agreement for the canal. "I would remind the President and all members of the Council that at the 682nd meeting I spoke of the shipping agreement concluded between the two parties. I read it out, concluding with the phrase which appears on..."[101] At that moment, Azmi slurred his words and then slumped forward in his chair. Diplomats from other delegations—including a doctor from the Israeli delegation—rushed to attend to him. Azmi was ushered from the council chamber to a suite of offices next door and then to the UN infirmary, where guards struggled to revive him. At 5:30, he was pronounced dead of a heart attack.[102] Suez had claimed its first diplomatic victim, but not its last.

The canal was one part of a complicated and shifting regional diplomacy. Arab nationalism was in full bloom, and Egypt's charismatic young leader, Gamal Abdel Nasser, had ambitions to lead the Arab world. He envisioned a strong and united region that would not be beholden to either side of the Cold War. To achieve that political freedom to maneuver, Nasser played the great powers against each other. In 1954, he signed an agreement with the British that allowed them continued rights to use the Suez Canal in exchange for the departure of British troops. The next year, he concluded a major arms deal with the Soviet bloc. The West competed for Nasser's affections in the way it knew best—with its wallet. Working through the Western-dominated World Bank, the United States and Britain dangled financing for one of Nasser's cherished public works projects, the Aswan Dam. But negotiations stalled, and Nasser's rhetoric became increasingly anti-Western. By the summer of 1956, the Americans and the British had tired of the courtship. On July 19, John Foster Dulles informed Egypt's ambassador that the U.S. government had withdrawn its support for the Aswan project. The British conveyed the same message the next day.

Nasser's response came quickly. On July 26, he gave a bombastic speech in Alexandria, and as he spoke Egyptian police and military took control of the canal's facilities. The canal had been nationalized. The move stunned Paris and London. It was, said British prime minister Anthony Eden, "a thumb on the windpipe" of Europe. In addition, control of the canal would embolden and empower a man whom the European powers considered to be very dangerous. France, which was battling an Algerian independence movement, worried that a more powerful Nasser would expand his support for the rebels. If the nationalization were allowed to stand, said French foreign minister Christian Pineau, "it would be useless to pursue the struggle in Algeria. France considers it more important to defeat Colonel Nasser's enterprise than to win ten battles in Algeria."[103] For their part, British politicians drew analogies between Nasser and the dictators of the 1930s. Eden feared a scenario that began with the nationalization of the canal and ended with an economically choked and defenseless Britain. Nasser was not Hitler, Eden acknowledged, but he could easily be a new Mussolini, working at the behest of the Soviet Union.[104]

For the next three months, a confrontation developed in slow motion between the European colonial powers and the Egyptian strongman, though neither side called the council into session on the issue. The rhetoric in Paris and London became heated, and a consensus quickly emerged that the nationalization must not stand. In early August, British and French military planners began examining their options. The United States was less alarmed, and it cautioned its allies to exhaust diplomatic means before resorting to force. In August and September, Eden and Eisenhower exchanged a series of candid letters on the crisis. "We must be ready, in the last resort, to use force to bring Nasser to his senses," Eden wrote on the day after nationalization. Eden's tone alarmed Eisenhower, who was convinced that threats of force would backfire. On July 31, the president responded, "I have given you my personal conviction, as well as that of my associates, as to the unwisdom even of contemplating the use of military force at this moment."[105]

At other levels as well, British and American officials were cautiously sounding each other out. On September 11, Lodge invited his British counterpart, Pierson Dixon, to lunch. The U.S. ambassador conveyed Eisenhower's deep hesitation about the use of force against Nasser. The United States "was unalterably opposed to the use of force or to any action at the United Nations which would imperil the Organization." It was a frank but cordial exchange between two very different ambassadors. Lodge was a politician, Dixon a professional diplomat.[106]

Their relationship was never overly warm, but it was, by necessity, close.[107] Britain and the United States worked hand in glove on almost everything that came before the council.

In late September, Britain and France finally decided to bring the slow-moving crisis to the council. For weeks, they had hesitated, doubting that it could play a constructive role and wary that opening the discussion would give the Soviets an opportunity to meddle. The Americans agreed and favored the use of a large international conference to resolve the issue. Egypt, which could have forced the council to take up the case earlier, saw no reason to concede that the nationalization had created a crisis worthy of the council's attention. In essence, the main actors in the crisis were searching for a diplomatic forum that would suit their particular needs, and the council did not seem to offer it.

In the end, however, the council proved to be impossible to avoid. Whether the protagonists liked it or not, the council had pride of place. The resort to force without at least a show of council diplomacy was not acceptable to Western publics. "British liberal opinion," acknowledged senior British politicians, "would have been shocked by the use of force without a prior appeal to the U.N."[108] The arguments used by Western statesmen during the Berlin crisis about the council's indispensable role now pushed Britain and France toward a diplomatic session they did not want. Even after only a decade of existence, the council had begun to develop an almost gravitational pull that drew international crises into the chamber.

In early October, three foreign ministers—Selwyn Lloyd of Britain, Christian Pineau of France, and Mahmoud Fawzi of Egypt—flew to New York for the long-awaited council meeting. Lloyd began by conceding the obvious. "The Canal is geographically part of Egypt. It is under Egyptian sovereignty." But, he continued, "that does not mean the absence of international rights."[109] Leaving such a vital waterway at the mercy of an Egyptian government that had carelessly violated international agreements was not an option. Pineau joined the chorus. Nasser's nationalization speech, he said, was full of "appeals to violence, incitement to hatred and glorification of anti-foreign feelings." Such behavior might threaten "the whole flow of trade between Europe and Asia."[110] Fawzi, for his part, took pains to demonstrate that Egypt was a capable and reliable guardian of the canal. In the more than two months since nationalization, he pointed out, 3,000 ships had passed through the canal without trouble.[111] British and French alarm was a symptom of "the collapse of the thoroughly corrupt imperialist colonial system, a system which has outlived itself."[112] The Egyptian predicted that the British and French would use the council as little more than a procedural stepping-stone on the way to war.

The real action was on the sidelines of the council meeting. At the urging of the Americans, Dag Hammarskjöld convened long private meetings with Lloyd, Pineau, and Fawzi. They wrestled with how the canal might be operated to everyone's satisfaction, and, after much back and forth, they agreed on six principles, including free and open access to the canal and respect of Egypt's sovereignty, which the council as a whole then endorsed.[113] The ministers agreed to meet again soon in Geneva. On October 13, Lloyd told the council that "a beginning has been made in the process of finding a basis for negotiation."[114] To London, he reported that "the results were better than we could have expected."[115] Worried observers, including Eisenhower and Dulles, could be forgiven for concluding that the council session had moved the crisis toward a peaceful resolution.

"There Will Be a Veto"

Privately, Eden and French prime minister Guy Mollet were convinced that the council could offer them no satisfaction. Military planning accelerated, and on October 14 the French added a twist. Why not include the Israelis in the operation to take back the canal and unseat Nasser? Israel, after all, feared Nasser as much as they did, and it possessed a capable military practically next door to the canal. Even better, Israeli action against Egypt would give British and French intervention good cover: it would be a peacekeeping mission to separate the Israelis and the Egyptians.

The idea intrigued Eden, who was determined to punish Nasser but worried about how it would appear. He authorized senior British officials to follow up the idea. On October 22, the British, French, and Israelis met secretly in a French mansion outside Paris. The meeting was almost comically cloak-and-dagger. Israeli prime minister David Ben Gurion wore a broad hat so as to avoid recognition at the airport. British foreign minister Selwyn Lloyd told his staff that he had a cold and then flew secretly to an out-of-the-way airport near Paris.[116] The meeting was tense and awkward, but it accomplished its purpose. Israel agreed to attack Egypt, clearing the way for a British and French "peacekeeping" intervention that would leave them in control of the canal.

In the midst of the secret talks came startling news from Eastern Europe. On October 23, a rebellion broke out in Soviet-dominated Hungary. Tens of thousands of Hungarians crowded into downtown Budapest to demand political reform and the departure of Soviet troops. Instead, more Red Army forces entered Hungary the next day. In the council, the Americans prepared to make political hay of the revolt and any Soviet effort to put it down. Lodge consulted with Dixon and France's UN ambassador, Bernard Cornut-Gentille, about how to make their case before the council. On October 27, the Western allies together requested that the council consider the Soviet suppression of the revolt. Dixon and Cornut-Gentille joined the Americans in condemning Soviet interference. "Nothing can hide the fact that foreign troops have intervened on a mass scale in Hungary," Dixon told the council the next day. "Such an action is subversive of the whole foundation on which the United Nations is built. Our hearts bleed for the sufferings of the Hungarian people in their struggle for freedom."[117]

The very next day, Israeli forces began advancing quickly down the Sinai peninsula; they had fulfilled their part of the bargain. Word of the assault reached the U.S. East Coast in the afternoon. That evening, decked out in white tie, Lodge was at the opera. Pierson Dixon sat in a nearby box. Their minds were not on the performance, however. In the imaginations of British planners, the world's leaders would be confused by the sudden events in the Middle East and would take time to respond. The British knew that the Americans would be uncomfortable with the Israeli move and their planned response, but they expected at least a grumbling acquiescence. As such, the British did not imagine that they would be flouting the will of the council; they would merely be acting while it dithered.

It was a bad miscalculation. Eisenhower had no patience for what he saw as naked aggression, particularly so close to the American presidential election. When Dulles told the president of the Israeli move, the old general reacted furiously. "All right, Foster, you tell 'em that, goddamn it, we're going to apply sanctions, we're going to the United Nations, we're going to do everything that there is so we can stop this thing."[118] If the United States didn't move fast in New York, the president worried, the Soviet Union might complain to the council first and score a public relations victory.

Throughout the opera, Lodge and Dixon exchanged increasingly exasperated notes. Dixon did not know about the secret agreement and did not understand the role that the Israeli invasion was playing in Anglo-French plans. Douglas Hurd, Dixon's private secretary (and a future foreign secretary), later recalled that the British UN team was in the dark but knew that London would not support the call for an emergency council meeting. "I had carried to the opera instructions from the Foreign Office that we were to do no such thing. There was no accompanying explanation, no background, no analysis, nothing that would enable Dixon to hold a rational conversation with Lodge."[119] With only that vague mandate, Dixon pushed back against Lodge's insistence on a quick condemnation of Israel. "Don't be silly and moralistic," he scribbled to Lodge from his box. "We have got to be practical." Lodge was stunned by the attitude and demeanor of his British colleague. "[T]he mask fell off and he was virtually snarling," he reported to Dulles.[120]

The council met the next morning in an atmosphere of high tension. Lodge moved quickly to put the U.S. government on the record.

The Government of the United States feels it is imperative that the Council act in the promptest manner to determine that a breach of the peace has occurred, to order that the military action undertaken by Israel cease immediately and to make clear its view that the Israeli armed forces should be immediately withdrawn.

Other delegations joined in the growing chorus of condemnation. Britain and France kept quiet. French ambassador Cornut-Gentille whispered to Israel's ambassador, Abba Eban, "[D]on't worry, there will be a veto."[121]

The Soviets, always sensitive to Western conspiracies, sniffed out the plot first. "It is plain from everything that is happening that Israel could not have made this attack without encouragement and help from those aggressive circles which are not interested in the preservation of peace in the Middle East and are trying to find some pretext for moving their troops into this area." Then, switching from Russian to his fluent English, Sobolev read aloud a wire story that had just arrived, reporting news of the British and French "ultimatum" to the warring parties.

Dixon and Cornut-Gentille were left fumbling for a response, and the council quickly adjourned so that the members could find out what was happening. At the beginning of the afternoon session, Dixon read aloud Anthony Eden's statement in Parliament confirming the ultimatum. Britain and France's collusion with Israel was exposed. The admission, wrote Eban, "acted like oil on fire."[122] By this point, the strain had become too much for the French ambassador. He collapsed shivering on a couch and was replaced by his deputy.[123]

That evening, the council voted 7–2 in favor of a resolution condemning the Israeli action and calling on all states to avoid the use of force. Britain and France voted against the resolution, in what was Britain's first-ever use of the veto power. From New York, Dixon cabled the Foreign Office to report on the proceedings. "Lodge did his best," he wrote, "but he was clearly under instructions to oppose us at every point."[124] As the British and French endured abuse and isolation, Lodge enjoyed celebrity status at the United Nations; America's stand on principle against its long-time allies was very popular with the small states and with the UN bureaucracy. Lodge reported that even busboys, elevator operators, and typists working at the United Nations were congratulating him.[125]

As Lodge soaked up the praise, British and French bombers were winging their way toward Egyptian airfields. As expected, the Egyptians rejected the ultimatum, and the military assault ensued. The first British bombs fell on Cairo on the evening of October 31. Meanwhile, British and French paratroopers made final preparations for an assault on Egypt's Port Said, and British troop ships steamed ever closer to the Egyptian coast. After months of anxiety and scheming, control of the canal was tantalizingly close.

Back in New York, the diplomatic battle was all but lost. The United States employed the Uniting for Peace tactic it had developed during the Korean War to move the crisis out of the council and into the General Assembly. The British concern about the tactic had been prescient; now, Britain and France were facing a hostile assembly without a veto and without the support of the United States. An ill and exhausted John Foster Dulles appeared at the assembly to speak for the United States. "I doubt that any delegate ever spoke from this forum with as heavy a heart as I have brought here tonight," he began, his hands trembling at times. "We speak on a matter of vital importance, where the United States finds itself unable to agree with three nations with whom it has ties, deep friendship, admiration, and respect, and two of whom constitute our oldest, most trusted and reliable allies."[126] On November 2, the assembly voted 65–5 to condemn the use of force and to demand that all foreign forces withdraw from Egypt.[127]

The next day, Eden spoke to a nation bewildered by the events and unnerved by the American opposition. "We put the matter to the Security Council," he reminded his compatriots. "Should we have left it to them? Should we have been content to wait and see whether they would act?" Instead, he said, Britain had taken decisive action. "We acted swiftly and reported to the Security Council, and I believe that before long it will become apparent to everybody that we acted rightly and wisely." Eden was at pains to convince the public that Britain was not deserting the United Nations nor flouting the council. "I have been a League of Nations man and a United Nations man, and I am still the same man, with the same convictions, the same devotion to peace."[128]

Eden's protestations did not stem the torrent of criticism at home and abroad, which spread as the British and French ground assault began on November 5. American outrage was palpable, not least because Suez had distracted attention from the Soviet moves in Hungary. When Lodge introduced another resolution condemning the expanding Soviet crackdown, he did it without consulting the British or the French. It was a stinging rebuke, and the American isolation of the British diplomats extended into the lower ranks. A junior British diplomat recalled the environment.

> The extraordinary way in which the American delegation treated us, I'll never forget.... We had run the UN together, you know. They had the best whisky sours in the bar at the UN which we drank with our American delegation friends. We used to make arrangements: "You control that

committee, I'll control this one," that sort of thing. Here they were, turning their backs on us, literally. Cabot Lodge, who was a politician, his relations with Dixon were sorely tried to put it at the least. They tried to pass motions late at night without informing us, and all that. It was very bad.[129]

"In the present circumstances," Dixon cabled to London, "the Americans thought it better not to be identified too closely with Britain and France in this matter." By this time, interactions between Lodge and Dixon had become "frigid." An exhausted and almost frantic Dixon cabled the Foreign Office that "we are inevitably being placed in the same low category as the Russians in their bombing of Budapest. I do not see how we can carry much conviction in our protests against the Russian bombing of Budapest, if we are ourselves bombing Cairo."[130]

The French were willing to endure the uncomfortable parallels; they wanted to complete the intervention, seize the canal, and then negotiate from a position of strength. But British alarm at the American reaction—and, as important, American financial pressure—made them desperate for a compromise. In a matter of weeks, the British and French agreed to withdraw from the Suez in favor of a UN force—the first peacekeeping mission of any size—composed of troops from small and medium-sized countries. Hammarskjöld and Canadian foreign minister Lester Pearson worked feverishly to assemble the innovative multinational expedition, known as the United Nations Emergency Force (UNEF), and to establish a doctrine for it.

What emerged were the basic principles of UN peacekeeping: the dispatch of a neutral force that would position itself between combatants and monitor a ceasefire impartially and without using force, except in immediate self-defense. It was a striking measure of the council's disunity and consequent marginalization that the United Nations' most important innovation in the realm of peace and security was developed by the Secretary-General in a mission blessed by the General Assembly rather than the council.

By Christmas, UNEF was arriving and the British and French troops were gone. There was no disguising the humiliation. The power of public opinion, concentrated to devastating effect in the council and the assembly, had forced two former empires to halt a major military operation designed to defend their colonial privileges. The strain of the fiasco proved to be too much for Eden; his doctors advised him to rest, and he left London on November 24 for a two-week respite in Jamaica. His ministers were left to pick up the pieces of the diplomatic catastrophe. A year later, Pierson Dixon confided to his diary the toll the crisis had taken.

Even today, a year after the event, I recall the sick-at-the-stomach feeling with which I defended our case here. It came of the conviction that the operation was misconceived and probably would fail. The effort of concealing these feelings and putting a plausible and confident face on the case was the severest moral and physical strain I have ever experienced.[131]

The two powers took quite different lessons from the fiasco. Britain, though bitter, emerged even more determined to maintain its ties with the United States and to work through the council whenever possible. "The one overriding lesson of the Suez operation," reflected the British military commander of the expedition later, "is that world opinion is now an absolute principle of war and must be treated as such."[132] In the years after Suez, the British voted with the United States on the council even more frequently than it had in the past.[133]

The Suez experience was less traumatic for France, which did not bruise as easily—or, at least, as obviously—in the face of American opposition. While Eden was forced to resign, French premier Guy Mollet in December got a fresh vote of confidence from the national assembly.[134] France's political establishment blamed the Americans for objecting so strenuously and the British for yielding so easily.[135] The episode helped to reawaken French unease at being so enmeshed in the Atlantic alliance; the country needed an independent foreign policy that did not rely on the council, which it had always suspected was a vehicle for American domination. While Britain tied itself ever closer to the Americans, the French began to strike out on their own. The days when the three Western powers automatically stood together on the council had ended.

Ironically, their disharmony may have helped to keep the council intact. The Soviets, who had often muttered about pulling out of the Western-dominated body, realized that the council could be something other than a clubhouse for powerful capitalists: it could be a place where the capitalists publicly battled each other. Moscow was "intensely gratified by the sight of the 'imperialist whales' falling out—the United States voting with the U.S.S.R. against Britain and France."[136] The Western squabble could not have happened at a more propitious time for Moscow. The Soviets "regard Suez as a heaven-sent distraction from Hungary," reported Britain's ambassador in Moscow. "It also gives them a chance to recover their moral standing by posing as the champion of the United Nations and of an Arab country."[137] The Soviet Union was never as sensitive as the Western powers to the public pressure the council could bring to bear, but Suez helped to dilute even that modest influence. Together with the changing General Assembly membership, the council's performance on Suez shifted the Soviet attitude toward the organization.[138] And with Soviet frustration tempered, the council emerged from its turbulent first decade whole, although certainly not healthy.

CHAPTER 3

THE COURT OF WORLD
OPINION (1957–1967)

IN THE LATE 1950s, French diplomats in New York were reeling from criticism of their colonial policies in North Africa. Tunisia complained to the council about French military forays into its territory, which were designed to disrupt the support bases for Algerian rebels. Arab diplomats, already angry about the Algerian war, were livid. "The losses suffered by the Tunisians as a result of this aggression can be added to the deaths of thousands and thousands of innocent Algerians who are being killed daily at the hands of the French army for no crime except their right to and their fight for independence and freedom," thundered Iraq's ambassador at a typical Security Council meeting in 1958.[1] The atmosphere was even less comfortable in the General Assembly. African and Asian countries regularly introduced resolutions condemning France's Algeria policy, which would send French diplomats rushing to head them off. Together with the Suez crisis, the Algerian war poisoned relations between France and many Arab and African states, and the Soviet Union was only too happy to offer support for the attacks on a Western power.

The violence in Algeria wreaked havoc on French domestic politics as well. By April 1958, turmoil had become insurrection, as French military officers in Algeria rebelled against the Paris politicians whom the officers feared were preparing to abandon the cause. As the republic teetered, the country turned to Charles de Gaulle, who in 1946 had quit the presidency in disgust and retired from politics. The general agreed to return from self-imposed political exile, but on very specific terms: a new constitution and a new, more powerful presidency. He got what he demanded.

De Gaulle wasted no time in dramatically realigning French foreign policy. Surprising many observers and bitterly disappointing French settlers in Algeria, he adopted a conciliatory tone toward Tunisia and Algeria and began moving the French public toward an acceptance of Algerian independence. He demanded the same independence for France on the world stage. The world, he said, was divided between "the Anglo-Saxons and the Soviets," not between West and East.[2] He dashed off a memo to President Eisenhower and British prime minister Harold Macmillan questioning the utility of the NATO alliance and signaling that France would no longer subordinate its interests to the needs of an American-dominated alliance. At the United Nations, he made clear, France would chart its own course. In July 1958, de Gaulle rebuffed the strategy that American and British diplomats had developed for using the Security Council to address the political crisis in Lebanon. He recommended instead a quieter setting, where the issue could be discussed in "objectivity and serenity."[3]

The general had a special distaste for the organization, which he habitually referred to as the "so-called United Nations."[4] His skepticism was not entirely new in Paris. The French had never felt as invested in the United Nations as were the Americans and the British. Still, de Gaulle's animosity toward the institution went well beyond that of his predecessors. The opprobrium that had been directed at France in the council and the General Assembly no doubt colored his views. In de Gaulle's eyes, the organization had become a spectacle, a "scene of disturbance, confusion, and division" where "wild or fanciful currents" motivated debate and "perpetual invective" dominated.[5]

De Gaulle's view of the United Nations had deeper roots than bitterness at France's inability to keep its colonial troubles off the agenda. The general viewed nation-states as the natural and indispensable units of international relations. "For him, history is in the last analysis the history of nations," one scholar has written. "They are the supreme driving force."[6] Supranational bodies like the United Nations, in de Gaulle's view, must not attempt to compete. To the extent that the council acted as a simple concert of great powers that kept out of the internal affairs of sovereign states, it was useful and proper. But anything more was unacceptable. De Gaulle agitated repeatedly for summit meetings of the great powers outside the council chamber, without the meddlesome nonpermanent council members and without Chiang Kai-shek's China, which de Gaulle never considered a worthy member of the great-power club.

The frequently expressed French preference for great-power gatherings outside the United Nations reflected de Gaulle's view that the organization had become unmoored. The great-power concert embedded in the Security Council had ceded initiative to the General Assembly. The United States had invited and encouraged that activism by championing the Uniting for Peace maneuver. As newly independent states joined the organization, the assembly was becoming a hotbed of anticolonialist sentiment. The council itself had been invaded by loud and meddling Lilliputians.

> Today, it must be said that the United Nations really does not in any way resemble what it was or ought to have been at the start. First of all, the Security Council no longer comprises—it is far from comprising—only the big powers, but also several powers elected in turn, and then there is an undetermined number of delegations attending all debates of the Security Council, depending on the subjects under discussion. . . . So that now the meetings of the United Nations are no more than riotous and scandalous sessions where there is no way to organize an objective debate and which are filled with invectives and insults.[7]

Whatever solution France chose for the Algerian crisis would be a French solution and not the product of pressure from the meddling world organization. "We would pay no attention to any overtures from any capital, to any offer of 'good offices,' to any threat of 'agonizing reappraisals' in our foreign relations, to any debate in the United Nations," the general later summarized his position.[8]

As troubling to de Gaulle as the new and unruly membership was the permanent bureaucracy the United Nations was developing. The Suez crisis, and the peacekeeping mission that helped to end it, had forced the organization to become operational. Thousands of soldiers patrolling the Sinai wore the United Nations' light-blue helmets, and an expanded staff of officials in New York helped to run the operation. That novel peacekeeping mission had been cobbled together through the diligent efforts of Secretary-General Dag Hammarskjöld. A compromise candidate for the post, the Swedish diplomat was emerging as an independent force in international politics. He revitalized and bestowed a sense of mission on the growing UN bureaucracy in New York. As important, he restored hope among many Western observers that the United Nations could play a positive role despite the Cold War divide.

In 1953, Hammarskjöld flew to China and negotiated the release of an American flight crew that had been held there since being shot down during a mission over Korea. He played a key role in mediating the 1958 political crisis in Lebanon, during which the United States dispatched troops to bolster the Lebanese and Jordanian governments. When a Soviet veto blocked Security Council action, the secretary-general on his own authority expanded a group of UN monitors already serving in the country.[9] Hammarskjöld's activism, his quiet charisma, and his almost mystical sense of mission did not sit easily with de Gaulle's effort to restore French fortunes. A meeting between the two men in 1959 was reportedly cold and unproductive.[10]

De Gaulle's vision of a minimalist United Nations deferential to national sovereignty and with power focused in the council bore a strong resemblance to the organization the Soviet Union had supported at Dumbarton Oaks. The parallel was not surprising. The Soviet Union then had assumed it would be outnumbered and isolated in the Western-dominated organization; by the mid-1950s, France felt increasingly alone in an organization animated by anticolonialism. De Gaulle's critique was a product of his own brand of French nationalism, but it also demonstrated something akin to a diplomatic law: a country that is isolated and subject to incessant attack will react against the forum attacking it.

French discontent foreshadowed a broader Western disenchantment with the United Nations, and de Gaulle was not alone in his view that the organization was often best avoided. The high likelihood of Cold War–inspired vetoes meant that neither the other Western powers nor the Soviet Union looked to the council as a reliable tool for making policy or resolving crises. Between 1946 and 1950, the council averaged about eighteen resolutions a year. Between 1951 and 1959, it averaged fewer than five, and many of those were routine resolutions admitting new members. The body met only sporadically, sometimes going a whole month without a formal session. In all of 1959, the council met just five times.

Nation Building, Take One

In June 1960, Dag Hammarskjöld was one of the few people in New York closely watching events in the Belgian Congo. That summer, the vast colonial territory, which was roughly the size of Western Europe, was careening toward independence. The Belgian government had abruptly decided that resisting an independence movement was beyond its capacity. The small European power no longer had the will or the resources to run an African empire. An independence ceremony was hastily arranged, and Belgian forces withdrew to a few bases, from which they would continue to advise the Congolese military.

Hammarskjöld anticipated that sudden independence would be dangerous, and he dispatched Ralph Bunche, an American who was one of his top troubleshooters, to monitor the country's first days of independence. Bunche's increasingly alarming cables vindicated Hammarskjöld's concern.[11] Within days of independence, the country experienced a wave of unrest. Congolese soldiers rebelled against the Belgian officers still serving as their superiors. European homes were ransacked, and reports of assaults and rapes circulated. Thousands of European settlers fled across the Congo River. On July 9, Belgian paratroopers moved off their bases and began an often brutal attempt to restore order. Two days later, secession was added to disorder when the resource-rich province of Katanga declared that it was splitting off from the new country.

By the afternoon of July 13, Hammarskjöld had heard enough. On his own initiative, the secretary-general called for a meeting of the council. Article 99 of the UN Charter gave him that power, but this was the first time it had been used.[12] It was a sign of Hammarskjöld's standing and confidence that he decided to lead rather than follow the council. At an evening meeting, he briefed the gathered diplomats on the breakdown of order in the new nation and laid out a plan for technical assistance, including the dispatch of UN forces to help train the Congolese Army and calm the country. Chaos and disorder in Congo, he argued, "have an important international bearing as they are of a nature that cannot be disregarded by other countries." He pleaded with the council to act "with utmost speed."[13]

Working until almost 3:30 in the morning, the council members tried to sort out their positions on the novel question of whether the United Nations should help a new nation get on its feet. Henry Cabot Lodge was urgent in his support; the Americans feared that chaos in Congo would increase the chances for Communist meddling. "Speed is essential," he said. "[T]he longer the present state of near anarchy continues, the heavier the toll of lives, the greater the prospect of hunger and epidemic, and the greater the difficulties in future economic

FIGURE 3.1. United Nations peacekeepers during the Security Council–authorized mission in Congo.

FIGURE 3.2. Demonstrators in the Security Council gallery denounce the United Nations' policy in Congo.

development."[14] The Soviets were wary of American enthusiasm for the project, but nonetheless felt compelled to endorse a mission that had strong African support and an anticolonial flavor. A week earlier, the Soviets had celebrated Congo's independence as "another powerful blow to the rapidly crumbling system of colonialism."[15] Moscow could not now reject that nation's request for UN assistance.

Britain and France, still active colonial powers, defended the honor of their European colleague. Belgium's efforts, argued the French ambassador, "have been directed solely towards saving the lives of Belgians and other nationals who have been threatened." Belgium's ambassador rejected all charges of misconduct by his country's troops. "Not a single Congolese house has been looted, not a single Congolese citizen has been maltreated or harassed."[16] Together, Britain and France fended off amendments that would have condemned the Belgian role. The final version of the resolution cast no blame and simply authorized the secretary-general to provide the Congolese authorities with military and technical assistance until they were ready to carry out their duties. The vote was 8–0, with China, Britain, and France abstaining.

The long night was not over for Hammarskjöld and his staff. They began the dozens of phone calls necessary to turn the council's resolution into an actual mission. Over the next twenty-four hours, the United Nations' most ambitious operation yet took shape. Several African countries offered troops, and both superpowers pledged aircraft to ferry them into Congo. Remarkably, the first blue helmets arrived in the country just two days after the council's resolution.

On the ground, however, the UN force struggled to establish itself and explain its role. One UN official, Brian Urquhart, remembered a puzzled Congolese asking him, "The UN? What tribe is that?"[17] It was a prescient question. The peacekeepers were soon forced to choose sides between the country's president, Joseph Kasavubu, and its firebrand prime minister, Patrice Lumumba. In September, Kasavubu fired Lumumba, who in turn tried to fire Kasavubu. Their schism soon took on Cold War overtones, as the Soviets championed Lumumba's cause. The Soviets also pressed the United Nations to actively oppose the secession of Katanga, something Hammarskjöld was reluctant to do because it might involve armed intervention in a domestic dispute. The secretary-general was forced to steer a middle ground between competing political movements in Congo even as he struggled to keep the support of a divided Security Council.

The task proved too much even for him. Soviet outrage grew as the UN force increasingly aligned itself against Lumumba and as Hammarskjöld steadfastly refused to use force against breakaway Katanga. With increasing vitriol, Moscow accused Hammarskjöld and the UN mission of siding with reactionary forces against "progressive" elements. The United Nations, with the support of Western powers, had established a "regime of illegality and terror."[18] Soviet outrage peaked when Patrice Lumumba was killed in disputed circumstances. The Soviet ambassador accused the UN force, which his country had helped to create, of being complicit in Lumumba's death.

> The criminal farce which has been played out in the last few days before the whole world has now been fully revealed and exposed. The crimes committed by the colonialists against the colonial peoples have been many, but this new crime is exceptional in that it was perpetrated from first to last under cover of the blue flag of the United Nations.[19]

France followed the Soviets into outright opposition, although the substance of its complaint was somewhat different. De Gaulle was alarmed at the increasingly complicated intervention in Congo's domestic affairs and accused Hammarskjöld of "set[ting] himself up as a supreme and excessive authority."[20] At the council, France emerged as a strict constructionist and a defender of the sovereign rights of the small states. "It is for the Congolese people to decide their own destiny," the French ambassador argued. Excessive UN meddling "would be likely to set a dangerous precedent, particularly in the case of the newly independent states."[21] The Soviets and the French began using their vetoes on resolutions relating to Congo, shattering the fragile consensus that had authorized the mission.

The political toll on the United Nations' leadership was also heavy. After Patrice Lumumba's death, Nikita Khrushchev demanded Hammarskjöld's resignation and announced that Soviet diplomats would no longer recognize him. In 1961, the Soviet Union proposed replacing the post of secretary-general with a three-person executive, one from the capitalist world, one from a Communist country, and one from a nonaligned state. This "troika" proposal won little support, but it signaled the severity of the breakdown between the Soviets and the UN bureaucracy.[22]

The council's frequent sessions on Congo were as lively as any it had held since the twin crises of 1956. The public lined up for seats at the meetings, almost all of which were open. In February 1961, several members of the public tried to take a more direct role in the deliberations. More than fifty activists burst into the public gallery and began denouncing the United Nations' policy toward Lumumba. Dozens of UN security guards tried to subdue them, and a near riot broke out. The public was excluded from the council proceedings for the rest of the day, and UN guards were issued billy clubs.[23]

Hammarskjöld did not survive the mission that he had championed. On the night of September 17, 1961, the plane ferrying him around the region crashed in northern Rhodesia. Shocked by the loss of the charismatic secretary-general, the United Nations' top leadership struggled to persevere. U Thant, Burma's UN representative, was named acting secretary-general, and he immediately faced the question of how to deal with the Katangan rebels. In December 1962, UN troops at long last put down the secession movement. It was victory enough for the organization, which was by now eager to be done with the mission. Congo might not be well run, but at least it was in one piece. By 1964, most peacekeepers had left the country. Constitutional rule did not survive long after their departure. In November 1965, army chief of staff Joseph Mobutu took over Congo; he would rule despotically and corruptly for the next thirty years.

The Congo operation has been dubbed the "UN's Vietnam," and the foray into nation building exacted a high price. It instilled a deep sense of caution in the organization and rattled the nerves of even stalwart UN supporters. Harlan Cleveland, the U.S. assistant secretary of state for international organizations, described the reaction.

> I shall not soon forget the political shock wave produced in our politics by the Congo crisis when Americans suddenly discovered that soldiers on a peace-keeping mission sometimes had to shoot back at people who insisted on shooting at the peace-keepers. It was more comfortable to think of "peace" as a cartoonist's image, a vaguely female figure in a pure white gown, mouthing sweet nothings and clutching her olive branch. But

when this ethereal creature, adjusting her halo to a rakish angle, whipped out her six-shooter to defend her right to walk a policeman's beat on the streets of Elisabethville, most Americans did a double take.[24]

Nor was the mission reassuring from the perspective of organizational management. Congo introduced a lamentable phenomenon that would reappear in later periods of UN activism: the tendency for the Security Council to authorize operations without the ability or the will to manage them as the situation developed. Member states, notably the United States, sometimes had better communications with the field than UN headquarters did. Harlan Cleveland recalled a typical conversation with Ralph Bunche, the UN point person in Congo.

CLEVELAND: "Ralph, do you know where your troops are today?"
BUNCHE: "Well, I think I know."
CLEVELAND: "Did you know that they crossed the Kolwezi River this morning?"
BUNCHE: "Oh my god, they're not supposed to do that. The Security Council has not said that's all right yet."[25]

Discerning precisely what the council had authorized was often a complicated task. "I have a right to expect guidance," the secretary-general had said shortly after the operation began. "[I]f the Security Council says nothing I have no other choice than to follow my conviction."[26] A year before his death, a frustrated Hammarskjöld asked the council to "shoulder its responsibility."[27] As it struggled to respond to events on the ground, the UN leadership was often without effective support or guidance from the badly divided council and was forced to make important decisions about operations on its own. The secretary-general and his staff did their best to divine the council's mood and intent and then sent orders directly to the peacekeepers in the field. As in Korea, the council had shown itself to be incapable of managing large field operations; delegating authority—to the United States in the case of Korea, to Hammarskjöld in Congo—was the best it could do.

The Congo operation also produced the organization's most severe financial crisis. The United Nations' expenditures began to increase dramatically after 1956 as it took on large-scale peacekeeping in the Suez. With the added expense of the Congo operation, many small states bridled, and in 1961 the General Assembly, which controlled most budgetary matters, decided that the permanent Security Council members had a special obligation to cover peacekeeping costs. The Soviet Union and France felt no such obligation and refused to pay their share, arguing that the United Nations was engaged in illegitimate interference in the internal affairs of a sovereign state. By 1962, the United Nations was almost $29 million in the red for the Congo operation alone and had to tap reserve accounts and borrow to meet operational expenses. It took years of political effort and innovative accounting for the organization to navigate out of the crisis.[28]

The experience carried sobering lessons for the council. Hammarskjöld had goaded its members into the Congo operation, convinced that the body had a responsibility to prevent a breakdown of order in the huge new nation. The United States endorsed the mission in large part because it believed that a UN presence might forestall Soviet meddling in the region. But it is possible that the council's foray into nation building was counterproductive in terms of both establishing order locally and managing superpower relations. From Congo's perspective, the best that can be said about UN involvement is that the country remained whole; the Katangan secession was put down. The UN mission did not produce democracy or even competent governance.

As bad, the operation may have inflamed already raw superpower relations by forcing the United States and the Soviet Union to take positions on factional feuds in Congo that they otherwise might have been able to ignore. Khrushchev was reportedly obsessed with the twists and turns of the UN mission and became personally hostile to Hammarskjöld. In effect, the United Nations' involvement elevated Congo's struggle to the international stage and forced the Five to confront it.

However dramatic, the Congo mission was an aberration. No operation even remotely as ambitious was attempted again during the Cold War. Instead, the council by the early 1960s had become a place for the great powers to make public stands and attempt to sway world opinion, which was increasingly determined by what *Time* magazine called the "small, excitable new nations."[29] A propaganda war on a global scale was playing out in the council.

Props and Principles

On May 1, 1960, Francis Gary Powers took off from an airbase in western Pakistan bound for Norway. Along the way, he would traverse the Soviet Union, and the cameras in his aircraft would snap thousands of photographs. Powers, a Kentucky native working for the CIA, had made similar flights a half dozen times, all without mishap. A few hours into this flight, however, something went wrong. Powers heard a thump, and his craft jerked suddenly. A Soviet surface-to-air missile had exploded just below his fragile plane. Within seconds, the U-2 was disintegrating. Powers managed to extricate himself from the cockpit and parachuted into the atmosphere over Soviet territory. As he descended slowly, he removed from his flight suit the poison injection all U-2 pilots were issued and encouraged to use if captured. Before Powers hit the ground, he put the needle carefully back into his pocket.[30]

The United States had begun sending reconnaissance planes over Soviet territory in the mid-1950s. The U-2s flew above the reach of Soviet missiles and planes, although Soviet radar could usually track the flights. The intrusions were maddening to Soviet leaders, but they dared not advertise their impotence by publicly complaining. Despite misgivings, President Eisenhower had personally approved Powers's mission. He was under heavy pressure from the CIA and the Pentagon to authorize such flights, which gave the United States critical insight into the state of the Soviet missile program.

For Eisenhower, the news that a plane had been lost was a nightmare realized. In quiet conversations at the White House, the president admitted that the United States had been caught in an activity that was "illegal, and, in fact, immoral."[31] In Moscow, Khrushchev was elated that the Soviet military had finally managed to down one of the spy planes, but he also felt a sense of personal betrayal. The premier had made a dramatic trip to the United States in 1959. The Soviet's meeting with Eisenhower went smoothly, and Khrushchev had left American soil determined to ease relations with the United States and to turn instead to the Soviet Union's crushing domestic problems.

Khrushchev wanted a public apology from the Americans, and at the Security Council, the Soviet ambassador was instructed to exploit the incident. A televised meeting of the council was called, and Andrei Gromyko, who flew to New York just for the session, launched into a lengthy denunciation of American recklessness. "On 1 May 1960, as the members of the Security Council are already aware, a United States military aircraft, acting on a direct order from United States authorities, invaded the Soviet Union to a depth of more than 2,000 kilometres and was brought down by Soviet rocket units." The U-2 incursion, Gromyko warned, could lead the superpowers down the slippery slope to war.

> What will international relations come to if attempts to trample underfoot that fundamental principle of relations among States are not resolutely rebuffed? Today we are concerned with a high-handed invasion of the air space of a sovereign state, tomorrow warships will be dispatched to invade its territorial waters and the day after tomorrow one pretext or another will be used to land divisions on its territory; one step leads to another.

Gromyko proposed a resolution condemning America's "aggressive acts," which "create a threat to universal peace."[32]

The Soviets did not count on the American penchant for theatrics. As the debate entered its third day, Lodge again rose to respond to the attack, and he tried to place the U-2 flights in the context of Soviet secrecy about its missile program. "When such a government insists on secrecy," he said, "it is in effect also insisting on preserving the ability to make a surprise attack on humanity. If the free world failed to attempt to protect itself against such a danger, it would be inviting destruction." What's more, he argued, the Soviets were no strangers to espionage of all kinds. "It so happens that I have here today a concrete example of Soviet espionage so that you can see for yourself." With that, Lodge reached down and pulled from under the table a wooden Great Seal of the United States, which had been presented to the U.S. embassy in Moscow by the Soviet-American Friendship Society. Placing the seal on the council table, Lodge demonstrated how the Soviets had buried an electronic bug deep inside the wood under the eagle's beak.[33] The revelation was a diversion, but it was an effective one. A draft Soviet resolution to condemn the United States was soundly defeated. Lodge's rebuff of the Soviet offensive on the council was typical of the time. The Soviets were able to make their point, but they had little chance of besting—or even humiliating—the Americans.

FIGURE 3.3. Henry Cabot Lodge exposes Soviet espionage during a council debate on the U-2 affair in 1960.

In January 1961, the burden of foiling Soviet diplomacy fell to a new American ambassador. President John F. Kennedy chose the venerable Democratic politician Adlai Stevenson as his man at the United Nations. Stevenson was welcomed warmly at the council. His low-key style and sense of humor—he once quipped that the United Nations survived on "protocol, alcohol, and Geritol"— won him accolades.[34] But Stevenson had a traumatic introduction to UN diplomacy. For several years, the CIA had been planning to depose Cuba's Fidel Castro by training and deploying teams of Cuban exiles. With the new president's reluctant approval, the plan finally went into motion. On April 15, a group of planes piloted by Cuban exiles attacked Cuban Air Force bases before landing in Miami. At the United Nations, Cuba immediately charged the United States with complicity. The Cuban foreign minister held aloft pictures of alleged U.S.-run training camps for exiles and demanded that Stevenson concede that the United States was training and supporting armed exile groups. Stevenson, unaware of U.S. involvement, called the charges "lurid" and displayed his own set of photographs, which the CIA had provided. They purported to show that the planes involved in the bombing were actually Cuban Air Force planes that had defected from Castro. "The fundamental question," he assured the delegates, "is not between the U.S. and Cuba but among the Cubans themselves."[35]

The American cover story soon fell to pieces. Stevenson cabled the State Department in frustration. He was "greatly disturbed" at mounting evidence of U.S. involvement. "No one will believe the bombing attacks on Cuba from outside could have been organized without our complicity."[36] The fingerprints of the CIA were all over the operation, and on April 21, President Kennedy took responsibility for the botched mission. Stevenson was "absolutely sunk at having misled the United Nations."[37] He worried that his credibility had been ruined, and he contemplated resigning. His confidence in Kennedy's team was shaken. "I never thought they'd do this to me," he reportedly complained.[38]

"Until Hell Freezes Over"

Stevenson soon had an opportunity to test the resiliency of U.S. credibility, once again courtesy of Cuba. In October 1962, American intelligence officials became convinced that the Soviets were deploying nuclear missiles to the island. The president was briefed, and a week later he publicly accused the Soviet Union and demanded that the missiles be withdrawn. Senior U.S. officials fanned out to convince U.S. allies of the seriousness of the threat. Former secretary of state Dean Acheson was recruited to visit de Gaulle in Paris. He found the French leader surprisingly receptive to the American position. De Gaulle had little use for the idea of bringing the issue to the Security Council, but he did believe that America's response had to be firm. At the State Department, Secretary of State Dean Rusk began briefing dozens of foreign ambassadors, most of whom were shown reconnaissance photos of the missile sites.[39]

Kennedy's team knew that these meetings were not enough; the United States had to make the case more dramatically, and the Security Council was the place to do it. Whether they had the right man in New York was less clear; Kennedy's aides worried that Stevenson might not be tough enough. In the initial deliberations on the crisis, he had opposed all military options and advocated immediate compromise. Attorney General Robert Kennedy was outraged at Stevenson's weakness. "We have to get someone better at the United Nations or put some starch in the son of a bitch's back," he said at one meeting.[40] The president agreed that Stevenson needed support and dispatched the hawkish veteran troubleshooter John J. McCloy to New York.[41] Arthur Schlesinger was sent to help with speechwriting. The CIA designated a specialist, Colonel David Parker, to brief Stevenson on the photographic evidence of Soviet missiles. With the Bay of Pigs in his mind, Stevenson greeted the CIA man skeptically. "I hope you are in a position to prove beyond a shadow of a doubt that the missiles exist in Cuba," he said coldly.[42]

Adlai Stevenson first presented the American complaint to the council on October 23, the day after Kennedy's speech to the nation. He placed the

FIGURE 3.4. A standing-room-only audience views aerial photographs of Soviet missile sites during the Cuban missile crisis.

deployment of Soviet missiles in the context of what he described as decades of Soviet aggression and offered a resolution that called for the immediate dismantling of the missiles and for a UN inspection corps to verify their removal.[43] Stevenson had set the scene, but he intentionally held back the surveillance photographs. During the next two days, as all council members had their say, Parker and the White House aides worked with Stevenson and his staff to hone a sixty-five-page speech to the council that would include all of the evidence. By this time, Stevenson had become convinced that the intelligence was genuine and was eager to make the case.[44]

In the Caribbean Sea, meanwhile, events were reaching a climax. The U.S. Navy had been tracking dozens of Soviet-flagged ships as they approached the American vessels ringing the island. Throughout the evening of October 24, the Soviet ships steamed steadily toward the blockade line. When President Kennedy's executive committee met the next morning, there were conflicting reports about what was happening at sea. Meanwhile, UN secretary-general U Thant was awaiting the Soviet and American responses to a public message he had sent the previous day calling for a cooling-off period and offering his services as a mediator.

Kennedy and his advisors debated how to manage the UN diplomacy. The idea of inserting UN inspectors into Cuba had been discussed, and Secretary of Defense Robert McNamara proposed forcing a Soviet veto in the council as the prelude to air strikes on the missile sites. "If the Security Council has turned down by veto our proposal—by which we send in UN inspectors—this might set up the circumstances in which we can go in and take those missiles out." Kennedy listened but did not endorse the suggestion to use a Soviet veto as the trigger for military action.[45]

As the scheduled time for the climactic council meeting approached, the president apparently became nervous that the aggressive speech that Stevenson had drafted might damage the chances of a Soviet retreat. Just as Stevenson was set to depart for the council chamber, Arthur Schlesinger called him to say that the president was reconsidering the speech. Stevenson was outraged. He had stayed up nights preparing it, and the council meeting was only minutes away. He headed for the council chamber, intent on delivering the speech as prepared. "God damn it," he yelled, "tell Kennedy I can't talk to him; the meeting is about to begin."[46]

Stevenson's aides prevailed on him to take the call on a phone just outside the council chamber. As the president explained that Stevenson had to scale back his speech, U.S. diplomat Joseph Sisco approached Soviet ambassador Valerian Zorin, who was serving as council president that month, and asked for a brief delay in the proceedings. Zorin promised not to start the meeting until the Americans were ready. Sisco then hurriedly edited Stevenson's address, omitting whole sections, including the narrative to accompany the carefully prepared slides and photographs.[47] Shortly after 4:00 p.m., the meeting began.

As Stevenson was delivering his truncated remarks, however, the White House reversed course and decided to ratchet up the diplomatic pressure on Khrushchev. It was clear that Zorin had no specific instructions and was not prepared to rebut the detailed presentation.[48] Word went out to the council that Stevenson was now free to fire with both barrels. "Stick him," Robert Kennedy said.[49] Zorin himself opened the door for Stevenson to give his full presentation. "The government of the United States," he contended, "has no such facts in hand except the falsified information for review in the halls and which are sent to the press. Falsity is what the United States has in its hands—false evidence." Stevenson took the floor a few moments later and spoke directly to the Soviet ambassador. Their exchange was beamed around the world.

STEVENSON: Do you, Ambassador Zorin, deny that the U.S.S.R. has placed and is placing medium- and intermediate-range missiles and sites in Cuba? Don't wait for the translation! Yes or no?

ZORIN: I am not in an American courtroom, sir, and I do not wish to answer a question put to me in the manner of a prosecuting counsel. You will receive the answer in due course....

STEVENSON: You are in the courtroom of world opinion right now and you can answer yes or no. You have denied that they exist, and I want to know whether I have understood you correctly. I am prepared to wait for my answer until hell freezes over, if that's your decision. I am also prepared to present the evidence in this room.[50]

The council's gallery burst into cheers and laughter. Zorin tried gamely to recover the initiative. As council president, he could recognize any members who had placed their names on the speakers' list, and he quickly called on the Chilean ambassador, hoping to deflect Stevenson's assault. But Chile offered no shelter. "I should prefer to speak after you have replied, if you deem it necessary, to the comments or questions addressed to you by the United States representative. I should be glad to yield the floor to you for that purpose." The gallery again broke into laughter.

Stevenson leaped to seize the advantage. "I doubt whether anyone in this room, except possibly the representative of the Soviet Union, has any doubt about the facts," he began.

[B]ut in view of his statements and the statements of the Soviet government up until last Thursday, when Mr. Gromyko denied the existence of or any intention of installing such weapons in Cuba, I am going to make a portion of the evidence available right now. If you will indulge me for a moment, we will set up an easel here in the back of the room where I hope it will be visible to everyone.[51]

With that, Colonel Parker opened the chamber door and brought in the carefully prepared slides. Moments before, as he waited nervously, Parker had realized to his horror that Stevenson's staff had changed the order of the blown-up photographs. With the eyes of the world upon him, he improvised.

> There was nothing I could do except take them all out when my time was called, put them on the floor in front of the briefing stand, and as Ambassador Stevenson went from one to another, I would have to take my cue from what he was saying and my knowledge of the photography to make sure that I got the right board upon the stand at the proper time.[52]

Nobody could tell. Stevenson methodically introduced photos showing the hasty Soviet construction of missile bases in Cuba.

Forced to take the floor, Zorin stumbled. He tried to taunt Stevenson with the false evidence he had presented during the Bay of Pigs debate. "What is the value of all your photographs? He who lies once is not believed a second time. Therefore, Mr. Stevenson, we do not propose to look at your photographs."[53] But Stevenson turned even this gambit into a winning point.

> I wonder if the Soviet Union would ask their Cuban colleagues to permit a United Nations team to go to these sites. If so, Mr. Zorin, I can assure you that we can direct them to the proper places very quickly. And now I hope that we can get down to business, that we can stop this sparring. We know the facts, Mr. Zorin, and so do you, and we are ready to talk about them. Our job here is not to score debating points: our job, Mr. Zorin, is to save the peace. If you are ready to try, we are.[54]

In the White House, President Kennedy doodled on a legal pad while watching the debate; he wrote the word "veto" over and over again, even circling it.[55] He was relieved by the presentation. "Terrific, I never knew Adlai had it in him," he said. "Too bad he didn't show some of this steam in the 1956 [presidential] campaign."[56] For all of the hours of preparation that had gone into the photographs and Stevenson's speech, what stuck with the public was the direct questioning of Zorin, which was spontaneous. The Soviet ambassador cabled to Moscow that night that he had "ridiculed the maneuver which Stevenson had made... in showing the photographs which had been fabricated by American intelligence." The American attempt "to turn the Council into a tribune for base propaganda," Zorin reported, "met no support from other members of the Council."[57] It does not appear that his dispatches reassured Moscow. Zorin was relieved as UN ambassador just a few weeks after the confrontation.[58]

Judging the effect of the debate on the council members is not easy; the body adjourned that day without even taking a vote on the various draft resolutions that had been offered. However, several key players believed that the council contributed measurably to the resolution of the crisis. Dean Rusk saw its value primarily as a brake on the pace of events.

> Although the Cuban missile crisis was directly resolved between Washington and Moscow, it was very important that the Security Council [took] it up. Prolonged discussion lessened the chance that one side would lash out in a spasm and do something foolish. The UN earned its pay for a long time to come just by being there for the missile crisis.[59]

Others pointed to the effect on world public opinion. The debate, concluded presidential aide Arthur Schlesinger, "dealt a final blow to the Soviet case before world opinion."[60] British prime minister Harold Macmillan saw a similar effect. He wrote later that the exchange "had a profound effect in Britain and throughout the world."[61] There is reason to be skeptical about these claims, however. One journalist covering the United Nations concluded that American officials overestimated the impact of the presentation. "Not only the non-aligned but many Westerners doubted (in private) whether any Soviet rockets really were in Cuba," he wrote. "Mr. Stevenson's photos did nothing to convince them. They were convinced only by Khrushchev's [subsequent] admission."[62]

It would not be surprising if Stevenson's presentation changed few minds. Those in the council chamber and watching on television were no better positioned to assess the validity of the evidence the American ambassador displayed than they were during the Bay of Pigs invasion. Some important players staked out positions without even viewing the evidence. De Gaulle famously declined to look at the reconnaissance photographs. "These would only be evidence," he said. "[A] great nation like yours would not act if there were any doubt about the evidence."[63] Whatever its true effect, Stevenson's presentation burned itself into the American psyche as an example of effective public diplomacy.

The Newcomers

For all of its drama, the Stevenson-Zorin confrontation was the last contribution that the council as a whole made to the Cuban missile crisis. It did not meet again in formal session until the end of November. Secretary-general U Thant continued his diligent mediation, and for several days he was at the center of efforts to end the crisis. Stevenson and McCloy helped to negotiate some of the final details of the settlement with the Soviets. In the end, bilateral communication between the superpowers proved more fruitful than council diplomacy. The loud debate had helped to set the tone, but the crisis was resolved in quiet meetings between intermediaries.

The prospect of a Soviet presence in the Caribbean continued to preoccupy the Kennedy and Johnson administrations. In April 1965, the United States dispatched marines to prevent a leftist rebel movement from taking power in the Dominican Republic. President Lyndon B. Johnson alleged that a "band of Communist conspirators" had hijacked the protest movement and intended to establish a Communist state.[64] At the council, the Soviets insisted, "American imperialism is barbarously dealing with the people of a sovereign country which has arisen against a blood-soaked dictatorship."[65]

The Adlai Stevenson who had so deftly skewered Zorin now found himself in the awkward position of defending what appeared even to some close allies as an act of aggression or, at least, armed interference with a sovereign state. In the chamber, Stevenson mocked the "loud and self righteous" Soviet criticism and insisted that the United States had no intention of "impos[ing] a military junta or any other government."[66] He cobbled together enough support to avoid having to use the American veto. In private, he complained that the invasion was a mistake and that defending U.S. action in the council "took several years off my life."[67]

The Dominican intervention went down poorly in many quarters of the United Nations, particularly with the organization's newest members, which were mostly from Africa and Asia. Many of these diplomats saw a gloomy pattern emerging in the council's work: the great powers could get away with whatever they pleased. The ambassador from the Ivory Coast put it this way:

When there was a dispute between two small powers, the dispute eventually disappeared.

If there was a dispute between a small power and a great power, the small power disappeared.

And if there was a dispute between two great powers, the Security Council disappeared.[68]

This ambassador was part of a growing force at the United Nations. The world and the organization's membership had changed dramatically since the San Francisco conference. Total membership had increased from 76 in 1955 to

117 in 1965. The United Nations' corridors were awash with delegates from new African and Asian states.

In the midst of this roiling change, however, the make-up of the Security Council had remained fixed; its membership was overwhelmingly white and European. Non-Western delegates struggled to make their influence felt. The charter gave nonmembers the right to appear before the council when it was debating conflicts in which they were involved, and nonmembers tried to make the most of that access. Krishna Menon, India's long-time envoy in New York, was often a dramatic presence. During council debates on Kashmir in 1957, he insisted on appearing despite poor health. Once, he collapsed at the council table only to return later in the afternoon and hold forth for almost an hour. On another occasion, a worried physician monitored the diplomat's pulse while he spoke.[69] A joke circulated in the UN corridors that the surest way to revive Menon should he collapse was to wave a microphone under his nose.[70]

But these were cameo appearances. Throughout the early 1960s, the United States and its Western allies retained significant control of the council agenda. The United States could usually muster the seven votes it needed to determine what the council would debate and what resolutions it would consider. Issues on which the United States believed the council could play a constructive role were brought before it, while less convenient topics were shunted aside. American leaders often struggled to decide when the council should be used, and the growing conflict in Vietnam presented a particularly acute dilemma. By early 1965, thousands of American combat troops were battling North Vietnamese forces and Viet Cong irregulars.

Arthur Goldberg, the former Supreme Court justice who succeeded Adlai Stevenson as UN ambassador, beseeched the administration to make its case on Vietnam in the council. As one of the most aggressive proponents of a negotiated solution to the conflict, Goldberg believed that America could use the council to help extricate itself from Vietnam. At a White House meeting in July 1965, as the U.S. troop buildup was proceeding, he presented the argument. "What would be the worst that could happen to us in the Security Council? Are we so lacking in friends that we won't be applauded [for bringing up the issue]?" It would be better, he argued, for the United States to bring Vietnam to the council than for another country to confront America. "I want us to be the plaintiff, not the defendant."[71] The State Department and many influential Johnson advisors preferred to stay out of court altogether. The conflict was unpopular abroad, and U.S. diplomats saw no reason to give other council members the chance to meddle. Goldberg's advice was rejected, and he was instructed to keep Vietnam off the agenda whenever possible.

A few months later, the United States changed tack. In January 1966, as it prepared to end a month-long bombing pause, the administration decided to couple its renewed military pressure with a very public push for a negotiated solution. Dean Rusk recommended to the president that "once our bombing of the North has resumed, it will be especially important that it be clear to the world that our peace offensive is still being vigorously pursued; also such a move would meet the persistent domestic criticism that the full resources of the UN have not been brought to bear on the Viet Nam problem."[72] Henry Cabot Lodge, by now ambassador to Vietnam, cabled the State Department to support the idea. No stranger to council theatrics, Lodge recommended a dramatic show.

> A colorful, somewhat emotion-stirring showing is needed to dramatize the fact that the Communists are in truth flagrant aggressors and not the moralistic, patriotic civil war fighters which Communist propaganda has, with considerable success, made them out to be. The Security Council meeting provides a great chance for this, and, as I have reported, we have dramatic materials here in the way of NVN [North Vietnamese] uniforms, Chinese firearms, etc., with which to document a strong speech by Amb. Goldberg that this is a clear case of aggression.[73]

On February 2, 1966, Goldberg presented a draft resolution to the council. But the newfound American eagerness for using the body to address Vietnam was not reciprocated. The French opposed placing the issue on the agenda. The British were not enthusiastic. The Soviets, who might have welcomed the chance to put America on the defensive, instead loudly rejected the proposal. Behind the rhetoric lay a diplomatic dilemma for Moscow. Relations between the Soviet Union and China had deteriorated since the late 1950s, and the Soviets were locked in a battle with the Chinese for the affections of the North Vietnamese. In this context, Moscow apparently viewed council diplomacy as too risky. The Chinese had already suggested that the Soviets might sell out the North Vietnamese to improve relations with Washington.[74] Goldberg's initiative fizzled. He succeeded in placing Vietnam on the council's agenda, but within a week he conceded that nothing else would be possible.

The South Rising

To many small states, the fact that the council could not bring itself to seriously debate a major conflict involving the great powers revealed a deep flaw in the institution and undercut the rationale for a small, great-power-dominated body. As decolonization swelled the ranks of the United Nations, an eleven-member

Security Council dominated by the feuding superpowers appeared increasingly anachronistic and futile. Beginning in the mid-1950s, the Five came under pressure to expand the ranks of the council so that representatives of the new states could more regularly have a seat at the table. Latin American countries were the first to formally propose expanding the council. Given the region's strong representation on the council, the proposal seemed odd. But the Latin American states realized that, without expansion, the new African and Asian states would soon reapportion the nonpermanent seats on their own, perhaps leaving Latin America with nothing.

For several years, the Soviets effectively throttled any expansion by linking the issue to the admission of Communist China. The Soviet ambassador insisted:

> [I]t would be a flagrant and unthinkable violation of the Purposes and Principles of the Charter to engage in any discussion of [amending the charter] so long as 600 million Chinese people were not represented in the United Nations and the lawful representative of the Chinese people was denied the right to his seat in the Organization.[75]

The uncompromising Soviet stance allowed the rest of the Five to keep a low profile on the issue, but it was clear enough that none wanted the expansion. The British Foreign Office worried.

> [T]he Afro-Asians (joined not infrequently by the Latin-Americans) are still all too ready to use their weight of numbers to push through irresponsible and extreme resolutions, which those they are directed at cannot be expected to comply with, and which, accordingly, serve only to undermine the authority of the United Nations and to bring it into disrepute.

The principal British objective was "the maintenance of the strongest possible voting strength in the Council for the West as a whole."[76] A CIA analysis expressed concern that a growing sense of solidarity among the smaller UN members might "force the great powers into countermoves to strengthen their own community of interests."[77]

When the issue finally reached a full debate in a 1963 session of the General Assembly, the great powers trotted out well-practiced arguments about the need for an efficient and responsive council that could act quickly in a crisis. But the pleas to maintain a small council rang hollow. The Cold War, after all, had rendered the body incapable of action in many crises. In the heady days of 1946, the small states could be convinced that only a small council could be effective. By the 1960s, it was a hard case to make. Would adding a few more nonpermanent members really cripple the body? And wouldn't a fairer allocation of seats increase the council's legitimacy in Africa and Asia? Given the body's all-too-apparent limitations, the great-power arguments were not persuasive to most states.

Still, the Five likely would have prevailed had the Afro-Asian bloc not held a trump card: the procedure for electing nonpermanent members to the council. Since the council began operating, nonpermanent seats had been apportioned along geographical lines. One of the six rotating seats was reserved for British Commonwealth countries, one for Eastern Europe, one for Western Europe, two for Latin America, and one for Africa and Asia. The breakdown had made some sense in 1946, but it was manifestly unfair after rapid decolonization yielded dozens of new African and Asian countries. In 1946, an eleven-member council represented almost 20 percent of the organization's membership; by 1964, it represented just 10 percent.

Nowhere was the geographical division of nonpermanent seats set down in writing; like much else at the United Nations, it was a matter of custom established in the organization's early days. If the Five would not agree to expand the council, the Afro-Asian bloc could use its voting power in the General Assembly to radically alter that custom. They had the votes in the assembly; by the end of 1963, African and Asian states together comprised 50 of the United Nations' 112 members, and they could count on support from many states in Latin America and the Middle East. Western diplomats realized that an expanded council was better than one dominated by African and Asian states. An internal State Department assessment in late 1963 concluded that the United States "would do better to acquiesce in enlargement than fight it."[78] The Soviets and the French, traditionally most insistent on great-power privilege, resisted longer, but they too yielded.

The debate on the council expansion did produce one point of tacit agreement among the Five: the utility of the General Assembly in security matters was greatly reduced. That body had simply become too large and unpredictable to play as active a role as it had in the 1950s and early 1960s. A memo from the U.S. National Security Council conceded the point. "It is in the long-range interest of this country, as well as the USSR, that important matters such as peacekeeping go through the Security Council channel due to the present nature and composition of the General Assembly."[79] The United States never disavowed entirely the Uniting for Peace tactic, but it quietly moved away from a reliance on the assembly.

In August 1965, proposed revisions to the charter secured the needed ratifications. The council would now have fifteen members, and nine votes were now needed to pass a resolution. The veto power remained untouched, but the grip of the great powers on the council had become less certain. If they acted together, the nonpermanent members of the council commanded the votes to pass resolutions and determine the agenda. In strictly East-West issues, the three Western powers and Taiwan now needed support from five nonpermanent members to pass a resolution. By the time the council convened in January 1966, UN staff had adjusted the horseshoe table and installed extra seats in the chamber. The council became a more crowded and less predictable place as the global "South" broke into the great-power citadel.

Firefighting

The council agenda, thin for much of the 1950s, grew crowded too, as flare-ups around the world pressed in. Using their voting power, the new states were often able to insist that the council debate issues that its permanent members would have preferred not to confront. And yet, even in the midst of East-West and North-South tension, there were moments when the council could be effective—in part because it allowed countries to publicly vent and then quietly compromise. The conflict over Cyprus and the dispute between India and Pakistan were such occasions. Fighting broke out in late 1963 between the Greek and Turkish communities in Cyprus, and the issue came before the Security Council a few weeks later. With the strong support of Britain and the United States, the council authorized a peacekeeping mission to monitor a "green line" between the hostile communities. The Soviet Union, fearful that the alternative to UN peacekeeping would be a NATO intervention force, grudgingly approved the plan.[80] Envisioned as a stopgap to prevent wider conflict, the peacekeepers in Cyprus have entered their fifth decade of service.

In South Asia, the disputed territory of Kashmir also triggered conflict. In April 1965, Pakistan sent hundreds of militants across its border to conduct operations in the disputed region. A few months later, India reacted with a full-scale assault. The conflict did not serve the interests of the Five. The United States had provided economic and military aid to both parties and was eager to maintain good relations with both. The Soviets, too, had been courting the rivals. Moscow also feared that China—no longer a Soviet ally—might become involved.

The United States was chairing the council when it considered the crisis in September. The U.S. ambassador, Arthur Goldberg, called a meeting of the permanent members to coordinate strategy, and they agreed to pressure the warring parties to accept a peace settlement by 3:00 that morning at the latest. When the Pakistani foreign minister arrived for the council meeting, he had a brief discussion with Goldberg. "Would you do me a favor?" the American diplomat recalled him asking. "This is very painful for me. Would you allow me to make a long speech? It will be a terrible speech. It's going to excoriate the Indians. However, at one minute to three, I'll announce that we accept [the proposed ceasefire]." That was exactly what happened. The Pakistani minister gave a scathing speech during which he described the Indians as "rats." India's diplomats walked out of the chamber in protest. But, as promised, Pakistan agreed to the ceasefire moments before the deadline.[81]

The India-Pakistan duel and the Cyprus imbroglio were little more than warm-ups for the council as it grappled with new trouble in the Middle East. By the spring of 1967, the fragile peace brokered in the wake of the Suez crisis was coming undone. Egypt's Nasser was under intense pressure from other Arab leaders to take the fight to Israel. The once-venerated Egyptian leader was now ridiculed in the Arab press for allowing Israel to go unpunished. In April and May, the rhetoric from Arab regimes became extreme. A government-run newspaper in Syria wrote that "our heroic people, singing songs of war, is [*sic*] longing to begin the final battle. There is no way to remove occupation other than by smashing the enemy's bases and destroying his power."[82] The goading was effective. Nasser ratcheted up military preparations and began mobilizing for war. Only UNEF, the UN peacekeeping force in the Sinai, stood in his way. For more than a decade, its roughly 3,000 troops had patrolled the border between Israel and Egypt on the Sinai peninsula. Troops from UNEF were stationed on the Egyptian side of the ceasefire line only, as Israel would not acquiesce to the presence of UN troops on its soil.

On the night of May 16, an Egyptian courier approached the UN commander in the Sinai and presented him with a written request that he withdraw his forces as soon as possible. Egyptian forces, the dispatch said, were already on their way to replace them. The UN commander accepted the letter but did his best to temporize. The request, he told the Egyptian, would have to go directly to the secretary-general. Nasser's move placed UN secretary-general U Thant in a delicate position. The UN buffer force in the Sinai was there with Egypt's permission. It had been created by the General Assembly, not by the council acting under its mandatory chapter VII powers. The legal case for keeping the force in Egypt without the government's consent was weak. Practical realities also militated in favor of acceding to Nasser; the largest troop contributors to the UN force, India and Pakistan, wanted no part of a mission that did not have Egypt's approval.

Thant's room for maneuver was narrowed further by the Security Council's lethargy and division. The council could have seen in the Egyptian request the warning signs of renewed conflict and seized control of the issue. Nasser's move worried the United States, but it decided not to force the issue on the council. The Soviets sided with their Egyptian ally. A few nonpermanent members tried to galvanize the council, but they made little headway. The whole unpleasant matter was left to the secretary-general.[83] On the evening of May 18, Thant ordered UNEF to withdraw.[84]

As the crisis developed, Thant came under withering criticism for that decision. A *New York Times* columnist wrote that the secretary-general had "used his international prestige with the objectivity of a spurned lover and the dynamism of a noodle."[85] The criticism is only partially fair. Thant certainly could have made a determined stand on the issue and raised the alarm to a higher volume than he did. As former senior UN official Brian Urquhart has written:

> [Thant could have] refused the original demand for UNEF withdrawal, convoked the Security Council immediately to deal with a threat to the peace, and let the responsibility and blame fall on the members of the Council rather than on the Secretary-General. Disaster would not have been avoided by such a tactic, but the scapegoat would have escaped.[86]

Without firm backing from the council, Thant likely would have been compelled to withdraw the peacekeepers in any case. At the very least, large contingents of UN troops would have been pulled. Those troops who remained might have faced the prospect of conflict with Egyptian troops, something they were ill equipped to handle. Averting a UN withdrawal would have required something akin to heroism from the secretary-general. Dag Hammarskjöld might have been capable of it; U Thant was not.

The Sinai saga presented a dynamic that would become all too familiar in later years. Faced with difficult political and military decisions, the divided council would become adept at shifting hard decisions to the United Nations' permanent officials. Blame for the ensuing failure could then be passed to the organization's bureaucracy, which would not always cover itself with glory. Senior UN officials—and particularly the secretary-general—are generally selected for their low profiles and political palatability, not for their leadership skills. They are ready-made scapegoats.

By May 20, most of the UN observer force had been replaced by Egyptians. There was no confrontation; the UN troops simply melted away. Israel's diplomats were livid. "Before shooting at [the Egyptians] at least you could have shouted at them," Israeli ambassador Gideon Rafael angrily told U Thant.[87] Israel rejected requests to move the observer force to its territory, fearful that observers would inhibit its ability to respond to infiltration and would create a precedent for international control of disputed territory.

The next domino soon tumbled. On May 22, Nasser ordered a blockade of the Gulf of Aqaba, effectively closing Eilat, Israel's only Red Sea port. The move, together with an Egyptian military buildup in the Sinai, put Israel in a state of panic. Yitzhak Rabin, the Israeli Army's chief of staff, was close to a nervous breakdown and was administered a tranquilizer.[88] As the clock ticked down to war, the council behaved as if it, too, had been sedated. It met desultorily on May 24, but the Soviet ambassador complained that there was no reason for such a "hasty convening of the Security Council" and Egypt's ambassador concurred.[89]

The nationality of the council president for the month of May might have contributed to the council's sluggishness. It was nationalist China's turn at the head of the table. Seven members of the council had no diplomatic relations with Taiwan, and several close observers have contended that the council president was unable to play his traditional role of organizing debate and arranging informal talks.[90] The council met again on May 29 and May 30, but most of the meeting time was consumed with speeches by the parties rather than deliberations by the council members. The next day, the French ambassador asked for a two-day adjournment, and the council agreed. On Saturday, June 3, the group convened for a short session. "The situation with which the Council is confronted today has deteriorated since the Council first met on this question," said Gideon Rafael. "What is required is action, concrete steps to forego [sic] all acts of belligerence and to withdraw the armies back to their previous position[s]." His words had little effect. The session adjourned at 2:20 in the afternoon, and the next meeting was set for Monday.[91]

Israeli warplanes moved much faster. Early Monday, almost 200 planes took off from an airfield in Israel. Flying low, they headed for the Mediterranean before banking sharply toward Egypt. At about 7:30, the planes struck Egyptian airfields, destroying runways and strafing planes on the ground. A second wave of Israeli planes picked up where the first had left off. By 9:00 that morning, almost three-quarters of the Egyptian Air Force had been destroyed.[92]

Before dawn in New York, Rafael received a terse phone call from Israel. "Please take paper and pencil and write down: 'Inform immediately the President of the Security Council that Israel is now engaged in repelling Egyptian land and air forces.'" Rafael tracked down Hans Tabor, the Danish diplomat serving as council president in June. A few minutes later, Egypt's ambassador called Tabor with the same news. Tabor immediately scheduled a 9:00 meeting. Before it began, Rafael recalled later, he received one more message from the foreign ministry. It was a telegram that began, "For the Ambassador, Personal—For Your Eyes Only." It contained news of the air strike's stunning success and strict instructions that he must not communicate the news to anyone yet. "It was apparently meant as a booster shot for the head of the mission to get him in good trim for the forthcoming fierce UN debates," Rafael reflected.[93] It would be needed. The howls of protest at the Israeli strike were loud, and not only from

Israel's traditional enemies. "Angry as hell" was how Secretary of State Dean Rusk described the U.S. reaction to the Israeli preemptive strike.[94]

A startled and uncertain council convened that morning. Everyone felt that a meeting was necessary, but nobody knew quite what to say. The military situation was still unclear, and most council ambassadors were not privy to the Israeli information on the success of their air sorties. Egypt was claiming that it had inflicted serious losses on Israeli forces. Facts on the ground mattered much more than speeches, and the council quickly adjourned so that its members could track events more closely. The Soviet ambassador disappeared inside the Soviet mission and could not be reached.[95]

As Israel's startling success became obvious, Soviet diplomats emerged from seclusion and raced to arrange a ceasefire for their beleaguered allies. The Arab losses were a shock to the Politburo, which saw its alliance with the Arab world as "the biggest geopolitical achievement of Soviet foreign policy since the end of World War II."[96] Soviet hesitation about engaging the council had turned to an almost panicked insistence on achieving a ceasefire through it. On the evening of June 6, the council unanimously adopted a simple resolution calling for an end to the fighting.

For the advancing Israelis, however, every extra hour meant new territory and a better position. Having flown all night from Israel, Foreign Minister Abba Eban arrived at the council that same evening to make the Israeli case. He had the good fortune of addressing the council in primetime on the American East Coast. The three major U.S. networks canceled their evening programming and carried the debate live. After the Iraqi and Syrian ambassadors spoke, Eban tried to convey the atmosphere in Israel in the weeks before the fighting. He described a beleaguered and blockaded country struggling to survive in a hostile environment.

> There was peril for Israel wherever it looked. Its manpower had been hastily mobilized. Its economy and commerce were beating with feeble pulses. Its streets were dark and empty. There was an apocalyptic air of approaching peril. And Israel faced this danger alone.[97]

Only now, by dint of military heroism, was Israel removing the noose from around its neck, he argued. Eban's journey to New York paid dividends. The American public and press welcomed his speech warmly. The *New York Times* praised Eban's composure in the face of Arab outrage and called the live telecast "one of television's finest achievements."[98]

During the next several days, the council debates degenerated as Soviet and Arab alarm increased. The Soviets and their Eastern European allies frequently compared the Israelis to the Nazis. "Does the representative of Tel-Aviv have any moral right to sit at the Security Council table?" asked the Soviet ambassador.[99] Rafael fired back as fast as he could. "Neither Israel nor the Jewish people," he said at one point, "concluded a pact with Hitler's Germany, a pact which unleashed Nazi Germany's aggression against the world."[100] The Soviet ambassador had reached a "record low in vilification when he dared to refer in one breath to Israel and to the Nazi monsters, whose names I do not need to mention in the Security Council."[101]

The Americans, and Goldberg in particular, received almost as much fire as the Israelis. "United States policy," alleged the Syrian ambassador, "is geared and has been geared for the last quarter of a century, to say the least, to the fulfillment of the aims of Zionism."[102] Several Arab ambassadors charged that the Americans and British had intervened militarily on the side of Israel. The Soviets insinuated that Goldberg was acting as a proxy for his coreligionists. "Why does the United States representative's sense of objectivity and justice fall short in this respect?" he asked slyly. "We should like to hear an answer to our question."[103]

As the sparring continued at the council, American policymakers watched the fighting nervously. There was sympathy for Israel, and Eban's dramatic address had helped the Israeli cause with the American public. In this context, the Johnson administration was willing to see Israeli forces strengthen their position. When Goldberg asked Rafael what he needed in terms of diplomatic support, the answer was simple: "Time."[104] Washington obliged—for a while. The Americans fended off Soviet-sponsored resolutions labeling the Israelis as aggressors and demanding a return to prewar positions.

American patience was not unlimited, however. As Israel advanced, Moscow hinted that it might intervene militarily to protect its Arab allies. President Lyndon Johnson and Soviet premier Alexei Kosygin spoke for the first time on the telephone hotline created after the Cuban missile crisis, and Kosygin warned that a superpower clash leading to a "grave catastrophe" was possible.[105] To signal American determination, Johnson ordered the U.S. Sixth Fleet to sail closer to the conflict zone.

At all costs, the United States wanted to avoid the appearance that the fighting had ended because of a Soviet ultimatum, and American pressure on Israel intensified. Rafael phoned Jerusalem to warn that the diplomatic dam was breaking. "Not only [was] Israel's credibility at stake but we were in danger of being condemned by the Security Council, including [by] the United States."[106] By the afternoon of the sixth day, American patience was exhausted. In the delegates' lounge, Goldberg pulled Rafael aside and told him that the time had come to cease fire.[107] The Israeli cabinet finally assented, and by Saturday, June 10, most of the guns in the region had fallen silent. The Six-Day War had ended.

Constructive Ambiguity

Thus far, the conflict had been little short of an embarrassment for the council, which had shown itself incapable of averting a war telegraphed far in advance. That failure could not be blamed entirely on the conflicting political interests of the major powers. The historical record suggests that none of the permanent five desired a conflict. Instead, mutual suspicion and inadequate leadership were to blame. Exhausted and still bitter, the council that had been so negligent as war approached tried to construct a diplomatic framework for lasting peace in its aftermath. The key question became whether and under what conditions Israel would cede some or all of the territory it had captured. For weeks after the fighting ended, the council wrestled with that question. When it failed to produce a resolution, the General Assembly, called into emergency session, tried its hand. The assembly debate produced nothing, however, and the issue was firmly back in the council's hands by October.

Then, just as it appeared that the wheels of diplomacy had become irretrievably stuck, the ground shifted. Goldberg and Britain's ambassador, Lord Caradon, plodded away on a draft resolution that would establish a central quid pro quo: the Israelis would exchange captured land for lasting peace. Putting that simple principle into the form of an acceptable resolution required many long weeks of effort, however. Negotiations were made easier by a change in Soviet personalities. Deputy foreign minister Vasily Kuznetsov arrived from Moscow in the middle of October to replace Nikolai Fedorenko. The new ambassador proved to be pleasant and flexible, and it became clear that he carried with him a more accommodating set of instructions.[108]

The next six weeks passed in a flurry of council diplomacy, sometimes in formal meetings, often in informal huddles outside the council chamber. The rigid alignment that had dominated during the fighting began to break down. Goldberg lost patience with the Israelis, who seemed intent on formally annexing some of the land they had captured. Syria broke with other Arab states on the question of whether Palestinian rights were being adequately considered. Meanwhile, multiple draft resolutions circulated. By the middle of November, a British draft was getting the most attention, and it appeared that it might have the necessary support, although the Soviet vote was still in doubt.[109]

As the momentum grew, Britain's Caradon met alone with Kuznetsov, who asked for a delay of several days. Caradon expressed doubt that further delay would serve any purpose. "I am personally asking you for two days," Kuznetsov pleaded, believing that he could win over the Politburo. Caradon consented, and on November 22, his patience was rewarded.[110] The British draft was put to a vote, and Kuznetsov raised his hand in support. The resolution passed unanimously, and the gallery broke into loud applause.[111]

Resolution 242 was remarkably simple. It emphasized the "inadmissibility of the acquisition of territory by war and the need to work for a just and lasting peace in which every state in the area can live in security." It established two principles to guide a lasting settlement. First, Israel must "withdraw from territories occupied in the recent conflict." Second, it required all states to end their states of war and to accept the right of all other states in the region to exist. The resolution requested that the secretary-general appoint a mediator to begin negotiations with the parties.[112]

A few days after it passed, Lord Caradon celebrated the Soviet representative in verse.

> When prospects are dark and hopes are dim,
> We know that we must send for him;
> When storms and tempests fill the sky,
> Bring on Kuznetsov is the cry.
>
> He comes like a dove from the Communist ark,
> And light appears where all was dark;
> His coming quickly turns the tide,
> The propaganda floods subside.
>
> And now that he has changed the weather,
> Lion and Lamb can vote together.
> God bless the Russian delegation,
> I waive consecutive translation.[113]

Resolution 242 became perhaps the most famous resolution in the council's history. For more than four decades, it has been the starting point for discussions on Middle East peace. Henry Kissinger later described its virtues: "what it lacked in precision, it made up for in flexibility. It was well suited for beginning a negotiation in which reconnecting the different interpretations of the parties would be one of the objectives."[114] Its passage was a result of determined diplomacy and superpower compromise, and the diplomats involved have sometimes sparred over which of them deserves the most credit. For all of its notoriety, however, it is still little more than an aspiration. As has been the case since the council's very first contact with Palestine, the body lacks the will to impose a solution.

Still, the resolution was the product of deft draftsmanship and a case study in the value of ambiguity. It provided a basic principle to anchor often confused negotiations. Almost as soon as the resolution passed, the parties began squabbling over what it meant. The English version of the resolution called for Israel to withdraw from "territories occupied." The indefinite article "the" was notably absent. In French and in other official languages, however, it was clear that Israel was obliged to withdraw from all of the occupied territories. There is little doubt that the ambiguity was intentional—indeed, there likely never would have been a resolution without it. The text allowed all sides to read into the resolution what they wanted. It permitted the council to endorse an important principle—that land should be traded for peace—without stating how much land.[115] The lack of clarity in council resolutions, which could be so maddening during active operations, as in Congo, had distinct advantages when the council was trying to shepherd warring parties toward negotiations.

The Six-Day War placed in stark relief the Cold War council's capacities and incapacities. The body could not act quickly to head off a crisis and was too fractured to avoid even a conflict that none of the permanent members desired. It did not have the will to impose a permanent solution to the conflict. What the council could offer was a mechanism for the great powers to ensure that they were not drawn into the vortex, and it could articulate vague principles for an eventual settlement that, not coincidentally, allowed each superpower to claim that it had defended the interests of its allies. Israelis and Palestinians could be forgiven for concluding that the council's most powerful members were more concerned with saving face than with improving the lot of the millions affected by the conflict. In a world full of nuclear weapons on high alert, however, according the superpowers that flexibility was no small accomplishment.

CHAPTER 4

A HOSTILE ENVIRONMENT
(1968–1985)

G EORGE BALL DREADED Security Council meetings. The fifty-nine-year-old lawyer had enjoyed a remarkable career in business and government that included service as a presidential envoy and as undersecretary of state in the Kennedy and Johnson administrations. In the latter post, he had argued passionately against military escalation in Southeast Asia. Ball developed a reputation for cutting through official palaver. Disillusioned with the spiraling costs of the Vietnam war and intent on replenishing his own coffers, Ball had left government in 1967 for a lucrative position at Lehman Brothers in New York. Lyndon Johnson had other plans. The president flattered and bullied Ball into replacing Arthur Goldberg when he stepped down as UN ambassador in 1968. "I need you, George," the president told him. "No one else has ever disagreed with me as much as you but I need you." It took all of Johnson's persuasive power to drag Ball back from Wall Street and into the council chamber.[1]

By the time he arrived, the council had become even more trying for those averse to empty rhetoric. The 1966 expansion had ensured that more countries from the developing world would have council seats and limited the great powers' ability to control the agenda. The African and Asian states elected to the council were usually members of the Non-Aligned Movement (NAM), an organization designed to more effectively communicate and defend the interests of states not firmly allied with either superpower bloc. The brainchild of Yugoslavia's Marshal Josip Tito, India's Jawaharlal Nehru, and Egyptian president Nasser, the NAM took shape in the early 1960s and soon became a significant force in world politics, particularly at the United Nations.

In practice, the NAM tilted sharply toward the Soviet bloc. The group's most active members, including Cuba, had little fondness for the United States, its foreign policy, or its economic system. The movement's declarations made its sympathies clear. "The underlying cause of international tensions," read one statement, "is attributable to the forces of imperialism, colonialism, neo-colonialism, Zionism, racism and other forms of alien domination."[2] The Soviets and their satellites cultivated relationships with NAM members and usually voted with the bloc at the United Nations.

Sheer numbers gave the NAM major influence in New York. By coordinating positions on key issues and marshaling votes, these states often achieved diplomatic clout out of all proportion to their economic or military power. That influence soon extended into the council, long the preserve of the great powers. Many observers viewed the developing world's new clout as a sign that the council was modernizing and democratizing. The notion that the Five should control the agenda appeared increasingly outdated. The UN secretary-general, Kurt Waldheim, wrote in 1972:

> [E]ven if the Security Council were to acquire a new effectiveness through Great Power détente, the idea of maintaining peace and security in the world through a concert of great powers, although these powers obviously have great responsibilities in matters of peace and security, would seem to belong to the nineteenth rather than to the twentieth century.[3]

As if to underscore Waldheim's point, a resolution on the Middle East conflict passed in the council in 1973 without the affirmative votes of any of the Five. France, the United Kingdom, the Soviet Union, and the United States abstained, and China did not participate in the vote.[4] Twice in the early 1970s, the NAM pressured the council to decamp from New York and hold meetings in the developing world. The group of ambassadors trekked to Ethiopia and Panama for a series of meetings. Many ambassadors from the developing world saw the trips as psychologically important. "The Council members were now nearer to the realities of colonialism and racial discrimination," wrote Abdulrahim Abby Farah, Somalia's UN envoy at the time.[5] Western diplomats were far less enthusiastic. "No business was conducted at those meetings that could not have been better done in New York," complained British ambassador Colin Crowe. "The Council is too valuable a piece of international machinery to be turned into simply a vehicle for pressure and propaganda."[6]

Wherever the council was meeting, the nonaligned members spent much of their considerable speaking time on denunciations of the United States, neocolonialism, and the inequities of the international economic order. In the early 1970s, the nonaligned states elaborated the concept of a "new international economic order" to redress the injustices of colonial exploitation and took up the cause of national liberation movements in Africa, Asia, and the Middle East. The nonaligned had no hesitation about laying the world's economic and social disparities on the council table. What greater threat was there to the world's security, after all, then the chasm between the world's affluent "North" and its impoverished "South." The critique was an incisive one. Since it began meeting, the council had focused on the most extreme manifestation of discontent— violent conflict, usually between states. It darted from crisis to crisis but paid little attention to what many poor nations saw as the root cause of much conflict: disparities in economic development.

With their new access to the council, the developing world set out to right that imbalance. Relying on a generous interpretation of Article 31 of the UN Charter, which provides that all states may participate in council meetings when their interests are "specially affected," a parade of non-council members took turns speaking. Because inviting nonmembers is a procedural decision immune from the veto, the Western powers could do little to stop the practice. The Soviets, for their part, were pleased to welcome the generally anti-Western speakers. During the long speeches, George Ball would jot down stanzas, which he would surreptitiously share with his colleague in verse, Lord Caradon. While Caradon had written odes to cooperative Soviet diplomats, Ball often skewered the council for its often meaningless resolutions and tedious debates.

> Each time this august group *deplores*
> It's like a feral wolf that howls.
> I feel a chill in my pores;
> A fearful tremor in my bowels.
>
> My lungs would suffocate with phlegm,
> My mind recoil, my pulse race faster,
> If the Council should ever *condemn*,
> Since that would mean extreme disaster.
> For I can't think that any nation
> Could stand such deep humiliation.

Specific council personalities were not spared Ball's sharp pen. Yakov Malik, the Soviet ambassador in the council's early days, had returned for a second tour of duty in the late 1960s. In another ditty, Ball compared Malik to Moloch, a demon of legend.[7]

Less literary diplomats often leafed through documents, some of them classified, while the council speeches droned on. The incaution of these diplomats stunned a senior Soviet official at the United Nations. He knew that KGB operatives regularly snapped photos from the glass-enclosed translation booths above the council chamber, and he assumed that Western intelligence agents did the same.[8] The spies might have been among the most attentive observers. During many meetings, diplomats dozed and the public gallery housed only a few devoted souls.

Still, there were moments when the council once again became a focus of world politics. The Soviet invasion of Czechoslovakia in 1968 was one such occasion. In August of that year, hundreds of Soviet tanks rolled into Prague to put down a burgeoning reform movement. A few Czech protestors hurled bottles and fired antique rifles at Soviet troops, but the battle was lost almost as soon as it began. The propaganda fight in New York, however, still had plenty of life. At the council meetings called to address the crisis, U.S. diplomats assembled a coalition to condemn the invasion. Soviet diplomats, meanwhile, struggled to keep their talking points in order. At first, they insisted that the incursion was at the request of the Czech government. It was an untenable position, and in the midst of the council's first session on the crisis, more plausible instructions arrived from Moscow, clarifying that Soviet intervention had been requested by certain "party and state figures of Czechoslovakia."[9]

The American case was helped immeasurably by the spectacle of Czech diplomats breaking publicly with the Soviets. The reform movement, the Czech ambassador insisted, was about improving socialism, not destroying it. "Human rights and freedom," he argued, "must be an indispensable part of any socialist system." A mid-level Soviet diplomat at the meeting recalled whispering to a colleague, "sounds very reasonable," before noticing that Malik was staring at him.[10] On August 24, the Czech foreign minister himself appeared before the council. "We are deeply disappointed, offended and humiliated; and this is even more cruel because it came from such countries from which we had not expected it in the least, and from which we did not deserve it in the least."[11] Staring at the Soviet representative across the table, he said simply: "No one in the government of Czechoslovakia invited your troops. No one wanted your troops."[12]

When Malik insisted that the Soviet Union was simply providing "fraternal assistance" to its Czech colleagues, Ball fired back. "The kind of fraternal assistance that the Soviet Union is according to Czechoslovakia is exactly the same kind that Cain gave to Abel." Britain's Lord Caradon even feigned sympathy for his Soviet colleague, who was forced to defend the sordid invasion. "All of us must have felt a sense of compassion for Ambassador Malik who has today endeavoured to carry out such an unworthy task. We can picture his distaste, indeed his disgust, at having to defend such a disgraceful act. No wonder that in doing so he carried so little conviction." Suitably goaded, Malik chose to direct his vitriol at Ball.

When Mr. Ball speaks of freedom, he evidently has in mind freedom to kill many hundreds of thousands of wholly innocent people in Viet-Nam, freedom for political terrorism which has led to the destruction of many outstanding political leaders of the United States. When he speaks of freedom he apparently means freedom for the racists who have placed over 20 million people with "non-white" skin in a position where they are deprived of all rights, an unbearable position.[13]

The outcome of the debate was preordained: most council members would condemn the invasion, and the Soviets would scuttle the resolution. When the inevitable veto came, Ball was ready with a ringing peroration:

This is the 105th time that the Soviet Union has employed the veto to frustrate a decision by the Security Council.... no one is surprised that a Power which views Czechoslovakia as its private colonial domain and which has vetoed by naked and brutal force the right of the Czechoslovak people to breathe the air of freedom should undertake without apparent qualms or reservations to try to shut off and frustrate this solemn and serious body, the Security Council. Your veto, Mr. Malik, may stifle the legal vote of this Council, but it cannot suffocate the soul of a proud people.[14]

The debate was animated, but it was also ritualistic. Nobody expected results and none emerged. The protagonists themselves sometimes seemed to recognize the artificiality of the spectacle. Ball recalled encountering Malik after one long and acrimonious session. The Soviet pounded him on the back and grinned. "Well, I guess I kept you up late tonight, didn't I?" Ball knew the drill. "We were going through the motions and putting on a good show but there was nothing more we could do."[15] Even the American condemnation of the Soviet veto rang hollow: the United States itself was set to embrace the procedural tactic it had criticized for so long.

America Says No

The beating the Soviets took over Czechoslovakia was unusual. By the late 1960s, rhetoric at the United Nations had become increasingly anti-Western, and Americans grew weary of the abuse. As early as 1962, major political figures had begun to reassess the country's relationship with the organization. Senator Henry "Scoop" Jackson, a moderate Democrat and a leading authority on foreign affairs, argued that the United Nations should have a much less prominent place in American diplomacy.

The truth is that the best hope for peace and justice does not lie in the United Nations. Indeed, the truth is almost exactly the reverse. The best hope for the United Nations lies in the maintenance of peace [and] peace depends on the power and unity of the Atlantic community and on the skill of our direct diplomacy.[16]

In January 1970, a classified U.S. memo stated that U.S. policy at the United Nations was to hunker down, particularly on issues related to Africa.

Neither [the United Nations nor Africa] is central in any way to US foreign policy operations or interests. We deal with them because they are there, not because we hope to get great things out of participation. . . . What we really want from both is no trouble. Our policy is therefore directed at damage limiting, rather than at accomplishing anything in particular.[17]

Much as harsh criticism had inspired jeremiads from de Gaulle against the United Nations in the 1950s and early 1960s, U.S. political leaders began to vent their frustration at the organization. By March 1970, the United States was ready to do something it had never done before: veto a council resolution. Since 1946, the United States had always been able to use its sway to avoid the necessity of a veto. It normally had the votes necessary to keep issues it did not want to address off the agenda or at least to prevent hostile resolutions from achieving the votes required for passage. Because a veto is defined as a vote by a permanent member against a resolution that would otherwise have passed, the U.S. voting record remained clean, and it was free to chastise the Soviets for their tactics. The context of the first American veto suggests the degree to which the United States had lost control of the council's agenda. The issue was the white regime in Rhodesia, a frequent target of the United Nations' ire. A long-time British possession, Rhodesia had declared independence in 1965 after its white rulers rejected British pressure to share power with the black majority. Ian Smith, the regime's obdurate leader, rejected any possibility of compromise. With Britain's support, the council imposed economic sanctions on the regime in 1965, but Smith's government still clung to power. Its very existence was an outrage, particularly to members of the NAM.

On March 17, 1970, African and Asian members of the council formally proposed a resolution that would have condemned Britain for refusing to confront the Rhodesian regime even more directly than it had, with force if necessary. Lord Caradon made clear that he would not support a resolution that effectively required his country to invade Rhodesia. "It is a question of an invasion—an invasion in the middle of a continent. We know that once force is used escalation can quickly ensue. We know that the results of violent action can be incalculable."[18] British and American pleas for a delay in voting on the resolution were rebuffed.

The Americans, grasping at straws, resorted to a rare tactic. They insisted on consecutive translation of the council proceedings, as they were technically entitled to do. For years, it had been polite practice at the council to waive the procedural right, which slowed the pace of debate to a crawl as speeches were translated into the several official council languages, one after the other. The move outraged the African representatives, and resentment between them and the Western powers broke out with unusual ferocity as the resolution moved steadily toward a vote. The Zambian ambassador attacked the British ambassador directly. "I hope that from now on Lord Caradon will stop arrogating to himself the role of patriarch, the role of brother—shall I say, big brother?—of Africa and Asia. We are mature enough to take care of our destinies and our future."[19]

The resolution's African sponsors pushed relentlessly for an immediate vote on their draft. When it finally came, U.S. ambassador Charles Yost raised his hand alongside Caradon's to oppose the resolution, which had the nine votes needed for passage. Malik could barely contain his glee. Seeing the British and the Americans forced to rely on the veto was a wonderful turnabout from the days of Soviet isolation. He lectured the British ambassador.

> Throughout the history of the United Nations, you have been accustomed
> to controlling and manipulating the voting machinery. You did not have
> to use the veto then. Using your automatic majority you imposed your
> will on others and forced it down their throats. But times have now
> changed, and today you are in a position in which you have been obliged,
> with the support of the United States representative, to use the veto.[20]

It was an unceremonious end to America's streak of veto-free years. There was no great matter of principle or national interest at stake. The veto was not even necessary: Britain's own vote killed the draft resolution quite effectively. It was fitting that the first U.S. veto was almost nonchalant. The organization had fallen so far in American esteem that the move caused scarcely a ripple domestically. The second veto was not long in coming. On September 10, 1972, the United States startled even its close allies when it vetoed a resolution calling for an immediate cessation to all military action in the Middle East. The United States saw the resolution, prompted by a round of Israeli air strikes on Syria and Lebanon, as imbalanced. It contained no mention of the terrorist attack that had sparked the Israeli strikes.[21] During a visit to the United Nations a few weeks after that vote, Secretary of State William Rogers prepared the organization for a new American attitude on the council. The veto on the Middle East, he said, had been "good medicine." "If the resolution is a bad one," he pledged, "we will veto."[22] During the next two decades, the United States became increasingly willing to use its veto to fend off Soviet and nonaligned resolutions, particularly condemnations of Israel. A tactic that U.S. politicians and diplomats had once despised as obstructionist became a valuable tool. The American view of proper Security Council procedure, it turned out, depended very much on the vote count in the council; when the United States needed the veto, it did not hesitate to use it.

The American tone changed as much as the tactics. A new breed of ambassador—willing and able to lambaste the organization itself—appeared on the scene in the person of Daniel Patrick Moynihan, appointed by President Gerald Ford in June 1975. A Harvard professor and a Labor Department official in the Kennedy administration, Moynihan owed his appointment to an article he had written for *Commentary* magazine, "The United States in Opposition." The article made waves in conservative circles and at the United Nations. Why was it, Moynihan wrote, that the nation that had all but given birth to the United Nations was now so regularly pilloried and outvoted in it? "There has been a massive failure of American diplomacy," he concluded. But the remedy was not more concessions and kinder words. Nor was it opting out of the system entirely, as some critics demanded. To the contrary, the United States had to fight rhetoric with rhetoric. "It is time," Moynihan concluded, "that the American spokesman came to be feared in international forums for the truths he might tell."[23]

Traditional American internationalists observed in horror the implementation of this new style. The *New York Times* worried that Moynihan's appointment signaled a decision to abandon diplomacy. "Does Washington still view the United Nations as an essential if limited arena for constructive, collective diplomacy or—wounded by unfair criticism and a cascade of Assembly defeats through the 'tyranny of the majority'—is the United States now out simply to respond in kind?"[24] Moynihan did plenty of that. He unleashed choice salvos at the organization. When the Security Council adjourned a meeting on the Middle East and delayed voting on a pending resolution, Moynihan expressed astonishment. "Here we have a crisis, the Council meets, and nobody seems to have anything to say. Of course I am a newcomer, but the procedure surprises me."[25] Foreign leaders also blundered into his crosshairs. After Uganda's Idi Amin delivered a harsh speech against Israel, Moynihan called him a "racist murderer" and said it was no accident that the dictator had been selected to head the Organization of African Unity.[26] The professorial Moynihan often leavened his speeches with literary and cultural references. In one typical intervention at the council, Moynihan referenced the Swiss historian Jacob Burckhardt and a fourteenth-century Chinese novel in the space of a few moments.[27]

However literate, Moynihan's interventions were not always well received, even by friends of the United States. British ambassador Ivor Richard called Moynihan a "trigger happy Wyatt Earp" and complained that Moynihan's abrasive style was making constructive work at the United Nations that much harder.[28] At the State Department, the ambassador's flamboyant style annoyed Henry Kissinger, who preferred to have the United Nations remain as quiet as possible. "Don't bother me with that UN crap!" he once chastised an assistant.[29] Moynihan's penchant for generating headlines meant that UN matters landed on Kissinger's desk with unusual frequency.

China Arrives

Dramatic as it was, Moynihan's arrival at the United Nations was not the most consequential of the decade. That distinction went to the representatives of Communist China. Since 1950, debate over which government should hold China's UN seat had been an annual ritual on the East River. Year after year, the General Assembly would vote on a resolution proposed by a Communist-bloc country that the Communist government in Beijing replace the Taiwanese delegation. And year after year, the resolution would be defeated. The U.S. State Department and UN mission made winning the vote a priority, and its diplomats wooed and occasionally bullied smaller states into rejecting the Communist resolution. The effort to keep Communist China on the diplomatic sidelines was aided immeasurably by the Korean War, which saw Chinese troops in active combat against UN-authorized forces. Had China not joined that fight, it likely would have secured UN admission far earlier.

In the years after the fighting in Korea ended, and as the Communists' claim to be the effective government of China became unquestionable, Taiwan's grip on the UN seat began to slip. The U.S. contention that Communist rule in China was a passing phase appeared increasingly bizarre. One by one, UN members, including key U.S. allies, recognized Beijing. By the mid-1960s, the State Department was struggling to hold back the tide. "It now appears that a strong resolution calling for the seating of Peiping and the removal of National China from the UN will for the first time come precariously close to, or even achieve, a simple majority vote in the assembly." Far from alarming the UN membership, China's detonation of an atomic bomb in 1964 appeared to strengthen the conviction of many states that China had to be reckoned with. The test, concluded the State Department, "has enhanced Communist China's prestige among many non-aligned countries and could provide an additional incentive for certain wavering countries to vote for its admission."[30]

As states shifted recognition from Taiwan to Beijing, Taiwan's presence on the council complicated the body's day-to-day operations. When Taiwan assumed its regular slot as president of the council, it had to manage meetings at which many of the participants did not recognize its seat. The Soviets always threatened to embarrass the Taiwanese representative by publicly challenging his credentials, and Soviet diplomats refused to meet with the representatives of Taiwan in informal sessions. To avoid such awkwardness, the council rarely met in the months when Taiwan held the presidency.

Quietly, many senior American diplomats despaired at the U.S. position. Adlai Stevenson pressed Kennedy to shift position, and Arthur Goldberg tried to convince Johnson. But the perceived domestic price was always too high. What American president wanted to expend political capital for Chairman Mao? Kennedy put the political calculation to Stevenson bluntly when they discussed the issue in 1961.

> It really doesn't make any sense—the idea that Taiwan represents China. But, if we lost this fight, if Red China comes into the UN during our first year in town, your first year and mine, they'll run us both out. . . . we can delay the admission of Red China till after the election.[31]

But there was always another election, and the State Department would dutifully round up the votes to oppose China's admission. As those votes became increasingly hard to find, the United States resorted to procedural gymnastics. It sought to designate the admission of China as an "important question" (as provided for in Article 18 of the charter). A simple majority vote on that preliminary question meant that two-thirds of the General Assembly had to approve the switch in Chinese representation.

The flagging U.S. effort to deny Beijing a seat benefited, however, from China's turbulent domestic politics and often erratic international posture. In the 1960s, the world watched in amazement as the Cultural Revolution spread through China. At one point, extremist Red Guards besieged and then ransacked the Foreign Ministry building, convinced that it was under the control of reactionary elements. In this context, it was not clear that Mao even wanted a UN seat. Indeed, China appeared to be searching for an alternative organization in which to exercise its influence. In January 1965, an official Chinese outlet contended that "more and more facts have shown that the United Nations has been increasingly reduced to a tool of imperialism and old and new colonialism headed by the United States." Another publication picked up the theme. "The UN is not the place where the Asian and African countries can uphold justice; it is the place where United States imperialism bullies and oppresses people. Can this be tolerated any longer?" Just as the Soviet Union had toyed with the idea of a

Communist alternative to the United Nations, the Chinese wondered whether their interests wouldn't be better served by a friendlier forum, a "revolutionary" United Nations.[32]

In the midst of the Cultural Revolution and the aggressive rhetoric of Maoism, the moment did not seem right to admit the unpredictable Goliath into the diplomatic inner circle. The heated rhetoric and the ritualistic votes in the General Assembly concealed, however, a seismic shift in China's global position. Since the early 1960s, China's relations with the Soviet Union had turned sour and even violent. In the spring and summer of 1969, Soviet and Chinese troops clashed along their shared border. Several hundred troops were killed or wounded.[33] The American government was slow to react to the split in the Communist world, and the Vietnam War doomed most U.S. approaches to China. But the winding down of that conflict in 1969 and 1970 finally created the needed diplomatic space. President Richard Nixon and his national security advisor, Henry Kissinger, began exploring a diplomatic opening soon after Nixon's election. After months of backchannel contacts, Kissinger arranged a secret trip to Beijing in July 1971.

Kissinger's Asian adventures placed America's new UN ambassador in a difficult position. At the request of the Republican Party, George H. W. Bush had given up his safe seat in the House of Representatives ro run for a Senate seat in 1970. He lost, but Nixon rewarded his sacrifice with the UN ambassadorship. Bush now faced a delicate dilemma. He knew that an American rapprochement with China was all but inevitable. But he also had instructions from the White House to at least keep Taiwan, America's loyal ally, in the organization, although it was understood that Beijing would take the council seat. At a White House meeting in September 1971, Nixon instructed Bush to "fight like hell to keep Taiwan in the organization." Warming relations with China were critical, he said, but "in this country there's a hell of a lot of people that don't want to see us just drag our feet and let Taiwan go down the drain." Kissinger agreed: the United States should simultaneously pursue rapprochement with Beijing and work to preserve a UN seat for Taiwan through procedural maneuvers at the United Nations. "Nobody understands those anyway," said Kissinger.[34] So Bush's team of diplomats drummed up support for a two-seat solution that would hand China's seat to Beijing while creating a new spot for Taiwan.

The goal of this maneuvering proved to be impossible. China would not accept Taiwan's continued presence in the organization. A Communist newspaper opined in September that, "without expelling the Chiang Kai-shek clique, restoration of the legitimate rights of the People's Republic of China is totally out of the question."[35] Taiwanese officials responded in kind. "Rhetoric and friendly gestures notwithstanding," Taiwan's foreign minister warned the

General Assembly, "there is no evidence that the [Communist] regime now intends to pursue a course of action consistent with the United Nations Charter. Indeed, all signs point the other way."[36]

In the General Assembly, however, all signs pointed toward growing support for Beijing, which had skillfully positioned itself as a champion of the Third World. Official Chinese media outlets insisted that, even if Communist China made it into the Security Council, it would not simply be another great power. "China will never seek the so-called big-power position," one editorial read. "We will forever stand side by side with all oppressed people and oppressed nations. The Chinese people will fight together with the people of the whole world to resolutely smash the doctrine of big-nation hegemony!"[37]

The end came abruptly for the Taiwanese delegation. On October 26, 1971, the General Assembly narrowly rejected the "important question" resolution, which would have required a two-thirds majority to replace Taiwan with the Communist government. Anticipating the inevitable next step, the Taiwanese delegation walked out of the General Assembly moments before the lopsided vote that formally evicted them. In that instant, Chiang Kai-shek's government lost all rights at the United Nations, including the coveted council seat. It was just as well that the Taiwanese had left. Many delegations broke into wild applause—and even dancing—as the results were announced.[38] Finally, after twenty-five years of exclusion, Communist China would be in the inner sanctum.

In Washington, congressional Republicans, in particular, were outraged. Senator Barry Goldwater argued that "the time has come [to] recognize the United Nations for the anti-American, antifreedom organization it has [become]." He suggested that the United States cut funding and ask the organization "to find a headquarters location outside of the United States that is more in keeping with the philosophy of the majority of voting members, some place like Moscow or Peking."[39] In Taipei, Chiang Kai-shek put a brave face on the defeat. "We are not small and weak," he insisted. "[W]e still intend to count in the world."[40] For the Soviet Union, China's admission was bittersweet. Moscow had long railed against Beijing's exclusion, but the Communist China about to enter the United Nations had become virulently anti-Soviet in the intervening years. After the vote, an American diplomat leaned over to congratulate a Soviet counterpart. "You introduced [the resolution] twenty years ago and you've won now. China is sitting in the U.N." The Soviet diplomat replied tersely, "Yes, we have won a heavy victory."[41]

On a blustery afternoon a few weeks later, two jetliners touched down at New York's Kennedy Airport. They carried the dozens of officials, translators, and aides who would be the new face of China at the 1971 General Assembly and then at council meetings. Delegates from almost two dozen countries met the Chinese at the airport. In the distance, a small but vocal group waved Chinese flags and portraits of Chairman Mao. Even farther away, a knot of protestors struggled to be noticed.

Over the scream of jets, the delegation attempted to hold a press conference.

> The people of the United States are a great people and there exists a profound friendship between the peoples of China and the United States. We would like to take this opportunity to convey our good wishes to the people of all walks of life in New York City and the American people.

Police escorted the delegation into the city and to their hotel—fittingly, the Roosevelt—where they were ushered through a crowd of press and curious onlookers.[42]

A few weeks later, a much quieter greeting took place in an East Side apartment that the U.S. government had located for the Chinese delegation. Accompanied by Bush and General Alexander Haig, Henry Kissinger arrived for a secret meeting with Huang Hua, the new Chinese ambassador to the United Nations. Kissinger had met Huang during his secret visits to Peking, and the purpose of this visit was to coordinate the two countries' positions at the United Nations and on the council. Kissinger instructed an aide to provide the Chinese with a direct phone number to his office at the White House. He asked them to use a code name when they called. "If you give your real name," he warned, "every operator at the White House will listen to the conversations." Kissinger gestured toward the female Chinese interpreter. "If she calls me and gives a girl's name, they will pay no attention." Kissinger promised that the United States would avoid polemics against China at the United Nations, and he expressed appreciation for the restrained tone that the Chinese had adopted since their arrival. Vietnam, he reminded the Chinese somewhat unnecessarily, "is a particularly sensitive point."[43]

The conversation then turned to the crisis of the moment: the dangerous dispute between India and Pakistan over eastern Pakistan. That territory, dominated by ethnic Bengals, had long felt estranged from the Pakistani elite, which was based in the west of the country. The 1970 national elections had provoked a crisis in the relationship, and full-scale civil disobedience in the east had led to a military crackdown. India was eager to weaken its archrival and did all it could to fan the flames of Bengali separatism, including training and equipping a resistance force. As the dispute escalated, the major powers picked sides. The Chinese and much of the NAM backed Pakistan. The Soviets supported India, a longtime ally. The United States desperately tried to stay neutral. In December, the crisis reached a climax. Pakistan's air force bombed Indian military bases, and

India retaliated by wiping out Pakistani airbases in the east. Indian and Pakistani tanks and troops clashed directly, and millions of refugees flowed into India.[44] The secession of its eastern territories and their nearly 80 million people was a cataclysm for Pakistan, and the conflict led to a series of heated council meetings.

Pakistani foreign minister (and, later, president) Zulfikar Ali Bhutto flew to New York to make the case that the council had to intervene. It was a hopeless mission; the permanent members were divided and none had any desire to get enmeshed in the conflict. At one point in the debate, as it became clear that his pleas were in vain, Bhutto appeared to depart from his notes. "Mr. President, I am not a rat. I've never ratted in my life. I have faced assassination attempts, I've faced imprisonment. Today I am not ratting, but I am leaving your Security Council." With that, he tore up his notes and strode out of the chamber, tears streaming down his face. Outside the chamber, he addressed the media. "I hate this body. I don't want to see their faces again. I'd rather go back to a destroyed Pakistan."[45]

The Chinese joined the fray, alleging that the Soviets, by backing India, were engaging in their own form of imperialism. The charge outraged the Soviets. "Now it is clear," responded Malik, "why the People's Republic of China wanted to join the UN—so that it could spread monstrous lies about the first socialist country in the world." The war of words continued for months. In August 1972, the council debated whether to admit Pakistan's eastern territories to the organization as the new state of Bangladesh. The Chinese demanded that all foreign forces leave Bangladesh before it would support its admittance. The Soviet Union "has stopped at nothing in confounding black with white and reversing right and wrong, reaching the height of truculence," charged Huang.[46]

The Sino-Soviet animosity extended well beyond the India-Pakistan dispute. Huang Hua refused to shake Malik's hand when they were first introduced, causing the Soviet to turn "a livid shade of purple."[47] At a meeting on the Middle East in 1971, the Chinese and Soviet ambassadors began screaming at each other over a procedural issue, first in their native languages and then in English.[48] Malik repeatedly portrayed the Chinese as false friends to the Palestinians.

> The Soviet Union is helping the Arab countries not by empty, vacuous, demagogic, slanderous statements such as we hear from the mouth of China and its representatives, not by hypocritical conjurations and mere words such as the Chinese indulge in but real, genuine efforts aimed at strengthening the military readiness of the armed forces of the Arab states.[49]

The squabbling was humiliating for the Soviet Union, which had long been the undisputed leader of the Communist camp, and the Soviets did the only

FIGURE 4.1. The U.S. ambassador, George H. W. Bush, greets Chinese ambassador Huang Hua in 1971.

thing they could: they accused the Chinese of having sold out to the West. Malik referred to Huang as a "slanderous man from the socialist betrayal camp" who was "aspiring to the role of an imperialist jester."[50] The Americans, Malik warned, were "sitting there, rejoicing, laughing, smiling, smirking, and rubbing hands" at the sight of the intra-Communist dispute.[51] The Sino-Soviet tension added complexity to the relationships among the Five. But the Chinese soon learned that a seat on the council did not necessarily imply influence on all matters that came before it. On critical issues, and particularly in crisis diplomacy, the Soviets and the Americans remained in a different league. Two years after the Chinese joined the United Nations, the Middle East offered further evidence of that reality.

The Moscow Draft

A phone rang in the Soviet diplomatic compound at Glen Cove, New York, early on Saturday, October 6, 1973. A Soviet desk officer for the Middle East was reporting that fighting had broken out between Israeli and Arab forces. Seeking to surprise their adversary, Syria and Egypt had waited until Yom Kippur, Judaism's holiest day, to strike. At the compound, Malik, the tough, veteran ambassador, was gleeful, and he braced himself for combat in the council. Once again, he expected, the Soviets would have a chance to skewer the Americans for their support of Israel and prove that the Soviets were the Arab world's most reliable ally. It was a dynamic that the Soviets had used to considerable advantage for years, and Malik knew the script by heart. When instructions arrived from Moscow later that day, however, there was no mention of calling a council meeting. Syrian and Egyptian forces appeared to have the element of surprise, and the Kremlin saw no reason to apply pressure for a ceasefire just yet.[52]

As in 1967, many council members wanted to test the fortunes of war before stepping in to demand peace. There was an even more important factor that led Moscow to keep Malik on a short leash: the fragile détente between the superpowers. Since 1968, Kissinger and his Soviet counterparts had worked to establish a modus vivendi that would acknowledge fundamental differences while easing Cold War tensions. The 1973 war was a severe test for the improved superpower relationship. For several weeks, the superpowers would struggle together to end the fighting, using the Security Council as a principal instrument.

From a White House consumed by the metastasizing Watergate scandal, Kissinger instructed UN ambassador John Scali to stall. With neither superpower eager for a quick council meeting, the diplomats in New York bided their time. They met informally and hunted for nuggets of information on the course of the fighting. Meanwhile, Kissinger worked the phones and tried to keep a distracted President Nixon apprised of developments. American intelligence expected that Israeli forces would quickly blunt the Arab offensive and perhaps even advance beyond the prewar lines. Confident that events would move in the Israeli direction, Kissinger was content to wait until they did. He strongly urged the Soviets to forge a joint approach on the council and, above all, to avoid a debate in the General Assembly, which was dominated by the Non-Aligned Movement.[53]

Washington's confidence about Israel's prospects soon began to dissolve. Israeli losses were severe, and alarmed Israeli officials told the Americans that dozens of tanks and fighter aircraft had been lost. Israel's prime minister, Golda Meir, considered flying to Washington to beg for more weapons. Kissinger discouraged her, afraid that the visit would signal to the moderate Arab states that their enemy was in panic. Nixon ordered the Pentagon to accelerate the flow of military supplies to assuage Israeli concerns. It would have been an ideal moment for the Soviets and the Arabs to press for a ceasefire resolution in the council. The United States, Kissinger believed, would have been hard pressed to veto a resolution calling for the opposing forces to cease fire in their positions, a posture that would have left Arab forces occupying significant recaptured territory.[54]

The council finally met in formal session on October 9, three days after the fighting had begun, and Malik had a chance to engage in the theatrics he had been denied. As the Israeli representative expressed condolences for any innocent civilians killed in the bombing of Damascus, the Soviet exploded. "The Soviet delegation," he yelled across the table, "does not wish to hear excuses from a representative of murderers and international gangsters!"[55] Malik walked out of the chamber as applause echoed around him. Australian diplomat Laurence McIntyre, who had the misfortune of serving as council president during the conflict, slammed his gavel down to restore order, and Israel's diplomat quickly responded.

> I'm not surprised that the delegate of the Soviet Union walked out of the room. His country must assume a great share of the responsibility for what has happened. The Soviet Union has identified itself with barbaric hatred and has supplied all kinds of weapons of war to the Arab states.[56]

It was the kind of exchange that the Kremlin had long encouraged. In this case, however, Malik's bosses were not pleased. Gromyko reportedly called it a "cheap show" and passed word that Malik should tone down the rhetoric. The Soviet press, normally keen to highlight such dramatics, paid almost no attention. Malik might have been eager to do ideological battle, but Moscow hoped to keep détente alive. In Kremlin meetings, Soviet premier Leonid Brezhnev fended off suggestions that the Soviets intervene directly. Flying arms to the Arabs was one thing; sending in troops was far too dangerous.[57]

The Israelis gradually recovered the initiative. By October 10, they had regained the Golan Heights and were advancing toward Damascus. In the Sinai, the Israeli Air Force began to inflict severe losses on Egyptian armor. The Egyptian Third Army, which had crossed the Suez Canal, was bogged down and in danger of being cut off entirely by the advancing Israelis. The unexpectedly successful Egyptian advance risked becoming a strategic disaster.

Soviet and Arab enthusiasm for a quick ceasefire grew as the military picture darkened, but Washington was content to see Israel recover its bearings. For the next week, diplomatic efforts sputtered. Finally, with Israel's military position much improved, Kissinger decided that the time had come to strike a deal through the council. But there was a catch. The details of a ceasefire resolution were too important, he decided, to be left to the council's often unwieldy multilateral drafting process.[58] He would draft the text himself, in coordination with the Soviets.

Late on October 20, Kissinger flew to Moscow for direct talks. Inside Brezhnev's Kremlin office, Kissinger and Soviet diplomats hammered out a council resolution to bring an end to the conflict. The superpowers quickly agreed on terms. What would become Resolution 338 was simple enough: it called for a ceasefire no later than twelve hours after the adoption of the resolution, reaffirmed the arduously negotiated Resolution 242, and called on the parties to immediately begin negotiating on how to implement its terms. Kissinger and Gromyko agreed to tell their UN missions that no changes to the draft would be accepted without their mutual consent.

All that was left was to communicate the text to the American diplomats in New York so that they could prepare the ground for a council meeting. This proved surprisingly difficult. The initial dispatch from the U.S. embassy failed to reach New York, precipitating a temper tantrum from Kissinger. Frantic, the American team sent Kissinger aide Lawrence Eagleburger to Moscow's airport to use *Air Force 2*'s communication system. That failed as well. The delegation in New York received word that a ceasefire resolution had been agreed to, but the text itself was not transmitted. Eagleburger then raced back to the American embassy to try again. Almost four hours after the text had been drafted, it finally reached American diplomats in Washington and New York. In his memoirs, Kissinger speculated that the Soviets might have somehow jammed American communications to complicate American diplomacy, although there is no direct evidence to support the theory.[59]

At the United Nations, the odd couple of U.S. ambassador John Scali and Yakov Malik sat down to review the drafts they had each received. They checked to make sure they were identical and then quickly called for a meeting.[60] The superpower-blessed resolution passed 14–0 (with China abstaining) just before 1:00 a.m. on October 22. Malik was stunned at the orders he was receiving from Moscow. "The instruction [from Moscow] was excellent, but there was one omission," he joked bitterly. "It did not say whether I should clear with Scali my going out to the restroom during the meeting of the Security Council." The same Soviet diplomat who reported Malik's reaction wrote that he could not "remember such harmony in words and deeds of the two superpowers at the United Nations throughout the entire period of the Cold War."[61]

Remarkable as it was, Resolution 338 did not have the intended effect of ending the fighting immediately. In fact, in the twenty-four hours after it passed, events lurched briefly toward a full-blown superpower crisis. Kissinger had told the Israeli leadership that they could take some additional time "implementing" the ceasefire to improve Israel's position on the ground. He almost certainly did not anticipate the consequences of his leniency: Israeli forces cut off the Egyptian Third Army entirely, threatening to turn a barely acceptable military outcome for Egypt into a rout. On October 23, the superpowers struggled to contain the crisis by passing yet another council resolution, this one demanding that the warring parties return to the positions they had occupied when Resolution 338 passed.[62]

By now, the close U.S.-Soviet cooperation had become too much for the Chinese. In a raucous meeting, deputy Chinese ambassador Chiao Kuan-Hua angrily condemned the superpower consensus. "China firmly opposes that the Council should be used as a tool of the two superpowers," he said. "We cannot tolerate such a practice." When Malik tried to interrupt the Chinese speech, Chiao exploded. "You should wait," he yelled, arms waving. "What does it matter if you wait a few moments? You should do things with style. I've known you for decades—you've never changed your habits."[63] The exchange became so heated that Australian Laurence McIntyre took the unusual step of ordering the proceedings to a halt. During the forced recess, Malik and Chiao stood next to the council table, surrounded by onlookers and still yelling.[64]

Even this new resolution did not prevent the fighting between Israeli and Egyptian units from continuing in the Sinai. Then, U.S.-Soviet cooperation began to break down. The alarmed Soviets put several airborne units on standby and hinted in letters to Nixon and Kissinger that they might intervene directly to stop the fighting. Israel, wrote Brezhnev to Nixon, "is brazenly challenging both the Soviet Union and the United States since it is our agreement with you which constitutes the basis of the Security Council decision."[65] With Soviet support, Egypt's president, Anwar Sadat, called for a joint Soviet-American force to monitor the ceasefire. The proposal horrified Kissinger, who was determined to keep Soviet forces out of

FIGURE 4.2. Soviet ambassador Yakov Malik and deputy Chinese foreign minister Chiao Kuan-Hua quarrel after a meeting on the Middle East.

the Middle East. Convinced that Soviet intervention in the region was possible, Kissinger called an emergency meeting of U.S. senior officials on the night of October 24 and then ordered the first change in America's wartime alert system since the Cuban missile crisis. The U.S. armed forces moved to Defcon III.[66]

The superpowers stepped back almost as quickly as they had moved toward confrontation, again by working through the council. The morning after the American strategic alert, the Soviets accepted a U.S.-sponsored resolution authorizing a new UN peacekeeping force for the Sinai without Soviet or American troops. In Washington, Kissinger exulted. He was convinced that increasing the alert level had cowed the Soviets and salvaged the joint approach on the council. But he also had to field some angry calls. The French and Chinese ambassadors both complained about the lack of consultation in the council.[67] Huang, a frequent recipient of Kissinger's blandishments about the need to counter the Soviets, was particularly angry and told Kissinger so.

> Very honestly speaking, I would like to say that the practice of the United States and the Soviet Union that they were doing during the Security Council meetings of the 22nd and 23rd, of putting in a resolution agreed upon by themselves, but not letting other countries consult or receive instructions from their governments, is a practice we find intolerable.[68]

The crisis had effectively turned the fifteen-member council into a two-player body. The United States and the Soviet Union used the council as a focal point for their own meeting of the minds on the conflict, and those watching from the outside were not pleased. French and Chinese discontent must have appeared comical to many of the smaller powers outside the council, who had long complained about the body's exclusivity. The council had a charmed circle within the charmed circle.

The Outcast

The United States emerged definitively during the 1973 war as Israel's most important ally. The American military aid that had poured into Israeli airports was critical in bolstering the country's embattled forces, and the Israeli public knew it. An enthusiastic crowd greeted the American secretary of state when he landed in Israel after the conflict.[69] In the ensuing months, Kissinger's frenetic shuttle diplomacy helped the parties to take critical steps back from a war footing. But his peregrinations could not alter the increasingly anti-Western and anti-Israel dynamic at the United Nations. Israel's cause had never been popular with the broad UN membership. The sheer numbers in the Arab bloc—and the increasing importance of Middle East oil—meant that its position carried significant weight in the General Assembly. That weight increased many times over as the Non-Aligned Movement began after 1973 to direct its energies toward UN diplomacy.

It was a winning strategy. As long as the movement maintained a modicum of unity, it would dominate many debates at the United Nations. The General Assembly was putty in the hands of the PLO's supporters in the NAM. On almost any issue related to the dispute, the assembly could be counted on to return a sizable majority in favor of the Palestinian position. The PLO chairman, Yasser Arafat, was invited to address the assembly for the first time in 1974. The visit became a major political event. Arafat was accorded the honors of a head of state, and he arrived wearing his trademark green fatigues and keffiyah. When Arafat finally ascended to the rostrum in the General Assembly hall, he spoke in triumphal terms. "Despite abiding world crises," he said, "despite even the gloomy powers of backwardness and disastrous wrong, we live in a time of glorious change. An old world order is crumbling before our eyes, as imperialism, colonialism, neocolonialism and racism, whose chief form is Zionism, ineluctably perish."[70]

The next year, the assembly overwhelmingly endorsed a resolution equating Zionism and racism.[71] That resolution—one of the most notorious in UN history—passed by a lopsided vote of 72–35, with 32 abstentions. A series of annual resolutions heaped ever more condemnation on Israel, and many Arab diplomats walked out of the assembly hall when the Israeli delegate rose to respond. Only the threat of an American withdrawal of funding prevented the assembly from revoking Israel's credentials and forbidding its participation in assembly debates.

The Security Council was less pliant, but it too was influenced by nonaligned activism and intense anti-Israel feelings. The NAM normally had at least four members on the council at any one time and sometimes as many as six—enough to exercise a decisive influence over the council agenda—and these members met frequently to coordinate strategy. The members of NAM serving on the council owed their election to the votes the movement could generate, and they usually hewed closely to the NAM consensus. A PLO representative addressed the council in January 1976 and became a regular participant in council meetings on the Middle East, over the repeated objections of the United States. "The PLO will never be absent from a discussion that affects the future of its people," pledged the Syrian ambassador in 1976.[72] From 1973 to 1983, the council would meet to discuss Israel and Palestine dozens of times. The dispute appeared on the council's agenda more frequently than any other issue.

At this point, the council became the forum for a multilevel game. At one level was an effort by the council members, and particularly the superpowers, to prevent tensions in the region from again sparking open conflict. For all of their differences, none of the permanent members had an interest in another war. On several occasions, the council served as a bully pulpit from which the Five could chide parties in the region when they strayed beyond the vague boundaries of acceptable behavior. The United States voted for a series of resolutions criticizing Israel's incursions into Lebanon. In 1981, when Israeli warplanes swept into Iraq and bombed Saddam Hussein's fledgling nuclear facilities at Osirik, the United States voted with the rest of the council for a resolution condemning the Israelis for going too far.[73]

More often, however, the council served as an outlet for various states and groups to vent their displeasure, curry favor with allies, and satisfy domestic constituencies. Most council resolutions on the Middle East had limited policy relevance. After the 1973 war, the United States kept the mediation efforts it led well away from the United Nations. When President Jimmy Carter brokered the Camp David Accords, which normalized relations between Israel and Egypt, the council played no direct role. Perhaps in part because of the body's limited impact, the rhetoric in the council was often extreme. Comparisons between the Zionists and the Nazis became commonplace. During a January 1976 meeting, the Libyan ambassador asked:

What should the world do with a racist movement and with a racist entity? Should they be treated differently from Nazism and apartheid? ... While it may be our fate to face the challenge of Zionist colonialism and to bear its atrocities and aggressions, sometimes we wonder if these people are really the survivors of Bergen-Belsen, Auschwitz or Treblinka.[74]

During the Israeli incursion into Lebanon in 1982, the Syrian ambassador offered his Israeli counterpart, Yehuda Blum, a holiday greeting: "Happy Rosh Hashanah, Mr. Blum, as you eat and drink over Arab corpses, Palestinian and Lebanese alike."[75]

A few diplomats forged their reputations through speeches on the Middle East. Saudi Arabia's long-time ambassador, Jamil Baroody, was one of the period's most notable orators. When he strode into the council chamber, word would go out and people would stream in to watch the performance. Usually invited to speak by a sympathetic council member, Baroody would walk slowly and deliberately to the horseshoe table, arms behind his back.[76] He would often speak for more than an hour from a single sheet of notes. He ranged easily from Israel's depredations to the evils of modern capitalism. He had a lighter touch than some of the other Arab ambassadors and was even occasionally introspective. At a meeting in the summer of 1976, he tried to place Israel in historical context. "We Arabs had three empires, but we got drunk with power and wealth and lost our heads, and our empires crumbled—and rightly so. So I feel sorry for the Zionists, because sooner or later, if not by war, they will be assimilated like those who have been assimilated before them."[77]

Baroody could improvise as well as lecture, and he enjoyed poking fun at the American ambassadors, who would often wander in and out during the long sessions. Once, Ambassador Bush entered the chamber while Baroody was in full swing. Without missing a beat, the Saudi greeted him: "I'm glad to see you, Mr. Bush. Come in and sit down. I'm having a few things to say about the oil companies. I want you to hear this."[78] On another occasion, he needled Moynihan for being absent. "I was hoping that my good friend Mr. Moynihan would speak," he said during a 1976 meeting, "but he has put his alternate in his seat. I do not know whether my voice irritates his eardrums or whether he is busy elsewhere."[79]

The Saudi would often bring his rhetoric to the edge of outright anti-Semitism before innocently backing away. The American mass media, he said in 1974, "are to a large extent controlled by Zionist interests." A few years later, he noted that Jews have "permeated all Western society and have become very powerful—bankers, traders. They clothe the United States. Go to Seventh Avenue. More power to them. We like them to prosper, but not at our expense." Baroody was always quick to deny any racial or religious animosity. "We do not hate the Jews. I do not hate my enemies. Why should I hate them? They are guests in this world. We are all guests."[80]

Baroody and other Arab and African ambassadors took special pleasure in linking Israel to the organization's other bête noire, South Africa. "The Afrikaner regime in South Africa and the Zionist regime in Palestine have many features in common and have had right from the beginning," said the Syrian ambassador in 1976. "They are both settler regimes based on exclusivism, racism, oppression and exploitation."[81] The tactics the nonaligned states used to marginalize Israel were employed to even greater effect against South Africa. In the General Assembly, the Non-Aligned Movement successfully stripped South Africa of its credentials. No South African delegate had the right to address the body without the explicit permission of the membership. Britain, the United States, and France halted a similar initiative in the council, but the council did pass a slew of resolutions condemning both apartheid itself and South Africa's frequent interventions in southern Africa.

Israel angrily rejected the parallel. The council was betraying its purpose, the Israeli ambassador argued, by becoming an echo chamber on the issue of Palestine. "If the Council acquiesces in becoming an instrument for satisfying the whims of what is, as must by now be obvious, an immature and barren political approach, there is nothing I can do except truly to regret that the Organization has descended to this unhappy pass."[82] Could it really be, Israel's envoys asked, that the Middle East deserved to consume so much of the council's time? "Some of us have had the feeling over the past few weeks that there may be other international problems confronting the international community," said Israeli ambassador Yehuda Blum in January 1982. "This Council, it would seem, is not aware of their existence. Not for the first time there seems to be a certain divergence between the real world and the world as experienced and viewed by this Council."[83]

As nonaligned and Communist states queued up to condemn the evils of Zionism, Israeli diplomats targeted their accusers individually. During a debate over Lebanon, Blum bristled at criticism from the Soviet Union and Poland. The Polish ambassador, he told the Soviets, "comes from a country that you have enslaved." Sudan's record, said Blum, "is shocking and best not be repeated here." When the Yemeni ambassador criticized Israel, Blum reminded the council of Yemen's own bloody civil war. "It was reassuring to see that the representative of Yemen could take time out from his country's difficulties at home and be with us here today." Pilloried at one point by the ambassador from Khmer Rouge–controlled Cambodia, the Israeli ambassador responded, "I am tempted to comment that this is a case of Pol Pot painting the kettle black."[84]

For several weeks in 1982, Israel and Jordan descended to grade-school tactics. Seeking to make the point that Palestinians already had a home in Jordan, Israel insisted on referring to Jordan as the "Palestinian Arab State of Jordan." In turn, Jordan's ambassador, Hazem Zaki Nuseibeh, called Israel the "Israeli entity." The two ambassadors interrupted each other repeatedly. The transcript from the April 16 meeting was typical:

MR. NUSEIBEH (Jordan): . . . and yet the representative of the Israeli entity has the temerity to complain, with his acknowledged and bellicose theatrics, that Israel is singled out for complaint at the United Nations. We do not initiate—

MR. BLUM (Israel): Point of order.

THE PRESIDENT (interpretation from French): I would ask the representative of Israel not to interrupt the statement of the representative of Jordan. He will soon have an opportunity to speak. I would ask the representative of Jordan to continue his statement.

MR. BLUM (Israel): Point of order. I should again like to request that the representative of Jordan be instructed to refer to my country by its proper name, under which it was admitted to the United Nations.

MR. NUSEIBEH (Jordan): I continue: And yet the representative of the Israeli entity has the temerity to complain—

MR. BLUM (Israel): Point of order.[85]

Israeli ambassadors on the council could feel confident that the United States, at least, shared their exasperation with the intense focus on Israel's sins. Indeed, the United States became so solicitous of Israel's interests that other council members began referring to Israel as the sixth permanent member. Between 1970 and 1985, the United States exercised its veto seventeen times to thwart criticism of its ally. In most cases, the United States objected to the lack of balance in the draft resolutions, which often condemned Israel for a reprisal without mentioning the security problems Israel was facing. At certain times, the votes were more than simple objections to the specific draft resolutions; they were signals to the council that it should stay out of the conflict. "They don't want to give the Security Council the idea that it's back in business," said long-time Israeli diplomat Abba Eban of the U.S. approach. "If you allow the Council to make one condemnation, then every three weeks it will condemn some action of Israel."[86]

America's staunch defense of Israel often angered traditional U.S. allies. When Israeli forces invaded Lebanon in June 1982, the council began what would become a marathon session of meetings. France was chairing the council and proposed a resolution calling for the immediate withdrawal of Israeli forces. After 3 a.m., when the vote finally came, the United States vetoed the French-sponsored resolution. "It became clear that provoking a U.S. veto, rather than working with the United States for a change in policy, was the object of French efforts," an American diplomat recalled. "What seemed to matter most to France was the appearance of independence from the United States."[87] From the French perspective, the American insistence on sheltering Israel from condemnation was just as incomprehensible.

The demands of defending Israel at the council sometimes caused America's diplomatic machinery to seize up. Andrew Young, a veteran civil rights campaigner and ordained minister who was President Jimmy Carter's first UN ambassador, was particularly uncomfortable in the role of Israel's shield-bearer. Along with many in the Carter administration, he believed that the United States had unnecessarily alienated the Third World, and he struggled to repair the breach. Eventually, his penchant for off-the-cuff remarks and freelance diplomacy caught up with him. He once said that Cuban troops were a stabilizing force in Angola and alleged that the United States was holding hundreds of political prisoners. News that Young had met privately with a representative of the PLO—a violation of stated U.S. policy—eventually forced his resignation. He spoke with uncommon frankness in his farewell address to the council.

I've said that it's a ridiculous policy not to talk to the PLO, and I think it is a ridiculous policy. But if it's ridiculous not to talk to the PLO on the part of the United States and the nation of Israel, it's also ridiculous for many of you around this table not to have good relations with the nation of Israel. For ultimately, if we are going to have peace in that region, people have got to approach each other as friends and as brothers and not as enemies, blood-thirsty for the destruction of each other.[88]

Young's successor, Donald McHenry, was also singed by the Middle East. On March 1, 1980, acting on instructions from the State Department, he abstained on a council resolution that criticized Israel's settlement policy and included references to East Jerusalem as "occupied territory." With no U.S. veto, the resolution passed easily. Within hours, the White House was besieged with angry phone calls. Carter, partially on the advice of his campaign advisors, quickly reversed course and disavowed the American vote.[89] McHenry, a capable and experienced Foreign Service veteran, was forced to explain the embarrassing shift to his surprised council colleagues.

The council's rancorous Middle East debates took their toll on diplomats and on relations among council members. As with U.S.-Soviet debates, they gradually became ritualized exchanges with limited relevance to the lives of people on the ground. On a few occasions, however, individuals directly affected by the conflict found their way into the council chamber. In December 1980, the council debated Israel's expulsion of two Palestinian mayors from the West Bank. The Palestinians came to New York to personally plead their case, and the council voted unanimously to condemn Israel's action. Apparently emboldened by the vote in their favor, the men then began a hunger strike in a small room near the council chamber. They pledged to drink nothing but salt water until Israel allowed their return. To Israel's chagrin, UN officials provided blankets and pillows for the men, who for five days camped just steps from the council chamber. Finally, on Christmas Day, the Palestinians were persuaded to vacate the room.[90]

The protest may have inspired imitators. A few months later, a group of Lebanese Christians broke away from their tour group, hopped over the partition separating the public gallery from the chamber floor, and began a loud demonstration. The security guards were more prepared this time. "Syrian pigs out of Lebanon," the demonstrators shouted as they were dragged out of the chamber.[91]

Backroom Dealing

By 1980, the formal chamber that had been the site of so much drama over the years was being used less and less often. A much-needed round of renovations in the late 1970s, funded primarily by the West German government, transformed the physical space around the formal council chamber. On one side of the chamber, an area that had held small offices was converted into a conference room for informal council meetings. In its first thirty years, the council had often met informally in the council president's small office or in one of the many conference rooms in the UN headquarters building. But the practice had never been regularized, and the absence of an established space for anything other than formal meetings in the chamber gave the procedure an ad hoc feeling. The construction of a special room, just steps from the formal chamber, changed that. Almost immediately, the room became the site for much of the hard negotiating on council activities.

Complete with an interpreters booth, the space provided a sanctuary for council members away from the glare of television lights and the demands of the news media. The council members sat at a U-shaped table that mimicked far more modestly the formal chamber's version. With fifteen ambassadors, various advisors, and the Secretariat staff, the room was cramped. It was, quite literally, a smoke-filled room. The table was usually "littered with boxes of the international brands—Dunhill, Benson & Hedges, Du Maurier and Gitanes."[92] One long-time UN official described it as a "hot and airless little room" where diplomats sat "perched on narrow seats and jostled by the endless coming and going [of aides and staff]."[93] The West German government also funded the construction of a comfortable lounge next to the consultation room. Called the "quiet room," but quickly dubbed the German Lounge, it became an even more informal spot for council politicking. The new rooms were completed in November 1978, and some council diplomats noticed a change in the working atmosphere. At one early meeting in the consultation room, Donald McHenry recalled, a Communist-bloc diplomat launched into a denunciation of the United States laced with classic propaganda lines. The Soviet ambassador leaned over to his colleague and said, in his fluent English, "we don't talk that way in here." The propaganda speeches, he made clear, were for the formal chamber.[94]

Conversations in the consultation room were supposed to be for council members only. No press was permitted, and states not on the council were excluded. The relative confidentiality of the discussions allowed ambassadors to test the diplomatic atmosphere without binding their governments. "It was very important," recalled British ambassador John Thomson, "because it was possible to take positions there from which you could retreat or advance without committing your government's prestige to it."[95] In practice, little that was said in the room remained private. Non-council members often huddled in the lobby outside the room, waiting to consult with the insiders. One diplomat stepped out of the room during a meeting in the 1980s to discover Iraqi diplomats listening to the debate through the door in the translators booth.[96] Security in the area around the council chamber was lax by today's standards. A UN official recalled unlocking the council president's office one morning to discover a college student passed out on the floor. He had apparently disembarked from an East River cruise and climbed through an open window.[97]

A few UN insiders worried that the use of the consultation room would simply drive the council behind the scenes and, worse, allow it to evade its responsibilities. Brian Urquhart, the United Nations' undersecretary-general for political affairs, was particularly skeptical of the development.

> Sometimes [informal] consultations maximize the Council's reluctance to meet to the point where it decides not to meet publicly at all. On such occasions it is in effect reduced to mumbling behind closed doors on issues affecting international peace and security—which does little to increase its prestige or the public respect in which it should be held.[98]

Urquhart's critique was a powerful one, and it echoed a suspicion of "secret diplomacy" that had long been present in the United Nations and, before it, the League of Nations. Conventional wisdom in Europe held that secret treaties had pushed the world into war in 1914, and the league's supporters believed that the organization should expose international diplomacy to the light of day. That belief in the power of transparency and public opinion endured as the United Nations was created, and many diplomats at San Francisco rejected the idea that the council could meet behind closed doors. By 1978, however, the council's low level of debate had disillusioned most of those who believed in the power of open debate to resolve conflicts. If working behind the scenes could reduce the vitriol, it seemed a small price to pay.

There were a few notable signs that the council was working more effectively in the late 1970s. The permanent Western powers on the council, along with nonpermanent members Canada and West Germany, negotiated a comprehensive resolution of Namibia's status. They conducted the diplomacy with the knowledge of the full council and presented their plan to the council for consideration in 1978. The resolution declaring Namibia to be independent passed 13–0, with the Soviet Union and its ally Czechoslovakia abstaining. That year, for the first time in almost a decade, there were no vetoes.

The council's newest permanent member also showed signs that it was becoming more comfortable in its seat. Since it had joined in November 1971, Beijing had adopted what one China scholar described as a "low-key and apprentice-like posture" in the council.[99] Its occasional noisy clashes with the Soviets notwithstanding, Beijing preferred to stay out of most council disputes. "We are not interested in publicity," said Huang Hua.[100] Unlike the U.S.S.R. and the United

States, China was sparing in its use of the veto. In 1976, China initially voted against Kurt Waldheim's bid for a second term as secretary-general but yielded after it had made clear its preference for a candidate from the Third World. On many other council votes, China simply chose not to participate, a practice which had been used a few times by other members but which China developed into an art form. Between 1971 and 1976, China chose not to participate in nearly 30 percent of the substantive questions that the council considered.[101]

Peacekeeping issues were particularly sensitive, in part because China objected on principle to any missions that were authorized while Taiwan held the seat and in part because of China's historical distrust of UN military forces. The Chinese played no part in votes on the peacekeeping missions to Cyprus or Lebanon. Policy in Beijing was shifting, however. Mao died in 1976, and as Deng Xiaoping consolidated power over the next several years, Beijing's international posture changed. Within a few years, China had abandoned its principled objection to peacekeeping and had begun participating in council votes. In small but significant ways, China was becoming part of the system.

Slip Sliding Away

The improved atmosphere in the council's meeting room could not compensate for a darkening international landscape. In 1979, the world appeared to lurch toward instability and confrontation. In January, Vietnamese troops crossed into Cambodia and deposed the bloody Khmer Rouge regime, which was backed by China. In November, Iranian extremists broke into the U.S. embassy in Tehran and took fifty-two hostages. Barely a month later, the Soviet Union invaded Afghanistan, executed the sitting president, and installed a puppet government. Afghan rebels took to the hills and began what would be a decade-long fight to expel the Soviets, fueled by Saudi and American money and weapons.

In 1980, Saddam Hussein sent thousands of Iraqi troops into Iran. The Iraqi dictator was determined to cut Ayatollah Khomeini down to size and to establish Iraq as the preeminent Arab power. Instead, he began a war of attrition that would last the better part of a decade and claim almost a million lives. In Angola, thousands of Cuban troops arrived to help that country's leftist dictatorship in its struggle against U.S.-backed rebels. As the world grew more dangerous, the United States took a sharp turn politically; in January 1981, Ronald Reagan took office, pledging to call Soviet tyranny by its rightful name and resist it wherever possible. Détente was a distant memory. In the Middle East in 1982, old tensions erupted as Israeli troops advanced into Lebanon to root out militants using that country as a base for strikes against Israel.

The council could do very little to contain the spread of conflict. Iran's hostage seizure was such a breathtaking violation of diplomatic norms that the council managed to condemn it unanimously.[102] That unity quickly dissolved, however, and the body could not agree to impose sanctions on Tehran. The council held several long meetings at which states condemned the Soviet invasion of Afghanistan, but the certain Soviet veto of any resolution meant that it was all for show. Meaningful action on the invasions of Cambodia and Lebanon was also squelched by differences among the permanent members.

The council did no better on the Iran-Iraq conflict, which was emerging as the world's bloodiest. The revolutionary regime of Ayatollah Khomeini recovered from the shock of the Iraqi invasion and embraced the war as a religious mission. Not only would Iran repel the invaders, it would rid Iraq of its corrupt and irreligious government. Saddam, declared the Ayatollah, "is fighting to destroy Islam."[103] Thousands of Iranian teenagers were pressed into service defending it, often with little training or equipment. Iran's war effort was complicated by the widespread animosity it faced in the region. Arab states, alarmed at the specter of a revolutionary Shia regime that claimed to speak for Islam, lined up behind Saddam Hussein. "There is no way to thwart [Iranian] plans and foil them," Saudi Radio announced, "except by supporting Iraq financially and militarily in order to destroy the Iranian war machine."[104] It often seemed that Iran was fighting the entire Arab world.

Iran had few allies in the council chamber. With the hostage crisis a fresh and bitter memory, the United States was happy to see Iran bloodied and amenable to improving relations with Iraq. Ronald Reagan dispatched an envoy, Donald Rumsfeld, to speak directly with Saddam in 1983, and the United States established formal diplomatic relations with Iraq in 1984. The Soviet Union at first tried to stay neutral in the conflict, but as Iraq's military fortunes ebbed, Moscow funneled weapons and money to Saddam. France had significant economic interests in Iraq and sold Baghdad high-end military equipment throughout the war, infuriating Tehran. Britain and China had the least turbulent relations with Iran, but they were not willing to consistently argue its case in the council. Nor did Iran have much influence with the nonpermanent members of the council. The nonaligned caucus deferred to the Arab states on Middle East issues and accordingly was sympathetic to Iraq.

In this environment of tacit support for Iraq, the council called for a ceasefire but pointedly declined to identify Iraq as the aggressor. Instead, it blandly urged both parties to "settle their dispute by peaceful means."[105] The next year, as fighting raged, the council said nothing. This neutrality outraged Tehran, which refused to accept the ceasefire resolutions and declined even to communicate directly with the council. For most of the war, Iran would communicate only with the secretary-general. One typical letter asked whether Iran was wrong to doubt "the impartiality and objectivity of this distinguished body [the council] which had remained silent for more than 22 months of Iraqi occupation of our territories, and started deliberations only after the Islamic Republic of Iran was succeeding in forcing the aggressors to retreat."[106]

Far from stopping wars, the council was barely able to perform such basic housekeeping tasks as selecting a new secretary-general to lead the organization. In one of its most assertive moments on the council, China vetoed Kurt Waldheim's 1981 bid for a third term on sixteen separate occasions. Beijing often styled itself as the developing world's permanent representative on the council, and it insisted that an individual from the Third World serve as the organization's new leader. It took months of ugly wrangling—"total buffoonery," one ambassador called it—and dozens of closed-door meetings for the council to choose Javier Pérez de Cuéllar, a veteran Peruvian diplomat who had served as his country's UN representative.[107] The newly minted secretary-general did not wait long before pointing out the council's dysfunction. In his first annual report, Pérez de Cuéllar charged that the body that had elected him was failing in almost every respect.

> [W]e have strayed far from the Charter in recent years.... The Security
> Council, the primary organ of the United Nations for the maintenance of
> international peace and security, all too often finds itself unable to take
> decisive action to resolve international conflicts and its resolutions are
> increasingly defied or ignored by those that feel themselves strong enough
> to do so.[108]

At least one ambassador on the council fully shared his distaste for the way the council was operating. In 1981, Jeane Kirkpatrick had arrived to serve as the new American UN representative. Kirkpatrick shared Daniel Patrick Moynihan's willingness to expose the organization's absurdities and dysfunction. "What takes place in the Security Council," she said once, "more closely resembles a mugging than either a political debate or an effort at problem-solving." She insisted that the United States needed to exact a price for hostile rhetoric, particularly when it emanated from countries that received U.S. military or economic support. "We operate as though there were no difference between our relations with supporters and opponents," she wrote, "with no penalties for opposing our views and no rewards for cooperating."[109]

A letter circulated by the NAM in September 1981 gave her a chance to unveil the new strategy. Viewed in the context of Third World radicalism, the letter's content was unremarkable. It contained the normal tirades against capitalism, Western colonialism, and Israel. Kirkpatrick refused to let it pass. She

FIGURE 4.3. The U.S. ambassador, Jeane Kirkpatrick, presides over a council meeting in March 1982.

fired off a letter of her own that went to almost all the original letter's signatories. It expressed surprise that the country "would or could associate yourselves with a document composed of such base lies and malicious attacks upon the good name of the United States."[110] Like Moynihan, Kirkpatrick generated strong reactions, particularly from Americans. During one council debate, an observer in the gallery stood up and began yelling at her, "Don't lecture the United Nations! I'm an American citizen—you're a disgrace!"[111] Kirkpatrick seemed to welcome the brickbats thrown her way. She was not in New York to win friends but to aggressively defend America, particularly against what she saw as the unholy alliance of the nonaligned nations and the Soviets.[112]

Her best opportunity to skewer the Soviets arrived in late 1983. On the evening of August 31, a Korean Airlines Boeing 747 took off from Anchorage, Alaska, on a regularly scheduled flight to Seoul. Somewhere near the Kamchatka peninsula, it strayed off its designated course and into Soviet airspace. The Soviet Air Defense Command dispatched fighter planes, and after a confused series of communications with ground control, the fighters shot down the jet. All 269 passengers and crew members perished. The attack startled the world, and the Reagan administration hustled to capitalize on the opportunity to expose Soviet cruelty.

In the days after the incident, the Soviets struggled to explain what had happened and issued a series of confusing statements. Kirkpatrick was ready to apply the coup de grâce. In Washington, a producer with the U.S. Information Agency was summoned to a secure room in the State Department and presented with an audiotape that contained radio intercepts of the Soviet pilots who shot down the jetliner. A small team of diplomats and technicians quickly produced a professional-looking videotape that included a transcript to accompany the garbled voice recordings.[113]

When the council met on September 6, the presentation was ready. Kirkpatrick played the grainy recording and the accompanying videotape. Television monitors had been set up around the room so that council diplomats could read as well as hear the intercepts of the Soviet communications. The American delegation took care to situate one monitor near the Soviet ambassador, and the American team also provided transcripts to the translators in the booths over the council, a wise move since the recording was barely decipherable even to those fluent in Russian.

Kirkpatrick set the scene deftly, cataloging the confusing and contradictory Soviet explanations for the disappearance of the Korean airliner. "The United States Government, in co-operation with the Government of Japan, has decided to spread the evidence before this Council and the world." Nothing had been cut from the tape, she assured the council members. For the next fifteen minutes, the council listened and watched as the tape played and the chilling translation flashed onto the monitors.

"Now I will try a rocket."

"Missile warheads locked on."

"I have executed the launch. The target is destroyed."

The tape, Kirkpatrick argued, made clear that "the Soviets decided to shoot down a civilian airliner, shot it down, murdering the 269 persons on board, and lied about it." The Soviets "have spoken as though a plane's straying off course is a crime punishable by death." She reminded the audience that this was not the first time that Soviet misdeeds had been dramatically exposed in the council. "Adlai Stevenson too had evidence to back up his charge, photographic evidence as irrefutable as the audio tapes we have heard today. The fact is that violence and lies are regular instruments of Soviet policy."[114]

It fell to Oleg Troyanovsky, the Soviet ambassador since 1976, to fight back. Educated in the United States and fluent in English, Troyanovsky was an unusually open Soviet ambassador who generally shied away from the diatribes that had been a staple of Soviet diplomacy on the council. He also possessed a quick wit. During a break in one early 1980s meeting, a protestor posing as a journalist hurled a container toward Troyanovsky and a nearby American diplomat. The stunned Soviet ambassador looked down and found that he was covered in red paint. "Better red than dead," he reportedly quipped.[115]

But Troyanovsky's charm and skill could only take him so far. Like many Soviet diplomats over the years, he had to make do with incomplete information from Moscow. As the Korean airline saga dragged out, Troyanovsky became frustrated at the confused story coming from Moscow and the absence of clear instructions on how to defend against American charges.[116] He resorted to generalized attacks on American credibility and Cold War boilerplate. "It is well known that American propaganda has no equal when it comes to the job of disinformation," he argued. The doomed airliner was a pawn in the broader Cold War. "Those people lost their lives not because of the Soviet Union, as is so loudly proclaimed in the West: they are additional victims of the Cold War whose apologist and pursuer is the present United States administration."[117]

For the U.S. team on the council, the Korean airliner incident and the condemnation it brought to Moscow offered a respite from the obloquy and isolation it usually encountered. The Reagan administration's foreign policy was unpopular with much of the world, and its willingness to criticize the United Nations made relations in New York especially tense. The American respite did not last long, however. At 5 a.m. on the morning of October 25, U.S. Marines and Army Rangers landed on the tiny Caribbean island of Grenada. They quickly deposed the Marxist-inspired military government and bustled to safety a group of hapless American medical students. A series of long council meetings on the invasion provided a forum for a new round of harsh criticism. Grenada's soon-to-be-unseated ambassador led the charge. "It is very clear that in today's world, the United States has decided that might is right, that nobody has the right to decide its own destiny." The Mexican ambassador agreed. "What we have here is a clear violation of the rules of international law." France "deeply deplore[d]" the invasion. A draft resolution condemning the U.S. incursion received eleven votes in favor and forced the United States to exercise a lonely veto.[118] "We don't feel the slightest bit isolated," an American diplomat insisted. "We have many, many friends. We have many friends in the Caribbean. We have many friends throughout Central and South America."[119]

Those friends were often hard to spot in New York. "It's open season on the U.S.," said a UN official after witnessing a council meeting which Libya packed with speakers hostile to the United States. America's adversaries were gleeful. "The United States has no friends," crowed Libyan ambassador Ali Treiki after a council debate on American involvement in Nicaragua. "The word 'Yankee' in Latin America is synonymous with evil and Satan."[120] The harsh criticism exacerbated the already significant American frustration with the organization. During one debate, the Soviet ambassador suggested that the United States might no longer be an appropriate venue for the world body. Perhaps it was time for the organization to move elsewhere. It was an irresistible opening for one of Kirkpatrick's aggressive aides. "We will put no impediment in your way," he thundered, "and we will be at the dockside bidding you a farewell as you set off into the sunset."[121] It was hyperbole, but it reflected the mindset of a powerful political constituency that was influencing policy toward the United Nations. In 1985, the United States threatened to stop paying large portions of its UN dues, ostensibly because of concerns about bureaucratic waste and what was perceived as an unfairly high U.S. assessment. Congress passed legislation that year demanding that the United States have voting power on budget issues to match its contribution.

Particularly on the political Right, abandoning the organization altogether was not out of the question. The influential Heritage Foundation churned out a series of reports documenting UN excesses and marshaling evidence that the organization was foundering. The oft-heard argument that the council at least provided a useful forum for states to vent—"it is far better to jaw-jaw than war-war," Winston Churchill famously said—no longer seemed convincing. Particularly on the Middle East, the council seemed to be doing little more than escalating rhetoric and forcing countries to vote on ineffectual but divisive resolutions. "Steam is no longer released into the atmosphere," concluded a Heritage Foundation report, "but is circulated, under pressure, until the corporate body is dangerously overheated. Jaw-jaw gives way to war-jaw."[122]

For an organization that had endured forty years, it was a dangerous moment. Fewer and fewer observers believed that the United Nations and its council were making a positive difference. A survey that asked almost 200 UN delegates to rate the effectiveness of the Security Council gave it failing marks, lower even than the General Assembly.[123] As important, the nation that more than any other had breathed life into the organization—the United States—had little good to say about it. When Britain called for an emergency council meeting to criticize Argentina for its looming invasion of the Falklands, the Americans were bewildered. Why even bother resorting to the council, Kirkpatrick demanded. The United States had good relations with Argentina and saw no possible value in placing before the council a dispute between two friendly nations. The British ambassador insisted that he would call the meeting nonetheless. Kirkpatrick never appeared, and a junior U.S. diplomat took her place with instructions not to actively assist the British.[124] With superpower relations deteriorating and the United States openly skeptical of the council's utility, the chances that the council could do anything constructive were dissipating fast.

Even the tourists seemed to realize that the air had gone out of the building. By the early 1980s, the number of visitors to the headquarters had dropped almost 40 percent from the levels of the 1960s. "Perhaps some of the aura of U.N. activity has been lost," a UN spokesperson conceded.[125] Long-time UN official Brian Urquhart, who had joined the organization in its earliest days, wondered whether interplanetary intervention might be necessary to ease the great-power deadlock. "There are moments when I feel that only an invasion from outer space will re-introduce into the Security Council that unanimity and spirit which the founders of the Charter were talking about."[126]

In September 1985, a huge tapestry of Picasso's *Guernica* was unveiled in the hallway outside the council chamber. Its images of violence, fear, and anguish stood in sharp contrast to the hopeful mural of a phoenix rising from the ashes that dominated the interior of the chamber. The tapestry seemed to be as much an indictment as an adornment. The Five had been given great power and responsibility after the Second World War, and this is what they had done with it?

CHAPTER 5

THE ICE BREAKS (1986–1993)

I N EARLY DECEMBER 1986, the Maltese oil tanker *Free Enterprise* was sailing in the Persian Gulf near Iran's Kharg Island when Iraqi jets streaked overhead. Seconds later, a missile plowed into the ship, which was forced to limp into a nearby port.[1] It was the second attack on the tanker in less than three months and part of a disturbing expansion of the Iran-Iraq conflict into the Persian Gulf. In 1985, there were more than sixty documented attacks on shipping in the gulf.[2] In 1986, some ninety merchant ships were attacked, with numerous casualties. Both combatants were deploying new technologies purchased abroad to harass ships trading with its enemy, and the tit-for-tat strikes were reaching ever closer to the Strait of Hormuz, a critical bottleneck for international commerce. Iranian officials warned Iraq's allies in the region that Iran would be within its rights to close the strait.[3] The toll at sea was serious, but it paled next to the losses on land. By late 1986, the war had already taken nearly 250,000 lives. Iraq regularly bombed major Iranian cities and used chemical weapons to blunt Iranian infantry advances. Iran retaliated as best it could, lobbing missiles inaccurately into Iraqi cities and using its superior troop strength to wear down Iraqi forces.

All the while, Iran's bitterness at the council's inaction festered. The dynamics on the council, however, were shifting rapidly. The Soviets, in particular, were reevaluating their attitude toward the organization and its role in conflict resolution. Over the decades, the Soviets had realized that the body could be useful for dividing and embarrassing its Western rivals and for cultivating relations with the developing world, but its suspicion of the council as a Western-dominated institution had never disappeared. The Soviet leadership rarely attempted to use the council to pursue substantive policy goals. At most, the council was a place to expose Western hypocrisy.

A dramatic shift in the country's fortunes put the institution in a new light. By the mid-1980s, Soviet economic growth, once regularly in the double digits, had declined precipitously. Elements of the Soviet leadership realized that the country risked falling ever more quickly behind the United States, particularly in technology. In March 1985, Mikhail Gorbachev became secretary-general of the Communist Party; by the standards of recent Soviet leaders, he was young, energetic, and progressive. The Soviet economic crisis, he conceded, "has clutched us by the throat."[4] In fits and starts, he reined in Soviet adventurism abroad and inched toward accommodation with the Reagan administration. The United Nations and the council in particular offered the Soviets a convenient mechanism for extricating themselves from the many expensive regional conflicts they had helped to stoke.

Gorbachev did not wait long to signal the new approach. At the funeral for his predecessor, Konstantin Chernenko, the new Soviet leader told Pérez de Cuéllar that his country's attitude toward the United Nations was warming. "I think the Soviet Union, from now on, will be very supportive of the United Nations because we think that in the future all problems should be solved through your organization. You can rely on me."[5] Other hints of a new Soviet attitude appeared in New York. After years of abstaining grumpily, the Soviet delegation for the first time supported the peacekeeping force in Lebanon—and expressed willingness to help pay for it. In September 1986, the Soviet Union used its turn as council president to arrange a bilateral meeting with Israel's prime minister, the first in several decades. Soviet foreign minister Eduard Shevardnadze and Israel's Shimon Peres conversed quietly in the small council president's office, steps away from the formal chamber.[6]

In early 1987, Pérez de Cuéllar decided to test the new atmosphere by encouraging the council to resolve the gulf conflict. At a press conference, he gently scolded the Five for their inaction and reminded them of what he described as the UN Charter's implicit contract.

> The five permanent members have an obligation to try to reach agreement on the solution of problems related to peace and security. That is their duty. Of course, they could start by having differences, but that is why they have to work until they agree on a solution to international problems. That is why they have the veto power. It is not something given to them generously by the membership of the United Nations. The veto power implies that they have to work in order to reach agreement for the peaceful solution of international problems.[7]

A few days later, at the customary monthly council luncheon, the secretary-general invited the ambassadors of the Five to meet in his office for tea, and he proposed that they consider regular consultations on the Iran-Iraq war. In February, British ambassador John Thomson contacted the other delegations with an invitation to continue the dialogue. To his surprise, they all accepted.[8]

Their initial meetings were quiet and relaxed. The ambassadors chose to meet at Thomson's residence rather than at the United Nations, so as to avoid attracting attention. One ambassador described it as "an atmosphere of tea, muffins, and sympathy."[9] The ambassadors refrained from formal speeches and made no statements to the press. They spoke entirely in English to avoid the need for interpreters. As the contacts became routine, a second and even more productive working group emerged, composed of the political advisors to the ambassadors. They met weekly in the U.S. mission over coffee and cookies. With no press attention, they explored formulations, isolated areas of difference, and sketched out the details of a possible binding council resolution that would demand an end to the conflict.

The new spirit of cooperation among the Five sprang from a confluence of circumstances, ably summarized by U.S. diplomat Cameron Hume in his account of the period.[10] None of the Five desired a clear victory by either Iran or Iraq, and all feared the further disruption of shipping in the gulf. The Reagan administration badly needed a diplomatic achievement in the region to help it recover from the debilitating Iran-Contra scandal. The U.S. team at the United Nations was

FIGURE 5.1. Secretary-General Javier Pérez de Cuéllar briefs the Five on the Iran-Iraq conflict.

well suited for a more pragmatic approach. Jeane Kirkpatrick and most of her team exited in 1985, and in her place came Vernon Walters, a veteran trouble-shooter, former army general, and accomplished linguist. Where Kirkpatrick could be acidic, Walters was avuncular and a raconteur.

Britain and France, realizing that the United States might soon be the sole superpower, saw in the council's revitalization a chance to constrain the American tendency toward unilateralism. Since they were second-tier powers, elevating the Security Council had the effect of inflating their own status. The active French hostility toward the United Nations had cooled considerably since the 1960s as decolonization moved off the agenda, as the unpredictable General Assembly faded in importance, and as the organization's secretaries-general became more modest in their ambitions. The French had always liked the idea of exclusive great-power roundtables. Finally, the council was starting to act like one.

A sense of geopolitical caution prevailed in Moscow and Beijing. The Soviet Union wanted to keep relations with the West cordial as it struggled with eco-nomic and political reform. As Soviet political and economic power declined, moreover, the council was a reassuring reminder that the Soviet Union was still a great power. China in 1987 tended to approach most council issues as a regional rather than as a global power. The resolution of the Iran-Iraq war did not impli-cate Beijing's immediate interests and it was content to stand aside. Moreover, the peaceful resolution of conflict between two recognized states, without any flavor of intervention in internal affairs, was the type of UN diplomacy that least offended sensibilities in Beijing.

The burgeoning council diplomacy did not mean that the Five eschewed more traditional methods. Most of them continued to pursue bilateral contacts of various sorts with the warring parties, forays which sometimes complicated the joint initiative. The United States and the Soviets still doubted each other's motives, and the superpowers jousted over whether it was appropriate for the United States to deploy warships to protect shipping in the gulf. In June, even as negotiations were proceeding in New York, an official Soviet publication com-plained that the United States was "usurping the role of protector" in the gulf and warned that Moscow "could not stay indifferent" to the presence of U.S. war-ships in the region.[11]

Nor was there easy agreement on the content of the resolution that the Five were slowly drafting. Discord broke out over whether the council should actu-ally coerce the parties into peace. The United States insisted that the council be ready to impose sanctions on the parties if they failed to agree, but China and Russia balked. They were suspicious of U.S. zeal and unwilling to endorse such blunt pressure. Still, over the next six months, over innumerable pots of tea, and in dozens of meetings, the permanent members fashioned a draft resolution that they all could support. The nuances of the UN Charter offered ground for compromise on the central question of how to enforce the resolution. The draft resolution did not explicitly mention any measures the council might take to force the parties into peace, but it did allude to further measures and state that the resolution was being adopted under Articles 39 and 40 of the charter, provisions which rendered the resolution mandatory under international law.

Only when the Five had reached agreement on a complete text did they move their discussion across the street to the consultation room and the full council. Although the Five had been remarkably discreet, the other council members by now knew that the permanent members had been meeting separately. The Chinese ambassador, who was serving as council president for the month, read aloud a statement to which the Five had agreed. It was an odd moment for the small states on the council, particularly those from the Non-Aligned Movement. They had long called for greater cooperation between the superpowers and bemoaned the Cold War paralysis. It was apparent, however, that great-power consensus might imply the marginalization of the nonaligned.

The fact that China was transmitting the views of the Five was particularly ironic. Beijing had often railed against "secret diplomacy" within the council, most vocally during the 1973 Middle East crisis. Now, it was acting as the spokesperson for the great powers. Faced with the unanimity of the permanent members, the rest of the council haggled over a few words, but the resolution emerged from the consultation room intact. Not since the San Francisco conference had the Five worked together so effectively on an issue of war and peace.

On July 20, 1987, the council convened in the formal chamber to unanimously approve the resolution. It was an unusually high-level session. The foreign ministers of six countries, including the United States, Britain, and France, sat at the horseshoe table to express support for Resolution 598, which demanded that the parties cease fire immediately and "withdraw all forces to the international[ly] recognized boundaries without delay." It called on the parties to work with the secretary-general to implement the ceasefire and reach a lasting settlement.[12] The U.S. secretary of state, George Shultz, declared that the council "has functioned in the collegial spirit envisioned by the founders of the United Nations at its creation."[13] The British foreign secretary pledged that a failure to comply with the council's demands would have consequences. "If one or both of them choose to disregard their obligations under the Charter, then let the world hear this, and hear it clearly: this Council will use all its powers under the Charter to make the resolution effective."[14]

At first, the council's demand appeared to have little impact in the region. Saddam Hussein welcomed the resolution, but this was no surprise. He had been seeking a way out of the costly war for years, and he had confidence that the council was not hostile to him. But there was no euphoria in Tehran. Iran's leaders remained deeply suspicious of council diplomacy, and the influence of the United States on the resolution made them more so. Iran's UN ambassador labeled the resolution "a vicious American diplomatic maneuver."[15] Hashemi Rafsanjani, then speaker of Iran's assembly, called the council members "liars" and insisted that it had again avoided its duty of condemning Iraqi aggression. "Without the trial and punishment of the aggressor," he insisted, "this war will not end."[16]

It took another full year and thousands of lives for the parties to yield to the council's pressure. Javier Pérez de Cuéllar and a small team of UN diplomats worked tirelessly to turn the council's resolution into an actual ceasefire. An incident in July 1988 underlined the danger of the continued fighting to commerce in the Persian Gulf. The cruiser USS *Vincennes* shot down what it thought was an incoming fighter plane. It turned out to be an Iranian passenger jet, and all 290 people on board died. A few weeks later, Iran finally accepted the council's ceasefire resolution, and in late August, face-to-face negotiations between Iranian and Iraqi diplomats began in Geneva. For the first time in nearly a decade, the border between the countries was quiet.

How critical was the council's involvement? By 1987, Iran and Iraq were exhausted, and there was no sign that either one could achieve a military breakthrough. No major powers had a strong interest in the war continuing, although most of them derived income from weapons sales. It is possible that Tehran and Baghdad would have reached an understanding even without a push from the council. Cameron Hume argues that the council managed to capture "latent cooperation" in the international system. There were few structural reasons for the conflict to continue, but until the council initiative, there was no ready mechanism for ending it. A diplomatic push by one of the great powers alone would have aroused the suspicion of the others, and the council's involvement allowed the diplomacy to appear as a joint initiative. By providing a forum where the great powers could regularly compare notes, the council structure also reduced the ability of the parties to play the great powers against each other, as they had often sought to do.[17]

In the wake of the successful gulf diplomacy, a host of conflicts that were untouchable during the Cold War became eligible for resolution. Beginning in 1988, the council pivoted from the Persian Gulf to Central America and southwestern Africa, where Cold War proxy battles had been simmering for years. The council sent ceasefire observers to Nicaragua and El Salvador to assist in decommissioning the Contra rebel forces in the region.[18] Meanwhile, the council approved a long-delayed peacekeeping mission to Namibia. It dispatched thousands of troops, civilian police monitors, and election observers from dozens of countries to implement a political settlement between the rebel movement and the South Africa–imposed authorities.[19] In January 1990, the council began intensive meetings about a possible solution to the lingering conflict in Cambodia between the Khmer Rouge and forces led by the Soviet-backed strongman Hun Sen. The tentative tea parties at the British ambassador's residence had grown into a concentrated effort to clean up some of the world's most damaging conflicts.

These diplomatic initiatives had a strong Western flavor. U.S. and British diplomats were usually the key players and drafted most of the council resolutions. For the moment, the U.S.S.R. and China were willing to play along. Just as the Soviet Union's economic vulnerability inclined it toward flexibility on the council, political unrest in China muted the concerns that Beijing might otherwise have had about the council's active involvement in internal conflicts. The 1989 Tiananmen Square uprising and the subsequent government crackdown shook China's foreign policy and unnerved its diplomats. A British diplomat working on the council at the time, Christopher Hum, recalled the dramatic effect of the crisis on the Chinese delegation. As the crackdown unfolded in Beijing, the Chinese ambassador disappeared from sight. "We learned afterward that he was so appalled by the whole thing that he'd locked himself in his office and no one could get at him."[20] After recovering from the shock, Beijing's posture on several issues before the council appeared to soften. That year, for the first time in its history, China participated directly in a peacekeeping operation by dispatching several dozen unarmed observers to help supervise the Namibian elections.[21]

The council's political renaissance did not yet mean that it was playing the assertive role that many of the United Nations' founders had intended. In the Iran-Iraq conflict, its role was primarily hortatory. The references to the enforcement provisions of chapter VII in Resolution 598 marked an important step, but the council balked at actually imposing sanctions or, more dramatically, compelling the parties to comply through military force. In Central America and in Namibia, the council was helping parties to implement peace terms they had already negotiated. The council's potentially powerful tools had rusted considerably during decades of disuse. Korea and Congo were the last times the council had even indirectly authorized military force. The Military Staff Committee— envisioned as the command center for council-authorized military operations— had over the decades become a bureaucratic relic. It had offices at UN headquarters and met monthly, but only because the council could not agree to formally disband it. In its place, the UN Secretariat had built up a small and overworked staff to manage peacekeeping operations, but it lacked the capacity to plan and oversee complicated operations that involved the use of force.

The council's experience with mandatory sanctions was minimal too. In 1965, it had imposed economic sanctions on Rhodesia that were only lifted when the country threw off white rule and became Zimbabwe in 1979. The council had approved a mandatory arms embargo on South Africa in 1977. Neither measure was particularly effective. Rhodesia's tight economic links with South Africa, as well as widespread smuggling, had helped it to resist economic pressure. South Africa had a vibrant domestic arms industry which kept its security forces well provisioned despite the arms embargo. In a few short years, the council's political flexibility had increased dramatically. But it would take another crisis in the Middle East for the council to uncover the mettle that the United Nations' founders had given it.[22]

Saddam's Gamble

On the evening of August 2, 1990, Thomas Pickering, America's UN ambassador, was in a New York restaurant with Crispin Tickell, his British colleague. Both men were professional diplomats, and they were excited to be serving at the United Nations during what appeared to be a minor renaissance in its fortunes. Tickell had served in Mexico, the Netherlands, and France and along the way had developed an intense interest in climate change, even authoring a book on the subject in the 1970s. Pickering was popular at the United Nations for his willingness to listen and his attention to detail. Unlike the political appointees that Washington often sent, he knew the mechanics of the United Nations well and spent most of his time in New York rather than in Washington. He had served as U.S. ambassador to Israel, El Salvador, Nigeria, and Jordan and spoke Arabic, French, Spanish, and Swahili.

Halfway through the meal, the restaurant staff received an urgent phone call for Pickering, which the diplomat took in the restaurant's kitchen. As waiters clattered by, he absorbed the news that Iraq had invaded Kuwait. Pickering drove straight to the U.S. mission, where he assembled a team of advisors. In consultation with Washington, they began hurriedly drafting resolutions condemning Iraq's invasion and demanding its immediate withdrawal. Soon, the full council assembled in the consultation room. It was a disorderly scene. With only a few, early-model cell phones in use, diplomats raced back and forth between the consultation room and the bank of phones in the corridor, struggling to contact their foreign ministers even as they negotiated the text of the resolution.[23] At least one ambassador could not reach his capital and had to operate without instructions. After eight hours, the council emerged from its emergency meeting with a resolution demanding that Iraq withdraw "immediately and unconditionally."[24] Britain and France firmly backed the United States. China's ambassador was reticent but gave no indication that he would oppose a council response to the invasion. The nonpermanent members lined up behind the draft resolution, with the lone holdout being Yemen, whose ambassador confided that his president felt some personal loyalty to Saddam Hussein.[25]

Pickering flew to Washington early that morning to meet with President George H. W. Bush's national security team, and he received support for continued activism at the United Nations. The president then flew to Colorado for a planned conference that included British prime minister Margaret Thatcher. The two leaders spent hours discussing how to respond to the invasion. While supportive of a firm response, Thatcher did not share the American enthusiasm for managing diplomacy through the council. In a reversal of long-standing positions, she contended that relying too much on the council threatened Western freedom of action. Thatcher argued that, once the United States had secured basic resolutions condemning Iraq and recognizing the principle of collective self-defense, it should pull back.

> I did not like unnecessary resort to the UN, because it suggested that sovereign states lacked the moral authority to act on their own behalf. If it became accepted that force could only be used—even in self-defence—when the United Nations approved, neither Britain's interests nor those of international justice and order would be served. The UN was a useful—for some matters vital—forum. But it was hardly the nucleus of a new world order. And there was still no substitute for the leadership of the United States.[26]

Thatcher recognized that the conflict could represent an inflection point in the council's trajectory and that decisions on how to use the Security Council could have important consequences. Years of disuse, particularly during the 1970s and 1980s, had pushed the institution to the periphery of international politics. America now faced the choice of how energetically to pull it back to the center. A simple resolution condemning the invasion and recognizing Kuwait's right to self-defense, as Thatcher envisioned, would have given the body a moderate boost but not made it the center of attention. On the other hand, building a coalition and managing the war through the council would establish an important precedent. Converting the council into the international community's political command center might make it hard to ignore at less convenient moments. By asking the Americans to consider the long-term institutional implications of their strategy, Thatcher was reprising a role the British had played often with their more powerful ally. During the Korean War, the British attempted to temper American ardor for bypassing the council and using the General Assembly, presciently pointing out that the assembly might not be hospitable for long.

Thatcher's reluctance had to yield in the face of America's newfound enthusiasm for council diplomacy. During the next several months, Pickering kept his colleagues working at a brisk pace. "It became my strategy never to let the Council have a day without focusing on Iraq," he recalled.[27] After Resolution 660 came a flurry of additional measures declaring the annexation of Kuwait null and void, condemning Iraq's treatment of foreign nationals and Kuwaiti civilians, and demanding protection for foreign embassies and consulates.[28] The frequent and harsh criticism of Iraq took a toll on that country's veteran ambassador. After another in a series of stinging rebukes, recalled Britain's Crispin Tickell, the Iraqi envoy left the council chamber in tears.[29]

Pickering had a more parochial motive for churning out resolutions. As much as possible, he wanted to keep the U.S. assistant secretary of state for UN matters, an intense lawyer named John Bolton, from becoming too involved.[30] Bolton, based at the State Department in Washington, had developed a reputation among America's UN diplomats for being intensely ideological. By generating the text of resolutions in New York, Pickering could minimize Bolton's influence. The texts were normally drafted by the American or British missions, shared informally with the French, and then discussed at one of the frequent meetings of the Five. Only when the Five had agreed among themselves would the resolutions be brought to the council as a whole for informal consultations.

The most significant of these early resolutions may have been 661, which was adopted on August 6. It imposed a comprehensive sanctions regime on Iraq and established a special committee to monitor compliance. The creation of that committee was a small but notable step toward an active governance role for the council. The council, after all, might have delegated the function of monitoring sanctions to the secretary-general and his staff, just as the council had long delegated the management of peacekeeping operations. Instead, it chose to carry out the task itself. Diplomats from all of the council states were assigned to the sanctions committee, which met for the first time two days after the sanctions resolution passed.[31]

Working so intensively through the council carried risks, and America's policymakers sometimes forgot that relying on the council's authority implied an obligation not to move faster than the body was willing to go. A week into the crisis, the Bush administration announced that U.S. Navy ships were planning to interdict ships carrying goods to and from Iraq. Several Iraqi tankers were steaming through the gulf, and Bush was under pressure from his military advisors to seize them as a sign of American determination. On August 20, Pickering was told to push through a resolution authorizing naval seizures—even if it took all night. Many council members bridled at the American pressure, however, and after intense internal debate, the administration agreed to wait. Several U.S. warships shadowed the tankers until they entered Yemen's territorial waters but did not attempt to board them.[32] Over the next several days, as Pentagon officials stewed, American diplomats convinced the Soviets, Chinese, and several wavering nonpermanent members to support military enforcement of the sanctions regime. At 4:00 a.m. on August 25, the council finally assented.[33]

American reliance on the council's authority also forced American flexibility on other issues, notably the Israeli-occupied Palestinian territories. The always simmering issue inconveniently boiled over in the midst of Persian Gulf diplomacy. On October 8, violence broke out in Jerusalem's Temple Mount after Palestinians rained stones on Jewish worshippers. During nearly an hour of rioting, Israeli police opened fire, leaving nineteen Palestinians dead.[34] The NAM states on the council demanded a resolution condemning Israel. For Saddam Hussein and his few allies on the council, it was a precious opportunity to fracture the coalition that was mustering to repel the aggression. For Pickering and his team, it was a delicate challenge. The Americans wanted at all costs to avoid using their veto, which might derail the council's unity on Iraq. But the traditional U.S. policy of sheltering Israel from harsh condemnation could only bend so far.

In long consultation-room sessions, the ambassadors haggled over the wording of a resolution that would upbraid Israel for its excessive use of force. The Americans readily agreed to criticize Israel. The sticking point was how East Jerusalem would be referred to in the text. The PLO and those sympathetic to its cause wanted a clear statement that East Jerusalem was part of the "occupied territories" and thus covered by Resolutions 242 and 338. This, the Americans resisted. The status of Jerusalem was a delicate issue, and the Bush administration was not willing to place it in the category of "occupied territory."

Pickering's insistence on precisely calibrating the resolution drove some nonaligned ambassadors to distraction. Robert Grey, the American political counselor at the time, recalled that one nonaligned diplomat was almost reduced to tears of frustration by Pickering's word parsing.[35] On October 12, the long-debated resolution passed. The council condemned the "acts of violence committed by the Israeli security forces" during the unrest in Jerusalem and called upon Israel to scrupulously adhere to the Geneva Conventions.[36] The pressure angered Israel. "The United States has the goal of maintaining a coalition against Saddam Hussein in the Gulf," said Israel's UN ambassador as the resolution was being debated. "To maintain that coalition some principles are being sacrificed."[37] Israel refused to cooperate with a UN delegation to the region, prompting another critical council resolution two weeks later.[38]

From the American perspective, the benefits of council diplomacy outweighed these complications. As the crisis in Jerusalem passed, the council moved steadily toward a crucial vote on whether to authorize military force against Iraq. With the British, the Americans drafted a resolution that endorsed "all necessary means" to oust the Iraqi forces from Kuwait. The United States wanted the council to pass the resolution by the end of November, the month during which the United States held the presidency of the council. On December 1, the presidency would pass to Iraq's ally Yemen, significantly complicating council diplomacy. On November 3, U.S. secretary of state James Baker began circumnavigating the globe to secure approval for the resolution. He worried that deliberations in New York alone would take too long and might veer in unexpected directions. "I was determined to meet personally with the head of state or foreign minister of every Council member in the weeks before the vote," he wrote later. "U.N. ambassadors are notorious for their freelancing."[39]

That assessment may have been aimed at Pickering as much as at foreign ambassadors. During the hectic diplomacy, Baker's entourage in Washington grew frustrated that Pickering was attracting so much attention. John Bolton described Pickering as "hyperactive" and recalled frequent calls from Baker inquiring about what "that cowboy in New York was up to."[40] The friction between New York and Washington was not new. America's UN ambassadors had often had difficult relationships with secretaries of state, in part because of the American tradition of appointing political figures with their own constituencies and ambitions rather than career diplomats to the post. Henry Cabot Lodge had a close relationship with Eisenhower and sometimes resisted when the State Department gave him instructions.[41] Moynihan routinely annoyed Kissinger with his antics in New York, and Jeane Kirkpatrick clashed several times with Reagan's secretary of state, Alexander Haig.[42] The tension with Pickering may have been less a personality clash than an inevitable side effect of diplomacy being so concentrated in New York. Baker and his staff wanted to take the UN route, but they did not want the UN ambassador in the limelight.

As Baker began his sojourn in search of council votes, the permanent members were the priority. Because the Bush administration had prohibited high-level visits to Beijing after the Tiananmen Square massacre, Baker huddled with the Chinese foreign minister in a VIP lounge at the Cairo airport. The foreign minister expressed unease with the prospect of the United Nations' involvement in a war, but Baker left encouraged that Beijing would not stand in the way, particularly if Washington agreed to speed the resumption of normal diplomatic relations. In a dacha outside Moscow, Baker spent more than a dozen hours meeting with Gorbachev and his foreign minister, discussing how much time Saddam should be given to comply and how many resolutions the council should consider.

In London and Paris, Baker found strong support but different views on whether a use-of-force resolution was even necessary. Thatcher once again expressed the view that the right of self-defense—safeguarded in Article 51 of the charter—was more than enough.[43] French president François Mitterrand, by contrast, wanted another resolution. "Article 51 doesn't mind public opinion," Baker recorded him saying. "Fifty-five million French people are not international lawyers."[44] The French president understood that council resolutions are more about public opinion than about the fine points of international law and that a resolution clearly authorizing force was essential.

As he was courting the Five, Baker did not neglect the nonpermanent members. American diplomats were eager to achieve overwhelming support for the use of force, and they chased every vote. In Geneva, Baker sat down with the foreign ministers from three nonaligned members of the council—Ivory Coast, Ethiopia, and Zaire—to discuss their concerns. It is one of the odd features of council diplomacy that poor and weak states will not infrequently be feted by the great powers. This superpower pressure could be an inconvenience for the nonpermanent members, some of which would have preferred not having to pick sides on controversial global issues. But the vote chasing could also be a boon. The U.S. secretary of state carried with him a list of "sweeteners"—including foreign aid packages and trade concessions—that President Bush had authorized him to offer. The phenomenon of Security Council members, particularly those from the developing world, reaping economic rewards for their votes was hardly unprecedented. Two economists have found that poorer countries experienced significant aid boosts when they served on the council, particularly during years when there were major issues before the body. "Aid payments sharply increase in the year in which a country is elected to the Security Council," the economists reported, "remain high throughout the two-year term, and return to their earlier level almost immediately upon completion of the term."[45]

The toughest challenge for Baker was the so-called Gang of Four: Yemen, Cuba, Colombia, and Malaysia. They saw the U.S. approach to the crisis as belligerent and proposed instead to send the secretary-general to negotiate directly with Saddam. Baker stopped in Yemen for friendly but inconclusive discussions with its president. Back in New York, Baker met with Cuban foreign minister Isidoro Malmierca at a downtown hotel, the first such high-level meeting in almost thirty years. The meeting could have been considered a departure from standing U.S. policy not to meet with members of the Castro regime. Baker avoided that distinction by claiming that he was meeting the Cuban in his capacity as president of the Security Council, not as the U.S. secretary of state.[46]

In the days leading up to the critical vote, a council meeting was held to showcase the atrocities committed by Iraqi forces in Kuwait. Planned and organized with the help of a public relations firm hired by the Kuwaiti government-in-exile, the presentation included testimony from Kuwaiti refugees, poster-sized photographs of victims, and a videotape of Iraqi forces opening fire on Kuwaiti civilians.[47] The combination of quiet diplomacy and public relations was a success, and the use-of-force resolution gained momentum. Iraq appeared stunned by the change in the diplomatic landscape. "If we still had the Soviets as our patron, none of this would have happened. They would have vetoed every U.N. resolution," Iraqi foreign minister Tariq Aziz reportedly complained.[48] Whatever hope the Iraqis had for a break in the great-power consensus disappeared on November 29, when the council met to vote on the use-of-force resolution. Continuing the public relations offensive to the end, Baker arrived at the United Nations for the meeting and promptly presented the secretary-general with a check for $185 million—a substantial portion of what the United States owed to the organization.[49]

The council meeting that day had been carefully choreographed. Kuwait's ambassador spoke first, and he praised the council for vindicating the doctrine of collective security, for which he found support in the Koran. "If two parties among the believers fall into a quarrel, make ye peace between them," he quoted. "But if one of them transgresses beyond bounds against the other, then fight ye (all) against the one that transgresses until it complies with the command of God." Iraq's ambassador spoke next, and he lashed out at the United States for coddling Israel while it punished Iraq and at the council for falling in line behind the Americans. "The current crisis has shown, among other things, that the United States totally dominates the Security Council and its arbitrary and biased procedures," said the Iraqi ambassador.

Yemen's envoy noted the oddity of the American position that sanctions were not working fast enough. "It is a little surprising that those who used to lecture us on the need to be patient for sanctions to work when they had to do with Rhodesia or South Africa are today in such a hurry to declare that those comprehensive and enforceable sanctions imposed on Iraq are simply not working."[50] The speech, which ended with a plea to "give peace a chance," won scattered applause in the packed council chamber, and as the Yemeni ambassador spoke, Baker passed a note to a colleague. "Yemen's permanent rep. just enjoyed about $200 to $250 million worth of applause for that speech." Yemen's substantial U.S. aid package, Baker made clear, would not survive the vote.[51] With these discordant notes out of the way, the council formally voted on the resolution. It passed 12–2, with Cuba and Yemen voting against and China abstaining.

Baker reached for a less vindictive tone in his speech after the vote. He cast the Iraqi challenge as an opportunity for the organization to vindicate itself. "History now has given us another chance. With the cold war behind us, we now have the chance to build a world which was envisioned by this organization, by the founders of the United Nations," he said. "We must not let the United Nations go the way of the League of Nations." Soviet foreign minister Shevardnadze echoed Baker's view that the invasion represented a key moment in international relations.

> We have just started overcoming the mutual hostility, suspiciousness and alienation that used to breed frictions and conflicts.... What has taken place in the Persian Gulf region is a blow dealt to a nascent world of civilised behaviour. That is why it is so important to parry this blow and to prevent it from inflicting irreparable damage to the institutions of freedom and democracy and plunging humankind into chaos.... The fact that today we respond to these challenges in a different way than we did yesterday is extremely important. We give preference to law, to acts based on the UN Charter, at the Security Council, and collective efforts.[52]

The council had not encountered such sustained media attention since the early 1960s when the debates on Congo and Cuba often led newscasts. To help the council to navigate in the age of cable news, Secretariat officials installed a television set tuned to CNN in the lounge adjoining the consultation room, and council members would often watch breaking news together. To their amusement, they could view reporters in the hallway just outside opining—often incorrectly—on what the council was doing behind closed doors. On the evening of January 16, after several last-minute peace initiatives fizzled, the council members stood together in the lounge to watch coalition bombs and cruise missiles explode in Baghdad.[53] The first council-authorized war since Korea had begun. "In conjunction with the forces of our coalition partners," announced the White House spokesperson, "the United States has moved under the codename 'Operation Desert Storm' to enforce the mandates of the United Nations Security Council."[54]

As the first reports of civilian casualties surfaced, a group of Arab states called for a council meeting to discuss the war's victims. Most members, including the United States, successfully resisted. It was unusual for the council to refuse a meeting that several of its members wanted. The rules provided that any council member could request a meeting and that the council president should call one expeditiously. Almost a month after the air campaign began, the allies finally relented. The council convened for a formal debate on the issue of civilian casualties, and representatives of more than sixty countries spoke. But the United States and Britain insisted that the debate occur behind closed doors, a rare procedure for an official meeting. "We must ensure that the presence of the media does not influence and even distort the course of the debate," said British ambassador David Hannay. Pickering seconded the view. "We must not send signals which Iraq will misuse and misperceive that the council is not firm in its decisions and is not intent on seeing them implemented," he said.[55]

The contrast with the council's prewar, stage-managed session on Iraqi atrocities was notable, and the double standard outraged Cuba's ambassador. "What is there to conceal and from whom are we to conceal it?" He accused the council of having become afraid of the daylight, preferring to meet behind closed doors. Once the meeting began, Yemen's ambassador chastised the council members who had voted in favor of closing the doors. "The war is not the property of the fifteen states around this table," he said.[56]

In fact, the war was primarily the property of the U.S. military. The council itself had nothing to do with the conduct of the fighting. The Military Staff Committee, briefly revived for consultations on naval interdiction in the Persian Gulf, had returned to its slumber. The United States resisted all efforts by other council members to modify the military campaign, including a last-minute Soviet attempt to avoid the use of ground troops. On February 24, the coalition's ground forces went into action. One hundred hours after that, the war was over. As U.S. troops entered Kuwait City, the last Iraqi forces fled north, back across the border.

Aftermath and Afterglow

The Iraqi military collapse signaled the beginning of a new period of council activity. In April 1991, the council passed Resolution 687, a complex document drafted almost entirely by the Americans, which established specific criteria for the cessation of hostilities with Iraq. It demanded that Iraq compensate victims of abuses in Kuwait, accept monitors on the border with Kuwait, and pledge not to develop nuclear weapons. The United Nations' International Atomic Energy Agency (IAEA) was responsible for inspecting Iraq's nuclear program. But the United States was determined not to leave the weapons inspections in the hands of career UN bureaucrats, whom Washington in particular distrusted.

Resolution 687 created an unusual body, the United Nations Special Commission (UNSCOM), to handle the hunt for chemical and biological weapons. UNSCOM reported directly to the Security Council rather than to the Secretariat. "There was a positive effort to deny that the Secretary General should play any substantive role in the process," remembered Thomas Pickering, who feared that the Secretariat was too politicized to carry out the delicate task.[57] UNSCOM's funding came from Security Council countries and from seized Iraqi assets, depriving the General Assembly of its normal budgetary influence. The unusual arrangement led to immediate friction with the UN bureaucracy, which moved slowly to accommodate the inspectors' requests for office space and logistical support.[58]

For its part, Iraq bridled at the web of conditions that Resolution 687 imposed and accused the council of creating a "new colonial period."[59] In the weeks that followed the resolution's adoption, it became evident that ensuring Iraqi compliance would be a prolonged struggle. In July, Iraq missed a deadline for declaring all of its weapons of mass destruction, and the United States suggested that it would consider using air strikes to enforce the terms of the ceasefire. "We are deadly serious about [Iraq] coming into compliance," said defense secretary Richard Cheney.[60] Evidence of Iraqi obfuscation continued to surface. UNSCOM's inspectors located large quantities of chemical weapons, several times more than Baghdad had declared. And in August 1991, just as the council was considering whether to finally lift the economic sanctions, Iraq was forced to admit that it had enriched small amounts of plutonium.[61]

Iraq's often clumsy skullduggery persuaded the council to keep the sanctions in place. The council's Iraq sanctions committee, which had been meeting quietly throughout the run-up to the war, took on a new importance. The economic pressure that the council wielded had become a principal tool for compelling Iraqi compliance. In the bowels of UN headquarters, representatives of the fifteen council members regularly reviewed economic activities related to Iraq to determine whether they violated the sanctions and what exceptions could be made on humanitarian grounds. Medicines clearly fell outside the sanctions regime. But what about books, clothes, construction materials, and agricultural equipment? And how should the council respond to requests for sanctions exemptions from states heavily dependent on Iraqi oil? Case by case, the sanctions committee struggled to manage the mechanics and politics of the economic isolation it was imposing on Iraq.[62]

A complex game between Saddam and the council had begun. In theory, it should have been no contest. Iraq was prostrate economically and battered militarily. The Five, meanwhile, appeared determined to enforce the provisions of Resolution 687, and Iraq's initial challenges were met with firm resistance from the entire council. Saddam had several distinct advantages, however. The first was time. Iraqi security forces had brutally suppressed the challenges to Saddam's authority from the Shiites in the south and the Kurds in the north. The sanctions were biting, but they were not threatening Saddam's rule, and he could afford a long-term strategy. Iraq's second advantage was information. Iraqi leaders almost always knew what went on behind the closed doors of the consultation room, likely via sympathetic nonpermanent members. When a U.S. representative on the council inadvertently softened the language of a draft resolution, the Iraqis heard about it almost immediately. "We know every word which is spoken in the closed session of the Security Council," Tariq Aziz boasted to the weapons inspectors.[63]

The postwar struggles with Saddam Hussein did not diminish what was a remarkable triumph for the council. For most of its members, particularly the Western powers, the liberation of Kuwait was a high point. It was not lost on the diplomats involved that the council's revival had been orchestrated by a man who had labored in the chamber. "If we hadn't had Bush as president, someone who actually knew and liked the UN and had worked there, it never would have happened," said Alexander Watson, the U.S. deputy ambassador in New York at the time.[64] In dramatic fashion, the council members had repelled aggression, vindicated the founders' vision of the organization, and rescued it from what had appeared to be a long slide into irrelevance. "There is no question that the successful bringing to an end of the state of hostilities in the Gulf war is a feather in the cap of the Security Council," said David Hannay.[65] Bush himself was far more expansive. "[W]e can see a new world coming into view," he declared in a speech to Congress shortly after the war ended. "A world in which there is the very real prospect of a new world order.... A world where the United Nations, freed from Cold War stalemate, is poised to fulfill the historic vision of its founders. A world in which freedom and respect for human rights find a home among all nations."[66]

This vision of an assertive Security Council righting wrongs and defending human rights around the world caused unease in some quarters, which began to manifest itself as the council considered how to help the victims of Saddam's postwar wrath. As Iraqi forces cracked down on Kurdish separatists, thousands of refugees fled through mountain passes into Turkey. France insisted that the council address their plight and suggested that the time was right to establish a "duty to intervene" in the face of internal repression, possibly by amending the charter. "When new crimes are committed," said French foreign minister Roland Dumas, "why should the rule of law not acquire the resources to respond?"[67] The Soviet Union and China balked at direct interference in Iraq's internal affairs. The final draft split the difference. It condemned Iraq's repression of its own civilians, which had consequences that "threaten international peace and security in the region," but did not authorize enforcement measures and did not reference Chapter VII."[68]

The draft resolution contained an important, though not unprecedented, acknowledgment that a state's internal policies could become the business of the Security Council. South Africa had received a similar warning in the 1980s over its apartheid policy. Even in its weakened form, the resolution generated significant resistance from states not eager to set a precedent for humanitarian intervention. China and India abstained, while Cuba, Yemen, and Zimbabwe voted against it. The resolution, which passed in April 1991, secured only ten votes, just one more than the minimum needed to pass it.[69]

A growing number of voices warned that the council had become a mechanism for the great powers to foist their preferences on the rest of the world. "Since the renaissance at the United Nations is closely linked to the strengthened role of the permanent Security Council members, it raises fears in the south of an hegemonic directorate," said Olga Pellicer, Mexico's deputy representative at the United Nations. "It is always their agenda, not ours."[70] Some in the developing world wondered whether, in focusing so intensely on peacekeeping and military intervention, the Five had forgotten about the economic inequities that many poor countries believed were the principal cause of insecurity.

The nonaligned also worried that the Five were using the council to unfairly isolate and punish leaders whom the West had deemed "rogues." In March 1992, Britain, France, and the United States introduced a resolution imposing sanctions on Libya for its failure to extradite suspects accused of bombing Pan Am flight 103 in December 1988. The proposal made several of the nonaligned states on the council uneasy, relying as it did on the findings of Western intelligence agencies rather than international bodies. With the Five operating harmoniously, however, the nonaligned were unable to resist the political pressure to punish Libya, and the measure passed easily.[71] Libya took the matter to court, protesting to the International Court of Justice that the council had no authority to impose sanctions and that the dispute was covered by existing international treaties. Unsurprisingly, the world court refused to interfere.[72] Libya discovered what Australia's Herbert Evatt had realized in the council's earliest days: aside from political will, there are few limits to the body's authority.

Exit the Soviet Union, Enter Russia

The way the Five handled the collapse of the Soviet Union did not ease concerns about the council's accountability. By the middle of 1991, it had become clear that the Soviet Communist Party's grip on power was slipping. The clumsy and short-lived coup launched by Kremlin hardliners in August 1991 only served to accelerate the system's collapse. Mikhail Gorbachev emerged from his brief captivity as a wounded and confused figure, and Boris Yeltsin quickly pushed him aside. On December 21, 1991, the Soviet Union ceased to exist. For the Security Council, it was a potentially revolutionary moment. One of the organization's founding members had collapsed. There were strong legal arguments for amending the charter to address the U.S.S.R.'s disappearance. The charter specifically named the Union of Soviet Socialist Republics—not Russia or the Russian Federation—as a permanent council member.[73] The process of amending the charter would have inevitably opened the door to reforming the council membership to reflect new political realities.

The Five quickly stamped out any such ideas. With scarcely a whisper of debate, they closed ranks and decided that Russia should replace the Soviet Union on the council, with no need for a broader reorganization. Yuli Vorontsov, the U.S.S.R.'s ambassador to the council in December 1991, sat down in the chamber in January 1992 as the ambassador of the Russian Federation. Behind the scenes, some voices of protest were heard. "The argument was raised that legally this doesn't make any sense—they have no right to this," recalled then deputy U.S. ambassador Alexander Watson. "The Soviet Union no longer exists, that's the one that's supposed to be here. Shouldn't we talk about a rotation or something like that? But in the final analysis, people said, 'what's the real alternative?'"[74] The Five seemed to realize that they had played fast and loose with the charter. "We were lucky the General Assembly wasn't in session," a Western diplomat told the *New York Times*. "Otherwise we might have had howls of fury to contend with."[75]

The quick acceptance of Russia as one of the Five made sense from the perspective of managing the Soviet collapse and smoothing relations among the major powers. The successor states to the Soviet Union agreed (some grudgingly) that Russia should maintain the council seat, and any effort to open debate would have been a further humiliation of the already humbled power. But it is also clear that the moment was a missed opportunity to realign and perhaps expand the council. Just as the end of the Second World War had opened space for the council's creation, the end of the Cold War might have allowed adjustment to reflect new realities and to refresh the council's legitimacy with the rest of the world. That the council members did not seize the opportunity—or even seriously discuss it—reflected their priorities. Managing Russia's descent from superpower status easily trumped considerations of bolstering the council's long-term health.

On January 31, 1992, Yeltsin, now the president of the Russian Federation, tried out his country's seat at the table in person. The council was meeting for the first time in its history at the level of heads of state. It was Britain's month to serve as council president and Prime Minister John Major gaveled the meeting to order. "We are meeting at a time of momentous change," he began.

> Just a year ago, the Council met the challenge of Iraq's invasion of Kuwait, and the Council did that with great success. But today we face new challenges, and to set a new course in tackling them, it is right, I believe, that we should meet for the first time ever at the level of Heads of State or

FIGURE 5.2. The U.S. ambassador, Thomas Pickering, President George H. W. Bush, and Secretary of State James Baker during the Security Council summit in January 1992.

Government. Today, we must show that the Security Council is working with a common purpose.

The meeting prompted a number of dramatic gestures. French president François Mitterrand announced that his country was ready to place 1,000 peace-keepers at the organization's disposal. Yeltsin declared the pardoning of the last ten political prisoners in Russia. "There are no longer any prisoners of conscience in free Russia," he said.[76]

It seemed fitting that a brand-new secretary-general presided over this unprecedented council meeting. A few months earlier, the council had selected and the General Assembly had ratified Boutros Boutros-Ghali, a veteran Egyptian diplomat, as the organization's sixth chief administrator. Fluent in French, Boutros-Ghali enjoyed Paris's strong support and was acceptable to the Americans. A Coptic Christian, Boutros-Ghali never reached the post of Egyptian foreign minister, which always went to a Muslim, but he had been effectively running Egypt's foreign policy for many years and had an extensive network of contacts in foreign ministries around the world. He was the first secretary-general from Africa, and he brought to the organization a sharp focus on the needs of the developing world, as well as a sharp tongue.

He arrived at the most optimistic moment since the United Nations' founding. A senior British diplomat described the atmosphere. "We thought we were living in the golden age," said Thomas Richardson, Britain's deputy ambassador at the time. "We thought we had a chance to resolve all these nasty little civil wars supported by outsiders for Cold War reasons."[77] But alongside the optimism was an understanding that the post–Cold War period would have its own fearsome challenges. A spate of civil wars and ethnic conflicts was breaking out around the world, as governments that had been propped up by the superpowers crumbled and as rivalries that had been subsumed by ideological struggles resurfaced. The council immediately tasked Boutros-Ghali with drafting a plan for how the United Nations could use its new momentum to promote international security and tamp down what some observers were already calling the "new world disorder."

The secretary-general released his study, titled *An Agenda for Peace*, in June 1992. Traditionally, reports from the UN secretary-general were consigned almost immediately to filing cabinets. This one made news around the world, and at its heart was a bold call to finally equip the council with the tools envisioned by the charter.

> The United Nations was rendered powerless to deal with many of these crises because of the vetoes—279 of them—cast in the Security Council, which were a vivid expression of the divisions of that period. With the end of the Cold War there have been no such vetoes since 31 May 1990, and demands on the United Nations have surged. Its security arm, once disabled by circumstances it was not created or equipped to control, has emerged as a central instrument for the prevention and resolution of conflicts and for the preservation of peace.

Boutros-Ghali recommended that UN members finally negotiate the charter's Article 43 agreements to place forces at the disposal of the council and suggested that the council activate the Military Staff Committee to advise it on forceful military operations.[78] Picking up on the stated willingness of several council members to designate troops for UN service, he envisioned a UN force that might stand ready to intervene on the council's orders. "I'm asking all members to let me have up to 1,000 trained troops within 24 hours," Boutros-Ghali said. "That's the most useful number of troops and it would really change my life."[79] His vision resonated in many parts of the world. "Why not have a standing army in blue helmets that is available to keep the world peace?" Australia's UN ambassador asked. "I am talking about a far more effective UN, seen on a much more daily basis."[80] The *New York Times* helpfully drafted a job description.

> WANTED: Small, highly mobile army, able to respond overnight to civil disorder. Must be able to enforce cease-fires, cope with natural disasters,

facilitate relief and deal impartially with all belligerents. Reply to United Nations, N.Y.[81]

Nation Building, Take Two

To the diplomats serving on the council, the summer of 1992 offered little of the relaxation that summers had sometimes granted their predecessors. The council was in almost continuous session as it struggled to manage both the continuing fallout from the Gulf War and the multiple peacekeeping operations it had authorized. Peacekeeping itself was nothing new for the council, which had approved missions to hotspots, including the Suez, Lebanon, and Cyprus, during the Cold War. But those peacekeepers generally confined themselves to monitoring ceasefire lines and acting as a buffer between warring parties. This new generation of operations was much closer to the controversial operation the council launched in Congo in 1960. They included election monitoring, military and police training, and even civil administration. In essence, the council was attempting to salvage failing states. Where local governments had failed, the council members appeared willing and often eager to step in and provide order and a pathway to effective governance. The ambition of these missions accelerated the council's post–Cold War shift from a limited political concert toward an expansive governance role that included not only traditional collective security but also regular interventions in civil conflicts. With little planning or preparation, the council was testing how far its new unity would take it.[82]

The undertaking in the southern African territory of Namibia in 1989 offered grounds to believe that this more ambitious form of peacekeeping might succeed. For more than a decade, South Africa had prevented the deployment of a planned UN mission and refused to grant independence to the territory it had long controlled. A low-level struggle between South African forces and Namibian rebels operating from bases in Angola continued. In early 1989, as the world political climate changed, South Africa finally consented to the UN deployment. The mission almost failed as soon as it began. Thousands of rebel fighters crossed into Namibian territory before the designated time, leading to clashes with South African security forces. The council pressured the parties to keep the peace process alive, and UN mediators hustled to bolster fraying confidence. Over the next several months, peacekeepers and civilian officials successfully guided South Africa and Namibia away from conflict and toward democratic elections, which took place without violence in November. In March 1990, the hated South African flag was pulled down and replaced with that of an independent Namibia. In neighboring Angola, several hundred UN military observers were sent to supervise a peace accord between the Angolan rebels and the leftist government and to help prepare for national elections.[83] The success in Namibia made the council optimistic that a resolution of Angola's related conflict was within easy reach.

The peacekeeping floodgates were opening, and one of the council's most ambitious missions was in Asia. In Cambodia, thousands of peacekeepers dispatched by the council in 1991 monitored an agreement signed by the country's competing political factions and prepared to shepherd the country through elections. Civilian employees of the United Nations moved into offices in Phnom Penh, where they monitored and advised Cambodian officials trying to create a unified government. The Cambodia mission was not a forcible intervention. The council sent peacekeepers to Cambodia with the consent of the country's principal factions, and it was authorized under chapter VI of the charter. But even in this environment of consent, the peacekeepers soon faced the dilemma of how to assert themselves. In July, the Khmer Rouge refused to fulfill its agreement to allow peacekeepers into areas under its control. The United Nations briefly considered confronting the holdouts but ultimately chose to simply ignore the Khmer Rouge. Preparations for elections went ahead in other areas of the country, and the United Nations was spared a direct confrontation.

In the Balkans, which was beginning to consume the council's attention, the context was more menacing. Fighting broke out in the former Yugoslavia in June 1991, when the westernmost republic of Slovenia declared independence. The Serb-dominated federal army briefly but unsuccessfully attempted to drag the breakaway republic back. Shortly thereafter, neighboring Croatia launched its own independence bid, but it would not escape so easily. The republic had a large Serb minority that had no interest in living under Croat domination. With help from the Yugoslav Army, they seized control of traditionally Serb areas, often expelling Croats who lived there. In September 1991, the council imposed an arms embargo on the whole of the former Yugoslavia.[84] As was quickly pointed out, that embargo hit hardest the republics bearing the brunt of the Serb offensive. They often had little access to weapons, while Serb forces had all they could use, courtesy of Yugoslavia's Serb-dominated army.

In February 1992, the council authorized an 8,000-person peacekeeping mission for Croatia, called the UN Protection Force (UNPROFOR). The blue helmets took positions between the Serb enclaves and the rest of Croatia. But the Balkan crisis was quickly spreading to Yugoslavia's most ethnically mixed republic, Bosnia and Herzegovina. Serb militias and regular units of the Serb-dominated federal army began expelling non-Serbs from swathes of eastern and northern Bosnia. In Bosnia's cosmopolitan capital, Sarajevo, residents realized that they, too, were vulnerable to the escalating violence. In March, armed militias constructed roadblocks, and full-scale fighting broke out when Bosnia declared independence in early April. Determined to crush the nascent Bosnian state, Serb forces in the hills began lobbing shells into the city and sniping at the residents.

Alarmed at the spreading violence, the council voted to extend UNPROFOR into Bosnia. That decision came in the face of opposition from Boutros-Ghali and his advisors, who thought the conditions for successful peacekeeping were not present. The deployment was an important departure from accepted peacekeeping practice in several ways. There was no peace agreement on the ground and no consent from one of the key combatants—the Bosnian Serbs. Second, the mission involved significant numbers of troops from the Five. It had been standard peacekeeping practice to avoid the involvement of permanent council members, as it was feared that they might import great-power competition directly into local disputes. States without strong Cold War allegiances, such as Sweden, India, and Nepal, provided most Cold War peacekeeping troops. With the Cold War over, that concern was muted, and the military resources of the Five could now be hitched more directly to the missions the council authorized. The intense pressure of events was reshaping tools the organization had developed in a very different political environment.

Boiling Point

Thousands of miles away from Bosnia, and with far less international attention, Somalia was descending into anarchy. Its long-time dictator, Siad Barre, was overthrown in 1991. The militias that ousted him, however, were incapable of consolidating their hold on the country. Vicious clan warfare broke out which, combined with a prolonged drought, produced mass starvation. The relief supplies that did arrive in the country were usually diverted by militias for their own use or to be sold. The lone remaining Somali diplomat at the United Nations pleaded for assistance. "I am emotionally affected—and ashamed—by what is happening in my country," she wrote to the president of the council. "The situation cries out for the help of the United Nations."[85]

For several months, the council had little to offer. It imposed an arms embargo on Somalia in January 1992, a largely meaningless step as the country was awash with weapons.[86] It called for negotiations between the feuding factions, which yielded only a temporary ceasefire. Reports from aid agencies grew increasingly alarming. By April, observers reported that Somalis were dropping dead on the streets from malnutrition and disease. At the United Nations, the contrast between the intense activity on the Balkans and the sluggishness on Somalia had become too obvious to ignore. "It is clear that the only crisis that matters to the powers-that-be in the Security Council is the crisis in Eastern Europe," said Botswana's UN ambassador. "People are dying by the thousands in Africa, but no one here is convening urgent consultations. Our crises don't spark that kind of response."[87] To Boutros-Ghali's outrage, the council refused for several months to authorize the dispatch of 500 troops to safeguard the delivery of food. Officials from the United States balked at the plan, worried that Congress would refuse to fund yet another peacekeeping operation during an election year.[88]

The secretary-general's mounting frustration at the council crested in July when mediators from the European Community attempted to assign the United Nations responsibility for monitoring a temporary—and, as it turned out, short-lived—ceasefire in Bosnia without consulting him. When the council endorsed that idea, Boutros-Ghali dispatched a blistering letter to British ambassador David Hannay, who was council president at the time.

> I must express my considered opinion that it would have been preferable if the Security Council, as has been the usual practice heretofore, had requested and awaited a technically grounded opinion by UNPROFOR, before taking such a position....I am, of course, at the service of the Security Council. At the same time, however, I would hope that my views would be ascertained in areas which are clearly within my competence.[89]

For an organization accustomed to the secretary-general giving public obeisance to the council, the statement was startling. "I've never seen the Secretary-General take on the Security Council like this," said one council diplomat.[90] Hannay did not respond, and he urged his council colleagues to let the matter rest. But the incident evidenced several growing tensions.

The first was a struggle between the council and the permanent UN bureaucracy, particularly over the management of peacekeeping operations. Hammarskjöld's championing of large, Secretariat-managed peacekeeping operations in the 1950s and 1960s had altered the charter's vision of how the organization would deploy forces. The UN civil servants, not the council's Military Staff Committee, managed day-to-day field operations. The council still authorized the missions, and as they became more complex and controversial, it felt pressure to manage ongoing operations through resolutions and statements. It was a cumbersome and ineffective form of oversight. The council's often intricate wordsmithing did not lend itself to effective crisis management. A savvier and less jealous secretary-general would have worked to make sure the council fully understood the operational dilemmas by making available to it UN experts and peacekeeping commanders and insinuating himself into its debates.

Instead, Boutros-Ghali weakened the ties between the Secretariat and the council. In early 1993, he stopped attending most of the council's informal consultations and designated a representative, the veteran Indian diplomat Chinmaya Gharekhan, to attend in his stead. The move made some sense; the council was meeting almost every day, and attending every session would have consumed the secretary-general's time. Still, Boutros-Ghali's decision was a sharp break from past practice and was seen by several council members as "an affront to their importance."[91] Worse, Boutros-Ghali prohibited many of his subordinates from briefing the council directly. He and a close circle of advisors jealously guarded the information flow between the Secretariat and the council.

The July squabble over Bosnia also suggested a brewing competition between the United Nations and regional organizations, such as the European Community, for primacy on peace and security issues. As a matter of international law, there was little doubt that the Security Council had the lead. The charter stipulated that regional organizations could play a role in security matters, but only with the council's blessing. Churchill's vision of regional security councils that would handle most issues had been decisively rejected in favor of a centralized organization. As a matter of practical politics, however, the Security Council's primacy was far less certain. The EC, in particular, was enjoying a renaissance, and several leading European politicians saw the Balkans crisis as an opportunity for the organization to assert itself on security issues. "The hour of Europe has dawned," proclaimed Jacques Poo, the Luxembourgian minister serving as president of the European Council, as Yugoslavia's dissolution began. To Boutros-Ghali, it appeared that Europe wanted to handle the important issues and use UN peacekeepers as hired labor. He told the council directly, "I cannot agree that the UN should become merely the executing agency for regional organizations."[92]

Perhaps most important, the confrontation over Bosnia reflected Boutros-Ghali's frustration at what he saw as the council's double standard. "If the Europeans wanted more activism on Bosnia," Boutros-Ghali reflected later, "they should do more themselves, not expect the United Nations to divert critical resources to a conflict in Europe at the expense of conflicts in Africa, Asia, and Latin America."[93] On several occasions, Boutros-Ghali had expressed his view that Bosnia's sorrows paled next to those in many other parts of the globe. Inexplicably, he made the case while visiting besieged Sarajevo, where he told a Bosnian reporter, "you have a situation here that is better than in 10 other places in the world."[94]

However maladroit, Boutros-Ghali had a valid argument: the suffering in Somalia easily eclipsed that in Bosnia. But did that end the debate about where the council should concentrate its efforts? In the post–Cold War period, humanitarian need often became the standard by which the council's performance was judged. This reflected a particular interpretation of the council's mandate to maintain "international peace and security," but it was certainly not the only plausible one. The effect of a given conflict on other countries and on international commerce, the danger of regional escalation, the possibility of great-power entanglement, and whether the combatants possessed weapons of mass destruction could all be relevant factors for the council to consider. Viewed in this light, it was possible to argue that, while Somalia's crisis was more dire from a humanitarian perspective, the Balkan conflict more gravely threatened international peace and security. The Balkans, after all, had been the trigger for one great-power conflict, and a number of analysts worried that the new fighting there might trigger a regional war, perhaps even dragging in Turkey and Greece. Much more than Bosnia seemed to be at stake. "The whole concept of a multiethnic Europe has been undermined," a senior Greek official warned. "We're tearing apart what we've built over the last 50 years in Europe."[95]

Boutros-Ghali was plainly skeptical that strategic wisdom rather than regional or even racial prejudice was animating the council's disparate responses. "The situations in Bosnia and Somalia are basically similar," he argued, "except for the fact that the parties in Somalia are not sophisticated and did not wish the UN to become involved, whereas those in Bosnia are sophisticated, welcome the UN, but violate the agreement the UN helps them conclude."[96] Through his reports and recommendations to the council, the secretary-general could pressure its members to see the world the way he did. But in the case of strong differences, his real influence was the bully pulpit. The UN Charter made it the council's role—not the secretary-general's—to determine the relative danger of conflicts and the appropriate response to them. Unfortunately, Boutros-Ghali was not adept at using the media to go over the council's head. He often appeared acerbic, and, as his disastrous trip to Sarajevo showed, he had a penchant for angering the audiences he was trying to convince.

The media belatedly took up Somalia's cause. In the fall of 1992, images of starving children appeared regularly in the Western press. Compared to Bosnia's complex ethnic conflict, Somalia's crisis appeared eminently soluble. In the final months of his term, having lost his reelection bid, George H. W. Bush decided that the United States would not continue to stand aside as thousands of Somalis starved to death. By November 1992, he was ready to send troops. The rescue operation was put together hastily. Senior American military officers arrived to coordinate with the UN peacekeeping staff. American diplomats and UN officials were pulled abruptly from meetings on other topics to plan the intervention. For the United Nations' peacekeeping staff, which was in the midst of launching a much smaller mission to Mozambique, the pace was almost overwhelming.

FIGURE 5.3. A Mogadishu resident argues with a U.S. Marine during a weapons confiscation patrol.

A two-pronged operation emerged for Somalia. A U.S.-led intervention force of almost 20,000 troops would land, secure Mogadishu, and ensure food distribution channels—all with council authorization. As the force secured the ground, the United Nations would recruit a reinforced UN peacekeeping operation to stabilize the political environment and to begin reconstruction of the shattered country. Once order was restored, the United States would hand over responsibility to the peacekeepers. It was all arranged in a matter of days, and the council approved the plan on December 3. The resolution authorizing the force was, wrote British ambassador David Hannay later, "probably the most astonishing single document to be agreed in the immediate post–Cold War period at the UN.... It swept aside the whole notion, or fiction in the case of Somalia, of consent by the host nation."[97] The U.S. Marines stormed Somalia's beaches in early December 1992, and the council's first armed humanitarian intervention was under way. Another troubled corner of the globe had come under the council's wing.

Safe Areas and Field Trips

By the winter of 1992, many Bosnians wondered whether the council's attentions were worth having. The siege of Sarajevo began to produce shortages of food, water, and medicine, and the city that had proudly hosted the 1984 Winter

Olympics was running short of heating oil and bread. With public outrage mounting, fissures emerged in the council chamber. The members had very different notions of what the UN peacekeepers it had authorized should be doing and what the council's posture should be toward the warring parties.

The United States and several of the council's elected members were eager to punish Serbia for its transgressions and unwilling to countenance the division of Bosnia, which they saw as rewarding ethnic cleansing. The young administration of President Bill Clinton took several months to refine its position, but it soon advocated lifting the arms embargo on the Bosnian Muslims and using air strikes to roll back the Serb acquisitions. In May 1993, the new U.S. secretary of state, Warren Christopher, traveled to Europe to make the case for what was being called the "lift and strike" option. He encountered stiff resistance. Britain and France together had several thousand troops serving in UNPROFOR, and with soldiers in harm's way, they emphasized continued diplomacy, maintaining decent relations with all of the warring parties, and facilitating the delivery of humanitarian aid. British and French politicians did not want their troops in combat, and the American notion of lifting the embargo and pouring more weapons into the inferno appeared to be irresponsible moral grandstanding.

Humanitarian relief remained the one mission on which all council members could agree. In June 1992, the council insisted that Serb forces open Sarajevo's airport to relief flights, and on the eve of the deadline, the Serbs agreed. Small victories like that could not obscure the reality that humanitarian relief was a substitute for the more difficult decisions that would have been required to end the war. The relief operation, wrote a senior UN official, was "a substitute for political action. Ensuring its success, and its perception of success, was important to key governments."[98] The perception that the United Nations was responding adequately to the crisis faded quickly. The millions poured into humanitarian relief while fighting raged prompted bitter remarks that the United Nations was doing little more than keeping Bosnians alive for the snipers. Over the next year, Serb forces skillfully exploited the divisions on the council and the vulnerabilities of the UN command structure. They repeatedly tested the council's patience before defusing building pressure with limited concessions. Meanwhile, the ethnic cleansing of Bosnia continued. Convinced that a permanent ethnic partition was imminent, Bosnia's Muslim and Croatian populations, loosely aligned when the conflict began, turned on each other, sparking new fighting and fresh atrocities.

In the face of this critical situation, the council cast about for additional measures short of forceful intervention. It met more often and passed more resolutions on the former Yugoslavia than it had done for any crisis in history. In October 1992, it declared a no-fly zone over Bosnia. A few months later, it demanded the closure of detention camps, particularly those where systematic rapes were occurring. Many of the council's resolutions and statements were impotent and quickly forgotten calls for the warring parties to stop fighting, comply with international law, and behave like civilized people. In the consultation room, ambassadors sometimes seemed stunned at their own inability to control events. "Here we have 15 countries with big military machines, but not a single military machine is available for use by [the] Security Council," exclaimed Russian ambassador Vorontsov. "There are big military forces around Bosnia, like big tigers just lazing around. It is time that those tigers are put to use."[99]

One resolution, passed in late February 1993, was more significant than most. It called on the secretary-general to establish a criminal tribunal to punish the conflict's worst crimes. It was a significant innovation and a sign of the council's expanding reach. The UN Charter grants the council the right to establish subsidiary bodies that it deems to be necessary, and over the years the council had created a few small technical commissions. The war crimes tribunal was a much more dramatic step. Using its powers under chapter VII, the council created an international court that had the power to try individuals, including high government officials, for war crimes, genocide, and crimes against humanity committed in the former Yugoslavia. Not all council members were comfortable with the step. China and several nonpermanent members initially argued that any court should be established by an international conference, not by the council. And many observers dismissed the tribunal as little more than a fig leaf to cover the council's inability to stop the Bosnian atrocities.

Relationships on the council were often rubbed raw by the strain of the emerging Bosnia debacle. The Anglo-American partnership reached one of its lowest points since the Suez crisis. Just as Henry Cabot Lodge and Pierson Dixon had dueled then, U.S. ambassador Madeleine Albright and her British counterpart, David Hannay, squared off repeatedly over the Bosnian conflict and the proper council response. Both diplomats were forceful presences, though they had very different styles.

Albright was a Democratic Party foreign policy eminence and university professor whose career had been almost entirely in Washington. Like other American ambassadors in this period, Albright suffered in the eyes of her council colleagues by comparison with Thomas Pickering. As ambassador, she was frequently in Washington rather than New York and had limited patience for the painstaking negotiations in the consultation room. She tended to speak from prepared statements rather than engaging extemporaneously with her colleagues. Boutros-Ghali complained that "she seemed to have little interest in the difficult diplomatic work of persuading her foreign counterparts to go along with the positions of her government, preferring to lecture or speak in declarative sentences, or simply to read verbatim from her briefing books."[100] Hannay had a very different background. A career diplomat who had been posted in Kabul, Tehran, and Brussels, he was a master of detail who enjoyed dueling over fine points in the consultation room. He paired his substantive expertise with often cutting wit and he had little patience for those not as prepared. Behind her back, Hannay referred to his American counterpart as "Half-bright."[101]

As the Five struggled to coordinate their positions on Bosnia, a group of nonpermanent council members grew frustrated. As it had with increasing frequency since the end of the Cold War, the council tended to operate in concentric circles. The Western powers would normally consult together on draft resolutions, then discuss them with the Five, and only then with the broader council. Hungary's representative, André Erdos, found the process maddening. His government and that of Austria, also on the council at the time, had deep historical connections with Bosnia and believed they had insight to contribute. "The whole atmosphere around Bosnia was very bizarre. I was flabbergasted by the ignorance of my colleagues about the historical and geographical realities on the ground. European ambassadors were just drifting along, not analyzing and wishing to know what was happening in the former Yugoslavia." Erdos at one point brought into the consultation room a 1911 text on the Balkans to show that Bosnia had a historical basis and was not merely a creation of Tito, as was sometimes alleged.[102] Erdos insisted on his voice being heard, and he once chastised Albright and Hannay for carrying on a private conversation while he was speaking.[103]

As the divisions among the Five persisted, the nonpermanent members acquired uncommon influence. Improbably, one of Bosnia's most effective advocates on the council was the ambassador from Venezuela, Diego Arria, who had joined the council in January 1992. A veteran politician and one-time presidential candidate, Arria was a charismatic personality. He walked with a limp and spoke during deliberations with unusual passion. Typically, council ambassadors are in regular contact with their respective foreign ministries to receive instructions on how to vote. Arria had a close relationship with Venezuelan president Carlos Andrés Pérez and did not require or accept regular instructions from the Foreign Ministry.[104] His personality and room to maneuver made him an unusually influential nonpermanent ambassador. On Bosnia, he worked closely with the Islamic states on the council, including Pakistan, which feared that the United Nations was permitting the slow destruction of Bosnia's Muslim community. Jamsheed Marker, Pakistan's ambassador, often argued that UN commanders on the ground cared more about their cherished neutrality than about protecting the conflict's principal victims.

During the deliberations on Bosnia, Arria—who had by now won the sobriquet "Don Diego of Sarajevo"—became convinced that the council was getting information from too few sources.[105] Like many small-state ambassadors, he did not have detailed reports from national intelligence services and had to rely on the Secretariat for most of his information about the peacekeeping operations. Increasingly frustrated with UN officials, Arria initiated a new procedure for the council to meet directly with representatives of nongovernmental organizations and with victims of the conflicts they were investigating. While bringing outsiders into official meetings was not acceptable to the council, Arria arranged for informal briefings that council members could attend. The first one occurred in 1992, when Arria brought in a Bosnian priest to discuss the conflict in his country. These meetings, dubbed "Arria formula" sessions, became a regular feature of the council's work.[106]

Arria and Marker also championed an initiative to designate several besieged Bosnian towns as "safe areas." The idea faced strong opposition. The British, French, and Russians, as well as the Secretariat, were skeptical. How would these areas be defended? And if the peacekeepers repelled attacks with force, wouldn't they become a party to the conflict? The proposal acquired urgency as Bosnian Serb forces approached the embattled town of Srebrenica in April 1993. Observers feared a massacre of the Muslim inhabitants, and in a series of emergency meetings, the council declared Srebrenica a safe area on April 21. Reports filtering in from the ground indicated that Serb forces had stopped at the edge of the town. "It might have been the 13th hour," said a relieved Jamsheed Marker, "but we did it."[107]

With one safe area already declared, Britain, France, and Russia acquiesced to a resolution several weeks later granting five other Bosnian cities and towns the same status. Still, the wording of the resolutions left many questions. Could peacekeepers use force to defend the safe areas from attack or just to defend themselves? When could they call in air strikes? Senior peacekeeping officials were intensely frustrated by the ambiguities.

> [The resolutions] deployed UN troops in [the safe areas] but expected their mere presence to "deter attacks," carefully avoided asking the peacekeepers to "defend" or "protect" these areas, but authorized them to call in air power "in self defence"—a masterpiece of diplomatic drafting but largely unimplementable as an operational directive.[108]

Arria pressed the council ambassadors to see with their own eyes the conflict they were attempting to manage. There was little precedent for the fact-finding mission he proposed. Council members were not in the habit of unseating themselves from New York for visits to the field; that was the work of national diplomats in embassies, UN peacekeepers, and representatives of the Secretariat. The Five were cool toward Arria's idea of traveling to the region in person. The

Secretariat was also skeptical. Particularly under Boutros-Ghali, it jealously guarded its prerogatives and believed that little good could come of council ambassadors roaming the war zone. Arria would not be deterred, however, and at the last moment the French and Russian ambassadors decided to join the trip. The delegation left New York in late April and flew to Sarajevo via Croatia's capital, Zagreb. Arria quickly concluded that he was not welcome. A UN military commander complained openly about the stream of "wooly-headed" resolutions emanating from New York. Arria had the impression that UN officials planned to treat the council delegation as glorified tourists rather than as serious interlocutors.[109]

The next day, Arria and his colleagues flew by helicopter to Srebrenica. Their helicopter was forced to land in Serb-controlled territory to pick up a minder, and the journalists accompanying the delegation were told that they could not travel with the ambassadors to the town. It soon became clear why. In the report submitted to the full council, the ambassadors described Srebrenica as an "open jail," where Serb forces prevented surgeons from tending to the sick and where residents rioted for the few available spots on trucks going to other parts of Bosnia. The gap between the council's lofty resolutions and the reality on the ground was startling to Arria. Peacekeepers in Bosnia were forced to make decisions every day about which the council knew nothing. Viewed from ground level, the council's warnings, pleas, and demands seemed almost comically irrelevant. The council may be important, a Canadian peacekeeper told the delegation, but "it is of no importance to the Serbs in the area."[110]

It was not until June that the council debated whether and how these safe areas would be protected. When it did, the now-familiar passive-aggressive dynamic between Boutros-Ghali and the council reappeared. The council asked the secretary-general to provide a plan for protecting the safe areas, and he responded that more than 30,000 troops would be needed. It was an impossible figure, and Boutros-Ghali knew it. But the estimate made his point: the safe areas would not be safe without a massive troop presence, and the council should never have committed itself to a project it could not fulfill.[111] The council, of course, insisted that Boutros-Ghali come up with another option, and he promptly offered a "light" version that involved only 7,500 troops, which was approved. But even the light option proved to be too much of a burden for the council and the UN membership. Four months after the troops were authorized, they had still not arrived.[112]

The Bosnian Serbs were constantly testing the council's commitments, but the most dramatic attack on its authority during the summer of 1993 occurred in Somalia, where the U.S.-led operation to help feed the population was rapidly becoming more complex. When the Clinton administration took office in January

1993, it insisted that the handover from the U.S.-led force to a new UN peace-keeping force take place as soon as possible, even though the UN force was not fully staffed. The warlord Mohamed Farah Aidid decided that the UN presence he had initially countenanced no longer served his interests. His forces attacked a group of Pakistani peacekeepers on June 5, killing twenty-four. Startled, the council swiftly passed a resolution condemning Aidid's attacks and authorizing military action to apprehend him.[113]

By the fall of 1993, the Security Council was supervising three large and complicated peacekeeping operations that involved more than 80,000 troops. It had authorized the creation of the first international criminal tribunal since the end of World War II. It was monitoring a no-fly zone over Bosnia and a comprehensive sanctions regime against the entire former Yugoslavia. Another sanctions regime was in place against Saddam Hussein's Iraq, and dozens of arms inspectors were prowling around that country and reporting back to the council. Since the end of the Cold War, the council had also imposed economic sanctions or arms embargoes on Somalia, Libya, and Angola, where a peacekeeping mission had failed to end that country's civil war.

The volume and pace of the council's activity were intense. Between 1984 and 1988, the council passed 80 resolutions. In the next five years, it passed 246. In 1986, the council held 96 formal meetings and convened for 72 informal consultation sessions. In 1993, those numbers jumped to 171 and 253, respectively. The council's schedule for the week of June 14–18 was typical of the period.

Monday, June 14

- Consultations on Cambodia, Haiti, Somalia, Bosnia, and North Korea

Tuesday, June 15

- Consultations on Haiti
- Resolution on Cambodia passed

Wednesday, June 16

- Consultations on Haiti, North Korea, Bosnia (including the UNPROFOR mission), Iraq, and Rwanda
- Resolution on Haiti passed

Thursday, June 17

- Consultations on Bosnia, the status of Macedonia, Rwanda, Somalia, and the council's annual report to the General Assembly

Friday, June 18

- Consultations on Bosnia, Iraq and Kuwait, Somalia, and UNSCOM inspections in Iraq
- Two resolutions passed on Macedonia
- One resolution passed on the former Yugoslavia
- One resolution passed on Bosnia[114]

In the space of five years, the council had gone from an often sleepy club for high politics to a frenetic world governance body that was struggling to contain conflict, mete out punishment for crimes against humanity, and end civil strife around the world.

CHAPTER 6

GROWING PAINS (1994–2001)

THE U.S. MILITARY transport that took off from Fort Bragg, North Carolina, in August 1993 carried some of America's most highly trained warriors. As Mohamed Farah Aidid's challenge to UN authority in Somalia stood unanswered, the Clinton administration dispatched the country's elite forces to bring the warlord to heel. Once established in Somalia, the Delta Force and Army Rangers conducted a series of raids around Mogadishu that netted some of Aidid's lieutenants, but not the warlord himself. Then, on October 3, an American operation went awry. The American units found themselves embroiled in a prolonged firefight and cut off from assistance. Eighteen American soldiers and hundreds of Somalis died. The bodies of several Americans were dragged through the streets by angry Mogadishu residents.[1]

The Pentagon dispatched temporary reinforcements, but the battle of Mogadishu effectively ended the peacekeeping effort. The United States had no stomach for prolonged engagement, and without American commitment, the rest of the UN mission crumbled. Mogadishu marked a clear pause in the council's dramatic post–Cold War rise. A local warlord had attacked peacekeepers, tangled with the superpower's army, endured the outrage of the council, and lived to tell the tale. The insidious doubts about the council's effectiveness that had been partially subsumed in the success of the Iran-Iraq mediation and the Gulf War resurfaced.

As important, the briefly close relationship between the United Nations and the United States was in tatters. The United Nations was accused of having dragged America into a nation-building operation it did not intend and of bungling the response once the fighting began. The *New York Times*, normally a staunch defender of the organization, accused the United Nations of enmeshing the United States in a quagmire.[2] Among more practiced UN skeptics, the mission was evidence of multilateralism's potential to sap American strength. "The U.N. has the potential of entrapping the U.S. in costly failures," read a report from the Heritage Foundation. "It is doubtful whether Washington would have shifted from relief operations to intervening with 25,000 troops had the U.S. not been working closely with the U.N. Moreover, it is unlikely that the U.S. would still be in Somalia were it not for the U.N.'s nation-building agenda."[3] Few American politicians had an incentive to temper the invective. For conservatives, the United Nations had long been a favored target. And for the Clinton administration, the organization could be used to deflect blame for Washington's own missteps.

Cooler heads pointed out that the military operation that precipitated the debacle was American-planned and -executed and that there had been little consultation with UN commanders. Nor did the notion that the United Nations had somehow snookered the United States into nation building withstand scrutiny. The United States had been involved at every stage of the deliberations on the Somalia mission. Washington had even insisted that the UN special representative in Somalia be an American diplomat and former military officer. However blame was apportioned, it was clear that the Mogadishu battle ushered in an era of marked caution on the council. The council had relearned painfully the lessons of the 1960 Congo operation. It was far easier to launch missions than to successfully complete them. Interventions that appeared uncontroversial, neutral, and purely humanitarian from Washington, London, or Moscow often looked very different through the eyes of local leaders.

There was little time for the reverberations from the Somalia debacle to settle. The pace of work on the council continued to be intense, and challenges to its authority mounted. The council struggled to put back on track the Angola peace agreement between the government and the UNITA rebels that had collapsed spectacularly in 1992. In Haiti, a military regime had unseated the government of Jean-Bertrand Aristide, and the council wrestled with the questions of how to restore him to power and whether doing so was even its responsibility. By the time the council authorized a Haitian mission to oversee a return to democratic rule, supporters of the military junta had already absorbed the lesson of Mogadishu. A threatening mob gathered to meet the American ship carrying the first peacekeepers, and the vessel promptly turned around.[4] In eastern Bosnia, Serb forces increased pressure on several of the remaining Muslim enclaves. And in February 1994, a shell slammed into a Sarajevo marketplace and killed several dozen civilians. It was a bloody reminder that, for almost two years, the council had failed to lift the siege of a major European city.

The Rwandan in the Room

General Romeo Dallaire, a French Canadian army officer experienced in peace-keeping, landed in the tiny African nation of Rwanda for the first time in August 1993. A group of senior Rwandan diplomats, including the country's UN ambassador, Jean-Damascène Bizimana, were on hand to greet him. Dallaire had just been appointed commander of the United Nations' newest peacekeeping force, the United Nations Assistance Mission in Rwanda (UNAMIR). Its purpose was to help push the Rwandan government and the opposition Rwanda Patriotic Front (RPF) toward political compromise and unified government. For years, the Hutu-dominated government and the RPF had battled for control. From its bases in neighboring Uganda, the RPF launched periodic forays across the border, the most serious in February, when its forces reached the outskirts of Kigali, the capital city. That incursion scared the Hutu-dominated government to the negotiating table, and a plan to share power was signed that summer in Arusha, Tanzania.

That the council had authorized a peacekeeping mission to Rwanda at all was notable. After the Mogadishu battle, the Clinton administration viewed most proposed missions skeptically. A U.S. policy directive on peacekeeping, which was in draft form at the time of the crisis, was hastily revised to put much stricter limits on U.S. participation in and authorization of future missions. Reduced in size and with its mandate trimmed, the proposed mission to Rwanda slipped through the council's tightening net. The Arusha peace accord helped to convince Washington and the council that the mission might be simple and clean. "I don't think anyone was thinking of a major new commitment on the level of Bosnia, Somalia, Cambodia," recalled Michael Sheehan, a White House official responsible for peacekeeping. "It was a smaller mission. There seemed to be some progress on the political front at the time, and that mission was basically there to help give that political process a little space."[5] France, always keenly interested in Francophone Africa, strongly supported the deployment, which it thought might help to keep its traditional Hutu allies from being overthrown by the RPF. As a French-speaking officer, Romeo Dallaire was a good political fit for the mission.

During the initial meeting at the Kigali airport, Dallaire wrote later, Ambassador Bizimana maintained a strange silence. "He watched and listened intently and said nothing, his sombre silence more than a little disturbing, as he was Rwanda's man in New York and an important interlocutor on our behalf in front of the media that day."[6] In the hectic and optimistic beginning to UNAMIR, the odd encounter faded. Over the next several months, Dallaire attended to the myriad logistical problems of establishing his 4,000-person force, composed mainly of Belgian, Bangladeshi, and Ghanaian troops. Dallaire reached out to a host of Rwandan politicians and military officials—and he gradually began to develop his own sources of information.

In January 1994, he stumbled across something startling. A confidential informant reported that a group of Hutu extremists were stockpiling weapons and planning for large-scale massacres of Tutsis and moderate Hutus. Dallaire immediately cabled the information to the peacekeeping office in New York, then headed by a long-time UN official from Ghana, Kofi Annan. The general wanted permission to raid the arms caches and to offer protection to the confidential source. The answer from New York came quickly: the proposed operation was out of the question. Armed raids were not in the job description of a peacekeeper. "The overriding consideration," read the cable from Annan's office, "is the need to avoid entering into a course of action that might lead to the use of force and unanticipated repercussions."[7] Instead of taking action, Dallaire was instructed to brief the Rwandan president and the U.S., French, and Belgian embassies, which he did.

It appears that neither Dallaire's cable nor the reply made it to the Security Council.[8] In the context of UN peacekeeping operations, this was not surprising. The Secretariat received dozens of cables from peacekeepers every week, and the council had no interest in reviewing them. And given the political climate after Somalia, there is little reason to believe that dissemination of the cable would have altered the course of events. Had the council considered the matter, however, at least one member would have been keenly interested: Ambassador Bizimana. Rwanda had been chosen months earlier by the African caucus to fill one of the nonpermanent council seats allocated to the region. Like most other regional caucuses, the African states selected their candidates for the council long in advance and then presented their choice to the full General Assembly for approval. Keeping a united regional front helped to avoid messy contested ballots in the full assembly, and Rwanda was elected overwhelmingly in October 1993.

The UN Charter insists that a state's "contribution . . . to the maintenance of international peace and security and to the other purposes of the Organization" should be relevant criteria for election to the council. In practice, nonpermanent council seats are often allocated based on regional horse trading that has little to do with how effective a state can be on the council. It was unusual, though not unprecedented, for the recipient of a UN peacekeeping operation to have a council seat, and nobody gave the issue much thought at the time. Rwanda even touted its own recent history of conflict as an advantage in advancing peace around the world.[9] In early 1994, Bizimana began reporting to the consultation room for the almost daily meetings of the council.

The situation in Rwanda became increasingly tense in February and March, with occasional assassinations and rumors of an impending breakdown in the peace process. The storm finally broke on the evening of April 6, when the plane carrying Rwanda's president, Juvénal Habyarimana, was shot down as it approached Kigali's airport. Within hours, extremist Hutus began arming their followers, tracking down and killing moderate politicians, and seizing control of radio stations. The extremists made clear that the peacekeepers were not immune. Ten Belgian peacekeepers were surrounded, disarmed, and killed. Their battered bodies were delivered hours later to Kigali's hospital.

The next day, the council reacted to the reports of violence by appealing to "all Rwandese and to all parties and factions to desist from any further acts or threats of violence."[10] Meanwhile, the United States, France, and Belgium wasted little time in evacuating their nationals. Hundreds of French and Belgian troops seized control of the main Kigali airport and ensured safe passage to and from their embassies. A small American military team escorted U.S. citizens to neighboring Burundi by road. Desperate Rwandans, some of whom had worked for foreign embassies, climbed on board several of the foreign convoys. At frequent checkpoints, the regime's gunmen pulled them off. Most were executed, sometimes on the spot.[11]

In New York, pressure grew to extract the peacekeepers as well. After the killing of its soldiers, the Belgian government decided to withdraw the entire contingent. And at the United Nations, Belgian diplomats urged the council to scrap the whole mission. A unilateral Belgian withdrawal would look cowardly; a council decision would make retreat more palatable. The Belgians found considerable support, particularly in Washington, where the Clinton administration, traumatized by Mogadishu, wanted nothing to do with another round of African civil strife. Secretary of State Warren Christopher cabled Albright with instructions to vote accordingly.

> Our opposition to retaining a UNAMIR presence in Rwanda is firm. It is based on our conviction that the Security Council has an obligation to ensure that peacekeeping operations are viable, that they are capable of fulfilling their mandates, and that UN peacekeeping personnel are not placed or retained, knowingly, in an untenable situation.[12]

For its part, the Secretariat was initially indecisive. Boutros-Ghali was traveling in Europe during the first several weeks of the crisis, and he suggested from afar that the United Nations should examine the logistics of a pullout. With the Belgians departing and Bangladesh suggesting that it might pull out its own troops, UNAMIR was in danger of disintegrating. Eventually, Boutros-Ghali presented the council with several options, including total withdrawal and large-scale reinforcement. But the secretary-general's report made clear that he favored maintaining only a minimal presence. Perhaps remembering his costly clashes with the council over Somalia and Bosnia, Boutros-Ghali decided not to extend himself to save UNAMIR.[13]

Late in the evening of April 21, as massacres accelerated in Rwanda, the council members shuffled the few short steps from the consultation room to the formal chamber and voted to reduce UNAMIR to a token 270 troops. It was, coincidentally, a year to the day since the council had declared the Bosnian town of Srebrenica to be a safe area. Most council ambassadors believed that they had no choice but to extract the peacekeepers, and no one on the council made the case for bolstering the force. From Rwanda, General Dallaire tried futilely to change the political climate. He pestered New York with phone calls and granted interviews to all of the reporters he could interest. But it became clear to the general and his staff that the council was not willing to bolster UNAMIR nor rescue the thousands of Rwandans who saw it as their only hope. "We could have packed up dead bodies, put them on a [transport aircraft], flown to New York, walked in the Security Council and dumped them on the floor in front of the Security Council, and all that would have happened was we would have been charged for illegally using a U.N. aircraft," said Dallaire's deputy. "They just didn't want to do anything."[14]

As the council sounded the retreat, a few human rights groups sought ways to influence its closed-door deliberations, and they found willing conduits in

FIGURE 6.1. The U.S. ambassador, Madeleine Albright, leads a council session in the consultation room a few months after the Rwanda genocide.

several of the nonpermanent members, who were frustrated by the scant information on Rwanda available to them. Colin Keating, New Zealand's UN ambassador and the council president during April, met several times with representatives from the Red Cross and other private relief agencies and passed on their findings to the council. The Czech ambassador, a first-time diplomat named Karel Kovanda, read a *New York Times* letter to the editor on Rwanda by the advocacy group Human Rights Watch and called the organization for more information.[15] He was passed to Alison des Forges, a Rwanda specialist, who briefed him for several hours. Kovanda then arranged for her to speak with several other nonpermanent council members over tea at his residence.[16] Kovanda knew very little about Rwanda, did not trust the information coming from the Secretariat, and was not afraid to reach outside the UN building for guidance. "It was really an act of tremendous responsibility on his part," said des Forges.[17]

In part because of those interactions, the council grappled directly with the question of genocide at the end of April. In his last days as council president, Keating pushed for a council statement that used the term "genocide" and warned that it was a crime punishable under international law. The ensuing debate was one of the most heated that the council had on Rwanda. Kovanda strongly backed Keating and questioned the council's intense focus on achieving a new ceasefire, which he likened to asking Hitler to reach a ceasefire with the Jews. But the draft encountered immediate resistance from most of the permanent members. Hannay worried that the council would be a "laughing stock" if it called the crisis a genocide but did nothing to stop it. The United States, France, and China also opposed using the word.[18] The acrimonious meeting ended with a strained compromise: instead of a resolution, the council issued a presidential statement that used key words and phrases from the definition of genocide—but not the term itself. In the corridor outside the council chamber, American officials approached Kovanda and reminded him that the term genocide implied a legal responsibility to act. Perhaps it would be better, they suggested, not to use the inflammatory word in public.[19]

Keating, Kovanda, and a few other nonpermanent ambassadors took on the role of the council's conscience during the crisis. Nonpermanent members, particularly small states, can be well suited for the part. They often lack the complex—and sometimes compromising—entanglements of the major powers. And as temporary council residents, they are often eager to achieve as much as possible during their short tenures. But in this case, their activism struck some of the permanent members as posturing. It was not troops from the Czech Republic or New Zealand, after all, who would do the hard work of stopping the killing. The U.S. peacekeeping specialist Michael Sheehan, who attended most of the council sessions on Rwanda, described the tenor.

I recall one of the deputies in the margins of discussions of the Security Council making to me a sanctimonious speech about how the people were dying, and I screamed at him that we were very aware of people dying. I still had the dust on my boots from Mogadishu that I had just come back from.... We were trying to do what we could; we certainly didn't need any more sanctimonious speeches from people that weren't willing to put forces on the ground.[20]

By mid-May, the council's decision to reduce UNAMIR appeared increasingly irresponsible. Chastened, it hastily approved a new, larger force for Rwanda of up to 5,500 troops and imposed an arms embargo on the country.[21] Impressive on paper, the resolution was a hollow gesture. Only a few countries had expressed a willingness to send troops, and it was not clear how they would deploy to Rwanda. None of the major powers pledged troops, nor did they make available their air forces to ferry the troops who had been offered. Keating was stunned at the amateurish quality of the military discussions on the council. "The situation cried out for professional military and technical advisers to sit together with the Secretariat's chief military adviser and quickly work through the military issues," he wrote later.[22] All but meaningless on the ground, the resolution merely gave the appearance of action.

Rwanda itself was the only country to vote against the May 17 resolution. Throughout the crisis, Ambassador Bizimana—the representative of the regime organizing the genocide—had been sitting placidly in the consultation room. At one point, he circulated a letter blaming the violence on outrage at the president's assassination and insisting that the authorities were restoring control. He huddled with African ambassadors and the nonaligned caucus when they met separately, but he said little in the council's meetings, particularly after the first week of the violence. Hannay described him as a "sullen but largely silent spectator."[23] However awkward his presence, no one on the council confronted him. One member of the U.S. delegation recalled that diplomatic niceties were observed.

Nobody said, "Stop it." Nobody said, "Your presence here disgusts me." Nobody said, "Why don't you just get out of the room?" There was never a real moment in which they dressed him down because if you did, you would be breaking the rules of the club.[24]

It appears that Bizimana provided Rwanda's authorities with regular reports on the closed council deliberations. Dallaire was startled to find that government officials in Kigali often knew details of the deliberations in New York that he did not. "There I was with my small team of intelligence officers who were risking their lives for crumbs of information while the extremists had a direct pipeline to the kind of strategic intelligence that allowed them to shadow my every move," he wrote later, describing his frustration during the tense weeks before the killing began. The chaos of the days following the president's assassination may have made regular communications between New York and Kigali difficult, but Dallaire believes that satellite phones enabled the regime's leaders to maintain contact with Bizimana as the council struggled to react to the violence.[25] If the ambassador was in regular contact with his superiors once the massacres started, the message would have been simple: this council has no will to intervene.

One force was ready and willing to do the job: the opposition Rwanda Patriotic Front. As soon as the killings began, the RPF began marshaling its forces to drive the Hutu authorities out of power. They did so with remarkable speed. The RPF had seized much of the country by June, and thousands of Hutus—including many perpetrators of the genocide—fled westward, most toward Goma, on the eastern edge of Zaire. Finally, the Five stirred. France offered to lead an expeditionary force that would establish humanitarian corridors in western Rwanda and safeguard the refugees. Washington backed the plan, which appeared to be risk-free. The so-called Operation Turquoise, blessed by a council resolution, began in late July.

As the French belatedly protected several thousand fortunate Rwandans and as the RPF mopped up the remnants of Hutu rule, the council did its own bit of housekeeping. Alphabetical order required that Rwanda take over the presidency of the council in September. While Bizimana was still haunting the UN hallways, the rest of the council decided that they could not tolerate him in the president's seat. He was asked not to appear at any more council meetings. Shortly thereafter, a new Rwandan delegation composed of RPF supporters took over the country's UN mission. They found the offices stripped bare. The mission's bank accounts had been emptied and its furniture was gone. Nobody could find Bizimana. The Rwandan ambassador slipped away from New York and disappeared.[26]

The council's Rwanda debates—and many others during this hectic period—featured frequent references to the council's credibility and standing in the world. Hannay worried that using the term "genocide" without taking action would make the council appear ridiculous. The United States demanded that the council not again issue meaningless resolutions. There was a clear sense that the council had acquired a store of credibility through its post–Cold War activism that the body had a responsibility not to squander. At the same time, there was a strong pull toward consensus. Ibrahim Gambari, Nigeria's ambassador, recalled a powerful though often unspoken pressure for the council to remain united, whatever course it chose.[27] And in public, it was united. The key votes on Rwanda in April and May were lopsided. Perversely, the desire to preserve the council's credibility and unanimity served the cause of inaction. Those on the council who might have publicly shamed its powerful members were cowed into silence or convinced that public disharmony was worse than unified inaction.

Inaction in the face of atrocity was becoming a common posture for the council. Almost precisely a year after the genocide ended in Rwanda, the first "safe area" in Bosnia came under renewed assault. Since 1993, the besieged town of Srebrenica had been tense but mostly calm. Then, in early July 1995, the Serbs decided to make a move. Their forces unleashed an artillery and rocket barrage. They surrounded and disarmed the Dutch peacekeepers stationed on the edge of the safe area. The offensive placed senior UN officials in Sarajevo, Zagreb, and New York in a quandary. The council had declared Srebrenica safe but never had provided enough troops to defend it. It had authorized the use of NATO air power, but it had also created a complicated decision-making system—referred to as the "dual key"—that left military commanders uncertain as to when and how they could call in air strikes. The Serbs were calling the council's bluff.

At several points during the Serb advance, the Dutch peacekeepers requested air support. The UN commanders temporized; they were not sure the conditions were right and they worried that strikes might lead to retaliation against the peacekeepers. Several days after the assault began, the secretary-general's representative, Chinmaya Gharekhan, briefed the council, but he had limited and inaccurate information. He reported that the Serb advance had stopped, when it had not. He was unable to explain to the council when or even whether air strikes had been requested.[28] Meanwhile, Serb forces tightened their grip on the town, and UN commanders finally authorized the use of air power. A grand total of two bombs were dropped before the strikes were called off because of concerns for the safety of the peacekeepers. The remaining Dutch peacekeepers were disarmed without firing a single shot.

Reacting to criticism, a UN spokesperson pointed to the council. "It is up to the Security Council to decide whether a safe area is no longer a safe area."[29] In New York, the French representative on the council pushed for a resolution clarifying that air power could be used to protect the town. But by then, the battle was over. On the afternoon of July 11, the Bosnian Serb commander, General Ratko Mladic, entered the town. "We present this city to the Serbian people as a gift," he said. "The time has come to take revenge on the [Muslims] in this region."[30]

A few days later, reports filtered out that Serb troops had herded hundreds of Muslim men and boys onto buses. Later in July came word that the prisoners were all dead. On August 10, the council met in the consultation room. Madeleine

Albright brought with her a sheaf of classified reconnaissance images that showed what appeared to be mass grave sites at a soccer field near Srebrenica. "As the photographs circulated," she wrote later, "the council room—scene of so many noisy debates—grew still. I could hear fingers brushing the stiff photographs as they passed from hand to hand."[31] In the span of fourteen months, one of the twentieth century's worst genocides and the largest massacre in Europe since the Second World War had occurred on the watch of peacekeepers sent by the council.

The Rwanda genocide and the Srebrenica massacre highlighted several fundamental flaws in the council's new efforts to restrain conflict. As Boutros-Ghali frequently pointed out, there was a startling gap between the council's resolutions and the resources it provided to enforce them. With few exceptions, the council members were not willing to commit their own troops and resources to ensure that its resolutions had meaning. It is hardly surprising that states not on the council were even less enthusiastic, particularly when the mission involved possible combat. The spectacle prompted David Owen, the lead European mediator for Bosnia, to propose that council members commit forces as a condition of serving on the body, a reform that would allow "power and responsibility [to] come together on the Council."[32]

There was also a conceptual and even an ethical flaw in the organization's approach to Rwanda and Bosnia: a hesitancy or inability to appropriately distinguish between the perpetrators of violence and the victims. Both crises were complex and no side was pure, but the United Nations often seemed to lose itself in the shades of grey. This tendency was pronounced in the organization's permanent bureaucracy, which had been weaned on the doctrine of impartiality and which had grown callous to the victimhood claims of warring parties. When criticized for this tendency, UN staffers often pointed to the council. Discussing Bosnia, one UN official defended the organization's conduct to journalist David Rieff.

> Blame your own governments for what has gone on; they could have given us a different mandate.... But it is pointless to blame us. The UN is not the world's government. It is an organization of the world's governments. And peacekeeping is only an instrument that we in the UN can make available if called upon to do so by the Security Council. You think we are hiding behind the mandate, but the fact is that it provides us with the only legitimacy we have.[33]

It was a fair response. The impartiality that was so maddening in certain UN officials on the ground was often fostered and reinforced by the council. For the first several weeks of the Rwanda genocide, the council regularly issued calls for

FIGURE 6.2. Secretary-general Boutros Boutros-Ghali pays
his respects at a massacre site in Rwanda.

political negotiations between the parties, as if the problem were a conflict
between mutually stubborn parties rather than a deliberate campaign of extermi-
nation. Rhetorically, the council was more willing to lay blame in Bosnia, but it
created a peacekeeping structure that all but forced UN personnel to bargain
with and sometimes supplicate themselves to the forces committing the worst
atrocities.

The council's preference for avoiding the concepts of aggressor and victim
was not new. Given the prominence of aggression in the United Nations' founding, the concept had played surprisingly little role in statements and resolutions
throughout its history. As Iran discovered to its chagrin in 1980, even outright

cross-border invasion would often not produce a finding of aggression. And when the council actually *did* take sides—in Korea in 1950 and Iraq in 1990—it usually avoided the loaded term "aggression" and opted instead for "breach of the peace." At certain moments, the council's unwillingness to formally take sides served it well. In 1967 and 1973, it pushed the warring parties in the Middle East toward ceasefires without taking a position on the merits of the parties' causes. As the council evolved from talking shop to its new and much more ambitious role, however, the shortcomings of this approach were becoming apparent. Policing the world, it turns out, often requires taking sides.

Some saw in the twin failures of Bosnia and Rwanda the effective death of the United Nations in international security. Michael Lind wrote in 1995 that "in the eyes of perceptive observers the United Nations and the philosophy of collective security that it embodies have been finally and completely discredited." The organization, he concluded, "should be allowed to wither away into irrelevance."[34]

The Five Out of Step

The Srebrenica massacre and perhaps lingering guilt over Rwanda pushed the three Western powers toward a more unified and muscular approach in Bosnia. With American support, the British and French assembled a 12,000-person rapid reaction force that had the military wherewithal that UNPROFOR lacked. More quietly, the three countries agreed to simplify the cumbersome dual-key rules that had been established for deploying NATO air power. As they took these steps, the Western powers agreed not to involve the council any more than necessary. Existing resolutions, they believed, provided all of the authority necessary for more aggressive air strikes. Beginning in late August 1995, waves of NATO planes pounded Serb artillery positions, arms depots, and command centers. Sarajevo residents watched in amazement as the jets streaked overhead, finally punishing the forces that had tormented them for more than three years.

Many Russians watched the NATO air strikes through a different lens. There was a widespread belief in Russia that the Orthodox Serbs had been unfairly isolated as the villains of the conflict, and the Russian government reacted angrily to the strikes. As the West increased military pressure on Serbia and the Bosnian Serbs, Russian frustration mounted. "Russia is not a banana republic but a fullfledged member of the UN Security Council," railed a Russian Foreign Ministry official after an early round of NATO air strikes.[35] As if to prove the point, Moscow vetoed a resolution in December 1994 that would have tightened economic sanctions on Serbia. It was the first substantive veto for the Russians in a decade, and one council diplomat likened the move to "a guard dog's growl."[36]

As NATO became more assertive in 1995, Albright rushed to New York from meetings in Washington on several occasions to head off unexpected Russian resolutions condemning the alliance's action. The Dayton Peace Accords, signed in November 1995, finally ended the Bosnia war, and NATO troops replaced the beleaguered UN peacekeepers. Eager to be rid of the crisis, the Russians agreed to a council resolution endorsing the NATO mission. The Bosnian struggle had ended, but managing Russian sensitivities had become a major preoccupation for Western diplomats on the council.

Moscow's ambassador on the council at this time was well suited to articulate its increasingly independent stance. Sergei Lavrov had labored in the Soviet UN mission for much of the 1980s. He was elevated to deputy foreign minister in 1992 and then to the UN ambassadorship in late 1994. Lean and angular, with close-cropped dark hair, Lavrov exuded competence, and he emerged as a potent force in the consultation room. His dogged style and sensitivity to any perceived slights were a marked contrast with his more amiable predecessor. Britain's long-time ambassador, Jeremy Greenstock, described Lavrov as "highly political, articulate, strategic, and tactically acute."[37]

Lavrov's skill and preparation won him grudging admiration from even those who clashed with him. He spoke fluent English and, when speaking Russian in council sessions, frequently corrected the simultaneous interpreters if he felt that they had not captured his precise meaning. During his turns as council president, he ruthlessly restrained what could often be long and windy debates in the consultation room. One ambassador recalls him chiding speakers for unnecessary repetition. "Thank you for that long and interesting intervention," he would say dryly after a speaker finally concluded. "Has anyone got anything to add that we haven't heard before?"[38] Lavrov could skewer his colleagues with a pen as well. He was an accomplished doodler and caricaturist. During long sessions, he often sat with his head down, drawing elaborate sketches that included stylized renderings of the particular UN operation or program under discussion. On a few occasions, he drew caricatures of his colleagues, complete with bubble quotes. As word of his talent spread, colleagues lingered near his seat to collect the works of art he left behind.

The differences between Russia and the West on Bosnia reflected a broader reality: the close consultations among the Five that had occurred during the Iran-Iraq diplomacy, the Gulf War, and Cambodia were breaking down. The resentment of the council's elected members to the hegemony of the Five also contributed to the breakdown of close and regular coordination. Several

FIGURE 6.3. One of dozens of doodles drawn by Russian ambassador Sergei Lavrov during council sessions.

nonpermanent members became so agitated when they heard of separate meetings of the Five that the practice was sometimes more trouble than it was worth. Greenstock recalled that the Canadians, in particular, bridled at the practice of private meetings of the Five.[39] Diverging policies, however, were much more important. The Five had forged their remarkable post–Cold War unity on the question of Iraq, but by 1994 their policies toward that country were increasingly dividing them. For several months after the Gulf War ended, the Five maintained a united front, insisting that Iraq comply fully with the terms of Resolution 687 and deciding to maintain the sanctions imposed after the invasion of Kuwait until Iraq had complied. By the middle of 1994, their unity had dissolved. "A mistake once made should not keep this nation in a constant regime of punishment," Lavrov insisted.[40]

Sanctions proved to be the most divisive topic. In early 1995, Russia, France, and China circulated a draft resolution that would have partially lifted the sanctions. A clear philosophical difference had emerged. Russia, France, and China conceived of sanctions as a temporary measure that should be removed, or at least eased, as Iraq made progress in complying with the council's demands. An all-or-nothing approach to sanctions relief, they argued, gave Iraq no incentive to marginally improve its behavior. Iraq, after all, had taken several steps toward compliance. It had recognized Kuwait's sovereignty in 1993, allowed the destruction of tons of prohibited weapons, and grudgingly compensated Kuwait's victims. In their formal statements, Britain and the United States conceded that Saddam might ultimately win a reprieve from economic isolation. In less formal settings, American and British policymakers made clear that the sanctions should remain in place as long as Saddam Hussein did.[41]

The sanctions regime could withstand the opposition of three permanent members because the original resolutions stated that the measures would remain in place unless affirmatively removed. In other words, one vote from among the Five could prevent the council from lifting the sanctions. The procedure was unusual. Peacekeeping missions, for example, had to be regularly reauthorized by an affirmative council vote. The absence of such a "sunset provision" drove Lavrov to distraction. During one debate, a council diplomat recalled, the Russian ambassador looked across the consultation room and pointed his finger at Albright. "Madeleine, I will tell you this now and you can count on it. Russia will never agree to a Council resolution like this again. Never!"[42]

The mounting political discord over Iraq had important implications for the various monitoring initiatives under the council's supervision. The task of ensuring Iraqi compliance with the ceasefire conditions had spawned a mini-bureaucracy under the council's leadership, including UNSCOM and the Iraq sanctions committee. Given the breadth of the sanctions regime and the political importance of the issue, that committee in particular was an important test case for the council's new governance responsibilities. To function properly, it required constant attention and cooperation, particularly from the Five. Almost from its inception, the committee was hobbled. It operated by consensus, meaning that any of the fifteen representatives could hold up a decision. Moreover, its chairperson was always a nonpermanent member of the council, which meant that the committee's leadership changed frequently as nonpermanent members left the council and were replaced. To the growing frustration of the Russians and the French, the U.S. representatives on the committee scrutinized the contracts that were submitted, sometimes taking weeks to approve them.[43]

At the same time, the United States acquiesced to significant violations of the sanctions. When Jordan, which was highly dependent on imports of Iraqi oil, approached the Security Council in 1991 about a possible exemption, the committee took note of the request but never issued a decision. Confident that it had a green light, Jordan proceeded to import large quantities. A pattern of tacit exceptions and unwritten agreements had been established.[44] In 1995, the committee's task grew even more complicated. After months of negotiations, the Security Council approved and Iraq finally agreed to participate in an "oil-for-food" program, through which Iraq could export certain quantities of oil. The proceeds would flow into escrow accounts that could be used to purchase food, medicine, and other necessities for the Iraqi people.[45] The program was the result of mounting pressure, particularly from humanitarian organizations, to ease the burden of sanctions on ordinary Iraqis.

Politics and corruption intruded even as the program was being established. Private-sector expertise was needed to administer an escrow account and to inspect the oil leaving Iraq and the humanitarian goods entering. One UN procurement officer, a Russian named Alexander Yakovlev, saw in the rushed bidding process a chance for personal gain. He secretly faxed companies with inside information on the bidding in the hopes of receiving a payoff. The broader pattern, however, was of UN officials attempting to anticipate the preferences of the Five as they assembled the complex program. A French bank's bid was accepted for running the escrow account. Then, another French company submitted the lowest bid for the job of inspecting humanitarian goods entering Iraq. This put UN officials in a difficult position. They knew that it would be unacceptable in Washington and London to have French companies filling both roles. One UN staffer, a Cypriot named Joseph Stephanides, alerted the British mission to the situation. He hoped that British diplomats could convince the British company to lower its bid, which it ultimately did. The procedure, which later came under intense scrutiny, reflected the stew of political, economic, and administrative interests involved in managing the sanctions regime. The council members, particularly the Five, did not hesitate to champion their own companies in ways that skirted standard UN procurement rules.[46]

The Iraqi sanctions program was a festering issue, but the most dramatic break among the Five during the mid-1990s came over the future of Boutros Boutros-Ghali. By mid-1995, the relationship between the secretary-general and Madeleine Albright, in particular, had become unrecoverable. Albright, her close aide Jamie Rubin, and White House advisor Richard Clarke launched what they called Operation Orient Express, designed to ensure that Boutros-Ghali did not receive another term. In public, Washington remained quiet on the question of a second term for Boutros-Ghali, but behind the scenes, the United States was carefully coordinating his removal.[47]

Fresh animosity between Albright and Boutros-Ghali broke out at the end of 1995 over the details of a new peacekeeping mission in Croatia. Boutros-Ghali released a report critical of the council's plan, which was strongly backed by the United States, and Albright in turn chided the secretary-general for shying away from risky missions. Once again choosing confrontation over conciliation, Boutros-Ghali responded during a council session by accusing the United States of *vulgarité*.

The fight over Boutros-Ghali's reappointment became one of the nastiest of Albright's tenure. While other council members agreed that Boutros-Ghali had shortcomings, none were as outraged as the Americans. The French remained solidly behind Boutros-Ghali, and the rest of the Five were willing to grant him the second term that had become customary for secretaries-general. When it came time to take formal positions, France, Britain, Russia, and China lined up against the United States, and several sent messages of support to Boutros-Ghali. French president Jacques Chirac and South African president Nelson Mandela called on Clinton to intercede, prompting the Orient Express operatives to take quick action. Clarke recalls hustling to the Oval Office whenever he was alerted that a foreign leader had called to discuss the issue.[48] Boutros-Ghali was stunned by the American intransigence. "Surely you cannot just dismiss the secretary-general of the United Nations by a universal diktat of the United States!" he exclaimed to Warren Christopher. "What about the rights of the other Security Council members?"[49]

Washington was firmly in diktat mode when the council met in November 1996 to take its first straw polls. The first came out with thirteen votes for Boutros-Ghali, the United States against, and Britain abstaining. On the next vote, the British also voted for Boutros-Ghali. "There is only one delegation opposed to Boutros[-Ghali]," said British ambassador John Weston, shortly after the council members voted.[50] Boutros-Ghali was reportedly buoyant as he watched the United States chastised by commentators around the world for its arrogance. Undeterred, Albright vetoed Boutros-Ghali again and again. In the midst of the standoff, her stock rose when President Clinton nominated her to be the next U.S. secretary of state. Finally, the rest of the council blinked. Other candidates emerged, including Washington's favorite, Kofi Annan.

France was still determined to make the United States pay for its rejection of Boutros-Ghali. The French ambassador vetoed Annan on the first several ballots after Boutros-Ghali's name had been omitted. Then, making a virtue of necessity, France traded its veto on the issue for the right to have a French national as the head of UN peacekeeping.[51] When it became apparent that a deal had been struck, the council ambassadors switched quickly from deal makers to media personalities. John Weston sneaked out of the council chamber to brief the press first, annoying Albright and enraging the council president, Italy's Paolo Fulci.[52] Still, Fulci achieved the most theatrical announcement, borrowing papal imagery. "White smoke," he declared, "has finally emerged from the chimney of the

Security Council's Sistine Chapel."[53] The secretary-general who had most directly challenged the infallibility of the permanent members had paid the price.

Expansionism

Razali Ismael watched the council impatiently as it selected the next secretary-general. Business at the United Nations all but ground to a halt as the organization waited for its new chief, and Razali was eager to get back to work. The veteran Malaysian diplomat had assumed the presidency of the UN General Assembly in October 1996. The year-long post had often been symbolic, but Razali was determined to achieve something of substance: reforming the Security Council. Like the representatives from many developing countries, he believed that the organization had too often been a pawn for the great powers. "The whole history of the UN for the last 50 years, leading on to the sorry state it is in now, has been that it has been used by the major powers," he said.[54] For Razali, expanding the Security Council would be a major step toward a more effective and representative organization.

The procedural barriers to change were daunting. Like any formal amendment to the charter, a change in council membership required two-thirds of the General Assembly and the approval of the council, including the acquiescence of the Five. The 1966 expansion to fifteen members from eleven had occurred in large part because the broader UN membership had threatened to fill the existing elected seats with developing countries often hostile to the Western agenda, something they could achieve without the council's approval. With the non-aligned already well represented among the ten elected members, achieving a new round of reform would be trickier. Razali was determined to marshal the necessary support, and he set for himself the goal of meeting with every ambassador in New York.

The Malaysian had chosen a promising moment to take on council reform. Pressure for expansion had been building since the end of the Cold War, and Germany and Japan had thrown their considerable weight behind the idea in late 1992. As leading financial contributors to the organization and key American allies, their opinions were critical. They also decided to make themselves candidates for permanent seats, not a simple decision in either capital. There was urgent debate in both countries about whether their pacific post–World War II constitutions would permit them to serve as permanent council members. Traditional peacekeeping operations were not controversial, but participating in chapter VII enforcement missions might be more than domestic opinion would stand.

A handful of other countries sought to position themselves as permanent members in waiting. Indian diplomats reminded counterparts that their country was the world's largest democracy and that Indian troops had been a mainstay of peacekeeping missions for decades. "If any country has a right to be on the Security Council, India does," its foreign minister proclaimed in 1994.[55] Brazil touted its status as Latin America's largest country and declared itself ready to assume the responsibilities of permanent membership, responsibilities that Franklin Roosevelt had quixotically tried to give it a half century before. Nigeria, South Africa, Indonesia, and Egypt also signaled their interest in being considered.

Most UN members needed little convincing that the time had come to revise the council's membership, and the body's return to the center of world politics only heightened the desire of less powerful states for more frequent access to the council table. Addressing the nonaligned caucus in 1992, Indonesia's president pledged, "[W]e shall not be mere spectators, nor accept to be sidelined in the currents of historical change now sweeping across the globe."[56] The General Assembly created a permanent working group on council reform in 1993 to draft a specific plan for expansion. "It is absolutely clear that the Security Council we have today is yesterday's Security Council," said Richard Butler, Australia's UN ambassador. "It cannot do the job we need done today and will certainly need in the future."[57] Advocates insisted that appropriate reform would produce concrete results. "We have no doubt that a Security Council enlarged in a fair way would have more legitimacy, and would therefore be more effective in promoting peace and security," argued the Brazilian foreign minister, whose government reportedly hired a public relations firm to help make its case.[58]

The claim that expansion would increase the council's legitimacy was frequently heard during the debates on reform. If the council looked more like the world, the argument ran, it would command more respect from the world. It is a difficult claim to assess. A broader and more diverse council might persuade more states to participate in peacekeeping, to comply with sanctions, and to settle their disputes peacefully. The oft-heard complaint that the council is a tool of the West would be harder to sustain. But many of the council's post–Cold War struggles had involved face-offs with nonstate actors resistant to international pressure, and it is hard to credit the notion that council reform would have altered the equation. Would the Bosnian Serbs have pulled back at the gates of Srebrenica had Indians, Brazilians, and South Africans been permanent members? Would a council with Japan and Germany have been more effective in addressing Somalia or Rwanda? Nor did the advocates of expansion grapple with the question of whether expansion might introduce as many legitimacy problems as it solved. To take but one of many possible examples, would Pakistan view a council with India as a permanent member as more or less legitimate? The concept of legitimacy is a notoriously slippery one that blends issues of representativeness, effectiveness, power, and procedural propriety.[59] During the debates on expansion, legitimacy often became a slogan.

FIGURE 6.4. A Chinese petition opposing Japan's bid for a permanent Security Council seat.

The Five were initially quite skeptical of any membership changes, and they had their own slogans. "It ain't broke, so don't fix it," said a U.S. official in early 1992, concisely reporting the U.S. position at the time. "The organization cannot afford to engage in an overhaul of machinery which not only is not broken but is in fact in good working order," said the Soviet representative.[60] Britain and France, in particular, worried that broaching the subject might put into question their continued hold on permanent seats, though this fear was rarely stated explicitly. "Our constant concern on this complex question is to insure that the Security Council retains maximum efficacy," a French spokesperson insisted.[61]

In part to defuse pressure for expansion, the council agreed to make its proceedings more transparent. The increased use of the closed consultation room in place of the formal chamber had generated resentment. In response, the council president started the practice of briefing non-council states after certain informal consultations. The council released schedules of its planned meetings and a tentative monthly agenda. It produced more information about the sanctions committees it supervised and beefed up the reports that the council submitted to the General Assembly. At a political level, the friction that developed among the council's permanent members during the 1990s might have had the effect of assuaging concerns in the General Assembly that the council was developing into a great-power bloc that would impose its will on the rest of the world. The fear of concerted great-power hegemony appeared much more plausible in 1992 than it did in 1995.

The assembly showed no signs of being reassured, and by the mid-1990s, most of the Five were willing, if still not eager, to discuss membership reform. The years since the Gulf War had undercut some of the strongest arguments for the status quo, in particular the notion that the council was operating too effectively to change. That claim had carried some weight after the Iran-Iraq success, the Cambodia and Namibia operations, and the successful defense of Kuwait. It was a harder argument to make after several years of muddling in Bosnia and the abject failures in Somalia and Rwanda. The United States was the first permanent member to publicly support expansion. In 1993, it endorsed the German and Japanese candidacies and expressed willingness to consider an expansion up to twenty-one members. Britain and France reluctantly followed the American lead. Russia and China said the least about expansion, but they were not committed to opposing it.

As negotiations progressed, advocates of council reform coalesced into two broad groups: those who believed that the council should take on new permanent members and those focused on adding additional elected seats. Unsurprisingly, the first group included those states with the best chance of acquiring permanent membership: Japan, Germany, Brazil, and India. The second group, usually led by Italy and Pakistan, rejected the idea of adding permanent members and saw itself as defending the interests of the small and medium states. In the European Union, Italy had proposed that the British and French seats be consolidated into one EU seat and that the other seat be freed up for Japan. Ambassador Paolo Fulci continued the Italian activism during one of Italy's turns as a nonpermanent member. He was particularly adamant that Germany not be placed in a different category than Italy. During one consultation-room meeting, he strode up to Madeleine Albright, who had just reiterated American support for German and Japanese membership. "We lost the Second World War too!" he shouted.[62]

With debate about the council's future simmering, Razali formally introduced his plan in March 1997. He proposed adding five permanent members and four rotating members to the council. Of the five new permanent members, three would come from the developing world and two from the industrialized world. The four new nonpermanent members would all come from the developing world. Razali rejected the idea of extending the veto power to the new permanent members, arguing that doing so would only "compound an inequity." One of the innovations of the plan was its phased approach. It asked the General Assembly first to vote on the structure of the council reform, and only then to select the countries that would fill the new permanent and nonpermanent seats.

It quickly became clear that Razali faced deep skepticism—and some outright hostility. The nonaligned group met in April, and most of its members saw his plan as too favorable to the industrialized world. "There shall be no partial or selective expansion or enlargement of the membership of the Security Council to the detriment of developing countries," read a joint communiqué issued after the meetings. The Italians and the Pakistanis also blasted the plan, which they argued would "undermine democracy and aggravate an already elitist, antidemocratic and anachronistic system." Fulci said the result would be a train with 175 nations "crowded into third class."[63] He and his Pakistani counterpart set about organizing a group of mid-size states, which included Canada, Argentina, Mexico, Egypt, and Spain, to work with the Non-Aligned Movement in opposing the plan.

The Razali plan had become a flashpoint for the perennial question of the council's identity. Should the council remain a body primarily for the great powers or should it become something else—perhaps a miniature version or working committee of the assembly? The tension had existed since the council's creation, when several small states at San Francisco pushed for more elected seats and a more transparent council. The 1966 expansion had tilted the balance of power considerably in the direction of the broader membership, and the Non-Aligned Movement in particular had acquired significant influence in the council's deliberations as a result. By adding five permanent seats to only four elected ones, the Razali plan would have reversed that trend.

A group of about thirty states, including the leading candidates for new permanent seats, did their best to salvage the proposal. Germany and Japan circulated letters to all of the UN delegations, but to no avail. By September, Razali was forced to admit defeat. "I believe that we have come pretty close, tantalizingly close, to a package which could win the support of at least two-thirds of the General Assembly members," he said.[64] In some ways, the failure of the Razali proposal was a relief to the Five, though none of them said so publicly. Had the General Assembly united around a plan, they would have been hard pressed to oppose it. Favorable as the plan was to them, the status quo was far better. Moreover, the spectacle of the assembly struggling to agree reinforced one of the most powerful arguments against council expansion: a too-large council risked becoming another assembly—loud, fractious, and ultimately incapable of achieving anything.

Bypass Operations

On the afternoon of December 16, 1998, the Security Council was debating the latest report from the chief weapons inspector for Iraq, Australian diplomat Richard Butler. Russia's Sergei Lavrov was harshly criticizing the inspectors for exceeding their mandate when an aide strode hurriedly into the chamber and

FIGURE 6.5. Russian ambassador Sergei Lavrov before a council meeting on Iraq.

whispered something to Kofi Annan. Media outlets were reporting explosions in Baghdad and at other sites in Iraq. An American-led air campaign to punish Iraq for its resistance to weapons inspectors had begun. The bombing did not come as a complete surprise. For weeks, Washington and London had been threatening to strike if Baghdad did not fully cooperate. In November, only a last-minute Iraqi concession had kept American bombers on the ground. However, many council ambassadors had expressed hope during the day that the threatened air strikes could be avoided.

The meeting broke up in confusion as the ambassadors rushed out to watch the latest news. "It looks like the United States is determined to go for a military strike regardless of what the Security Council membership feel[s] about it, and that's very bad," said Iraq's ambassador. China's ambassador left the chamber fuming. "There is absolutely no excuse or pretext to use force against Iraq," he said. "The use of force not only has serious consequences for the implementation of Security Council resolutions but also poses a threat to international as well as regional stability." For his part, the secretary-general was mournful. "This is a sad day for the United Nations and for the world."[65]

Annan had particular reason to be gloomy. He had invested a great deal of his office's prestige in trying to achieve a diplomatic resolution to the crisis. Despite American and British misgivings, Annan had traveled to Baghdad in February—on a plane provided by Jacques Chirac—to convince Saddam to comply with the council's previous resolutions. Annan had wavered on whether to attempt personal diplomacy, but the council's own deep division had convinced him that he might have a role to play. Russia, China, and France had become deeply skeptical that further military measures were justified or would be effective in pushing Iraq toward full compliance. They had made clear to the Americans and British that they should not expect a resolution authorizing new strikes. For a moment, it seemed that Annan had saved the council from itself; he returned from Baghdad with an Iraqi pledge to cooperate that satisfied even the skeptical Americans. A crowd of UN employees greeted him like a conquering hero.[66] But the deal fell apart even as Annan was collecting praise, and the matter returned to the fractured council.

Operation Desert Fox lasted for three days. Cruise missiles and bombs rained down on military facilities throughout Iraq. In the council chamber, the ambassadors debated whether the strikes were permissible under international law. Sergei Lavrov charged that the bombings threatened the international legal order. "No one is entitled to act independently on behalf of the United Nations," he argued, "still less assume the functions of a world policeman." The United States and Britain countered that the council resolutions authorizing force before the 1991 Gulf War had never expired and that the ceasefire was contingent on Iraq's full compliance with weapons inspections.[67] The legal debate ran on inconclusively, but Desert Fox had one clear practical consequence: the UNSCOM inspection regime had ended. Iraq refused to allow the inspectors back, and the Americans and the British had to be content with the damage their bombers and missiles had inflicted on Iraq's military machine.

Desert Fox signaled a new willingness in Washington and London to work around the council when necessary. From the U.S. perspective, Russia was emerging as a consistent obstacle to council consensus. "We go out of our way to consult with Russia," an administration official explained. "But on some key issues, as the United Nations Charter clearly allows, we must protect our national interests."[68] Beijing was less of a concern. China was skeptical of many American initiatives, but it was usually willing to abstain rather than veto when the other four had reached agreement. The one issue on which China was willing to expose itself on the council was Taiwan. In 1997, China deployed its first veto in a quarter century to oppose sending peace observers to Guatemala (a few weeks later, it reversed course). Then, in February 1999, Beijing vetoed another routine resolution reauthorizing the small UN force serving in Macedonia as a firewall against ethnic conflict. In both cases, the Chinese explained their votes in terms of doubts about the missions in question, but the real reason was clear to all: Guatemala and Macedonia had diplomatic relations with Taiwan, and Beijing wanted to punish them.

China's Macedonia veto came at an awkward moment. Another crisis in the Balkans was brewing, and Macedonia would be on the frontlines. In early 1998, the simmering tension in the Serbian province of Kosovo escalated as an ethnic Albanian militia attacked Serb-dominated security forces. Serbian forces responded brutally, attacking Albanian villages and engaging in activities reminiscent of the ethnic cleaning seen in Bosnia. The Kosovo crisis was a clear failure of preventive diplomacy. Experts in the region had warned for years that conflict was likely, and the international community had never grappled effectively with the province's status. For the United States and Europe, the outbreak of fighting became a chance to exorcise some of Bosnia's ghosts. By responding quickly and firmly, they could prevent the bloodletting they had permitted in Bosnia. Madeleine Albright and British prime minister Tony Blair advocated a strong Western response through NATO, and in late 1998, the alliance for the first time in its history instructed its members to prepare for possible combat.

In a near replay of the debate over Iraqi repression of the Kurds in 1991, Russia and China were willing to condemn Serb excesses through tough council resolutions, but they refused to explicitly authorize the use of force. Both countries saw the Western push as a dangerous violation of Serbia's sovereignty. "If you take it to the UN, we'll veto it," promised Russian foreign minister Igor Ivanov. "If you don't we'll just denounce you."[69] The Americans were not troubled by the notion of going around the council. But the Russian and Chinese refusals to acquiesce created an acute dilemma for many other NATO countries. Council approval was seen as the sine qua non for the legitimate use of force in many parts of Europe, particularly within Left-leaning political parties. And yet Kosovo appeared to be ethnic cleansing in the making. The doctrine of humanitarian intervention was colliding with the strictures of the UN Charter, producing severe discomfort.

A few Western politicians and legal scholars contended that the council's previous resolutions on Kosovo constituted authorization for the use of force, but it was a strained argument that did little to help Western politicians evade the dilemma.[70] German foreign minister Joschka Fischer embodied the tension. A member of the Green Party and a peace campaigner during the Cold War, Fischer argued at the early stages of the crisis that a council resolution would be required for military action. Acting without the council, he argued, would create a dangerous precedent that powerful countries could abuse.[71] A Green Party spokesperson declared flatly that war without the council would be illegal. Yet a few months later, Fischer found himself making the case for air strikes without the council's imprimatur. "I was a peace activist against colonial wars," he explained. "But this is not a colonial war I think. This is an aggressive confrontation against aggressive nationalism."[72] Fischer preferred to say as little as possible about the implications of bypassing the council. Others simply acknowledged that Kosovo was an extraordinary case. As French president Chirac explained, "[T]he humanitarian situation constitutes a ground that can justify an exception to a rule, however strong and firm it is."[73]

Some Western diplomats were willing to draw more ambitious conclusions. Canadian foreign minister Lloyd Axworthy argued that the crisis demonstrated the "obsolescence" of the council veto. "The fact that [China and Russia] use a veto means that they have emasculated the Security Council in its role and you almost have to find a functional equivalent," he argued.[74] Canada briefly toyed with the idea of reviving the Uniting for Peace formula devised in the 1950s as a means of seeking approval from the General Assembly, but the idea was quickly dropped. None of the Five wanted to reestablish a precedent that would empower that unwieldy body.

When the bombing began, on March 24, 1999, China's UN ambassador described the use of force without council approval as "a severe violation of the U.N. Charter and established principles of international law." Russian president Boris Yeltsin declared that the action made Russia "morally higher" than the West. Sergei Lavrov was personally angered by the move and, on Moscow's insistence, forced a council vote on a draft resolution condemning NATO and demanding that it immediately halt the bombing. It was defeated 12–3, a vote that some Western observers saw as backhandedly legitimizing the operation. The air campaign continued, and the situation in Kosovo deteriorated as Serb forces expelled hundreds of thousands of Albanians. Massive refugee camps sprang up in Macedonia and Albania.

The diplomatic strain caused by the crisis was real. Kosovo exacerbated the sense of marginalization that Russia and, to a lesser degree, China had often felt in the post–Cold War era. The Russian Parliament passed a resolution labeling the United States and its allies "international terrorists." Telephone calls between Clinton and Yeltsin were frosty and, at times, alarming. During one conversation, the Russian president yelled at Clinton, "Don't push Russia into this war! You know what Russia is! You know what it has at its disposal! Don't push Russia into this!" In this environment of harsh words and bruised egos, there was also a strong desire in the West and in Russia to ease the crisis and achieve some tangible sign of cooperation. "Somehow, somehow, we've got to keep diplomacy alive," Russian foreign minister Igor Ivanov told Albright.[75]

The council, or at least the mechanism of a council resolution, helped to do that. Even as the bombs fell, senior American officials expressed interest in working with the Russians on a resolution that would create a new framework for

Kosovo. "We valued the role Russia played in the 14 months up to the beginning of the bombing, and we hope it will be part of the diplomacy afterward," said Deputy Secretary of State Strobe Talbott, who served as the lead negotiator with the Russians throughout the crisis.[76] The process of seeking a council resolution allowed the West to seek an after-the-fact blessing from Moscow and Beijing and in so doing confer international legitimacy and legality on the mission. For Russia and China, it would be at least an acknowledgment that their consent mattered. The key differences were over when the bombing would stop and who would police the province when the Serbs withdrew. The Russians wanted a bombing pause for negotiations and a strong UN role in the province, while the West insisted that the bombing continue until Serb forces withdrew and that a NATO-led security force take their place.

The early discussions on a draft resolution took place far from New York. U.S. and Russian diplomats, accompanied by senior Finnish officials who often acted as mediators, met intensively to arrange a framework for post-conflict settlement. At the same time, German diplomats suggested that a scheduled meeting of the Group of Eight industrialized countries (G8) in Germany should serve as the forum for broader negotiations. Comprising the United States, Great Britain, France, Italy, Germany, Canada, Japan, and Russia, the G8 had a number of advantages. "You don't have fifteen sitting around a table you have eight," recalled Paul Heinbecker, Canada's envoy to the session. "It's informal and it's out of the public eye. Even in the consultations in the Security Council you're sitting there with fifteen countries. Nothing stays very secret very long."[77] The G8's environment was what it had been hoped the council consultation room would be: a place where diplomats could speak freely, try out ideas, and make hard compromises away from the limelight. Since its opening in 1978, however, consultation-room discussions had gradually become more formal and, many diplomats thought, less helpful. Spontaneous debate and the free exchange of ideas had been replaced by cumbersome prepared statements.

In addition to the helpful atmospherics, the G8's roster of members included four of the five permanent members, including Russia, which had just been added, and several of the other key players in NATO, such as Germany and Canada. At the same time, members of the council whose relationship to the crisis was tangential were excluded. "[The G8] avoids the minor players on the Security Council while involving everyone who really matters on this one," a Western diplomat explained.[78] That formulation would not have been well received in China, which was not a member of the G8 and was not pleased that deliberations on a resolution were taking place without its participation. The episode echoed what had happened a quarter century before, just as China joined the council. During the 1973 Middle East conflict, Soviet and American officials drafted what became Resolution 338 in the Kremlin. Once again, it had proved to be convenient to transport deliberations on a council resolution well away from the council chamber—and, in so doing, push China and the council's non-permanent members to the sidelines.

In early May, at a meeting in Bonn, the G8 foreign ministers agreed on a set of principles to end the crisis, including the withdrawal of Serb security forces, the creation of an interim administration for the province, and the arrival in the province of a UN-mandated peacekeeping force. Both in Russia and in the West, there was relief that the path to eventual reconciliation in the council was now open. "The real advantage is that this has unblocked the path of the UN Security Council," said British foreign minister Robin Cook. "The only thing that has blocked us until now has been the prospect of a Russian veto."[79] For a moment, it appeared that the decision to take for granted China's acquiescence might backfire. On the evening of May 8, just after the G8 diplomatic breakthrough, several U.S. bombs hit the Chinese embassy in Belgrade, killing three Chinese citizens. The United States hastily apologized and explained that an outdated targeting map had led to the mistake, but riots broke out in Beijing and several other Chinese cities. Western diplomats feared that China would respond by blocking any agreement in the council, and they rushed to minimize the damage. They were relieved to find that Beijing was not inclined to retaliate with its veto.

In early June, as signs emerged that Serbia's endurance in the face of NATO's air campaign was cracking, the G8 ministers met again to finalize the details of a resolution. On the evening of June 9, a completed text was sent from Germany with instructions that the ambassadors in New York not alter it. Only one country attempted to do so. China insisted on a prolonged debate and on several relatively minor changes to the draft. "The Security Council must have a full and thorough discussion," said a Chinese spokesperson. "No one should expect the Security Council to rubber stamp anything."[80] As in 1973, China grumbled about being left out of the inner circle, but it eventually endorsed the G8's handiwork. Resolution 1244 passed on June 10, with China abstaining. For Russia's leaders, working through the council eased the pain of being unable to defend its ally. "Formulated as a resolution of the UN Security Council," Yeltsin reflected later, "the [Serbian] surrender ceased to be humiliating."[81]

This "Kosovo formula"—working through the council as far as possible, bypassing it to use military force, and then reverting to it after the fact—represented a compromise between a maximalist view that demanded council approval for all uses of force and an outright rejection of the council's status. As such, it was a distinct retreat from the belief in some quarters that the council could on its own manage international peace and security. The council had operated during the crisis less as a governing body assertively managing international security than as a diplomatic tool for easing differences and forging compromise among the major powers. It was a constructive role, but it was far from the hopes of many of the organization's advocates after the Cold War. In some respects, the council had retreated to its more traditional concert function. Nor was this crisis likely to be an exceptional case. The bloody repression of separatist movements by sovereign governments is a frequent occurrence, and the question of how to respond was emerging as a consistent point of tension between the West and the incipient anti-intervention bloc of Russia and China.

Taking Stock

In June 1999, NATO troops rolled into Kosovo without blue helmets but with the last-minute council resolution authorizing their presence. During the long negotiations that ended the conflict, the Western powers, particularly the United States, had insisted that NATO rather than the UN command the postconflict stabilization force. Memories of hapless blue helmets in Bosnia were fresh. The United Nations would have the lead on civilian affairs in Kosovo, but NATO would keep order. That same month, the number of UN peacekeepers around the world reached its lowest level in more than five years. In 1993, some 70,000 blue helmets were on duty. By the middle of 1999, that number had dropped to just over 9,000. The huge mission in Cambodia was over, and the operation in Somalia had collapsed. The peacekeepers sent to Mozambique in late 1992 had wrapped up successfully by 1994. Smaller missions were still under way in Angola, Haiti, and Bosnia, and perennials such as Cyprus and the Golan Heights remained, but the peacekeeping boom had subsided.

The sharp contraction in UN peacekeeping in part reflected a reckoning with the missteps of the early-1990s. Through painful experience, the council had refined the tools it could use to impose its will. Military force directly under the council's supervision was increasingly disfavored. Even when the council had the political will to endorse the use of force, it seemed wiser to delegate the mission to an outside actor. The council's reaction to a crisis in East Timor in late 1999 was indicative of the new approach. The United Nations had a team of civilians on the island to monitor and to help administer a long-delayed referendum on its independence from Indonesia, which had ruled the territory in often brutal fashion for decades. When the independence vote won in September 1999, militias loyal to Indonesia unleashed a wave of violence that sent thousands of refugees fleeing.

Reacting with unusual speed, a delegation of five council ambassadors dashed to the region to mediate. America's freshly minted ambassador, Richard Holbrooke, arrived in New York too late to join the mission, but upon its return he helped to push through a resolution authorizing a well-armed multinational force for East Timor led by Australia. Holbrooke, the lead author of the Dayton Accords that had ended the war in Bosnia, was acutely aware of the limitations of UN peacekeeping. In Sierra Leone in 2000, the council deputized British troops to restore order after peacekeepers came under attack. In both cases, a more traditional peacekeeping operation was involved, but established national militaries operating outside of UN command did the heavy lifting.

Other council methods were also coming in for tough scrutiny. Since 1990, sanctions and arms embargoes had become an almost reflexive council reaction in the face of violence and human rights violations. Many observers thought the trend had gone too far. The Iraq sanctions, in particular, inspired a powerful backlash. In late 1998, the head of the UN humanitarian program in Iraq resigned in protest. The sanctions regime, he said, was a "totally bankrupt concept" that was responsible for the deaths of thousands of Iraqi children each month.[82] In 2000, Canada pressured the council to convene a working group that would examine how to improve UN sanctions and ensure that they did not inflict more suffering than necessary on the population.

As troubling as the ethical questions were the administrative ones. The Iraq experience had demonstrated how difficult it was for the council to manage a complicated program while navigating political differences. Almost as soon as the oil-for-food program began, Iraq sought ways to manipulate it. Iraqi officials began directing oil contracts toward companies in Russia, France, and China— all skeptical of the sanctions regime. Baghdad even devised ways to offer influential individuals, including prominent politicians in France and Russia, the chance to benefit from the program. Jean-Bernard Merimee, who served as France's UN ambassador when the oil-for-food program was launched, received almost $200,000 through oil concessions after he left his post and began working for the United Nations in a different capacity.[83] Iraq granted the Russian Communist and Nationalist parties—staunch opponents of sanctions—millions in oil concessions. Emboldened by their success, Iraqi officials devised other ways of subverting the sanctions, including imposing "port fees" and "surcharges" on companies receiving Iraqi oil. The revenue from these fees went to the Iraqi government without passing through the oil-for-food system.

The Iraq sanctions committee, which had been meeting regularly since August 1990, proved to be incapable of keeping up with the Iraqi ploys and rising above its own differences. The committee declined to address the extra charges that Iraq was imposing on oil sales, which was generating revenue outside the oil-for-food channels. It also ignored clear evidence that Iraq was selling oil for below-market prices and receiving kickbacks. Only the United States regularly scrutinized the contracts into which Iraq was entering, and its frequent requests for "holds" on certain contracts outraged the French and Russian representatives. The Dutch ambassador, who chaired the sanctions committee in 1999, remembered that "it almost looked as though France was engaged in a competition with Russia to be recognized as Iraq's most devoted friend, with France simply having to work harder as a former member of the Gulf War coalition."[84]

As the Iraqi effort to subvert the oil-for-food system became increasingly aggressive, the council's monitoring tools deteriorated. The sanctions committee had hired four oil "overseers," experts in oil trading whose job it was to monitor the contracts Iraq was signing for the sale of oil. The first inspectors came from France, Russia, Norway, and the United States. By late 1998, both the U.S. and Norwegian inspectors had stepped down, however, and the Five could not agree on their replacements. China wanted one of the slots, but the United States would not agree to a roster of inspectors from France, Russia, and China. Finally, in 2000, the council gave up and asked the secretary-general to appoint two new inspectors, which he did (they came from the Netherlands and Denmark). That small stalemate was broken, but the larger policy divide remained. In the summer of 2001, Russia blocked an attempt by the other four permanent members to make the sanctions "smart," by targeting them more narrowly at the Iraqi leadership. Moscow wanted to lift the sanctions, not improve them.

Russia at least had the satisfaction of dismantling one long-standing council sanctions regime. With Kosovo securely in NATO hands, the council agreed to lift the last of the sanctions on Serbia. For a decade, the Five had struggled to contain the reverberations from the former Yugoslavia's collapse and Europe's worst fighting since the Second World War. It had been a clumsy, often unprincipled, and dangerous effort, but it had at least been a peaceful one among the great powers. The vote to lift the sanctions took place on September 10, 2001. It was quick and unanimous, and the council turned back to other items. The council's remarkable post–Cold War unity had ended—and, with it, the notion that the council could easily assume the governance role that many of its supporters fervently hoped it would play—but its agenda was still full.

CHAPTER 7

A MORE DANGEROUS WORLD
(2001–2006)

ANDRÉS FRANCO, COLOMBIA'S deputy UN ambassador, enjoyed the ten-block walk from his country's mission on East Fifty-seventh Street to the UN headquarters. His often leisurely walks became more hurried in late 2000, after the General Assembly elected Colombia to a seat on the council. The mission's small staff nearly doubled as Colombia prepared to take positions on the full range of issues before the council, including sanctions in Angola, peacekeeping in Congo, and the disarmament of Iraq. For Colombia, as for most elected members, getting up to speed on the council agenda required time, effort, and additional diplomats.

On the morning of September 11, 2001, Franco was headed to a meeting with several other council ambassadors on policy toward Sudan. That country's regime in the early 1990s had sheltered a number of extremists, including Osama bin Laden. In 1996, the council had imposed a travel ban on several Sudanese leaders for their failure to hand over individuals suspected of an assassination attempt in Egypt. By early 2001, however, many observers had become convinced that Sudan was cutting its links to terrorist groups, and the United States signaled that it would not oppose lifting the travel ban.

Franco noticed some commotion on the streets at about 8:45, and he heard from passersby that a small plane had struck the World Trade Center. He entered the UN building without incident, proceeded up one flight of stairs to the offices next to the council chamber, and met his colleagues in a small conference room. A few minutes into the session, UN guards opened the door and reported that the building was being evacuated. The electronic alarm that would normally signal an evacuation was not functioning, and guards ran from room to room to spread the word. The ambassadors walked downstairs into a chaotic scene, as hundreds of employees streamed toward the exits. Franco heard a few screams in the background. Word was circulating that the UN building was itself a terrorist target.[1]

French ambassador Jean-David Levitte, who was the council president for the month, hurried from a separate morning meeting with European colleagues back to the French mission and began tracking down the other council ambassadors. For the rest of the day, the diplomats communicated as best they could by phone and fax. That evening, Levitte issued a statement condemning "the horrifying terrorist attacks which have taken place today in New York, Washington, D.C., and elsewhere in the United States." The attacks, he said, are "a tragedy for and a challenge to all humanity."[2]

The next day, with fires still burning at the World Trade Center site, Levitte convinced Secretariat officials to prepare the council chamber and consultation room and to locate a skeleton crew of interpreters. He convened a formal meeting in the nearly deserted UN building, and the Security Council stood together for a moment of silence. "It was close to prayer, it was very emotional," remembered Franco.[3] As the ambassadors made somber speeches in the formal chamber, their deputies and political counselors huddled in the consultation room and drafted a resolution. A few hours later—lightning speed, by council standards—the text was ready. The council condemned the attacks, recognized that terrorism was a threat to international peace and security, recalled the inherent right of self-defense, and pledged to "take all necessary steps" to combat terrorism.[4] The resolution made clear that those who aided and supported terrorism could be legitimate targets. Several ambassadors signed the document without even receiving instructions from their foreign ministries, so eager were they to respond promptly.[5]

The council's efficiency derived from genuine shock and outrage at the attacks, but it also had a pragmatic dimension. It was clear that there would be an aggressive American response, and the other members wanted to ensure that the United States worked through international institutions as it struck back. Statements from key council members in the days after the attacks betrayed a nervousness that the wounded superpower might break free of institutional restraints. "Any military action must comply with the objectives and principles of the U.N. Charter as well as widely recognized norms in international law," said Chinese president Ziang Zemin a week after the attack.[6] The next day, French president Jacques Chirac and Russian president Vladimir Putin urged the United States to take advantage of international institutions, "first and foremost the UN and its Security Council."[7]

In one respect at least, the United States was eager to comply. Just hours after the attacks, the State Department began drafting a comprehensive resolution that would require all states to prevent, combat, and punish terrorism. Only the British assisted in the drafting, which was done at a high level in Washington. At the end of September, a complete draft was presented to the council, and a few days later, the council passed a resolution that required states to cut off funds flowing to terrorists, punish or extradite terrorists on their soil, and share the information needed to investigate terrorist activities. The council established a counterterrorism committee to supervise the effort and asked all member states to submit reports detailing their compliance.[8] For the first time, the council was confronting a transnational threat comprehensively and requiring all member states to do the same by enacting domestic legislation. "In effect," Canadian diplomat David Malone has written, "the Council here took on a legislating role, imposing domestic regulatory requirements that previously had been the preserve of the treaty-making process at the UN and elsewhere."[9]

It was a potentially dramatic expansion of the council's powers. The council had often required member states to obey sanctions regimes or arms embargoes, but it had not been in the business of telling them what domestic legislation to enact. The measure occasioned surprisingly little debate. A few council members sought minor adjustments, but none questioned the premise that the council had the power to impose these sweeping obligations on all member states.[10] In a normal environment, the broader UN membership would have been outraged at the council's power play, and the elected members, always sensitive to the concerns of the General Assembly, would have resisted. In the immediate post–9/11 environment, however, the United States had the run of the council. Andrés Franco recalled an unusual silence about national sovereignty and the proper limits on the council's power.

> Who would dare to say anything at that moment? The context wasn't there for a normal negotiation. It just wasn't conducive for anyone to raise the classical issues about why this resolution should be so strong. It was quite a moment in terms of the U.S. working through the UN.[11]

The threat of global terrorism had the potential to strengthen the council's political unity and to give the body a concrete governance mission—stamping out nonstate terrorists—behind which the permanent members could unite. All of the permanent members were threatened by terrorists, and none of them used terrorist groups as a significant element of national policy. It was a more immediate and concrete mission than the enormous but also quite diffuse task of stabilizing failed states and alleviating humanitarian crises that the council had often set for itself after the Cold War.

When it came to military operations, however, the stunned and angry superpower was in no mood for council deliberations or additional resolutions. Instead, the United States took the minimalist course that Margaret Thatcher had urged a decade before, after Iraq's invasion of Kuwait. The George W. Bush administration welcomed the council's recognition of the right of self-defense and sought nothing more. On October 9, the United States sent the body a simple letter announcing that "the United States of America, together with other states, has initiated actions in the exercise of its inherent rights of individual and collective self-defense following armed attacks that were carried out against the United States on Sept. 11, 2001."[12] Ireland had the council presidency for the month and its ambassador, Richard Ryan, urged U.S. ambassador John Negroponte to at least appear before the council to announce the beginning of military operations. "My job is to get you in," Ryan told Negroponte. "This is good for you. It will give you something of the legal and moral authority represented by the Council and being associated with the Council."[13] Negroponte hesitated. The Bush administration did not want to suggest that it needed permission, but it finally agreed. The American and British ambassadors appeared before the council to discuss the letter and the incipient military operations, and Ryan issued a statement acknowledging the exchange.[14] It was formalistic consultation, but preserving the forms mattered.

In the next few days, American aircraft and special operations forces led a campaign to unseat the Taliban. The world's attention shifted from New York to Mazar-i-Sharif, Jalalabad, and Kandahar. By mid-November, when the United Nations belatedly held its General Assembly session, the Taliban was reeling and Al Qaeda's leaders appeared to be on the run. American military operations had generated the expected concerns about civilian casualties, but it was still possible to see the war on terror as a joint struggle against those determined to destroy the international order. Osama bin Laden reinforced that impression with a message timed for the UN meetings. "Those who want to solve our problems at the United Nations are hypocrites who [try to] deceive God, his prophet and believers, because our suffering is caused by the U.N.," he said. "It is an instrument of crime."[15]

For a brief moment, the diplomats assembled at the United Nations wondered whether bin Laden had a more lethal message in mind. On November 12, news broke that an airliner had crashed in Queens, New York, moments after takeoff. The United Nations' headquarters was hastily sealed off, stranding several foreign ministers who were trying to attend a council meeting.[16] The combination of the security scare and the news that Taliban rule was crumbling gave the council meetings that week an electric feeling. There were no clear plans for what would replace the Taliban, however, and the United Nations' special representative to Afghanistan, Lakhdar Brahimi, urged the council to somehow fill the vacuum. A few weeks later, a political conference of Afghan leaders in Bonn,

Germany, selected an interim Afghan government. And at the end of December, the council unanimously authorized an international security force, initially under British command, to secure Kabul and its surroundings. Little thought was given to sending in traditional UN peacekeepers, and the pattern of delegating to coalitions of willing countries prevailed.

In general, a notable unity had prevailed on the council since the terrorist attacks. With the exception of one U.S. veto on a Middle East resolution in December 2001, all resolutions for nearly six months after September 11 passed without dissenting votes. Even a new outbreak of fighting between Israeli and Palestinian forces in April 2002 did not sunder the council's solidarity. Combat near the Jenin refugee camp had sparked international outrage and put Israel on the defensive. It was a situation tailor-made for division between the United States and the other council members; similar flare-ups in the past had often been occasions for the Arab states to provoke American vetoes. Deft diplomacy and a still palpable sense of common purpose avoided public division. Speaking with one voice, the council endorsed a fact-finding mission by the secretary-general.[17]

Disorder over the Court

A few months later, however, a diplomatic storm that had been brewing for several years hit the council. It had little to do with the war on terror and instead revolved around the council's role in the development of international law. In April 2002, the International Criminal Court was born. For the first time, the world had a permanent court devoted to prosecuting individuals for war crimes, crimes against humanity, and genocide. The movement for international accountability that had begun at Nuremberg had achieved a milestone. The ICC's creation provoked jubilation—and not a little hyperbole—among its advocates. "A page in the history of humankind is turning," said one senior UN official.[18] For influential human rights groups and for many Western governments, the ICC represented a critical step toward a world governed by law rather than force. And in many respects, the ICC was the logical conclusion of a process that the United States itself had championed. In the early 1990s, U.S. diplomats had worked through the council to create international tribunals for the former Yugoslavia and Rwanda. Though both courts began slowly, they ultimately investigated and indicted senior military and political leaders, including the sitting president of Serbia, Slobodan Milosevic, and the former prime minister of Rwanda, Jean Kambanda.

There was, however, a key distinction between the Yugoslav and Rwanda tribunals and this new court. The ICC was not created by the Security Council and was not subordinate to it. Its prosecutor could initiate cases without the council's approval and could prosecute citizens of any state, including the Five; the veto offered no real protection. The council did have some influence with the new court. It could request that the prosecutor investigate certain cases and could temporarily delay prosecutions that it believed were interfering with diplomatic efforts. But in important respects, the ICC was independent. For most supporters, this independence from the council was a virtue. As an inherently political institution, the council might taint the impartial application of international justice. "If prosecutions before the ICC are dependent on prior approval of the UN Security Council," argued a UN human rights official, "the prosecutions will be politicised and the Court will not be perceived as independent."[19]

For the United States, particularly for the Bush administration, however, the ICC was dangerous. With troops deployed around the world, the United States viewed as unacceptable even the abstract possibility that an American soldier or official could be hauled before an international court. The United States had unique global responsibilities and would be uniquely vulnerable to politicized prosecutions. As important, the ICC marked a departure from the accepted hierarchy of international relations, with the Security Council at the apex. Secretary of State Colin Powell and other senior officials argued that the court would dilute the council's authority by creating a parallel and politically unaccountable body that would be involved in many security crises.

With the court set to open its doors in the Hague, Undersecretary of State John Bolton launched a campaign to put Americans beyond the court's reach. With great relish, he penned a letter renouncing the U.S. signing of the ICC's founding statute—accomplished in the last days of the Clinton administration. Bolton traveled to dozens of countries to negotiate bilateral agreements immunizing U.S. personnel. And on the council, U.S. diplomats warned that they would not authorize new peacekeeping operations or reauthorize existing ones unless Americans serving with them were given immunity from ICC prosecution.

European envoys bristled at what they saw as an attempt to undermine the new court. France's ambassador insisted that acceding to the U.S. call for immunity would violate his country's international legal obligations. Russia and China, which had both expressed concerns about the ICC, kept a low profile, content to let the Western states battle. In June 2002, the dispute escalated. "If there is not adequate protection for U.S. peacekeepers," an American diplomat stated bluntly, "there will be no U.S. peacekeepers."[20]

The U.S. stance put at risk a UN police-training mission in Bosnia, which included a number of Americans and which was due for reauthorization at the end of June. The council met throughout the last weekend of the month but was unable to reach a compromise. On Sunday afternoon, the United States called the rest of the council's bluff and vetoed the reauthorization of the Bosnia mission. The United States would not ask its citizens "to accept the additional risk of politicized prosecutions before a court whose jurisdiction over our people the government of the United States does not accept," said Negroponte.[21] Nearly the entire council voted against the United States, which was as isolated as it had been since Madeleine Albright fought against Boutros-Ghali's reappointment.

Two weeks after the American veto, the council patched together a compromise. Participants in peacekeeping missions from states that had joined the ICC secured a year-long exemption from its jurisdiction. The deal left no one happy, and several council diplomats recalled the episode as one of the most difficult of their tenure. Canada, a leading supporter of the ICC, was livid. Its ambassador called the compromise an "abuse of power" and argued that the Security Council had no right "to interpret treaties that are negotiated somewhere else."[22] Germany's justice minister condemned what she called "special rules for strong countries."[23] America's image abroad suffered from the perception that the United States wanted to place itself above the law that bound other countries. "Washington daily demands that other nations hew to international norms and standards...and rightly claims that the world would be a better place if they were respected," opined the *Japan Times*. "The U.S. cannot demand their adherence to those norms and then simultaneously assert that it is free from those same constraints."[24]

The debate in many ways mimicked the exchanges that had taken place over the decades about the special rights granted to the Five. In essence, the United States was seeking to deploy the great-power privileges it enjoyed on the council to restrain the developing field of international criminal law, and it was meeting fierce resistance. In the chaotic wake of the September 11 attacks, the council had unanimously expanded the body's powers related to terrorism and in so doing had usurped some of the traditional treaty-making power of states. As the ICC debate showed, however, that move in many respects cut against the tenor of the times.

Since the end of the Cold War, the web of international treaties and institutions had grown increasingly dense and complicated. The ICC was just one manifestation of this trend. Countries signed a slew of new human rights treaties and acquiesced to limits on the traditional immunity of high government officials from criminal prosecution. Meanwhile, the powers of the European Union grew, and supranational European courts began deciding issues that used to be the exclusive province of national courts. In the economic realm, most of the world agreed that international officials at the World Trade Organization could resolve major trade disputes and that even the most powerful member states would be bound by their decisions. In this increasingly legalistic environment, the special political prerogatives of the Five—fundamentally the product of power—were hard to defend, even within the council.

The UN Route

The ICC debate produced hard feelings among the Western states at an awkward moment. At the same time that the United States was dueling with some of its closest allies over the court, it was preparing to seek their support for a controversial next stage in the war on terror. By early 2002, Washington had decided that the status quo with Iraq was not acceptable in a post–9/11 world. In his January 2002 State of the Union address, Bush warned of an "axis of evil" that included Iraq, Iran, and North Korea. "I will not stand by," he pledged, "as peril draws closer and closer."[25]

As the Bush administration set its sights on Saddam Hussein, a debate emerged within the president's cabinet over how to pursue the quarry. Vice President Dick Cheney and Secretary of Defense Donald Rumsfeld contended that seeking further authorization from the United Nations served little purpose and would commit the United States to what might be an interminable process of haggling over texts and timetables. In late August 2002, Cheney made that case publicly in a speech to the Veterans of Foreign Wars.

> Saddam has perfected the game of cheat and retreat, and is very skilled in the art of denial and deception. A return of inspectors would provide no assurance whatsoever of his compliance with U.N. resolutions. On the contrary, there is a great danger that it would provide false comfort that Saddam was somehow back in his box.[26]

Colin Powell, meanwhile, advocated a diplomatic campaign at the United Nations. He believed that the United States could muster support for its policy and ultimately legitimize whatever action was necessary. "As a first step," he said in early September, "let's see what the inspectors find, send them back in."[27] For several weeks, the debate between the two factions appeared to be at equipoise.

British prime minister Tony Blair tipped the balance. He had flown to Washington a few days after the September 11 attacks and was a guest of honor at Bush's speech to Congress on September 20. His oratory in the weeks after the attack created a deep bond with the president and his team. "We were with you at the first," he said of the United States in early October. "We will stay with you to the last."[28] The commitment went deeper than words. Blair shared the president's view that the combination of rogue states and weapons of mass destruction was unacceptable, and he, too, was determined to confront Saddam. Blair's support came with conditions, however. The prime minister insisted on seeking additional resolutions from the council. The alignment was ironic in light of the debates between Washington and London when the Iraq saga began. In 1990, Margaret Thatcher had warned George H. W. Bush that relying heavily on the council as it dealt with Iraq might shackle the United States to the institution and confer on the council too central a role. A dozen years later, another prime minister was insisting that another President Bush work through the council to maintain international support.

In September 2002, President Bush arrived in New York for the United Nations' annual General Assembly session with a speech that was still being edited. The tug-of-war between Powell and Cheney had been narrowed down to a few phrases in the draft. Would the president commit to seeking additional council resolutions on Iraq or would he opt for more general language? Powell believed that, with an assist from Blair, he had convinced the president to call for additional resolutions. As the president spoke in the General Assembly, his secretary of state followed along with a printed version. According to journalist Bob Woodward, when Bush reached the point in the text at which he was supposed to mention new council resolutions, he skipped over the key sentence. Powell was alarmed and wondered for a moment whether he had been outmaneuvered. It turned out to be a Teleprompter problem, not a political one. Bush realized that the line was missing and inserted it extemporaneously.[29]

Immediately after the president's address, Powell went to work on the fourteen other council members, whose role in the process he had defended. Reaction to the speech was generally favorable at the United Nations. "I believe the president's speech galvanized the international community," Kofi Annan said.[30] The prospects for tough council action looked favorable among the Five. French president Jacques Chirac suggested giving Iraq a several-week period to disarm, with military action to follow if it refused. The prevailing sentiment in Washington was that Moscow, not Paris, posed the most serious obstacle to united council action. "The key to this is not the UN, it's not the Security Council, it's one nation—Russia—and one man, Vladimir Putin," former UN envoy Richard Holbrooke said at the time, "and we'll find out soon enough what the Bush-Putin relationship is worth."[31] If Russia and France could be convinced not to veto, the United States was certain that China would abstain and that the nonpermanent members would fall in line.

On September 16, 2002, Saddam Hussein scrambled the diplomatic puzzle. In a letter to Annan, he accepted the return of inspectors for the first time since the 1998 coalition bombings. "The Government of the Republic of Iraq has based its decision concerning the return of inspectors on its desire to complete the implementation of the relevant Security Council resolutions," the letter read, "and to remove any doubts that Iraq still possesses weapons of mass destruction." The United States dismissed the move as a tactical ploy, but the letter had an immediate impact on deliberations among the Five. Russian foreign minister Igor Ivanov suggested the next day that a new resolution might not be necessary, and France, too, questioned whether the council still needed new measures.

The Iraqi gambit and the doubt it sowed among the Five led the United States and Britain to emphasize that, while they wanted action by the council, they did not require it. "The United Nations Security Council must work with the United States and other concerned parties to send a clear message that we expect Saddam to disarm," Bush said. "If the United Nations Security Council won't deal with the problem, the United States and some of our friends will."[32] On September 19, the White House sent Congress a draft resolution that would authorize the president "to use all means that he determines to be appropriate, including force, in order to enforce the United Nations Security Council Resolutions[,]...defend the national security interests of the United States against the threat posed by Iraq, and restore international peace and security in the region." During the 1990 gulf conflict, George H. W. Bush had secured UN authorization before he went to Congress. His son's administration made clear that it already had the legal authority it needed. In London, the language was more tempered, but the message was similar. "We think it is desirable, not least politically, to have a new resolution. But if you go through the existing resolutions, there is ample power there and ample evidence of a material breach," Foreign Minister Jack Straw told members of Parliament.[33]

The distinction between the political and legal meaning of council approval was not an easy one to maintain. In effect, Washington and London were relying on the legal authority of past council resolutions while pursuing additional measures for political effect. In the global debate, however, that fine point was often lost. Council approval had become the critical test of legitimacy and legality. The council's centrality was a remarkable shift from the Cold War, when council approval for military action was rarely sought or considered to be essential. That the world's sole superpower—and an administration quite skeptical of the United Nations—felt compelled to seek council approval was a telling gauge of how the world had changed.

Some viewed the focus on winning the council's imprimatur as unfortunate. "It is perverse, and profoundly dangerous, that the United Nations is being encouraged to place upon its own brow a garland of laurels it has woven for itself as the sole legitimizer of force in international affairs," wrote columnist George Will.[34] "We can never subject our security interests to the United Nations or the Security Council of the United Nations on the ground that somehow that's a moral objective force out there," said Republican senator Jon Kyl. "That's a group of nations with their own self-interest just as we have our own self-interest."[35] Ironically, Kyl's reasoning was similar to that of the ICC's supporters, who argued that the council's decisions were fundamentally political and therefore not impartial. Both sides of the political spectrum, it turned out, could exploit the council's dual political and legal nature. Many of the United Nations' champions saw no inconsistency in demanding that a "politicized" council stay out of the administration of international justice yet be the final word on the legality of the use of force. For their part, Washington and London drew freely on the legal power of past resolutions while presenting the ongoing UN debate as legally inconsequential.

Even as debate swirled about the significance of council authorization, the diplomatic struggle for a new resolution continued. At the end of September 2002, Washington and London presented a draft resolution to the rest of the council. It was remarkably tough. It demanded that Iraq submit a full declaration on its weapons programs and that inspectors be given unlimited access, including to presidential palaces. Failure to comply in all respects would automatically trigger action, and council members could use "all necessary means"—council-speak for military action—to enforce compliance. As they unveiled the draft, senior American and British emissaries were dispatched to Paris and Moscow to make their case.

The reception was chilly in Paris. President Chirac's lead advisor, Jean-Marc de la Sablière, told the Americans that the draft could never attract the necessary nine votes. In the diplomatic equivalent of a stiff-arm, he said it might not even be a basis for negotiation. What was being termed "automaticity"—language that would permit force without additional council action—emerged as the critical issue. France advocated a two-resolution structure: the first would set a deadline for Iraqi compliance, and a second resolution would authorize a response in case of noncompliance. The approach had the advantage of maximizing support for tough new conditions on Iraq while forcing down the road the much more difficult question of authorizing force. "The problem for the Americans is that a two-step resolution is more likely to get everybody on board, but once they are on board they all have their hands on the tiller," a British diplomat was quoted as saying.[36] French foreign minister Dominique de Villepin preferred a different analogy. "We cannot go for two hares at the same time. We should look for one, and we get one. If we look for two, we won't catch any one."[37]

As has happened often in the council's history, intentional ambiguity created space for compromise. The United States and Britain insisted that the text accommodate their view that the 1990 authorization of force against Iraq was still active and that Saddam was getting one final opportunity to comply with dozens of subsequent resolutions. France, Russia, and China wanted a clear reference to an additional council meeting after the report of the international inspectors was received; in other words, no automaticity. The challenge was to craft language that could satisfy both camps. "Semantics and linguistics mattered a lot and sometimes political compromise had to violate the very rules of grammar and proper language," a French official involved in the drafting recalled.[38]

The final negotiations on the text were primarily a Franco-American affair, with the British, Russians, and Chinese consulted regularly. Colin Powell and Dominique de Villepin spoke on the phone at least a dozen times. The two diplomats could scarcely have been more different, although both were legitimate celebrities. Powell was a career soldier who spoke crisply and thought pragmatically. De Villepin, a professional diplomat who had served previously in India and Washington, had flowing silver locks and an oeuvre that included several volumes of poetry, expositions on French culture, and a biography of Napoleon.

Their telephone diplomacy gradually produced consensus. The emerging draft recalled the 1990 authorization of force and emphasized that the resolution ending the Gulf War "imposed obligations on Iraq as a necessary step for achievement of its stated objective of restoring peace and security in the area." It deplored Iraq's failure to comply and determined that Iraq remained in material breach of its obligations. It imposed strict requirements for access that Iraq was to give the new inspectors and required inspectors to report to the council within sixty days on Iraq's compliance. The last two paragraphs in particular were the subject of intense negotiation.

> 12. *Decides* to convene immediately upon receipt of a report [from inspectors]... in order to consider the situation and the need for full compliance with all of the relevant Council resolutions in order to secure international peace and security;
> 13. *Recalls*, in that context, that the Council has repeatedly warned Iraq that it will face serious consequences as a result of its continued violations of its obligations.

One last phone call between Powell and de Villepin late on November 6 sealed the deal, and both sides communicated the good news to Moscow. With the prime movers in agreement, approval by the full council was assured. On November 9, the draft passed 15–0 as Resolution 1441. Even the skeptical Syrians voted for it. The council's unity had been preserved, and inspections had been given a new lease on life. The chief weapons inspector, Hans Blix, recalled that "differences in interpretation faded into the background in the general delight that the Council had come together and had come out strong."[39] Jacques Chirac declared that the resolution reaffirmed "the central role and the responsibilities of the UN Security Council in the field of peace and security."[40] President Bush celebrated the achievement in a Rose Garden ceremony with Powell. The UN route still looked promising.

The Second Resolution

The passage of Resolution 1441 ushered in an intense four months during which the council members fenced repeatedly over whether Iraq was complying with its terms. The UN weapons inspectors returned to Iraq in late November, and their every move and utterance provided fresh grist for disagreement. Even the physical handling of Iraq's written declaration—submitted to the inspectors in early December—proved contentious. The council initially decided that the UN weapons inspectors should review the declaration before any of the council members saw it. Several of the permanent members worried that any nuclear secrets in the declaration might fall into the hands of non-nuclear council members— "the innocents," as they were sometimes called.

But as the Iraqi declaration was en route from Baghdad, the Bush administration changed its mind. It now wanted the Five, but not the other council members, to have immediate access to the document. "There was great pressure on our delegation from Washington to get access to the declaration immediately," recalled John Negroponte. "I've never been put under greater pressure from Washington on any single subject than to get ahold of that document ASAP."[41] Colombia held the council presidency for the month, and Negroponte hurried to the Colombian residence on a Sunday afternoon. He and the Colombian ambassador worked the phones. After a few hours, all council members but Syria had agreed to give the Five immediate access.[42]

Procedurally, the Syrian holdout placed the Colombian diplomats in a bind. The proper move was to call for council consultations that night to resolve the issue. But Colombian president Alvaro Uribe had no patience for the niceties of council procedure. Cementing relations with Washington was his top priority. Give the Americans whatever they want, he instructed his UN team. At about 8:30 that evening, the Colombians went to the UNMOVIC (United Nations Monitoring, Verification and Inspection Commission) offices and handed over the declaration, which was still in the black duffel bag in which it had been transported from Baghdad. An American diplomat hustled the package to Washington, where it was copied and distributed to the other permanent members. The next day, Colombia faced sharp criticism for its concession to the Americans. The Syrians called the move "a grave violation of the procedures of the Council," and Norway's foreign minister complained that the Five were treating the other members as "B-list" nations.[43]

Even as the United States bent the council's procedures, top American officials contemplated using the body as a forum to convince the world of the danger that Iraq posed. The administration wanted its own "Adlai Stevenson moment," and it began to assess the evidence that could be assembled. In late December, CIA director George Tenet met with Bush and the senior members of his national security team. After the standard daily briefing, they began a special session on Iraq's weapons of mass destruction material. Tenet recalls the president being unimpressed. "Nice try," he told the CIA briefer. According to Bob Woodward's account of the meeting, the president thought the evidence would not sway the public. "I don't think this is quite—it's not something that Joe Public would understand or would gain a lot of confidence from."[44] The president wanted a case that would convince average citizens around the world.[45]

The slide toward a public showdown on the council alarmed at least one senior French diplomat. As France's UN ambassador, Jean-David Levitte had helped to fine-tune Resolution 1441, working closely with his American, British, and Russian colleagues. In December, he became ambassador to Washington, and in the next few months he tried to convince several senior U.S. officials to avert a council clash. He suggested that the Kosovo model of bypassing the council and then returning to it had much to offer. "We understand that you will push for war. We think it's a big mistake, but don't add another mistake. Just do what we did for Kosovo—act on the basis of existing resolutions, and you go. And then it will be easier after the war to come together."[46]

The ambassador's gambit remains somewhat mysterious, and it does not appear to have been part of a coordinated or sustained French strategy. Even as Levitte tried to avoid a clash, Chirac insisted that any next steps be determined by the council as a whole. "It's the responsibility of the Security Council and the Security Council alone to make a decision regarding the report, and also the requests of the inspectors," said Chirac on January 15. "If one country or another were to take a step that did not conform to what I just said, it would purely and simply be contravening international law. This is a position that of course France would not be able to support."[47]

The next week, the French stance became even more assertive. The French assumed the council presidency in January, and they scheduled a meeting at the foreign minister level on counterterrorism. It was agreed with Washington that there would be no discussion of Iraq. On January 19, de Villepin and Powell met privately at the Waldorf Hotel. The French team left that meeting convinced that the Americans were determined to go to war and that there was no remaining diplomatic space.[48] The next day, after the formal council meeting, de Villepin lashed out at the United States to the press. "We believe today that nothing justifies envisaging military action. If the United States were to decide to take unilateral military action against Iraq, the first question we would ask is, 'What is the legitimacy of that action?' "[49] Powell was outraged at what he felt was a diplomatic ambush. French officials adamantly resisted the charge, pointing out that France had abided by the agreement not to raise the Iraq issue in the formal council meeting, and that, in any case, it was the Americans who had slammed the door on real diplomacy.

Whatever the French intent, Powell returned from New York angry and depressed. Marc Grossman, the State Department's third-ranking official, saw the de Villepin press conference as decisive. It confirmed the fears of those in the administration who had opposed relying on the United Nations and weakened the already shaky ground that Powell occupied in arguing for persistence.

> As soon as the news crossed my desk that the French had said "never" to a second resolution, I said to my staff "that's it, there's now going to be war. This is over." Because what had happened was that in a bizarre way Chirac and de Villepin had allied themselves with Don Rumsfeld and the vice president and had finished Powell. Powell was toast.... It was from that day that I tried to turn the department around to doing whatever was necessary to get ready to fight.[50]

The prospect that the French would veto a second resolution forced a reckoning in London as well. In Parliament, Tony Blair was asked whether Britain would support military action without a second resolution. "We would support it," he responded, "where it was clear there was a breach by Saddam and there was an unreasonable blockage of a Security Council resolution."[51] Blair was echoing the language that had been used fifty years before when the United States sought to bypass the council during the Korean War. The council should be the arbiter of the use of force, Blair contended, except when a permanent member was being "unreasonable."

Some Americans held out hope that the French would yield. Colin Powell at one point suggested to aides that de Villepin, with his flair for the dramatic, was "batting above his weight" and wondered whether Chirac might ultimately restrain him.[52] American diplomats could not understand the French strategy. "What are they going to do, render the Security Council irrelevant?" a U.S. official was quoted as saying. "They can't do that. It's the basis of French authority. It's their forum for global relevance. If it is meaningless, they are meaningless."[53]

The weapons inspectors, who might have broken the deadlock, showed no desire to take sides in the dispute. Hans Blix, the head of UNMOVIC, and Mohamed ElBaradei, chief of the United Nations' Atomic Energy Agency, briefed the council several times in January on their progress. Their statements, which were carefully parsed by the media and diplomats, offered morsels to all sides. On January 27, Blix told the council, "Iraq appears not to have come to a genuine acceptance—not even today—of the disarmament which was demanded of it and which it needs to carry out to win the confidence of the world and to live in peace." ElBaradei was more sanguine. The nuclear inspection process, he reported, was "steadily progressing and should be allowed to run its natural course."[54]

Showtime

When Bush and Blair met at the White House in late January 2003, the prime minister made clear that he still needed to follow the UN route as far as it would go by seeking a second resolution. Bush agreed. He realized that Blair's domestic political situation was precarious and was willing to play out the UN process, even though he had little faith it would yield anything. The formal decision to pursue a second resolution came as the United States prepared its council presentation, which would showcase the evidence against Iraq.

Even if the chance of avoiding a veto appeared slim, the United States could make its case and perhaps sway public opinion. Given the stakes, several administration officials argued in favor of a multiday presentation, with one day devoted to WMD, one to human rights, and one to Iraq's links to international terrorism. Powell reportedly rejected the idea out of hand. "I can't go up there and stop the world for three days. Adlai Stevenson did not have an Adlai Stevenson week. He had an Adlai Stevenson moment. I can only do this once."[55] Not all senior U.S. officials were convinced that the Council was the right forum for the presentation. John Negroponte recalled that he was skeptical about making the presentation to the Council. "It's not because I thought that there weren't any WMDs, but I thought we should do it at a hearing or in a speech," he said. "I didn't think you should tie up the Council. [Washington was] looking for a 'Stevenson moment' and I didn't think much of that idea."[56]

On January 29, Powell appeared in the office of Lawrence Wilkerson, his chief of staff, with marching orders. He handed Wilkerson a collection of highly classified material from the White House and told him to assemble a team, proceed to CIA headquarters, and draft the presentation to the council. Wilkerson and a select group of advisors spent almost a week at the CIA's Langley headquarters. With only a few days before the council presentation, the atmosphere was intense and, at times, almost panicked. Staffers snatched a few hours of sleep on couches in the hallway but otherwise worked around the clock.[57]

The first task was deciding what belonged in the presentation. After only a few hours, Powell's team dispensed with the White House draft, which they decided contained too much speculative material, and instead used the CIA's national intelligence estimate as their starting point. The debates on the speech's content were often animated. At one point, a senior CIA official brought a reinforced aluminum tube into the conference room and rolled it on the table to dramatize his point that its only use could be for a nuclear program. Powell, who came to Langley in the evenings and on the weekend, insisted that the CIA back everything in the speech. Several key portions, including the material on Saddam's links to terrorists, were drafted primarily by CIA analysts. Powell was quite literal about his desire to have the CIA behind the speech. He asked Tenet to come to New York and sit behind him in the council chamber as he spoke. Tenet was reluctant but agreed. "If he wanted me there, I was going to be there, even if my presence was more than a little odd for a serving [CIA director]."[58]

Even as the team struggled over substance, they realized that the speech was a public performance. Powell insisted that the presentation remain concise and lively. He read through several drafts with a stopwatch in hand and worried out loud that they were long and dry. "I'm falling asleep during my own presentation," he complained at one point. Just as Adlai Stevenson had his oversized reconnaissance photographs, Powell's presentation would have props, although updated for the twenty-first century. The plan was to show schematics of mobile weapons laboratories and satellite imagery of suspected weapons sites and to play excerpts of recorded conversations. When the CIA's audiovisual experts had trouble producing the needed visuals, the White House dispatched the president's own graphics team to Langley.[59]

On February 4, Powell and his sleep-deprived team traveled to New York. The speech was still being edited, and his advisors faxed drafts and supporting material back and forth to Washington. A mock-up of the Security Council table had been set up in the U.S. mission for a final rehearsal. In the Security Council chamber itself, technicians installed two large video screens to show the slides and the video clips. They placed monitors in the booths overlooking the council so that the simultaneous interpreters could see precisely what Powell was referencing in his speech.

Teams from the Pentagon and CIA arrived, and security agents swept the premises. Outside the council chamber, in the hallway where diplomats briefed the press, a large UN-blue curtain was placed in front of the tapestry of *Guernica*. Some observers saw the redecoration as a bit of American image control—was *Guernica* the best backdrop for a call to arms?—but UN officials insisted that the change was made at the request of camera operators concerned about the lighting, not at the behest of Washington.[60] Adlai Stevenson had been harassed by last-minute instructions from Washington, and Powell's aides got the same treatment; their cell phones were ringing until the moment they entered the council chamber.

Powell's speech was broadcast around the world. German foreign minister Joschka Fischer chaired the meeting, but all eyes were on the American secretary of state. The chamber was packed, and many observers were forced to stand. For

FIGURE 7.1. Secretary of State Colin Powell presents evidence on Iraqi weapons to the council in February 2003.

FIGURE 7.2. President George W. Bush watches Colin Powell's council presentation.

an hour and twenty minutes, the council heard excerpts of intercepted Iraqi radio messages discussing nerve agents and viewed schematics of a supposed mobile weapons lab. At one point, Powell held up a vial to demonstrate how little nerve agent would be required to wreak havoc. "Leaving Saddam Hussein in possession of weapons of mass destruction for a few more months or years is not an option," he declared, "not in a post–Sept. 11th world."[61] Several American officials were convinced that he had nailed the presentation, and the betting on the American side was that France would come on board. The mood on the secretary's flight back to Washington was satisfied, even buoyant. "We were convinced that we had made the case," one member of the speechwriting team recalled.[62]

In some quarters, Powell had succeeded. Senator Joseph Biden, a leading Democratic voice on foreign policy and future vice president, called the presentation "powerful and irrefutable."[63] The *New York Times*, consistently critical of the administration's approach, described it as "the most powerful case to date that Saddam Hussein stands in defiance of Security Council resolutions and has no intention of revealing or surrendering whatever unconventional weapons he may have."[64] Council diplomats already supportive of the U.S. position, such as the Bulgarian ambassador, Stefan Tafrov, found the speech compelling, although not easy to assess.

> It was so technical in a way. All those conversations and trucks, it was difficult to analyze on the spot. But I thought it was serious. . . . It came from somebody like Colin Powell, a tremendously respected man. Somebody like Colin Powell wouldn't say nonsense—that was the assumption of everyone.[65]

But Powell's powers of persuasion did not sway council skeptics. As he listened, French ambassador de la Sablière became convinced that the presentation was a show for the benefit of the American public. He was surprised that the Americans had chosen the council as the site for a presentation so clearly directed to a domestic audience. The intelligence material that he had seen did not support several of the claims Powell had made, particularly on the mobile weapons laboratories. At one point, he leaned forward and whispered to de Villepin. "Nobody believes what he's saying—and maybe he doesn't believe it himself." Nearby, German ambassador Gunter Pleuger was similarly incredulous. "We were convinced that everything was wrong—that was our immediate impression." From the French and German perspectives, Powell's speech changed nothing.[66]

The speech did not appear to convince the undecided states either. For Chile's Juan Gabriel Valdés, the presentation did not match the expectations it had generated.

> During the previous five or six days at the UN rumors were that we would be absolutely overwhelmed by the type of information that he would

provide. I remember speaking to the Mexican ambassador in terms of what we are we going to do if [the Americans] provided proof that was so clear that there was no way to continue our policy of promoting inspections. . . . The reaction after the meeting was that there is nothing we have been told that we didn't know or that had not been suggested by the American delegation in the weeks before. Therefore, we were not surprised and not impressed.[67]

It did not take long for the Americans to realize that little had changed on the council. A week after the presentation, France and Germany were close to open revolt against the U.S. and British position. At a security conference in Munich, Donald Rumsfeld and German foreign minister Joschka Fischer traded barbs. "In a democracy, you have to make the case," Fischer said. "Excuse me, but I am not convinced."[68]

Powell's presentation was one of an unusual number of council meetings at the level of foreign ministers. A series of interim reports from the weapons inspectors brought the council's foreign ministers to New York on an almost weekly basis. For a short period, the vision of regular council meetings at the level of foreign ministers was being realized. When the foreign ministers came to town, however, it was not for quiet deliberations. The Iraq debates reintroduced a phenomenon that had all but disappeared since the end of the Cold War: open and contentious council debates. Formal council meetings had become set-piece affairs, with little drama or spontaneity; all the hard work was done behind the closed doors of the consultation room. Briefly, the Iraq debates changed that; passionate speeches and pointed barbs were back.

Some UN ambassadors wondered if the public spectacle was helpful. "Here we go," Negroponte reportedly exclaimed when it was announced that the foreign ministers would again convene in the council, "the weekly ministerial meeting coming to town."[69] Bulgaria's Tafrov recalled that the public meetings did little good. "They were a show."[70] As political figures, the foreign ministers were more inclined to play to their publics than to forge compromise. "[The public meetings] crystallized the differences," de la Sablière recalled. "You give your position—you do not try to compromise. It's not a negotiation. If you want to negotiate, you better negotiate out of the room as Powell and de Villepin did on 1441."[71]

At the council's open session on February 14, the chamber witnessed the most direct public debawwte on Iraq to date. "No one can say today that the path of war would be shorter than the path of inspections," said Dominique de Villepin. "No one can claim either that it might lead to a safer, more just and more stable world. For war is always the penalty of failure." In his peroration, Villepin played on Donald Rumsfeld's characterization several weeks before of France and Germany as "old Europe."

It is an old country, France, of an old continent such as mine, Europe, that speaks before the Council today, that has known war, occupation, barbarity—a country that does not forget and that is aware of all it owes to the fighters for freedom who came from America and elsewhere. And yet France has always stood upright in the face of history and before mankind. Faithful to its values, it wants to act resolutely with all members of the international community. We believe in our ability to build a better world together.[72]

The council chamber burst into applause as increasingly isolated American diplomats fumed. De Villepin may have become carried away with his own rhetoric. At a council luncheon shortly after that speech, one ambassador remembered, Villepin insisted repeatedly and at high volume that "war never solved any problem." German foreign minister Fischer, a staunch opponent of military action in Iraq, felt compelled to remind his French counterpart that military force had in fact served the useful purpose of stopping Hitler.[73]

George Bush and Tony Blair were also taken with the analogy of the Second World War, particularly with the failed League of Nations. Throughout the debate on Iraq, they sought to portray the diplomatic battle as one for the future of the United Nations and the council. "The decision is this for the United Nations: when you say something, does it mean anything?" President Bush said

FIGURE 7.3. French foreign minister Dominique de Villepin speaks to the press outside the council chamber in 2003.

in mid-February. "Free nations will not allow the United Nations to fade into history as an ineffective, irrelevant debating society."[74] Blair had argued in similarly apocalyptic terms. "If, at this moment, having found the collective will to recognize the danger, we lose our collective will to deal with it, then we will destroy not the authority of America or Britain, but of the United Nations itself."[75] Saddam's war with Iran and his invasion of Kuwait had, in many respects, pulled the council out of the Cold War doldrums. Failure to force Iraqi disarmament, the Americans and British warned, might again consign the body to the margins of international relations.

In the private meetings of the council in February and March, the ambassadors usually managed to avoid the pyrotechnics of their superiors, but the strain showed. British ambassador Jeremy Greenstock tirelessly made the case for a resolution authorizing force. John Negroponte, according to observers, supported him but exhibited little of his British colleague's fervor or energy. In deference to Tony Blair, Washington continued the struggle for a second resolution, but it was clear that only London was desperate for it. "The British were on the front line," said de la Sablière. Chile's Valdés recalled that "the main actor in the Council was Jeremy Greenstock, not John Negroponte. The British provided all the main arguments."[76]

They also took much of the flak. One council ambassador recalled a session during which Greenstock reported to his colleagues that Iraqi police had stopped the weapons inspectors from searching a hospital and suggested that a significant cover-up might be under way. Sergei Lavrov reacted furiously. He demanded to know whether the British had special access to information from the inspectors, and a few days later the Russian directly accused the British of feeding the council misinformation.[77]

As the council divide persisted, the United States, Britain, and Spain circulated a very simple resolution for consideration. It was designed to be as inoffensive as an authorization of force could be.

> Acting under Chapter VII of the Charter of the United Nations, Decides that Iraq has failed to take the final opportunity afforded to it in resolution 1441 (2002). Decides to remain seized of the matter.[78]

The foreign ministers of Russia, Germany, and France met and offered a competing statement. "The military option should only be a last resort," they concluded. "So far, the conditions for using force against Iraq are not fulfilled. While suspicions remain, no evidence has been given that Iraq still possesses weapons of mass destruction or capabilities in this field." They pledged to work together to block a resolution authorizing force.[79]

Swing States

To this point, de Villepin had managed to steal the council spotlight several times with his grandiloquent rejections of war. World public opinion, the French realized, was on their side, and the public council sessions were helping to solidify the opposition to the U.S. approach. On March 7, the council's foreign ministers gathered for yet another open debate, and British foreign secretary Jack Straw sought to stem the tide with a passionate and apparently impromptu speech of his own. He stared at de Villepin throughout and—dispensing with council formalities—called him by his first name.

> Dominique said that the choice before us was one between disarmament by peace and disarmament by war. That is a false choice. I wish it were that easy, because then we [would] not be obliged to have this discussion; we could all put up our hands for disarmament by peace and go home. The paradox we face is that the only way we are going to achieve disarmament by peace of a rogue regime . . . is by backing our diplomacy with the credible threat of force.[80]

Straw's oratory won some applause of its own in the council chamber and was celebrated by the British press. "So often the grey man of British diplomacy, Jack Straw last night let rip at the French foreign minister in front of a shocked UN Security Council," the *Daily Telegraph* recounted excitedly. The session "was the most heated public spat between a senior British and French official in recent times."[81] Straw may have boosted spirits in London, but the vote count offered no solace. Spain and Bulgaria had committed to support a second resolution, but Chile, Mexico, Angola, Cameroon, Guinea, and Pakistan remained publicly on the fence. Germany, France, Syria, Russia, and China appeared to be firmly opposed. Blair several times called Greenstock to check on the state of play. "How many votes can you guarantee me for the second resolution?" Blair asked. "Four," Greenstock replied. "Crumbs," said the prime minister.[82]

The prime minister attributed the difficulty that Washington and London were having in winning over the nonpermanent members to France's suggestions that it would vote against a second resolution, using its veto if necessary. "If it wasn't for the French," Blair told the Polish prime minister, "we would have the swing countries behind us."[83] Negroponte concurred in that assessment. If the French had indicated that they would abstain, he was certain that Moscow and Beijing would have done the same, and enough nonpermanent members would have voted with Washington to ensure passage of a second resolution. "It came down to what was going on in the mind of Jacques Chirac," he said later. "That was the game."[84]

The dynamic appeared differently when viewed from Paris. Most of the council's nonpermanent members told French diplomats that they firmly opposed war. But these states faced intense pressure from Washington, and they wanted political cover. A French official involved in the negotiations recalled that the message from the nonpermanent members was often the same: "You want us to go along with you so that the U.S. doesn't get a majority? OK, we can do that, but you have a much bigger stick. You can veto. Assume your responsibility and we'll assume ours."[85]

As early as the San Francisco conference that created the United Nations, the French had exhibited a diplomatic persona that emphasized defending the rights of the small states, often against Anglo-American dominance. The Iraq debate was an irresistible opportunity to reprise the role. The Americans and the British saw France's wooing of the council's nonpermanent members as evidence of perfidy. The French believed that they were ensuring the right of the weaker members to vote their consciences. The less powerful needed protection from American bullying, and Jacques Chirac was ready to provide it.

For all the public focus on France, several American diplomats recalled the German role with particular bitterness. Germany had assumed a Council seat in January and emerged as a staunch opponent of the use of force. Germany's ambassador, Gunter Pleuger, helped coordinate opposition to a second resolution, and his activism angered American diplomats. Their reaction did not surprise Pleuger. "We were not as needed as the French or the Russians because they were permanent members and they would be needed on other issues beyond the two-year term that Germany had. The [permanent members] do not get as confrontational with each other as they do with the 'tourists,' as they call the nonpermanent members."[86]

Indeed, the pressure on the council's nonpermanent members became intense. Whatever France and Russia decided, the votes of the other council members would shape the perceptions of the council split. Nine votes in favor of authorizing war stopped by a French veto would give Washington and London a moral victory. At the United Nations, the uncommitted ambassadors often received conflicting intelligence briefings. "It was a great complication to us when we listened to Ambassador Negroponte give us information and then when we left the room and the German or the French ambassador came to tell us exactly the contrary, based on their own intelligence services," recalled Valdés.[87]

The campaign for votes went to the highest levels. Blair spoke to Chilean president Ricardo Lagos a half dozen times. Bush telephoned Mexican president Vicente Fox repeatedly and encouraged Spanish president José Maria Aznar, a committed U.S. ally, to make the case to Fox in person. The council's African members—Guinea, Cameroon, and Angola—were courted by senior British,

American, and French diplomats. In Washington, Colin Powell spent time closeted in his private office with the foreign minister of tiny Guinea.[88] De Villepin and senior American and British diplomats crisscrossed Africa, chasing the three votes. Walter Kansteiner, the U.S. assistant secretary of state for African affairs, believed that he had secured at least two and likely all three of the African votes.

The swing states received other, less public attention. In early March, a report in the British newspaper the *Observer* alleged, "[T]he United States is conducting a secret 'dirty tricks' campaign against UN Security Council delegations in New York as part of its battle to win votes in favour of war against Iraq."[89] It described a spying campaign designed to uncover dirt on Security Council members who opposed the Iraq war. Most council members shrugged. They assumed that multiple intelligence services bugged their UN offices and phones. "You'd have to be very naïve to be surprised," said a Pakistani diplomat.[90] Indeed, there is a long and rich history of espionage at the United Nations. Intelligence agents have often tried to recruit—and occasionally bribe—diplomats, particularly those from smaller countries. In the 1970s, the CIA even planted a Russian-speaking journalist in the gallery above the council to read the lips of Soviet diplomats as they conversed with one another. In this environment of pervasive surveillance, Bulgaria's Stefan Tafrov joked that he would have been offended if no one was recording his conversations. Still, some of the council ambassadors took precautions. Several informal meetings of undecided ambassadors took place in the German mission, which had a secure room that had been checked for listening devices.[91]

An incident in the frenzied last days of diplomacy reminded the council's diplomats just how closely their moves were being watched. In mid-March, six of the undecided ambassadors met in a small room in Chile's mission. They were discussing a possible new draft resolution that would delay the use of force while, they hoped, satisfying the United States and Britain. The possibility of a new draft resolution that might muddle the choice facing the council alarmed Washington and London. A few minutes into the meeting, several of the diplomats received calls on their cell phones. Leave the meeting immediately, they were told by their superiors: the United States has heard about the meeting and considers it "an unfriendly act."[92] The session broke up, and the ambassadors never managed to agree on a compromise resolution. A few weeks later, at the request of the ambassador, Chilean security officers swept the embassy for bugs. They found that the phones were tapped and that a powerful microphone outside the building was aimed at the ambassador's office.[93]

The British struggled to strike a last-minute compromise that would involve specific and strict "benchmarks" for the Iraqis to meet, but the effort was doomed. Washington was noncommittal, and Paris opposed the initiative almost immediately. Greenstock, who was by this point isolated, noted bitterly that the French had rejected the compromise before even the Iraqis had. On March 17, the United States, Britain, and Spain formally withdrew their draft resolution. However maddening French rigidity was to Greenstock in New York, it was becoming a political blessing for the embattled Tony Blair. His political team adroitly exploited the perception that France had become obstructionist. Relatively few Britons were convinced of the wisdom of the war, but plenty could agree that the French were behaving obnoxiously. On March 18, Blair's government survived a harrowing vote of confidence in Parliament.

By that time, there was an odd calm around the council chamber. Most foreign ministers had left town. The weapons inspectors had no more briefings to offer. The council still met, but Iraq was not on the agenda. For the United States and Britain, the UN route had ended in public relations calamity. The remarkable achievement of Resolution 1441 was a distant memory, and instead of going into battle with a contested but at least plausible imprimatur from the council, the coalition fought under the cloud of diplomatic defeat. A strategy designed to bestow legitimacy on a campaign to unseat Saddam had instead made it appear illegal and illegitimate to much of the world.

Many thought that the council as an institution had suffered a debilitating blow. Richard Perle, an influential Bush administration advisor, saw in the episode the end of the United Nations' role in security issues.

> The chronic failure of the Security Council to enforce its own resolutions is unmistakable: it is simply not up to the task. We are left with coalitions of the willing. Far from disparaging them as a threat to a new world order, we should recognise that they are, by default, the best hope for that order, and the true alternative to the anarchy of the abject failure of the UN.[94]

Certainly, the council had been unable to craft a strategy for disarming Iraq that satisfied all of its members, and it had failed dramatically in its mission to preserve peace and security. The very public disagreement rubbed raw the relations among the Five. The saving grace of the council for many decades had been its ability to smooth the edges of great-power relations. It had arguably done just the opposite on Iraq. By forcing the Five into public debates on the war, it aggravated differences that might otherwise have been downplayed. As bombs exploded in Baghdad on March 20, the council's tense and tired diplomats turned back to the comparatively quiet and uncontroversial work of managing the peacekeeping operations in Congo and Sierra Leone.

The Return to Relevance

A week after the military campaign began, the council was back in action on Iraq. On March 28, it unanimously authorized the secretary-general to use the funds in the oil-for-food accounts for humanitarian aid. The question of what political role the organization should play in Iraq was more fraught. Paris and Moscow initially opposed any steps that would retroactively legitimize the invasion. They also called for a substantial UN role in the administration of the country; somehow, they argued, the United Nations' authority had to be restored. Russian foreign minister Igor Ivanov insisted that the international system is a "pyramid topped by the United Nations and its Security Council." He warned that "there is no alternative to the United Nations."[95]

Fresh off its military triumph, the Bush administration was not inclined to hand an organization it deeply distrusted any significant influence. Powell conducted a fresh round of diplomacy that included a trip to Moscow for direct talks on the shape of a new council resolution. In the weeks of negotiation, diplomats tried out a variety of formulations to describe the role that the United Nations should play in postwar Iraq: among those attempted were "a central but not the central role," a "very, very important role," a "robust" role, and a "vital role." By late May, agreement had been reached on a resolution that gave the Americans most of what they wanted: the troops occupying Iraq were recognized as the temporary authority in the country and a key player in the establishment of a new Iraqi government. The United Nations was asked to coordinate with the coalition on humanitarian, economic, and political matters, but it had no clear authority. The measure passed without a dissenting vote and with only Syria abstaining. The resolution, said Jack Straw, "shows that the international community is coming back together."[96]

The council may have been coming together, but Iraq was falling apart. The United Nations' small postwar team of political, development, and humanitarian experts was dispatched into an environment of increasing lawlessness and violence. Since the traumatic missions of the 1990s, the Secretariat had tried to steer the council away from sending UN personnel into environments unsuitable for them, and senior UN officials were frustrated at the role the organization was being asked to play in Iraq. "I could not get the coalition to tell us what was the substance of the vital role that they said they wanted us to play," said Kieran Prendergast, a senior advisor to Kofi Annan. "We were not asked for advice on anything, we were not asked to play a role in anything. We were just there for decoration."[97] That frustration turned to raw outrage in late August when a bomb tore through the UN headquarters in Baghdad, killing twenty-one people, including the secretary-general's talented and charismatic special representative, Sergio Vieira de Mello.[98]

The Baghdad bombing deepened an already powerful sense of crisis among the organization's senior staff. Not only was the political utility of the Security Council in doubt, but the organization's integrity was being questioned. In the weeks after the war, a series of media reports exposed mismanagement in the oil-for-food program. "Where are Iraq's missing oil billions?" demanded the *Sunday Telegraph*, which ran a lengthy investigation of the program.[99] Council diplomats had known for years that the sanctions regime was porous. The Americans had most consistently sought to hold the line, but even they acquiesced to sanctions busting by several allies. The public was about to learn just how skillfully Saddam had manipulated the system—and how he had managed to curry favor with businesspeople, politicians, and even a few UN officials. Kofi Annan's own son came under scrutiny for dealings related to the oil-for-food program.

Annan believed that the organization itself was in peril. "We have reached a fork in the road," he told the General Assembly in September 2003.

> This may be a moment no less decisive than 1945 itself, when the United Nations was founded. Now we must decide whether it is possible to continue on the basis agreed then, or whether radical changes are needed. And we must not shy away from questions about the adequacy, and effectiveness, of the rules and instruments at our disposal.[100]

Annan insisted that the United Nations address urgently the question of unilateral military action, how to respond to humanitarian crises, and how to bolster the Security Council's legitimacy through reform. The secretary-general's solution was to convene a collection of international wise men and women to devise ways to reform and redirect the organization. A year later, the so-called High Level Panel on Threats, Challenges and Change produced its report. It was a thoughtful compendium of proposed reforms that spanned management, personnel, and budgeting. It tackled difficult questions, including the composition of the United Nations' controversial Human Rights Council and the evolving "responsibility to protect"—a doctrine that would clear the way for humanitarian intervention in many cases. The report also suggested two specific plans for reforming the council, both of which would increase the membership to twenty-five.

The fears that the council would be unable to recover from the political breach on Iraq proved to be exaggerated. Most council diplomats reported that the tension over Iraq did not impede for long the council's work. In fact, the Iraq debate's protagonists joined forces soon after the diplomatic debacle. In May 2003, the council responded promptly to an outbreak of violence in eastern

Congo, authorizing a French-led force. And in early 2004, the United States and France worked hand in hand to authorize a peacekeeping force in Haiti, where supporters of Jean-Bertrand Aristide's government were battling rival factions. American and French diplomatic pressure persuaded Aristide to abandon the island, and U.S. Marines and French soldiers together helped to maintain order once he did.[101]

Nor was there any sign that the world had lost interest in the council. As the postwar situation in Iraq deteriorated, some observers even argued that the council's status had been elevated by the diplomatic clash. The body's refusal to acquiesce to military action by its most powerful member gave it a measure of added credibility with states wary of American power. "The UN actually worked," argued Paul Heinbecker, Canada's UN ambassador at the time. "The fact that the Council would not give the Americans and the British the authority to do it probably added to the credibility of the institution. The institution didn't cave in under enormous pressure from the most powerful country on earth."[102]

In 2003 and 2004, states competed as vigorously as ever for council seats. The sections of the high-level panel's report that dealt with council reform were widely read and hotly debated. The report's publication gave a new impetus to council expansion, and the states with the strongest prospects for permanent seats—Brazil, Japan, Germany, and India—seized on its recommendations to advance their cause. The UN officials were sometimes frustrated that the other elements of the report got little attention. Notwithstanding the dire predictions that Iraq had rendered the council irrelevant, it often seemed that diplomats in New York wanted to talk about nothing else.[103]

The relative speed with which the council returned to normal reflected an important truth about the Iraq debate. The heated exchanges between Washington and Paris, in particular, often gave the impression of an all-consuming diplomatic crisis. But the dispute was not, in fact, a clash of vital great-power interests. Russia and, to a lesser degree, France had modest economic interests in Iraq, and they disagreed with the United States about the scale of the threat and the likely consequences of an occupation. As a general principle, they wanted to keep U.S. power tethered to international institutions. But there was not even a hint that the dissenting council members would seek to punish the United States economically or actively oppose U.S. military action once it began.

The contrast with many of the crises the council had handled in its history was stark. During the Berlin airlift, the Suez crisis, the Cuban missile crisis, and the Middle East wars of 1967 and 1973, a real possibility of military conflict between the permanent members had existed. In those cases, the council served as a forum for debate and compromise on the underlying dispute. By contrast, the dispute over Iraq was in many respects *about* the council: Washington and London wanted the body's blessing, and the rest of the Five did not want to give it. The council's imprimatur mattered, and the Five were willing to squabble over it, but the diplomatic fight was not comparable to the most serious Cold War clashes.

For all of its drama and gravity, the Iraq debate was structurally similar to the debates about Operation Desert Fox against Iraq and the NATO offensive in Kosovo, neither of which had doomed the council. As in those cases, Washington and London advanced their case, went as far as the process would bear, then bypassed the council before once again seeking its approval after major military operations ended. Kofi Annan believed that the Iraq war posed an existential threat to the organization, but the Security Council's members did not appear to share his sense of alarm.

From the American side, the dire predictions of the council's irrelevance faded. On several fronts, Washington determined that the body still had value. The Bush administration had worked hard to achieve a peace agreement between northern and southern Sudan, and it worked through the council to dispatch a UN peacekeeping force to monitor that agreement. As the fighting in Sudan's Darfur region expanded, the council again took center stage. Despite Russian and Chinese reluctance, the council eventually condemned Khartoum's policy in Darfur, initiated an investigation into war crimes, and imposed an arms embargo. In March 2005, with American acquiescence, if certainly not enthusiasm, the council referred the case of Darfur to the International Criminal Court. The American use of the council to address humanitarian crises in Africa was not a surprise. African issues, including a number of active peacekeeping operations, had emerged since the end of the Cold War as a particular focus of council activity. More unexpected was the U.S. decision to seek council action on the nuclear programs in Iran and North Korea. This was precisely the kind of challenge the council had, by Washington's lights, failed in Iraq. And yet, just two years after Baghdad fell, Washington was using the council to pursue the remaining members of what Bush had termed the "axis of evil."

Missiles and Messages

These nonproliferation challenges arrived in the council just as a new American ambassador did. In March 2005, Bush nominated John Bolton as UN ambassador. The move was jarring for a council that had been accustomed to the discreet John Negroponte and his almost gentle successor, the former senator and ordained Episcopalian minister John Danforth. From his post at the State Department,

Bolton had spearheaded the unpopular effort to immunize Americans from the International Criminal Court. He had long experience with the United Nations—he had served as the assistant secretary for UN affairs during the first Bush administration—but he was also a fierce critic.

A prolific writer and a leading conservative thinker on foreign policy, Bolton criticized not only the United Nations' management woes and political biases but also what he saw as a dangerous trend toward supranationalism in international relations. Bolton was a committed nationalist and defender of state sovereignty whose view of the United Nations had much in common with de Gaulle's. He had little use for the permanent UN bureaucracy and saw the council as the organization's most useful arm—or, perhaps, its least useless. His often uncompromising rhetoric and bristling mustache rounded out the image of a man who would go to New York to do battle with the institution.

After a bruising and unsuccessful confirmation battle—Bolton was ultimately appointed on a temporary basis while Congress was out of session—he arrived in New York in early August 2005. In the tradition of Daniel Patrick Moynihan and Jeane Kirkpatrick, he often acted as if the United Nations were a delinquent schoolchild in need of discipline. When his turn came as council president, Bolton insisted that the notoriously late meetings begin as scheduled. "Starting on time is a form of discipline," he told the press. "I brought the gavel down at 10. I was the only one in the room, though."[104]

Bolton did not manage to impose punctuality on the council, but he had some modest success in extracting resolutions from it. In the face of Russian and Chinese skepticism, the United States, Britain, and France pushed for sanctions on Sudan and managed to authorize peacekeepers for the Darfur region. But Bolton's most notable and most cherished success came on nuclear proliferation. On July 4, 2006, North Korea launched several ballistic missiles into the Sea of Japan. The tests alarmed Japan and the United States, and Bolton pressed for an immediate condemnation and the imposition of sanctions. China demurred. It had close ties to Pyongyang and no desire to publicly confront the regime. Beijing's priority was preventing an economic and social implosion in North Korea, not confronting the regime over weapons unlikely to threaten China. After a week of painful negotiations, Bolton achieved a condemnation of the tests, but not the sanctions he wanted. He encountered a similar frustrating dynamic on Iran, which the United Nations' nuclear watchdog agency referred to the council in February 2006. The Five could not agree on measures to increase economic pressure on Tehran, despite its refusal to end uranium enrichment. Russia and China were unwilling to sever their lucrative energy and technology ties with that country and worried that sanctions might open the door to military action.

The nuclear proliferation debates entered a new and more urgent phase in October 2006, when North Korea conducted a small atomic test. Bolton consulted intensively with the other members of the Five; there were nearly two dozen meetings among the permanent members in the space of a week. But China was the key, and Bolton and his Chinese counterpart, a London School of Economics graduate named Wang Guangya, retreated to quiet spaces at UN headquarters to chat. Wang smoked incessantly, and Bolton often found him with a cigarette in the lounge near the council chamber.[105]

China's centrality during the North Korea debate was natural; geography and ideology gave it pride of place in most discussions about the reclusive regime. But China's heightened profile on the council was also the product of its changing global status. For most of its nearly four decades on the council, China had behaved as a regional power with narrow interests. Chinese diplomats almost never introduced resolutions of their own, preferring to react to the initiatives of others. U.S. diplomats often counted on Beijing's demonstrated willingness to abstain, even on resolutions it disliked, rather than appear isolated or stand in the way of agreement among the other permanent members.

As China's economic fortunes boomed, its diplomacy acquired new confidence. In June 2005, China publicly threatened to veto a plan to expand the council's permanent membership and include Japan. Wang Guangya was even occasionally outspoken about council measures on the Middle East, in part

FIGURE 7.4. The U.S. ambassador, John Bolton, and his Chinese counterpart, Wang Guangya, confer before a July 2006 session on North Korea.

because Chinese personnel were serving in UN observer missions there. With Russia, China consistently opposed punitive sanctions against Sudan's government. Running through many of the Chinese positions was an insistence on limiting interference with countries' internal affairs.[106] By the time Bolton arrived in New York, that perspective was being heard even more forcefully on the council. "I could see the difference in their approach between Bush 41 and Bush 43 very clearly," said Bolton. Chinese diplomats spoke more assertively and often in very good English.[107]

Together with Russia's skepticism about many American initiatives, the new Chinese confidence complicated council diplomacy. The halcyon days of the early 1990s, when the Western powers could push through their agenda with little opposition, were gone. In part, this was because the West, in certain cases, did not have a common agenda. The Iraq war debate, for example, was essentially a fight among the Western powers. But that intramural squabble obscured a more important trend: growing Russian and Chinese assertiveness. Many of the debates after the Iraq war—on Sudan, Iran, and North Korea—had a distinct flavor of West against East, interventionism against traditional national sovereignty, and individual human rights against collective interests.

This heightened ideological tension made achieving results through the council difficult but not impossible. Bolton had known Wang for years, and they had negotiated on proliferation issues before. Their concentrated diplomacy—and parallel efforts between Washington and Beijing—paid dividends. A few days into the negotiations, Wang informed Bolton that there would be no Chinese veto. Moscow followed suit, and on October 14, 2006 the council unanimously condemned the North Korean nuclear test and imposed new restrictions on commerce with Kim Jong Il's regime.[108] Secretary of State Condoleezza Rice declared that the measure would be a "powerful tool" for increasing pressure, and Bolton was satisfied that the major powers had finally sent a strong message, which he hoped would be an important precedent.

He was quickly disabused of that notion. On the day the resolution passed, Russia's UN ambassador communicated a personal message to Bolton from former UN ambassador Sergei Lavrov, who had recently been elevated to the post of Russian foreign minister. From Moscow, Lavrov had been following the council negotiations and had finally approved Russia's vote for the resolution. But Lavrov wanted to make clear that Russia's approval did not signal a broader shift in its nonproliferation strategy. "Iran will not be this easy" was the message passed to Bolton.[109]

THE COUNCIL IN CONTEXT

WHEN FORMER NEW YORK CITY mayor Rudolph Giuliani addressed the Republican National Convention in August 2008, part of his mission was to demonstrate the superior foreign policy acumen of the Republican candidate, Senator John McCain. Twenty minutes into the speech, Giuliani compared the responses of the presidential candidates to the Russian military offensive in Georgia. Russian forces had advanced into Georgia a month before the convention, decimating the tiny country's military and alarming many in the West. As Russian tanks rolled through Georgian towns, the Security Council held several rancorous but inconclusive meetings.

Giuliani juxtaposed McCain's strong statement in support of Georgia with what he described as Senator Barack Obama's vacillation. Obama's legions of advisors and supporters, the former mayor argued, could not compensate for the candidate's debilitating lack of foreign policy experience. Animated and sarcastic, Giuliani was reaching the punchline. "Later, after discussing this with his 300 foreign policy advisers, [Obama] changed his position, and he suggested the United Nations Security Council could find a solution." The crowd booed lustily at the mere mention of the institution. "Apparently, none of his 300 foreign policy security advisers told him that Russia has a veto power in the United Nations Security Council," he said, to more cheers and laughter.[1]

Giuliani's derision toward the council, and the United Nations generally, has long and healthy roots in American politics. In part, it is the product of a deep skepticism of international institutions and a concern for preserving American freedom of action in a dangerous world. The UN skeptics insist that the United States should not have to ask permission before acting in defense of its interests.

But the animosity toward the United Nations also draws on a sense of disappointment and even betrayal. After the Second World War, Americans across the political spectrum invested their hopes in the new project for world organization. For the first time, the United States threw its full weight and prestige behind a major international organization, and the United Nations was in many respects the product of American idealism and legalism.

Disillusionment came fast. The early flurry of Soviet vetoes led many to shed whatever hopes they had harbored for the organization. And in later decades, the angry and insistent criticism of American policy at the United Nations outraged many more, not least because much of the criticism came from dictators and despots. The few moments when the UN machinery rose to the challenge of preserving peace and security—Korea and the Gulf War are usually cited—have been false dawns that led only to renewed disappointment. The Suez crisis and the invasion of Hungary exposed the council's paralysis soon after Korea, and the debacles in Bosnia and Rwanda followed the council's success in the Gulf War. The Russian rampage through Georgia—and the inability of the council to stop it—provided fresh evidence of the body's impotence. With each failure has come a new round of obituaries for the institution.

For a body so often declared lifeless, however, the Security Council shows odd signs of vitality. It meets almost daily to debate a range of issues and is a focal point for crises from Darfur to Congo to Iran. It supervises sanctions on a half dozen countries, and nearly 100,000 peacekeepers around the world respond to its orders. Powerful countries send their most accomplished diplomats to represent them in the body, and countries without permanent seats fight fiercely for the council's rotating slots. In 2008, for example, Turkey made winning a council seat one of its top diplomatic priorities and launched an international charm offensive to achieve it. None of this behavior makes sense if the council is as moribund as the skeptics charge. More than sixty years after it began operating, the council is very much alive.

International institutions should do more than exist, however; they should serve some useful purpose. If the council's meetings do not yield firm action and if its resolutions are often ineffective, what value does it add? The historical record suggests that the council has been most useful as a loose concert of the world's major powers. It is a mechanism for regular and sustained contact, for negotiating compromises on security issues, and for alerting each other to sensitivities and priorities. At times, as during the Berlin blockade and the Iran-Iraq war, the regular proximity of top diplomats can yield diplomatic breakthroughs. Because envoys to the council see each other almost daily, negotiations can take place with little of the publicity and distraction that accompany formal negotiations.

More broadly, the council structure forces the permanent members to engage routinely on issues that they might otherwise not discuss in detail. "There is a special relationship among [the Five]," one long-time French ambassador said. "Bilateral relations between the permanent members are influenced by their common status. We often discuss from capital to capital issues on the council agenda, trying to reach agreement or at least to narrow the gap."[2] A veteran German ambassador has argued that the Five treat each other differently because of their shared Council privileges.

> If you sit in a forum like the Security Council, and if you wield real power there that can be used against you, then you are a little more cautious with each other because you need each other. You have to make constant deals, whether it's the election of the new Secretary General or a Chapter VII resolution. You need each other all the time and I think it affects also the way you behave in bilateral relations.[3]

A British UN ambassador contended that serving together on the Council "adds further impetus to cooperation" between the permanent members.[4] There is some evidence for that assertion. Since 1990, U.S. secretaries of state have traveled to a combined 80 bilateral meetings with the four other permanent members of Council, nearly twice as many as with four major powers without permanent Council seats (Japan, Germany, Brazil, and India).[5] As with most elite clubs, the council creates a diffuse but meaningful sense of identity and common interest.

This effect should not be exaggerated, however. Many critical political and economic issues among the major powers are not on the council agenda and are not touched by council diplomacy. Moreover, forced engagement on sometimes peripheral issues can have its disadvantages; there are several episodes in the council's history—including Congo in the 1960s and the 2003 Iraq war—when it has appeared that the elevation of issues to the council agenda harmed relations among the Five. But the benefits of routine and institutionalized consultation among the great powers outweigh the costs. Governments can sometimes be lazy about maintaining important bilateral relations, and the council's structure creates a check on diplomatic and political negligence. Because Washington routinely needs Beijing's vote on council matters, for example, it is harder for the United States to ignore Chinese concerns and interests.

The council also offers important services in managing crises that might draw in the great powers. The perceived necessity of appearing before the council can slow crises that might otherwise escalate dangerously. During the Cuban missile crisis, a series of scheduled council meetings gave President Kennedy an additional means to resist pressure for immediate military strikes. The council played no formal role in resolving that crisis, but the council *process* created valuable additional time. In the wake of diplomatic ruptures, the council can ease the humiliations that even powerful states must endure. The process of negotiating a council resolution in 1999 soothed Russian sensitivities even as NATO troops seized control of Kosovo. China has at several moments used the process of negotiating council texts to insist that its viewpoint be accommodated.

Perhaps most important, the council provides a fixed address for diplomacy. During the 1967 and 1973 Middle East conflicts, the superpowers always acted on the assumption that council resolutions would mark the end of the fighting and help to restore peace. That certainty about the negotiating mechanism saved time and energy, provided a focal point for diplomacy, and reduced the chances of miscommunication among the superpowers. The vague and intentionally ambiguous resolutions the council passed in the wake of those conflicts did little to resolve the underlying issues, but they at least allowed the superpowers to signal their common desire to avoid future clashes. Other diplomatic venues or ad hoc groups will sometimes be more appropriate, but the council in many cases will remain the right place for diplomacy.

That diplomacy is often best conducted behind closed doors rather than in the council's formal chamber. The temptation to use the council as public theater is strong, as Colin Powell can attest. Adlai Stevenson's "moment" during the Cuban missile crisis captured the American imagination—and it has been distorting expectations for what can be done through the council ever since. There is little evidence that even dazzling and dramatic council presentations actually change many minds, particularly in other countries, and the habit of playing to the public gallery rarely helps to forge compromise and agreement. The council's closed consultation room was a valuable innovation, and it is where the body's most productive moments will continue to occur.

The council's modest but significant contributions to great-power comity should not obscure its lackluster record in enforcing and protecting peace and security more broadly. The delays, word parsing, and ambiguity that help to smooth relations among the veto-wielding permanent members often cripple its efforts to assertively manage global security. The council has not often succeeded in ending regional conflicts, rebuilding failed states, managing sanctions, or avoiding humanitarian catastrophe. In a few cases, it has taken preventive steps that may have avoided major conflict; the missions it authorized in Cyprus during the 1960s and in Macedonia thirty years later likely helped to avert prolonged bloodshed. Council diplomacy helped to end the decade-long Iran-Iraq war and may have averted catastrophe in East Timor.

Unfortunately, these governance successes are the exception. Perhaps most damning, the council has failed utterly to craft a lasting political solution to the conflict in the Middle East. It abdicated its responsibility in the 1940s and has continued to do so ever since. Its governance record is little better in other regions. The council's largest and most ambitious undertakings—in Congo during the 1960s and in Bosnia, Somalia, and Cambodia during the 1990s—either collapsed or produced few sustainable results. Since the late 1990s, the council has failed to respond to genocide in Rwanda, ethnic cleansing in Bosnia, and massive crimes in Darfur. Its efforts to restrain nuclear proliferation have been intermittent and ineffective.

If the council is useful in its concert mode but poor at more ambitious global governance, why not abandon the conceit that it is managing international peace and security? A host of other organizations, many at the regional level, might fill the governance vacuum. Winston Churchill's vision of a decentralized network of regional organizations keeping the peace, which was rejected at the time of the United Nations' founding, remains plausible and even promising. The European Union and NATO are expanding and taking on new responsibilities in places as distant as Chad and Afghanistan. The African Union has dispatched troops to several of that continent's crisis zones.

The dilemma is that there is a symbiotic relationship between the council's governance and concert functions. The council meets regularly precisely because of its responsibility to maintain international peace and security and to manage the dozens of active UN operations in the field. If those burdens were formally or informally shifted elsewhere, the energy would go out of the body, and its utility as a great-power concert would all but disappear. Moreover, international law privileges the Security Council, and altering that hierarchy would require a massive diplomatic initiative with very uncertain prospects. There is no getting around the council.

There are specific reforms that might improve the council's performance both as a concert and as a governance body. Activating the Military Staff Committee, which was designed as the council's arm for managing military operations but which has lain dormant for most of the United Nations' history, could help to bridge the gap between the council's resolutions and the reality of its peacekeeping and stabilization operations. Having a group of experienced military planners from the Five and other key members meet to regularly review the tactical and strategic challenges that peacekeeping operations face might instill a greater sense of responsibility among the permanent members, which have often authorized missions without providing the resources necessary for their success. The UN Secretariat, responsible for the day-to-day management of peacekeeping, would likely resist that interference, but the council can insist.

A more active Military Staff Committee would have the ancillary benefit of creating an additional forum for military-military exchanges among the major powers in a neutral setting.[6] Just as the council itself has allowed for quiet political exchanges at various moments, a more active Military Staff Committee might permit great-power military representatives to communicate quietly and informally in moments of tension.

The most important reforms, however, are not in structure but in mindset. Policymakers must decide how to use the council and what to expect of it. It is particularly important to steer between twin fallacies: that the Security Council does not matter at all and that it is the only thing that matters. Both are dangerous. Ignoring the council—or, worse, actively delegitimizing it—could weaken and eventually destroy a valuable institution. Policymakers must do more than employ the council instrumentally; they must also pay some attention to how their actions and rhetoric affect its long-term viability. "International organization is but a means to an end," the scholar Inis Claude wrote a half century ago. "[H]owever it cannot be an effective means unless it is in some degree treated as an end in itself."[7] The American and British rhetoric in the months preceding the Iraq war was a study in corrosive hyperbole. The alarmist predictions of the council's imminent demise likely deepened public skepticism about a body that both governments knew would be important in the future.

The United States, in particular, has often paid too little attention to the institution's long-term value. America's unparalleled power gives it the luxury of using the council tactically and ignoring the implications of its maneuvers. The decades-long American struggle to keep China off the council and its effort in the 1950s to bypass the council through the General Assembly are examples of policies that served immediate political and diplomatic needs but hampered the council's broader utility. The rhetoric about the council during the Iraq debate was similarly shortsighted.

Increasingly, European leaders and publics have made the opposite mistake—elevating council unity above even most substantive goals. Polls suggest that many Europeans view Security Council approval as a prerequisite to the legitimate use of force. Major European leaders convinced themselves that the humanitarian intervention in Kosovo, launched without council approval, represented a unique exception, and America's traumatic experience in Iraq has reaffirmed their view that the use of force without the council imprimatur is unacceptable and unwise. Some observers believe that this insistence derives from a conviction that the world is moving beyond dangerous anarchy and toward governance by rules and law. As Robert Kagan has written, "Europeans have stepped out of the Hobbesian world of anarchy into the Kantian world of perpetual peace."[8]

Europe may be there, but the whole world is still not. The major powers will—and, in some cases, should—bypass the council again, for reasons of both principle and strategic interest. Russia and China resist the expanding Western doctrine of humanitarian intervention and will, in many cases, be reluctant to approve forceful measures to end atrocities. There are also stark differences among the Five on the seriousness of nuclear proliferation and the measures that should be taken to forestall it. It is fanciful to imagine that the council members will be able to forge consensus on all of these issues. And any minimal consensus that could be achieved might do unacceptable damage to interests and values. In this environment, leaders should employ the Security Council whenever possible. In those few cases when council diplomacy becomes stuck on a matter of critical importance, they should bypass it gently and return to it expeditiously. They should bear in mind the council's genuine political value while at the same time resisting the legalistic view that the council offers the only possible route to legitimate or productive international action.

Leaders have a further responsibility: to do no harm as they reform the council. Some change is essential. The council no longer accurately reflects the realities of world power, which is its principal value. Emerging powers, including Brazil, India, and perhaps South Africa, merit seats at the table. Japan, which trails only the United States in financial contributions to the organization, also deserves a permanent seat. If Europe continues to forge a common security agenda, the British and French seats should eventually be consolidated into one seat for the European Union, a change that would finally give a regular voice to Germany.

Persuading the broader UN membership to accept additional permanent seats will not be easy. From its birth, the council has faced the resentment of those states excluded from its deliberations. The spectacle of permanent members operating on a different plane from the rest of the UN membership has always been hard to accept. "The five permanent members are like Brahmins," said former British ambassador David Hannay. "They move around in a different world to the world of the great unwashed out there who aren't members of the Security Council."[9] Accordingly, many proposals for council reform compensate for the addition of new permanent members by offering six, eight, or even ten additional rotating seats open to the general membership. These changes would boost total council membership to twenty-five or more. In part, these reform proposals reflect organizational politics. Amending the charter requires the support of two-thirds of the General Assembly, and most states are unlikely to support an expansion plan that does not offer them greater access to the council. But the push to increase the number of rotating council seats also employs principled arguments. The legitimacy of the council, it is often said, will steadily erode unless it includes more, and more diverse, voices.

Too often, council expansion is presented as cost-free. The reality is that whatever increased legitimacy expansion bestows on the council will matter little if the body ceases to be an accommodating environment for major-power diplomacy. At fifteen members, the council is already close to its maximum effective capacity. Its informal sessions—designed to create space for the candid exchange of views—have often become long and unproductive exercises in which each of the assembled ambassadors feels compelled to make a formal statement. Effective reform should amplify the council's strengths rather than exacerbate its weaknesses, and that will mean keeping the council small and dominated by the major powers.

Doing so may be especially important at this moment. Great-power diplomacy is becoming significantly more complex. As a global economic power, China now has interests in parts of the world it was often content to leave to others. The Chinese tradition of abstaining on many council resolutions it does not like may soon yield to a more assertive posture that suits a global player. Meanwhile, Russia is seeking to revive its strategic profile by forging economic and military ties outside its region, including in America's backyard. At times, Moscow and Beijing have linked arms in their effort to counter American ascendancy, and they share a rudimentary geopolitical ideology that emphasizes state sovereignty and nonintervention and downplays many Western concerns, including human rights, democratization, and nonproliferation. Ensuring that these differences do not become conflicts will require constant vigilance, and the council can be a vital forum for that effort.

Giuliani's convention speech played upon the council's most glaring incapacity: its powerlessness when one of the Five is determined to pursue a course of action that others oppose. That limitation, embodied in the veto arrangement, is intentional, and it means that the council in certain cases will have no influence on the trajectory of the great powers or on relations among them. It is not a fatal flaw, however, and at many moments it has kept the council intact. The relative peace among the world's strongest powers that has endured for more than a half century is not inevitable and must not be taken for granted. "The only hope for the world is the agreement of the Great Powers," wrote Churchill as the Second World War ended. "If they quarrel, our children are undone."[10] It remains true. The Security Council helps at the margins to preserve peace among those powers—and they need all the help they can get.

NOTES

Introduction

1. The scholars Charles Kupchan and Clifford Kupchan have succinctly described some of the key characteristics of a concert. "A concert entails no binding or codified commitments to collective action," they write. "Rather, decisions are taken through informal negotiations, through the emergence of consensus." A concert does not seek to eliminate power politics or competition among the major powers, but it does hope to control that competition and prevent it from "escalating to overt hostility and conflict." Kupchan and Kupchan, "Concerts, Collective Security, and Europe," *International Security* 16, no. 1 (Summer 1991), 120.

2. Several scholars have approached analyses of the council in a similar way. Erik Voeten has examined the council as an "elite pact" among its members. Voeten sees in this type of pact many of the benefits and characteristics of a concert of powers and contrasts it with more traditional views of the council's utility. "The Political Origins of the UN Security Council's Ability to Legitimize the Use of Force," *International Organization* 59 (Summer 2005), 527–557. As the Cold War ended, Richard Rosecrance wondered whether the Security Council might not play the role of a new concert of powers. See "A New Concert of Powers," *Foreign Affairs* (Spring 1992), 241–276.

3. Thomas G. Weiss et al., *UN Voices: The Struggle for Development and Social Justice* (Bloomington: Indiana University Press, 2005), 340.

Chapter 1

1. Richard Griffiths, *Pétain: A Biography of Marshall Philippe Pétain of Vichy* (Garden City, NY: Doubleday, 1972), 240.

2. Quoted in Joel Larus, *From Collective Security to Preventive Diplomacy: Readings in International Organization and the Maintenance of Peace* (New York: Wiley, 1965), 30.

3. Quoted in E. H. Carr, *The Twenty Years' Crisis, 1919–1939* (New York: Harper & Row, 1964), 35. Carr's account of the utopian confusion in the interwar period is a powerful case for "realism" in international politics.

4. F. S. Northedge, *The League of Nations: Its Life and Times* (New York: Holmes & Meier, 1986), 243.

5. Quoted in Northedge, *League of Nations,* 163.

6. See Douglas Gageby, *The Last Secretary General: Sean Lester and the League of Nations* (Dublin: Town House and Country House, 1999), 193.

7. John Keegan, *The Second World War* (London: Pimlico, 1989), 399.

8. Richard J. Overy, *The Air War, 1939–1945* (Washington, DC: Potomac, 2005), 150.

9. Adam B. Ulam, *Expansion and Coexistence: The History of Soviet Foreign Policy, 1917–1967* (New York: Praeger, 1968), 316.

10. Wendell L. Willkie, *One World* (New York: Simon & Schuster, 1943), 125.

11. Ruth B. Russell, *A History of the United Nations Charter: The Role of the United States, 1940–1945* (Washington, DC: Brookings Institution Press, 1958), 51.

12. See, for example, Townsend Hoopes and Douglas Brinkley, *FDR and the Creation of the U.N.* (New Haven, CT: Yale University Press, 1997), 78–82.

13. For accounts of the differences between Hull and Welles on postwar planning, see Russell, *History of the United Nations Charter,* 98–99; Hoopes and Brinkley, *FDR and the Creation of the U.N.,* 50–51; Cordell Hull, *Memoirs of Cordell Hull* (New York: Macmillan, 1948), vol. 2, 1640 (Hull labels Welles a "convinced advocate of regional organization"). Hull and his allies employed rather ruthless methods to oust Welles from his post. See Hoopes and Brinkley, *FDR and the Creation of the U.N.,* 78–82.

14. U.S. Department of State, *Foreign Relations of the United States* (Washington, DC: GPO, 1943) (hereinafter FRUS), I:756.

15. Russell D. Buhite and David W. Levy, *FDR's Fireside Chats* (Norman: University of Oklahoma Press, 1992), 278.

16. Diane Clemens, *Yalta* (New York: Oxford University Press, 1970), 47.

17. Anthony Eden, *The Reckoning* (Boston: Houghton Mifflin, 1965), 431.

18. Robert E. Sherwood, *Roosevelt and Hopkins* (New York: Harper, 1950), 717.

19. Eden, *The Reckoning,* 437.

20. Sherwood, *Roosevelt and Hopkins,* 846.

21. Hoopes and Brinkley, *FDR and the Creation of the U.N.,* 115.

22. Hoopes and Brinkley, *FDR and the Creation of the U.N.,* 128.

23. Quoted in David Dilks, ed., *Diaries of Sir Alexander Cadogan, O.M., 1938–1945* (New York: Putnam, 1972), 582.

24. Dilks, *Diaries of Sir Alexander Cadogan,* 578.

25. Quoted in Adam Roberts, "Britain and the Creation of the United Nations," in *Still More Adventures with Britannia: Personalities, Politics and Culture in Britain,* ed. Wm. Roger Louis (London: Tauris, 2003), 232.

26. Dilks, *Diaries of Sir Alexander Cadogan,* 627.

27. Interview with Lord Gladwyn Jebb, 35a, United Nations Oral History Project Transcripts, Manuscripts and Archives, Yale University Library.

28. Dilks, *Diaries of Sir Alexander Cadogan,* 653–654.

29. For a good discussion of the political currents in postwar Britain regarding colonial policy, see John Darwin, *Britain and Decolonisation: The Retreat from Empire in the Post-War World* (New York: St. Martin's, 1988), esp. 69–75.

30. See, e.g., Brian Thomas, "Cold War Origins: II," *Journal of Contemporary History* 3, no. 1 (Jan. 1968), 189.

31. See L. G. Shaw, "Attitudes of the British Political Elite towards the Soviet Union," *Diplomacy & Statecraft* 13, no. 1 (Mar. 2002), 55–74.

32. Donald W. Treadgold, *Twentieth Century Russia* (Boulder, CO: Westview, 1990), 292; Ulam, *Expansion and Coexistence,* 134.

33. Robert Rhodes James, *Anthony Eden* (New York: McGraw-Hill, 1987), 258–259. Eden probably should not have been so shocked. Later in the war, Churchill and Stalin sat down over a map to crudely sketch out possible spheres of influence in Eastern Europe and the Balkans. "Let us burn this paper," Churchill said when they were done. "No, you keep it," responded Stalin.

34. Eden, *The Reckoning,* 335.

35. In his memoirs, U.S. diplomat Charles Bohlen, who was present at the Tehran and Yalta conferences, argues that Stalin was convinced by Roosevelt's arguments on this point at Tehran. See Charles E. Bohlen, *Witness to History* (New York: Norton, 1973), 151.

36. Quoted in Daniel Yergin, *Shattered Peace: The Origins of the Cold War and the National Security State* (Boston: Houghton Mifflin, 1977), 56.

37. Sherwood, *Roosevelt and Hopkins,* 778.

38. Dilks, *Diaries of Sir Alexander Cadogan,* 581.

39. Vladislav Zubok and Constantine Peshakov, *Inside the Kremlin's Cold War: From Stalin to Khrushchev* (Cambridge, MA: Harvard University Press, 1996), 25.

40. Adam B. Ulam, *Stalin: The Man and His Era* (New York: Viking, 1973), 596; Bohlen, *Witness to History,* 158.

41. Hiss was accused of being a Soviet agent in August 1948 and was later convicted of perjury (though not of espionage). As Soviet documents and U.S. intelligence intercepts have come to light, the case against Hiss has become stronger. It is not clear, however, what information, if any, Hiss was providing to the Soviets during the negotiations on the founding of the United Nations. See Edward G. White, *Alger Hiss's Looking Glass Wars: The Covert Life of a Soviet Spy* (New York: Oxford University Press, 2004). For an argument against Hiss's guilt, see Kai Bird and Svetlana Chervonnaya, "The Mystery of Ales," *American Scholar* (Summer 2007).

42. UN Oral History Interview with Lord Gladwyn Jebb, 35, Yale University.

43. Dilks, *Diaries of Sir Alexander Cadogan,* 654.

44. Yergin, *Shattered Peace,* 49.

45. Andrei Gromyko, *Memoirs* (Garden City, NY: Doubleday, 1989), 77–79.

46. Robert Hilderbrand, *Dumbarton Oaks* (Chapel Hill: University of North Carolina Press, 1990), 69.

47. Russell, *History of the United Nations Charter,* 440.

48. Charles K. Webster, "The Making of the Charter of the United Nations," *History* 32, no. 115 (Mar. 1947), 25.

49. Dumbarton Oaks, Washington Conversations on International Peace and Security Organization, Oct. 7, 1944, chapter VI, available at www.ibiblio.org.

50. Thomas M. Campbell and George C. Herring, eds., *Diaries of Edward R. Stettinius, Jr., 1943–1946* (New York: New Viewpoints, 1975), 113.

51. Campbell and Herring, *Diaries of Edward R. Stettinius,* 113, 111.

52. Hubert Miles Gladwyn Jebb, *The Memoirs of Lord Gladwyn* (New York: Weybright & Talley, 1972), 148.

53. Dilks, *Diaries of Sir Alexander Cadogan,* 663.

54. Russell, *History of the United Nations Charter,* 470–472.

55. Gromyko, *Memoirs,* 116.

56. Jonathan Fenby, *Chiang Kai-shek* (New York: Carroll & Graf, 2003), 395–396.

57. UN Oral History Interview with Lord Gladwyn Jebb, Yale University.

58. Stephen G. Craft, *V. K. Wellington Koo and the Emergence of Modern China* (Lexington: University Press of Kentucky, 2004), 117.

59. Craft, *V. K. Wellington Koo,* 182.

60. W. W. Kulski, *De Gaulle and the World: The Foreign Policy of the Fifth French Republic* (Syracuse, NY: Syracuse University Press, 1966), 4.

61. Quoted in Russell, *History of the United Nations Charter,* 107.

62. For accounts of the episode, see Hull, *Memoirs of Cordell Hull,* 1129–1133; Raoul Aglion, *Roosevelt and de Gaulle: Allies in Conflict* (New York: Free Press, 1988), 66–67.

63. Sherwood, *Roosevelt and Hopkins,* 685. Hopkins thought the Secret Service's precautions were comical. "To me," he wrote, "the armed Secret Service was unbelievably funny and nothing in Gilbert and Sullivan could have beaten it. Poor General de Gaulle, who probably did not know it, was covered by guns throughout his whole visit."

64. Franklin D. Roosevelt, *F.D.R.: His Personal Letters* (New York: Duell, Sloan and Pearce, 1950), 1400, 1453.

65. Hull, *Memoirs of Cordell Hull,* 961; Dilks, *Diaries of Sir Alexander Cadogan,* 640.

66. Aglion, *Roosevelt and de Gaulle,* 133.

67. Francois Kersaudy, *Churchill and de Gaulle* (New York: Collins, 1981), 346.

68. Campbell and Herring, *Diaries of Edward R. Stettinius,* 90.

69. Sherwood, *Roosevelt and Hopkins,* 781.

70. "Connally Urges Peace Plan Unity," *New York Times,* Oct. 10, 1944, 13.

71. "The United Nations," *New York Times,* Oct. 10, 1944, 22.

72. Reinhold Niebuhr, *The Children of Light and the Children of Darkness* (New York: Scribner's, 1944), 163–164.

73. Hilderbrand, *Dumbarton Oaks,* 213.

74. Prime Minister's Personal Minute, quoted in Martin Gilbert, *Road to Victory: Winston S. Churchill, 1941–1945* (London: Heinemann, 1986), 1170.

75. Piers Dixon, *Double Diploma: The Life of Sir Pierson Dixon* (London: Hutchinson, 1968), 136.

76. Bohlen, *Witness to History,* 173.

77. Clemens, *Yalta,* 116.

78. Quoted in Steven Merritt Miner, "His Master's Voice: Viacheslav Mikhailovich Molotov as Stalin's Foreign Commissar," in Gordon A. Craig and Francis L. Loewenheim, eds., *The Diplomats,* (Princeton, NJ: Princeton University Press, 1994), 85; an account of the exchange can also be found in Albert Resis, ed., *Molotov Remembers: Inside Kremlin Politics* (Chicago: Dee, 1993), 51.

79. Charles McMoran Wilson, *Churchill: Taken from the Diaries of Lord Moran* (Boston: Houghton Mifflin, 1966), 242.

80. Sydney Bailey and Sam Daws, *The Procedure of the UN Security Council* (Oxford: Oxford University Press, 1998), 457.

81. Sherwood, *Roosevelt and Hopkins,* 857.

82. UN Oral History Interview with Alger Hiss, 19, Yale University.

83. Sherwood, *Roosevelt and Hopkins,* 870.

84. Dixon, *Double Diploma,* 148.

85. Eden, *The Reckoning,* 619.

86. Sherwood, *Roosevelt and Hopkins,* 879.

87. David McCullough, *Truman* (New York: Simon & Schuster, 1992), 234.

88. "Locksley Hall," reprinted in Alfred Tennyson, *The Poetical Works of Alfred Tennyson* (New York: Thomas Crowell, 1890), 92.

89. First Address of President Truman to Congress, April 16, 1945, full text available at the Harry S Truman Library, www.trumanlibrary.org.

90. Declassified excerpts from the Venona Project suggest that the Soviet intelligence services transferred several agents to San Francisco for the conference. Excerpts are available via the Web site of the U.S. National Security Agency, http://www.nsa.gov/public_info/declass/venona/index.shtml. See also Stephen C. Schlesinger's history of the San Francisco conference, *Act of Creation* (Boulder, CO: Westview, 2003), 102.

91. Quoted in Russell, *History of the United Nations Charter,* 629.

92. In his memoirs, Anthony Eden states that Stalin sent Molotov as "a gesture of respect" for the deceased president. *The Reckoning,* 609.

93. Accounts differ as to how precisely the exchange occurred. Truman recalled the conversation this way, but Truman's translator, Charles Bohlen, did not. See McCullough, *Truman,* 376; Bohlen, *Witness to History,* 213.

94. Bohlen, *Witness to History,* 214–215.

95. See, for example, A. W. Deporte, *De Gaulle's Foreign Policy, 1944–1946* (Cambridge, MA: Harvard University Press, 1968), 105–108; John W. Young, *France, the Cold War and the Western Alliance, 1944–1949* (New York: St. Martin's, 1990), 43, 52–53; Schlesinger, *Act of Creation,* 101–102.

96. FRUS, 1945, I:404.

97. UN Oral History Interview with Alger Hiss, 27–28, Yale University.

98. Quoted in Joseph C. Grew, *Turbulent Era: A Diplomatic Record of Forty Years, 1904–1945* (Boston: Houghton Mifflin, 1952), vol. 2, 1516n5.

99. Jean Lacouture, *De Gaulle* (New York: Norton, 1993), 92; Young, *France, the Cold War and the Western Alliance,* 56.

100. Escott Reid, *On Duty: A Canadian at the Making of the United Nations, 1945–1946* (Kent, OH: Kent State University Press, 1983), 54.

101. UN Oral History Interview with Professor Leland Goodrich, Yale University.

102. Dilks, *Diaries of Sir Alexander Cadogan,* 742.

103. Russell, *History of the United Nations Charter,* 716.

104. Herbert Vere Evatt, *The United Nations* (Cambridge, MA: Harvard University Press, 1948), 14.

105. Dilks, *Diaries of Sir Alexander Cadogan,* 745.

106. Schlesinger, *Act of Creation,* 193–200.

107. Arthur Hendrick Vandenberg and Joe Alex Morris, *The Private Papers of Senator Vandenberg* (New York: Houghton Mifflin, 1952), 200.

108. Paul Hasluck, *Workshop of Security* (London: Cheshire, 1948), 129–130.

109. Tom Connally, *My Name Is Tom Connally* (New York: Crowell, 1954), 283.

110. Hoopes and Brinkley, *FDR and the Creation of the U.N.,* 201.

111. Quoted in Adam Chapnick, *The Middle Power Project: Canada and the Founding of the United Nations* (Vancouver: University of British Columbia Press, 2005), 137.

112. United Nations Charter, Art. 51.

113. Quoted in Chapnick, *The Middle Power Project,* 126.

114. Russell Porter, "Small Countries Gain Wider Role," *New York Times,* May 7, 1945, 10.

115. See F. P. Walters, *A History of the League of Nations* (New York: Oxford University Press, 1952), vol. 2, 815.

Chapter 2

1. Grew, *Turbulent Era,* 2:1445–1446.

2. Quoted in Gaddis Smith, *American Diplomacy during the Second World War, 1941–1945* (New York: McGraw-Hill, 1985), 141.

3. Quoted in Alan Bullock, *Ernest Bevin: Foreign Secretary, 1945–1951* (New York: Norton, 1983), 110.

4. A Canadian diplomat preparing for the United Nations' opening wrote in his diary, "as soon as the bomb fell all the security articles in the Charter became archaic." See Reid, *On Duty,* 77.

5. See *Report of the Preparatory Commission of the United Nations* (London: His Majesty's Stationery Office, 1946), 126–129.

6. Reid, *On Duty,* 99.

7. For a discussion of the efforts by New England cities and towns to host the United Nations, see Charlene Mires, "The Lure of New England and the Search for the Capitol of the World," *New England Quarterly* 79, no. 1 (Mar. 2006), 37–64.

8. Security Council Official Records, First Meeting (Jan. 17, 1946) (hereinafter SCOR).

9. SCOR, First Meeting (Jan. 17, 1946).

10. At one trial of impure Bolsheviks, Vishinsky demanded that "dogs gone mad should be shot—every one of them." Most of them were. See Ulam, *Stalin,* 414.

11. Victor Israelyan, *On the Battlefields of the Cold War: A Soviet Ambassador's Confession* (University Park: Pennsylvania State University Press, 2003), 16.

12. James B. Reston, "Britain, U.S. Urge Iran Study by UNO," *New York Times,* Jan. 26, 1946, 1.

13. Trygve Lie, *In the Cause of Peace: Seven Years at the United Nations* (New York: Macmillan, 1954), 32.

14. Bohlen, *Witness to History,* 255.

15. James B. Reston, "Russian Vetoes U.N. Levant Plan; Council Closes," *New York Times,* Feb. 17, 1946, 1.

16. Hasluck, *Workshop of Security,* 143.

17. "Horseshoe Table for Security Council to Give Sessions a More Intimate Air," *New York Times,* July 25, 1946, 3.

18. Bernard Moore, *The Second Lesson: Seven Years at the United Nations* (London: Macmillan, 1957), 121.

19. Edward Montgomery, "United Nations: East and West," *New Republic,* Apr. 1946, 571.

20. James B. Reston, "Council Proceeds; Soviet Delegate Walks Out of UNO," *New York Times,* Mar. 28, 1946, 1.

21. UN Oral History Interview with Pauline Frederick (part 1), 21, Yale University.

22. Bailey and Daws, *The Procedure of the UN Security Council,* 231–232.

23. James B. Reston, "Votes and Vetoes," *Foreign Affairs* 25, no. 1 (Oct. 1946), 19.

24. Rupert Emerson and Inis Claude, "The Soviet Union and the United Nations: An Essay in Interpretation," *International Organization* 6, no. 1 (Feb. 1952), 1–26.

25. Quoted in Emerson and Claude, "The Soviet Union and the United Nations," 8–9.

26. For a discussion of the American deliberations on the issue, see James Chace, "Sharing the Atom Bomb," *Foreign Affairs* (Jan.–Feb. 1996), 129–144.

27. Cord Meyer, Jr., "Peace Is Still Possible," *Atlantic Monthly*, Oct. 1947, 32–33.

28. Brendan Gill, "Black Sheep," *New Yorker*, Apr. 13, 1946, 24.

29. "Australia Fights U.N. Trieste Plan," *New York Times*, Jan. 8, 1947, 7.

30. Hasluck, *Workshop of Security*, 45.

31. For a good discussion of how the right of abstention developed, see Sydney D. Bailey, "New Light on Abstentions in the U.N. Security Council," *International Affairs* 50, no. 4 (Oct. 1974), 554–573.

32. Official Records of the Second Session of the General Assembly, Supplement No. 11, A/364, Sept. 3, 1947.

33. Lie, *In the Cause of Peace*, 164.

34. Alexander Cadogan diary entries for Tuesday, Mar. 9, 1947, and Wednesday, May 19, 1947, viewed at Churchill College Library, Cambridge University.

35. Quoted in William J. Durch, ed., *The Evolution of UN Peacekeeping* (London: Macmillan, 1994), 88.

36. Correspondence quoted in Robert D. Accinelli, "Pro-U.N. Internationalists and the Early Cold War: The American Association for the United Nations and U.S. Foreign Policy, 1947–1952," *Diplomatic History* 9, no. 4 (Fall 1985), 356.

37. See Allida Black, ed., *The Eleanor Roosevelt Papers*, vol. 1, *The Human Rights Years, 1945–1948* (New York: Thomson Gale, 2007), 774.

38. Bullock, *Ernest Bevin*, 607.

39. "Text of the Western Powers' Reply to the Proposals of the Soviet," *New York Times*, Sept. 27, 1948, 6.

40. Anne O'Hare McCormick, "Abroad," *New York Times*, Sept. 18, 1948, 16.

41. "Vishinsky Rouses Syrian Sleeping during His Talk," *New York Times*, Oct. 6, 1948, 3.

42. SCOR, 361st meeting (Oct. 4, 1948), 20–21.

43. Dean Acheson, *Present at the Creation: My Years in the State Department* (New York: Norton, 1969), 269.

44. For accounts of the U.S. deliberations on whether and how to negotiate with the Soviets on Berlin, see Bohlen, *Witness to History*, 480; Acheson, *Present at the Creation*, 261–270; Philip C. Jessup, "Park Avenue Diplomacy—Ending the Berlin Blockade," *Political Science Quarterly* 87, no. 3 (Sept. 1972), 377–400.

45. Lie, *In the Cause of Peace*, 218.

46. Lie, *In the Cause of Peace*, 254.

47. SCOR, 459th Meeting (Jan. 10, 1950), 3.

48. Lie, *In the Cause of Peace*, 251.

49. Zubok and Peshakov, *Inside the Kremlin's Cold War*, 64.

50. Harry S Truman Library, Third Oral History Interview with John D. Hickerson.

51. UN Oral History Interview with James Nevins Hyde, Apr. 18, 1990, 7–8, Yale University.

52. SCOR, 473rd Meeting (June 25, 1950), 4, 8.

53. SCOR, 473rd Meeting (June 25, 1950), 13.

54. See Alexander Dallin, *The Soviet Union at the United Nations: An Inquiry into Soviet Motives and Objectives* (Westport, CT: Greenwood, 1976), 36.

55. Ulam, *Expansion and Coexistence*, 521; Zubok and Peshakov, *Inside the Kremlin's Cold War*, 64.

56. William Stueck, *The Korean War: An International History* (Princeton, NJ: Princeton University Press, 1995), 47.

57. FRUS, 1950, VII:208–209.

58. Victor S. Kaufman, "Chirep: The Anglo-American Dispute over Chinese Representation in the United Nations, 1950–1971," *English Historical Review* 115, no. 461 (Apr. 2000), 354–377.

59. "U.N. Meeting to Be a Sellout," *New York Times*, July 29, 1950, 4.

60. SCOR, 480th Meeting (Aug. 1, 1950), 1.

61. SCOR, 480th Meeting (Aug. 1, 1950), 3.

62. SCOR, 480th Meeting (Aug. 1, 1950), 9.

63. SCOR, 480th Meeting (Aug. 1, 1950), 19.

64. SCOR, 480th Meeting (Aug. 1, 1950), 15.

65. SCOR, 481st Meeting (Aug. 2, 1950), 4.

66. SCOR, 486th Meeting (Aug. 11, 1950), 8.

67. Jebb, *Memoirs of Lord Gladwyn*, 234.

68. Churchill College, Cambridge University, British Diplomatic Oral History Programme, Interview with Sir Peter Ramsbotham, 20.

69. British Foreign Office, Doc. FO 371/88446 (Sir Gladwyn Jebb to Sir Pierson Dixon, July 8, 1950).

70. See the discussion of Uniting for Peace in Bailey and Daws, *The Procedure of the UN Security Council*, 229–230.

71. Dean Acheson, *The Korean War* (New York: Norton, 1971), 52.

72. United Nations General Assembly (hereinafter UNGA) Resolution 377 (Nov. 3, 1950).

73. The United States had previewed the strategy for bypassing the Soviet veto on the council several years earlier during the dispute over British involvement in Greece. In that case, the council, with Soviet approval, appointed an investigative commission. When the Soviets vetoed resolutions based on the commission's findings, however, the Western powers moved the dispute to the assembly. See the discussion in Durch, *Evolution of UN Peacekeeping*, 77–83.

74. UNGA Resolution 376 (Oct. 7, 1950).

75. Stueck, *Korean War*, 88.

76. See, for example, Stueck, *Korean War*, 119.

77. George Barrett, "Peiping Is Invited to Council Hearing," *New York Times*, Sept. 30, 1950, 1.

78. A Nov. 9, 1950, cable from the Soviet archives suggests that the Soviets wanted the Chinese to refuse the invitation. The communication, from Andrei Gromyko to Chinese foreign minister Chou En-lai, concedes that Soviet UN ambassador Malik was under instructions to oppose the invitation, on the grounds that its scope was too narrow, but that he became "carried away" with the tactical victory he had won over the Americans. Available at Cold War International History Project virtual archive, http://www.wilsoncenter.org/index.cfm?topic_id=1409&fuseaction=va2.browse&sort=Collection

79. FRUS, 1950, vol. VII (Korea), 1237.

80. SCOR, 527th Meeting (Nov. 28, 1950), 2, 4.

81. FRUS, 1950, vol. VII (Korea), 1255, 1272.

82. Moore, *The Second Lesson*, 188.

83. See Stueck, *Korean War*, 90–91.

84. Edith Iglauer, "The UN Builds Its Home," *Harper's Magazine*, Dec. 1947, 562.

85. George A. Dudley, *A Workshop for Peace: Designing the United Nations Headquarters* (Cambridge, MA: MIT Press, 1994), 132.

86. Dudley, *Workshop for Peace*, 146.

87. Dudley, *Workshop for Peace*, 93–94.

88. Dudley, *Workshop for Peace*, 142–143.

89. British Foreign Office, Doc. FO 371/95621 (letter from D. F. Duncan to J. D. Fraser, Ministry of Works, Feb. 1, 1951).

90. "Security Council Ends 6 Years of Wandering, Enter Permanent Quarters on East River," *New York Times*, Apr. 5, 1952, 4.

91. Bill Henry, "By the Way," *Los Angeles Times*, Oct. 3, 1952, A1.

92. Moore, *The Second Lesson*, 97.

93. UN Oral History Interview with James Nevins Hyde, 19, Yale University.

94. UN Oral History Interview with James Nevins Hyde, 21–22, Yale University.

95. William J. Miller, *Henry Cabot Lodge* (New York: Heinemann), 270.

96. A. M. Rosenthal, "Debate Is Bitter," *New York Times*, June 21, 1954, A1.

97. UNSC Resolution 104 (June 20, 1954).

98. Central Intelligence Agency, "Operation PBSuccess: The United States and Guatemala, 1952–1954," available via the National Security Archive, George Washington University.

99. FRUS, 1952–1954, vol. IV (American Republics), 1182–1183.

100. FRUS, 1952–1954, vol. IV (American Republics), 1185.

101. SCOR, 684th meeting (Nov. 3, 1954), 10.

102. "Egyptian U.N. Delegate Stricken during Debate on Israel and Dies," *New York Times*, Nov. 4, 1954, 1.

103. Quoted in Maurice Vaisse, "France and the Suez Crisis," in *Suez 1956: The Crisis and Its Consequences*, ed. Wm. Roger Louis and Roger Owen (Oxford: Oxford University Press, 1989), 137.

104. Eden worked hard to convince a skeptical Eisenhower of the danger Nasser posed. On September 6, 1956, he wrote to the president that "the seizure of the Suez Canal is, we are convinced, the opening gambit in a planned campaign designed by Nasser to expel all Western influence and interests from Arab countries." Peter G. Boyle, ed., *The Eden-Eisenhower Correspondence, 1955–1957* (Chapel Hill: University of North Carolina Press, 2005), 165.

105. The correspondence and many other important documents from the crisis are excerpted in Anthony Gorst and Lewis Johnman, *The Suez Crisis* (New York: Routledge, 1997), 61–67.

106. An account of the meeting can be found in Dixon, *Double Diploma*, 260.

107. It appears that Dixon thought Lodge was too direct and aggressive. See Edward Johnson, "The Diplomats' Diplomat: Sir Pierson Dixon, Ambassador to the United Nations," in Saul Kelly and Anthony Gorst, eds., *Whitehall and the Suez Crisis* (London: Cass, 2000), 193.

108. FRUS, 1955–1957, vol. XVI (Suez Crisis), 521–522.

109. SCOR, 735th Meeting (Oct. 5, 1956), 3.

110. SCOR, 735th Meeting (Oct. 5, 1956), 20–21.

111. SCOR, 736th Meeting (Oct. 8, 1956), 4–5.

112. SCOR, 736th Meeting (Oct. 8, 1956), 17.

113. UNSC Resolution 118 (Oct. 13, 1956). For a discussion of Hammarskjöld's meetings with the foreign ministers, see Urquhart, *Hammarskjöld*, 166–168.

114. SCOR, 742nd Meeting (Oct. 13, 1956), 3.

115. Selwyn Lloyd, *Suez 1956: A Personal Account* (New York: Mayflower, 1978), 162.

116. Lloyd, *Suez 1956*, 180–181.

117. SCOR, 746th Meeting (Oct. 28, 1956), 12–13.

118. Kennett Love, *Suez: The Twice Fought War* (New York: McGraw-Hill, 1969), 503.

119. Douglas Hurd, "Half a Century On, the Ghosts of Suez Return," *Spectator*, July 22, 2006.

120. FRUS, 1955–1957, vol. XVI (Suez Crisis, July 26–Dec. 31, 1956), 841.

121. Abba Eban, *An Autobiography* (New York: Random House, 1977), 214.

122. Eban, *An Autobiography*, 214.

123. "Aide to French Delegate Heads Council Session," *New York Times*, Nov. 1, 1956, 15.

124. Foreign Office cable excerpted in Gorst and Johnman, eds., *The Suez Crisis*, 108.

125. Cole C. Kingseed, *Eisenhower and the Suez Crisis of 1956* (Baton Rouge: Louisiana State University Press, 1995), 104; see also FRUS, 1955–1957, vol. XVI (Suez Crisis, July 26–Dec. 31, 1956), 887.

126. "Remarks in the United Nations General Assembly Debate on the Invasion of Egypt," *New York Times*, Nov. 2, 1956, 6.

127. UNGA Resolution 997 (ES-1) (Nov. 2, 1956).

128. "'Police Action' in Egypt," *Times* (London), Nov. 5, 1956, 4.

129. Churchill College, Cambridge University, British Diplomatic Oral History Programme, Interview with Sir Peter Ramsbotham, 23.

130. Foreign Office document quoted in Johnson, "Diplomats' Diplomat," 190.

131. Dixon, *Double Diploma*, 278.

132. Quoted in Keith Kyle, "Britain and the Crisis, 1955–1956," in Louis and Owen, *Suez 1956*, 130.

133. See James E. Todd, "An Analysis of Security Council Voting Behavior," *Western Political Quarterly* 22, no. 1 (Mar. 1969).

134. See, for example, the discussion in Jean-Pierre Rioux, *The Fourth Republic, 1944–1958* (Cambridge: Cambridge University Press, 1987), 275.

135. See Kulski, *De Gaulle and the World*, 331.

136. Dallin, *The Soviet Union at the United Nations*, 118.

137. British Foreign Office document quoted in Peter G. Boyle, "The Hungarian Revolution and the Suez Crisis," *History* 90, no. 300 (Oct. 2005), 561.

138. Some Soviet warming toward the organization occurred in the months before the Suez crisis. See Dallin, *The Soviet Union at the United Nations*, 40.

Chapter 3

1. SCOR, 811th Meeting (Feb. 18, 1958).

2. Charles de Gaulle, *Major Addresses, Statements, and Press Conferences of General Charles de Gaulle* (New York: French Embassy, 1964), 27.

3. See Robert C. Doty, "De Gaulle against Holding Summit Parley at U.N.," *New York Times*, July 23, 1958, 1.

4. President de Gaulle's Eleventh Press Conference, Feb. 4, 1965, quoted in Robert S. Wood, *France in the World Community: Decolonization, Peacekeeping, and the United Nations* (Leiden: Sijthoff, 1973), 65.

5. *Major Addresses, Statements, and Press Conferences of General Charles de Gaulle*, 119–121.

6. Quoted in Kulski, *De Gaulle and the World*, 13.

7. *Major Addresses, Statements, and Press Conferences of General Charles de Gaulle*, 120–121.

8. Charles de Gaulle, *Memoirs of Hope*, trans. Terence Kilmartin (New York: Simon & Schuster, 1971), 46.

9. The UN Department of Peacekeeping Operations' official history of the Lebanon mission provides a concise summary of its evolution. It is available at http://www.un.org/Depts/dpko/dpko/co_mission/unogil.htm.

10. Brian Urquhart, *Hammarskjöld* (New York: Knopf, 1972), 385.

11. Urquhart, *Hammarskjöld*, 391–392.

12. Urquhart, *Hammarskjöld*, 396.

13. SCOR, 873rd Meeting (July 13, 1960), 3.

14. SCOR, 873rd Meeting (July 13, 1960), 15.

15. SCOR, 872nd Meeting (July 7, 1960), 11.

16. SCOR, 873rd Meeting (July 13, 1960), 36.

17. Brian Urquhart, *A Life in Peace and War* (New York: Harper & Row, 1987), 149.

18. SCOR, 930th Meeting (Feb. 2, 1961), 23.

19. SCOR, 933rd Meeting (Feb. 13, 1961), 3.

20. Kulski, *De Gaulle and the World*, 388.

21. SCOR, 942nd meeting (Feb. 20, 1961), 9.

22. See Richard N. Gardner, "The Soviet Union and the United Nations," *Law and Contemporary Problems* 29, no. 4 (Autumn 1964).

23. See "Riot in Gallery Halts U.N. Debate," *New York Times*, Feb. 16, 1961, 1; "The Bear's Teeth," *Time*, Feb. 24, 1961; James Feron, "U.N. Takes Steps to Prevent Riots," *New York Times*, Feb. 17, 1961, 1.

24. Harlan Cleveland, *The Obligations of Power: American Diplomacy in the Search for Peace* (New York: Harper & Row, 1966), 71.

25. UN Oral History Interview with Harlan Cleveland, Apr. 22, 1990, 7, Yale University.

26. SCOR, 888th Meeting (Aug. 21, 1960).

27. Andrew W. Cordier and Wilder Foote, eds., *Public Papers of the Secretaries-General of the United Nations*, vol. 5, *1960–1961* (New York: Columbia University Press, 1978), 173–174.

28. For a helpful discussion of the financial crisis, see Norman J. Padelford, "Financing Peacekeeping: Politics and Crisis," *International Organization* 19, no. 3 (Summer 1965), 444–462.

29. "A Week of Reason," *Time*, Feb. 9, 1962.

30. Michael Beschloss, *Mayday: Eisenhower, Khrushchev, and the U-2 Affair* (New York: Harper & Row, 1986), 26–27.

31. Beschloss, *Mayday*, 311.

32. SCOR, 857th Meeting (May 23, 1960), 4–19.

33. SCOR, 860th Meeting (May 26, 1960), 14.

34. Alden Whitman, *Portrait: Adlai E. Stevenson: Politician, Diplomat, Friend* (New York: Harper & Row, 1960), 224.

35. "Excerpts from Statements Made by Roa and Stevenson to U.N. Political Committee," *New York Times*, Apr. 18, 1961.

36. FRUS, 1961–1963, X:230.

37. John F. Kennedy Library Oral History Program, Interview with Francis Plimpton, 12.

38. United Nations Oral History Interview with Pauline Frederick (part 1), 24, Yale University.

39. Dean Rusk, as told to Richard Rusk, *As I Saw It* (New York: Norton, 1990), 235.

40. Dino A. Brugioni, *Eyeball to Eyeball: The Inside Story of the Cuban Missile Crisis*, ed. Robert F. McCort (New York: Random House, 1991), 318.

41. Brugioni, *Eyeball to Eyeball*, 393.

42. Brugioni, *Eyeball to Eyeball*, 395.

43. SCOR, 1022nd Meeting (Oct. 23, 1962), 16.

44. John F. Kennedy Library Oral History Program, Interview with Charles W. Yost.

45. Ernest May and Philip Zelikow, *The Kennedy Tapes: Inside the White House during the Cuban Missile Crisis* (New York: Norton, 2002), 403–404.

46. John F. Kennedy Library Oral History Program, Interview with Joseph Sisco.

47. Oral History Interview with Joseph Sisco, 21, Yale University.

48. One Soviet official who worked at the United Nations contends that Zorin was losing his mental faculties at the time of the Cuban missile crisis. See Arkady N. Shevchenko, *Breaking with Moscow* (New York: Knopf, 1985), 114.

49. Brugioni, *Eyeball to Eyeball*, 427.

50. SCOR, 1025th meeting (Oct. 25, 1962), 11–12.

51. SCOR, 1025th meeting (Oct. 25, 1962), 12–13.

52. Brugioni, *Eyeball to Eyeball*, 426.

53. SCOR, 1025th meeting (Oct. 25, 1962), 16.

54. SCOR, 1025th meeting (Oct. 25, 1962), 17.

55. Michael Dobbs, *One Minute to Midnight: Kennedy, Khrushchev, and Castro on the Brink of Nuclear War* (New York: Knopf, 2008), 131.

56. Kenneth P. O'Donnell and David F. Powers, *"Johnny, We Hardly Knew Ye"* (Boston: Little, Brown, 1972), 334.

57. "Telegram from the Soviet Representative to the United Nations, Valerian Zorin, to the USSR MFA," Oct. 25, 1962, available via the Cold War International History Project.

58. "Zorin Is Returning to Post in Moscow," *New York Times*, Dec. 24, 1962, 1.

59. Rusk, *As I Saw It*, 236.

60. Arthur Schlesinger, *A Thousand Days* (Boston: Houghton Mifflin, 1965), 824.

61. Harold Macmillan, *At the End of the Day: 1961–1963* (New York: Harper & Row, 1973), 196.

62. Philip Ben, "U Thant and the Cuban Crisis," *New Republic*, Nov. 17, 1962, 7.

63. Quoted in Douglas Brinkley, *Dean Acheson: The Cold War Years, 1953–1971* (New Haven, CT: Yale University Press, 1994), 167.

64. "News Summary and Index," *New York Times*, May 3, 1965, 35.

65. SCOR, 1196th meeting (May 3, 1965), 3.

66. "Excerpts from Speeches at the U.N.," *New York Times*, May 4, 1965, 16.

67. Whitman, *Portrait: Adlai Stevenson*, 269.

68. Quoted in Thant, *A View from the UN* (Garden City, NY: Doubleday, 1978), 374.

69. Kathleen Teltsch, "Exhaustion Stops Indian's U.N. Talk," *New York Times*, Nov. 12, 1957, 4; Amy Janello and Brennon Jones, eds., *A Global Affair: An Inside Look at the United Nations* (New York: Jones & Janello, 1995), 290.

70. Andrew Boyd, *Fifteen Men on a Powder Keg: A History of the UN Security Council* (New York: Stein and Day, 1971), 136.

71. FRUS, 1964–1968, vol. III (Vietnam), 245.

72. FRUS, 1964–1968, vol. IV (Vietnam), 191.

73. FRUS, 1964–1968, vol. IV (Vietnam), 196.

74. For a description of the complications that Vietnam created for Soviet diplomacy, see Anatoly Dobrynin, *In Confidence* (New York: Times Books, 1995), 135–136.

75. UN Doc. A/SPC/SR.197, pars. 14 and 17 (1960).

76. British Foreign Office, Docs. FO 371/172636, FO 371/172644.

77. FRUS, 1964–1968, XXXIII:677.

78. FRUS, 1961–1963, XXV:641.

79. FRUS, 1964–1968, XXXIII:619–620.

80. See the excellent discussion of the Cyprus operation in Durch, *Evolution of UN Peacekeeping*, 206–236.

81. Goldberg's recollection of the incident is recorded in Linda Fasulo, *Representing America: Experiences of U.S. Diplomats at the UN* (New York: Praeger, 1984), 101.

82. Michael Oren, *Six Days of War: June 1967 and the Making of the Modern Middle East* (New York: Oxford University Press, 2002), 42–43.

83. The council was occasionally capable of united action on the Middle East. In November 1966, it voted unanimously to condemn a severe Israeli reprisal against Palestinian forces operating from Jordanian territory. The censure, and American support for it, reportedly startled Israeli politicians. See Oren, *Six Days of War*, 34–35.

84. Thant, *A View from the UN*, 226–227.

85. C. L. Sulzberger, "Foreign Affairs: The Deadliest Game," *New York Times*, May 31, 1967, 43. U Thant discusses the criticism he received in his memoir, *A View from the UN*, 229–231.

86. Urquhart, *A Life in Peace and War*, 215.

87. Gideon Rafael, *Destination Peace: Three Decades of Israeli Foreign Policy* (New York: Stein and Day, 1981), 140. Thant does not mention the exchange in his memoirs.

88. Oren, *Six Days of War*, 91.

89. Sydney D. Bailey, *Four Arab-Israeli Wars and the Peace Process* (New York: St. Martin's, 1990), 409.

90. Bailey, *Four Arab-Israeli Wars*, 202–203.

91. SCOR, 1346th Meeting (June 3, 1967).

92. Oren, *Six Days of War*, 176.

93. Rafael, *Destination Peace*, 155.

94. Rusk, *As I Saw It*, 386.

95. For an account of the reaction in the Soviet UN mission, see Shevchenko, *Breaking with Moscow*, 133–134.

96. Vladislav M. Zubok, *A Failed Empire: The Soviet Union in the Cold War from Stalin to Gorbachev* (Chapel Hill: University of North Carolina Press, 2007), 199.

97. SCOR, 1348th Meeting (June 6, 1967), 15.
98. Jack Gould, "TV: Spotlight on Crisis," *New York Times*, June 7, 1967, 95.
99. SCOR, 1354th Meeting (June 10, 1967), 4.
100. SCOR, 1352nd Meeting (June 9, 1967), 13.
101. SCOR, 1356th Meeting (June 10, 1967),12.
102. SCOR, 1348th Meeting (June 6, 1967), 20.
103. SCOR, 1354th Meeting (June 10, 1967), 6.
104. Rafael, *Destination Peace*, 157.
105. "Hot-line Diplomacy," *Time*, June 16, 1967; Oren, *Six Days of War*, 297.
106. Oren, *Six Days of War*, 296.
107. Rafael, *Destination Peace*, 164–165.
108. Bailey, *Four Arab-Israeli Wars*, 267–268.
109. Sydney D. Bailey, *The Making of Resolution 242* (Dordrecht: Martinus Nijhoff, 1985), 146–148.
110. Lord Caradon, "Reflections and Hopes," in *Paths to Peace: The UN Security Council and Its Presidency*, ed. Davidson Nicol (New York: Pergamon, 1981), 77–78.
111. A long-time UN official recalled the reaction to the vote in United Nations Oral History Interview with F. T. Liu, 29, Yale University.
112. UNSC Resolution 242 (Nov. 22, 1967).
113. Boyd, *Fifteen Men on a Powder Keg*, 37.
114. Henry Kissinger, *Crisis: The Anatomy of Two Major Foreign Policy Crises* (New York: Simon & Schuster, 2003), 273.
115. In his memoirs, Israeli foreign minister Abba Eban described the importance of the precise wording. See Eban, *An Autobiography* (New York: Random House, 1977), 451–452.

Chapter 4

1. George Ball, *The Past Has Another Pattern* (New York: Norton, 1982), 437.
2. "Fifth Conference of Heads of State or Government of Non-Aligned Countries," reprinted in Odette Jankowitsch and Karl P. Sauvant, *The Third World Without Superpowers: The Collected Documents of the Non-Aligned Countries*, vol. 2 (Dobbs Ferry, NY: Oceana, 1978), 753.
3. Quoted in Cameron Hume, *The United Nations, Iran, and Iraq: How Peacemaking Changed* (Bloomington: Indiana University Press, 1994), 36.
4. UNSC Resolution 344 (Dec. 15, 1973).
5. Abdulrahim Abby Farah, "The Council Meets in Africa," in Nicol, *Paths to Peace*, 108.
6. Colin Crowe, "Some Observations on the Operation of the Security Council including the Use of the Veto," in Nicol, *Paths to Peace*, 97.
7. Ball, *The Past Has Another Pattern*, 442–443.
8. Shevchenko, *Breaking with Moscow*, 229.
9. Israelyan, *On the Battlefields of the Cold War*, 151.
10. Israelyan, *On the Battlefields of the Cold War*, 153.
11. SCOR, 1445th Meeting (Aug. 24, 1968), 19.
12. Quoted in Seymour Maxwell Finger, *Your Man at the UN* (New York: New York University Press, 1980), 191.
13. SCOR, 1443rd Meeting (Aug. 22, 1968), 18.

14. SCOR, 1443rd Meeting (Aug. 22, 1968), 29.

15. Quoted in Fasulo, *Representing America*, 122.

16. "Jackson Assails U.S. Policy on UN," *New York Times*, Mar. 21, 1962, 1.

17. FRUS, 1969–1972 (Foundations of Foreign Policy), 163.

18. SCOR, 1534th Meeting (Mar. 17, 1970), 2–3. Caradon was quoting from a statement he had made in the council in June 1969.

19. SCOR, 1534th Meeting (Mar. 17, 1970), 17.

20. SCOR, 1534th Meeting (Mar. 17, 1970), 24.

21. Robert Alden, "U.S. Casts a Veto in U.N. on Mideast, Citing Terrorism," *New York Times*, Sept. 11, 1972, A1.

22. M. A. Farber, "U.S. Won't Shun Use of U.N. Veto," *New York Times*, Oct. 15, 1972, 4.

23. Daniel Patrick Moynihan, "The United States in Opposition," *Commentary*, Mar. 1975, 31–44.

24. "New Man at Turtle Bay," *New York Times*, May 3, 1975, 17.

25. Paul Hoffmann, "Moynihan Chides U.N. on Israel Issue," *New York Times*, Dec. 7, 1975, 14.

26. "Moynihan Assails Uganda President," *New York Times*, Oct. 4, 1975, 59.

27. SCOR, 1870th Meeting (Jan. 12, 1976).

28. Finger, *Your Man at the UN*, 244.

29. Seymour Maxwell Finger, *Inside the World of Diplomacy: The U.S. Foreign Service* (Westport, CT: Praeger, 2002), 129.

30. FRUS, 1964–1968, XXXIII:678.

31. Walter Johnson et al., eds., *The Papers of Adlai E. Stevenson*, vol. 8, *Ambassador to the United Nations, 1961–1965* (Boston: Little, Brown, 1979), 119.

32. Quoted in Byron S. Weng, "Communist China's Changing Attitudes toward the United Nations," *International Organization* 20, no. 4 (Autumn 1966), 696–700.

33. See, for example, Thomas W. Robinson, "The Sino-Soviet Border Dispute: Background, Development, and the March 1969 Clashes," *American Political Science Review* 66, no. 4 (Dec. 1972), 1175–1202.

34. "Conversation between President Nixon and National Security Adviser Kissinger, followed by Conversation among Nixon, Kissinger, and U.N. Ambassador George Bush, 30 September 1971," National Archives, Nixon White House Tapes, Conversations 581–1 and 582–2, transcribed by the National Security Project at George Washington University.

35. "Resolutely Oppose the U.S. Scheme of Creating 'Two Chinas'", *People's Daily* (Sept. 25, 1971), reprinted in *Hsinhua Selected News Items* (Hong Kong: Hsinhua News Agency, 1971).

36. Henry Tanner, "Taiwan Warns U.N. Peking Is Peril to It," *New York Times*, Oct. 9, 1971, 1.

37. Quoted in Samuel S. Kim, *China, the United Nations, and World Order* (Princeton, NJ: Princeton University Press, 1979), 133.

38. One of the delegates who danced in the aisles was Tanzania's talented ambassador, Salim Ahmed Salim. Almost a decade later, the United States repeatedly vetoed his candidacy for secretary-general, in part because of this incident. See Urquhart, *A Life in Peace and War*, 331–332.

39. John W. Finney, "Sentiment Developing in Congress to Reduce Financial Support to U.N. Agencies," *New York Times*, Oct. 27, 1971, 16.

40. Tillman Durdin, "Nationalists Determined to Make Best of a 'Tough but Not Irreparable' Situation," *New York Times*, Oct. 28, 1971, 14.

41. Fasulo, *Representing America*, 178.

42. Henry Tanner, "Peking Delegation in U.S.: Greets a 'Great People,'" *New York Times*, Nov. 12, 1971, A1.

43. Memorandum from Winston Lord to Henry A. Kissinger, Nov. 29, 1971, available via the National Security Archives at George Washington University.

44. A concise account of the conflict can be found in Hussain Haqqani, *Pakistan: Between Mosque and Military* (Washington, DC: Carnegie Endowment for International Peace, 2005), 51–86.

45. Henry Tanner, "Bhutto Denounces Council and Walks Out in Tears," *New York Times*, Dec. 16, 1971, A1.

46. SCOR, 1660th Meeting (Aug. 25, 1972), 8.

47. George Bush (with Victor Gold), *Looking Forward* (Garden City, NY: Doubleday, 1987), 118.

48. Fasulo, *Representing America*, 179.

49. SCOR, 1874th Meeting (Jan. 15, 1976), 10.

50. UN Doc. S/PV 1608 (Dec. 6, 1971).

51. SCOR, 1608th Meeting (Dec. 6, 1971), 20.

52. Shevchenko, *Breaking with Moscow*, 253.

53. Henry Kissinger, *Years of Upheaval* (Boston: Little, Brown, 1982), 471–473.

54. Kissinger, *Crisis*, 160.

55. SCOR, 1744th Meeting (Oct. 9, 1973), 11.

56. Robert Alden, "A Soviet Walkout Marks U.N. Debate," *New York Times*, Oct. 10, 1973, 1.

57. Victor Israelyan, *Inside the Kremlin during the Yom Kippur War* (University Park: Pennsylvania State University Press, 1995), 70.

58. For an excellent account of the diplomatic and military developments, see Bailey, *Four Arab-Israeli Wars*, 305–342.

59. Kissinger, *Years of Upheaval*, 557.

60. Interview with John Scali in Fasulo, *Representing America*, 197.

61. Israelyan, *Inside the Kremlin during the Yom Kippur War*, 138.

62. UNSC Resolution 339 (Oct. 23, 1973).

63. Robert Alden, "Security Council to Send Observers to Suez Front," *New York Times*, Oct. 24, 1973, 97.

64. The photo accompanied a *New York Times* story. See Robert Alden, "Security Council to Send Observes to Suez Front," *New York Times*, Oct. 24, 1973, 97.

65. Document available via National Security Archives, George Washington University.

66. See, for example, Walter Isaacson, *Kissinger: A Biography* (Simon & Schuster, 1992), 529–531.

67. Documents via the National Security Archive, George Washington University. A record of the conversation with the French ambassador is available at http://www.gwu.edu/~nsarchiv/NSAEBB/NSAEBB98/octwar-75.pdf. A record of the conversation with the Chinese ambassador is available at http://www.gwu.edu/~nsarchiv/NSAEBB/NSAEBB98/octwar-72.pdf.

68. U.S. Department of State, Memorandum of Conversation between Secretary Kissinger, Ambassador Huang Chen, et al., Oct. 25, 1973. Document available via the National Security Archive, George Washington University.

69. Isaacson, *Kissinger*, 527.

70. "Transcripts of Addresses to the U.N. Assembly by Arafat and Israeli Delegate," *New York Times*, Nov. 14, 1974, 22.

71. UNGA Resolution 3379 (Nov. 10, 1975).

72. SCOR, 1871st Meeting (Jan. 13, 1976), 7.

73. UNSC Resolution 487 (June 19, 1981).

74. SCOR, 1877th Meeting (Jan. 21, 1976), 6.

75. UN Doc. S/PV.2396 (Sept. 19, 1982).

76. Author interview with former UN official (interview conducted on a background basis).

77. SCOR, 1928th Meeting (June 18, 1976), 12.

78. Fasulo, *Representing America*, 173.

79. SCOR, 1873rd Meeting (Jan. 15, 1976), 15.

80. SCOR, 1873rd meeting (Jan. 15, 1976), 14–15.

81. SCOR, 1917th Meeting (May 5, 1976), 6.

82. SCOR, 1922nd meeting (May 26, 1976), 6.

83. SCOR, 2328th meeting (Jan. 14, 1982), 42.

84. SCOR, 2131st meeting (March 19, 1979), 10.

85. UN Doc. S/PV.2355 (Apr. 16, 1982), 21–22.

86. UN Oral History Interview with Abba Eban, Apr. 16, 1990, 55, Yale University.

87. Alan Gerson, *The Kirkpatrick Mission: Diplomacy without Apology* (New York: Free Press, 1991), 160.

88. Janello and Jones, *A Global Affair*, 299.

89. See John M. Goshko, "Glitch in a U.N. Vote May Be Embarrassing in the Short Run, Damaging in the Long Run," *Washington Post*, Mar. 16, 1980, A15.

90. Bernard Nossiter, "2 Palestinians End U.N. Hunger Strike," *New York Times*, Dec. 25, 1980, 4.

91. John Usher, "Lebanese Briefly Occupy Security Council," United Press International, Apr. 7, 1981.

92. Gerson, *The Kirkpatrick Mission*, 136–137.

93. Marrack Goulding, "The UN Secretary-General," in *The UN Security Council: From the Cold War to the 21st Century*, ed. David Malone (Boulder, CO: Rienner, 2004), 275.

94. Author interview with Ambassador Donald McHenry.

95. Author interview with Sir John Thomson.

96. Author interview with former Security Council diplomat (conducted on background basis).

97. Author interview with UN official (conducted on background basis).

98. Brian Urquhart, "International Peace and Security: Thoughts on the Twentieth Anniversary of Dag Hammarskjöld's Death," *Foreign Affairs* (Fall 1981), 14.

99. Kim, *China, the United Nations, and World Order*, 196.

100. Quoted in Kim, *China, the United Nations, and World Order*, 196.

101. Kim, *China, the United Nations, and World Order*, 210.

102. UNSC Resolution 457 (Dec. 4, 1979).

103. Dilip Hiro, *The Longest War: The Iran-Iraq Military Conflict* (New York: Routledge, 1991), 53.

104. Quoted in Shahram Chubin and Charles Tripp, *Iran and Iraq at War* (London: Tauris, 1988), 165.

105. UNSC Resolution 479 (Sept. 28, 1980).

106. Javier Pérez de Cuéllar, *Pilgrimage for Peace* (New York: St. Martin's, 1997), 136.

107. UN Oral History Interview with Sir Anthony Parsons, 45, Yale University.

108. General Assembly Official Records, Supplement No. 1 (Sept. 7, 1982), 1.

109. Seymour Maxwell Finger, "The Reagan-Kirkpatrick Policies and the United Nations," *Foreign Affairs* 62, no. 2 (Winter 1983–1984), 441.

110. The letter is reproduced in Richard L. Jackson, *The Non-Aligned, the UN, and the Superpowers* (New York: Praeger, 1983), 299.

111. Elaine Sciolino, "U.S. Vetoes Resolution on Israel in the U.N.," *New York Times*, Mar. 13, 1985, A3.

112. Kirkpatrick's assertive policy stances accompanied an often gentle personality. Clovis Maksoud, the Arab League's representative to the United Nations, recalled encountering Kirkpatrick at the council at a time when Maksoud's wife was on a hunger strike to protest Israeli policy in Lebanon. "Tell your wife to at least have salt," Kirkpatrick counseled. Author interview with Clovis Maksoud.

113. See Alvin A. Snyder, *Warriors of Disinformation* (New York: Arcade, 1995), 69–71. Snyder subsequently alleged that the videotapes shown to the council omitted important sections that suggested that the Soviet fighter pilots believed that they were tracking a Western spy plane.

114. Security Council Provisional Records, S/PV.2471 (Sept. 6, 1983), 3–18.

115. Mara D. Bellaby, "Soviet Diplomat Oleg Troyanovsky Dies at Age 84," Associated Press, Dec. 22, 2003. There have been different accounts of this episode. For a version that attributes the quip to an American diplomat, see Janello and Jones, *A Global Affair*, 292.

116. After retiring, Troyanovsky complained in his memoirs (published only in Russian) that Soviet diplomacy during the episode was "clumsy." But he also accused the United States of duplicity in its presentation of the Soviet aircraft communications. See Oleg Troyanovsky, *Cherez gody i rasstoyaniya* (Moscow: Vagrius, 1997). (translation for author by Alexandra Kapitanskaya, M.A. candidate, American University).

117. Security Council Provisional Records, S/PV.2471 (Sept. 6, 1983), 7–8.

118. Richard Bernstein, "U.S. Vetoes U.N. Resolution 'Deploring' Grenada Invasion," *New York Times*, Oct. 29, 1983, 1.

119. Associated Press, Oct. 28, 1983.

120. John Usher, "U.S. Isolated Again at United Nations," United Press International, Apr. 3, 1983.

121. Quoted in Edward C. Luck, *Mixed Messages: American Politics and International Organization, 1919–1999* (Washington, DC: Brookings Institution Press, 1999), 64.

122. Report quoted in John Usher, "Blowing an Off-Key U.N. Trumpet," United Press International, July 15, 1984.

123. Thomas M. Franck et al., *An Attitude Survey: Diplomats' Views on the United Nations System* (New York: UNITAR, 1982), 8–14.

124. UN Oral History Interview with Sir Anthony Parsons, 4, Yale University.

125. "U.N. Is Losing Its Attraction for Tourists," *New York Times*, Oct. 10, 1982, 23.

126. Elaine Sciolino, "U.N.'s Internal Conflict: Reality Edging out Vision," *New York Times*, Sept. 23, 1985, A12, quoted in Hume, *The United Nations, Iran, and Iraq*, 54.

Chapter 5

1. "Iranians Shell Basra and Southern Iraq Towns," Associated Press, Dec. 8, 1986.
2. Pérez de Cuéllar, *Pilgrimage for Peace*, 149.
3. Robert Fisk, "Iran Threatens Gulf States with Closure of Hormuz," *Times* (London), Aug. 30, 1986.
4. Quoted in Zubok, *A Failed Empire*, 299.
5. Oral History Interview of Javier Pérez de Cuéllar, Apr. 4, 2002, in the Oral History Collection of the United Nations Intellectual History Project, Graduate Center, City University of New York, 21–22.
6. Bernard Gwertzman, "Peres Meets with Soviet Official; Says They Agreed to Consider Ties," *New York Times*, Sept. 23, 1986, A1.
7. Pérez de Cuéllar, *Pilgrimage for Peace*, 152.
8. Author interview with Sir John Thomson.
9. Sir Crispin Tickell, "The Role of the Security Council in World Affairs," *Georgia Journal of International and Comparative Law* 18, no. 3 (1988), 307, 314.
10. The discussion of the political dynamics surrounding UN diplomacy draws heavily on Hume's account. See Hume, *The United Nations, Iran, and Iraq*, 55–102.
11. *BBC Summary of World Broadcasts*, June 26, 1987.
12. UNSC Resolution 598 (July 20, 1987).
13. "Security Council Calls for Ceasefire in Iran-Iraq Conflict," *U.S. Department of State Bulletin*, Sept. 1987.
14. UN Doc. S/PV.2750 (July 20, 1987), 17.
15. Alan Cowell, "Iraq Is Warm to Truce Call; Iran Is Harsh," *New York Times*, July 22, 1987, A10.
16. "Iran's Rafsanjani Attacks Security Council's 'Liars,'" *BBC Summary of World Broadcasts*, July 27, 1987.
17. Author telephone interview with Ambassador Cameron Hume.
18. UNSC Resolution 644 (Nov. 7, 1989).
19. UNSC Resolutions 629 (Jan. 16, 1989) and 632 (Feb. 16, 1989).
20. Author telephone interview with Sir Christopher Hum.
21. "China Ready to Contribute to Greater Success of U.N. Peace-Keeping Operations," Xinhua General News Service, Oct. 31, 1989. For a broader discussion of China's attitude toward UN peacekeeping, see Yongjin Zhang, "China and UN Peacekeeping: From Condemnation to Participation," *International Peacekeeping* 3, no. 3 (Fall 1996), 1–15.
22. For a succinct discussion of the council's experience with embargoes and sanctions, see Edward C. Luck, *UN Security Council: Practice and Promise* (New York: Routledge, 2006), 58–67.
23. Author interview with Ambassador Thomas Pickering.
24. UNSC Resolution 660 (Aug. 2, 1990).
25. Author interview with Ambassador Thomas Pickering.
26. Margaret Thatcher, *The Downing Street Years* (New York: HarperCollins, 1993), 821.
27. Author interview with Ambassador Thomas Pickering.
28. See UNSC Resolutions 662 (Aug. 9, 1990), 664 (Aug. 18, 1990), 667 (Sept. 16, 1990), and 670 (Sept. 25, 1990).
29. Author interview with Sir Crispin Tickell.

30. Author interview with Ambassador Thomas Pickering.

31. For an excellent description of the sanctions committee's work, see Paul Conlon, *United Nations Sanctions Management: A Case Study of the Iraq Sanctions Committee, 1990–1994* (Ardsley, NY: Transnational, 2000).

32. Terry Leonard, "Iraqi Tanker, Shadowed by U.S. Warship, Reaches Aden," Associated Press, Aug. 22, 1990.

33. For an account of the deliberations surrounding that resolution, see Elaine Sciolino and Eric Pace, "Putting Teeth in an Embargo: How U.S. Convinced the U.N.," *New York Times*, Aug. 30, 1990, A1.

34. Jackson Diehl, "Israeli Police Kill 19 Palestinians in Temple Mount Confrontation," *Washington Post*, Oct. 9, 1990.

35. Author interview with Ambassador Robert Grey.

36. UNSC Resolution 672 (Oct. 12, 1990).

37. Paul Lewis, "U.S. Presses the U.N. to Condemn Israel," *New York Times*, Oct. 10, 1990, A1.

38. UNSC Resolution 673 (Oct. 24, 1990).

39. James A. Baker, *The Politics of Diplomacy* (New York: Putnam's, 1995), 305.

40. Author interview with Ambassador John Bolton.

41. See Arnold Beichman, *The "Other" State Department: The United States Mission to the United Nations* (New York: Basic, 1968), 106–107.

42. See, for example, Fasulo, *Representing America*, 204; Gerson, *The Kirkpatrick Mission*, 110–111.

43. See Thatcher, *Downing Street Years*, 828.

44. Baker, *Politics of Diplomacy*, 315.

45. Ilyana Kuziemko and Eric Werker, "How Much Is a Seat on the Security Council Worth? Foreign Aid and Bribery at the United Nations," *Journal of Political Economy* 114, no. 5 (2006), 907.

46. Baker, *Politics of Diplomacy*, 321.

47. Victoria Graham, "Kuwaiti Refugees Tell Tales of Murder, Torture," Associated Press, Nov. 27, 1990.

48. Thomas L. Friedman and Patrick E. Tyler, "From the First, U.S. Resolve to Fight," *New York Times*, Mar. 3, 1991, A1.

49. Pérez de Cuéllar, *Pilgrimage for Peace*, 250.

50. Security Council Provisional Records, S/PV.2693 (Nov. 29, 1990), 18–38.

51. Baker, *Politics of Diplomacy*, 325–326.

52. Security Council Provisional Records, S/PV.2693 (Nov. 29, 1990), 92.

53. See Chinmaya Gharekhan, *The Horseshoe Table: An Inside View of the UN Security Council* (New Delhi: Dorling Kindersley, 2006), 48.

54. Text of Statement by President Bush, Associated Press, Jan. 16, 1991.

55. John M. Goshko, "U.N. to Hold Private Debate on War," *Washington Post*, Feb. 14, 1991, A34.

56. Deborah Cameron, "Security Council Draws the Curtain," *Sydney Morning Herald*, Feb. 15, 1991, 8.

57. Quoted in Jean E. Krasno and James S. Sutterlin, *The United Nations and Iraq: Defanging the Viper* (Westport, CT: Praeger, 2003), 5.

58. Krasno and Sutterlin, *The United Nations and Iraq*, 19–22.

59. Paul Lewis, "U.N. Votes Stern Conditions for Formally Ending War," *New York Times*, Apr. 4, 1991, A1.

60. Eric Schmitt, "U.N. Deadline to Baghdad Passes, but U.S. Rules Out Attack Soon," *New York Times*, July 26, 1991, A1.

61. R. Jeffrey Smith, "Baghdad Surreptitiously Extracted Plutonium; International Monitoring Apparently Failed," *Washington Post*, Aug. 6, 1991, A11.

62. For a good account of the sanctions regime, see Sarah Graham-Brown, *Sanctioning Saddam: The Politics of Intervention in Iraq* (New York: Tauris, 1999), 56–104.

63. Quoted in Krasno and Sutterlin, *The United Nations and Iraq*, 13.

64. Author interview with Ambassador Alexander Watson.

65. Jonathan Schachter, "The UN's New Image," *Jerusalem Post*, Mar. 8, 1991.

66. George Bush and Jim McGrath, *Heartbeat: George Bush in His Own Words* (New York: Scribner, 2001), 134.

67. Robert Cottrell, "Crisis in the Gulf: Paris Calls for New UN Laws to Help Kurds," *Independent*, Apr. 5, 1991, 10.

68. UNSC Resolution 699 (Apr. 5, 1991).

69. Operation Provide Comfort, as the humanitarian mission was termed, began the next day. American, British, and French cargo planes dropped tons of supplies for Kurdish refugees.

70. Paul Lewis, "The United Nations Comes of Age, Causing Some Anxiety," *New York Times*, Aug. 5, 1990, sec. 4, 3.

71. UNSC Resolution 748 (Mar. 31, 1992).

72. The case is *Questions of Interpretation and Application of the 1971 Montreal Convention Arising from the Aerial Incident at Lockerbie (Libyan Arab Jamahiriya v. United Kingdom)*, Provisional Measures, Order of Apr. 14, 1992, I.C.J. Reports 1992, 3. For a helpful discussion of the case's implications for judicial review of Security Council decisions, see Vera Gowlland-Debbas, "The Relationship between the International Court of Justice and the Security Council in the Light of the Lockerbie Case," *American Journal of International Law* 88, no. 4 (Oct. 1994), 643–677.

73. For a discussion of some of the legal issues raised by the maneuver, see Yehuda Blum, "Russia Takes Over the Soviet Union's Seat at the United Nations," *European Journal of International Law*, no. 3 (1992), 354–361.

74. Author interview with Ambassador Alexander Watson.

75. Paul Lewis, "West Acts to Defer Issue of New U.N. Council Seats," *New York Times*, Jan. 3, 1992, A6.

76. Security Council Provisional Records, S/PV.3046 (Jan. 31, 1992), 2, 18, 46.

77. Author telephone interview with Sir Thomas Richardson.

78. UN Doc. A/47/277, *An Agenda for Peace, Preventive Diplomacy, Peacemaking and Peace-Keeping* (June 17, 1992).

79. Paul Lewis, "U.N. Chief Asks for 1,000-Troop Units," *New York Times*, June 20, 1992, 5.

80. Quoted in Adam Connolly, "UN May Raise Standing Army," *Advertiser*, June 12, 1992.

81. "The New World Cops," *New York Times*, June 28, 1992, E16.

82. For an excellent insider account of these first post–Cold War UN operations, see Marrack Goulding, *Peacemonger* (Baltimore, MD: Johns Hopkins University Press, 2003).

83. See UNSC Resolutions 626 (Dec. 20, 1988) and 696 (May 30, 1991).

84. UNSC Resolution 713 (Sept. 25, 1991).

85. Robert M. Press and Lucia Mouat, "United Nations Takes Lead in Somalia Crisis," *Christian Science Monitor*, Feb. 12, 1992, 6.

86. UNSC Resolution 733 (Jan. 23, 1992).

87. Quoted in Reed Kramer, "Suffering Rises as Civil Strife Persists: New Initiatives to End Wars in Somalia and Mozambique," *Africa News*, July 20, 1992.

88. Paul Lewis, "Reined in by U.S., U.N. Limits Mission to Somalia," *New York Times*, Apr. 26, 1992, 15.

89. Boutros Boutros-Ghali, *Unvanquished: A U.S.-UN Saga* (New York: Random House, 1999), 43.

90. Linda Hossie, "Boutros Ghali, Security Council Locked in Battle," *Globe & Mail*, July 23, 1992.

91. Gharekhan, *The Horseshoe Table*, 25. See also Goulding, *Peacemonger*, 317–318.

92. Gharekhan, *The Horseshoe Table*, 111.

93. Boutros-Ghali, *Unvanquished*, 44.

94. Susan Linnee, "U.N. Chief Jeered on Visit to Sarajevo," Associated Press, Dec. 31, 1992.

95. David B. Ottaway, "The West Watches for the Ripple Effect," *Washington Post*, Dec. 26, 1993, A33.

96. Boutros-Ghali, *Unvanquished*, 55.

97. David Hannay, *New World Disorder: The UN after the Cold War—An Insider's View* (London: Tauris, 2008), 109.

98. Nicholas Morris, former special envoy of the UN High Commissioner for Refugees in the Balkans, quoted in David Rieff, *A Bed for the Night* (New York: Simon & Schuster, 2002), 137.

99. Quoted in Gharekhan, *The Horseshoe Table*, 120–121.

100. Boutros-Ghali, *Unvanquished*, 68.

101. Author interviews with senior U.S. and British diplomats (conducted on background).

102. See Adam LeBor, *Complicity with Evil: The United Nations in the Age of Modern Genocide* (New Haven, CT: Yale University Press, 2006), 30. Marrack Goulding argues that the Austrian and Hungarian ambassadors "brought to the Council a passionate bias which did not help the Council to find a way through the very difficult problems it was to encounter in Bosnia." Goulding, *Peacemonger*, 310.

103. Author interview with Ambassador Robert Grey.

104. Author telephone interview with Ambassador Diego Arria.

105. See Gharekhan, *The Horseshoe Table*, 32.

106. See Bailey and Daws, *The Procedure of the UN Security Council*, 73–74 For perspective on how the Arria-formula meetings have contributed to discourse on the council, see Ian Johnstone, "Security Council Deliberations: The Power of the Better Argument," *European Journal of International Law* 14, no. 3 (June 2003), 460–462.

107. Peter Pringle, "UN Holds Its Fire until the 13th Hour," *Independent*, Apr. 18, 1993.

108. Shashi Tharoor, "Should UN Peacekeeping Go 'Back to Basics'?" *Survival* 37, no. 4 (1995), 60, as quoted in Rupert Smith, *The Utility of Force: The Art of War in the Modern World* (New York: Knopf, 2007), 344.

109. Author telephone interview with Ambassador Diego Arria.

110. Report of the Security Council Mission Established Pursuant to Resolution 819, S/25700 (Apr. 30, 1993), 8.

111. Goulding has argued that Boutros-Ghali's capitulation on this point was a "mistake with disastrous consequences." See Goulding, *Peacemonger*, 290.

112. Mats Berdal, "Bosnia," in Malone, *The UN Security Council*, 455.

113. UNSC Resolution 837 (June 6, 1993).

114. Weekly schedule provided by Norma Chan of the UN Secretariat, Security Council Affairs Division.

Chapter 6

1. See Mark Bowden, *Black Hawk Down: A Story of Modern War* (New York: Penguin, 2000).

2. "Spell It Out to the U.N. on Somalia," *New York Times*, Oct. 6, 1993, A20.

3. Heritage Foundation, "No More Somalias: Reconsidering Clinton's Doctrine of Military Humanitarianism," Backgrounder No. 968, Dec. 20, 1993.

4. See Douglas Farah, "Haitians Block U.S. Troop Arrival; Move Threatens U.N.-Mediated Accord," *Washington Post*, Oct. 12, 1993, A1.

5. "Ghosts of Rwanda," interview with Michael Sheehan, *PBS Frontline*, available at http://www.pbs.org/wgbh/pages/frontline/shows/ghosts/interviews.

6. Romeo Dallaire, *Shake Hands with the Devil: The Failure of Humanity in Rwanda* (Toronto: Random House Canada, 2003), 58.

7. United Nations, *Report of the Independent Inquiry into the Actions of the United Nations during the 1994 Genocide in Rwanda*, Dec. 15, 1999.

8. Gharekhan, *The Horseshoe Table*, 239–240.

9. "Rwanda's War Experience Will Help It Foster Peace Elsewhere: President," Reuters, Oct. 6, 1993.

10. UN Doc. S/PRST/1994/16 (Apr. 7, 1994).

11. Linda Melvern, *A People Betrayed: The Role of the West in Rwanda's Genocide* (New York: Zed, 2000), 141.

12. Quoted in Samantha Power, *"A Problem from Hell": America and the Age of Genocide* (New York: HarperCollins, 2003), 368.

13. See *Report of the Independent Inquiry*, 22. For a searing indictment of the Secretariat's lack of leadership, see Michael Barnett, *Eyewitness to a Genocide: The United Nations and Rwanda* (Ithaca, NY: Cornell University Press, 2003), 118–124.

14. "Ghosts of Rwanda," interview with Brent Beardsley, *PBS Frontline*.

15. It appears that the letter to the editor was published in the *Times* on April 20 under the headline "Don't Write Off Rwandan Violence as Ethnic" and was written by Human Rights Watch, Helsinki, executive director Jeri Laber.

16. Author telephone interview with Ambassador Karel Kovanda.

17. "Ghosts of Rwanda," interview with Alison des Forges, *PBS Frontline*.

18. See Melvern, *A People Betrayed*, 180.

19. Author telephone interview with Ambassador Karel Kovanda.

20. "Ghosts of Rwanda," Sheehan interview, *PBS Frontline*.

21. UNSC Resolution 918 (May 17, 1994).

22. Colin Keating, "Rwanda: An Insider's Account," in Malone, *The UN Security Council*, 509.

23. Hannay, *New World Disorder*, 171.

24. Michael Barnett, quoted in "The Triumph of Evil," *PBS Frontline*, Jan. 26, 1999.

25. See Dallaire, *Shake Hands with the Devil*, 195, 357; Linda Melvern, *Conspiracy to Murder: The Rwandan Genocide* (London: Verso, 2004), 202. In response to written questions from the author, Dallaire contended that Bizimana was aware of the plans for the genocide and was in contact with the regime throughout the crisis.

26. Stewart Stogel, "Rwanda Returns to Nothing at U.N.," *Washington Times*, Aug. 18, 1994, A11. An expert on Rwanda contacted by the author reported that Bizimana might at one point have applied for asylum in the United States, although it has not been possible to confirm this.

27. Author interview with Ambassador Ibrahim Gambari.

28. See UNGA, *Report of the Secretary-General Pursuant to General Assembly Resolution 53/35* (1998), par. 282.

29. "UN Says Security Council Must Decide Srebrenica Is Still 'Safe,'" Deutsche Presse Agentur, July 11, 1995.

30. David Rohde, *Endgame: The Betrayal and Fall of Srebrenica* (Boulder, CO: Westview, 1997), 167.

31. Madeleine Albright, *Madam Secretary* (New York: Miramax, 2003), 188.

32. David Owen, *Balkan Odyssey* (New York: Harcourt Brace, 1995), 396.

33. David Rieff, *Slaughterhouse: Bosnia and the Failure of the West* (New York: Simon & Schuster, 1995), 172.

34. Michael Lind, "Twilight of the U.N.," *New Republic*, Oct. 30, 1995.

35. Sergei Tsekhmistrenko, "Slap In The Face From Partners May Cost Dearly To 'Partnership'," *Russian Press Digest*, Apr. 13, 1994.

36. Julia Preston, "Russia Shows Testy New Assertiveness at U.N.," *Washington Post*, Dec. 29, 1994, A20.

37. Author interview with Sir Jeremy Greenstock.

38. Author interview with Ambassador Richard Ryan.

39. Author interview with Sir Jeremy Greenstock.

40. Lee Michael Katz, "Perry Rejects Dole's Call on Return of Haiti Troops," *USA Today*, Nov. 15, 1994.

41. See Krasno and Sutterlin, *The United Nations and Iraq*, 152–155.

42. Author interview with Ambassador Edward Gnehm.

43. See, for example, Peter van Walsum, "The Iraq Sanctions Committee," in Malone, *The UN Security Council*, 187; Jeffrey A. Meyer and Mark G. Califano, *Good Intentions Corrupted: The Oil-for-Food Scandal and the Threat to the U.N.* (New York: Public Affairs, 2006), 177.

44. Meyer and Califano, *Good Intentions Corrupted*, 150–164.

45. UNSC Resolution 986 (Apr. 14, 1995).

46. Meyer and Califano, *Good Intentions Corrupted*, 150–164.

47. See, for example, Thomas W. Lippman, *Madeleine Albright and the New American Diplomacy* (Boulder, CO: Westview, 2000), 24–28.

48. Richard Clarke, *Against All Enemies: Inside America's War on Terror* (New York: Free Press, 2004), 201–202.

49. Boutros-Ghali, *Unvanquished*, 270.

50. Quoted in David Usborne, "US Defies the World to Block Boutros-Ghali," *Independent*, Nov. 19, 1996.

51. Author interviews with former Security Council diplomats (conducted on a background basis).

52. Author interview with Sir John Weston.

53. Zainul Arifin, "France Loses Vote but Wins Big in UN," *New Straits Times*, Dec. 16, 1996.

54. "Razali—Man of the Hour—Takes Up His Final Test," *New Straits Times*, Sept. 18, 1996, 12.

55. Eric Weiner, "India Lobbies for Permanent Seat in UN Security Council," *Christian Science Monitor*, Oct. 3, 1994, 2.

56. James Bone, "German UN Claim Unsettles Britain," *Times* (London), Sept. 26, 1992.

57. Barbara Crossette, "At the U.N., a Drive for Diversity," *New York Times*, Oct. 24, 1994, 6.

58. Annika Savill, "Inside File: Brazil's Fancy Footwork May All Be in Vain," *Independent*, July 21, 1994, 13.

59. For a superb discussion of how the council's legitimacy should be analyzed and assessed, see Hurd, *After Anarchy*.

60. Quoted in Dimitris Bourantonis, *The History and Politics of UN Security Council Reform* (New York: Routledge, 2005), 36.

61. Paul Lewis, "U.S. to Push Germany and Japan for U.N. Council," *New York Times*, June 13, 1993, 5.

62. Author interview with Ambassador Edward Gnehm. Madeleine Albright also recounted the exchange. See Albright, "Think Again: United Nations," *Foreign Policy*, Sept.–Oct. 2003.

63. Paul Lewis, "U.N. Panel Proposes Expanding Security Council to 24 Members," *New York Times*, Mar. 21, 1997, A13.

64. Anne Penketh, "UN Security Council Reform Deadlocked on Numbers, Veto," Agence France Press, Sept. 15, 1997.

65. BBC Texts and Transcripts, "'A Sad Day:' Full Text of Annan Iraq Statement," Dec. 17, 1998.

66. James Traub, *The Best Intentions: Kofi Annan and the UN in the Era of American World Power* (New York: Farrar, Straus and Giroux, 2006), 85.

67. SCOR, 3955th Meeting (Dec. 16, 1998).

68. Judith Miller, "Security Council Relegated to Sidelines," *New York Times*, Mar. 14, 1999, 14.

69. Quoted in Tim Judah, *Kosovo: War and Revenge* (New Haven, CT: Yale University Press, 2002), 183.

70. See Ian Black, "War in Europe: Allies Argue a Humanitarian Case for Action," *Guardian*, Mar. 25, 1999, 4. A good summary of NATO's struggles on the question of legality is in Catherine Guicherd, "International Law and the War in Kosovo," *Survival* 41, no. 2 (Summer 1999), 19–34.

71. BBC Monitoring Europe, Oct. 3, 1998.

72. PBS, *NewsHour*, May 25, 1999, available at http://www.pbs.org/newshour/bb/europe/jan-june99/fischer_5-25.html.

73. Quoted in Ivo H. Daalder and Michael E. O'Hanlon, *Winning Ugly: NATO's War to Save Kosovo* (Washington, DC: Brookings Institution Press, 2000), 44.

74. Mike Blanchfield, "Axworthy: Veto Provision 'Gets in the Way,'" *Ottawa Citizen*, Mar. 29, 1999, A3.

75. Strobe Talbott, a key figure in the diplomacy with Russia at this stage, reported both of these exchanges in his book *The Russia Hand* (New York: Random House, 2002), 306, 311.

76. Barbara Slavin, "Albright Tries to Mend Relationship with Russia Leaders to Seek Diplomatic 'Common Ground,'" *USA Today*, Apr. 13, 1999, 5A.

77. Author telephone interview with Ambassador Paul Heinbecker.

78. Paul Koring, "Russia and NATO Close in on Kosovo Deal," *Globe & Mail*, May 6, 1999, A1.

79. Ian Black and Ian Traynor, "Russia Agrees Peace Deal; Kosovo Pact Goes to UN but Gaps Remain," *Guardian*, May 7, 1999.

80. "Security Council Talks Will Not Be Rubber Stamp: China," Agence France Presse, June 8, 1999.

81. Boris Yeltsin, *Midnight Diaries* (New York: Public Affairs, 2000), 265.

82. "Middle East UN Official Blasts Iraq Sanctions," *BBC Online,* http://news.bbc.co.uk/2/hi/middle_east/183499.stm, Sept. 30, 1998.

83. See, for example, Charles Bremner, "Envoys admit taking Iraqi oil payoffs," *Times* (London), Oct. 14, 2005, 50.

84. Van Walsum, "The Iraq Sanctions Committee," in Malone, *The UN Security Council*, 191.

Chapter 7

1. Author telephone interview with Ambassador Andrés Franco.

2. UN Press Release 7141 (Sept. 11, 2001).

3. Author interview with Andrés Franco.

4. UNSC Resolution 1368 (Sept. 12, 2001).

5. Author interview with senior French official (conducted on background basis).

6. Nicholas Kralev, "China, Iran Seek U.N. Role in Retaliation," *Washington Times*, Sept. 19, 2001, A1.

7. Anton La Guardia, "Putin and Chirac Suggest That UN Leads the Allies," *Daily Telegraph*, Sept. 21, 2001, 13.

8. UNSC Resolution 1373 (Sept. 28, 2001).

9. David Malone, *The International Struggle over Iraq: Politics in the UN Security Council, 1980–2005* (New York: Oxford University Press, 2006), 186.

10. The U.S. delegation attempted to include language in the resolution about "bringing justice to the terrorists," an echoing of President Bush's speech to Congress. According to Ambassador Richard Ryan, the Irish delegation opposed the formulation, and it was eventually changed to "bringing terrorists to justice."

11. Author telephone interview with Andrés Franco.

12. "United States Officially Informs United Nations of Strikes," *Washington Times*, Oct. 9, 2001, A14.

13. Interview with Ambassador Richard Ryan.

14. UN Press Release, AFG/152, SC/7167 (Oct. 10, 2001).

15. Colum Lynch, "Extraordinary Security Greets U.N. Delegates," *Washington Post*, Nov. 11, 2001, A22.

16. James Bone, "Straw Stranded as UN Locks Doors," *Times* (London), Nov. 13, 2002.

17. UNSC Resolution 1405 (Apr. 19, 2002).

18. The UN undersecretary, General Hans Corell, as quoted in Gerald Nadler, "World's First Permanent War Crimes Court to Come into Force July 1 Despite U.S. Opposition," *Associated Press*, Apr. 11, 2002.

19. The UN Special Rapporteur for the Independence of the Judiciary, Param Cumaraswamy, quoted in "UN Forfeiting International Leadership with ICC Withdrawal: UN Expert," *Agence France Presse*, May 8, 2002.

20. Serge Schmemann, "U.S. Links Peacekeeping to Immunity from New Court," *New York Times*, June 19, 2002, 3.

21. Serge Schmemann, "U.S. Vetoes Bosnia Mission, Then Allows 3-Day Reprieve," *New York Times*, July 1, 2002, A3.

22. John Ibbitson, "Canada Condemns World Court Compromise," *Globe & Mail*, July 13, 2002, A11.

23. Patrick Smyth, "UN Mandates Renewed after Compromise on US Troops," *Irish Times*, July 15, 2002, 9.

24. "The Ugly American Again," *Japan Times*, July 10, 2002.

25. President's State of the Union Speech, Jan. 29, 2002.

26. White House, Office of the Press Secretary, "Vice President Speaks at VFW 103rd National Convention," Aug. 26, 2002.

27. Glenn Kessler, "Powell Treads Carefully on Iraq Strategy; Weapons Inspection Urged before Action," *Washington Post*, Sept. 2, 2002, A1.

28. Tony Blair speech to the Labour Party Conference, Oct. 1, 2001.

29. Bob Woodward, *Plan of Attack* (New York: Simon & Schuster, 2005), 183–184.

30. Julia Preston and Todd S. Purdum, "U.N. Inspectors Can Return Unconditionally, Iraq Says," *New York Times*, Sept. 17, 2002, A1.

31. Julian Borger and Ian Traynor, "Bush Sets the War Clock Ticking," *Guardian*, Sept. 13, 2002, 1.

32. Todd S. Purdum and Elisabeth Bumiller, "Bush Seeks Power to Use 'All Means' to Oust Hussein," *New York Times*, Sept. 20, 2002, A1.

33. Fraser Nelson, "Straw: Britain Does Not Need UN Approval," *Scotsman*, Sept. 26, 2002, 1.

34. George Will, "Stuck to the U.N. Tar Baby," *Washington Post*, Sept. 19, 2002, A27.

35. Robert Schlesinger, "Lawmakers Eye Narrowing of Iraq Resolution," *Boston Globe*, Sept. 23, 2002, A1.

36. Anton La Guardia, "Powell Confident of Ultimatum to Iraq within Days," *Telegraph*, Sept. 17, 2002.

37. Julia Preston and Todd S. Purdum, "U.N. Inspectors Can Return Unconditionally, Iraq Says," *New York Times*, Sept. 17, 2002, A1.

38. Author interview with French Foreign Ministry official (conducted on background basis).

39. Hans Blix, *Disarming Iraq* (New York: Pantheon, 2004), 89.

40. "UN Resolutions a Chance for Iraq to Disarm in Peace: Chirac," *Agence France Press*, Nov. 8, 2002.

41. Author interview with Ambassador John Negroponte.

42. Author telephone interview with Ambassador Andrés Franco.

43. Edith Lederer, "Facing U.N. Criticism, U.S. Defends Deal to Take Possession of Iraq's Weapons Declaration," *Associated Press*, Dec. 11, 2002.

44. Woodward, *Plan of Attack*, 249.

45. George Tenet, *At the Center of the Storm: My Years at the CIA* (New York: HarperCollins, 2007), 361.

46. Quoted in Malone, *International Struggle over Iraq*, 196.

47. Elaine Sciolino, "UN Inspectors to Ask for More Time in Iraq; In Rebuff to U.S., Chirac Supports Move," *International Herald Tribune*, Jan. 18, 2003, 4.

48. Author interview with Ambassador Jean-Marc de la Sablière.

49. Joe Lauria, "U.S. on Collision Course with Security Council over Iraq Action," *Gazette*, Jan. 21, 2003, A18.

50. Author interview with Ambassador Marc Grossman.

51. James Bone, Richard Beeston, and Charles Bremner, "Germany Blocks the Road to War," *Times* (London), Jan. 23, 2003, 1.

52. Author interview with former U.S. State Department official (conducted on background basis).

53. *Age*, Jan. 31, 2003.

54. SCOR, 4692nd meeting (Jan. 27, 2003), 3, 12.

55. Woodward, *Plan of Attack*, 291.

56. Author interview with Ambassador John Negroponte.

57. Author interviews with Colonel Lawrence Wilkerson and former senior State Department officials (conducted on background basis). Drawing in part on conversations with Wilkerson, journalist Karen DeYoung provides a vivid account of the preparation for the speech in her excellent biography of Powell, *Soldier: The Life of Colin Powell* (New York: Knopf, 2006).

58. Tenet, *At the Center of the Storm*, 375.

59. Author interviews with Colonel Lawrence Wilkerson and a senior State Department official (conducted on background basis).

60. For different views of the *Guernica* "cover-up," see David Cohen, "Hidden Treasure: What's So Controversial about Picasso's *Guernica*?" *Slate*, Feb. 6, 2003, http://www.slate.com/id/2078242/; Claudia Winkler, "The 'Guernica' Myth," *Weekly Standard* online, Apr. 16, 2003, http://www.weeklystandard.com/Content/Public/Articles/000/000/002/556paocc.asp.

61. UN Doc. S/PV.4701 (Feb. 5, 2003), 17.

62. Author interview with senior State Department official (conducted on background basis).

63. "Irrefutable," *Washington Post*, Feb. 6, 2003, A36.

64. "The Case against Iraq," *New York Times*, Feb. 6, 2003, 38.

65. Author telephone interview with Ambassador Stefan Tafrov.

66. Author telephone interviews with Ambassador Jean-Marc de la Sablière and Ambassador Gunter Pleuger.

67. Author telephone interview with Ambassador Juan Gabriel Valdés.

68. Andrew Buncombe, "Rumsfeld Condemned for Insulting Germans during Fence-Mending Jaunt into 'Old Europe,'" *Independent*, Feb. 10, 2003.

69. Julian Coman and David Wastell, "The Parting of the Ways," *Sunday Telegraph*, Feb. 16, 2003, 18.

70. Author telephone interview with Ambassador Stefan Tafrov.

71. Author telephone interview with Ambassador Jean-Marc de la Sablière.

72. SCOR, 4707th Meeting (Feb. 14, 2003), 13.

73. Author telephone interview with Ambassador Stefan Tafrov.

74. Bill Sammon, "Bush Urges U.N. to Show 'Backbone,'" *Washington Times*, Feb. 14, 2003, A1.

75. "We've Made a Good Start, but We've Not Been Bold Enough," *Daily Telegraph*, Oct. 2, 2002, 10.

76. Author telephone interview with Ambassador Juan Gabriel Valdés.

77. Interview with Ambassador Juan Gabriel Valdés.

78. "U.S.-British Draft Resolution Stating Position on Iraq," *New York Times*, Feb. 25, 2003, A14.

79. Elaine Sciolino, "France and Germany Call for Long Inspections," *New York Times*, Feb. 25, 2003, A14.

80. United Nations, Doc. S/PV.4714 (Mar. 7, 2003).

81. Marcus Warren and Robin Gedye, "Straw Takes War to the French in Vitriolic U.N. Tirade," *Daily Telegraph*, March 8, 2003, 5.

82. This exchange was reported by Julian Coman, "The Blunt Response of Britain's UN Ambassador . . . ," *Sunday Telegraph*, Mar. 16, 2003, 19. Jeremy Greenstock confirmed the account in an interview with the author.

83. Peter Stothard, *Thirty Days: Tony Blair and the Test of History* (New York: HarperCollins, 2003), 41.

84. Author interview with Ambassador John Negroponte.

85. Author interview with senior French official (conducted on background basis).

86. Author interview with Ambassador Gunter Pleuger.

87. Author interview with Ambassador Juan Gabriel Valdés.

88. Richard Wolffe and Tamara Lipper, "Powell in the Bunker," *Newsweek*, Mar. 24, 2003, 30.

89. Martin Bright, Ed Vulliamy, and Peter Beaumont, "Revealed: US Dirty Tricks to Win Vote on Iraq War," *Observer*, Mar. 2, 2003, 1.

90. Quoted in Colum Lynch, "Spying Report No Surprise to U.N.," *Washington Post*, March 4, 2003, A17.

91. Author interview with Ambassador Gunter Pleuger.

92. Heraldo Munoz, *A Solitary War: A Diplomat's Chronicle of the Iraq War* (Golden, CO: Fulcrum, 2008), 57–58.

93. Author telephone interview with Ambassador Juan Gabriel Valdés.

94. Richard Perle, "Thank God for the Death of the United Nations," *Guardian*, Mar. 21, 2003.

95. Andrei Zolotov, Jr., "Ivanov Plays Down Differences on Iraq," *Moscow Times*, May 13, 2003.

96. Jon Smith, "UN Resolution Marks a 'Good Day for Iraqis,'" *Birmingham Post*, May 23, 2003.

97. "Interview with Sir Kieran Prendergast, Former UN Under-Secretary General for Political Affairs," *Fletcher Forum of World Affairs* 30, no. 1 (Winter 2006), 66.

98. The journalist and scholar Samantha Power has written a remarkable biography of Sergio Vieira de Mello. See *Chasing the Flame: Sergio Vieira de Mello and the Fight to Save the World* (New York: Penguin, 2008).

99. Edward Simpkins, "Where Are Iraq's Missing Oil Billions?" *Sunday Telegraph*, May 18, 2003, 8.

100. Secretary-General, Address to the General Assembly, Sept. 23, 2003.

101. See Christine Ollivier, "Bush, Chirac Find Common Ground in Haiti," Associated Press, Mar. 3, 2004; Antonio Rodriguez, "Iraq War Foes Align with U.S. on Haiti," Agence France Presse, Mar. 6, 2004.

102. Author telephone interview with Ambassador Paul Heinbecker.

103. Traub, *The Best Intentions*, 313–314.

104. Warren Hoge, "United Nations: Bolton's 'Discipline' Is Rejected," *New York Times*, Feb. 3, 2006, A8.

105. Author interview with Ambassador John Bolton.

106. "Some wayward stranger from another planet, doing a content analysis of the annual UN debate on the state of the world," one scholar has written, "could easily take sovereignty as a quintessentially Chinese idea." Samuel S. Kim, "Sovereignty in the Chinese Image of World Order," in *Essays in Honour of Wang Tieya*, ed. Ronald St. John Macdonald (Dordrecht: Martinus Nijhoff, 1994), 428.

107. Author interview with Ambassador John Bolton.

108. UNSC Resolution 1718 (Oct. 14, 2006).

109. John Bolton, *Surrender Is Not an Option: Defending America at the United Nations and Abroad* (New York: Threshold, 2007), 309.

Conclusion

1. Cameron Brown, et al., "Rudolph W. Giuliani's Speech at the Republican National Convention," *New York Times*, Sept. 3, 2008.

2. E-mail correspondence from Ambassador Jean-Marc de la Sablière.

3. Author telephone interview with Ambassador Gunter Pleuger.

4. E-mail correspondence from Ambassador John Sawers.

5. Calculations based on the list of travels by U.S. Secretaries of State compiled by the Office of the Historian, U.S. State Department, available at http://www.state.gov/r/pa/ho/trvl/c7388.htm. Travels for multilateral conferences and private visits were excluded from the tabulation.

6. Curiously, the permanent members that are least enthusiastic about reviving the Military Staff Committee are those that are, in many respects, most inclined to develop the council as an institution: Britain and France. Because these countries have secured for their nationals important positions in the UN Secretariat—a French citizen heads the peacekeeping department and a British official normally leads the United Nations' Department of Political Affairs—they may be uncomfortable with granting a body outside the Secretariat a greater role. For a concise argument in favor of activating the Military Staff Committee, see Abraham D. Sofaer, "International Security and the Use of Force," in *Progress in International Law*, ed. Russell Miller and Rebecca Bratspies (Leiden: Martinus Nijhoff, 2008), 552–554.

7. Inis L. Claude, Jr., *Swords into Plowshares: The Problems and Progress of International Organization* (New York: Random House, 1956), 94.

8. Robert Kagan, "Of Power and Weakness," *Policy Review*, June–July 2002, 3.

9. British Diplomatic Oral History Project, Interview with Sir David Hannay, July 22, 1999, conducted by Malcolm McBain.

10. Prime Minister's Personal Minute, quoted in Martin Gilbert, *Road to Victory: Winston S. Churchill, 1941–1945* (London: Heinemann, 1986), 1170.

SOURCES AND
FURTHER READING

FOR GOOD REASONS and less good ones, this book has an American and British tilt. In part, this focus reflects the importance of the United States and the United Kingdom on the council. These two states forged the council, and, at many key moments in its history, U.S. and British diplomats have assembled coalitions and drafted key resolutions. But this tilt is also the product of the raw materials available for research. The British and U.S. archives tend to be more complete and accessible than the Russian and Chinese archives, in particular. My language limitations have narrowed the scope of my research; many French, Russian, and Chinese documents, memoirs, and diaries have not been translated. I have tried to compensate by relying on secondary materials. In researching this book's more contemporary chapters, I have interviewed diplomats and observers from the permanent members and from many of the states that have served on the Security Council as elected members. Their insights have provided important perspectives on the council's deliberations.

In my research, I benefited from a number of excellent existing works on the Security Council. The indispensable volume on the procedure of the council is Sydney Bailey and Sam Daws, *The Procedure of the UN Security Council,* now in its third edition. The Canadian diplomat and scholar David Malone has produced several outstanding books on the council, including an edited volume that includes firsthand accounts from council diplomats. The best short work on the council is by Columbia University's Edward Luck and is part of the Routledge series on international institutions. Ian Hurd has explored the important issue of the council's legitimacy, most fully in *After Anarchy.* French diplomat Pascal Teixeira assessed the council's ability to meet contemporary challenges in *The Security Council at the*

Dawn of the 21st Century. More than three decades ago, the journalist Andrew Boyd wrote an engaging history of the Security Council, *Fifteen Men on a Powder Keg*.

Articles

Accinelli, Robert D. Pro-U.N. Internationalists and the Early Cold War: The American Association for the United Nations and U.S. Foreign Policy, 1947–1952. *Diplomatic History* 9, no. 4 (Fall 1985), 347–362.

Albright, Madeleine. Think Again: United Nations. *Foreign Policy*, Sept.–Oct. 2003, 16–24.

Bailey, Sydney D. New Light on Abstentions in the U.N. Security Council. *International Affairs* 50, no. 4 (Oct. 1974), 554–573.

Ben, Philip. U Thant and the Cuban Crisis. *New Republic* 147, no. 20 (Nov. 17, 1962), 6–7.

Blum, Yehuda. Russia Takes Over the Soviet Union's Seat at the United Nations. *European Journal of International Law* 3, no. 2 (1992), 354–362.

Boyle, Peter G. The Hungarian Revolution and the Suez Crisis. *History* 90, no. 300 (Oct. 2005), 550–565.

Chace, James. Sharing the Atom Bomb. *Foreign Affairs* 75, no. 4 (Jan.–Feb. 1996), 129–144.

Cohen, David. Hidden Treasures: What's So Controversial about Picasso's *Guernica? Slate*, http://www.slate.com/id/2078242/, Feb. 6, 2003.

Daws, Sam. Seeking Seats, Votes and Vetoes. *World Today* 53, no. 10 (Oct. 1997), 256–259.

Emerson, Rupert, and Inis Claude. The Soviet Union and the United Nations: An Essay in Interpretation. *International Organization* 6, no. 1 (Feb. 1952), 1–26.

Finger, Seymour Maxwell. The Reagan-Kirkpatrick Policies and the United Nations. *Foreign Affairs* 62, no. 2 (Winter 1983–1984), 436–457.

Gardner, Richard N. The Soviet Union and the United Nations. *Law and Contemporary Problems* 29, no. 4 (Autumn 1964), 845–857.

Gill, Brendan. Black Sheep. *New Yorker*, Apr. 13, 1946, 23–24.

Gowlland-Debbas, Vera. The Relationship between the International Court of Justice and the Security Council in the Light of the Lockerbie Case. *American Journal of International Law* 88, no. 4 (Oct. 1994), 643–677.

Guicherd, Catherine. International Law and the War in Kosovo. *Survival* 41, no. 2 (Summer 1999), 19–33.

Hurd, Ian. Legitimacy and Authority in International Politics. *International Organization* 53, no. 2 (Spring 1999), 379–408.

———. Legitimacy, Power, and the Symbolic Life of the UN Security Council. *Global Governance* 8, no. 1 (2002), 35–51.

Iglauer, Edith. The UN Builds Its Home. *Harper's Magazine* (Dec. 1947), 562–572.

Jessup, Philip C. Park Avenue Diplomacy—Ending the Berlin Blockade. *Political Science Quarterly* 87, no. 3 (Sept. 1972), 377–400.

Johnstone, Ian. Security Council Deliberations: The Power of the Better Argument. *European Journal of International Law* 14, no. 3 (June 2003), 437–480.

Kagan, Robert. Of Power and Weakness. *Policy Review*, no. 113 (June–July 2002), 1–19.

Kaufman, Victor S. Chirep: The Anglo-American Dispute over Chinese Representation in the United Nations, 1950–1971. *English Historical Review* 115, no. 461 (Apr. 2000), 354–377.

Kupchan, Charles A., and Clifford A. Kupchan. Concerts, Collective Security, and Europe. *International Security* 16, no. 1 (Summer 1991), 114–161.

Kuziemko, Ilyana, and Eric Werker. How Much Is a Seat on the Security Council Worth? Foreign Aid and Bribery at the United Nations. *Journal of Political Economy* 114, no. 5 (2006), 905–930.

Meyer, Cord. Peace Is Still Possible. *Atlantic Monthly* 170, no. 4 (Oct. 1947), 33–39.

Mires, Charlene. The Lure of New England and the Search for the Capitol of the World. *New England Quarterly* 79, no. 1 (Mar. 2006), 37–64.

Montgomery, Edward. United Nations: East and West. *New Republic* (Apr. 1946).

Moynihan, Daniel Patrick. The United States in Opposition. *Commentary* 59, no. 3 (Mar. 1975), 31–44.

Padelford, Norman J. Financing Peacekeeping: Politics and Crisis. *International Organization* 19, no. 3 (Summer 1965), 444–462.

Reston, James B. Votes and Vetoes. *Foreign Affairs* 25, no. 1 (Oct. 1946), 13–22.

Robinson, Thomas W. The Sino-Soviet Border Dispute: Background, Development, and the March 1969 Clashes. *American Political Science Review* 66, no. 4 (Dec. 1972), 1175–1202.

Rosand, Eric. Security Council Resolution 1373, the Counter-Terrorism Committee, and the Fight against Terrorism. *American Journal of International Law* 97, no. 2 (Apr. 2003), 333–341.

———. The Security Council's Efforts to Monitor the Implementation of Al Qaeda/Taliban Sanctions. *American Journal of International Law* 98, no. 4 (Oct. 2004), 745–763.

Rosecrance, Richard. A New Concert of Powers. *Foreign Affairs* 71, no. 2 (Spring 1992), 64–82.

Shaw, L. G. Attitudes of the British Political Elite towards the Soviet Union. *Diplomacy & Statecraft* 13, no. 1 (Mar. 2002), 55–74.

Szasz, Paul C. The Security Council Starts Legislating. *American Journal of International Law* 96, no. 4 (Oct. 2002), 901–905.

Tharoor, Shashi. Should UN Peacekeeping Go "Back to Basics"? *Survival* 37, no. 4 (1995), 52–64.

Tickell, Crispin. The Role of the Security Council in World Affairs. *Georgia Journal of International and Comparative Law* 18, no. 3 (Winter 1988), 307–317.

Todd, James E. An Analysis of Security Council Voting Behavior. *Western Political Quarterly* 22, no. 1 (Mar. 1969), 61–78.

Urquhart, Brian. International Peace and Security: Thoughts on the Twentieth Anniversary of Dag Hammarskjöld's Death. *Foreign Affairs* 60, no. 1 (Fall 1981), 1–16.

Voeten, Erik. The Political Origins of the UN Security Council's Ability to Legitimize the Use of Force. *International Organization* 59, no. 3 (Summer 2005), 527–557.

Webster, Charles K. The Making of the Charter of the United Nations. *History* 32, no. 115 (Mar. 1947), 15–35.

Weiss, Thomas G. The Illusion of Security Council Reform. *Washington Quarterly* 26, no. 4 (Autumn 2003), 147–161.

Weng, Byron S. Communist China's Changing Attitudes toward the United Nations. *International Organization* 20, no. 4 (Autumn 1966), 677–704.

Winkler, Claudia. The "Guernica" Myth. *Weekly Standard* online, http://www.weeklystandard.com/Content/Public/Articles/000/000/002/556paocc.asp, Apr. 16, 2003.

Zhang, Yongjin. China and UN Peacekeeping: From Condemnation to Participation. *International Peacekeeping* 3, no. 3 (Fall 1996), 1–15.

Books and Reports

Acheson, Dean. *Present at the Creation: My Years in the State Department.* New York: Norton, 1969.
———. *The Korean War.* New York: Norton, 1971.

Aglion, Raoul. *Roosevelt and de Gaulle: Allies in Conflict.* New York: Free Press, 1988.

Albright, Madeleine. *Madam Secretary.* New York: Miramax, 2003.

Allison, Graham T. *Essence of Decision: Explaining the Cuban Missile Crisis.* Boston: Little, Brown, 1971.

Baker, James A. (with Thomas M. DeFrank). *The Politics of Diplomacy: Revolution, War, and Peace, 1989–1992.* New York: Putnam's, 1995.

Bailey, Sydney D. *The Making of Resolution 242.* Dordrecht: Martinus Nijhoff, 1985.
———. *Four Arab-Israeli Wars and the Peace Process.* New York: St. Martin's, 1990.

Bailey, Sydney, and Sam Daws. *The Procedure of the UN Security Council.* Oxford: Oxford University Press, 1998.

Ball, George. *The Past Has Another Pattern.* New York: Norton, 1982.

Beichman, Arnold. *The "Other" State Department: The United States Mission to the United Nations.* New York: Basic, 1968.

Bellamy, Alex J. *Kosovo and International Society.* New York: Palgrave, 2002.

Beschloss, Michael. *Mayday: Eisenhower, Khrushchev, and the U-2 Affair.* New York: Harper & Row, 1986.

Black, Allida, ed. *The Eleanor Roosevelt Papers, vol. 1, The Human Rights Years, 1945–1948.* New York: Thomson Gale, 2007.

Blix, Hans. *Disarming Iraq.* New York: Pantheon, 2004.

Bohlen, Charles E. *Witness to History.* New York: Norton, 1973.

Bolton, John. *Surrender Is Not an Option: Defending America at the United Nations and Abroad.* New York: Threshold, 2007.

Bourantonis, Dimitris. *The History and Politics of UN Security Council Reform.* New York: Routledge, 2005.

Boutros-Ghali, Boutros. *Unvanquished.* New York: Random House, 1999.

Boyd, Andrew. *Fifteen Men on a Powder Keg.* New York: Stein and Day, 1971.

Boyle, Peter G., ed. *The Eden-Eisenhower Correspondence, 1955–1957.* Chapel Hill: University of North Carolina Press, 2005.

Brugioni, Dino A. *Eyeball to Eyeball: The Inside Story of the Cuban Missile Crisis,* edited by Robert F. McCort. New York: Random House, 1991.

Buhite, Russell D., and David W. Levy. *FDR's Fireside Chats.* Norman: University of Oklahoma Press, 1992.

Bullock, Alan. *Ernest Bevin: Foreign Secretary, 1945–1951.* New York: Norton, 1983.

Bush, George (with Victor Gold). *Looking Forward.* Garden City, NY: Doubleday, 1987.

Bush, George, and Jim McGrath. *Heartbeat: George Bush in His Own Words.* New York: Scribner, 2001.

Butler, Richard. *The Greatest Threat.* New York: Public Affairs, 2000.

Campbell, Thomas M., and George C. Herring, eds. *The Diaries of Edward R. Stettinius, Jr., 1943–1946.* New York: New Viewpoints, 1975.

Carr, E. H. *The Twenty Years' Crisis, 1919–1939.* New York: Harper & Row, 1964.

Central Intelligence Agency. *Operation PBSuccess: The United States and Guatemala, 1952–1954,* available via the National Security Archives, George Washington University, http://www.gwu.edu/~nsarchiv/NSAEBB/NSAEBB4/cia-guatemala5_a.html.

Chapnick, Adam. *The Middle Power Project: Canada and the Founding of the United Nations.* Vancouver: University of British Columbia Press, 2005.

Chubin, Shahram, and Charles Tripp. *Iran and Iraq at War.* London: Tauris, 1988.

Clarke, Richard. *Against All Enemies: Inside America's War on Terror.* New York: Free Press, 2004.

Clemens, Diane. *Yalta.* New York: Oxford University Press, 1970.

Cleveland, Harlan. *The Obligations of Power: American Diplomacy in the Search for Peace.* New York: Harper & Row, 1966.

Conlon, Paul. *United Nations Sanctions Management: A Case Study of the Iraq Sanctions Committee, 1990–1994.* Ardsley, NY: Transnational, 2000.

Connally, Tom. *My Name Is Tom Connally.* New York: Crowell, 1954.

Cordier, Andrew W., and Wilder Foote, eds. *Public Papers of the Secretaries-General of the United Nations.* New York: Columbia University Press, 1978.

Craft, Stephen G. *V. K. Wellington Koo and the Emergence of Modern China.* Lexington: University Press of Kentucky, 2004.

Craig, Gordon A., and Francis L. Loewenheim, eds. *The Diplomats.* Princeton, NJ: Princeton University Press, 1994.

Daalder, Ivo H., and Michael E. O'Hanlon. *Winning Ugly: NATO's War to Save Kosovo.* Washington, DC: Brookings Institution Press, 2000.

Dallaire, Romeo. *Shake Hands with the Devil: The Failure of Humanity in Rwanda.* Toronto: Random House Canada, 2003.

Dallin, Alexander. *The Soviet Union at the United Nations: An Inquiry into Soviet Motives and Objectives.* Westport, CT: Greenwood, 1976.

Darwin, John. *Britain and Decolonisation: The Retreat from Empire in the Post-War World.* New York: St. Martin's, 1988.

De Cuellar, Javier Perez. *Pilgrimage for Peace: A Secretary General's Memoir.* New York: St. Martin's, 1997.

De Gaulle, Charles. *Major Addresses, Statements, and Press Conferences of General Charles de Gaulle.* New York: French Embassy, 1964.

———. *Memoirs of Hope: Renewal and Endeavor,* translated by Terence Kilmartin. New York: Simon & Schuster, 1971.

De Porte, A. W. *De Gaulle's Foreign Policy, 1944–1946.* Cambridge, MA: Harvard University Press, 1968.

DeYoung, Karen. *Soldier: The Life of Colin Powell.* New York: Knopf, 2006.

Dilks, David, ed. *The Diaries of Sir Alexander Cadogan, O.M., 1938–1945.* New York: Putnam, 1972.

Dixon, Piers. *Double Diploma: The Life of Sir Pierson Dixon.* London: Hutchinson, 1968.

Dobbs, Michael. *One Minute to Midnight: Kennedy, Khrushchev, and Castro on the Brink of Nuclear War.* New York: Knopf, 2008.

Dobrynin, Anatoly. *In Confidence.* New York: Times Books, 1995.

Dudley, George A. *A Workshop for Peace: Designing the United Nations Headquarters.* Cambridge, MA: MIT Press, 1994.

Durch, William J., ed. *The Evolution of UN Peacekeeping.* London: Macmillan, 1994.

Eban, Abba. *An Autobiography.* New York: Random House, 1977.

Eden, Anthony. *The Reckoning.* Boston: Houghton Mifflin, 1965.

Evatt, Herbert Vere. *The United Nations.* Cambridge, MA: Harvard University Press, 1948.

Fasulo, Linda. *Representing America: Experiences of U.S. Diplomats at the UN*. New York: Praeger, 1984.

Fenby, Jonathan. *Chiang Kai-shek: China's Generalissimo and the Nation He Lost*. New York: Carroll & Graf, 2003.

Finger, Seymour Maxwell. *Your Man at the UN: People, Politics, and Bureaucracy in Making Foreign Policy*. New York: New York University Press, 1980.

————. *Inside the World of Diplomacy: The U.S. Foreign Service*. Westport, CT: Praeger, 2002.

Franck, Thomas M., et al. *An Attitude Survey: Diplomats' Views on the United Nations System*. New York: UNITAR, 1982.

Franda, Marcus. *The United Nations in the Twenty-first Century: Management and Reform Processes in a Troubled Organization*. Lanham, MD: Rowman & Littlefield, 2006.

Gageby, Douglas. *The Last Secretary General: Sean Lester and the League of Nations*. Dublin: Town House and Country House, 1999.

Gerson, Alan. *The Kirkpatrick Mission: Diplomacy without Apology*. New York: Free Press, 1991.

Gharekhan, Chinmaya R. *The Horseshoe Table*. New Delhi: Dorling Kindersley, 2006.

Gilbert, Martin. *Road to Victory: Winston S. Churchill, 1941–1945*. London: Heinemann, 1986.

Goodwin, Geoff. *Britain and the United Nations*. New York: Manhattan Publishing, 1957.

Gorst, Anthony, and Lewis Johnman. *The Suez Crisis*. New York: Routledge, 1997.

Goulding, Marrack. *Peacemonger*. Baltimore, MD: Johns Hopkins University Press, 2003.

Graham-Brown, Sarah. *Sanctioning Saddam: The Politics of Intervention in Iraq*. New York: Tauris, 1999.

Grew, Joseph C. *Turbulent Era: A Diplomatic Record of Forty Years, 1904–1945*. Boston: Houghton Mifflin, 1952.

Griffiths, Richard. *Pétain: A Biography of Marshall Philippe Pétain of Vichy*. Garden City, NY: Doubleday, 1972.

Gromyko, Andrei. *Memoirs*. Garden City, NY: Doubleday, 1989.

Hannay, David. *New World Disorder: The UN after the Cold War*. London: Tauris, 2008.

Haqqani, Hussain. *Pakistan: Between Mosque and Military*. Washington, DC: Carnegie Endowment for International Peace, 2005.

Hasluck, Paul. *Workshop of Security*. London: Cheshire, 1948.

Hilderbrand, Robert. *Dumbarton Oaks*. Chapel Hill: University of North Carolina Press, 1990.

Hiro, Dilip. *The Longest War: The Iran-Iraq Military Conflict*. New York: Routledge, 1991.

Hiscocks, Richard. *The Security Council: A Study in Adolescence*. New York: Free Press, 1973.

Hoopes, Townsend, and Douglas Brinkley. *FDR and the Creation of the U.N.* New Haven, CT: Yale University Press, 1997.

Hull, Cordell. *Memoirs of Cordell Hull*. New York: Macmillan, 1948.

Hume, Cameron R. *The United Nations, Iran, and Iraq: How Peacemaking Changed*. Bloomington: Indiana University Press, 1994.

Hurd, Ian. *After Anarchy*. Princeton, NJ: Princeton University Press, 2007.

Isaacson, Walter. *Kissinger: A Biography*. New York: Simon & Schuster, 1992.

Israelyan, Victor. *Inside the Kremlin during the Yom Kippur War*. University Park: Pennsylvania State University Press, 1995.

————. *On the Battlefields of the Cold War: A Soviet Ambassador's Confession*. University Park: Pennsylvania State University Press, 2003.

Jackson, Richard L. *The Non-Aligned, the UN, and the Superpowers*. New York: Praeger, 1983.

James, Robert Rhodes. *Anthony Eden*. New York: McGraw-Hill, 1987.

Janello, Amy, and Brennon Jones, eds. *A Global Affair: An Inside Look at the United Nations*. New York: Jones & Janello, 1995.

Jankowitsch, Odette and Karl P. Sauvant, eds. *The Third World Without Superpowers: The Collected Documents of the Non-Aligned Countries*, vol. 2. Dobbs Ferry, NY: Oceana, 1978.

Jebb, Hubert Miles Gladwyn. *The Memoirs of Lord Gladwyn*. New York: Weybright & Talley, 1972.

Johnson, Walter, et al., eds. *The Papers of Adlai E. Stevenson*. Boston: Little, Brown, 1979.

Judah, Tim. *Kosovo: War and Revenge*. New Haven, CT: Yale University Press, 2002.

Keegan, John. *The Second World War*. London: Pimlico, 1989.

Kelly, Saul, and Anthony Gorst. *Whitehall and the Suez Crisis*. London: Cass, 2000.

Kennedy, Paul. *Parliament of Man: The Past, Present, and Future of the United Nations*. New York: Random House, 2006.

Kersaudy, Francois. *Churchill and de Gaulle*. New York: Collins, 1981.

Kim, Samuel S. *China, the United Nations, and World Order*. Princeton, NJ: Princeton University Press, 1979.

Kingseed, Cole C. *Eisenhower and the Suez Crisis of 1956*. Baton Rouge: Louisiana State University Press, 1995.

Kissinger, Henry. *Years of Upheaval*. Boston: Little, Brown, 1982.

———. *Crisis: The Anatomy of Two Major Foreign Policy Crises*. New York: Simon & Schuster, 2003.

Krasno, Jean E., and James S. Sutterlin. *The United Nations and Iraq: Defanging the Viper*. Westport, CT: Praeger, 2003.

Kulski, W. W. *De Gaulle and the World: The Foreign Policy of the Fifth French Republic*. Syracuse, NY: Syracuse University Press, 1966.

Lacouture, Jean. *De Gaulle*. New York: Norton, 1993.

Lall, Arthur. *The UN and the Middle East Crisis, 1967*. New York: Columbia University Press, 1968.

Larus, Joel. *From Collective Security to Preventive Diplomacy: Readings in International Organization and the Maintenance of Peace*. New York: Wiley, 1965.

LeBor, Adam. *Complicity with Evil: The United Nations in the Age of Modern Genocide*. New Haven, CT: Yale University Press, 2006.

Lie, Trygve. *In the Cause of Peace: Seven Years at the United Nations*. New York: Macmillan, 1954.

Lippman, Thomas W. *Madeleine Albright and the New American Diplomacy*. Boulder, CO: Westview, 2000.

Lloyd, Selwyn. *Suez 1956: A Personal Account*. New York: Mayflower, 1978.

Louis, Wm. Roger, ed. *Still More Adventures with Britannia: Personalities, Politics and Culture in Britain*. London: Tauris, 2003.

Louis, Wm. Roger, and Roger Owens, eds. *Suez 1956: The Crisis and Its Consequences*. Oxford: Oxford University Press, 1989.

Love, Kennett. *Suez: The Twice Fought War*. New York: McGraw-Hill, 1969.

Luard, Evan. *A History of the United Nations*. New York: St. Martin's, 1982.

Luck, Edward C. *Mixed Messages: American Politics and International Organization, 1919–1999*. Washington, DC: Brookings Institution Press, 1999.

Luck, Edward c. *UN Security Council: Practice and Promise*. New York: Routledge, 2006.

Macdonald, Ronald St. John, ed. *Essays in Honour of Wang Tieya*. Dordrecht: Martinus Nijhoff, 1994.

Macmillan, Harold. *At the End of the Day: 1961–1963*. New York: Harper & Row, 1973.

Malone, David, ed. *The UN Security Council: From the Cold War to the 21st Century*. Boulder, CO: Rienner, 2004.

———. *The International Struggle over Iraq: Politics in the UN Security Council, 1980–2005*. New York: Oxford University Press, 2006.

May, Ernest, and Philip Zelikow. *The Kennedy Tapes: Inside the White House during the Cuban Missile Crisis*. New York: Norton, 2002.

McCullough, David. *Truman*. New York: Simon & Schuster, 1992.

Melvern, Linda. *Conspiracy to Murder: The Rwandan Genocide*. London: Verso, 2004.

Meyer, Jeffrey, and Mark G. Califano. *Good Intentions Corrupted: The Oil-for-Food Scandal and the Threat to the U.N.* New York: Public Affairs, 2006.

Miller, Russell, and Rebecca Bratspies, eds. *Progress in International Law*. Leiden: Martinus Nijhoff, 2008.

Miller, William J. *Henry Cabot Lodge*. New York: Heinemann, 1967.

Moore, Bernard. *The Second Lesson: Seven Years at the United Nations*. London: Macmillan, 1957.

Munoz, Heraldo. *A Solitary War: A Diplomat's Chronicle of the Iraq War*. Golden, CO: Fulcrum, 2008.

Nicol, Davidson, ed. *Paths to Peace: The UN Security Council and Its Presidency*. New York: Pergamon, 1981.

Niebuhr, Reinhold. *The Children of Light and the Children of Darkness*. New York: Scribner's, 1944.

Norris, John. *Collision Course: NATO, Russia, and Kosovo*. Westport, CT: Praeger, 2005.

Northedge, F. S. *The League of Nations: Its Life and Times*. New York: Holmes & Meier, 1986.

O'Donnell, Kenneth P., and David F. Powers, *"Johnny, We Hardly Knew Ye."* Boston: Little, Brown, 1972.

Oren, Michael. *Six Days of War*. New York: Oxford University Press, 2002.

Overy, Richard J. *The Air War, 1939–1945*. Washington, DC: Potomac, 2005.

Owen, David. *Balkan Odyssey*. New York: Harcourt Brace, 1995.

Pérez de Cuéllar, Javier. *Pilgrimage for Peace*. New York: St. Martin's, 1997.

Power, Samantha. *"A Problem from Hell": America and the Age of Genocide*. New York: HarperCollins, 2003.

———. *Chasing the Flame: Sergio Vieira de Mello and the Fight to Save the World*. New York: Penguin, 2008.

Rafael, Gideon. *Destination Peace: Three Decades of Israeli Foreign Policy*. New York: Stein and Day, 1981.

Reid, Escott. *On Duty: A Canadian at the Making of the United Nations, 1945–1946*. Kent, OH: Kent State University Press, 1983.

Resis, Albert, ed. *Molotov Remembers: Inside Kremlin Politics*. Chicago: Dee, 1993.

Rieff, David. *Slaughterhouse: Bosnia and the Failure of the West*. New York: Simon & Schuster, 1995.

———. *A Bed for the Night*. New York: Simon & Schuster, 2002.

Righter, Rosemary. *Utopia Lost: The United Nations and World Order*. New York: Twentieth Century Fund, 1995.

Rioux, Jean-Pierre. *The Fourth Republic, 1944–1958*. Cambridge: Cambridge University Press, 1987.

Rohde, David. *Endgame: The Betrayal and Fall of Srebrenica*. Boulder, CO: Westview, 1997.

Roosevelt, Franklin D. *F.D.R.: His Personal Letters*. New York: Duell, Sloan and Pearce, 1950.

Rusk, Dean. *As I Saw It*. New York: Norton, 1990.

Russell, Ruth B. *A History of the United Nations Charter: The Role of the United States, 1940–1945*. Washington, DC: Brookings Institution Press, 1958.

Russert, Bruce, and Ian Hurd. *The Once and Future Security Council*. New York: St. Martin's, 1997.

Schlesinger, Arthur. *A Thousand Days*. Boston: Houghton Mifflin, 1965.

Schlesinger, Stephen C. *Act of Creation*. Boulder, CO: Westview, 2003.

Sheeny, Thomas P. *No More Somalias: Reconsidering Clinton's Doctrine of Military Humanitarianism*. Washington: Heritage Foundation, 1993.

Sherwood, Robert E. *Roosevelt and Hopkins: An Intimate History*. New York: Harper, 1950.

Shevchenko, Arkady N. *Breaking with Moscow*. New York: Knopf, 1985.

Smith, Courtney B. *Politics and Process at the United Nations: The Global Dance*. Boulder, CO: Rienner, 2006.

Smith, Gaddis. *American Diplomacy during the Second World War, 1941–1945*. New York: McGraw-Hill, 1985.

Smith, Rupert. *The Utility of Force: The Art of War in the Modern World*. New York: Knopf, 2007.

Snyder, Alvin. *Warriors of Disinformation*. New York: Arcade, 1995.

Stothard, Peter. *Thirty Days: Tony Blair and the Test of History*. New York: HarperCollins, 2003.

Stueck, William. *The Korean War: An International History*. Princeton, NJ: Princeton University Press, 1995.

Talbott, Strobe. *The Russia Hand*. New York: Random House, 2002.

Tenet, George. *At the Center of the Storm: My Years at the CIA*. New York: HarperCollins, 2007.

Thakur, Ramesh, ed. *What Is Equitable Geographic Representation in the Twenty-first Century*. Tokyo: United Nations University, 1999.

Thant, U. *View from the UN*. Garden City, NY: Doubleday, 1978.

Thatcher, Margaret. *The Downing Street Years*. New York: HarperCollins, 1993.

Traub, James. *The Best Intentions: Kofi Annan and the UN in the Era of American World Power*. New York: Farrar, Straus and Giroux, 2006.

Treadgold, Donald W. *Twentieth Century Russia*. Boulder, CO: Westview, 1990.

Troyanovsky, Oleg.*Cherez gody i rasstoyaniya*. Moscow: Vagrius, 1997.

Ulam, Adam B. *Expansion and Coexistence: The History of Soviet Foreign Policy, 1917–1967*. New York: Praeger, 1968.

———. *Stalin: The Man and His Era*. New York: Viking, 1973.

United Nations. *Report of the High Level Panel on Threats, Challenges, and Change*. New York: United Nations, 2004.

———. *Report of the Independent Inquiry into the Actions of the United Nations during the 1994 Genocide in Rwanda*. New York: United Nations, 1999.

Urquhart, Brian. *Hammarskjöld*. New York: Knopf, 1972.

———. *A Life in Peace and War: Memoirs*. New York: Harper & Row, 1987.

U.S. Department of State. *Foreign Relations of the United States*. Washington, DC: Government Printing Office, 1945–1973.

Vandenberg, Arthur Hendrick, and Joe Alex Morris. *The Private Papers of Senator Vandenberg*.
New York: Houghton Mifflin, 1952.

Waldheim, Kurt. *In the Eye of the Storm: A Memoir*. Bethesda, MD: Adler & Adler, 1986.

Walters, F. P. *A History of the League of Nations*. New York: Oxford University Press, 1952.

Weiss, Thomas G., et al. *UN Voices: The Struggle for Development and Social Justice*.
Bloomington: Indiana University Press, 2005.

———. *The United Nations and Changing World Politics*. Boulder, CO: Westview, 2007.

Whitman, Alden. *Portrait: Adlai E. Stevenson: Politician, Diplomat, Friend*. New York: Harper
& Row, 1965.

Willkie, Wendell L. *One World*. New York: Simon & Schuster, 1943.

Wilson, Charles McMoran. *Churchill: The Struggle for Survival, 1940–1965, taken from the
diaries of Lord Moran*. Boston: Houghton Mifflin, 1966.

Wood, Robert S. *France in the World Community: Decolonization, Peacekeeping, and the United
Nations*. Leiden: Sijthoff, 1973.

Woodward, Bob. *Bush at War*. New York: Simon & Schuster, 2002.

———. *Plan of Attack*. New York: Simon & Schuster, 2005.

Yeltsin, Boris. *Midnight Diaries*. New York: Public Affairs, 2000.

Yergin, Daniel. *Shattered Peace: The Origins of the Cold War and the National Security State*.
Boston: Houghton Mifflin, 1977.

Young, John W. *France, the Cold War and the Western Alliance, 1944–1949*. New York:
St. Martin's, 1990.

Zubok, Vladislav. *A Failed Empire: The Soviet Union in the Cold War from Stalin to Gorbachev*.
Chapel Hill: University of North Carolina Press, 2007.

Zubok, Vladislav, and Constantine Peshakov. *Inside the Kremlin's Cold War: From Stalin to
Khrushchev*. Cambridge, MA: Harvard University Press, 1996.

Oral History Collections and Archives

Churchill College, Cambridge University, British Diplomatic Oral History Programme,
Cambridge.

City University of New York, UN Intellectual History Project, New York.

Cold War International History Project, Washington, D.C.

Dag Hammarskjöld Library, United Nations, New York.

George Washington University, National Security Archive, Washington, D.C.

Harry S Truman Presidential Library, Independence, Missouri.

John F. Kennedy Presidential Library, Boston.

United Kingdom National Archives, Kew Gardens.

United Nations Archives, New York.

United Nations Information Center, Washington, D.C.

United Nations Oral History Project Transcripts, Manuscripts and Archives, Yale University
Library, New Haven.

Author Interviews

Nationality provided for diplomats and government officials.

Diego Arria (Venezuela, former permanent representative to the United Nations)

Neylan Bali (former member of UN Secretariat)

Olivier Belle (Belgium, deputy permanent representative to the United Nations)

John Bolton (United States, former permanent representative to the United Nations)

Norma Chan (UN Secretariat)

Romeo Dallaire (former commander of UNAMIR)

Sam Daws (President, United Nations Association of the United Kingdom, former member of the UN Secretariat)

Stewart Eldon (United Kingdom, former deputy permanent representative to the United Nations)

Andrés Franco (Colombia, former deputy permanent representative to the United Nations)

Ibrahim Gambari (Nigeria, permanent representative to the UN)

Edward Gnehm (United States, former deputy permanent representative to the United Nations)

Jeremy Greenstock (United Kingdom, former permanent representative to the United Nations)

Marc Grossman (United States, former undersecretary of state for political affairs)

David Hannay (United Kingdom, former permanent representative to the United Nations)

Paul Heinbecker (Canada, former permanent representative to the United Nations)

Kim Holmes (United States, former assistant secretary of state for international organization affairs)

Christopher Hum (United Kingdom, former political counselor in the U.K. mission)

Cameron Hume (United States, held various positions in the U.S. mission)

Karl Inderfurth (United States, former deputy permanent representative to the United Nations)

Walter Kansteiner (United States, former assistant secretary of state)

Sergey Karev (Russia, UN Counterterrorism Committee, former member of Russian mission to the United Nations)

Colin Keating (New Zealand, former permanent representative to the United Nations)

Ole Peter Kolby (Norway, former permanent representative to the United Nations)

Karel Kovanda (Czech Republic, former permanent representative to the United Nations)

Barry Lowenkron (United States, former State Department official)

Edward Luck (scholar, member of the UN Secretariat)

Clovis Maksoud (Arab League, former representative to the United Nations)

David Malone (Canada, scholar and former official at the Canadian mission to the United Nations)

Donald McHenry (United States, former permanent representative to the United Nations)

John Negroponte (United States, former permanent representative to the United Nations and deputy secretary of state)

John Norris (United States, former adviser to deputy secretary of state)

Herbert Okun (United States, former deputy permanent representative to the United Nations)

Olara Ottunu (Uganda, former permanent representative to the United Nations)

Thomas Pickering (United States, former permanent representative to the United Nations and undersecretary of state)

Gunter Pleuger (Germany, former permanent representative to the United Nations)

Thomas Richardson (United Kingdom, former political counselor to British mission to the United Nations)

Eric Rosand (United States, former adviser to U.S. mission to the United Nations)

Nicholas Rostow (United States, former adviser to U.S. mission to the United Nations)

Richard Ryan (Ireland, former permanent representative to the United Nations)

Jean-Marc de la Sablière (France, former permanent representative to the United Nations)

Vladimir Safronkov (Russia, senior counselor to the mission to the United Nations)

John Sawers (United Kingdom, permanent representative to the United Nations)

Abraham Sofaer (United States, former legal adviser to the State Department)

Alfredo Suescum (Panama, deputy permanent representative to the United Nations)

George P. Shultz (United States, former secretary of state)

Wegger Chr. Strommen (Norway, former permanent representative to the United Nations)

Stefan Tafrov (Bulgaria, former permanent representative to the United Nations)

Pascal Teixeira (France, adviser to the French mission to the United Nations)

John Thomson (United Kingdom, former permanent representative to the United Nations)

Crispin Tickell (United Kingdom, former permanent representative to the United Nations)

Roland Timerbaev (U.S.S.R., former deputy permanent representative to the United Nations)

Jorge Urbina (Costa Rica, permanent representative to the United Nations)

Juan Gabriel Valdés (Chile, former permanent representative to the United Nations)

Alexander Watson (United States, former deputy permanent representative to the United Nations)

Thomas G. Weiss (scholar, former member of the UN Secretariat)

Joanna Weschler (Director of Research, Security Council Report)

John Weston (United Kingdom, former permanent representative to the United Nations)

Lawrence Wilkerson (United States, former State Department official)

Alejandro Wolff (United States, deputy permanent representative to the United Nations)

INDEX

Castro, Fidel, 92, 160
Central America, 153–154
Chad, 1, 253
Chauvel, Jean, 53
Cheney, Richard, 164, 223–224, 230
Chernenko, Konstantin, 149
Chiang, Kai-Shek, 24, 81
    flees to Taiwan, 54
    friction with the United States, 25
    and Palestine, 48
    reaction to Korean War, 56
    removal from UN of, 122–123
Chiang, Meling, 24–25
Chiao, Kuan-Hua, 130
*Children of Light and the Children of
    Darkness,* 28
Chile, 95, 234, 237–239
China, 3, 28, 100, 154, 178, 215
    during Iran-Iraq diplomacy, 151–152
    during Korean War, 61–62
    during World War II, 24–26
    Hammarskjold in, 82
    and Kosovo, 211–212
    and North Korea, 246–247
    and policy on Palestine, 48
    position on Iraq, 198–99, 207
    representation question regarding, 6, 8,
        54, 57–58, 101, 120–123
    and Security Council reform, 205
    sovereignty concerns of, 165–166, 213
    tension with Soviet Union, 100, 125, 130
    use of abstention, 139–140
    use of veto power in Security Council,
        142, 208–209
    See also Taiwan
Chirac, Jacques, 208, 217, 224, 226, 229,
        230, 238
    and Boutros-Ghali reappointment
        dispute, 201
    and Kosovo, 210
    and nonpermanent members, 239
    and passage of Resolution 1441,
        227–228
Christopher, Warren, 177, 188, 201
Churchill, Winston, 19, 22, 41, 146, 174,
        253, 256
    during San Francisco Conference, 34–35
    during WWII, 13
    during Yalta Conference, 29–31
    opposition to Brazil as permanent
        member, 28

support for France as permanent member,
        26
    vision of the UN, 16–17, 18
CIA, 93, 231–232, 240. *See also* U.S. Central
        Intelligence Agency
Clarke, Richard, 200–201
Claude, Inis, 254
Clay, Lucius, 51
Cleveland, Harlan, 87–88
Clinton, Bill, 185, 221
Cable News Network (CNN), 162
collective security, 5, 15, 161, 170, 196
Colombia, 68, 160, 216, 228
colonialism (including anticolonialism), 17,
        28, 35, 67–68, 116, 121, 164
    and Congo operation, 85–86
    and French North Africa policy, 80–83
    Kosovo operation distinguished from,
        209–210
    and nonaligned movement, 113, 142
    and Suez Crisis, 72–73, 78–79
Congo, 1, 111, 154, 160, 162, 170, 185,
        192, 250, 251, 253
    council's post–Cold War involvement in,
        216, 241, 243
    UN force sent to in 1960, 83–89
Connally, Thomas, 28, 35
consultation room. *See under* UN Security
        Council
Cook, Robin, 212
Cornut-Gentille, Bernard, 76, 77
Croatia, 171, 177, 181, 200
Crowe, Colin, 113
Cuba, 40
    Bay of Pigs invasion of, 92
    during Gulf War diplomacy, 160–163, 166
    involvement of in Angola, 136, 140
    as member of non-aligned movement,
        112–113
Cuban missile crisis, 6, 93–97, 108, 131,
        244, 251–252
Cyprus, 103–104, 140, 170, 213, 252
Czech Republic, 190
Czechoslovakia, 115–116, 139

Daily Telegraph, 238
Dallaire, Romeo, 186–187, 189, 191–192
Danforth, John, 245
Darfur. *See* Sudan
Dayton Peace Accords, 197, 214

Lagos, Ricardo, 239
Lake Success, council meetings at, 43–44
Lavrov, Sergei, 7, 197–199, 206, 208, 210, 237
law, international, 14, 145, 152, 160, 178, 190, 210, 229
  council's relation to, 8, 208, 220
  and judicial review of council decisions, 166
Le Corbusier, Charles-Edouard, 63–64
League of Nations, 3, 10–12, 14, 17, 236
  American failure to join, 14
  British support for, 17
  closing of, 37–38
  council of, 3, 10–11
  lessons of, 41
  Yalta Formula and, 30
Lebanon, 43, 81, 118, 149, 170
  discussed during San Francisco conference, 35
  involvement of Hammarskjöld in, 82–83
  Israel invasion of, 133, 136–137, 140
legitimacy. *See under* UN Security Council
Lester, Sean, 12, 38
Levitte, Jean-David, 217, 229
Libya, 145, 166, 182
Lie, Trygve, 55, 65, 67
  on Berlin Crisis, 53
  and Korean War, 55
  and Palestine, 49
  and position on Chinese representation, 54
  and resignation of, 67
Lind, Michael, 196
Lloyd, Selwyn, 74
Lodge, Henry Cabot, 84, 91, 100, 159, 178
  and Congo operation, 84
  and Guatemala coup, 68–70
Los Angeles Times, 67
Luce, Henry, 24
Lumumba, Patrice, 86–87
Luxembourg, 174

MacArthur, Douglas, 56, 60–62
Macedonia, 182–183, 208–210, 252
Macmillan, Harold, 81, 97
Major, John, 167
Makin, Norman, 41
Malaysia, 160, 202
Malenkov, Georgi, 68

Malik, Yakov, 53–54, 114, 118
  during Berlin crisis, 53–54
  during the Korean War, 56–58
  during the 1968 Czechoslovakia crisis, 115–116
  during the 1973 Middle East conflict, 125–130
Malmierca, Isitoro, 160
Malone, David, 218
Manchuria, invasion of, 11
Mandela, Nelson, 201
Mao Tse Tung, 48, 121, 124, 140
Marker, Jamsheed, 179–180
Marshall, George, 20, 50
Marshall Plan, 50
McCain, John, 249
McHenry, Donald, 137–138
McIntyre, Laurence, 128, 130
McNamara, Robert, 94
Meir, Golda, 127
Menon, Krishna, 61
Merimée, Jean-Bernard, 214
Mexico, 41, 206, 234, 238, 239
Middle East, 196, 211, 244, 246, 252
  1948 conflict in, 48–50
  1967 conflict in, 104–111
  1973 conflict in, 126–131
Military Staff Committee, 154, 163, 169, 253, 254
Milosevic, Slobodan, 220
Mitterand, Francois, 160, 168
Mladic, Ratko, 193
Mobutu, Joseph, 87
Mollet, Guy, 74
Molotov, Viacheslav, 20, 29
  confrontation with Ernest Bevin, 43
  at San Francisco conference, 34
Monnet, Jean, 27
Motta, Giuseppe, 10
Moynihan, Daniel Patrick, 119, 120, 134, 142, 143, 159, 246
Mozambique, 175, 213

NAM. *See* Nonaligned Movement
Namibia, 139, 153–154, 170–171, 204
Nasser, Gamal Abdel, 71–72, 74, 122
NATO. *See* North Atlantic Treaty Organization
Negroponte, John, 219, 222, 228, 231, 235, 237–239
Nehru, Jawaharlal, 112

SINKING

— IN THE —

SWAMP

HOW TRUMP'S MINIONS AND
MISFITS POISONED WASHINGTON

LACHLAN MARKAY
& ASAWIN SUEBSAENG

VIKING

VIKING

An imprint of Penguin Random House LLC

penguinrandomhouse.com

LIBRARY OF CONGRESS CATALOGING-IN-PUBLICATION DATA

Names: Markay, Lachlan, author. | Suebsaeng, Asawin, author.
Title: Sinking in the swamp : how Trump's minions and misfits poisoned Washington / Lachlan Markay, and Asawin Suebsaeng.
Other titles: How Trump's minions and misfits poisoned Washington
Description: New York : Viking, [2020]
Identifiers: LCCN 2019038462 (print) | LCCN 2019038463 (ebook) | ISBN 9781984878564 (hardcover) | ISBN 9781984878571 (ebook)
Subjects: LCSH: Trump, Donald, 1946– —Influence. | Trump, Donald, 1946– —Friends and associates. | Presidents—United States—Staff. | Presidents—Press coverage—United States—History—21st century. | United States—Politics and government—2017– | Washington (D.C.)—Social life and customs—21st century.
Classification: LCC E912 .M38 2020 (print) | LCC E912 (ebook) | DDC 973.933092—dc23
LC record available at https://lccn.loc.gov/2019038462
LC ebook record available at https://lccn.loc.gov/2019038463

Printed in the United States of America
1   3   5   7   9   10   8   6   4   2

Designed by Cassandra Garruzzo

For Richard Henszey,
the most brilliant man I've ever known.

Lachlan

For my father's mom—Khun Ya Sanit.
I'm sorry I couldn't be there for you
as much as you were for me.
I love you, now and always.

Asawin

CONTENTS

ANOTHER SHITSTORM
IN FUCKTOWN

Asawin's chest puffed up. Lachlan rested his head in his hand and sighed. A hairsplitting dispute over a months-old news story looked as if it was about to turn into an all-out brawl in the lobby of the Trump International Hotel between a senior White House official and a reporter covering the West Wing.

It was both an absurd spectacle and a perfect encapsulation of our escapades as journalists in the Trump era in Washington, D.C. We were surrounded by the gilded splendor that is the Trump hotel lobby, flanked by a crew of mobbed-up-in-Trumpworld luminaries with whom we'd been having farcically overpriced cocktails and very amiable conversation just a few minutes earlier. And suddenly the whole thing was degenerating into a screaming match, with each party looking increasingly likely to throw a punch to the teeth.

The evening had kicked off after work at the Newseum on Pennsylvania Avenue, an ostentatious, now-defunct monument to the journalism profession that, when it wasn't singing the praises of reporters for "comforting the afflicted," rented out its glitzy rooftop lounge and patio to host receptions for the city's political elite. It was April 24, 2018, and the former FBI director James Comey, whom President

Donald Trump had famously canned the year prior, was hosting one of those receptions: an open-bar party and book signing for his autobiography, *A Higher Loyalty*. We were two of the political reporters who came for the free alcohol and food and maybe to ask the fired FBI chief a dumb question. It was clear from the outset that nobody was going to be getting any news or provocative responses from a buttoned-up, on-script Comey that evening.

Asawin—already a couple drinks in and buoyant—waited in line to ask him to sign a copy of his book for "Donald J. Trump." Comey let out a polite chuckle and demurred. Instead, he signed the book for Asawin's parents. The Thai American *Daily Beast* reporter felt like being cute, so he asked Comey if he wanted to join the two of us at the Trump International Hotel, situated roughly equidistant from the Newseum and the White House, to "do some Fireball shots." Again, Comey delivered a robotic giggle or two and politely declined. Lachlan, the more conservative and less willing to make an ass out of himself of the duo, stood a few feet away from Comey and Asawin, literally face-palming. He had to remind Asawin that the Trump hotel "does not serve Fireball. I keep telling you this."

When we reached the lobby of "Trump D.C.," Comey was of course nowhere to be found, but all was not lost. Our cocktail companions ended up including an assortment of Trumpworld regulars such as Richard Grenell, a veteran Republican operative who would soon be confirmed as Donald Trump's ambassador to Germany. Everything had been friendly until Cliff Sims showed up.

Sims is best known these days as the author of *Team of Vipers*, a tell-all book about his time in the White House. But back then, he was still working in the West Wing as the director of message strategy. He was friends with the crew we were hanging out with, but we're not sure whether they mentioned, in inviting him over, that we were there as well.

A few months earlier, we had written a story about which Sims was clearly still seething. The piece (which we'll get into in more detail later) reported that two Trump aides, Andrew Surabian and Sims, would likely be tapped as two of the White House's new point men on crisis communications related to all things Russia. To this day they deny that it was accurate (it was). We'd taken our share of the shouts of "fake news!" that had become routine in covering the Trump White House, and while they continued to criticize the piece months later, Surabian at least had come to laugh about it, and we'd rib each other over the piece virtually every time we ran into each other.

Sims, though, was a different story. Our relationship was still on the outs when he sauntered up to our table, a knee-height glass one surrounded by couches adjacent to the Trump hotel lobby bar. Multiple people sitting at the table knew things hadn't been smoothed over with Sims, and they decided to stir shit up. Two people quickly made a point of bringing up our disputed story about Surabian and Sims, prompting us to insist that, actually, the story was completely factual.

We thought it was all fun and games at this point. Sims didn't like that and made his feelings clear. The next thing anyone knew, he and Asawin (or Swin as his friends call him) were standing inches apart, noses nearly touching, and screaming their cases as others in attendance attempted to break things up. Sims decided he didn't want to deal with this anymore and extended his right hand to shake Swin's goodbye. (Swin and Sims would speak in the weeks after this incident. Each would say, over a laugh, that he essentially wanted to rip out the other's throat at that particular moment at the hotel. Relations have thawed between the reporter and the former Trump adviser; in fact, Swin would honest to God prefer it if more Trump officials and associates would get in his face instead of ratfucking behind his back.)

Sims is a lifelong teetotaler, and was as sober at the time as Donald

J. Trump always claims to be. Swin, on the other hand, was a few rum and Cokes deep and thoroughly pissed off. He rejected Sims's overture, loudly stating at least three times, "I'm not shaking his fucking hand!" Sims threw up his hands and headed for the door. At one point between the couches and the lobby exit, Sims turned around and made eye contact with Swin in one final taunt. The *Daily Beast* reporter took the bait and pursued him across the lobby, yelling the whole time. One of Sims's friends, in an effort to defuse the situation, tried to lure Swin back to the table. He placed a hand on his shoulder. Swin whirled, pushed him, and nearly knocked him over a piece of furniture.

By that time, Sims had made it to the exit, and no real blows had been thrown. Still, the shouting and drunken emotions didn't stop, and hotel security soon appeared, ready to eject Swin. Grenell, grinning widely, motioned to security that things were under control, and they backed off. Swin walked over to the bar to order more booze. Lachlan was thoroughly embarrassed and talked to Grenell for the rest of the evening, dodging whenever possible his idiot, truculent colleague.

Eventually, we both needed to get home to our respective girlfriends. In our shared cab ride home, Lachlan flatly stated, "I think my new favorite memory of us covering Trump together is you almost getting into a fistfight with a White House official at Trump hotel."

It was a casually ridiculous episode typical in our three years covering Donald Trump and his era in Washington. And it helped underscore just how thoroughly the old rules had gone out the window.

By that time, the Trump hotel itself had already become a symbol of the bare-naked corruption and gaudy opulence that defines the forty-fifth president's tenure. We were there mingling with people with whom we'd become friendly, even though they think we're part of a borderline-treasonous disinformation apparatus and we think they're part of an incompetent graft machine. This irreconcilable conflict had nearly resulted in a physical altercation at the center of political power in Trump's Washington.

And in true Trumpian fashion, though tempers flared, threats were made, and heated words were exchanged, in the end not much was accomplished.

THERE used to be a different geographic center of the American political universe. A block from the White House, just across the street from the Treasury Department, sits the storied Willard InterContinental Hotel. It's a historic place, dating back to 1850; the building itself was actually constructed thirty years earlier. Abraham Lincoln lived in the Willard for ten days before his stint in the White House. Martin Luther King Jr. prepared his "I Have a Dream" speech in the hotel. And if you believe the Willard staff, it's where the term "lobbying" was coined, by President Ulysses S. Grant, to refer to the special interests congregated in the hotel lobby, hoping to bend the ear of government officials who frequented the place.

The story is apocryphal—the term dates back over a century earlier, and to the British House of Commons—but in the Washington of Grant's day the Willard lobby was indeed a place where political business was done, mostly informally through D.C. social networks and handshake deals over high-end cocktails. Eventually, the term "lobbying" took on a meaning of its own, divorced from the physical structure from which it ostensibly originated, at least in American political parlance. A century and a half later, few would associate lobbying with an actual building lobby.

Until, that is, the era of President Donald Trump.

In Trump's Washington, the physical locus of political power isn't the Willard. And it isn't even the White House. It's that damned lobby in the Trump International Hotel down the street, at 1100 Pennsylvania Avenue. Administration officials, members of Congress, cable news personalities, political influence peddlers, corporate executives, the president's legal teams, chaos agents, and foreign diplomats all regularly flock to its sprawling, gilded atrium to mingle, suck up, be seen, bask in the omnipresent political glow that pervades the place. Omnipresent, at least, until a certain someone is out of office.

Sharply dressed hosts and waitstaff shepherd visitors into plush, low-seated couches and love seats throughout the sprawling lobby. Cocktail prices run into the three figures. Bar food includes strips of thick-cut, candied bacon served hanging from a plated clothesline. A giant American flag adorns the wall behind the crystal-covered bar, right above an array of large flat-panel televisions, two of which are perpetually tuned to CNN and Fox News. The sound is only ever turned up on the latter, at least whenever we've been around.

The hotel occupies one of Washington's oldest and most historic structures, the Old Post Office, and its clock tower offers one of the most stunning panoramic views of the capital's skyline. But prior to the Trump Organization's renovation, it had descended into a depressing state of disrepair. The only publicly accessible portion was a dingy food court. Even his most vehement detractors must concede that Trump did, in fact, make that place great again.

The hotel's quintessentially Trumpian hallmarks were evident early. Abutting the southern end of D.C.'s bustling downtown business district, the hotel sits right on the commuting route of many professional Washingtonians. Just as Trump's presidential campaign kicked into gear, and scared the shit out of much of D.C.'s professional class, those commuters began seeing a new, very large sign on Pennsylvania Avenue. It read "TRUMP: Coming 2016." The sign referred to the hotel, but no one in a city built on and obsessed with politics could miss the electoral double entendre. (It even drew a complaint to the Federal Election Commission alleging it was effectively a campaign sign. The FEC disagreed and let the sign stay.)

We visit the hotel often, simply because there is no better place in Trump's Washington to meet and talk with the most plugged-in people in the president's orbit. Corey Lewandowski virtually lives there. Ryan Zinke was frequently seen holding court when he led the Department of the Interior. Eric Bolling, one of the president's favorite pundits, routinely makes the rounds, beaming and shaking hands with a litany of fans and acquaintances. Rudy Giuliani, Wilbur Ross, Stephen Miller, David Bossie, Sean Spicer, Donald Trump Jr., Steven Mnuchin, William Barr, Brad Parscale, Lindsey Graham—walk in on any given weeknight, and chances are better than decent you'll see several of them dining and partying. The night Anthony Scaramucci was fired from his brief stint as White House communications director, we headed to the Trump hotel, figuring there was no place in D.C.— including the White House—that we'd be more likely to spot him. And sure enough, shortly after we arrived, he wandered out of the hotel's steak house over to the elevators, pale as a ghost, declining to comment on the way.

Reporters know that the hotel is the place to mingle with the people running the country and those who have their collective ear. So too do the legions of people—from lobbyists to foreign dignitaries—seeking to influence the president and those around him. The whole place is a mecca of (legal!) corruption, where the powerful can hobnob with one another and be feted by those seeking to break off a piece of their influence with the president.

And the best part about it, if you're President Donald Trump, is the whole thing is making you richer. The president can still draw profits from the trust he created upon taking office and into which he deposited his extensive assets. And when he leaves office, even that thin veneer of recusal won't be an issue any longer. So every dollar spent on Trump hotel cocktails while schmoozing a White House aide in the hopes of getting in the president's good graces is a dollar added to the president's balance sheets. He's created the incentive for that influence-seeking, and the venue for it, and he's collecting on the back end. No one ever said he wasn't shrewd, at least when it comes to a simple grift.

All of this is to say that we are fully aware of our complicity in Trump's monetization of the presidency. Just as the capital's influence-industry professionals mingle at the Trump hotel to win favor with the administration, we mingle to meet sources and in the hopes of building relationships and getting good, useful information. That inevitably requires the purchase of significant volumes of libations and an occasional meal. In the summer of 2017, we perched up on the patio of the hotel during a political fund-raiser, which drew throngs of protesters outside. One protester angrily demanded to know why we were financially supporting the president. We explained that it's part of the job. Swin told the protester he understood and sympathized with what she was saying but that he was tired and if he didn't have a drink while being forced by his bosses to go to the Trump hotel on a weeknight, he might blow his brains out before he turned thirty.

Our patronizing of the hotel is a microcosm of the degree to which Trump has subsumed Washington. Doing business in D.C. these days largely means doing business Trump's way—whether your business is government, lobbying, or journalism. That's true to a degree with every administration, which naturally alters the town's workings in dramatic ways. But Trump is such a uniquely narcissistic figure who demands unparalleled loyalty to himself personally that he, more than perhaps any prior president, individually defines and shapes the political environment in which he serves.

That has made for some very, very stupid times in the nation's capital. Fortunately for us, it has also meant no shortage of stories about the absurd ways in which the government and those Washingtonians who depend on and benefit from it have turned American politics into a circus of crookedness, incompetence, and rank dishonesty. (Well, more so than usual.)

To understand Washington in the Trump era, it is of course necessary to understand Trump himself. But after nearly five years of 24/7 media coverage, most Americans probably know more about our president than they care to. And we're far from the only journalists writing books attempting to dissect, explain, and reveal new details about this ridiculous moment in American political history.

To our minds, though, understanding this moment requires looking not just at the man at the top but at the people below him, the legions of minions and misfits who rode Trump's coattails to some of the most powerful political positions in the world. Many of them share his defining characteristics—narcissistic, corrupt, shallow, dishonest, shameless—and though Trump himself is the face of everything that happens in his administration, the D-listers, as we've come to call them, are in most cases those who actually put his will into effect.

It was a quirk of our approach to the Trump administration, as two reporters who had never covered any previous White House, that we ended up focusing as much on those surrounding the president as on the president himself. We suddenly found ourselves competing with some of the best reporters in the world for some of the craziest stories in modern American politics. And we're the first two to admit that we were regularly chasing some of our esteemed colleagues on some major scoops.

We were left to figure out what value we could bring to the increasingly insane daily political conversation. And we naturally settled into a role as storytellers for the people behind the headlines. *The Daily Beast* is a small newsroom that routinely punches above its weight. But when *The New York Times* or *The Washington Post* shifted the tectonic plates of Washington with a groundbreaking exclusive, we'd approach it with a different goal in mind: What are the thousands of midlevel functionaries toiling away in relative obscurity thinking and doing about the increasingly shambolic state of the administration that employed them? Before long, we'd carved out a niche as two White House reporters bringing an unvarnished view of the state of Trumpworld from the perspective of aides and advisers who often weren't making the headlines but were forced to deal with their fallout.

A deeper understanding of the Trump presidency requires examining the unique, often comical, frequently disturbing goings-on in the corridors of power outside the Oval Office. We're aiming to take you inside the Trump sausage factory, where grifters, ideologues, hangers-on, and unquestioning foot soldiers put the Trump vision for America into effect and frequently attempt to leverage it for their own personal, petty ends.

Our story begins before Trump's political ascent and revisits his time as a New York real estate developer and reality-television star. We will take you through the campaign with the amateurish and ethically questionable crew that ushered him into office. We'll revisit the early days of the Trump White House, its utter dysfunction, leaking, backbiting, and internal witch hunts, and the inevitable recriminations that enveloped the West Wing. And we'll delve into the pro-Trump media apparatus, the lobbyists and influence peddlers seeking to cash in on his presidency, and the federal agencies trying to make policy under the weight of constant infighting and scandal. We'll check in with the crew of lawyers who, so far, have managed to keep the president in office and out of the clink. And we'll dig deep into the sketchy crew of foreign businessmen who have, as of this writing, landed the president on the verge of impeachment.

This story involves many people of whom you're no doubt aware—folks like Steve Bannon, Corey Lewandowski, Scott Pruitt, Hope Hicks, and Rudy Giuliani. Others may be characters you've never heard of—Trump's favorite teleprompter operator, the Fox producer who paved the way for the cable news presidency, the obscure environmental policy aide caught up in soap opera–style drama that effectively brought down a White House chief of staff. And where we recount stories that have already made it into the news, we will do so in ways that, hopefully, illuminate previously unknown details of the sagas that set the stage for and defined Trump's first term in office.

And we'll also try to make you laugh—in abject terror, at least.

WE also want to be very clear about something else.

Originally, we had asked our agents and our publisher if this book that you're currently flipping through could be titled "Another Shitstorm in Fucktown: The Donald J. Trump Odyssey." If we had our druthers, that would be the title. Alas, everybody in a position of power in making this decision told us we couldn't do that. For one, it would make it harder to sell a book with such a name at Walmart or Costco or any other kid-friendly retailer.

After nearly three years of covering and investigating what Swin once publicly described as an "autocratic game-show host personality cult," we thought it felt like the only title that fully captured the essence of what the Trump era was really like.

Too many reporters and books on the Trump years (including the bestseller *Fear*, which was ostensibly written by Bob Woodward but had the distinct feel of Rob Porter's strong influence) cover this era without the necessary combination of horror, tar-black humor, and gleeful disregard for "respecting the office" for which we believe the occasion has called.

We're Washington-based reporters for *The Daily Beast*, a New York–headquartered digital news outfit that we affectionately refer to as a highbrow tabloid. The institutional mantra is "nonpartisan but not neutral," and that's the attitude we've brought to our White House coverage and that we've tried to bring to this book. We're not going to insult your intelligence by pretending to play it down the middle. And we hope you're looking for a take on this ridiculous time in our country that doesn't try to pretend that everything is fine and normal. It isn't.

The initial inspiration for the premise of *Sinking in the Swamp* wasn't any work of political nonfiction; it was a book about gangsters, the one on which the Martin Scorsese classic *Goodfellas* is based. That 1985 book, titled *Wiseguy* and written by the veteran crime reporter Nicholas Pileggi (who later co-wrote the screenplay with Scorsese), told the story of the American Mafia through the eyes of Henry Hill, a gangster turned FBI snitch. Hill wasn't a marquee figure in gangland or a recognizable big name like a Gambino or a Siegel or a Luciano. He was, at least at one point, a total obscurity with no pop culture name ID.

"There'd been several books about mob *bosses*," Pileggi once said, describing how and why he wrote his book. "But [with *Wiseguy*], it was like getting ahold of a soldier in Napoleon's army. That's who I want. I want to know how it worked inside. Detail, detail, detail. Everything is detail."

This premise—telling the story of the famous boss and organization through the viewpoint of some foot soldier—seemed perfect not just for the mob but for the decadent political universe of Donald

Trump. When we initially discussed coauthoring a book on Trump-world, one thing neither of us wanted to do was write the story through the eyes of a Trump, a Kushner, or a Bannon. It'd been done many times, too often, and sometimes to very boring and useless effect.

We wanted to tell the story of Trump, but through the eyes and misadventures of his lieutenants, his cable news collaborators, his hangers-on, his diehards, the lobbyists, the "shadow lobbyists," the grunts, the fixers, the ratfuckers, the operatives, and the unknowns-but-influentials. To tell this story from the ground up—from the worm's-eye view—we needed to find dozens upon dozens of Trump-world's Henry Hills.

The idea of taking this storytelling template from gangland to the Trump orbit would probably make perfect sense to, of all people, Donald Trump himself.

"You have to treat 'em like shit," Trump told his buddy the architect Philip Johnson, according to a 1992 *New York* magazine piece. The "'em" in that sentence was referring to women.

"You'd make a good mafioso," Johnson told Trump, to which the future U.S. president replied, "One of the greatest."

Decades later, numerous critics, including Trump's fired FBI director, James Comey, would compare Trump to a mob boss, though less flatteringly so. This comparison also came up during a private meeting at the White House that we had with Sarah Huckabee Sanders, at the time still working in the West Wing as Trump's most senior spokesperson and as a treasured confidante.

We were meeting her at her office in early 2019 in part to discuss the prospect of arranging an interview with her boss for *Sinking in the Swamp*. We explained the above premise and the *Goodfellas* analogy to Sanders, who seemed at least superficially interested, given her stated fandom for the acclaimed film. At one point, Swin conceded that there are, in fact, differences between La Cosa Nostra and the Trump administration, to which Sanders mockingly thanked him for generously admitting there were distinctions between Trump and a gore-soaked mobster.

"It's true. You guys have stronger NDAs," Swin replied.

"Yeah, but in the mob they'll just kill you!" Sanders shot back. She scribbled down our interview request on a sheet of paper and at least said she would bring it up with the president.

As you can likely guess, despite our entreaties to Donald Trump's senior spokespeople, including the back-to-back White House press secretaries Sanders and Stephanie Grisham as well as his former media gatekeeper Hope Hicks, we did not, ultimately, get to interview the president for this book, or anything else. We've asked numerous times and regret not having the opportunity to ask him about all the things we're writing about that would invariably have made him mad to our faces. In the course of our investigations, interviews, and digging for the book that you're holding, we communicated with at least 174 knowledgeable sources—administration officials, lawyers, Trump friends, operatives, party apparatchiks, media figures, lobbyists, strategists, villains, victims, professional bullshitters, backstabbers and backbiters, campaign brass, the works—to bring you this story.

A number of people, perhaps some very powerful and very wealthy people, will want to tell you that this book is "fiction" or "fake." Our official position directed at anyone who tries to tell you that is "All our news is real, and every orgasm you ever thought you gave someone was fake."

Reading this book, you might walk away with the sense that we have been two little piglets in the Trump years, gleefully inhaling the muck and empty calories at the trough of President Trump's lunacy. Indeed, we tried to reflect as much of the dark humor of this presidency as possible and have painted a portrait of what we believe are some of the defining characteristics and depravities of the Trump universe. By no means should this be mistaken for a numbness to the human costs of the era, on which numerous reporters and advocates have done incredible work. For us, the use of humor is a form of professional and personal novocaine.

In the end, the American people get the elected government they deserve. And that is punishingly true, very much so, of the election and administration of the forty-fifth president.

TIC TACS AND UNCLE TOMS

Throughout Donald Trump's long-running history of legal threats and maneuvers, there has been rampant bluffing, oftentimes taking the shape of verbally violent bluster. In his earlier real estate days, he was known to privately threaten businessmen, lawyers, and other adversaries with "my friends in Jersey" if he felt someone had crossed him. It is unclear if his threats of Mafia violence were backed up by anything remotely actionable or within his power to authorize, or if he was just making a big-boy noise. Most people who heard this simply rolled their eyes and went about their day.

President Trump was never able to shed his affinity for mob-don lingo, or at least his pop culture approximation of it. He'd repeatedly blast his former fixer and attorney, Michael Cohen, for being a snitch and a rat for cooperating with the feds and making him look bad, for instance. And Trump sues, or more often emptily threatens to sue or inflict pain via the justice system, as if failing to do so will cause him erectile dysfunction.

But long before he tore from Hillary Rodham Clinton the title of "leader of the free world," and a decade before he shot to right-wing political stardom as a garrulous vessel for racist birtherism, Donald

John Trump was himself the target of some pettier, less high-profile legal action. This was due to the fact that during the late 1980s and early 1990s Trump was—allegedly!—busy ripping off some poor schmuck's board-game idea.

In 1990, around the time the tabloid press was having a field day with Trump's brutal split from his first wife, Ivana, a real estate and insurance agent in Michigan named Walter Brockington III (then in his late twenties) briefly became a blip in The Donald's long life. In a lawsuit that year, Brockington alleged that Trump had stolen his idea for a Monopoly-esque board game that the real estate mogul created with Milton Bradley and simply called Trump: The Game. For his alleged trouble and dispossession, Brockington sought $50,000 in damages.

It was one of a litany of lawsuits and legal actions, frivolous or otherwise, that have consumed seemingly the entirety of Trump's seven decades on the planet, including his characteristically litigious presidency.

According to the suit filed in U.S. District Court in Detroit, Brockington claimed he had written Trump a letter in 1988 requesting financial support to move his game, Mogul, from drawing board to reality. Brockington claims that he received a letter back from the Trump Organization stating it was not interested. But the following year, Trump unveiled a new product with Milton Bradley, with Trump: The Game being sold for twenty-five bucks a pop.

Brockington's lawsuit ended up going nowhere, and Trump's board game proved to be a poorly selling dud. But to this day, Brockington believes the similarities between Trump: The Game and his letter to Trump—"the instructions, and the mechanics of Trump's game," he said—defied coincidence, thus proving he must've been "ripped off" by a supposed titan of industry he once so admired.

"He is a character," Brockington said during the 2016 GOP presidential primary. "I don't think he has what it takes to be president. When you look at what he said about immigrants, when you look at what he said about President Obama, he's a bad example.

"I don't think he's gonna make it as president, or the nominee for the Republican Party," Brockington added, chillingly but without much prescience.

IN the years that paved the way for Donald Trump's ascendance to the presidency, he accumulated cultural power the old-fashioned way: through a potent combination of coastal tabloid intrigue, Hollywood star-fucking, weaponized baby-boomer racism, red-meat conservative media, and trashy, anesthetizing television.

In early 2004, the reality-TV kingpin Mark Burnett and the National Broadcasting Company gave Trump an extraordinary platform to bombard millions of American voters with pure, uncut pro-Trump propaganda: the big, fat lie that he was somehow a master of the universe. But if you blame NBC's *The Apprentice* and *The Celebrity Apprentice* for fueling President Trump's rise and the cult of personality that propelled him into the Oval Office, then logically you must first blame the butterfly effect of the cast of *Friends* deciding to throw in the towel after a mere ten seasons on the air.

In the closing months of 2002, the actors playing Monica, Phoebe, Rachel, Joey, Ross, and Chandler on the beloved NBC sitcom all decided, and publicly announced, that season ten, to wrap in 2004, would be their curtain call. At the time, Jeff Zucker—who would soon become a nemesis of *President* Trump's as president of CNN—was the head of NBC Entertainment; he and other top execs scrambled to lock down adequate filler to help close the void that was about to be exposed by the evaporation of "Must See TV" on Thursday nights.

The network, in what at the time seemed like a bold gambit, slotted a new reality show—Burnett's *Apprentice*—in for Thursday-evening family viewing. And the move paid off. The first season, in which unknown businesspeople competed in menial contests for the honor of Donald Trump's televised approval, was a hit and featured some of the more memorable characters such as Omarosa Manigault, who would become an ally on Trump's 2016 campaign, a senior official in the Trump administration, and finally a high-profile backstabber and antagonist.

"Who knew that the replacement for 'Friends' would be Donald Trump?" Zucker told *The New York Times* all those years ago. Or that the replacement for Barack Obama would be Donald Trump?

BEFORE *The Apprentice* took off on NBC, Trump, with his string of colossal real estate catastrophes and bullshit-artistry, was at risk of cementing his status as a perennial D-lister and pop culture also-ran. With the success of the reality-TV series, he rose to the more respectable B-list and got a mere taste of the full-throttle political adulation that in time would be his for the taking.

He ruled over the set and series as his own personal fiefdom, barking orders as a morally vacant patrician acting out without fear of consequence, on or off camera.

One disgusting habit to which he'd routinely submit staff and the cleaning crew involved Tic Tacs. The hard-mint product became part of the Trump canon when *The Washington Post* published the infamous "grab 'em by the pussy" tape in the final weeks of the presidential campaign. On the tape, Trump explains to Jeb Bush's cousin Billy that he popped some Tic Tacs before meeting the women he assaulted. It would lead to Tic Tac's jumping on the bandwagon to denounce

Trump, with a tweet reading "Tic Tac respects all women. We find the recent statements and behavior completely inappropriate and unacceptable." But there's another gross Tic Tac story hiding further back in Trump's past.

On the set of *The Apprentice*, as Trump would sit behind the boardroom table, getting more and more bored as he waited to shoot his scenes, he would busy himself by sucking on Tic Tacs. He would spit them out behind the table, leaving them on the floor for staff to discover and, to their horror, to clean up.

"Trump used to take Tic Tacs, and suck out the outer layer, and stick them on the floor of the set—it was fucking awful," one person who worked on Trump's NBC show told Swin during the election. (All *Apprentice* staffers and alumni had to speak anonymously so as to not run afoul of strict, intimidating nondisclosure agreements, a Trump hallmark even then.)

One *Apprentice* colleague "started this tradition of keeping Trump-used Tic Tacs, and it was one day our goal to take them to a genetic lab" with the aim of cloning him, or at least getting the half-dissolved candies analyzed by a professional, this person added.

In a particularly stomach-turning moment of reporting, Swin was actually shown a photo of a container of Trump's used Tic Tacs. It was as upsetting as it sounds.

DURING the tail end of the 2016 election, Swin, working closely with one of his *Beast* colleagues, Gideon Resnick, did a lot of reporting on Trump's reign of terror at *The Apprentice* and attempted to show what his starring role and involvement with the production said about how he'd tackle being chief executive of the United States. The pair spent weeks cold-calling and contacting numerous former and then-current

Apprentice staff, leading to many of them anonymously breaking their million-dollar-plus NDAs, all in the service of dishing revealing tidbits on the kind of man DJT really was.

Some of the stories Swin and Gideon broke included Trump repeatedly mocking one of his supposed friends and "celebrity apprentices," Marlee Matlin, an Oscar-winning actress who happens to be deaf, as "retarded." (President Trump would later use the term to habitually trash his first attorney general, Jeff Sessions, as a "retarded," "weak," incompetent apparatchik.) During tapings of the series, Trump often scribbled notes as he sat at the long table and judged contestants in "the boardroom," the climactic Trump Tower setting for his game show. One person familiar with these notes and who cleaned up the boardroom after tapings found one of the slips of paper, which read in Trump's handwriting, "Marlee, is she retarded??"

A different *Apprentice* staffer recounted, "In the boardroom, he would talk to her like she was 'special.' He took her deafness as some kind of [mental] handicap." This staff member recalled being in the control room for taping of an episode on which Matlin was a contestant and listening as Trump made an "insensitive" remark on the actress's deafness while she was seated opposite Trump. "She responded; she stood up for herself," this source recalled. However, this interaction was relegated to the cutting room floor of the episode. The *Apprentice* tapes of these cut scenes, potentially a treasure trove of clips and faux pas that would be humiliating to Trump, have been squirreled away from the public, with Trump's buddy Mark Burnett, the *Apprentice* honcho, sticking to his vow of silence.

"People would just laugh this [stuff] off; it was just the culture," the *Apprentice* staffer noted. "But now it's a little more serious because it's not a joke anymore!" Another witness said Trump "would kind of do these mock voices," approximating a deaf voice. "Marlee was a popular person on the show . . . He would take the low road and mock her disability."

The day after that report published in October 2016, Matlin responded with a written statement on Twitter, reading **"Recent media reports have circulated that Donald Trump allegedly referred [to me] as 'retarded.' The term is abhorrent and should never be used. The fact that we are talking about this during a very important moment in American history has upset me deeply."**

She continued, **"As a person who is Deaf, as a woman, as a mom, as a wife, as an actor, I have a voice. And I'm using that voice to make myself heard... and vote."**

Another *Apprentice* story Swin broke later that same month, when, citing multiple anonymous sources, *The Daily Beast* ran the headline "Donald Trump Kept Calling Lil Jon an 'Uncle Tom' on Celebrity Apprentice." While making the thirteenth season of his NBC show, Trump caught a glimpse of the rapper/contestant wearing an Uncle Sam getup to help advertise hair-care products. After spotting this, Trump began exclaiming that Lil Jon, a black man, was a real "Uncle Tom!"—seemingly unaware that "Uncle Tom" is a racial slur typically directed at black men accused of being hyper-subservient to white people. When staff tried to tell Trump that what he really meant was "Uncle Sam," not "Tom," and that the latter would be taken as rather offensive to the recording artist, Trump refused to back down.

"No, that's a saying, it's Uncle Tom," Trump said with a straight face. There are even several unaired takes in *Apprentice* footage of Trump trying to figure out the difference between "Uncle Sam" (*bueno*) and "Uncle Tom" (*no bueno*), with the TV host somehow not able to grasp what was and wasn't problematic. His stubbornness on the issue set off a mini-crisis among producers and others on the set, with multiple producers having tried, to no avail, to persuade him not to use the term. One of the executive producers even called Trump to plead with him to drop the "Tom."

None of this worked.

Their fears were realized when Trump, well, ended up calling Lil Jon an Uncle Tom to his face in the boardroom.

Shortly before publication of this story on a Friday night, Swin emailed Hope Hicks, one of Trump's top aides and his media gate-keeper, with a standard comment request. Hicks had, for the most part, ignored Swin's requests for comment during the many months of the campaign. Within twelve minutes of receiving Swin's inquiry, however, Hicks messaged back a terse statement: "This is simply un-true." (As a mildly amusing aside, when Hicks sent this, she thought she was emailing a female reporter. The following year, Swin and Lach-lan would meet Hicks face-to-face for the first time, for a meeting in what had become Donald Trump's West Wing. During the initial min-utes of our conversation, Hicks kept looking at Swin in a gently bizarre, inquisitive way that became abundantly clear as to why, when at one point she interrupted him midsentence to say, "I'm sorry, I thought you were a girl." Lachlan promptly began chortling his ass off in the chair beside Swin. Since 2015, Swin and Hope had communicated only in the form of written electronic comms. She had assumed "Asawin Suebsaeng" was a lady's name. Who—who isn't Thai—could possibly blame her?)

The Daily Beast published the article regardless. Before the clock struck midnight that Friday evening, Lil Jon himself helped knock down the Trump campaign's explicit denial, tweeting a statement con-firming the report. **"When this 'Uncle Tom' incident happened on Celeb-rity Apprentice in the boardroom several of my castmates and I addressed Mr. Trump immediately when we heard the comment,"** the rapper said. **"I can't say if he knew what he was actually saying or not, but he did stop** using that term once we explained [its] offensiveness. I also want to be clear that I don't agree with many of the statements Mr. Trump has said during his current run for President." (As president, Trump would later claim at a press conference, when asked by a reporter about his track record of racist behavior, that he had no idea who Lil Jon was, despite having hosted him on his *Apprentice* set and having tweeted about the rapper in the past.)

Several other *Apprentice*-related scoops came out that month, but one in particular has stuck with Swin for all these years. It was the one story in the batch that, more so than the rest, truly underscored what kind of commander in chief Donald Trump would be. The story, which ran after the torrent of sexual assault and harassment allegations against the 2016 Republican presidential nominee had already started, had Donald Trump engaging in an alleged cover-up of a sexual attack, all to protect one of his famous friends.

During the filming of the 2011 *Celebrity Apprentice* season, Trump welcomed the Oscar nominee Gary Busey into the fold. Busey, of course, came with his fair share of personal baggage. In 1999, the actor had been investigated for domestic violence after his wife alleged that he "grabbed her shoulders and wrestled her to the ground," according to the authorities. Busey was freed after posting bail. Two years prior to that, a United Airlines flight attendant accused Busey of hitting her. No subsequent criminal charges were filed.

But Trump has frequently felt compelled to stick up for his notorious acquaintances, even those accused or convicted of serious crimes, whether they be Mike Tyson, Don King, Paul Manafort, or Gary Busey. It didn't hurt that Busey, in 2012, had endorsed Trump for the presidency back when the real estate mogul had previously flirted with running to unseat Barack Obama. (Trump would instead align himself with the eventual GOP nominee, Mitt Romney, whose campaign had actively sought the birther businessman's imprimatur. Years after that, Romney was elected senator in the Trump era, during which he mainly made national headlines for gently criticizing something Trump said or did that made him feel personally uncomfortable.)

But during the shooting of the 2011 season, Busey allegedly did something on the set that Trump himself would consider "naughty." Others would consider the alleged act sexual violence. The alleged incident occurred when the celebrity contestants were tasked by Trump to sell some art at a New York gallery. At one point, the cast and crew were taking a break outside, where one female employee, who spoke to Swin under the condition of anonymity, was allegedly grabbed by Busey. "They had booze for the [gallery party]; I think Lil Jon ordered it," she said. "And so, a few of the celebrities wanted to do a shot together after we finished [setting up] for the show. We all took a shot together and then went to stand together for B-roll time. We were smoking cigarettes outside, and Busey was standing next to me. And then at one point, he grabbed me firmly between my legs and ran his hand up my stomach and grabbed my breasts. I didn't know what to do. So I made this joke, 'Oh, I've never been sexually harassed by a celebrity before!' Then he grabbed my hand and put it [over] his penis and said, like, 'I'm just getting started, baby.'"

At that point, her friend, visibly alarmed, said she intervened and jumped in between her and Busey to put a stop to it. Word traveled fast, and the alleged victim's colleagues and friends were absolutely livid. Some reportedly demanded that Busey be kicked off the show, and internal discontent grew so loud that it rippled up the chain of command, from management and executive producers all the way to Donald Trump himself.

The real estate TV star not only turned a blind eye but laughed it off while doing so. Busey was permitted to remain on the show for the duration of the season, until he was "fired" by Trump and finished in sixth place. His alleged victim told Swin that she didn't pursue the matter further for fear she would be blackballed or suffer professional consequences. (Two years after the alleged assault, Busey would return to Trump's *Apprentice* fiefdom, if you're wondering what kind of blow-back he suffered.)

According to multiple sources, when Trump welcomed Busey into the boardroom, he did little more than giggle about the incident. "Keep your hands to yourself," Trump instructed Busey. "Gary, did you do a bad thing? . . . Got your hands where they're not supposed to be? . . . Bad boy, a very bad boy."

Multiple people witnessed the two of them yukking it up as Trump was supposed to be punishing him. Through a representative, Busey emphatically denied the allegations at the time *The Daily Beast* first published them.

During the final weeks of the 2016 election, Swin spent a lot of time investigating Trump's era of reality-TV stardom. Some of the stories he came across were frivolous; others were darkly humorous. But this one showed you basically everything you need to know about Trump as leader of the free world. Here he was presented with serious, credible allegations of a sexual assault, on his watch, and he gladly opted to protect the alleged perpetrator, even having already deemed him guilty of the act. He brushed it aside. In doing so, he personally covered up the scandal.

What would a president Trump do, then? Swin asked himself. *What would he cover up as commander in chief? What if there was a massive sexual assault scandal in, say, the military during his presidency? How willing would he be to look the other way?*

Three years of the Trump administration did little to assuage Swin's concerns on this. When Roy Moore was accused of child molestation,

Trump didn't care. He privately slammed Moore's multiple accusers of spewing made-up bullshit, and he and the Republican Party ended up doubling down on Moore's Senate candidacy, hoping that Moore would defeat his Democratic opponent, Doug Jones, and that they could then start hurling the accusations down the memory hole. Moore, however, lost the Alabama race. Even with all the horrifying allegations against Moore, President Trump would still tweet in 2019, "I have NOTHING against Roy Moore."

Furthermore, the official position of the Trump White House is that literally all of the women who came forward since 2016 to accuse the president of sexual misconduct or sexual violence are simply lying.

When his Supreme Court nominee Brett Kavanaugh was hit with an on-record allegation of attempted rape, President Trump didn't just support him through the confirmation fight. He made Kavanaugh's victory over the accusation a cornerstone of Republican messaging during the 2018 midterm elections. To this very day, the alleged attempted rapist's lifetime appointment to the highest court in the land remains one of Trump's most treasured accomplishments in his life.

Simply put, there is no shortage of allegedly violent, brutal men whom President Trump—or *Apprentice* Trump—is utterly and giddily willing to shelter and reward.

IF you lived through American popular culture since the late twentieth century, it was exceedingly difficult not to stumble across example after example after example after wretched example of overpaid filmmakers and well-rated TV shows depicting The Donald as a charming fancy-lad and ultimate elbow-rubber. If you thought you could watch the Sandra Bullock–Hugh Grant rom-com *Two Weeks Notice* without getting an eyeful of Donald Trump, think again, because he shows up for a cute, thirty-second cameo to needle Grant's character and inti-mate that he'd steal away his one true love. Any consumer of television and Tinseltown flicks in the 1990s and early years of the twenty-first century couldn't get away from Donald Trump if his or her life de-pended on it.

In the most basic, stereotypical (or archetypal) sense, Trump is a flouncing glob of "Hollywood": the sleaze, the boorish self-aggran-dizement, the backstabbing, and the constant bullshitting—it was all there, in the least likable, cattiest meaning of the loaded term. Though far too many famous friends, and famous former friends, put up with The Donald's incessant star-fuckery and gala ass-kissing for decades, his craving for the approval of Hollywood's ruling class naturally earned him some celebrity enemies long before he entered the West Wing.

This included women who refused to sleep with him. In late October 2016, the Hillary Clinton presidential campaign organized a confer-ence call with reporters, the primary motive being to allow the pro-Clinton Mexican American actress Salma Hayek to tell journalists why she hated Trump so much.

"He calls us criminals, but who is the one who has a lawsuit for Trump University?" the *Desperado* star said on the call. "He calls us rapists, but who has a lawsuit [against him] for raping a young girl?" (The Hollywood actress was likely referring to an accuser, who used a pseudonym to file a suit in Manhattan federal court, who alleged that Trump had raped her when she was just thirteen years old, at a 1994 sex party at the estate of the pedophile billionaire Jeffrey Epstein.)

On the same conference call, Hayek also claimed that Trump had once tried to date her and, when she turned him down, retaliated by—anonymously, no fingerprints—planting a false and unflattering story about her in the *National Enquirer*, a Trump-aligned supermarket tabloid that would find itself in the crosshairs of federal investigators after Trump became president.

"Not my type!" Hayek exclaimed to reporters.

Hayek spoke for many in the business.

By March 2011, when Trump had only begun to transform into a national hero of the Far Right, the comedian Lewis Black did a riff on his semi-regular "Back in Black" segment on *The Daily Show with Jon Stewart*, knocking Trump for his "dictator"-like qualities. This segment was titled "Trump 2012."

"There's one candidate who's got me really excited: Donald Trump!" the comedian said with Stewart at his side. "Now, you might say he'd make a terrible president. I mean, the guy bankrupted his own casino. A casino! Where the house always wins! Unless it's Donald Trump's house."

Black went further. "What this country needs is a crazy Third World dictator, and Donald Trump has what it takes to be that," he continued. "He's already got a plane with his name on it, solid-gold buildings, a harem! . . . He's even got the look of a dictator! Now, is [Trump's] hair any less crazy than [Kim Jong Il's] hair? And he's got what every good dictator needs: a ridiculously oversized ego . . . This is what I've been waiting for my whole life! A president who's not afraid to tell the truth—about being a lying asshole."

Black had been making jokes about Trump from time to time for decades. But when he did it on Comedy Central, a notoriously thin-skinned Trump perked up.

"I did a piece about him in 2011 on how what America needs is a banana republic dictator," Black told Swin less than two months before Election Day 2016. "His assistant called my assistant, said he wanted to talk to me. At first, it was like, 'What? Why would he call me? No one ever called me about anything I ever did on *The Daily Show*. So I said I was too busy and couldn't talk to him. I thought, 'Wow, I'm a comic; he's an entrepreneur—a businessman. How is it that I'm more busy than he is? That's unbelievable.'"

But, Trump being Trump, he simply would *not. Let. It. Go.*

"A call came the next day, and I just said no," Black recounted. "I didn't want to talk to him to legitimize him. That's how I felt . . . If I accept his call, that legitimizes him. And I didn't want to give him any little sense of legitimacy that I could have given him by answering the phone."

For a frame of reference, this is what an angry call from Trump can sound like after he catches something on the TV that annoys him: In a piece published by *Politico* in January 2016, the Fox News host Tucker Carlson wrote about one especially memorable voice message he had once received from the real estate nepotism baby. "About 15 years ago, I said something nasty on CNN about Donald Trump's hair," Carlson recounted. "I can't now remember the context, assuming there was one. In any case, Trump saw it and left a message the next day. 'It's true you have better hair than I do,' Trump said matter-of-factly. 'But I get more pussy than you do.'"

"Click," Carlson wrote.

Trump never got his chance to leave Lewis Black any voice mail attacking the comedian's sex life. Black noted that he had only one other personal experience involving Trump. Unsurprisingly, it occurred in the middle of the George W. Bush administration and involved a star-studded gala dinner in Manhattan and Donald Trump whining loudly at the help. "I have been within ten feet of him at an event I was working, for some book event, at the museum—the big one, with the fucking whale thing," Black recalled. "He was upset because he didn't get the right table. He was yelling about it."

In the 2016 election, Black, a self-identifying socialist, was reliably an avowed Bernie Sanders supporter. (He quipped he'd rather vote for the Pillsbury Doughboy than Hillary Clinton, for instance.) By 2020, John Cusack, another loud and proud Bernie diehard occupying an upper echelon of Hollywood fame, was still pulling hard for Bernie 2020, confident that the democratic-socialist senator from Vermont was the only candidate in the entire, sprawling Democratic field who could actually vanquish Trump. Cusack, similar to Black, had long viewed Donald Trump as a grotesque manifestation of avarice, capitalism, racist barbarity, and American empire.

In the movie *War, Inc.*, a 2008 satire on war profiteering, the actor Ben Kingsley voices a disembodied stand-in for U.S. imperial designs, barking orders at Cusack's assassin character through a loudspeaker connected to a large TV. As Kingsley speaks, the screen projects different photos and images representing the American id. There's Ronald Reagan, of course. And then there's John Wayne. There's also Donald Trump. The use of his face earned The Donald a sarcastic special "thanks" in the closing credits of the film.

The year Trump was elected, Cusack would tweet at Swin that Trump made a "cameo" in his movie **"as a joke and as we used him as an absurdist Americana authoritarian strong man in the film."** American political life, Cusack believed, was "always darker" than "the most perverse satire."

Nearly three years later, Cusack found himself again in Washington, D.C., in part to attend a special screening and Q&A of his 2000 film, *High Fidelity*, in part to meet with Representative Jerry Nadler, the House Judiciary Committee chairman investigating Trumpworld. Swin met Cusack for the first time face-to-face in the lobby area of the noir-influenced Kimpton Hotel Monaco near Chinatown and asked him about his past run-ins with Donald Trump. Some of the most revealing anecdotes about Trump's personality, and regarding what makes him tick, can be found simply by asking famous people and Hollywood stars to dish on past experiences with the guy. The actor Tim Robbins (star of *The Shawshank Redemption*, and yet another Bernie Sanders booster) told *The New York Times* in early 2018 about the time he threw a private party for his friends at a Greenwich Village club one evening in the mid-1990s. Trump, uninvited and unwanted, crashed it, simply so he could get someone to snap a picture of him photobombing the ascendant Hollywood actor. "It was weird," Robbins said. "He wanted a photo with me because I was famous. He used to do that a lot, by the way. He wanted to be photographed with famous people all the time."

Cusack, for his part, had two lasting impressions of the then future president, based on two separate incidents over the past three decades. Neither painted a flattering portrait, and both convinced Cusack years ago that The Donald was a sociopathic sleazeball.

One incident, he told Swin, occurred at a heavyweight championship fight two decades prior. Cusack showed up and was escorted to the VIP section near the ring. He shuffled past well-established businessmen and various luminaries and supposed titans of industry on his way to his seat to watch the two professional fighters beat the hell out of each other. Sitting down, Cusack peered to his left, to discover to his dismay and great annoyance that right behind him, in the second row, was Donald Trump and the future First Lady Melania. Cusack did his best not to make eye contact with either of them, fearing that the businessman would initiate an awkward conversation about doing deals, or Candice Bergen, or a potentially fictitious yacht orgy Trump attended, or some other shit.

Soon enough, Cusack noticed Melania peeking at him and grinning widely. Then Cusack noticed that she . . . wouldn't stop smiling and staring at him. At that point, Donald took notice, leaned forward, looked at John, looked at Melania, looked at John, looked at Melania. Then Donald Trump cracked an obsequious grin, tipping his hat to John's fame, apparently.

"Hey, my girlfriend REALLY likes you," Donald told John.

Cusack shuddered, smiled, and waved politely—"Well, nice to meet you," he said—before turning away in quiet horror, having come face-to-face with a flirty, maybe-horny Donald Trump.

The other Cusack incident occurred several years earlier, when the actor was researching his role for the political drama *City Hall*, in which he shared top billing with Al Pacino and Bridget Fonda. Cusack was at the actual city hall in Manhattan, shadowing Democratic aides and politicians, when he found in his character research a thoroughly Trumpian anecdote about Donald Trump. (Lachlan and Swin have since heard this same story from two sources in New York politics and business.) Many years ago, Trump was at city hall talking to some senior aides, asking them if they would rename a prominent Manhattan street Trump Avenue to stoke his towering ego. The aides appeared perplexed and proceeded to gently explain to Trump that the city couldn't do that. New York City, they told Trump, had a tradition of not naming streets after people who are still alive. The city could name streets after famous and beloved individuals, but *after* they had passed on.

Trump didn't miss a beat or flinch in his reply.

"Oh, Fred's in his late eighties," the future president shot back.

Frederick Christ Trump would die in 1999, three years after *City Hall* came out. But here Donald was, standing in the middle of the real-life city hall, using the upcoming corpse of his rich daddy in a vain effort to get a street named after Donald J. Trump.

To this day, President Trump—having become the most powerful person on the face of the planet and perhaps the single most famous human being alive in this young century—still carries around a chip on his shoulder about all the famous actors, musicians, models, athletes, agents, and directors who now see him as little more than a fascist creep. During his first term in office, his stage mom–style lust for fame and recognition among the "elite" usually manifested itself in the form of ill-tempered online activity.

"Washed up psycho @BetteMidler was forced to apologize for a statement she attributed to me that turned out to be totally fabricated by her in order to make 'your great president' look really bad," the forty-fifth president tweeted in early June 2019. "She got caught, just like the Fake News Media gets caught. A sick scammer!"

At the time, Trump was in London, meaning the tweet was posted around 1:00 a.m. his time. The president was for a moment preoccupied with Bette Midler while overseas on a state visit to the United Kingdom. Maybe it was easier than facing up to what was actually happening on that side of the pond, where he was being disrespected by an entirely different set of famous people. The young royals—William, Harry, Kate—refused President Trump a photo op with them.

The celebrity snub likely stung hard, even if the president tried not to let it show. But since entering the White House, Trump has complained privately about media reports that portray the British royal family as despising, and not wanting to hang out with, him, but loving Barack Obama. In 2018, the U.K. publication *The Times* reported that "Prince Charles and Prince William were unwilling to meet Donald Trump on his visit to Britain, leaving the Queen to greet the US president alone." A Whitehall official told the paper that the queen's meeting that year with President Trump was "kept to the bare minimum. The Queen will do her duty, but among the wider family, they were not as enthusiastic as they were when [President Barack] Obama came over."

JOE, MIKA, AND "THAT BITCH WITH THE TRANNY DAD"

I t was the middle of the day on the fourteenth floor of Trump Tower, where, as the candidate's campaign to destroy Hillary Clinton's hopes and dreams of West Wing occupancy kicked into high gear in late 2016, a ragtag group of Trump loyalists monitored and synthesized the unending stream of news coverage about their candidate. Oftentimes, when most of the campaign's staffers had already gone home, Team Trump's skeleton crew of media watchers was left working the midnight shift in the campaign's so-called war room. War rooms are the rapid-response nerve centers of political campaigns, where staffers huddle around television sets, keeping tabs on any developments in the race or mentions of their candidates, ready to blast out a statement or a media pitch if a moment in the news cycle presents itself.

The news cycles of 2016 were consumed by Trump to a degree unusual even for a major-party presidential candidate. That made his campaign's war room a central component of the campaign apparatus. And it also meant long hours for those tasked with sifting through the streams of cable news coverage and drip drip of reporting on their candidate's various flaws, foibles, and outrageous campaign trail pronouncements and actions.

Trump himself rarely ever set foot in his own campaign offices. Staffers recalled fewer than half a dozen times throughout the campaign—including election night—when he was spotted roaming the fourteenth floor. So on this quiet, average day in Trump Tower, the war room's denizens were stunned when they turned their heads to see that DJT, as campaign staffers knew him, had quietly sauntered up next to them. Some of them had never actually met the candidate, and here he was, calmly surveying his political operation.

No one knew what to say to the candidate. But he soon piped up. As he stood in front of his staffers, Trump motioned toward the war room televisions, each tuned to a different cable news channel.

"Which do you think is worse," the future president asked, to no one in particular, "CNN or MSNBC?"

They were taken aback. Did he really want to know their opinions on the relative merits of various TV news channels? But one of the staffers chimed in.

"Well, sir," he said sheepishly, "I think CNN is worse. MSNBC at least admits that they're liberal. But CNN claims they play it down the middle, when they're actually just as bad."

Trump lit up. "Totally agree! Totally agree!" he exclaimed, hands raised in characteristic palms-forward gesticulation. He launched into a soliloquy about the misdeeds of what he would soon call the "fake news media," and CNN in particular. But he quickly turned his ire back to MSNBC, and specifically Joe Scarborough and Mika Brzezinski, the co-hosts of MSNBC's *Morning Joe* program. Longtime Trump friends and acquaintances, Joe and Mika provided him with one of the few non-Fox platforms on cable news during the campaign that occasionally defended him, or at least took his candidacy seriously.

If that had earned them any goodwill with Trump at the time, he wasn't showing it. He was more interested in gossiping about the two mainstays of the New York media scene. And, ooh boy, did he have some juicy gossip to share with these midlevel campaign staffers whose names he didn't even know.

"You know," he said, clearly amused with himself, "nobody else knows about it, but I know about Joe and Mika's little apartment in the Upper East Side." At the time, the longtime *Morning Joe* co-hosts were rumored to be engaged in a long-running affair. They would get married a couple years later, in late 2018. But during the campaign, their relationship was very much not officially public.

"One day, I'll tell you all about it," Trump promised his war room.

Here was the future president of the United States in his campaign headquarters, quizzing top staffers not on the latest polling data or the campaign's ad strategies but on the love lives of two pundits about whom he simply loved to dish gossip.

Days later, Trump took another rare swing through his campaign's offices. But this time he had a couple guests in tow.

He was giving a personal tour of his beloved war room to none other than . . . his dear pals Joe and Mika.

Multiple people recounted this story to us over the first two years of the Trump White House. For those present, and their campaign colleagues who inevitably heard about it through the unending stream of high-school-cheerleader-esque gossiping that ceaselessly consumes Trumpworld, it was a simultaneous illustration of a number of idiosyncrasies that, the whole country would soon learn in depressing fashion, define Donald Trump the man and have come to define his presidency.

Trump's relationship with Joe and Mika, and his larger relationship with the pundit press, is akin to a really bad marriage. Each party despises the other, constantly hurls insults, threatens, demeans, berates, and promises that, *goddamn it, this is the last time, I swear I'm going to leave you.* But neither of them leaves, because when it comes down to it, they're in love, and they need each other. Trump needs the media to hang on his every word, and if that means they put on an air of outrage and derision, well, that's better than being ignored. And the punditocracy needs Trump and his endless stream of slights and outrages. They provide unending fodder for mindless and banal panel discussions, inevitably stacked with Republican strategists and Democratic strategists, titles seemingly devised purely for cable news chyrons with which to banner these reliably unenlightening television shout-fests.

Ground zero for the Trump-media marriage during much of the campaign was *Morning Joe*, where Brzezinski and Scarborough would profess their disgust with Trump's more outlandish, sexist, and xenophobic comments while adding to-be-sure paeans to Trump's—and by extension their own—down-home, middle-American appeal. Trump supporters, "formerly called common-sense conservatives, are considered drug-addled losers who are too stupid to determine what is in their best interest," Scarborough wrote in an April 2016 column in *The Washington Post*. "The left-wing's 'What's the Matter With Kansas?' is now the GOP establishment's 'What the Hell's Up With Upstate New York?'"

The New York pundit burnishing his real-American credentials soon became a Trump coverage genre of its own. Sure, he wants to throw brown people in camps, but golly someone's finally listening to the blue-collar Appalachian coal miner. Yes, he's threatening to use the Justice Department to prosecute political opponents. A bit extreme, but you know what? Americans are sick and tired of business as usual in Washington.

Trump professed his appreciation for the efforts—"You guys have been supporters, and I really appreciate it," he told Joe and Mika on one occasion—but behind the scenes he was gossiping about their long-running affair. Beyond his immediate family, Trump has no relationship that he does not define, wittingly or unwittingly, in terms of his own impulsive satisfaction. He loves being praised, he loves to gossip, and above all he loves being talked about. And he'll share his thoughts with anyone who will listen—be it one of his tens of millions of Twitter followers or a lowly war room staffer in his campaign headquarters.

THE Joe and Mika episode illustrated another essential Trump characteristic—a feature, not a bug—that dominated his campaign and would go on to do so in his presidential administration. The candidate frequently concerned himself with issues at best tangentially related to matters at hand (in this case, getting himself elected president). He was prone to distraction and consumed by gossip and petty feuds. And he took any criticism as a personal slight against him and went scorched earth in response.

It fell to the crew of staff assembled on the fourteenth floor to try to manage those instincts. Those who worked for the campaign continue to believe that Trump was far smarter and more adept than anyone gave him credit for. His understanding of the type of campaign that would propel him to the White House was second nature. And ideas for running that campaign that seemed outlandish to political professionals were, these staffers felt, strokes of genius during a campaign that defied all conventional wisdom on the conduct of a presidential candidate.

But these same staffers are the first to admit—and, indeed, have done so in countless private conversations with us—that Trump's erratic behavior made it virtually impossible to stay on message and present a coherent, compelling political platform. Offhand remarks about Mexican rape fiends, deeply personal criticism of a Gold Star family, flippant pledges to dismantle crucial U.S. military alliances— these were all products of the same seat-of-the-pants political approach that ended up being so successful. (Once in the Oval Office, Trump seemed to take this approach toward everything, foreign and domestic, whether it came to Baltimore or Beijing.) But they also put Trump's campaign staffers in the position of trying to keep this freewheeling political apparatus from going off the rails.

That would've been a challenge for the most seasoned and respected political operatives in the business. Initially, Trump's team was . . . not that. When he got into the race for real, he faced a crowded Republican presidential field stacked with some of the party's most prominent names and most promising political contenders. And those competitors had sucked up virtually all of the top-notch Republican political talent in the country. Most of those who weren't committed to a candidate believed, as much of the political establishment did, that Trump didn't stand a chance in the general election. None of them were eager to sign on with a dead-end campaign that would saddle them with all the baggage of Trump's boisterous and caustic and potentially toxic brand.

That left Trump to draw from a limited pool of political operatives who ranged from the inexperienced to the fanatical to the downright corrupt. And few arms of the campaign illustrated the ad hoc nature of the effort's ranks of operatives better than those tasked with being the public voices of the campaign.

By late 2016, one of the more garrulous faces of the operation was the senior communications aide Boris Epshteyn, a loud, brash, hulking Republican staffer. The Russian-born Epshteyn had ridden Sarah

Palin's brief ascendance to moderate prominence in GOP circles. He'd taken an ill-fated run through some New York financial services firms before returning to politics. During his stint on John McCain's 2008 presidential campaign, where he was a Palin handler, staffers recalled him as a hanger-on with few official responsibilities and an outsize opinion of himself. One former colleague recalled that Epshteyn would frequently brag about how much he could bench-press, until his colleagues one day found a workout bench in the basement of their offices and challenged him to put his muscle where his mouth was. Epshteyn proceeded to put up something on the order of a colossal 350 pounds, the former colleague recalled.

We asked him about that story years later. "It was 425," Epshteyn insisted with a grin.

After the McCain campaign, on which Epshteyn had helped run the Palin team's rapid-response operation, he signed on as the vice president of legal affairs for a financial services firm called West America Securities. A few years later, the Financial Industry Regulatory Authority expelled the firm altogether. Epshteyn, though ostensibly overseeing compliance matters for the firm, wasn't accused of any wrongdoing.

He went on to found a boutique investment firm, TGP Securities, that soon found itself embroiled in litigation. A client accused TGP in federal court of accepting $100,000 in fees but failing to deliver financial backing for a theme park in Texas. The case was settled and dismissed in 2017. But the lawsuit shed some light on Epshteyn's view of himself as a connected, high-level political consultant. The plaintiff in the case recalled Epshteyn bragging about his extensive relationships with high-level Republican officials and claiming that he "carried a lot of clout within the party." He "suggested that the Plaintiff should Google him and watch his videos on YouTube" and "claimed that he was a regular guest on MSNBC, CNN, CNBC, Fox News, and radio programs nationwide and provided analysis on topics including political strategy, financial markets, international affairs, future elections, and party relations."

That rosy description of Epshteyn's influence would've come as a surprise at the time to virtually anyone working in Republican politics, where he was known, if at all, as a bumbling and marginally competent comms operative. But Trump's ascent brought his largely marginal crew up with him, and Epshteyn had quickly become one of the most prominent public faces of the Republican front-runner and eventual nominee. He was a constant presence on cable television, where he did what any good Trump surrogate was expected to do: go to the mat to defend Trump against any and all criticism, no matter its merits. Trump was caught on tape bragging about sexually assaulting women? Boris was there to rejoin with a total non sequitur: "You think the mothers of the Benghazi victims think about this banter from eleven years ago?" Trump viciously attacked the father of a slain U.S. serviceman? Criticism is just an effort "to obscure the fact that Hillary Clinton and Barack Obama have failed at keeping this country safe."

Boris is more of a blunt instrument than a subtle operative, and for a high-level political professional turned commentator—in 2017, Epshteyn would land one of the nation's highest-profile posts in opinion journalism at the local-media conglomerate Sinclair—he appeared woefully ignorant of some basic aspects of how the American government functions. That was plain during a Twitter exchange with Lachlan in 2018, when Epshteyn sought to defend the president's constitutional authority to impose tariffs on national security grounds against congressional efforts to roll back that authority. Lachlan pointed out that tariffs are squarely in Congress's constitutional domain and that the president has only statutory authority—that is, granted by Congress, which can rescind it—to unilaterally impose such measures. No, no, Boris insisted, "national security" is the prerogative of the president, and therefore affixing that label to a tariff or any other measure automatically confers authority over it on the president. It was a totally nonsensical, constitutionally illiterate argument but fairly representative of Epshteyn's tenuous grasp on the basic functions of the American political system.

But what Epshteyn lacked in basic knowledge of American civics, he more than made up for in the one characteristic that has always propelled people to success in the employ of Donald J. Trump: unquestioning, vehement loyalty to his boss. There was no outlandish statement that could not be justified, no criticism of Trump that wasn't rooted in malicious double standards and personal animus, no Trump policy proposal that wouldn't be an unqualified boon for the Republic.

No campaign surrogate can be expected to criticize his principal, of course, but most at least benefit from an understanding of the office to which their boss is aspiring. Epshteyn seemed to lack that, yet here he was, a very large cog in the veritable nerve center of the Trump campaign, the war room.

Epshteyn would also collect a stable of enemies during the campaign, those who found him to be an inconsequential oaf worthy of leaks, scorn, and subterfuge. At times, the feuding would resemble less a seasoned political operation and more a high school cafeteria. Epshteyn and Bryan Lanza, Trump 2016's deputy comms director, hated each other so much that Boris would run informal polls throughout the office, trying to determine who was better liked among Trump staffers and who had more friends.

Even placed in such a prominent post, Epshteyn couldn't help but let some of his more juvenile instincts flare from time to time. On one occasion, when some Trump family members were visiting the fourteenth floor, Melania and Tiffany both took seats among the war room desks, beside some of the staffers in the office. These comms officials were at this point surrounded by some of the candidate's immediate family and were trying their hardest to simply stare straight ahead at the TVs and remain professional in the esteemed presence of Trump royalty.

Boris got a good laugh out of that later. "You're sitting next to two of the most beautiful women in the world and you can't even look at them!" he ribbed his colleagues.

Andrew Surabian joined the campaign relatively late in the race, in August 2016, but quickly impressed some of its higher-ups. He had previously been running the U.S. Senate campaign of Louisiana's Rob Maness, a Tea Party–style Republican. And that's where Surabian's roots were. A more libertarian-minded Republican from a suburb of blue-collar Worcester, Massachusetts, he was previously the political director for the Tea Party Express, where he experienced most of his early political education.

Neighboring Surabian in the war room was Steven Cheung, a bi-coastal, Asian American operator with eclectic career tastes and, relative to much of the Team Trump hodgepodge, a certain amount of experience in presidential politics at the time. Prior to the Trump campaign, he was a Las Vegas–based promoter and public relations executive for the mixed martial arts league Ultimate Fighting Championship. In the summer of 2016, he cold-called the campaign looking for a gig on Trump's staff. He landed one and quickly earned a reputation as one of the hardest-working staffers on the fourteenth floor, a reputation that endeared him to the Trump family and earned him a White House post the following year. In the halls of the White House, President Trump, who could never seem to remember Cheung's name, would still take to stilted small talk whenever the two would bump into each other.

The sleep-deprived, media-addled compatriots of the Trump war room were paid another rare visit from DJT himself in early September 2016, this time on the night of Donald Trump's and Hillary Clinton's respective "commander in chief" forums hosted by NBC's Matt Lauer aboard the decommissioned USS *Intrepid*. Following the forum, Cheung, Surabian, senior comms adviser Jason Miller, and assorted members of Trump's campaign staff were still huddled and at work in the Trump Tower war room, blasting out emails and press releases and keeping watchful eyes on cable news coverage just a couple hours shy of midnight. Their eyes bloodshot, their veins not nearly pumped enough with caffeine.

Suddenly, around 10:00 p.m., entered the Republican nominee, the future First Lady Melania, and other members of the Trump clan. Right after arriving on the near-empty floor in the dead of night, Trump quizzed his aides on his performance and what the press was saying about his portion of the forum. "How was I? How did we do?" he'd inquire. "How's the coverage?" The campaign hands across the board, of course, told him he was world class as always and that the news coverage wasn't that bad, considering how much the press seemed to hate, hate, *hate* Donald Trump. It was well understood that if you gave the boss the wrong piece of bad news or pinned the blame on him, you'd risk getting shipped to a prison camp in Siberia.

Looking pleased with himself, the candidate nodded and proceeded to sit down at an empty table on an old black office chair situated directly behind his staffers. Melania dutifully sat near him, keeping almost totally silent, looking bored out of her mind. The Donald, meanwhile, was taking in all the coverage on the nearly dozen mounted TVs, all switched to CNN, Fox News, MSNBC, and the occasional local channel.

It was while watching his war room's wall of television sets that evening that Trump began doing something conspicuously, well, weird.

At one point, Trump started swinging around while seated in the desk chair, swiveling, doing multiple 180s, while staring down at the carpet and shuffling his feet like a child and tapping them against the floor. Campaign staffers noticed the swiveling and initially didn't know what to make of it. The GOP presidential nominee then said out of nowhere, as he kept tapping his foot, "This is some really good carpeting. Where did this come from?"

Tap, tap, tap.

"Great carpet, where did this come from?"

Swivel, tap, tap-tap.

"Really fantastic. Fantastic stuff," Trump continued.

Staffers present didn't know what to say, because there was literally nothing remarkable about the carpeting across that floor at Trump Tower.

It was ordinary blue corporate-office floor covering.

But for some reason, the future president's addled mind was absolutely *fascinated* by it. He had just come off an evening of weighing in on some topics of international and national importance, such as talking about how Secretary of State Hillary Clinton "made a terrible mistake on Libya" and how she and the rest of Team Obama "complicated the mistake by having no management once they bombed you-know-what out of Qaddafi."

Back at campaign HQ just a couple hours later, Trump was back focusing on something more his speed: cable news and his precious blue carpet.

He sat in the war room, swiveling, sighing, and watching TV for about fifteen minutes before telling Melania it was time to go to bed. On the way to the elevator, he thanked the handful of aides left working late in the war room.

The following year, after Donald and Melania officially made the move to Washington, he had thousands of meters of new carpeting installed in the White House, including in the West Wing lobby and the Roosevelt Room, the latter of which had its Obama-era beige carpet torn out and thrown away. This was part of the Trumps' redesign and redecoration of the White House, a process costing millions of dollars and earning condemnation from *The Guardian*'s design critic, who censured the new president, saying, "A boring carpet, greige wallpaper and two giant eagles won't make the White House great again."

About two years after that, President Trump again found himself in the U.K., doing his very best to impress the royal family and conservative leadership. At Westminster Abbey, according to a press pool report at the time, the president "paused at the white marble slab commemorating Lord Byron, the poet politician, and asked what stone the flooring was made from."

DURING the constant melees of the Republican presidential primaries, Donald Trump defined himself by his enemies: the Mexicans, the Muslims, the Low-Energy Jebs, the Little Marcos, the Lyin' Teds, the insufficiently subservient members of the media class.

One of these enemies who was especially adept at getting on Trump's nerves was the NBC News correspondent Katy Tur, who would go on to write a memoir of her time covering the campaign and land an MSNBC anchor gig during a prime daytime slot. In early July 2015, three weeks following the candidate's Mexican-rapist launch at Trump Tower, he sat down with Tur for a one-on-one interview at his eponymous tower, a thirty-minute taped conversation that quickly devolved into the Republican presidential candidate getting snippy about Tur's questions and her personality.

"Oh, give me a break, Katy, go ahead, next question," Trump said after Tur asked him about civilian casualties in Iraq that his "bomb the hell out of ISIS" foreign policy could cause.

"International diplomacy is a delicate thing. You have to watch what you say, and how can anybody expect that you're going to be able to get into the White House and watch your mouth, when you were so widely panned for these . . . Mexico comments? How are you going to be able to hold your tongue and not piss off other countries?" Tur asked, presciently.

"Do you want to change the word, are you allowed to use that word on television?" he responded.

When Trump resumed demagoguing his fake immigrant crime statistics and Tur pushed back, Trump told her she was being a "very naive person." When she seemed to lose her train of thought for a moment, a visibly annoyed Trump yapped, "Come on, try getting it out, try getting it out. I mean, I don't know if you're going to put this on television, but you don't even know what you're talking about. Try getting it out, go ahead."

This animosity continued well into the following year, and Trump clearly wasn't inclined to let it go. The following December, Trump called "Little Katy" a "third-rate journalist" in the middle of a campaign rally, prompting Trump supporters to look her way and lustily boo her. During the same event, Trump lumped her in the category of media "scum."

At a press conference in July 2016, Tur asked Trump if he had "any qualms about asking a foreign government" to "hack into the system of anybody's in this country," referring to Trump's famous public wish that Russian intelligence would find and distribute Hillary Clinton's "30,000 emails that are missing."

When she attempted to ask a follow-up question, the candidate shot back, "Be quiet, I know you want to, you know, save her . . . Now, if Russia, or China, or any other country has those emails, I mean to be honest with you, I'd love to see them."

In her book, *Unbelievable: My Front-Row Seat to the Craziest Campaign in American History*, Tur wrote candidly about how Trump routinely made her a prominent object of hatred and about how candidate Trump once planted an abrupt, unwanted kiss upon her cheek, shortly before his appearance on MSNBC's *Morning Joe* in November 2015. "Before I know what's happening, his hands are on my shoulders and his lips are on my cheek," she wrote. "My eyes widen. My body freezes. My heart stops."

In the years since, the hard feelings and animus on Trump's end have yet to abate. Starting during the campaign, Trump would privately assign her a six-word nickname that was . . . somewhat unique to the rest of the 2016 traveling press corps. To friends and advisers, he'd bitterly refer to the NBC News reporter simply as "that bitch with the tranny dad."

Her biological father is named Zoey Tur (born Robert Albert Tur), a pilot and journalist who garnered plaudits for work covering events such as the 1992 Los Angeles riots and the O. J. Simpson car chase. During the 2016 election, Zoey Tur called Trump a "fascist" and "mentally ill" in an interview with *The Hollywood Reporter* and referred to Trump campaign stops as "his Nuremberg rallies."

None of this went unnoticed by said "fascist," who held all of it against the Tur family.

Two years before Trump launched his presidential bid, Bob Tur started hormone treatment to become Zoey. And ever since the days of the 2016 race, she will forever be known in President Trump's mind as that "tranny" with the "bitch" kid who annoyed the billionaire demagogue so frequently during his big, loud run for office.

▶ TALKING THE TALK

One of the most important people in Donald Trump's life whom you probably never heard of is "Gabe."

To most people who have heard Trump shout his name, that's all they know him by: just "Gabe." The reason a lot of people—particularly meddlesome political reporters seeking to do profiles on Trump's inner sanctum—do not know who he is, what he looks like, or what his "deal" is, is that there is an unofficial protection racket, operating within and without Trump's West Wing, set up to keep Gabe's name out of the papers and glossy magazines. Multiple well-known Trumpworld personalities chided us throughout the course of our reporting on Gabe, even for some of our more mundane questions, such as "What's his last name?"

Some of these people lied to us and insisted that they knew nothing about Gabe, or didn't know his last name, or weren't sure what he's up to these days. Others responded indignantly, telling us to mind our own business and that Gabe doesn't want anything to do with us, that he's a private citizen and doesn't deserve to be dragged into the limelight.

Call him private if you like, but Gabe is perhaps the most powerful Trumpworld figure you've never heard of. That's due to his inordinate control over the words that come out of the president's mouth.

Gabe's last name is Perez, for what it's worth. One of the reasons we know this is through an offhand mention by one of Trumpworld's most reviled denizens, Corey Lewandowski, who briefly refers to Gabe in *Let Trump Be Trump*, a 2017 book credited to Lewandowski and his friend and fellow ex-Trump aide David Bossie, the latter of whom is markedly less of an asshole than the former.

So why is Gabriel so vital to the forty-fifth leader of the free world? In a certain respect, Gabe has mastered the art of controlling Trump's public statements—for major speeches, during political events with party bigwigs, and at the booming, rowdy campaign rallies that helped win Trump the presidency in the first place.

All throughout the Obama era, numerous conservative media figures and right-wing blowhards (including future president Donald J. Trump) ceaselessly critiqued President Obama's use of a teleprompter—one of the absolute dumbest conservative gripes of the Obama years, given that the display device's ubiquity in American politics is so self-evident that complaining about its use is on par with demagoguing Obama's use of a toothbrush or a waist belt.

So, the 2016 Trump campaign rolls around, and The Donald starts making good use of the teleprompter. As luck would have it, virtually every insufferable git on the right miraculously and suddenly found it in themselves to forget all about their collective, years-long jihad on the teleprompter.

But while Trump mimics his predecessors in his frequent use of the scrolling speech-text device, running Trump's machinery is far more difficult than running Obama's. Trump's tendency to go off script is obviously well known. He's renowned for his ability to read a crowd, and he loves getting applause. So if Trump senses during a campaign rally that he's losing the room, he has some go-to tactics for getting everyone fired up. During the campaign, that generally meant calling for one of two things: the imprisonment of Hillary Clinton and the construction of the southern border wall.

After a while they became predictable asides. But not so predictable that a normal teleprompter operator would be able to keep up. And that was where Gabe shined. Those who would speak with us about him said Gabe had an uncanny ability to edit the scrolling text in a way that fit seamlessly with Trump's unpredictable speaking style. He knew when to pause. He knew when to rewind to get Trump back on track. He could follow Trump's stream of consciousness effectively enough that the boss could get right back on track with his prepared remarks even after a not-uncommon ten-minute deviation from the written version of a speech. For a presidential candidate who relied on authenticity and crowd energy during his stump speeches, that skill was an invaluable asset.

Gabe's inclusion on Team Trump was almost a fluke. According to Bossie and Lewandowski's book, the campaign "found Gabe by Googling 'teleprompters.'" But once he was on the Trump Train, it didn't take long for the Republican presidential front-runner to grow increasingly infatuated with Gabe's mastery of the form.

To get himself in the zone to work the Trump-eprompter, Gabe was known to play Candy Crush on his smartphone to warm up his nimble fingers. In teleprompter-driven speeches, when Trump would improvise or do different sections of the prepared remarks before he'd actually reached that part of the address, Gabe would spring into action. He'd quickly scroll through the script, stealth-edit it in real time, and delete the section to accommodate Trump's meandering oratory, to ensure Trump wouldn't start reading words he'd already prematurely blabbed onstage.

Trump took notice and lauded Gabe for making him actually like using a teleprompter. From then on, Gabe was Trump's guy. It got to the point where Trump would actively complain if he saw anyone else touching his precious machine. (Gabe would ultimately continue his work for Trump once the latter ascended to the White House.)

"Where's Gabe? Get Gabe!!! *GET GABE DOWN HERE NOW!*" Trump would exclaim to whichever campaign lackeys were closest to him, when Gabe wasn't around to rehearse or perform his orchestral duties.

It became something of an in-joke among a number of Trump's campaign aides, who often didn't even know whom he was talking about. "*Who the fuck is Gabe???*" they would ask among themselves. Was Trump summoning a real person? Did he screw up someone's name (again)?

He might as well have. To the vast majority of Trumpworld beyond its own elite, Gabe is a ghost. Albeit one of President Trump's favorite ghosts.

THE intense hypocrisy of Trump's routine reliance on Gabe's teleprompter was obvious. He'd spent years suggesting that his predecessor was incapable of delivering a speech without reading from prepared remarks. And if Trump *could* do so, even during a campaign defined by his freewheeling rants and nonsensical asides, it was probably better for everyone if he himself didn't come up with his own public remarks.

One howler of an example of impromptu inanity (or insanity) came in September 2016, when Donald Trump and his team had announced that he was—ostensibly—prepared to put all that ugly, birther racism in the rearview mirror. Election Day was fast approaching, and it was time to at least do the pantomime of "presidential."

Trump had built his political career and conservative street cred, circa 2011, on his reckless questioning of Barack Obama's place of birth. It was an early lesson for Trump in the potency of press attention, even when the coverage itself was relentlessly negative. It's entirely possible—Lachlan, at least, suspects this is the case—that Trump never *actually* thought Obama was ineligible for the presidency by virtue of his place of birth. But harping on the issue would provide Trump with two very potent political benefits: He would fire up the contingent of the political Right, which was apparently far larger than many at the time believed, that harbored racist sentiments toward Obama and thought Trump was right on the merits, or at least assumed that the black president just had to be an Other of some kind. At the same time, Trump would ensure that he would make headlines. The press, he likely knew, wouldn't be able to resist criticizing him. To criticize him, they would have to talk about him. And the more they talked about him, the more powerful and prominent he'd become, and not just as a businessman and reality-TV star but as a voice in American politics. So what if the voice was a racist one. His original sin in the arena of national politics would also be his golden ticket.

By 2016, he apparently considered it a liability. But to jettison this from his arsenal would be to ignore what made Trump, well . . . Trump. Still, the decision was made by the future president and his senior staff that it was worth letting this one slide. In the days leading up to Trump's first presidential debate with the Democratic nominee, Hillary Clinton, held at Hofstra University on September 26, 2016, Team Trump tried to organize an event at the site of the Trump International Hotel in the nation's capital. There, he would—however tepidly—relinquish birtherism at long last.

But first, the campaign wanted Trump to release an official, written statement renouncing birther conspiracy theories and declaring once and for all that baby Barack was born in the United States. His aides asked him for a short and sweet statement—just a few sentences—so they could put this to bed quickly and hopefully without causing a big fuss.

Trump convened some of his top campaign brass, including Hope Hicks and Jason Miller, on a conference call that month as he was patched in from his executive perch at Trump Tower in Manhattan. He told them he wanted to dictate a statement.

At first, his aides weren't sure what he was going to say, and feared he would want to double down on his birther-ring leadership. After all, he had resorted to dodgy lines during the 2016 campaign when asked about the topic. "Well, I don't know," he'd say when pressed on whether Obama was or wasn't foreign born. "If you believe that, that's fine," when reminded of the birth certificate Obama's people released.

"Okay, are you ready?" Trump asked everyone on the call. "Okay, here it is . . ."

This kicked off what two people on the call independently described as a seven-minute, meandering spat of word-vomit during which Trump kept finding new ways to say that his birther crusade was, in fact, necessary, good, and proper. He repeatedly echoed his past comments on the matter, claiming credit for forcing President Obama to settle the issue by publicly releasing his original long-form birth certificate. He insisted this never would have happened without his incessant questioning of Obama's birthplace. He achieved what John McCain, Bill Clinton, and so many others could only dream of doing, he thought. He blamed Hillary Clinton for being the godmother of the racist birtherism craze and for starting it in the first place. (She didn't.) So really, Trump reasoned, what he did was a smashing success that warranted no apology, and he was happy he helped settle one of the great questions of our time.

Had this soliloquy been made public, it would have spanned two pages, single spaced.

"You get all that?" Trump asked.

At first, the Republican presidential nominee was met with dead, eerie silence, with those on the line confused as to what the optimal response could possibly be. Multiple advisers wanted to tell him that his dictated statement was far, far, *far* too long and would cause many more headaches for the campaign than it would resolve. If released, this would defeat the purpose of everything the campaign staff was trying to accomplish on this front. And yet, no one wanted to upset Trump, whose legendary hair-trigger temper could easily be set off by the slightest sign of perceived insolence.

Hope Hicks—a top confidante and a press and comms hotshot whom Trump had for years treated as a surrogate daughter and whom he affectionately called Hopey and Hopester—was the brave one. Hopey/Hopester went first.

"Uh, we can't do this," she said, explaining that it would predictably deliver Trump a self-inflicted blow. She recommended they go the route of a less obstreperous, and much shorter, statement to the media.

"Okay," Trump said, before polling the other members of the conference call on whether they agreed with Hicks, or if they preferred using the diatribe the boss had just dictated. No campaign official who chimed in sided with Trump, with each of them giving some pussy-footing version of *This is insane, why would we do this?* Each added a "sir" or two to be safe.

After each aide said his or her piece, the call was interrupted by yet another uncomfortable, pregnant silence. It lasted an interminable three seconds. Then the inevitable eruption came.

"I WANT THAT STATEMENT!!!! GET ME THAT FUCKING

STATEMENT!!!!!!" Trump roared into his phone—multiple recipients of his wrath recount—as his thundering voice crackled on the receiving ends. *"I WANT THAT GODDAMN FUCKING STATEMENT RIGHT NOW!!!!! WHERE THE FUCK IS IT, WHY IS . . . JASON! JASON! GET THE HELL UP HERE NOW!"*

Click.

By the time all the other participants of the birtherism call had hung up, Miller, Trump's trusted senior communications adviser, was already hustling up to DJT's twenty-sixth-floor office in the Tower. Behind closed doors, Miller—with a thick skin for verbal lashing and a calming voice—miraculously managed to walk Trump back off that ledge and strike a compromise: Miller would release a brief, innocuous statement in his own name, not Donald J. Trump's, and the Republican presidential nominee would get to have his own say at the Trump hotel event in Washington, D.C. The secret, internally infamous, gargantuan Trump statement would be canned, never to see the embarrassing light of day. When Miller emerged from Trump's office, he assured fellow campaign officials that he'd put out that fire, at least for the time being.

In the moment, Trump was bitter and vexed, still itching to one day unleash his lengthy and unalloyed comment on his birther past and present. As in so many other political conundrums before and after that conference call, Trump was like a small child who'd just been informed by the minimum-wage theme park worker that he wasn't yet tall enough to ride Space Mountain.

Yet barely twenty-four hours after showing so much fury and dejection, he had already started forgetting about it and soon moved on. He wasn't pestering his staff about it, and he was back to his "Crooked Hillary" and Lock-Her-Up shtick.

His violent mood swing on this topic reflects a large truth and reality well known at the upper echelons of Trumpworld—a juvenile attitude that persists even when the domestic and international stakes are outstandingly high. In the veteran journalist Bob Woodward's Trump book, *Fear*, the president is described at one point as recklessly and wrathfully ordering his then secretary of defense, James Mattis, to have the Syrian president, Bashar al-Assad, snuffed out.

"Let's fucking kill him! Let's go in. Let's kill the fucking lot of them," Trump reportedly told Mattis over the phone, not long after news had broken that the mass-murdering dictator launched a chemical-weapons attack on civilians in Khan Sheikhoun. The chemical attack occurred in early April 2017, just months after Trump was inaugurated. According to Woodward's account, Mattis assured Trump that he'd get "right on it." Comically, the defense secretary put down his phone and immediately told a subordinate, "We're not going to do any of that." Instead, the Trump administration soon opted for a limited missile attack that did little, if anything at all, to change the course of the war or Assad's butchering of Syrians. And in late 2019, President Trump would once again rejigger his Syria war policy, including green-lighting a Turkish massacre and the ethnic cleansing of Kurds.

During that phone call, when President Trump reportedly ordered what would have been a history-altering, potentially region-shaping assassination of a foreign leader, Mattis knew exactly what those on the birtherism call knew: just stall, and The Donald will quickly—hopefully—forget about whatever it was that had just hours ago been the most important, passion-inflaming thing in the world for him.

In each case, crisis was averted only because it slipped Trump's elderly mind. And that was that: no batshit written statement, no batshit assassination attempt.

Still, there will be times when the reprieve is tragically short-lived.

On September 16, 2016, Trump ultimately came around to rejecting birtherism in public—in the most cynical, unconvincing, and utterly meaningless way possible. On that day, he gathered the campaign press at his then-new Trump-branded hotel just blocks from the White House he'd soon win. He teased it as a "major announcement," which of course served as a barely veiled effort to trick the press into traveling with him to his garishly mediocre hotel lobby to get it some free advertising. It worked. "Nice hotel," he said into the mic, kicking off the event, which mostly consisted of him bragging about his property, as well as the supporters and military men he had assembled behind him onstage.

Trump gave at least half an inch of lip service to non-racism and non-lunacy. "President Barack Obama was born in the United States, period," he said quickly and as if he had his index and middle fingers crossed behind his back. "Now we all want to get back to making America strong and great again." Trump's senior campaign aides did not know he'd actually say that Obama was born in America until the moment he said it. Some genuinely feared he'd use the event to triple down on birtherism, just because he might feel like doing it. When he decided not to during the staged event that Friday morning, the sighs of relief, from his advisers looking on, were clearly audible.

But to anyone operating with a shred of good faith, the man who had just introduced Trump at the event had all but negated any authenticity the future president was hoping to convey. The man was the retired Air Force lieutenant general Thomas McInerney, himself *a fellow birther*. That the Trump campaign was so childishly incompetent that it couldn't even mount a supposedly anti-birther ceremony without giving no fewer than two birthers speaking roles yet again reinforced Trumpworld's reputation for turning the laziest possible satire into stark reality.

In more ways than one, McInerney and Trump, the man he endorsed for the presidency in 2016, are the perfect match made in a gaudy, right-wing-talk-radio-fueled hell. McInerney had written a 2010 affidavit challenging President Obama's authority, citing "widespread and legitimate concerns" regarding his place of birth. (McInerney used to be the number three commander of the air force.) Three months before Senator John McCain died, McInerney went on Fox Business Network and smeared a dying McCain with the inaccurate claim that torture "worked on" him during the Vietnam War: "That's why they call him 'Songbird John.'" This comment was so deranged and insulting that Fox News had to publicly denounce the Trump-loving military vet by assuring news outlets that he would never be invited back as a guest on Fox Business or Fox News.

Now, several years into the age of Trump, it's pretty clear that neither the president nor his endorser is all that repentant of his distaste for McCain or his hatred of Trump's predecessor. Well into his presidency, Trump continued bringing up his suspicions about President Obama's birth certificate and clung to the conspiracy theory during private conversations with friends. He continued associating with leading birthers such as the *WorldNetDaily* writer Jerome Corsi, who would eventually be included in a joint defense agreement with the president when the Mueller shit hit the fan. And Trump would even take direct policy advice from the Fox Business host Lou Dobbs, who previously dubbed the birther conspiracy theory a "perfectly common sense question."

During the final months of his presidential campaign, it would have saved everyone some time if Trump had just undercut his own staff and released his preferred statement, their warnings be damned. It goes without saying that this president and candidate was always as likely to be honest with voters about this (or anything else) as he was likely to willingly put on a condom full of silverfish.

"OKAY, LAD, THAT'S ENOUGH"

The speed with which Donald Trump had fallen out with American pop culture icons must have been jarring for the man who so craved the adulation of every American with a microphone and TV camera. In the twenty-five years before his presidential run, he was mentioned by name in more than seventy-five songs by prominent musical acts ("Get money like Donald Trump," rapped Lil Wayne in 2011, at the height of Trump's birther phase). He enjoyed famous cameos in movies and television series such as *Home Alone 2*, *The Little Rascals*, and *The Fresh Prince of Bel-Air*. The success of *The Apprentice* overshadowed his retrograde political views with much of the American public.

Still, his rising star on the xenophobic right quickly made him an outcast among those out of "Central Casting," as Trump loves to say.

Trump's run for president cemented his pariah status in the entertainment and media business. And that was something that he simply could not abide. But Trump's solution wasn't to change anything about his presidential run, his policy platform, or his unhinged public rhetoric. It was far easier to simply lie about the people supporting him.

During the long, brutal 2016 campaign, Trump would boast about his "celebrity" support, as though he'd landed the public affections of Tom Hanks, Taylor Swift, and Nelson Mandela's ghost combined. In his heart, however, he knew he'd always be relegated to scoring endorsements from the likes of *Duck Dynasty* stars, Chachi from *Happy Days*, and a former Calvin Klein underwear model and soap-opera actor who now believes that Hillary Clinton and Barack Obama should be jailed at Gitmo. Generally speaking, it was not exactly the A-list of anywhere—which is particularly funny, given how much Trump has long cared about star-fucking and the seal of elite approval.

Perhaps the most impressive of Trump's primary election lot was Jon Voight, the Oscar-winning Midnight Cowboy. Beginning in June 2016, Swin became *The Daily Beast*'s Chief Jon Voight Correspondent. It was the perfect side project for the *Beast* reporter. In the summer of 2014, John Avlon and Noah Shachtman at *The Daily Beast* had hired Swin from *Mother Jones* magazine's Washington, D.C., office, where Swin had reported on the nexus of politics and popular culture (particularly Hollywood, movies, and TV series). The *Beast* hired Swin to do, essentially, the same thing. For about a year, that's what he did, and then a reality-TV and celebrity-fixated gasbag named Donald John Trump announced his run for the presidency, creating a campaign emblematic of the logical conclusion, if not extreme, of the intersection of pop culture and politics. Swin had never intended on being a White House reporter of any kind. For years, he'd self-deprecatingly referred to his beat as mostly defined by "frivolous bullshit," and it was nothing if not surreal to see that frivolous bullshit lead him directly to the door of the West Wing. The only reason he became a White House reporter in 2017 was that Hillary Clinton and her team were incompetent enough to shit the bed and—against all odds—find a way to lose to *Donald Trump*.

Anyway, Swin started pitching in with Trump coverage not long after he declared his run beneath the escalator at his Manhattan

Trump Tower, with a focus on how Trump's campaign and history intersected with the conservative enclaves of liberal Hollywood. So, with Jon Voight's entry into the 2016 maelstrom as an unofficial Trump surrogate, Swin set out to corner the market on Voightworld. Soon enough, he managed to secure Voight's personal cell-phone number and decided to keep bothering Angelina Jolie's dad for the rest of the election and beyond.

"How'd you get my number, you son of a bitch?" Voight asked Swin the first time they spoke in June 2016. For whatever reason, the Oscar-winning Trump enthusiast stayed on the line. He talked about how "I'll be as helpful as I can be" and said that "we'll see come convention time if [the Trump campaign] wants me at the convention." He talked about how "I'm in touch with the campaign, and I fully support Donald. I think he's the man for the job." He said he discussed with senior officials on Team Trump "what I might be available to do for them in California," an obvious Democratic stronghold. During this chat, and all subsequent ones, Voight repeatedly called Swin "lad." The conversation resulted in the *Daily Beast* article titled "Jon Voight in Talks with Trump Campaign: 'Everything Is on the Table.'"

For the remaining months of the 2016 race, Swin continued calling and texting Jon Voight, and for whatever reason Jon Voight would answer, over and over again, to extol the virtues of Trump. For a stretch of months, Swin would text him no fewer than a dozen times a week and call an average of twice a week.

In their first phone conversation, Voight declined to tell Swin any names of the senior people on the Trump campaign with whom he'd conversed. A few months later, Swin accidentally found out the name of one of them. While crashing on deadline one evening, alone, overworked, and tired, in the *Beast* D.C. office, Swin got bored and decided to call Jon Voight again. *Maybe he'll have an interesting comment for this article,* Swin thought to himself, but really it was just another excuse to pester the aging actor, whom Swin had watched and admired so much in his teenage and college years. After a couple minutes, Voight was done tolerating Swin's generally aimless questions. "Okay, lad, that's enough, goodbye," the Hollywood titan said right before ending the call. Chuckling, Swin resumed work, trying to meet a deadline set by demanding editors.

An hour or two passed with Swin typing away at his office desk, when his phone buzzed and the caller ID read "Jon Voight."

Why the hell is he calling me? Swin wondered. *He usually can barely contain his displeasure when we talk.* Swin answered and stammered out a couple of confused attempts at "Hi?"

"Hello, it's Jon, Jon Voight, do you have a few minutes?" he replied.

"Yeah, sure, what's going on, Jon?"

"Sorry we didn't have time to talk much earlier."

"That's . . . That's fine, you're a busy guy. What can I do for you?"

"Are you sure you have time now? I can call back if . . ."

"Jon, I have time, what's up?"

Swin had no earthly idea what to make of this. Why was the snarling villain from *Anaconda* being so vigorously accommodating?

"I had a couple of ideas I wanted to go over with you. I was thi . . . Wait . . ."

"Yes, Jon?"

"Wait, is this . . . Steve? Steve Mnuchin???"

(Steven Mnuchin, a Trump friend and successful banker who also dabbled in executive producing major Tinseltown fare such as *American Sniper, The Lego Movie, How to Be Single,* and *Batman v Superman: Dawn of Justice,* was the 2016 Trump campaign's national finance chairman. He would later land a spot in President Trump's cabinet.)

The moment Voight asked Swin who he was, Swin was bound by

journalistic ethics to tell Voight the truth. To this day, Swin wishes Voight hadn't figured out something was amiss before he had the chance to tell *The Daily Beast* what he and Mnuchin were discussing.

"No, Jon, this isn't Steve Mnuchin. This is Swin. Asawin. Suebsaeng. The *Daily Beast* reporter. We literally spoke about an hour ago on the phone."

"Oh, sorry, bye, lad."

Click.

By early September 2016, Swin and Voight would finally have their first in-person encounter—of all places, at the annual social-conservative, Christian-right Values Voter Summit thrown at the Omni Shoreham Hotel in Northwest D.C. Voight was there to intro-duce the GOP presidential candidate and to talk God, culture wars, and Trump, Trump, Trump. ("If you're not for Trump, then you're not for me," Voight had once succinctly phrased his outlook to Swin.)

A couple of hours before Voight was scheduled to hit the stage, Swin ducked into a hallway to ring him to see if he had a moment to meet for a coffee or a drink. This time, Voight was far less accommodat-ing. He didn't stay on the line for a long time. He didn't agree to another interview. He didn't even mistake Swin's voice for Steven Mnuchin's. The jig was up: Voight had finally figured out that Swin leaned left.

"Oh, shit," Voight said. "Look, I have a lot of sympathy for you, lad, but I will not be doing an interview with you. I have no interest in [co-operating] with someone who's trying to make me look bad. *The Daily Beast* is not friendly to the conservatives."

Swin told Voight that he'd interviewed him before without making him "look bad" and that *The Daily Beast* treated Voight fairly. "Let me get off the phone," Voight pleaded. "You seem like a decent guy, and I wish you the best. If I see you, I'll shoot you a big smile."

Swin checked the time, his messages, his emails. He realized he had a good amount of time to kill, no pressing deadline, and zero editors asking for his status. This meant it was the ideal time for him to run around the Omni Shoreham, in an effort to encounter the aforementioned big smile. By the time Swin stumbled into the restaurant area of the sprawling hotel lobby, there was Voight—greeting conference attendees, snapping pics with fans, and bumping into the Breitbart editor Matt Boyle, with whom he agreed to do a radio interview on the spot. Swin jumped in before Jon could make a break for it.

"Hi, Mr. Voight, could I please get a photo," Swin asked. Voight agreed and shook hands as a friend of Swin's took a photo. As the camera flashed, Swin whispered into Voight's ear, "By the way, my name's Swin, you might know me from *The Daily Beast*; we spoke earlier today on the phone."

Voight's eyes promptly dilated as he grabbed both of Swin's shoulders and began comically shaking the reporter in the middle of the Omni Shoreham entrance hall. "You're *Swinnnnnn*????" Voight said, and he continued gently rocking Swin from side to side, having finally come face-to-face with the young D.C. reporter who had cold-called him all those months ago.

The actor and Trump acolyte patted Swin on the back as if to signal that there were no hard feelings. Then he walked off toward the main ballroom, ignoring Swin's shouted questions and requests for a sit-down. When Voight did hit the stage to lavish Trump with praise, he held up the prolifically womanizing, rapaciously party-hopping, biblically illiterate accused serial sexual assaulter and bigot and scam artist as nothing short of God's man on a mission. "We are all witness to Hillary Clinton's lies and corruption," Voight said during his brief prepared remarks. "My heart aches watching Donald Trump . . . How can anyone doubt his sincerity?

"He will lift the dark cloud hanging over us right now," Voight said, telling the audience that, Lord willing, The Donald would be the next leader of the free world. "Such a great actor [and] person," Trump told the crowd, following Voight's introduction. "I love his movies."

Voight and the rest of the Moral Majority contingent of American conservatism hit a mildly inconvenient, Trump-size bump in the road the following month—in the form of the now infamous "grab 'em by the pussy" tape. Voight, for his part, made like the vast majority of the Republican Party and conservative movement: he unapologetically sacrificed himself at the altar of Trumpism. In Voight's case, that meant attacking Robert De Niro, his old *Heat* co-star, who had just recorded a video declaring, "I'd like to punch [Trump] in the face."

"I am so ashamed of my fellow actor Bobby DeNiro's rant against Donald Trump. What foul words he used against a presidential nominee," Voight wrote on Twitter while running interference for Trump during the "pussy" tape news cycle. "I don't know of too many men who haven't expressed some sort of similar sexual terms toward women, especially in their younger years . . . Donald Trump's words were not as damaging as Robert DeNiro's ugly rant. Trump's words did not hurt anyone. Can you imagine if any Republican said words like Robert DeNiro used—against Hilary Clinton or Barack Obama? All hell would break loose."

A little over two years after Trump's inauguration, the president— known for keeping tabs on who did and did not stay loyal to him during his "pussy" tape crisis, and acting accordingly—rewarded his part-time campaign surrogate. In late March 2019, the White House announced that President Trump would be appointing Voight to the Kennedy Center's board of trustees. "Congrats," Swin dryly texted the arch Hollywood conservative the day the news broke. Voight never responded. Not even with a canned "thanks, lad."

▶ "GET HIM THE FUCK AWAY FROM ME"

R ule 1 of the Trump campaign: Absolutely do not fuck with the boss's tweets—not if you want to survive.

David Bossie wasn't the first person to learn this lesson the hard way, and he certainly wasn't the last. But in the closing months of the 2016 election, it was one of the miscalculations that cost him a cushy job in the administration.

In September 2016, Trump finally brought Bossie aboard his campaign staff to serve in the official capacity of deputy campaign manager. He'd been a longtime buddy of Trump's, as well as a key player in the conservative movement as the president of the advocacy group Citizens United, which in the early Obama era forever altered how American political campaigns are financed. Years prior to that, he was a well-known investigator of President Bill Clinton. Though his title had "deputy" in it, his now former Trumpland colleagues often speak of Bossie as someone who orchestrated the nuts and bolts of campaign operations during those final critical weeks. In other words, many viewed him as more of a campaign manager, per se, than they ever viewed Kellyanne Conway, who had the official manager title but whom many cohorts derided behind her back as chiefly a TV spokeswoman.

This was in large part because Bossie was so instrumental in the scorched-earth strategy near the finale of the general election to, in an attempt to draw focus away from the numerous sexual assault and harassment allegations leveled at Trump, throw a spotlight on Bill Clinton's alleged sexual violence. Bossie also had a heavy hand in moving resources to Michigan and Wisconsin in the critical weeks before Election Day and quickly shifting the Republican nominee's travel schedule as the Electoral College math called for in that period. For Team Trump's ultimately successful Hail Mary, it largely fell to Bossie to work in a frenzy with the finance department, digital team, communications staffers, and God knows who else to make a Trump upset possible—by chipping away at the Democratic "Blue Wall" as if he were breaking out of Shawshank.

By the time the presidential turnover hit, Bossie was given a seat at the table on the transition team as a senior official. Everything seemed to be coming up Bossie. He just helped make the *Apprentice* star a White House resident. There was chatter about a possible administration assignment or maybe a Republican National Committee chairmanship, in succession to soon-to-be White House chief of staff, Reince Priebus.

And then . . . nothing. No administration post. No corner office in the White House. No leading the RNC. Poof. Nothing. Instead, he had a Fox News contract and the consolation prize of "outside adviser."

One key reason for this is that Dave—with his brash, sometimes chafing style—had simply pissed off too many people who didn't want to play with him or even put in a good word for him. One of those guys was Reince Priebus.

Another one of them, at least for a while, was Donald Trump.

During the closing weeks of the long and frantic campaign season, as Trump made his closing pitch to voters all across the country, Bossie identified possible impediments, or at least inconveniences, to his boss's path to the White House. This included the @realDonaldTrump tweets, which Bossie believed to be "unpresidential" in their crude nature. He thought Trump's wild-man tweeting resembled flailing anger far more than it did assured victory. **"Did Crooked Hillary help disgusting (check out sex tape and past) Alicia M become a U.S. citizen so she could use her in the debate?"** Trump tweeted in the early morning of September 30, 2016, for instance.

That Friday morning, Trump was slut-shaming Alicia Machado, a former Miss Universe whom Trump had repeatedly assailed (for her weight, among other reasons) and whom Clinton had embraced as a talking point and as a supporter of her campaign. Machado, for her part, had previously called Trump a "Nazi rat." And not that it mattered to Trump or his team, but the alleged "sex tape" that he wanted his Twitter followers to "check out" didn't actually exist.

Still, it was tweets such as these that worried Bossie so much. And he wasn't alone; numerous other top Trump advisers had wished their candidate would cut it out with the chronic rage-tweeting, or at least dial it back to a six instead of an eleven. But Bossie was the only one puckish enough to repeatedly lecture Trump on why he needed to stop tweeting so much. He simply wouldn't let it go.

This climaxed in the final weeks of the race, aboard Trump Force One, when Bossie once again brought up how the tweets were a problem.

"Oh, this again?" Trump said, sighing and shifting his lips in displeasure.

As Bossie pushed harder and harder, not having yet realized that negotiating with a Twitter terrorist is a bad idea, Trump's anger began to simmer and then boil. He asked Bossie to stop talking. Bossie persisted on the topic. He asked Bossie to shut up. Bossie persisted. Then, suddenly, Trump had had enough. He got up, walked away, and started screaming for his other aides to get Bossie out of his sight, if not off the plane entirely.

"GET HIM THE FUCK OUT OF HERE!!! GET HIM THE FUCK AWAY FROM ME," the future president demanded, furiously gesticulating toward Bossie and the door behind him—all because Bossie had asked him to tweet less violently.

It was an episode that epitomized the decaying rapport between the candidate and his underling. Bossie would, soon enough, repair relations with Trump, only to risk destroying them all together. In the opening months of the Trump presidency, Bossie became one of the president's top informal advisers and phone buddies, with Trump's having allowed the bygones of the high-stress campaign to be bygones. And when it came time for Trump to pick his third chief of staff, this one to succeed John Kelly in late 2018, Bossie found himself on the short list—a dark horse who didn't end up making the cut, but on the list, no doubt.

By mid-2019, Bossie was once again on the cusp of pissing it all away. On May 5 of that year, *Axios* reported on how the former deputy campaign manager had spearheaded what appeared to be financial self-dealing under the guise of reelecting Trump. Bossie's political group, the Presidential Coalition, had raised roughly $18.5 million since Trump's first year in office but had spent a paltry $425,000 on actual political activity. Many donors believed that their money was going toward reelecting the president, and yet the organization had spent more buying Bossie's own books—a common tactic for political groups with the nice side benefit of enriching their principals—than it had on political activity.

Few things so quickly enrage Trump as someone, particularly a professed loyalist, using the Trump family name to make a buck— especially if Trump is deceptively not cut in on the action. It didn't take long for word of the *Axios* report to find its way to President Trump, who immediately grew livid. As he stewed in his own billowing resentment, he picked up the phone and ordered his 2020 campaign manager, Brad Parscale (who worked with Bossie on the 2016 run), to release a statement retaliating against Bossie's shenanigans.

"President Trump's campaign condemns any organization that deceptively uses the President's name, likeness, trademarks, or branding and confuses voters," the campaign's statement read, before going further and encouraging the authorities to investigate. "There is no excuse for any group, including ones run by people who claim to be part of our 'coalition,' to suggest they directly support President Trump's re-election or any other candidates, when in fact their actions show they are interested in filling their own pockets with money from innocent Americans' paychecks, and sadly, retirements. We encourage the appropriate authorities to investigate all alleged scam groups for potential illegal activities."

At the time, Bossie was also a Fox News contributor. In the direct aftermath of the *Axios* revelations, his regular column at FoxNews .com suddenly stopped being printed. He disappeared from the airwaves of Fox News and Fox Business Network, the president's two most beloved channels, for many weeks before reemerging from the doghouse.

Several people familiar with this disappearing act noted that it was no coincidence. It was part of an effort by those in charge of Fox opinion programming not to infuriate their pal Trump.

RAINING ON THE POTUS PARADE

As soon as he was elected on that night in November, Trump's team began planning what the winning candidate surely wished would be the party of the century: his inauguration weekend. And Hollywood began planning to subvert it.

On December 22, 2016, @realDonaldTrump exclaimed, "**The so-called 'A' list celebrities are all wanting [tickets] to the inauguration, but look what they did for Hillary, NOTHING. I want the PEOPLE!**" A month later, the president-elect was unable to identify who these supposedly existing A-listers were. "Many of the celebrities that are saying they were not going, they were never invited," he said during a January 18, 2017, interview with *Fox & Friends'* Ainsley Earhardt. "I don't want the celebrities; I want the people. And we have the biggest celebrities in the world there."

This was two days shy of the infamously poorly attended inauguration. And when the Fox host cited Trump as an example of a celeb attendee, Trump laughed and said, "Well, I won't say that." Asked to name check a celebrity who would deign to attend, Trump told Fox News, "We have President Obama," with whom he briefly tried to build a rapport during the transition.

Trump didn't know at the time that the dearth of talent on the guest list was partly the product of a Tinseltown conspiracy. And for a president who can spot a deep state or media-driven conspiracy behind nearly everything he finds annoying, this was a hell of a blind spot.

In the nearly three months between his shock victory and the inauguration in Washington, D.C., there was a covert effort launched among Democratic Party loyalists in Hollywood and among the pop-music industry elite to undermine and bleed Donald Trump's big soiree of star power. They despised the *Apprentice* creator and Trump's partner in crime, Mark Burnett, and sought to hobble his efforts to apply a veneer of glamour to the inauguration. According to a December 2016 article published by *TheWrap*, "Burnett, who produces 'Celebrity Apprentice' with Trump and has been overseeing entertainment for inauguration festivities, has brought in talent recruiter Suzanne Bender, a former 'Dancing With the Stars' and 'American Idol' booker, to end an effective freeze-out by Hollywood."

In the end, Mark Burnett couldn't save Donald Trump from the harsh reality that nobody wanted to play with Donald Trump.

From the start, Trump and his staff were negotiating from a position of crippling weakness. Virtually all of the president-elect's favorite acts had supported Bernie or Hillary in 2016 and didn't want to be caught dead toasting President Trump's fortunes. Still, the Republican victor had a wish list for who would perform for him. At the top was the Queen of Soul herself, Aretha Franklin.

In the days after election night, President-elect Trump ordered Tom Barrack, his longtime confidant who was chairing the Presidential Inaugural Committee, to reach out to the music icon or her people to see if she would sing at his inaugural concert. Trump, who knew Franklin leaned liberal and had sung for Obama, had for years claimed the legendary soul artist was his dear "friend" and desired it to be pitched to her as a chance to bridge the ideological chasm and to help heal the country following an emotional, unsparing general election. What Franklin never got the chance to tell Trump to his face is that around the time she had learned of Team Trump's overtures, she privately stressed to friends that "no amount of money" could make the singer, a committed Hillary Clinton supporter, perform at a Trump inauguration. More bluntly, in the year and a half before she passed away, Aretha Franklin would repeatedly call Donald Trump "despicable" and, even more pointedly, a huge "piece of shit."

Upon the occasion of Franklin's death in August 2018, Trump claimed that she was "a person I knew well" who "worked for me on numerous occasions." (It's not at all clear what President Trump was getting at when he boasted that she'd "worked for me," though she had appeared or performed at Trump-branded properties.)

In late 2018, Swin, together with the *Daily Beast* media reporter Maxwell Tani, began reporting on this and discovered other examples of these big names and their managers attempting to subvert Trump's enjoyment of his first weekend as the forty-fifth president of the United States of America. The funniest example would have to be the curious case of the informal, small collective of liberal, center-left Hollywood insiders and operators who deployed every dirty trick they could muster to ensure that Trump's inaugural festivities were as punishingly lame as humanly possible. We are, for now, withholding the names of the members of this shadowy cabal, on the condition of our reporting certain details. Just think of them as potentially forever anonymous, as you would a group of CIA analysts who helped a foreign death squad do a coup.

These people knew that Trump hadn't changed all that much since his days of carousing and begging for dates with the entertainment and motion-picture aristocracy. No matter what incoming president Trump said publicly, he still couldn't help but crave the attention and, preferably, the amorous approval of the glitterati. Sadly for the former *Apprentice* star, the glitterati were largely in the tank for Hillary Clinton and Barack Obama and abhorred him even more widely now than they already had before he became the Republican Party standard-bearer. Trump could deny it all he wanted, but he cared—he *really* cared. And these Hollywood insiders could sense it and wanted to hit him where it hurt.

The average profile of each of these guys is exactly what you might expect: the entertainment-industry manager class who dabbled in liberal politics and Democratic Party sycophancy. They were big Hillary and Obama people. They detested Trump and all for which his 2016 campaign stood. Near the tail end of the 2016 race, they quietly searched for the rumored "Trump tapes" that never materialized. They chased rumors of his physically assaulting his third wife, Melania, in an elevator at Trump Tower and of his blurting out the word "nigger" on buried footage from *The Apprentice*, and hit dead end after dead end. But these guys also had the ears of agents and other managers of marquee names in music and celluloid. The message conveyed by these insiders to agents and managers of top performers and the A-list was clear: *Tell your clients that if they perform, or get caught on camera looking happy, at the Trump inauguration, they can kiss that next big job or paycheck goodbye. If your star clients are going, it had better be to protest or attend the Women's March.*

For a short while close to the start of the transition, a handful of entertainment bigwigs had lightly pressured certain popular artists to perform—not out of any ideological commitment to the GOP or Trumpism, but out of pure business calculation. There were a lot of ostensible liberals in the pop-music business who wanted the incoming president—even if that president was named Trump—to support and sign obscure legislation that would effectively help pad the bottom line of concert hosts. As soon as the militantly anti-Trump insiders caught wind of this, they set upon their counteroffensive. They began leaking to friendly reporters the names of famous people who were thinking of—or who they thought were thinking of, at least—performing any Trump inauguration events, in an attempt to intimidate celebrities into not showing up or entertaining the Republican president-elect. They knew that a public outcry would be a powerful deterrent.

The group started whispering in journalists' and associates' ears—in a nakedly obvious attempt to apply some public pressure—that acclaimed singers such as Elton John and Andrea Bocelli were approached, or possibly leaning toward the gig. It was plausible because Trump and Elton John had rubbed elbows going back years. **"Taking piano lessons from my friend Elton John,"** Trump wrote in December 2013, tweeting an old pic of them posing together at a white grand piano. When Trump and his ex-wife Ivana were going through brutal divorce proceedings in 1990 (during which Ivana stated in a deposition that her husband had raped her), their celebrity pals were split into two camps. At the time, the tabloid press and New York gossip papers—which once counted The Donald among their chattiest anonymous sources—widely reported that the English "Rocket Man" singer-songwriter was on Donald's side. For instance, the *Daily News* reported in February 1990 that Team Ivana included Princess Diana, Prince Charles, Calvin Klein, and Oprah Winfrey. Along with Elton John, the future president reportedly got Frank Sinatra, Don Johnson, Mike Tyson, Melanie Griffith, Oscar de la Renta, Cher, and Liza Minnelli in the divorce.

Similarly, Donald Trump had long bragged about Bocelli as a close personal buddy. In 2010, he hosted an evening with the Italian tenor at his private Mar-a-Lago getaway in Florida. By December 2016, rumors and anonymously sourced news items cropped up that Bocelli was on the verge of booking his performance in honor of President Trump. A report on Page Six, for instance, blared that Bocelli "is being personally approached by President-elect Donald Trump to perform at the inauguration." It took one week for Bocelli to pull the plug. Following a wave of backlash from his fans on social media, the singer decided not to perform, with, again, Page Six quoting an unnamed source that "Bocelli said there was no way he'd take the gig . . . He was 'getting too much heat' and he said no." The chairman of the inaugural committee, Barrack, subsequently insisted on CNBC that "the Bocellis came to [Trump] and said, 'Look, if it would be helpful to you, if you would like us to perform, we would consider it,'" adding that Trump once allowed Bocelli to use one of his planes. Barrack's spin was that it was in fact *Trump* who let Bocelli, of whom Trump is a gigantic fan, off the hook for his big, glitzy weekend: "Donald said: 'You don't need to. We're not in that kind of a framework. Thanks very much for the offer. You're my friend. You are always welcome at the White House.'"

As for the Elton leaks, they didn't even have to get that far because the Mooch did most of the work for them. Long before Anthony Scaramucci started screwing up royally for Trump as a short-lived part of his West Wing, he was already screwing up royally and needlessly for Trump as a member of the inauguration team. In late November 2016, the Mooch went on the BBC's *HARDtalk* and declared that "Elton John is going to be doing our concert on the Mall for inauguration" and that "this will be the first American president in U.S. history that enters the White House with a pro-gay-rights stance." (Trump's presidency quickly launched rollback after rollback of LGBTQ gains of the previous era, but these are apparently minor details.)

Team Elton sprang into action, seeming to not know what the hell this daft Trump adviser was talking about. "Elton will not be performing a Trump inauguration," his publicist Fran Curtis rapidly emailed Swin just minutes after he reached out that Wednesday morning.

As story after story piled up in the national political and entertainment press that the Trump inauguration was building to a star-studless dud, the small huddle of Hollywood insiders felt their stealth campaign vindicated. "President-elect Donald Trump's team is struggling so hard to book A-list performers for his inaugural festivities that it offered ambassadorships to at least two talent bookers if they could deliver marquee names, the bookers told *TheWrap*," in another story that ran that same December. Boris Epshteyn, now an inaugural committee spokesman and an incoming White House official, tried to shoot down the *Wrap* story, telling the news site, "There is no truth to this insinuation," and swearing that "first-class entertainers are eager to participate in the inaugural events."

To this day, President Trump will get super-defensive if you bring up the lack of wattage at his inauguration.

Ultimately, those A-list top-of-the-pops stars 3 Doors Down and the Piano Guys played Trump's "Make America Great Again!" welcome celebration, thrown at the steps of the Lincoln Memorial. At that same concert, where the president-elect sat in the audience wearing a long black coat and one of his standard-issue bright blue neckties (with the tip of the tie, as Trump always wore it, nearly touching his toes), the lineup also included DJ RaviDrums, a Mohawk-styled drummer whom Trump likely did not care for and has not thought of in the years since the inauguration. The DJ's past credits included being part of the *Slumdog Millionaire* original-song performance at the 2009 Academy Awards. He told *Billboard*, "I had many friends begging or advising me to boycott. I even got offers of far more [money] to boycott. But if I put my word down, I do it. I was raised on hard work and ideals and the deep appreciation of America. So I wanted to celebrate that" by playing Trump's inaugural concert.

The Trump team extended an invitation to a surprised RaviDrums shortly before Christmas Day that year. The pro-Hillary cabal couldn't have been gladder. It was mean-spirited, but how else does one try to effectively combat Donald Trump, the cattiest, pettiest man alive? They took solace in their quiet, small victory as DJ RaviDrums performed before the Lincoln Memorial in Washington, D.C., to a joyless-looking Donald and Melania Trump. No Elton, no Bocelli, no Celine Dion, no Mick Jagger.

Nothing.

➥ "DID YOU SEE THIS CRAP?"

O n March 19, 2000, *The Simpsons* aired what would become the storied sitcom's most prophetic episode. Set in the year 2030, it imagined Lisa Simpson as "America's first straight female president." About halfway through the episode, President Simpson throws out this line: "As you know, we've inherited quite a budget crunch from President Trump."

We all laughed at the thought two decades ago. (Though, perhaps not all of us, given that it was a throwaway joke in what is also widely considered one of the most distinctly mediocre *Simpsons* episodes of the series run.) Yet on January 20, 2017, Trump fulfilled Lisa Simpson's prophecy.

As soon as Trump finished reading out his inaugural address on a cold day in late January 2017 in Washington, D.C.—a speech that insisted, "We will not fail. Our country will thrive and prosper again"— he and his country fell into a protracted state of deep anxiety.

His administration's original "Muslim ban" (or "travel ban," as we were all spun into accepting as nomenclature) shit the bed in a cacophony of legal challenge, protest, and bush-league plotting. The GOP and Trump team's signature legislative push to torpedo and replace Obamacare ranged from ham-fisted to missed orgasm. The border wall went unrealized, he escalated the "endless foreign wars" he regularly groused about, and his big, beautiful infrastructure spending never took off beyond the planning stage of lazy punch line.

President Trump's first days in the West Wing were very much like all his later days occupying the Oval Office—spent asking resplendently stupid questions and acting accordingly.

Trump has a propensity for asking moronic questions at a near-constant clip. And when the questions don't make him sound as if he were in the middle of violently asphyxiating himself and cutting off oxygen to his brain, they sound as if they were being asked by a mean and obsessive six-year-old. President Trump has asked, according to the Cliff Sims book, *Team of Vipers*, if his Disney World Hall of Presidents animatron could say that America invented the skyscraper. (America did not invent the concept of taller buildings.) In late April 2019, Trump hauled Twitter's CEO, Jack Dorsey, into the Oval Office, for a meeting in which the president devoted a shocking amount of time to grilling Dorsey about his lost Twitter followers, asking if the phenomenon was a product of some nefarious anti-Trump, anti-conservative tech bias. (Dorsey had to explain to the idiot, baby-boomer-brained president that numerous Twitter users regularly lose followers when the site purges fake accounts and bots. Dorsey's insight didn't take, and the president continued in the months ahead with his petulant jihad against Big Tech and Twitter.)

And, as has not been previously reported, President Trump would also badger his former White House chief of staff Reince Priebus about, well . . . badgers. Literally.

For years, Donald Trump has had a superficial, incredibly basic fascination with wildlife and outer space. As those who know him well have observed, conversations with "experts" on these topics often send him into states of toddler-like wonder. For instance, after entering the White House, Trump would grill his space policy advisers on trash.

Whether it was while discussing his precious "Space Force" or his administration's moves to plant his flag on Mars, Trump would ask for comprehensive updates on space junk and debris: *Where does it go? Where does it crash to earth? What, exactly, is up there, circling the globe? Who, or what, is creating all this space garbage? Is this a national security threat?*

When considering this president's silliest, most annoying inquiries, these actually rank on the smarter tier. In April 2019, America's top military officer in charge of protecting the United States from space threats traveled to Capitol Hill to warn legislators about the perils of space trash. "I've advocated for a long time for the development of some kind of international norms and behaviors in space," the U.S. Air Force general John Hyten said at a hearing before members of the Senate Armed Services Committee. "If we keep creating debris in space, eventually we are going to get to the point where it's very difficult to find a place to launch, very difficult to find a place to put a satellite, to operate a satellite without having to maneuver it all the time to keep it away from debris. All of those things are complicated and have to be worked in an international perspective."

In his space camp–style fixation on the issue, President Trump isn't so much worried about the "international norms" as he is about asking juvenile-sounding questions like "What's with all the garbage up there in space?" as he points to the White House ceiling.

It was far nuttier and way funnier when Trump would waste Priebus's time bothering him not about outer space but by subjecting his senior aide to sustained questioning about badgers, the state animal of Priebus's old stomping ground of Wisconsin. This would sometimes occur at moments when Priebus was attempting to brief the president on matters of health-care initiatives, foreign policy, or Republican legislative agenda. After Trump was reminded that the short-legged omnivore was practically synonymous with the Badger State, he'd make a point of bringing it up at seemingly random occasions to his beleaguered chief of staff.

"Are they mean to people?" Trump at least twice asked Priebus in the opening months of his presidency. "Or are they friendly creatures?" The president would also ask if Priebus had any photos of badgers he could show him, and if Priebus could carefully explain to him how badgers "work" exactly. He wanted Reince—resident White House badger historian, apparently—to explain to him Wisconsin's obsession with the animal, how the little critters function and behave, what kind of food they like, and how aggressive or deadly they could be when presented with perceived existential threats. Trump also wanted to know if the badger had a "personality" or if it was boring. What kind of damage could a badger do to a person with its flashy, sharp claws?

An obviously enthralled president would stare at Priebus as the aide struggled for sufficiently placating answers, all the while trying to gently veer the conversation back to whether we were going to do a troop surge in Afghanistan or strip millions of Americans of health-care coverage.

For a frame of reference, this was back during a time when a classified guidance was distributed to professional intelligence analysts, urging them to keep it as truncated and as simple as responsibly possible while collating materials for the President's Daily Brief on national security threats around the world. At the time, Trump was receiving roughly a quarter of the information President Barack Obama had received in comparable briefings. This was done to accommodate President Trump's notoriously slim attention span and his penchant for fidgeting and rebelling at the image of throngs of nameless lanyard nerds lining up to lecture him on foreign affairs.

President Trump couldn't be bothered with receiving an actual intel briefing but could seemingly harangue his chief of staff for hours on end about mundane details of Wisconsin's flagship grassland mammal.

DONALD Trump had dreamed of affixing the title "president" to his name since at least 2000, when he mounted an ill-fated presidential run on the Reform Party ticket. When he finally succeeded, it became clear that his conception about significant elements of the job came from watching movies about the presidency.

That was a bit problematic, because Trump seemed to be particularly keen on cinematic violence. He famously enlisted his eldest son to fast-forward through the Jean-Claude Van Damme movie *Bloodsport*, stopping only to watch the film's fight scenes. On the other end of the spectrum, the first movie Trump screened in the White House was *Finding Dory*, a 2016 Pixar animated film in which Ellen DeGeneres reprises her role as a brain-damaged fish. According to those in attendance, the flick quickly bored him and he walked out.

The president's fascination with action movies in particular might have explained one of the oddest quirks of his early time in the White House: Trump was terrified that he would be assassinated.

During the presidential transition and into his early days occupying and redecorating the West Wing, President Donald J. Trump would inquire numerous times about the quality of the U.S. Secret Service agents protecting him. He would ask if members of his detail had voted for him. He'd ask if individual agents were "tough" enough, or at least as tough as his personal bodyguard and pal Keith Schiller. He would ask about the number of threats that had been made against his life since he defeated Hillary Clinton for the presidency and if the number outpaced that of his predecessor and foe, Barack Obama.

He would ask if the windows in the White House were, in fact, bulletproof, as he had heard about in "the movies."

"You sure?" Trump asked after one adviser assured him they were.

"You *sure*?" he asked again.

For a president and political candidate who so prolifically bragged about how much the American people supposedly adored him, he was privately fairly up-front about his crippling fears of one of them trying to take a shot at him and self-aware about the intense hatreds he had inspired.

Like a bed-wetting child at a new, hazing-prone boarding school, the new president also seemed terribly, viscerally homesick.

In his first few months in office, Trump constantly asked various aides and associates who worked for him and visited him in Washington about people he dubbed his high-profile, wealthy friends in New York City and if they still said nice things about him. Or if they had forever "turned on" him following his demagogic rise.

There would be times that he'd be on the phone with the Democratic Senate minority leader, Chuck Schumer, a fellow boroughite, to talk legislation or political impasses, and Trump would instead insist on gossiping about what he'd seen in the New York tabloids and papers or about high-society types he assumed were mutual friends.

"Hey, you hear he's getting a divorce?" Trump once asked, to Schumer's confusion, regarding some wealthy New Yorker whom the president was convinced the Senate Democrat intimately knew. (Schumer did not.)

Oftentimes, the president would get the *Fox & Friends* co-host Pete Hegseth on the line, with the Fox News star trying to steer the conversation in the direction of policy matters, particularly regarding the Department of Veterans Affairs and privatization efforts, an issue near and dear to Hegseth, himself an Iraq War veteran.

Trump would routinely and abruptly say things like "yeah, well . . . ," only to steer that chatter immediately back to what he last saw on the conservative media behemoth or, better yet, grill Hegseth on what was going on behind the scenes at Fox News, in the personal lives of top on-air talent.

It was the same tendency that had Trump musing to campaign staffers about Joe and Mika's love life. And it was how the Page Six president would solicit gossip from his Fox buddies and how he found a way to feel even more comforted and connected to the right-wing media giant that once gave him a prominent perch as gasbag commentator and crank.

He kept tabs on weekly installments of the NBC sketch comedy staple *Saturday Night Live*—a show that had once viewed him as a vaguely lovable, if aloof and racist, oaf—and its routine weekly skewerings of him as a crotchety idiot. He hated Alec Baldwin's pout and pantomime, knocking the actor's impression of him as "garbage" and the actor himself as a "shithead." And he hated hated HATED how the series, in the Trump administration's dawn, would portray Steve Bannon as the devilish brains of the operation—The Donald's puppet master, and the true, shadow leader of the free world. Guerrilla art posters even began to spring up around Washington depicting a sinister profile of the former Breitbart chief's face above the hashtagged caption #PresidentBannon.

"Did you see this crap?" Trump once angrily quizzed a confidant, referring to an *SNL* cold open in which Bannon, the recently installed White House chief strategist, was portrayed as a Grim Reaper/Svengali–type character who manipulates Baldwin's Trump into launching diplomatic crisis after diplomatic crisis.

At the conclusion of the sketch, "Bannon" tells "Trump" to give him back his Oval Office desk and chair, with the president addressing the

Reaper as "Mr. President." Baldwin's Donald then shuffles off to play with children's toys.

(Yes, this stupid sketch actually managed to affect the most powerful person in the world on an emotional level, and at the very least helped contribute to his rapid souring on Bannon, which would culminate in his ouster in the first year of the Trump presidency. As you continue reading this book, keep reminding yourself that this is the level of fragility and self-parody that defines presidential power and world affairs in the age of an ascendant Trumpism.)

President Trump's other complaints at this time bordered on self-satirizing. He vented to close friends and officials about how Melania Trump and the White House chef and dining staff had "put me on a diet" and how he didn't get to order in McDonald's nearly as much as he wanted to, and did routinely back in New York. (The nearest McDonald's to the White House is less than a five-minute walk, and the Secret Service would never let the president himself wander over.)

It was during this time that we started working together, in the Washington, D.C., bureau of *The Daily Beast*, a political and pop culture news website that had billed itself, in the words of the former editor in chief John Avlon, as "the smartest tabloid on the web."

We had been friends for years, getting acquainted as drinking buddies way back, pre-Trumpism, when Lachlan was an investigative journalist at the neoconservative *Washington Free Beacon* (shortly after his stint at the right-wing Heritage Foundation) and when Swin was an entertainment and politics reporter at *Mother Jones*, the magazine named after a legendary socialist organizer and self-described hellraiser.

On the night of Trump's historic upset in November 2016, Lachlan was watching returns from the *Free Beacon* offices, where opinions were mixed on Trump but decidedly less so on Hillary Clinton. The mood was one less of a righteous victory than a righteous vanquishment. A former colleague, who maintained his antipathy to Trump throughout the campaign, later recalled dropping by the office of the *Beacon*'s editor in chief, Matt Continetti, son-in-law of the prominent Never Trumper Bill Kristol, after polls closed. The two poured drinks, looked at each other, and just started laughing.

On the same night, Swin was bouncing around different areas of Northwest D.C. and gloomily texting Run the Jewels member Killer Mike, a leftist rap artist and a campaigner for Bernie Sanders in the 2016 Democratic primary, who simply messaged back a flushed-face emoji (😳) in apparent despair.

Just weeks prior to that evening, during Swin's birthday dinner at a Mexican restaurant in the Mount Pleasant neighborhood of Washington, we had been out drinking margaritas with several D.C. Republicans, all predictably bemoaning the nightmarish, cartoon-grade authoritarianism of Trump, as well as the roster of sexual assault and misconduct allegations against him.

But in the end, what bound Trumpism to the Republican elite would always be stronger than the quality of his character that irked them. No amount of mean tweets could possibly keep the mainstream GOP from bowing to Trump-branded nativism, given the right opportunity and the right deregulatory priorities. As it happened, one of those Republicans present at Swin's birthday would soon become a very senior official in Trump's administration, proudly serving in a new, ascendant era of conservatism, and that person wasn't the only one struggling to make peace with the new reality in Washington.

FEW dynamics defined the early Trump White House more starkly than the divisions that had set in during the 2016 campaign. The

Trump campaign had been staffed with the dregs of political talent for the primary, and they had been forced to lean heavily on the RNC during the general election campaign. And the RNC, stacked with operatives who were, by and large, not of the party's Trumpian wing, had been forced to back the party's presidential nominee, regardless of any misgivings. Any staff member who wasn't aboard the Trump Train, the RNC made clear, should find new employment.

The tensions lingered from a campaign in which the Trump faithful saw RNC betrayals everywhere. And many career Republicans had flunked what became known as the October 8 test, referring to the day after *The Washington Post* reported that Trump, on an on-set crew bus for the show *Access Hollywood*, had bragged about sexually assaulting women. If you stuck by the president during the ensuing fallout, publicly defended him, and refrained from any second-guessing of his candidacy, you had passed the October 8 test. If you hadn't, you hadn't.

Months later, these two competing camps were working side by side. And if you've never had the pleasure of touring the White House, know that it is a very small, cramped space. The physical proximity wouldn't help with any lingering tensions.

As they tried to establish a decent working relationship, a number of former campaign hands would begrudgingly admit that the former RNCer Michael Short, for instance, was a skilled communications operative. But they would quickly add that he just couldn't be trusted after he was supposedly seen vacating his desk at Trump Tower when *The Washington Post* broke the news of Trump's behind-the-scenes pussy-grabbing comments. Short insists to this day that he did no such thing and was scheduled to head back to D.C. anyway. But the reputation set in, and it was a microcosm of the intense divisions in the early White House that kept its staff at each other's throats.

The fourteenth-floor crew was convinced that Reince Priebus and his RNC contingent were, at best, out to co-opt this political insurgent for their own very swampy ends. And the White House hiring process didn't put their minds at ease, with RNC staffers landing senior West Wing gigs as campaign hands languished, waiting and wondering if they'd even be invited in.

The resulting White House staff was largely divided into two distinct camps that would soon set off an internal power struggle. But first, they had to figure out how to work the phones.

White House staffers who showed up to their new offices in January found the place a disaster. In the Eisenhower Executive Office Building, where the vast majority of White House offices reside, incoming staffers found desks and chairs piled up against walls. Phone lines were not set up, and the arcane system required professional installation. Some staffers couldn't even figure out how to turn on the lights. During past administration transitions, some staffers in the outgoing White House stuck around to show their successors the ropes. No one from the Obama White House extended that courtesy.

For the first few weeks, a number of staffers recalled huddling in vacant offices or working on colleagues' couches, receiving little direction on how they should set up work spaces and the basic office functionality they'd require.

FOR the White House and the new administration, the widespread chaos, dysfunction, and internal backbiting was a disaster. It made a coherent policy strategy difficult and a coherent communications strategy out of the question. It was impossible for midlevel staffers, the types who do the actual grunt work, to get much done, simply because internal deliberation was no longer internal; it was not a possibility but a guarantee that any sensitive subject discussed with White House colleagues would wind up in the press.

The leaking started on day one. Internal cooperation was largely a joke. No one trusted anyone outside, and often within, their immediate office. Looping colleagues in on an internal project was just a way to exponentially increase the odds that those colleagues would leak your work to the press, shit-talk you to a superior, or perhaps both.

This was especially problematic for the communications department, the arm of the White House tasked with putting together a public-facing strategy for the new administration. During the transition, many incoming officials, particularly those who'd worked on the campaign, expected that Jason Miller would be heading up the comms shop. And sure enough, he was tapped for communications director in December. And then soap opera–style drama consumed the place once again.

During the presidential transition, the former Trump campaign adviser A. J. Delgado blew up Miller's spot on Twitter, revealing to the public that a married Miller had fathered her love child during the 2016 campaign. This led to Miller's quickly withdrawing himself from the list of incoming White House staff and kicked off a legal fight between Team Jason and Team A.J. that is still ongoing well into the end of 2019. Delgado herself was supposed to get a position in the Trump White House as a deputy assistant to the president. Titles such as "deputy press secretary" were thrown around as Delgado's prize for being a vocal supporter of Trump's early in the race. That all came crashing down for her when she started airing dirty laundry.

By all accounts, Delgado ended up on the losing end of the affair. Back in her home state of Florida, she began raising the child whom Miller fathered while he went on to a plum gig at the powerhouse global consulting firm Teneo. Miller's own professional prospects would collapse a couple years later when other sordid details about his personal life would emerge through a lawsuit he himself filed against a news outlet that reported details of claims made in a custody battle between him and Delgado. But at the time, Miller, though denied a role in the White House, was still very much in the president's good graces while Delgado was stuck raising a child, without a visible future in Republican politics. Shortly into the Trump era, Delgado was given— at the request of the Trump family—a cushy gig at a Trump super PAC to perform the duties of a MAGA media envoy, though that job evaporated almost as quickly as it materialized.

Perhaps it was understandable, then, that Delgado saw every interaction with either her or Miller through the lens of that dispute. But as tensions brewed within Trumpworld, and her onetime colleagues picked sides in an ever-escalating dispute, Delgado also developed a reputation in Trumpworld as someone who was more than happy to dish it out just as hard as she got it.

We found ourselves on the receiving end of just that side of Delgado as we reported stories from inside Trumplandia. She had been happy to speak to us early in our tenure covering the White House, but sometime in 2018, Delgado for some reason developed the impression—the certainty—that we were carrying Miller's water. So when we reached out to her to inform her that we were writing this book, and that she would be mentioned in it, Delgado responded with a twenty-three-hundred-word emailed tirade. "I realize you are thirsty and eager to please Miller," she fumed. "Damn, you sell yourself cheap . . . Nothing personal but gosh, you really do sell your ethics for peanuts."

After the dust settled on the first phase of the Miller-Delgado debacle, the top role in messaging and communications fell to Sean Spicer, who would soon enter the West Wing with his old RNC chum

Reince. And few of those Trump "loyalists" from the fourteenth floor had much respect for Reince Priebus—a nice guy, sure, but a consummate insider and, worse, the type of timid pushover anathema to Team Trump's burn-it-all-down, own-the-libs, killer ethos. (At least in their eyes.) But now these two guys, Priebus and Spicer, were basically running the show, and in particular staffing up the office where White House messaging would take shape.

The result was a communications shop stacked with RNC alums—Spicer up top, flanked by aides including Raj Shah, Michael Short, Adam Kennedy, Ninio Fetalvo, and Natalie Strom, who'd been Spicer's personal assistant at the RNC. Those and other RNC alums were graced with White House positions shortly after Election Day. Prominent campaign hands, in contrast, found themselves in January without firm job offers. When Spicer finally contacted several campaign loyalists, they largely found themselves deprived of coveted senior staff roles that they considered their due. With a few exceptions, they initially ended up in midlevel positions that afforded them little if any face time with the president.

All of this made for a tense, chaotic, and distrustful work environment. In the communications shop in particular, staff simply couldn't work through a messaging strategy, because every memo and email was liable to wind up in the press—sometimes word for word. One comms staffer recalled crafting a document detailing a list of the White House's accomplishments to date. The document was designed for internal use, to fill in spokespeople and surrogates on good talking points when pressed to rattle off some of the administration's positive agenda items. Within days, he read the same memo, in full and nearly verbatim, in the *Washington Examiner.*

That staffer soon instructed his colleagues and subordinates to never put anything in writing—not even in an internal email to a boss or co-worker. It would, the staffer warned, inevitably end up in the press.

No White House is leakproof. What set Trump's West Wing apart wasn't just the volume of press leaks but the petty smallness of those doing the leaking. These tips to the press weren't designed to affect White House policy or expose some internal wrongdoing. Neither were they all dramatic or consequential or limited to those with actual influence in the West Wing.

No, everyone leaked, and they leaked about everything. Low-level staffers attempted to kneecap internal competition for a higher post, or even to get in the good graces of a superior. It could be done by leaking damaging information about a colleague or leaking in a way that made it sound as though the information came from that colleague—a good way to get someone marginalized internally or even fired. There was no larger purpose to most of these leaks; they were self-serving and frequently accomplished little beyond giving staffers a bit of satisfaction to see their own opinions on the matter in print.

With the new regime struggling to cobble together a functional workplace, a number of staffers, in both the White House and the larger administration, were obviously very frustrated. Many of them were young Republican professionals who'd maybe just caught the last few years of the Bush administration but had largely been forced to toil away in the opposition during eight long years under Barack Obama. Finally they got to the White House . . . and it was miserable. They weren't getting anything done, and, worse, the president seemed incapable of avoiding repeated self-inflicted wounds. He'd just effectively ended Hillary Clinton's political career, a historic achievement in the annals of Republican politics. So why couldn't this guy stop stepping on his own dick?

The White House beat in journalism had, in administrations of the recent past, become a largely ceremonial and boring post, the type of place where newsroom veterans could relax, get a few on-camera moments during regular press briefings, and mostly avoid breaking any news in favor of a steady and largely uneventful four-hour workday. But when Spicer took the lectern for his first-ever press briefing, famously lying through his teeth about the size of Trump's inauguration crowd, it was immediately clear that the stodgy humdrum of White House reporting past was very much over. And before long, some of the best political reporters in the country would be vying for scoops on 1600 Pennsylvania Avenue.

This was the atmosphere into which the two of us were dropped, with not a minute of White House reporting experience between us. There was no road map to follow in covering this insane new administration, its endless leaks, its Caligulan chief executive, its motley band of grifters and hangers-on, and its rabid political base. But one thing became clear very quickly: the people working in the administration were just as aware as we were that the whole thing was off the rails. And many of them were happy to say so, as long as no one knew it was them saying it.

Major news organizations were largely covering the Trump administration as they had previous ones, with a focus on an emerging policy agenda, early staff hires, and internal jockeying. We found a different if often complementary angle. We covered the daily toils of the staffers forced to manage the unmanageable. Often this simply consisted of calling or texting White House and administration sources in the wake of the daily catastrophes that enveloped Washington. Sources' reactions soon became somewhat predictable: no, the president is not on script, and no one knew he'd tweet that insane thing; no, that is not administration policy, and I have no idea why he's saying it; yes, this indictment or investigation is terrible for us and is going to end very poorly; yes, the whole thing is supremely fucked up. We soon carved out a role for *The Daily Beast*'s White House coverage as an outlet where White House and administration staffers could freely vent their frustrations about the chaos and dysfunction that surrounded them.

They weren't saying anything that wasn't obvious from the outside. But as an insider, you're not supposed to admit any of this. The fact that our sources would give us their unvarnished opinion about the internal chaos that defined the early Trump White House was in a sense a credit to the administration and consistent with Trump's campaign rhetoric: Many on his staff weren't trying to put lipstick on this pig of a White House operation. They were telling it like it was, and it was quite bad.

Things came to a fever pitch in May 2017, which we still remember as the White House beat month from hell. In the course of a few weeks, Trump fired the FBI director, James Comey; revealed classified information to the Russian foreign minister at an Oval Office meeting covered solely by a Russian state news outlet; sought to reach out to the ousted national security adviser, Mike Flynn, despite a mounting counterintelligence case against him; and offered his unvarnished thoughts on all those controversies and others, routinely contradicting official White House talking points, occasionally within hours of when White House spokespeople publicly issued them.

On May 12, three days after Comey's firing, Swin happened to be on the phone with a White House source as the president unleashed a torrent of such tweets, raging about Comey, the Russians, China, and contradictory statements from his own staff.

"As a very active President with lots of things happening, it is not possible for my surrogates to stand at podium with perfect accuracy!" @realDonaldTrump tweeted. "Maybe the best thing to do would be to cancel all future 'press briefings' and hand out written responses for the sake of accuracy???"

That tweet happened to post as Swin discussed the day's events with his White House source. "Did you see the latest tweet?" Swin asked.

"What? No," the source said, clearly caught off guard. "Hang on one second." The staffer pulled up Twitter and simply responded, "Jesus."

Stories on those sorts of reactions from inside the White House made for colorful coverage during an extremely hectic period in the White House. They also, we felt, added a certain human element to a time of unbridled chaos. It's not clear that a staff of the utmost political professionals would have been able to keep a lid on things amid the president's frequent public outbursts. But the staffers he'd brought with him to Washington were obviously unequipped or unable to keep White House strategy on track. Trump himself was the major story in all that, of course, but a corollary to his own idiosyncrasies was this crew of D-listers who seemed hapless in the face of an increasingly unmanageable administration.

FOR journalists covering this White House, there's little more amusing than senior Trump officials railing against the damage done by internal leakers. That's because, more often than not, the officials doing so are routine, shameless leakers themselves. The not-uncommon sight of Kellyanne Conway decrying duplicitous White House staffers on some cable news show would be enough for any White House reporter to publicly cry hypocrisy if Conway weren't in all likelihood one of their go-to sources.

Trump himself, scourge of leaks and anonymous sources, is known to provide information to a select few reporters, provided they attribute the information to something like a "senior administration official" or "a source with direct knowledge" or a person "familiar with the president's thinking."

So much of the MAGA Right and its triumph is built on massive levels of irony. President Donald Trump spends his nights and days chastising "the fake news media" for, among other supposed injustices, frequently citing anonymous sources, even though he spent years in real estate and entertainment whoring himself out as a regular "well-placed," faceless source, particularly to the New York tabloids.

In a mildly clever way, Trump has long understood that being a source with juicy information for reporters can serve as a form of protection for the self-interested. The logic goes like this: the more the press relies on you, the more they'll go out of their way not to upset you. This worked out well for other demagogues of American history, including the red-baiting senator Joe McCarthy, who was protected by certain editors and journalists who knew the monster he was but who viewed his gossipy, dishy nature as too helpful to meeting their deadlines.

Back in the 1990s, Trump frequently used phrases like "off the record but you can use it" when dealing with journalists. (Not to get too pedantic here, but what Trump might have meant is "on background" or "on deep background," which in journo-talk means that the information and/or quotations can be used anonymously, with agreed-upon attribution. "Off the record" means it stays between the reporter and the subject/source, so "off the record but you can use it" is technically a contradiction.)

But as he got older, the common usage of anonymous sourcing simply became yet another bad-faith attack, routinely deployed by a president who knew the vast majority of his millions of supporters didn't know any better or didn't give a shit. **"When you see 'anonymous source,' stop reading the story, it is fiction!"** Trump tweeted in August 2018.

As a matter of public messaging, Trump despises leakers, and so his staff, rife with leakers itself, was forced, especially in the early days, to make a show of cracking down on unauthorized conversations with the press.

No one made a bigger show than Sean Spicer. Few reporters elicited more consternation from Spicer than *Politico*'s Alex Isenstadt. Their feud went back years but escalated dramatically in February 2017. Isenstadt and a colleague reported that Spicer was interrogating his own staffers in an effort to root out comms shop leakers, even grilling one staffer, the deputy comms director Jessica Ditto, so viciously that she was brought to tears.

Spicer went nuclear. Isenstadt had of course asked him about his Ditto tip, and Spicer insisted that she was crying over the recent death of a U.S. Navy SEAL during an early Trump administration raid in Yemen. Isenstadt laughed off Spicer's patently absurd attempt to downplay the incident. But on the day his *Politico* story dropped, a very strange piece appeared in the *Washington Examiner*. It was written by Paul Bedard, the same *Washington Examiner* columnist who published the leaked White House accomplishments. He was a frequent dumping ground for West Wing spin doctors, and Bedard claimed, citing an "informed official," that Isenstadt "started laughing about that SEAL." Who was the "informed official"? Well, Spicer had emailed Isenstadt after their phone conversation, pledging to "get that out." And get it out he did.

Behind the scenes, Spicer was determined to root out leakers in general, and in particular anyone leaking to Isenstadt. The reporter's account of Spicer's phone checks was correct. Spicer was randomly reviewing devices of a number of his staffers, looking for anyone who might be providing information to Isenstadt and other reporters.

That made for a particularly awkward moment for Steven Cheung, the White House's rapid-response director. In the wake of his public blowup with Isenstadt, Spicer instituted one of his now-routine phone checks. Cheung handed over his device as requested. As Spicer took the phone, it began ringing, and a familiar name popped up on the caller ID: Alex Isenstadt. This led Spicer to immediately, in front of Cheung and dozens of members of President Trump's press, comms, and legal teams, flip through Cheung's text message app and call log to determine if he had been in contact with the *Politico* reporter. Satisfied that Cheung wasn't the snitch he was looking for, Trump's press secretary handed the iPhone back to the rapid-response director.

As the Spicer-Isenstadt episode illustrated, leaks in the early Trump White House were not just a fact of life but the way business was done. Given that sensitive internal information would end up in the press, the question then became how to leverage that fact to advance the White House's agenda, or, more commonly, one's own agenda—or, occasionally, to embarrass the reporters routinely embarrassing them. In practice, that meant a whole lot of disinformation coming from White House sources. Few leaked out of a noble desire to improve things internally. The leaks generally fell into four categories: cathartic venting (this is frustrating, and I want to talk about it), accurate but self-serving information (I'm leaking you something to advance myself or screw over internal enemies), inaccurate and self-serving information (I'm leaking you bullshit to do the same), and inaccurate and destructive information (I'm leaking to screw over you, the reporter). The decision to publish leaked information required figuring out which of those four categories applied and whether the information's public interest or news value outweighed the certainty that the leaker was using you to achieve some other end.

Fortunately, early White House attempts to manipulate reporters were obvious and ham-fisted.

Cheung might have been a UFC promoter, but few would mistake him for a professional boxer. So it was a bit strange for Lachlan to see an anonymous "tip" land in his in-box in April 2017 claiming that the White House aide was secretly fighting in an underground bare-knuckle boxing ring in Wilmington, Delaware. The email came from a very on-the-nose email address, swampydcinsider@yahoo.com. The first email Lachlan received from that sender claimed Cheung had not signed ethics paperwork required of all incoming administration staffers.

Lachlan had actually heard about Cheung's ethics agreement issue from another source and decided to ask him about it. Cheung didn't answer directly; he just told Lachlan to circle back with his source. Lachlan checked with his actual source on the story, not this supposed anonymous tipster, who reiterated that, no, Cheung had not signed the ethics agreement required of incoming officials under Trump's "drain the swamp" executive order. Lachlan exchanged a few more emails with Cheung, who repeatedly refused to say that he'd signed the ethics pledge. He arranged for a call with the short-lived White House communications director Mike Dubke, who insisted that Cheung had signed it as required. Not much came of that tip, but it did provide some insight into who was sending these swampydcinsider emails.

Then there was the issue of Cheung's supposed underground boxing fights. "Found out Chung [sic] fights in Delaware in an old building called Wilmington Blue Printing company," swampydcinsider wrote in an early May email. That building and the underground fights that took place there were the subjects of a *60 Minutes* investigation a few years earlier. It was pretty obvious at this point that swampydcinsider was shoveling bullshit our way in an effort to get us to either run a bogus story or reveal who our White House sources were. (When Swin reached out to Cheung about this weird-as-hell email about him moonlighting as an underground cage-match fighter, or whatever, Cheung simply laughed, and said, "I have never heard that before in my life, and it's hilarious someone would send you that.")

We decided to play along, and sure enough, over the next few months, "anonymous tipster" made very obvious attempts to elicit the identities of our West Wing sources. Swampydcinsider would throw out suspects, claiming we were seen talking to some White House official or that some other official had been seen sending us information during meetings in the West Wing. "Your source about the warroom was part of a honeypot. Distraction. You'll see why later next week," claimed one email in response to the story that earned us Sims and Surabian's ire. "Your story set off a lot of alarms and outed your source." We never did see why, and our source for the story was never discovered.

We never used swampydcinsider as a source for any story, of course, and never seriously pursued any information that wasn't also provided by a White House source we knew personally. The "anonymous tipster" was very clearly an effort to mess with us and try to root out people providing us with information.

We were later informed that it wasn't an anonymous tipster but an email account that was indeed shoveling horseshit our way. Multiple Trump loyalists and White House staffers had been given access to, or the ability to view, the account and were laughing their asses off about it. We thought it was pretty amusing as well. In the vaunted annals of political dirty tricks, these guys weren't even trying. And who could blame them? When you're working a desk job, serving at the pleasure of the lizard-brain game-show host, you gotta do something to pass the time.

➤ "WHY WOULD I TALK TO YOU?"

While the White House press shop wallowed in dysfunction, top Trump aides were doing what they could to get a policy agenda on track in the face of a president who made grandiose promises of security and prosperity on the campaign trail but had little interest in the minutiae of policy or government. Trump's signature style seemed to be one of convening. He would assemble teams of experts—or people who he believed were experts—in a room in the White House, often on camera, and lavish praise on their brilliant ideas to improve the country. Often that's as far as the ideas went.

For those surrounding Trump, the challenge wasn't just a president who didn't understand the complex problems the country faced. It was that he seemed to have little interest in understanding them. And the roster of third-rate talent with which the president surrounded himself from the beginning meant that it often was not, in fact, the Best People trying to get him up to speed.

That's not to say there weren't highly intelligent and talented people on Trump's staff and in the upper echelons of his administration. But one of the president's defining characteristics is a distrust of anyone whom he perceives to be smarter than himself. Barbara Res, whom Trump hired to oversee construction of his flagship Trump Tower in New York, put it this way: "Although some [Trump Organization executives] were very competent, they were, by and large, weak... Trump could not take a chance in hiring his male equal, so he kept them in their place."

It was tough to simultaneously hire the Best People while ensuring that no one would overshadow the president himself. And it was the source of notorious clashes between Trump and aides such as Secretary of State Rex Tillerson, the chief executive of the country's largest oil company and certainly someone whose accomplishments and intellect could, in the president's eyes, rival his own. Tillerson ostensibly headed up the administration's foreign policy, but Trump routinely ignored the former Exxon chief's counsel. And with few political appointees confirmed to work under Tillerson, and career State Department bureaucrats eyed suspiciously by a White House ever concerned about the seditious "deep state," foreign leaders soon found that Tillerson—like Secretary of Defense James Mattis and National Security Adviser H. R. McMaster—held little sway over the president's decision making on crucial military and foreign policy matters.

Instead, those leaders found that their interests were better served by lobbying officials with no actual expertise but with the trust and ear of the president—people like Jared Kushner, who became a lead point of contact for NATO allies trying to figure out whether Trump planned to follow through on his threats to effectively dismantle the flagship military alliance.

But there was one major problem with Kushner's role as the administration's NATO point man: he didn't seem to know what NATO actually did.

In May 2017, Kushner's father-in-law was about to embark on a high-profile foreign trip, with the commentariat and political class wailing about how President Trump couldn't be counted on to defend NATO allies, particularly against Russian aggression and in support of the collective defense principle of Article 5, which stipulates that an attack on one treaty member is to be considered an attack on all members. It's been invoked only once: in the aftermath of the September 11 terrorist attacks.

In the days before kicking off the overseas trip, Kushner quietly convened several journalists from mainstream political outlets—the *Post*, the *Times*, whatever other legacy media—at the White House (we were not invited) for a background briefing on what to expect from the high-stakes visit. As Kushner went deeper and deeper into discussing the intricacies of NATO and what his father-in-law's administration meant for the alliance, senior officials in the room started wondering what the hell the thirtysomething senior adviser to the president was talking about.

It was a word salad reminiscent of the president's own rambling when it came to issues and minutiae with which he couldn't be bothered.

After Kushner finished his show for the reporters, he smiled, people shook hands, and the hotshot reporters left, having enjoyed another taste of access to executive power. Michael Anton, at the time a spokesman for Trump's National Security Council, followed Kushner on his way out the door. Anton respectfully asked Kushner about whatever it was that he had just muddled in the room moments earlier. Anton brought up Article 5.

"Oh, Article 5," Kushner replied politely. "What's that, again?"

THOSE Trump officials who did have actual political principles and knowledge of the policy matters with which they were tasked soon discovered that they were working for a man for whom such matters were at best irrelevant and more often an active impediment to his narcissistic governing style.

So discovered Mick Mulvaney in early 2017 when he was assigned to oversee the Office of Management and Budget. It was a perfect fit for the former South Carolina congressman, who'd earned a reputation as a conservative budget hawk determined to slash the entitlement state and cut down on the size of the federal leviathan. He was now in the employ of a president who had repeatedly hammered his predecessor over the federal government's red-ink-covered balance sheets.

Mulvaney must have been taken aback, then, when the president punted the issue so hard it would've made an NFL kicker whistle.

The OMB chief had come to a meeting with the president prepared to convey the gravity of the problem. He knew that the president liked visuals, so he brought a chart showing the nation's skyrocketing public debt.

Trump sat and took in the data Mulvaney presented to him. The chart's "hockey stick" curve appeared to show that the national debt would reach a critical mass in the late 2020s. Mulvaney confirmed that that was indeed the case, stressing that in actuarial terms that was a very tight timeline.

"Yeah," Trump responded. "But I won't be here."

The complete disregard for the future of the country and its people and baffling displays of supremely Trumpian buffoonery toward policy, politics, and outreach to outside groups were almost in pornographic abundance as the administration began figuring out which way was up and which down.

A jarringly stark example of this took place in the White House Roosevelt Room on March 17, 2017, when Trump met with various vets groups. Early in the Trump administration, the president for some unfathomable reason entrusted some of his most important tasks to Omarosa Manigault, the former *Apprentice* villain, now senior Trump administration official, who would soon turn on him and his family by secretly recording audio of the president and launching a whirlwind media tour lambasting her former boss and friend as a corrupt and insane racist. One of these tasks was veterans' issues.

For some reason, Trump thought this was a smart choice—causing a swift backlash from vets groups who correctly read this as a hard smack in the face and a betrayal of his campaign sweet talk of "taking care of our veterans."

Following a resounding chorus of public shaming from veterans and advocacy organizations, Trump and his senior staff succumbed and announced the March 17 White House meeting with the principals from various vets groups, giving them a chance to offer suggestions and air their grievances, hoping Trump might notice.

The subsequent gathering of vets advocates quickly degenerated into a prolonged argument between the president and war veterans about napalm, Agent Orange, and the movie *Apocalypse Now*.

The first part of the event was open to the press, and it went relatively smoothly. It was when the reporters, cameras, and microphones had been ushered out that the staggering imbecility was allowed to begin.

It started innocuously enough. Trump went around the table asking different envoys what each of them was doing and what he and his administration could do to better serve them.

Soon enough, he got to Rick Weidman, co-founder of Vietnam Veterans of America, who served as a medic in the late 1960s, during the height of that conflict. Weidman was one of multiple Vietnam vets in the room that day. (The president was not one of them, of course. Trump had famously dodged military service in that miserable war, supposedly due to his "bone spurs." Many years later, he would joke on Howard Stern's show that his promiscuous sex life was like his own "personal Vietnam.")

At this point, Weidman brought up Agent Orange—a powerful, extremely brutal herbicide deployed by U.S. forces against the Vietnamese, which would later saddle American veterans with horrible health effects—and beseeched the president to grant access to health benefits for a larger number of Vietnam War veterans who say they were poisoned by Agent Orange.

Trump replied, confidently, "That's taken care of."

His response confounded the attendees, who had no idea what in God's name he was talking about, a familiar theme for normal-brained humans who spend time within speaking distance of the forty-fifth U.S. president. The issue most certainly had not been "taken care of."

Several people present tried explaining to him that the Department of Veterans Affairs hadn't made sufficient progress on the matter to consider it "taken care of," clarifications that Trump reacted to by abruptly upending the meeting and asking everyone present if Agent Orange was, in his inquisitive terms, "that stuff from that movie."

There was a brief pause as the military veterans present shot glances and furrowed brows at one another, unsure of what exactly this had to do with an actual life-or-death topic for Vietnam vets.

At first, President Trump didn't identify "that movie" he was referring to, but it didn't take long to figure out, as Trump kept on babbling, that he was talking about the acclaimed 1979 Francis Ford Coppola war epic, *Apocalypse Now*—specifically, the iconic helicopter attack on a Vietnamese village thunderously set to Richard Wagner's "Ride of the Valkyries."

Multiple people seated around Trump in the Roosevelt Room— including the actual Vietnam War veterans—chimed in to enlighten the president that the *Apocalypse Now* air-attack sequence featured Lieutenant Colonel William Kilgore ordering a napalm strike, not deploying Agent Orange. They also pointed out that it was not a film that portrayed Vietnam service members in a particularly positive or, they felt, accurate light.

The president was unimpressed and undeterred in the face of the instant fact check. (One clue that could've tipped him off in the moment is that the oft-quoted and co-opted Robert Duvall line from the scene is "I love the smell of napalm in the morning," not "I love the smell of Agent Orange in the morning," but these are just details.)

Instead, Trump refused to accept the premise that he could have possibly gotten this wrong and kept saying things like "No, I think it's that stuff from that movie," to the roomful of veterans and senior administration officials (and moviegoers).

Trump then decided to start going around the room, polling aides and attendees about whether the "stuff" in the scene was, just for the record, Agent Orange or napalm, plunging the meeting into a pointless and surreal argument between the president and, well, everybody else about a Francis Ford Coppola movie.

Trump simply would not let this go.

Finally, Trump's eye and pointed index finger landed back on Weidman.

"What do you think?" the president asked, nudging him on napalm or Agent Orange.

Weidman calmly reiterated what several others in attendance had already said: it was napalm. He added that he didn't enjoy *Apocalypse Now* and saw it as an insult to Americans who served in the war in Vietnam.

Trump flippantly replied, "Well, I think you just didn't like the movie," before *finally* moving on to a different subject. At that point, the great debate in the Roosevelt Room had somehow lasted at least two minutes, according to estimates from several who suffered through its entirety. Because of this, the president did not end up having enough time to call on every veterans advocate at the roundtable on this occasion. One attendee would later succinctly characterize this meeting to Swin as "really fucking weird."

SUCCESSFUL presidents depend, by design, on a coterie of knowledgeable and sober advisers who are able and allowed to offer candid advice that informs sound decision making. Those advisers generally have experience in the fields on which they counsel their presidents, and successful chief executives can effectively delegate and defer to their advisers and overrule them when necessary.

Trump had . . . very little of that.

The famously narcissistic president placed little value on actual competence and expertise, and far more on two qualities that made Sebastian Gorka a perfect fit for the senior White House role he was awarded early in the Trump administration: unflinching personal loyalty, and a good presence on television news.

Gorka is, without a doubt, a superb pundit. With his deep baritone and sophisticated-sounding British accent, the Hungarian-descended national security thinker commands attention during his frequent Fox News appearances and at campaign rallies. At the latter, he's greeted as a celebrity, often garnering louder applause than the political candidates he appears to support. At conservative gatherings in Washington and around the country, Gorka is a perpetual draw for selfie-hungry young professionals. And his witty repartee makes him a cable news favorite. Arguing with CNN's Chris Cuomo in 2017 over an incendiary

Trump tweet about his Muslim travel ban, Gorka jibed, "You're talking about one tweet, Chris, should we spend the whole program on it?"

Cuomo shot back, "I think that to call it a tweet is to run away from significance."

"It is a tweet," Gorka said, laughing. "What else is it, a bowl of petunias?"

Gold, Jerry.

Donald Trump was so captivated by how Sebastian Gorka would zealously lay into TV hosts that one day he invited the deputy assistant to the president into the Oval Office, where Kellyanne Conway and Mike Pence were already meeting with Trump. "A star is born," Trump said, congratulating a beaming, blushing Gorka after having caught one of his television hits. At the time, Gorka was seen as a categorical joke among the national security brass. In early 2017, President Trump personally directed national security officials who loathed Gorka to give the former Breitbart staffer a seat at the table on actual decision making and foreign policy planning. It didn't take long for officials outranking Gorka to figure out how to sideline him, because they thought he contributed worse than nothing to meetings. Gorka was known to derail actual, substantive policy conversation with talk of what random historical figures did in dire situations. To everyone who wasn't Gorka (or President Trump, for that matter), it was akin to listening to a college freshman trying to impress fellow coeds in all the wrong ways.

Nevertheless, the president had other plans for Mr. Seb. "They tell me he's a national security adviser," Trump once said, simultaneously praising and knocking Gorka behind his back. "I don't give a fuck what he is. He should be on TV every day."

Gorka rose to prominence during the 2016 presidential race, when he was simultaneously an employee of Bannon's Breitbart and a paid adviser to the Trump campaign. For a few years now, the Dragon of Budapest, as he's been informally—and mockingly—dubbed, has gone to highly entertaining lengths to cultivate an image for himself as both a hardscrabble tough guy and an international man of mystery. He is instantly recognizable around Washington for his absurd mode of transportation, a black Ford Mustang—not the 5-liter V-8, but its far less powerful 2.3-liter EcoBoost model—adorned with 9/11 memorial license plates, customized to read "ART WAR." Gorka is extremely proud of his Mustang, which he has a lot of trouble parking. On one occasion, he pulled the car onto an Arlington, Virginia, sidewalk and simply . . . left. A Twitter user captured the moment, complete with Gorka in the distance, walking away from the car that he'd just "parked" on a pedestrian walkway.

And of course no caricature of a red-blooded American conservative would be complete without guns. Lots of them. So few who know Gorka were surprised when he told *Recoil* magazine that he regularly carries not one but two sidearms on his person. More entertaining was the rest of his "everyday carry" kit: a Zippo lighter modified into a butane torch, a knife, a flashlight, a copy of the U.S. Constitution, and a tourniquet. "I can deploy it with one hand," he bragged of the latter.

That penchant for weaponry caused Gorka a bit of a problem in Hungary, where he served as a government adviser to, among other officials, the anti-Semitic strongman prime minister Viktor Orban. At some point, Gorka appears to have ended up on the wrong side of the law. In early 2018, *BuzzFeed* noticed his name on a Hungarian police website listing fugitives from justice in that country, which noted that his offense related to "firearm or ammunition abuse."

Gorka's name was removed from that website shortly thereafter. But it wasn't his only Hungarian red flag. His frequent contacts with British military and intelligence officials prevented him from obtaining a security clearance in the country, effectively scuttling his career as a counterterrorism adviser there.

Instead, Gorka moved to the United States, becoming a naturalized U.S. citizen in 2012. He served a brief stint at the Gatestone Institute, a nonprofit once chaired by the former White House national security adviser John Bolton that warns that "Muslim mass-rape gangs" are transforming Britain into "an Islamist Colony." He also set up his own counterterrorism training consultancy and received a few contracts from U.S. law enforcement agencies, including the FBI. Gorka's training sessions largely consisted of anti-Islam jeremiads, according to agents who recalled the events to our *Daily Beast* colleague Spencer Ackerman. The bureau terminated their relationship in late 2016.

But Gorka had bigger things on the horizon. Trump absolutely loved him for the faux-sophisticate air he presented in his frequent cable news interviews and the fact that Gorka, like others who have earned the president's affinity through TV hits, could find no fault in anything Trump had ever or could ever do. He checked every box for potential Trump employment—well, both boxes really: he was good on TV, and he was a total sycophant.

Gorka routinely dazzled the president with on-air zingers, including one accusing CNN staff of "handing around a crack pipe of Trump hatred" during commercial breaks. They were the sorts of lines that would keep him in the president's good graces after his ignominious White House departure.

For the time being, though, his owning of the libs was earning Gorka a coveted role as a deputy assistant to the president, a title of "strategist," and a starting salary of $155,000 per year.

What it could not get him was a security clearance. Gorka rode Bannon's coattails in the White House, and as an ostensible counterterrorism expert he was brought into the fold of the Strategic Initiatives

Group, a small committee of senior White House aides, headed by Bannon and Kushner, that attempted to operate as a shadow National Security Council. But even if it was a largely off-the-books effort to undercut the suspected deep state apparatchik H. R. McMaster, Trump's second national security adviser, the work it was doing required that those in the room be cleared to handle highly classified material.

Gorka wasn't, and so he found himself largely cut out of the policy making he was ostensibly at the White House to affect. Instead, he was known to kill time in the White House mess hall, with few responsibilities and even less influence.

After a few months on the job, such as it was, Gorka's position was untenable. The White House began looking for other agencies in the federal government where he might be moved. And this is when we first crossed paths with the Dragon of Budapest.

We knew little about the guy when we received a tip in April 2017 that the White House was looking to give him the boot. A source at one agency where the West Wing was considering a relocation had clued us into the search, and we soon confirmed on the White House end that officials were indeed weighing a new position for him elsewhere in the administration, ideally somewhere that would not require a security clearance. We called up Gorka to ask for comment. He politely requested that we put our questions in an email, to which he never responded. It was the first and last time we would interact on a friendly basis.

A few days later, Lachlan attended an event at the National Press Club, where Gorka addressed a crowd of Republican lawyers about the threat of radical Islam. After the event, he peppered Gorka with questions about his status at the White House and potential future employment plans. Larry Levy, an official with the Republican National Lawyers Association, the hosting organization, literally boxed out

Lachlan, physically preventing him from approaching Gorka as the self-proclaimed alpha male made a dash for the press club elevators.

Few people in Trump's orbit entertain and thrill us to the degree Gorka does. He is undeniably witty (in his way), with a voice for radio and a carefully curated public persona that he has convinced himself exudes sophistication and general badassery. We decided to stay on the Seb beat if only for the pleasure of continuing to interact with this cartoonish character. We soon reported on Trump's personal intervention to keep Gorka on staff at the White House, but his retention was short-lived. In August, after Gorka had managed to get a security clearance, the newly minted White House chief of staff, John Kelly, revoked it while Gorka was on vacation. He returned and was told he no longer had a job.

Gorka tried to claim he'd quit and leaked a "resignation letter" to friendly voices at *The Federalist*. "It is clear to me that forces that do not support the MAGA promise are—for now—ascendant within the White House," he wrote in a characteristically conspiratorial tone.

A month later, Gorka found his next gig: he was paid $20,000 per month to advise a political group called the MAGA Coalition. We were once again on top of the story and reported that the group was founded and run by a crew of nutters who were among the leading boosters of conspiracy theories such as the underground pedophilia ring run by prominent Democrats out of a Northwest D.C. pizzeria (dubbed Pizzagate, the outlandish theory, which originated in internet forums dedicated to deciphering supposed coded messages in hacked Democratic emails in 2016, resulted in a shooting at the pizzeria shortly after Trump's election). Gorka's new employer soon sponsored a political rally for the accused child molester Roy Moore, then running for Senate in Alabama, headlined by Gorka himself and the former Alaska governor Sarah Palin.

Gorka left the MAGA Coalition after a couple months and hit up the campaign speaking circuit—usually not considered a circuit per se, except he collected thousands of dollars in speaking fees for each of his campaign rally appearances. He also slid into a Salem Radio slot vacated by Michael Medved, one of the few remaining Trump-skeptical voices on nationally syndicated conservative talk radio.

And for all—or perhaps because of—our coverage of Gorka's Trump-era exploits, he never seemed to warm to us. "Why would I talk to you?" was a characteristic reply to one of our comment requests, and caterwauling about the "fake news" *Daily Beast* on his Twitter account—which we've both been blocked from viewing—became fairly standard. On one occasion, Gorka even sent an unsolicited email to Lachlan asking about his apparent drug problem. "A journalist just asked me if you have a problem with cocaine addiction. I was shocked," he wrote. "It's not true is it?" (It was not.)

After refusing to respond to a request for comment on a story Swin wrote in March 2018, Gorka emailed Swin: "I saw the piece you wrote. You are sad person fueled by hatred. I will prayer [*sic*] for you and all your colleagues who attack others they know absolutely nothing about. However I will be blocking you from this email address and my phone since there is no merit to any contact with you. Hopefully, with God's grace, you will one day find your moral center again."

Signed, "Dr Sebastian Gorka," as always.

WITH talent like Gorka filling out the upper echelons of the White House staff structure during its first few months, and scandal after scandal engulfing an administration just trying to get off the ground, a ham-fisted kickoff to the Trump era was inevitable. But as the summer of 2017 kicked into gear, the true scale of the dysfunction really came into focus internally.

Kaelan Dorr got a taste of just how deep that rot went when he was summoned to Sean Spicer's office in June and informed that he'd been doing the wrong job. Dorr was a campaign war room hand who'd been brought into the White House to coordinate with federal agency appointees on administration-wide communications strategy. Or at least that's what he thought he'd been hired to do.

Spicer was conducting a communications-department-wide audit at the time, trying to root out the internal backbiting that was preventing any coherent comms strategy from taking shape. And much to Dorr's surprise, Spicer informed him that his job was not, in fact, cabinet communications but rather congressional communications. Spicer's friends on the Hill had informed him that they'd never even received an email from Dorr, let alone huddled to craft a joint messaging strategy. Spicer wanted to know what the hell he'd been doing with his time.

Dorr tried to explain that that wasn't his job, or at least wasn't the job he'd been assigned. He had even been reporting on his progress in daily comms meetings that literally included Spicer and other senior staffers. If this wasn't supposed to be his job, perhaps someone—Spicer, even!—should have informed him of this. It was yet another microcosm of the rank disorganization and shambolic nature of the early Trump West Wing. Spicer was having none of it. He had a list on his desk that clearly showed that Dorr was tasked with congressional communications, not cabinet communications. That was his job, and he'd better start doing it.

Dorr shrugged. "This means I'm getting a raise, right?" he asked.

➡ "GET ME A PLAN!"

S teve Bannon liked to talk about what he was working on, and his corner of the White House boasted a visual prop that helped illustrate the enormity of the fundamental transformation he hoped to foist on the country. Hanging on the wall of his West Wing office was a whiteboard filled with scribblings detailing the sweeping agenda he was working to enact. The board listed all the different policy items Bannon was pursuing.

The agenda was, to put it mildly, aggressive. In mid-2017, it rattled off dozens of goals, followed by check marks when they were accomplished to Bannon's satisfaction. The sweeping agenda—revealed to the public in part because visitors to Bannon's office, including Gorka and Dinesh D'Souza, kept taking selfies in front of it—covered immigration, trade, health care, infrastructure, and tax policy. The agenda wasn't exactly a secret—most of the items were issues Trump had campaigned on—but they nonetheless presented an unvarnished view of the key policies that the White House, or at least Bannon's faction of it, hoped to achieve.

But on May 10, 2017, Bannon wasn't thinking about any of that. He was sitting in an office, holding court with a high-dollar Republican donor, and the television was tuned to CNN. The day before, Trump had fired the FBI director, James Comey, setting off a wave of recriminations that would hound the administration for years afterward. But Bannon wasn't feeling sheepish or intimidated. He was just pissed off.

"THEY WANT TO TALK ABOUT RUSSIA? THEY CAN SUCK MY MOTHERFUCKING DICK!" he screamed while pointing at the TV in Reince Priebus's chief of staff suite, which had on a chyron related to Trump-Russia. "They want to talk about Russia? We'll fucking talk about Russia." Bannon turned to the aide Andy Surabian, whom he had summoned to the room. He wanted to go on offense on the Russia front. He wanted to hit back. He wanted, to use his preferred term, to go to war. And what better mechanism to wage war than a war room? "Now go!" he bellowed to his lieutenant. "Get me a plan by the end of the night!"

The task to un-fuck Trump's inundated, shitshow communications and press team fell to several campaign "originals," including the "war room" vets Cliff Sims and Andy Surabian and their colleagues Steven Cheung and Andrew Hemming.

To those who've been reading this book from its beginning, you might see where this is going!

Over the weekend, they sat down to start mapping out the plan. But what they devised was far more than a new arm of the White House's communications apparatus; it was a wholesale revamp of the department.

Nevertheless, news of the "Russia war room" spread, with Fox News reporting in late May on "Trump's Russia war room of legal 'A-Team,' street fighters and surrogates" that was taking shape in the West Wing. Rumors were even circulating, again, that Lewandowski and Bossie could be brought in to head up the "rapid response" operation in an effort to combat the White House's persistent leak problem and the growing headaches that the Russia narrative was creating for a White House looking to jump-start its legislative agenda.

We got wind of this "Russia war room" and started asking around among our White House sources. Before long, we got one to dish some details. Surabian and Sims were two of the people heading up the effort, the source said, while Bannon and Kushner were supervising. But no one we spoke with expected that the White House would be able to rein in a news cycle that was spiraling far out of its control—not because staffers charged with doing so weren't up to the job, but simply because the president's compulsive tweeting and tendency to run his mouth for the cameras made a coherent messaging strategy impossible.

We published that story on Friday afternoon under the headline "White House's Russia 'War Room' Built on Ticking Time Bomb." Lachlan left the office, got in his car, and began the two-hour drive to Charlottesville, Virginia, for the weekend. About fifteen minutes into the drive, he got a call from Sims. The story was total BS, Sims said. The comment request we'd sent to him earlier in the day wasn't suffi-cient, he added. He suspected we were just fishing for information and that we wouldn't report his involvement based on a single source (the source, it turned out, was solid). He demanded to speak to our editor. Lachlan provided Sims with her number. Sims never called.

Thus began our lengthy spat with two longtime Trump aides that would culminate in the near brawl in the lobby of the Trump hotel we recounted earlier. We're on good terms with Sims and Surabian these days, even though they continue to claim that our story was inaccu-rate. There was no "Russia war room," they insist every time the topic comes up. But they don't dispute that the White House crafted plans for a war room. Or that the revamped rapid-response strategy was devised in large part to address the White House's Russia-related problems. In June, *Politico* ran with the label as well. "White House ices Russia war room idea," the paper reported, adding that the plan envisioned "two former campaign aides [taking] over rapid response on Russia questions."

So, guys, if you're reading this: We still stand by our story. But in the interest of burying the hatchet, we'll stop calling it a "Russia war room" . . . starting now.

SIMS, Surabian, Cheung, and Hemming's proposed Russ—*ahem*—comms department revamp envisioned a totally reorganized communications apparatus designed to streamline and clarify how the White House's messaging strategy would take shape by establishing clear roles and lines of authority among the brutally fractious and disorganized staff. And the plan was a hit. Bannon loved it. For the next few weeks, he'd use a printed-out slideshow of the plan as his prop to underscore just how innovative and action oriented his team was. When he received notable visitors to his office, Bannon would grab the plan, furiously point to it, and exclaim, "Check this shit out right here! This is what we're doing!"

Even more important, Kushner loved it. And the First Son-in-Law's sign-off was going to be crucial if the plan was ever going to be implemented. Around the West Wing, Kushner began affectionately referring to Surabian, Sims, Hemming, and Cheung as "the killers." He seemed to be fully on board. But there was one problem: Kushner considered Reince Priebus feckless and ineffective and wanted him out of the West Wing. And he knew that Priebus was on his last legs at the White House at the time. The communications chaos was, therefore, beneficial for Kushner, and he was determined not to improve things until Priebus was gone. He would revisit the communications plan

GET ME A PLAN!"

when Priebus—and, hopefully, Spicer—were out the door. Then, under a competent White House leadership structure, including a new communications director, he could go about restructuring the comms shop.

That's not exactly how things worked out. Instead, Kushner and the rest got Anthony Scaramucci and arguably the craziest eleven days of the early Trump era.

The Mooch was, of course, a known quantity in political circles, having served as a Wall Street fund-raiser for a number of prominent Republicans. They included no fewer than three 2016 GOP contenders. Trump was, in fact, Scaramucci's last choice during the campaign. He initially backed the Wisconsin governor, Scott Walker, whose aides suspected the Mooch of leaking details from campaign fund-raising calls to the press. A Walker campaign aide described the leaks as just "stirring up drama with the donors." It wasn't even clear that he had an immediate goal in doing so beyond his insatiable need to share his unvarnished opinions with a reporter. It was that same impulse that would be his White House undoing.

When Walker dropped out of the race in late 2015, Scaramucci approached the Florida senator Marco Rubio's campaign. Team Rubio, cognizant of his reputation, wasn't interested in his support, so the Mooch signed on with the campaign of Rubio's chief rival, the former Florida governor Jeb Bush. After Bush dropped out, Scaramucci finally threw his support behind the eventual victor.

Given his own reputation as a leaker—one solidified as early as the 2012 presidential campaign—Republican politicos were a bit taken aback at the number one agenda item that dominated Scaramucci's raucous entry into the Trump White House. He would root out the internal leakers betraying the president's trust and imperiling his agenda, Scaramucci vowed. The first step in that agenda was to scare the shit out of his new colleagues.

Tact and subtlety were not exactly the Mooch's strong suits. In addition to his reputation as a willing source, he was known in some Republican circles for the hilarious but often outlandish comments he'd make in the course of friendly conversation. During one of our trips to the Trump hotel, Scaramucci came up in conversation with a group of Trump-backing black evangelical pastors who were in town for an event. It was shortly after Scaramucci's White House tenure, so he was bound to be a topic of discussion. These guys recalled a conversation with the Mooch in which he attempted to burnish his credentials in the African American community. He was very in tune with the concerns of black Americans, Scaramucci said, citing the fact that he was, in his words, "black from the waist down."

Naturally, we fell over laughing at that. Scaramucci was out at the White House, but we had to write that up. It was simply too good. We called up the Mooch the next day to ask about it. He denied up and down that he had ever uttered such a thing. It "sounds racist," he objected. We pitched editors on the story, but they didn't see the immediate news value in publishing a story on Scaramucci's endowment. More than a year later, we got wind that Sims would be recounting a similar anecdote in his book. Excerpts from political books are frequently leaked ahead of time to generate buzz before the book's release, and bombshell details from Sims's account were already showing up in major publications. But we just wanted one anecdote from it. Finally, we got our hands on the chapter at issue. And sure enough, Sims recalled Scaramucci making the "black from the waist down" joke in a conversation with a number of White House media technicians, who were largely African American. With Sims's book coming out, we at last had both corroboration and a news peg. We revisited the story, with the editors' sign-off.

And naturally we went back to Scaramucci to see if he'd like to comment. "Nah thanks though," he texted back.

After the announcement of his hiring, and the simultaneous resignation of his predecessor, Sean Spicer, whom Scaramucci was brought on to replace, the outgoing White House press secretary gathered communications department staff in his office for a heartfelt goodbye speech. The press secretary's office is massive by the standards of the West Wing, big enough to fit a large desk, a table, and four chairs and have plenty of uncovered floor space. But the office was packed with staffers gathered to hear Spicer's final words to his troops.

Steven Cheung happened to be standing near the office's door as Spicer bade farewell. And Cheung was a bit taken aback when, in the middle of Spicer's speech, someone sneaked up behind him and gave him a big, loud hug. He turned around to see a glowing Anthony Scaramucci.

For those of us covering the White House at the time, the Scaramucci era looked to be a gift from the heavens. Just for the sheer entertainment value of it, a Scaramucci-run communications department was going to be gold for the political news business. He seemed to be the perfect Trump spokesman: amiable, brash, over the top, a consummate New Yorker, with a deep and unfiltered hatred of Washington business as usual and the whisper campaigns and backstabbing that defined it. "Anthony Scaramucci is Trump's mini-me," as CNN's Chris Cillizza put it.

And Scaramucci love-hated the press, in the same fashion as Trump. He was vowing to crack down on leakers and trying to shame the fake news for going after his new boss. But the Mooch himself reveled in every minute in front of the cameras and passed up no opportunity to answer the media's questions. That was clear from the outset of his White House tenure, which kicked off with a marathon ninety-minute press briefing during which he pledged he would take every question that reporters in the room had for him. And he followed through—mostly. Lachlan raised his hand after every answer. But when the presser wrapped up, it seemed he was the only one in the room who didn't get a question in.

Nevertheless, part of the Mooch's strategy for cracking down on press leaks appeared to be turning the White House communications shop into a functional and responsive place. He quickly implemented new rules for the press shop, including requiring that they respond to every single outstanding media request before going home each day. Perhaps if reporters got official responses from the White House, they wouldn't need to resort to the unofficial ones, which were invariably far more damaging and, in Scaramucci's eyes, less truthful.

When we heard that, there were high fives in the newsroom. Would the White House press shop finally begin doing its actual job of communicating with the press in a less hostile manner? Would we finally get questions answered when we reached out through official channels?

We would not, it turns out. Scaramucci's new every-media-request-gets-a-response rule was completely, laughably unrealistic. The West Wing simply didn't have the manpower for that herculean task. But we appreciated the sentiment nonetheless and figured that Scaramucci would at least usher in a more constructive relationship between us and our official contacts in the White House.

If Scaramucci was putting on a friendly face publicly, inside the White House it was a reign of terror. White House staffers lived in fear that the new communications director would finger them as leakers and have them summarily fired.

This internal leak hunt was designed to stem a practice in place since Trump's inauguration: the use of leaked information to mess with or damage internal colleagues. But the vehemence with which Scaramucci went about it had the opposite effect. If a White House staffer wanted to kneecap an internal rival or simply someone he or she didn't like, that staffer no longer had to leak negative information about that person but simply to intimate internally that that person was herself a leaker. The Mooch began putting together lists of staffers suspected of unauthorized press contacts, lists that would determine who would be fired when the impending leaker purge came. But he was also soliciting names from colleagues. And they had their own lists. Before long, there were dozens of leaker lists flying around the White House. Everyone down to the junior staff level had her own list of culprits that should be purged. And virtually everyone was on at least one of these lists. Like a Stalinist satire, it was hoped that the mere allegation of infidelity would be enough to rid the West Wing of a despised rival.

That panic nearly ensnared some top White House aides. One staffer there estimated that Raj Shah, then the White House deputy comms director and, as an RNC alum, a common name on the Mooch's various shit lists, was literally hours from being fired before the whole Scaramucci mess imploded.

The Mooch had developed a paranoid, hair-trigger style when it came to leakers, so it didn't comfort his new colleagues that he appeared to be totally ignorant of some of the basic functions of the government in which he was now a senior official.

"In light of the leak of my financial disclosure info which is a felony, I will be contacting @FBI and the @TheJusticeDept," he tweeted five days into his White House tenure, tagging Reince Priebus in the tweet to boot. Scaramucci was angry about a *Politico* story that publicly posted a financial disclosure filing showing that he was worth tens of millions of dollars. But *Politico* had simply obtained a publicly available copy of the information Scaramucci had submitted to federal ethics officials when he was appointed to a post at the U.S. Export-Import Bank just weeks earlier. It wasn't a leak; this was publicly available information. But days later, even after that fact was explained at length in the press, he was still demanding a federal criminal investigation into how the media was able to obtain it.

Even more alarming, Scaramucci appeared to be hunting for the leakers of information that he himself had leaked. He had taken his position as director of communications on a Friday. The following Tuesday, he made his first concrete move to oust a supposed White House leaker, telling *Politico*—on the record!—in a story that went live at around 9:00 a.m. that he planned to fire Michael Short, the former RNC aide and Priebus ally who served in a senior communications post. Scaramucci had openly previewed the move on Tuesday morning, but by that afternoon he was pointing to *Politico*'s report on his on-the-record comments as evidence of the White House's leak problem.

"Let's say I'm firing Michael Short today. The fact that you guys know about it before he does really upsets me as a human being and as a Roman Catholic. I should have the opportunity if I have to let somebody go to let the person go in a very humane, dignified way," Scaramucci told CNN. "Here's the problem with the leaking, why I have to figure out a way to get the leaking to stop, because it hurts people."

Just to recap: Scaramucci publicly said he would fire Short, then complained that the "leak" of that news was unfair to Short and showed why press leaks were so damaging and immoral.

In the end, it was Scaramucci's fundamental lack of understanding of the basics of his job that got him canned after just eleven short days. The *New Yorker* reporter Ryan Lizza reported that Scaramucci was dining with Trump, Sean Hannity, and the Fox News executive (and future White House communications director) Bill Shine at the White House. Scaramucci was incensed that news of the dinner leaked. He called up Lizza in a rage, demanding to know his source so the culprit could be fired. Lizza declined to name the source, and Scaramucci proceeded to go on a tear against his White House colleagues, telling Lizza, "I'm not trying to suck my own cock" like Steve Bannon, and dubbing Chief of Staff Reince Priebus a "fucking paranoid schizophrenic."

When Lizza published a story on the interview, Scaramucci cried foul again, claiming the whole conversation had been off the record. Lizza denied that, and it soon became clear that the Mooch had just assumed that none of what he was saying would make it into print—a laughable assumption, as a paid press operative could attest, and not the type of mistake one hopes to see in the White House's top communications hand.

Between Lizza's story and the various other tumults of Scaramucci's brief White House tenure, even the president, who adored the Mooch, began to wonder if he had a hold on things. By the time Lizza's piece went to print, the Scaramucci news cycle was out of control. And the new comms director appeared not only unable to control it but to be intensifying it with his every public utterance. It got so bad that Trump began wondering aloud to aides and advisers if his communications director was on drugs.

After eleven insane days, it was too much to bear. Priebus offered to resign the day Lizza's interview ran as it became clear he had completely lost any ability to control the spiraling disaster he oversaw. Trump replaced him with the former Marine Corps four-star general John Kelly. And Kelly's first order of business was to fire Scaramucci.

John Kelly's selling point was military discipline. He promised to impose order on a laughably chaotic West Wing, to regiment and structure a freewheeling White House, and to professionalize what was by all accounts a disastrously disjointed and amateurish operation more than half a year into Trump's tenure. The challenge for Kelly was that there were high-profile people both inside and outside the White House who benefited tremendously from the West Wing's total lack of order or structure. The ability to saunter into the Oval Office and drop a printed news article on the president's desk made for a potent way to shift conversation and even policy in the White House. And some aides used that opportunity to tremendous effect. In cracking down on the revolving-door access to the Oval, Kelly was going to make some enemies who were very loud and had the ability to yell directly to the president.

Among his first targets was Omarosa Manigault Newman. As a longtime Trump friend and colleague, she considered her own stature in the White House unique and unrivaled. She could call up the president on his cell phone at three in the morning and he would pick up every time, she'd later brag to us. No one outside the Trump family itself, she insisted, knew the president as well as she did or had been as close to him for so long. Omarosa jealously guarded her self-appointed role as the Trump whisperer of the early administration and in particular sought to sideline other black women who might encroach on her nearly unique demographic standing in the White House. Kay Coles James, the president of the Heritage Foundation, the flagship conservative think tank, would later accuse Omarosa of blocking her from getting an administration gig in early 2017.

Omarosa's day-to-day job at the Office of Public Liaison was fluid; no one was ever really sure what, if anything, she was doing. But her sense of self-importance was unrivaled. She even began referring to herself in official White House correspondence with the title "the

Honorable," which is generally reserved for people who actually hold, or have held, public office, not simply White House staffers.

Omarosa was almost universally reviled by her White House colleagues, who said she added little to any internal discussion and would more often show up to meetings simply to throw a wrench in the works. She was also known to try to micromanage the White House's press and messaging operations. On one occasion, the White House press pool was gathered in the Oval Office for a public event. The White House assigns a junior staffer, known as a wrangler, to handle pool access to White House events. The wrangler shepherds the press to and from events and makes sure they're updated on the day's schedule. But Omarosa happened to be at this Oval Office event, and at one point she simply decided that the event was over and began ushering journalists out of the room, without any input from, or even warning given to, the wrangler or any other press staffer. For those in the press shop, whose actual jobs included handling media access, it was a constant point of annoyance. But Trump himself seemed to enjoy turning loose his famously short-tempered sidekick on the fake news media. On one occasion, as he grew impatient with the slow pace with which the press were evacuated from an Oval Office event, the president barked at Omarosa to get them the hell out. "Handle it like you handled it on *The Apprentice*," he instructed.

Omarosa seemed to revel in conflict with her perceived inferiors, and colleagues would frequently text each other during meetings that Omarosa attended to frustratedly vent about her presence. "She doesn't have any friends in high places, except the one place it matters," one White House official remarked during her West Wing tenure.

Particularly annoying for staffers who interacted with the president was Omarosa's frequent attempts to "trigger" Trump, as one White

House official put it, by depositing on his desk printed-out copies of negative news stories or gossip tabloid items regarding figures in media and entertainment whom she knew Trump despised. The stories would inevitably send Trump into a tizzy and distract him from the actual business of the day. It was a persistent problem caused by a broad cross section of White House staff, but no one knew how to trigger Trump like Omarosa, and few enjoyed such unfettered access to the president.

John Kelly quickly went about putting a stop to that. Free access to Trump was a major problem as he saw it, and Omarosa was patient zero when it came to derailing the White House's agenda and momentum on a given day.

Since the beginning of the Trump administration, Omarosa's office had been relegated to the Eisenhower Executive Office Building across the street from the White House. She would nonetheless set up camp in the West Wing, where, as first reported by *Washingtonian Magazine*, she kept a large cache of shoes scattered around the area of an empty desk, to the annoyance of her colleagues, who were forced to gather them up and kick them under the desk in order to avoid a safety hazard in the already cramped West Wing. Omarosa had always reviled Priebus and Spicer and was elated when the two were ousted just a couple of weeks apart. Finally, she hoped, a West Wing office was hers for the taking.

Not only didn't she get the office, but Kelly moved swiftly to ensure that her access to the president was dramatically curtailed.

Omarosa bristled at being shut out, but lashed out at any reporter who suggested that she didn't retain as much influence over the president as any West Wing employee without the last name Trump (or Kushner). When we reached out for a story on her Kelly-related travails, she defiantly bragged that no one, not even this general turned chief of staff, could stop the president from seeking her counsel. She remained, and would remain, the president's most trusted and loyal aide, and those seeking to kneecap her were doing so out of jealousy or a desire to replace her. But Omarosa would not be replaced.

And then she was replaced.

In late 2017, Kelly finally fired her. The last straw was Omarosa's routine use of the official White House car service to run personal errands. The administration was in the throes of numerous scandals involving high-level officials using government resources for personal tasks. Omarosa's conduct was strictly forbidden and a huge liability for a PR-besieged White House. Kelly finally had the ammo he needed to rid the administration of this nuisance.

But Omarosa was not about to go quietly—literally. She learned she was being sacked late on a Tuesday evening. The Secret Service had deactivated her access card, which, after she left the White House grounds, would have prevented her from getting back in. But she wasn't planning to leave. She was going to confront the president, who, she was convinced, couldn't possibly know just how unfairly she was being treated. Trump was in the White House residence, an area of the complex where even senior staff are not permitted to aimlessly wander. But Omarosa wanted to march right up to the front door and get what she felt she was owed.

What happened next was described to us by various White House officials as an attempted "storming" of the residence, a darkly comical "ruckus," and "the closest thing to reality TV [I'd experienced] since getting here." Omarosa had to be physically removed from the White House campus.

She had nonetheless been able to extract one last concession from John Kelly's White House, or so she thought. It was very important to her that she be able to say that she had spent one year in Donald

Trump's White House—not 358 days, but one year. So when the White House counsel's office began putting together her exit paperwork, Omarosa was distressed to find that it listed her departure date as January 13, 2018—a week short of that one-year milestone.

On December 13, the day of her termination, John Kelly had summoned Omarosa to the White House Situation Room, the conference room where some of the nation's most consequential national security decisions take place. This was not one of those decisions.

When Omarosa showed up, she was greeted by Kelly; two attorneys in the White House counsel's office, Stefan Passantino and Uttam Dhillon; and the White House human resources aide Irene Porada. They were there to break the news of Omarosa's firing—and to do their best to make sure she went quietly. "I'd like to see this be a friendly departure . . . and you can go on without any type of difficulty in the future relative to your reputation," Kelly told her in what Omarosa interpreted as a threat.

We know that Kelly made that comment, because it turns out that Omarosa was recording the whole thing. It was one of a litany of internal White House meetings and phone calls that she had captured and that she began releasing to much media attention after her departure. But this wasn't one of the clips that made it onto CNN after Omarosa's relationship with the president turned sour in very ugly and public fashion. This audio is now on file with a federal court in Washington because John Kelly just had to stick it to Omarosa one last time.

Kelly departed the Situation Room meeting early, and Omarosa made one crucial request to Passantino and Dhillon. "How do I make it to the one-year mark?" she wanted to know. "That's important to me . . . to make it to the one-year mark." Dhillon said they would see what they could do. "Yes, to the twentieth of January," he said about ten minutes later. "We're taking you until the twentieth." The next day, Sarah Sanders released a statement on Omarosa's termination. "Her departure will not be effective until January 20, 2018," Sanders said.

All senior administration officials who leave government service are required to complete ethics paperwork detailing their personal finances as of the date of their departure. In late January, Omarosa provided the counsel's office with an email address where that paperwork could be sent. White House ethics officials sent a series of emails to that address with reminders that Omarosa needed to fill out that paperwork, and received no reply. Then they tried sending the reminders to the email address she'd provided as well as to a second one they had on file for her. The first two of those attempts went unanswered, but finally, in March 2018, Omarosa replied.

She would not fill out her termination ethics paperwork, she told the White House, because it inaccurately listed her departure date as January 13, not January 20. In late March, she got a phone call from Passantino. And once again, she was sure to record it.

"There's an error on the report about my termination day. So, my last day is the twentieth and it's indicated the thirteenth," Omarosa complained. "You were in the room [meaning the Situation Room] when we all agreed to the twentieth, so once that's corrected, I can complete the report and everything will be done. But, with that discrepancy, I don't feel comfortable completing that report."

Passantino was conciliatory, and he appeared to suggest that it was Kelly who had ensured that Omarosa would not, on paper, make it to her much-coveted one-year milestone. "When I talk to the chief [Kelly] and the chief is like, 'No, we changed it from the twentieth to the thirteenth, it is the thirteenth.' If I hear that, I guess I'll just tell you," Passantino said.

"I don't think you'll hear that," Omarosa shot back, "because you were in the room when the twentieth was decided. . . . I don't know where the discrepancy would have come from."

Passantino tried his best to placate her. "Yeah. Right. No, no, no, no, no. I hear you and I was there for the conversation of the twentieth," he assured her. "There would be only, if subsequently, subsequent to that conversation [the date] changed. But again, that's not my issue, I'm not going to get in the middle of that."

But Omarosa would not let it go. Six months after that conversation, she still had not been provided with a version of her termination paperwork that declared her preferred exit date. And as a result, she still had not signed that paperwork. She was legally required to do so, regardless of whether it dictated that she had served in the White House for a full year or just shy of one. She refused to do it, so on June 25, 2019, the Justice Department brought a civil case against her for knowingly violating the Ethics in Government Act.

As of our writing this, that case is still ongoing. And as more details emerge in the case about the circumstances of her departure, it becomes ever clearer that Kelly, ostensibly the stern and stately leader, had intervened to deny Omarosa a personal victory that was obviously so important to her.

➥ "I WISH HIM THE VERY BEST"

Even in a town full of liars, where lying is in fact often the default state of professional conversation, there are only two people who are so irredeemably dishonest that we will never, under any circumstances, use them as sources. One of them is Corey Lewandowski (the other being Roger Stone), and he is, in our experience, the single most dishonest person in the upper echelons of Donald Trump's coterie of aides, advisers, and hangers-on. As a matter of policy over the last few years, we will not use any information he provides unless it's on the record. Even if he tells us something we've also heard from half a dozen other unnamed sources, the eventual story will attribute the information to six sources; Corey will never be the anonymous seventh.

The American public seems to be more attuned to political dishonesty these days than in the recent past. Sean Spicer and Sarah Sanders are pop culture fixtures the way Obama's press secretaries Josh Earnest and Jay Carney never were. And the ease and consistency with which Trump's spokespeople peddle dishonesty on a daily basis is enough to make a mob attorney blush. But when it comes to sheer, unadulterated untruth, spread without hesitation or remorse, no one in Trump's orbit can hold a candle to Lewandowski.

So when we began hearing, just a few months into the Trump administration, that Lewandowski, relegated to a D.C. consulting practice at the time, was sure of his imminent appointment to a senior White House role, we knew to take it with a few grains of salt. "Trump wants me there, just you wait," as one associate relayed his comments to us in May 2017. That associate was one of six sources we spoke with for the story, all of them recounting various versions of the same assurance from Lewandowski: Trump trusted him more than anyone short of his family (sound familiar?), and a White House replete with leakers and deep state Never Trumpers needed a loyal and firm hand to set it on the right course.

We wrote up the story incredulously, with the lede "Corey Lewandowski, Donald Trump's controversy-courting former campaign manager, really wants you to think he's about to land a job in the West Wing."

With every staff shake-up or high-level vacancy, there's been a Lewandowski whisper campaign—more often than not, spurred by Corey himself—that he's the perfect man for the job, the president knows it, and pretty soon he'll be running things in the West Wing, so you best stay on his good side. Every version of it hits the same notes: Corey knows Trump best and has always trusted his instincts, and DJT, as campaign originals know, reciprocates on both counts.

But it never happens. Lewandowski still has never served in any position in Donald Trump's administration, let alone a senior White House one. Ask him, and he'll tell you that he's perfectly happy, and indeed more effective, as an outside adviser and spokesperson, and in any case he has a family to take care of and doesn't mind the income of his lucrative political consulting business.

The truth is far simpler: virtually everyone of consequence in Trump's White House beyond the president himself despises and distrusts Lewandowski. Trump's own family members—Ivanka, Jared, Don junior—repeatedly voiced their suspicions, sometimes to DJT himself, that Lewandowski had been leaking damaging information or stories, concocted or otherwise, about them to the press.

Still, no one despised and distrusted him more than John Kelly.

The truth is that Lewandowski has retained significant influence with the president in spite of his lack of any official White House role. He still speaks with Trump regularly and drops by the Oval Office for meetings. And he's highly active on the political side of things, maintaining a steady consulting gig with the pro-Trump super PAC America First Action that nets Lewandowski a monthly paycheck of $10,000. And Trump continues to solicit his opinion on matters of administration policy as he pines for the glory days of the 2016 campaign.

As Kelly sought to crack down on the access and influence of Trumpworld's various gadflies, a confrontation with Lewandowski was inevitable. But few could have predicted that that confrontation would get physical.

After Omarosa was frozen out, one of Kelly's first official acts as chief of staff was to deactivate Lewandowski's access badge, throwing up a major roadblock to his Trump access. Lewandowski was livid, of course, but there wasn't much he could do at the time beyond privately gripe. Trump had brought Kelly in to make changes, and until there was some sign that things were not improving internally, the general was going to have the run of the place.

Fortunately for Lewandowski, yet another scandal was brewing that would hand him all the ammunition he needed to kneecap Kelly and reclaim his position beside and influence over the president.

SENIOR staffers for the Environmental Protection Agency administrator Scott Pruitt were in Morocco in December 2017, on a trip arranged by a lobbyist who would later register as an agent of the Moroccan government. It was one of a number of controversies that bedeviled Pruitt. But in the course of the junket, something happened that, at the time, struck staff as odd. Only months later did they realize exactly how consequential it was.

At one point during the trip, at the hotel where the EPA delegation was staying, a member of Pruitt's scheduling and advance staff was approached by Samantha Dravis, Pruitt's top policy adviser. This advance staffer, a Trump 2016 campaign alum, had never personally interacted with Dravis, who was clearly very agitated. And she didn't know what to say when Dravis began interrogating her about Hope Hicks, the longtime Trump communications hand and senior White House official.

Dravis was incensed with Hicks, multiple members of Pruitt's delegation later told us, for carrying on a relationship with a man whom Dravis had been seeing romantically—and with whom she was living. It was a bizarre exchange, according to sources who witnessed it, but few at the time thought it was much beyond a strange and intriguing bit of workplace gossip. Within a few months, though, the real fallout from it would become very clear.

Dravis, it turns out, had been dating a senior White House aide, the staff secretary, Rob Porter. But at some point, Porter had ended their relationship and struck up a new one with Hicks. Dravis was rightfully distraught, and her former colleagues told us the drama was soon common knowledge at the EPA, where she freely aired details of the domestic dustup. But more damning details of Porter's troubled personal life were soon to emerge—and thoroughly disrupt the entire Trump administration and derail the standing of the president's most senior aide.

Porter was a former chief of staff for Senator Orrin Hatch, the veteran Republican from Utah. He joined the White House right at the beginning. As staff secretary, he retained significant influence over the people and information that made it to the Oval Office, and after Kelly took over in mid-2017, Porter became a go-to deputy in Kelly's efforts to control access to the president. Porter would eventually become one of Kelly's most trusted and relied-upon allies in the West Wing.

Virtually everyone who worked with Porter in the White House and in Hatch's office had only good things to say about him. But the women in his life knew a darker side. He was twice divorced, and both of his ex-wives, it turns out, had accused him of various types of abuse. His first wife, Colbie Holderness, recalled Porter choking and striking her and forcefully pressing his limbs into her body in anger. On one occasion, she said Porter punched her in the face, giving her a black eye. She would later publicly release a photo of her face after that instance of abuse. Porter's second wife, Jennifer Willoughby, recounted extensive verbal and emotional abuse at his hands. After they divorced, she took out a temporary restraining order against him. From the start, Porter denied that he had abused either of them.

Dravis had become obsessed with her breakup with Porter and his subsequent relationship with Hicks. Colleagues at the EPA recalled her repeatedly bringing it up in a woe-is-me fashion, complaining that she'd never be able to maintain a social life in Washington due to the awkwardness that the broken-off relationship had caused her in mutual social and professional circles.

In late 2017, Dravis also began dropping hints of Porter's problematic personal life. Former colleagues recalled her making vague allusions to skeletons in his closet, but none knew the full extent of the controversy that would soon ensue. At one point, she reached out to the White House counsel, Don McGahn, to inform him of Porter's "anger issues," though it's not clear how much detail she shared. If she did relay specifics, McGahn never acted on them. Even Pruitt was aware of some details of the relationship, according to multiple former colleagues whom we spoke with. Dravis denies ever discussing it with the administrator, but her former colleagues say, one way or another, Pruitt became aware of the situation, and pressed to keep the drama from bursting into public view and upending the agency's relationship with the White House by embarrassing one of its most powerful and, internally, widely liked staffers.

To understand how deeply the Porter story shook the White House, one needs to understand the nature of news cycles in early 2018. This was in the heat of Special Counsel Robert Mueller's probe into Russian election meddling and potential Trumpworld ties to the effort. In December, the former national security adviser, Mike Flynn, had pleaded guilty to lying to federal agents investigating Russia-related matters. In February, the former Trump campaign hand Rick Gates pleaded guilty to the same as well, Mueller indicted thirteen Russian nationals, and he leveled an additional thirty-two charges against Paul Manafort. Meanwhile, scandals involving Trump cabinet secretaries were intensifying. The president was rolling out aggressive trade policies that roiled global markets. He had just signed the landmark Tax Cuts and Jobs Act into law.

Despite the near-daily barrage of major news events, or perhaps because of it, few of these major developments on high-profile national issues seemed to penetrate the national media conversation and remain at the forefront for very long. The Mueller saga was always lingering behind the day's events. News organizations focused significant resources on the policy front, but talking heads were always more fix-ated on breaking events. Few of these major news events appeared to have much staying power in an ever-shifting news cycle.

The Porter news was a major exception. The scandal dominated headlines for weeks, a nearly unheard-of degree of staying power at the time. Part of that had to do with the soap-opera nature of the allegations against the White House staff secretary. Sex and intrigue at the highest levels of political power have always been catnip for the news business, after all.

But that alone wasn't what kept the nation's newsrooms—and their audiences' attention—so intently focused on this controversy. The real culprits were in the White House itself, and at each step in the story their public statements only served to exacerbate and prolong a deeply damaging public narrative about the character of a senior White House official and the seeming indifference with which his superiors, including the president, treated such disturbing allegations against him.

Virtually every major development in the Porter story managed to contradict a previous White House statement on the matter. First it was Sarah Sanders giving a fabricated timeline of when the West Wing knew about the allegations. Then they tried to blame a slow FBI background check process, only for the FBI's director to contradict the story in congressional testimony. Then, when Porter finally left the White House, Kelly and the principal deputy press secretary, Raj Shah, both claimed he'd "resigned." Just minutes later, Shah said that Porter had been "terminated." The whole thing turned into a credibility crisis for a White House that already had a mutually antagonistic relationship with the press.

Kelly in particular was encouraging colleagues to publicly float falsehoods about the internal reaction in an attempt to tamp down the rapidly escalating Porter scandal. As a former White House official told *New York* magazine, "Not only did he lie, he tried to get everybody else to lie."

WHEN the *Daily Mail* contacted the White House to request comment on its initial Porter story, the West Wing quickly went into a defensive posture. The story it eventually ran contained statements from Sanders, Kelly, and Orrin Hatch, who professed the integrity of his former chief of staff. But Hatch aides would later tell us that the White House had misled them about what exactly the senator was responding to. The White House called Hatch's office and told them a story was incoming and that they needed a statement, but they suggested that the story would only recount allegations of verbal abuse—certainly a serious thing, but short of the extremely disturbing wife-beating allegations that ended up in the *Mail*'s piece.

And that wasn't all that the White House told them. They assured Hatch that the story was a fictional product of a concerted smear campaign. And at least one of the people behind that smear campaign, the White House claimed, was Corey Lewandowski.

We had already heard, and reported, that Lewandowski was quietly bad-mouthing Porter to friends and allies, and we surmised that it had less to do with his relationship with Porter than with his burning desire to see John Kelly take one on the chin. This whole debacle was turning into a disaster for the chief of staff, and anything that prolonged or deepened the Porter scandal was reflecting directly on Kelly. And the president was taking notice.

We called up Lewandowski to get his reaction to the news out of Hatch's office. As expected, he was not candid about it. "I've never had a bad word about Rob Porter," he claimed. "I think he did a very good job, and I wish him the very best." We already knew that he was talking shit behind the scenes. But he appeared to be caught off guard by news that White House officials themselves were fingering him as a culprit behind what they described as a "smear campaign."

Lewandowski's surreptitious involvement had an air of tabloid-esque jilted-lover drama in addition to the power politics that pitted him against the chief of staff. Hicks and Lewandowski, who is married, had long been rumored to have carried on a love affair during the 2016 campaign. *New York* magazine later reported, based on accounts by three sources, that the latter would, long after that relationship ended, try to keep tabs on Hicks's romantic interests. The Porter debacle, one of those sources said, kicked up plenty of raw emotion.

In January 2018, as the Porter abuse story percolated and prepared to burst into public view, Willoughby, Porter's second wife, began receiving frantic phone calls from her ex-husband. She had written a blog post on a personal website recounting her abuse at Porter's hands, and that post was about to cause Porter some major problems. He pleaded with her to remove it. A former colleague, he told her, was out to get him and was threatening to leak the post to the press. Porter didn't say who the colleague was, but told Willoughby that the culprit was angry with him for impeding his agenda—his "racist ideas," as Willoughby later recalled—at the White House. She initially assumed Porter was referring to Steve Bannon. But after the abuse allegations blew up Porter's White House job, she came to a different conclusion: the person Porter had been freaking out about was Corey Lewandowski.

As expected, Lewandowski denied involvement at every turn. But allegations of his involvement were hardly a secret. Indeed, Kelly himself knew, or at least suspected, that this longtime rival may have been trying to undermine him with the Porter situation. About two weeks after Porter resigned, students from Marjory Stoneman Douglas High School, the site of a horrific mass shooting a week earlier, were visiting the White House for a listening session with the president. Trump was in his office before the East Room event, and he was joined by Kelly and Lewandowski.

Kelly was making known his displeasure with the other. Lewandowski, he griped, was making money hand over fist through unscrupulous business and lobbying deals that capitalized on his relationship with the president. At the same time, Kelly alleged, he was undermining the White House on virtually a daily basis, in particular through a string of TV hits since Porter's resignation that passive-aggressively laid the blame for the scandal at Kelly's feet.

At some point, *The New York Times* later reported, the president put the meeting on hold to take a phone call. Kelly and Lewandowski left the office, and the former quickly instructed a subordinate to have Lewandowski escorted off the White House campus. A shouting match ensued, and Kelly grabbed Lewandowski by the collar and shoved him against a wall. Secret Service had to intervene and separate the two, leaving West Wing aides aghast at what they'd just witnessed.

Kelly had reason to be angry. The Porter debacle, fueled by Lewandowski's public shots at Kelly and his behind-the-scenes campaign to sow White House dissension, marked the beginning of the end of Kelly's tenure. The president had hired him to be a steady hand atop a chaotic West Wing, but he was presiding over more chaos than ever before. Kelly began receding from day-to-day operations, sitting out meetings and conference calls and kept out of the loop on key personnel decisions. He had spearheaded an effort to install his top deputy, Kirstjen Nielsen, as the secretary of the Department of Homeland Security (he succeeded; she was not so fortunate). When allies griped to the president that Nielsen wasn't enough of an immigration hard-liner,

Trump exploded at Kelly. "You didn't tell me she was a fucking George W. Bush person!" he raged, according to a *Washington Post* report. As the president went around Kelly to make his own high-level personnel decisions, such as sacking the Veterans Affairs secretary, David Shulkin, Kelly flew off the handle in private, venting that he was determined to get the hell out of the White House.

To the extent that Kelly was still involved in such decisions, his role generally consisted of simply passing along the president's orders to those affected—occasionally in a humiliating fashion more befitting the commander in chief than a stern Marine Corps general. When Trump decided he'd had enough of his secretary of state, the former ExxonMobil chief executive Rex Tillerson, he tasked Kelly with delivering the news that Tillerson had been fired. When Kelly called to inform him, the secretary of state happened to be on the toilet. The chief of staff for some reason decided to share that anecdote with reporters during an off-the-record conversation at the White House. We weren't invited, and hence weren't bound by the off-the-record ground rules. We got wind of that amazing anecdote and reported it out, resulting in the most awkward media request Lachlan ever had the displeasure of lodging with the State Department's press office. "Believe me when I tell you I feel as awkward asking you this as you probably feel being asked about it, but I'm obligated to ask in any case," he wrote to the then spokeswoman Heather Nauert. The press office would only respond off the record.

The story we published was a microcosm of Kelly's diminished stature in the administration. To the extent Lewandowski was involved in using the Porter mess to sideline his White House rival, the effort was tremendously successful. The White House did its best to control fallout from the scandal, of course. But they could only do so much, given the flippancy with which the president seemed to treat the whole thing.

The day that Porter resigned happened to be the day that CBS released a preview of its upcoming season of the reality show *Celebrity Big Brother*. That season starred the recently fired Omarosa, and in the preview she went to task on the president. "I was haunted by [Trump's] tweets every single day," she said of her time in the White House. "Like what is he going to tweet next?" Asked whether "it's going to be okay," she warned, "No, it's going to not be okay."

It also happened to be the day that Raj Shah, the White House's principal deputy press secretary, gave his first daily press briefing. He spent about an hour in the Oval Office before the briefing in what was supposed to be a strategy session with the president ahead of what everyone, and certainly Raj, expected to be a bruising round of press questions about Porter.

But the president seemed to have little interest in discussing the top aide who'd just been fired for alleged domestic abuse, or the dire questions facing the White House about what it knew about those accusations and when, or what the implications of the scandal might be on the White House security clearance vetting process. Instead, Trump just wanted to talk about Omarosa. He was livid that his former aide and friend was trash-talking him publicly, and he wanted Shah to stick it to her on camera. Of the hour that Shah spent in the Oval, Trump spent a cumulative twenty minutes, give or take, going over the official White House response to Omarosa. It was by far the largest amount of time he spent on any single topic during that briefing prep and the subject he inquired most comprehensively and deeply about. (Again, this is on a day when the Porter scandal is front and center.) He went back and forth with Shah several times, helping to draft what Shah should say to reporters later that day about how much Omarosa sucked. The two men would ultimately settle on something short and sweet.

It is unclear why President Trump ever thought Omarosa was

worth his trust and affections. For one thing, we would later learn that even as she played the part of his close chum and adviser in the administration, she would gossip and spread unsubstantiated rumors about the president's sex life. Some of those who heard Omarosa spreading the outlandish claims simply assumed she was making them up out of whole cloth.

Anyway, Shah stepped up to the lectern and read a statement on the Porter scandal. He took a series of questions on the situation, repeating defenses that would be called into question or outright contradicted by later events. And then he got the Omarosa question.

"Omarosa was fired three times on *The Apprentice* and this was the fourth time we let her go," he said, trying and failing to suppress a grin. "She had limited contact with the president while here. She has no contact now."

Trump absolutely loved it. Never mind that his White House was coming apart at the seams.

➧ "DEFINITELY SOMEBODY KNIFING HIM"

E ven in his reduced role, Kelly managed to hold on to his job for months more, outlasting regular and periodic bits of reporting based on White House sources who insisted that this time he was on the way out. But in the wake of the Porter debacle, others weren't so inclined to stick around.

Just a few weeks after Porter resigned, Hope Hicks followed him out the door. She was serving as the Trump White House's fourth communications director, a position she'd been in since August 2017. But 2018 brought the Porter scandal and found Hicks forced to testify before a congressional committee probing allegations of Russian meddling in the 2016 presidential election. Hicks showed up at the House Permanent Select Committee on Intelligence, flashed a knowing smile to news photographers on her way in, and told the committee that she had indeed told "white lies" for the president on occasion. She then resigned the next day. She went to ground for months before being tapped to lead corporate communications for Fox Corporation, the trimmed-down Murdoch media empire.

Hicks was the White House's foremost "Trump whisperer." Few in the West Wing understood the president as well as she did or had spent so much time at his side. She knew how to talk to him, how to translate issues into terms he'd understand and respond to, and how he'd react to a particular situation. This isn't to say she would steer the president's thinking; she knew better than to think anyone could do that, and she trusted his instincts enough in any case to, as the saying goes, let Trump be Trump. But Hicks understood the president at a level few outside the Trump family possibly could have.

That made her departure a significant blow to a White House that still had not figured out how to run a government with Trump at the helm. Hicks's departure was about to leave a power vacuum that other type A personalities in the administration would rush to fill. And with its Trump whisperer on the way out and its chief of staff relegated to the fringes of West Wing influence, the ensuing fight was about to go off the rails in a way that aides hadn't seen since the early days of the Trump administration. The adults were no longer in charge, and the rowdiest kids were about to have the run of the playground.

Two candidates quickly emerged to replace Hicks atop the West Wing comms shop. The first was Mercedes Schlapp, and she'd become one of the White House's go-to surrogates in her role as director of strategic communications. The other was Tony Sayegh, a brash and affable New Yorker who left a job in media to run communications for Secretary of the Treasury Steve Mnuchin. Both had been Fox News fixtures prior to Trump's election, and by all accounts they were on good terms and friendly in a say-hi-in-the-office-hallway fashion.

Any goodwill evaporated almost immediately. It was just days into the internal comms director jockeying, and the White House was already divided into Team Sayegh and Team Schlapp. And the latter wasted no time before unleashing an artillery strike.

In mid-March, the *Washington Examiner* published a story on the ongoing fight to replace Hicks, which the paper reported "has fed a sense of anxiety and strife within the West Wing." The *Examiner* recapped the internal positioning before dropping a bombshell that was as vague as it was revealing. "Sources close to and within the administration said Sayegh has a tendency to 'delegate too much,' to boss people around, and to manipulate others for his own benefit," the paper reported. "One senior administration official said such behavior has been particularly noticeable in Sayegh's interactions with female staff."

The story was published during one of the first great waves of the #MeToo movement of early 2018, when everyone from Hollywood moguls to government officials to media personalities were getting sacked and ostracized for various sexually charged misdeeds. So it was no accident that the *Examiner*'s source had added that bit about Sayegh's alleged attitude toward female co-workers. The *Examiner* story itself quoted another source saying that the allegations were "'definitely somebody knifing him' in the race to replace Hicks, but added that the claims could damage his chances regardless of their authenticity." The "but" in that sentence was an artful transition. Of course the claims could damage those chances; that was, obviously, the purpose of leaking them. The White House had just suffered through an intense and prolonged scandal involving a senior official's treatment of women. There were few other accusations that could be so damaging to an aspirant for a senior West Wing gig.

But was there anything to the allegations? Swin started chasing the story. He spoke with ten senior Trump administration officials about Sayegh, and every one of them said they had never seen or heard of such conduct from him. Two of those sources, both women, separately used the term "bullshit" to describe the allegations. "A hundred percent not true and a complete cheap shot," another source said.

The likely motive for the claim wasn't hard to figure out. Julie Roginsky, a Democratic strategist and former Fox News contributor who had accused the late Fox chief Roger Ailes of sexual misconduct, called the allegations against Sayegh "really off base. Whomever [the leakers] are describing here bears no resemblance to the person I know and worked with for a long time."

Inside the White House, it was abundantly clear that the *Examiner* piece was the opening salvo in an all-out war between Schlapp's camp and Sayegh's. And it was also seen as a massive own goal. Leaking and backstabbing were facts of life in this White House, but the *Examiner*'s story was seen as so brazen, so scorched-earth, that most of those we spoke with anticipated it would have the precise opposite of its intended effect and would turn off key White House decision makers to Schlapp's internal candidacy.

"If you were to ask me today who was most likely to get the White House communications director job between Tony and Mercy, I would say Tony," one source close to the White House told Swin. "But if you were to ask me who is most likely to get the job between Tony, Mercy, and 'Fox News Personality X,' I would go with Fox News Personality X."

Schlapp and Sayegh were encouraged internally to reconcile their differences. They scheduled a meeting over coffee to sit down and hash out what was quickly becoming an unbearably brutal power struggle. But the meeting never happened, leaving tensions to fester.

Neither of them got the job. The communications director post remained vacant for four months after Hicks's departure. And just as our source close to the White House predicted, it went to a Fox News personality—and not just any Fox News personality, but Bill Shine, the channel's once powerful, ousted co-president.

WITHIN weeks of Hicks's departure, Trump was already pining for his trusted former communications hand. The internal backstabbing had reached heights not seen since the campaign-RNC battles of early 2017. Kelly was a lame duck, the Mueller probe raged on, and no one seemed to have a handle on internal operations.

And then there were the leaks. The volume and tenor of West Wing press leaks remained out of control, and they were creating major headaches for the White House.

On the evening of Thursday, May 10, *The Hill* published a story that was on the one hand incredible and on the other perfectly in line with what one might expect of subordinates to a president known for denigrating prisoners of war. At the time, the White House was struggling to shepherd the nomination of the CIA chief, Gina Haspel, through the Senate. Republicans still had the majority, but two holdouts were making the task difficult: Rand Paul, an on-again-off-again civil libertarian, and John McCain, renowned for both his opposition to War on Terror–era CIA interrogation practices and the torture he'd endured at the hands of the North Vietnamese.

McCain, who had been diagnosed with brain cancer the previous year, came up in a White House communications meeting over the Haspel nomination. That's when Kelly Sadler, an aide in charge of outreach to White House surrogates and allies, chimed in about McCain's opposition to the appointment. "It doesn't matter," she said crudely. "He's dying anyway."

Even for a White House helmed by a man who never hesitated to deride McCain, it was a particularly cruel remark. But over the ensuing week, the West Wing appeared far less concerned about the comment itself than the fact that it had leaked to the press. Sadler called Mc-Cain's daughter, the television personality Meghan McCain, to apologize for the comment, but neither she nor the White House made any public statement of contrition.

Instead, they insisted that Sadler was the victim of the ordeal. Matt Schlapp, a White House surrogate and Mercedes's husband, used that precise word. Sadler was "a little bit of a victim here," he claimed. Asked about the controversy during a White House press briefing, Shah complained that "if you aren't able, in internal meetings, to speak your mind or convey thoughts or say anything that you feel without feeling like your colleagues will betray you, that creates a very difficult work environment."

Internally, the White House recriminations focused on the leak as much as the comment itself. "I am sure this conversation is going to leak, too. And that's just disgusting," said Sarah Sanders in a communications shop meeting that did indeed leak. "You can put this on the record," Mercedes Schlapp interjected at the meeting. "I stand with Kelly Sadler."

Before long, in an effort to stem the leaks, Sanders slimmed down attendance at all internal meetings of the comms department. And in late May, the president summoned his top aides to the Oval Office to try to put a plan in place to stop internal deliberative information from getting to the press or, even more ideally, to purge the White House of the leakers who continued to bedevil it.

In attendance at that meeting were Kelly, Schlapp, Shah, and Sadler. The president was in one of his reality-TV moods. He was ready to employ his signature tagline. Whom, he wanted to know, should he fire to stop this incessant leaking? Who were these seditious loudmouths in their midst? And the president really wanted to get Sadler's input, given the ordeal she'd just gone through.

No one in the room expected what came next. Asked to name colleagues whom she suspected of leaking, Sadler dropped a dime on Schlapp, the woman standing right next to her, who had just gone to bat for Sadler—"on the record"—in the comms shop meeting about stemming the leak problem. Schlapp recoiled in indignation at Sadler's accusation, angrily assuring the president that she was not a leaker and was being falsely accused. Schlapp also turned to Sadler to snipe at her that her allegation was simply "outrageous." Schlapp's pushback was so fierce that even Kelly, the supposedly stately general, looked taken aback by her remarks and the whole scene. The president reclined in his chair behind the Resolute Desk and took in the *Apprentice*-style scene playing out before him.

The meeting adjourned shortly thereafter, but the drama wasn't finished. Outside the Oval, Schlapp repeatedly hissed, "That bitch," in outbursts she'd later deny up and down. The West Wing is a small space, and colleagues couldn't help but notice the unfolding drama. Morale was already sagging under the weight of the brutal press the place was having to endure. And here were two top communications aides at each other's throats. Things were not improving.

The most telling part of the whole episode lay in Sadler's ouster. The White House never officially said whether she was fired or she quit. But by early June, less than a month after her McCain comment leaked, Sadler was gone. She wasn't pushed out because of her McCain remarks. Instead, it was her intensifying feud with Schlapp, who was technically Sadler's boss, that led to her departure.

Months later, after McCain passed away, the president couldn't resist taking a few more shots at the late statesman, publicly deriding him for voting against an Obamacare repeal measure and his supposed role in disseminating the notorious Steele dossier. The flare-up in Trump's still-burning hatred of McCain got us wondering what had become of Sadler. We called her to ask what she'd been doing since leaving the White House. "I don't think so, thank you, goodbye," she said before abruptly hanging up.

We called around to former colleagues and friends. Few had heard anything from her in the months since her ignominious ouster. She had disappeared from the proverbial political map. Those sources did recall to us that the White House had tried to land her in a comfortable administration gig somewhere, because naturally offending John McCain wasn't too great an offense.

As one source recalled, "They gave her that option, but she told them to fuck off."

Eventually, Sadler would land where so many other benighted Trump alumni would: in a senior role at a node of the constellation of political groups supporting the president. For those cast out of the White House under clouds of scrutiny and scandal, that seemed to be the only viable choice.

By April 2019, she had booked her next gig at the pro-Trump super PAC America First Action as its communications chief and appeared on cable news and radio to sing the president's praises. But the president's McCain feuding was far from over. And it would end up taking a very Trumpian turn.

▶ "SHE'S BEEN GETTING FATTER?"

Donald J. Trump, leader of the free world, thinks Meghan M. McCain, the TV-prone daughter of the president's dead archrival John, is a fat ass.

And a uniquely brainless and talentless one, at that.

During a hectic stretch of days in March 2019, not long before the Mueller report was finally delivered to the Department of Justice, President Trump couldn't or wouldn't stop picking fights with the late senator John McCain, in spite—or perhaps because—of the near-universal reverence accorded to the Senate veteran and Vietnam War hero in the wake of his passing. The president—on social media, while talking to journalists, and onstage in Ohio—renewed his attacks on McCain as a backstabber, a Trump hater, a deep state enabler, and a classroom dunce at Annapolis.

Meghan McCain responded from her perch co-hosting *The View* on ABC by calling the president's life "pathetic" and small compared with her dad's. "I don't expect decency from the Trump family," she said on the March 21, 2019, episode.

When the notoriously media-obsessed president caught wind of Meghan's comments, he picked up the phone at the White House and began calling longtime friends to see if they'd join in on his cathartic minutes of hate against the McCain daughter and other enemies real and perceived.

"She's been getting fatter?" Trump asked, before launching into a harangue about how she is somehow "dumber" than her father. One confidant to whom the president vented his grievances about the McCain family described a diatribe that lasted at least a minute and a half during which the president spoke without interruption. This person at one point put the phone on mute, hit the speakerphone button, and allowed others present to hear President Trump bash Meghan McCain's chubby cheeks and, to the president's eye (ever attuned to the basest aspects of entertainment and cable news), her ever-expansive waistline.

During the conversations, he aggressively fixated on how awful a TV host she was, both on *The View* and during her time as a Fox News contributor. He wondered why anyone would want to hire her. He rambled on and on about how nobody would care about who she was or what she had to say, if not for the genetic proximity to Senator McCain.

This was said without a hint of self-awareness, given the forty-fifth president's last name, the cushy White House jobs afforded to his daughter and son-in-law, the interventions on their behalves when they were unable to secure government security clearances, the nepotism undergirding Trump's own rise in New York real estate, to say nothing of the well-maintained fortunes of Tiffany, Eric, Don junior, and so forth.

It also offered a window into how the president prioritizes his time, his energy, and his grievance mongering. That week, Trump had just announced he was nixing the long-standing American policy on the

Israeli-occupied Golan Heights, declaring "it is time" for the United States to "fully recognize Israel's Sovereignty" over the area.

Shortly thereafter, he was back working the phones, bitching about Meghan McCain's weight to fellow members of a Trump-era ruling class.

It wasn't the first time he'd maligned the appearance of a television news host. It wasn't even the first time he'd done so for one of the women on *The View*.

"She's a slob, she talks like a truck driver," Trump, then in his reality-TV phase, told *The Insider* during a 2006 interview at his office, speaking of dear Rosie, toward the end of the George W. Bush era. This was during Rosie's brief stint as a controversial, Bush-loathing *View* co-host, when Trump and O'Donnell began feuding publicly, replete with Trump's prolific legal threats.

"How does she even get on television? . . . If I were running *The View*, I'd fire Rosie. I mean, I'd look her right in that fat, ugly face of hers, and say, 'Rosie, you're fired,'" he continued in his rant to *The Insider*. It would alarmingly mirror his broadsides made more than a decade later against, for example, world leaders and diplomats. "We're all a little chubby, but Rosie's just worse than most of us. But it's not the chubbiness; Rosie is a very unattractive person, both inside and out. Rosie's a person that's very lucky to have her girlfriend. And she better be careful, or I'll send one of my friends to pick up her girlfriend. Why would she stay with Rosie if she had another choice?

"She's trying to use ABC and *The View* to get even with me. But with me, we fight back," Trump said. "I'll probably sue Rosie . . . It would be fun. I'd like to take some money out of her fat-ass pockets."

Trump dramatically concluded, "Rosie . . . is a loser."

Everything you need to know about Trump, the president and the celebrity and the lump of flesh, is contained in that Rosie clip. It's a decoder ring just waiting to be picked up and utilized by every establishment-media dipshit who ever earnestly asked himself or herself, "Isn't this beneath the dignity of the Oval Office?" It sure is! This is Trump when the cameras turn off, when staff depart the Oval Office and he's left to work the phones with friends and allies and muse about the losers and haters polluting his airwaves, and the ugly faces and large waistlines that he can't believe are on television but nonetheless can't stop talking about.

The *View* co-host Abby Huntsman, a former Fox News anchor and the daughter of the former Republican presidential contender Jon Huntsman, also caught President Trump's eye for physical detail and examination. Though this case was markedly more lustful and less scornful than his assessment of the McCain daughter.

On June 1, 2018, Kim Yong Chol, a senior North Korean official and confidant of the totalitarian ruler and Trump's buddy Kim Jong Un, was in town to visit the U.S. president at the White House as the two governments continued down the path of ostensible negotiations on the future of nukes on the Korea Peninsula. During the high-profile swing through Washington, D.C., the official conversed with Trump for hours and delivered a personal letter to the president from the North Korean dictator himself. In remarks to reporters on the White House South Lawn following that meeting, Trump was buoyant, lauding the "very nice letter."

To mark the occasion of this visit and diplomatic love letter, the White House invited some of the administration's top brass to pow-wow and socialize with the excitable Donald that same week. The elder Huntsman, one of the GOP old guard's many Civility Preachers and by this point Trump's ambassador to Russia, was one of those dignitaries invited by the White House to shake his new boss's hand and kiss the ring for good measure.

Jon Huntsman made the mistake of bringing along a plus-one: his spouse.

As Huntsman and Trump glad-handed in the West Wing, the ambassador's wife captivated Trump's attention. For a moment, Trump locked eyes with Mary Kaye, a blond, gorgeous, self-possessed, and Kennedy-esque-looking force in the room. He glanced her up and down.

"Now I know how Abby lost all her baby weight so fast!" a smirking Trump said to compliment the proud grandparents.

For a split second, the Huntsmans didn't know exactly what to make of the president's passive lechery and his comment about their daughter Abby or her appearance.

Soon enough, though, they put two and two together. In one short sentence, the president had managed to ogle both the daughter and the wife of one of his most important diplomats.

Trump is—if nothing else—a chemical addict of *Fox & Friends*. He adores the show, both weekday and weekend editions of it, so much so that it once caused him to trigger widespread tumult within the corridors of power in Washington, D.C.—over the NSA's mass-surveillance schemes.

On the morning of January 11, 2018, the Fox legal analyst and civil libertarian Andrew Napolitano appeared on a *Fox & Friends* segment to discuss the spying authority afforded by Section 702 of the Foreign Intelligence Surveillance Act, which allows for warrantless collection of gargantuan levels of data and communications. The section's renewal was at the top of the legislative wish list for Trump's Department of Justice and the U.S. intelligence services.

Napolitano, given his libertarian proclivities, saw things differently and urged Trump, through the TV, not to go along with this national security charade.

Then, at 7:33 a.m. eastern time, President Trump tweeted in response to the Fox segment, "'House votes on controversial FISA ACT today.' This is the act that may have been used, with the help of the discredited and phony Dossier, to so badly surveil and abuse the Trump Campaign by the previous administration and others?"

That single, Fox-inspired tweet sent Trump's allies and lawmakers on Capitol Hill on a mad dash to privately reassure the president that all was well with the deep state and that he should get back on board. With a few hours of counsel, it worked, but not after some heartburn.

Adam Schiff, the House Intelligence Committee's top Democrat, told *The Daily Beast* at the time that Trump's Twitter outburst "certainly threw everything into turmoil this morning. I can only imagine that the reaction within the intelligence community and law enforcement and among his own cabinet was the same as it was here in Congress, which is hard to describe without the use of expletives."

That is the degree of the forty-fifth U.S. president's devotion to his favorite shows, on matters of national security, immigration policy, political strategy, foreign affairs, and life and death at home and abroad. That is what we are working with.

Anyway, Abby Huntsman, before her ascension to the wine-mom, gabfest popularity of *The View*, was a *Fox & Friends* weekend host who co-helmed the morning broadcasts for a time while pregnant with her first child. Before that era in her life, Abby was a regular on MSNBC and billed herself and other members of her family as the Tolerant, Hip Republicans—those who didn't harbor a seething bloodlust toward gays or brown people, and perhaps viewed the Tea Party as a gang of knuckle draggers, useful idiots, and bovine bumpkins, but who also still wanted to turn Medicaid into a Powerball lottery.

Throughout her career, Abby has had no real coherent or discernible ideology and no obvious moral compass. She, like Trump, has worshipped at the altar of the ideology of the Self.

And in his ample time bingeing *Fox & Friends* in the White House, the president apparently noticed the pregnancy and watched her belly grow. The mental note stuck with the president long enough that when Abby returned to the Fox airwaves following her stint of maternity leave, Trump couldn't help but be pleased and impressed with her snapback to her prior physique—the shedding of her baby weight.

By the summer of 2018, President Trump hadn't forgotten and made sure to pat his Russia ambassador on the head for the achievement of spawning a scalding-hot daughter who took after her mother in all the most important ways.

Soon, word got back to Abby. In her retellings of this story in casual conversation, those present have noted that Abby grimaces at the thought of Donald "grab 'em by the pussy" J. Trump using what he's dubbed his "super TiVo" to leer at her and grade her fluctuating weight.

➤ "LOVELY JENNIFER"

J ennifer Rauchet is the most important name you've never heard before. Without her, Trump might never have become president. Her work helped alter the course of American and world history without your even knowing about it. Hell, *she* probably didn't know she was about to change the course of history forever. And she did it all while doing nothing more than producing yet another piece of junk food for the brains of hundreds of thousands of aging viewers and culture-war obsessives.

You won't read much about Rauchet in the news, except for the occasional tabloid story, blog post, or offhand mention in a newspaper article. In October 2017, Donald Trump smiled for a photo of a private dinner at the White House with his guests of honor: Robert J. O'Neill, a Fox News favorite who claimed it was he who heroically fired the shot that killed Osama bin Laden in the famous Obama-era raid—a claim forcefully disputed by multiple special operations sources. Seated to O'Neill's left was his wife, Jessica. The president sat at the head of the table. On the other side of the table sat Pete Hegseth, a top Trump confidant, informal policy adviser, and *Fox & Friends* star.

Seated to Hegseth's right, in a photo posted to Instagram that October, was Rauchet, sitting closest to President Trump.

Rauchet found herself the subject of tabloid gossip in the early

Trump era when rumors swirled that she and a married Hegseth had carried on a secret affair. She would later give birth to their child. The gossip and reports around the relationship came up in Hegseth's vetting for a possible senior post in the Trump administration and led to top officials tapping the brakes on his consideration, despite all the goodwill he'd built up with the president.

Hegseth would quickly rise as one of the key players in Trumpworld and end up marrying Rauchet in 2019—at Trump's New Jersey club, no less. But Rauchet is the better half of the Fox News power couple who actually helped build Trump into what he is today. In fact, perhaps Rauchet was sitting closer to President Trump in that Instagram photo in part because she has known Trump longer than Hegseth has.

For years, Rauchet had served as a well-regarded executive producer on *Fox & Friends*. (She has since moved on to other positions in the network, largely to create some breathing room between her and her former illicit lover boy Hegseth.) In April 2011, Trump began appearing in a weekly Monday segment on Rauchet's show *Fox & Friends*, calling in to the program to riff on culture, Obama, and political news of the day. It was a recurring segment that continued until 2015, when it was suspended as Trump began his quixotic and ultimately victorious journey to executive power.

Rauchet was instrumental in setting up that segment, going back and forth with Trump to hammer out the details of his involvement and produce it week after week. Long before Hegseth was a devoted follower of Trumpism (in fact, he had previously supported Marco Rubio and Ted Cruz during the 2016 GOP primary, before ultimately settling on The Donald), Rauchet saw in Trump the potential for a massive hit—not as a joke or celebrity oddity, but as a towering political and cultural presence in American life. And by God, his elevation at *Fox & Friends* was one potent way to accomplish that. Rauchet was known to defend the Trump segments to naysayers she came across at the Fox network and rib them for their out-of-touch elitism—for not getting it.

Trump valued her input and her commitment so much that during the 2016 election, when he would call in from the campaign trail or Trump Tower to the Fox control room to comment, or to give critique and suggestions, one of the people he'd ask to speak to most frequently was his "Jennifer!"

But before he embarked on his presidential warpath, the Trump call-in allowed him to regularly connect with the Fox audience in a unique way and early on forged the unshakable bonds between Trump and the morning news and commentary program. In doing this, Rauchet was central in making *Fox & Friends* a primary source of influence and information for Trump as he navigated the remainder of the Obama era. The gamble paid off handsomely for both Trump and Fox. Trump, a pop culture oddity and crank, was able to cement his status as a cable news attraction and driver of conversation. It was the original sin that years down the line would birth his Fox News presidency and bestow upon him a vast propaganda network. By February 2017, *Fox & Friends* would enjoy not only a ratings spike as the Trump surrogate but also its newfound position as Most Influential Program in the World.

Rauchet, for her part, has consistently made her support for the president and former Fox contributor clear on her personal social media posts. In return, Trump has anointed her the affectionate nicknames of "beautiful Jennifer" and "lovely Jennifer."

➤ "I DON'T KNOW THE TRUTH"

I f Donald Trump's crass comments make him sound like that bully from high school or that demeaning boss who once made an inappropriate sexually loaded comment or that drunk guy at the end of the bar at your local watering hole—well, that's exactly what they are. Every modern entertainment cliché and every dark corner of our national id are on full display in the debauched hellhole that is modern television. Trump came from that world. He's obsessed with it. And now he's brought it into the White House with him. And all the green-room navel-gazing and *New York Times* op-ed column space devoted to hand-wringing over this thoroughly twenty-first-century American phenomenon has yet to come to terms with one very disturbing but illuminating fact: millions of Americans knew *exactly* whom they were electing in 2016. They were electing themselves.

The classic Kurt Vonnegut short story "Harrison Bergeron" imagines a near-futuristic dystopia in which all levers of society seek to elevate the mediocre. The most prized attribute in this society is averageness, and citizens are assigned jobs at random for fear of rewarding anyone out of sheer merit. In the 1995 film adaptation, Eugene Levy plays the president of the United States, a man chosen at random to be the leader of the free world. And he brings his everyman credentials to the fore as he threatens to hit a populous Moroccan city with a nuclear weapon.

"The nuclear fallout could be apocalyptic!" an aide warns.

"Well, that's what they get for building a T-bomb when we told them not to," the president fires back. "Those cocksuckers gotta learn not to fuck with us!"

Trump hasn't yet threatened to nuke a population center, notwithstanding his brief employment of the arch war hawk John Bolton. But that scene was a clever and prophetic warning about political populism. Sure, you can put an everyman in charge of the levers of power in the most powerful nation in the world. But for all the caterwauling about "elitism" in American politics, sometimes it's nice to have elites— you know, the people who are trained, educated, and accomplished in their respective fields, as opposed to the creepy boss or the drunk slob at the bar—running the nation.

Nowhere are the pitfalls of everyman government in the Trump era more evident than in his thoroughly American reverence for television and nonstop gossiping and catty sniping about the personalities that appear on his screen. More than discussing and gossiping about them, he turns to them for direct policy advice, both by just watching what his favorite cable newsers have to say and by inviting them to comment on administration policy making directly. It turns out that a president obsessed with the whims of cable news hosts is not exactly a stabilizing force.

THIS is the sort of thing that takes up an inordinate amount of the forty-fifth president's headspace. To be fair (though not necessarily charitable) to the president, it's not just the gossip, the hate mongering, and the groaning and sniping that keep bringing him back for more. He also channels his avaricious media diet into personal murder-boarding for the politics, rhetoric, strategic salvos, and policy that drive the planet's one remaining superpower.

Throughout the Trump era, it has been almost too easy for us to mine for stories on the command and influence that President Trump's TV box has over his desires and decision making. All you have to do is ask about whom he puts on speakerphone or conference call. Various business interests and advocacy organizations have factored this into their daily operations, to the point where they have poured millions of dollars into advertising during Fox shows that they know Trump prodigiously consumes. In their efforts to influence him, some of these commercials will feature a person or a disembodied voice directly addressing President Trump. (The irony here is that it's actually a colossal waste of money; those who know him will tell you that Trump doesn't watch TV commercials. If people are in the room with him, he'll mute the TV and start talking to whoever is closest. If he's alone and using his TiVo, he'll just fast-forward to the good parts, as he had been known to do while watching his VHS tape of *Bloodsport*.)

You simply cannot understand the Trump presidency, or his widespread appeal in the modern Republican Party, without first understanding Lou Dobbs, the star Fox Business Network host and one of the originators of a cable-TV-fueled, anti-immigrant conservatism that would become full-blown Trumpism.

For many years, Trump has made Dobbs's show appointment viewing. Dobbs is the MAGA Socrates to The Donald's Plato.

He regularly quizzes senior staff, longtime confidants, and near strangers alike if they've seen recent Dobbs segments. He calls "Lou" regularly to gossip and pulse him on ideas. And the president has patched him in on speakerphone during high-level gatherings in the White House.

Beginning in the early Trump era, the president started including Dobbs, via speakerphone, in (multiple!) Oval Office meetings so that Lou—the cable gasbag who's repeatedly raged against St. Patrick's Day and other "ethnic holidays"—can advise him and his senior officials.

The president will ask Dobbs for his analysis and counsel before and after his aides or cabinet members have given theirs. Sometimes he's actually interrupted an official in the room so the Fox Business personality can get a say in.

Meetings Dobbs has been patched into include ones on trade or tax policy, with top-ranking officials such as the nativist hate merchant Stephen Miller, the "globalist" tax slasher Gary Cohn, the nationalist anime villain Steve Bannon, the China-loathing avatar Peter Navarro, and the *Lego Batman* and *Collateral Beauty* hype man Steve Mnuchin. Dobbs fit right in. The only difference was that he took a paycheck cut by Fox, not the federal government.

During his ultimately successful tax-bill blitz, Trump would make sure to tell his White House personal secretary to get Dobbs on the horn. At the end of one particularly memorable meeting—at least it was for the puzzled officials surrounding the president—Trump bade farewell to his dear friend and ideological precursor Lou, disconnected the line, and lifted up his head to survey the faces in the room. The president smiled and simply told everyone assembled to discuss the politics and intricacies of tax cuts, "*Love Lou.*"

"**Department of Justice should have urged the Supreme Court to at least hear the Drivers License case on illegal immigrants in Arizona. I agree with @LouDobbs. Should have sought review,**" our commander in chief shit-posted on the morning of March 21, 2018.

Trump's Fox-to-Oval-Office pipeline hardly ends with Lou, of course.

By the middle of the Trump era, *so much* ink had been spilled covering the obvious sway the Fox News megastar Sean Hannity holds over Trump's mind and mayhem. If we're to be even mildly honest about it, this included ink from us at *The Daily Beast*. Swin alone spilled enough to swim and then violently drown in.

Donald Trump has, of course, gifted numerous "EXCLUSIVE" interviews to Hannity, on both the Fox host's TV show and his radio show. Hannity is so accommodating to his president and prime benefactor that he'll signal to his own radio producers to stall as he takes phone calls from Trump, even if the call comes in during inconvenient moments like, well, as the live show is being broadcast.

But even for President Trump—a man who demands devotion and fealty from his fans and allies as if it were an elixir boosting sperm count—Sean Hannity can sometimes prove too accommodating.

In our time covering the Trump years, we discovered, or learned incidentally, more about the president and the TV babbler's mutual affinities than we ever cared to know. For one thing, Trump has a slight tendency to trash-talk Hannity behind his back, primarily about the quality of the Fox News icon's ultra-sycophantic method of interviewing Trump.

When Hannity's not in earshot, the president has repeatedly—and sometimes for a prolonged, uncomfortable stretch of time—made fun of his interviewing skills, mocking the laziness of his questions and complaining that there isn't any thrill or tension for Trump to work with. On several occasions since his inauguration, Trump simply used the word "dumb" to characterize Hannity's prepared questions.

For any reader uninterested in looking up a clip on YouTube or

jumping on a search engine to bear witness, a Hannity question for Trump has for years boiled down to nothing more than *"Did you sprain anything when you fell from heaven?"* or *"Those Democrats, amirite?"*

There's a joke in national and political media circles about Hannity's frequent interviews and conversations with the president and how gobsmackingly impossible it seems that someone with that much access to power can come away, almost each and every time, without breaking a single morsel of news. To any reasonable observer, it's simpering propaganda, not even *fun* simpering propaganda.

When Swin asked Hannity about this, the Fox News host didn't respond. He didn't even bother to decry this reporting on Twitter as "#FakeNews," as he has done with our work in the past. It's unclear if Hannity knows, or believes, that his dear friend and Dear Leader disrespects him when he's not around. Still, there's practically nothing Hannity wouldn't do, or hasn't done, for this president, short of literally committing seppuku on live television.

During one of Trump's appearances on Hannity's radio program during the 2016 presidential campaign, the then candidate Trump repeated the *National Enquirer*–promoted, fringe conspiracy theory that Senator Ted Cruz's dad, Rafael Cruz, was with Lee Harvey Oswald shortly before the 1963 assassination of President John F. Kennedy, and thus might have had something to do with it.

"There was a picture a few weeks ago, and it was all over the place, about Lee Harvey Oswald and his father," Trump told an enthralled Hannity.

"Was that verified ever? I saw that there was something on the internet," the host credulously replied.

"It was a picture put in and [the *Enquirer*] wouldn't put it in if they could be sued, that I can tell you," Trump, hilariously, contended. "Ted Cruz, I don't think denied it . . . [and] if that were true, what was

[Rafael] doing having breakfast . . . three months before the JFK assassination?"

"I have seen it, but I never thought it was going anywhere," Hannity said, entertaining the psychotic notion. "I don't know the truth, the veracity of it."

When Swin asked Hannity to comment further, Sean emailed, "I was saying that photo was not verified."

Asked if he believed the *National Enquirer* is generally a reliable news outlet, Hannity demurred, writing, "If [you] want to interview me, contact Fox PR."

Swin thought that was it, yet Hannity just couldn't help himself.

"So is the picture authentic or not? You don't have a clue either," he later emailed Swin, unprompted. "Lol," Hannity wrote, concluding his note.

Swin had never spoken to Hannity before this exchange, and it stuck with him as a perfect, distilled example of Hannity's subjugation to Trump. The cable news star was willing to argue with a complete stranger over email about a manufactured debate over whether Ted Cruz's father murdered JFK. Hannity, one of the most powerful on-air personalities in all of political media, couldn't think of anything better to do with his time at that moment.

Because failing to do so might risk making Trump look bad, foolish, or misguided. And we can't have that, now can we?

HANNITY, however, is a one-man target-rich environment. Beyond Hannity and Dobbs, there's an embarrassingly large pool of Fox talent, behind and in front of the cameras, that President Trump draws from for counsel, as a sounding board, and for juicy gossip.

Take, if you will, the exemplar Pete.

Some might know Pete Hegseth, Rauchet's baby daddy, from chapters past. Some might know him as the guy who almost killed that guy with an ax on live TV, during an ax-throwing demonstration on *Fox & Friends* in June 2015. (Hegseth missed his target, instead striking a member of the West Point Band, an official musical group of the U.S. Military Academy, who were there celebrating Flag Day. The victim would later bring a lawsuit against Hegseth, his almost killer.) A few might remember him as chief of the right-leaning advocacy group Concerned Veterans for America.

Others might remember him as the man who freely admitted on Fox News in 2019 to having a personal policy of not washing his hands, adding, "Germs are not a real thing. I can't see them; therefore they're not real." (He subsequently insisted he was trying to make a funny.)

President Trump knows him as one of his absolute favorite *Fox & Friends* hosts and go-to dial-a-buddies. Since the dawn of the Trump era, Hegseth has been able to parlay that not only into having an outsize impact on the president's talking points and messaging but also into guiding Trump on policy matters. It could be argued that Hegseth has more of an influence on policy—rather than mere rhetoric—than any of his Fox News cohorts, topping even Trump's philosophical shepherd Lou Dobbs.

In March 2019, Trump personally intervened in the case of a U.S. Navy SEAL on trial over allegations that he had committed war crimes in Iraq, tweeting, "**In honor of his past service to our Country, Navy Seal #EddieGallagher will soon be moved to less restrictive confinement while he awaits his day in court. Process should move quickly!**" On this tweet, the president tagged "@foxandfriends."

Gallagher had quickly become a cause célèbre for conservative media figures and politicians: a heroic, quintessentially American hero who had been strung up by a politically correct and masochistic system of American apology-tourists.

Hegseth, an Iraq War vet, had discussed the matter vigorously on the airwaves, but what was left unsaid was that the *Fox & Friends* mainstay had campaigned behind the scenes and had spoken to President Trump about the situation multiple times on the phone, prior to the "#EddieGallagher" tweet, urging the president to take a stand and some action. Hegseth also organized and spearheaded an effort to persuade Trump in 2019 to consider pardoning an array of accused and convicted American war criminals, chief among them Gallagher. In their many conversations about potential pardons, the president seemed receptive to Hegseth's entreaties—at least, that is, until he wasn't.

Around the time of Memorial Day 2019, Trump pulled back from the brink, following what he saw as unexpected blowback from envoys of the military and veterans community. After *The Daily Beast* broke the news that Hegseth had been counseling Trump on this matter (without disclosing such informal lobbying to his viewers), he got chewed out by Fox News brass for being too blatantly obvious with his advisory role. After he got reamed out, Hegseth started telling friends that he would need to be more discreet about his position as an unpaid policy adviser to President Trump, to avoid getting yelled at at the office.

But all the guff he got from Fox would be well worth it for Pete. On November 15, 2019, President Trump formally announced that he had absolved three U.S. servicemen in their respective war crimes cases. Trump had kept his trusted Hegseth in the loop till the end and even gave him a heads-up that the presidential intervention was imminent. The president cleared the three accused or convicted war criminals in the face of significant military, political, and international outrage and objections. The fallout caused by the two pardons and Trump's reversal of Gallagher's demotion even cost the Navy secretary, Richard Spencer, his job. But Clint Lorance, Mathew Golsteyn, and Edward Gallagher got their day made by President Trump—and nobody was giddier for them than Hegseth, who hosted Lorance on his Fox News program mere days after the pardons came down. "I love you, sir," Lorance told Trump through the TV. "You are awesome!"

In early 2018, when the walls were closing in on the Department of Veterans Affairs secretary and Obama-era holdover David Shulkin—whom conservative critics saw as both an impediment to partial privatization of veterans' health care and a corrupt buffoon—Hegseth was once again on the line, privately pushing Trump to discard Shulkin as quickly as humanly possible.

At the time, Shulkin had lasted far longer than his internal enemies felt comfortable with, in large part because Trump liked the guy. Shulkin felt so besieged that it got to the point where he even ordered an armed guard to be posted outside his office on the tenth floor of the VA and abrogated tenth-floor access to multiple appointees whom he suspected of subversion and backstabbing.

That year, when the Trump White House organized a meeting with vets groups, Shulkin initially sent over a list of organizations to invite, with the roster specifically excluding Concerned Veterans for America, Hegseth's old stomping ground and a bastion of anti-Shulkin antagonism. By the time the meeting rolled around, Shulkin was bigfooted, and a CVA representative was invited to attend by White House staff, anyway.

Ultimately, the president sided with people like Hegseth, and Shulkin became yet another expendable person in Donald Trump's ever-growing long line of expendables and forgettables.

WHEN "Judge Jeanine" Pirro was reprimanded and suspended for two weeks by Fox News for making bigoted comments regarding the left-leaning Muslim congresswoman Ilhan Omar, Pirro reached out to Trump for a lifeline. Soon enough, he was calling her, assuring her of his support, and tweeting his demand that Fox put her back on the air. And why wouldn't he? The two have been chums for years and were nearly members of the same regime. During the presidential transition, Pirro interviewed for the role of deputy attorney general in the Trump administration.

That was around the same time that Laura Ingraham, another Fox host, had interviewed to become Trump's first White House press secretary, a role that ultimately went to Sean Spicer. In the heat of the 2016 campaign, Ingraham had an unofficial advisory role on Team Trump, helping the Republican presidential contender craft and massage his speeches in the right-wing, "America First" vernacular that Trump had adopted and Ingraham had honed in her career in conservative talk radio. During the transition, she was rewarded with continued access to the upper echelons of Trumpworld. She even interviewed for the top spokesperson slot, with Trump's son Eric doing the interviewing at Washington's Four Seasons Hotel.

At the time, she nominally presided over the conservative culture and politics website LifeZette, where employees were on high alert the week of her Trump interview, unsure if Ingraham—a notoriously tyrannical, uncaring, and vindictive boss in D.C. media circles—would return to the office with a new gig and leave everyone at LifeZette holding the bag.

Under Ingraham's watch, LifeZette became a cesspool of anemic web traffic and also a working environment where numerous sources told us that women felt sexually threatened and harassed. Some of LifeZette's prominently placed content included such titles as "What to Do if Your Teenager Is Promiscuous," courtesy of the MomZette vertical, and "Why So Many Women Don't Like the 'F-Word.'" The website promoted since-deleted pieces on the Clinton family "body count" conspiracy theories, which one such article charmingly titled "Could Crossing the Clintons Kill You?"

In early 2018, when Trump was deciding whom to invite to a quiet, intimate dinner at the White House for a random Monday night, the president could have picked from any of the brightest minds, the greatest statesmen, or even the best artists in the world (well, at least from the ones who can still stand him). Instead, he chose to fete the fratty, forty-year-old Fox News host Jesse Watters and the Fox contributor Sebastian Gorka, the latter having been sacked from Trump's White House, though not his television set.

Later that week, Watters would giddily tweet out a photo of a White House dinner menu—which featured a dessert of milk chocolate mousse—signed by Donald J. Trump, reading "To Jesse[,] You are great!"

➤ "FAKE NEWS SPECIALISTS"

This will no doubt come as a shock, but not everyone on cable television is a genius. To paraphrase the president, when the nation's cable news bookers send their people to our living rooms, they're not always sending their best. So a president who takes his emotional, personnel, and policy cues from the little box in his living room is inevitably giving two-bit loudmouths with less brains than bombast an unofficial but no less impactful role in the policy-making process. These are mouth-breathing commentators whom the average American probably has never heard of before, and perhaps never will. And yet the most powerful man in the world hangs on their every word.

Take the case study of Dan Bongino, a habitually mad-online former Secret Service agent and thrice-failed congressional candidate whose public political commentary more closely resembles someone stepping on a rake than making an argument. His public persona has anger issues and the emotional maturity of a five-year-old. He has said, without a hint of irony or joy, that he rededicated his life in 2018 to the religion of "Owning the Libs."

He's not someone whose opinion on anything should be taken seriously—unless, that is, you're Donald Trump, who can't get enough of the guy when he appears on Fox evening and early-morning programming.

During one of Bongino's guest appearances on Fox News in mid-2018, the (now former) NRATV host delivered one of his standard, full-throated defenses of President Trump and played wingman to Trump's dubious claim that the feds, under the spell of anti-Trump bias, embedded a "spy" in his presidential campaign. Inside the White House, Bongino's voice resonated.

"Did you see what Bongino said?" Trump gushed to his advisers. "He's so right; he's just so right about it all. You have to see it."

And "see it," he did—over, and over, and over again.

On the day that much of the Republican and Democratic parties' elite gathered to honor the memory of the late senator John McCain at Washington National Cathedral, President Trump was holed up in the White House, effectively banned by the McCains from attending. While the funeral goers mourned with three major political families—the Obamas, Bushes, McCains—who all openly despise Trump, the sitting president instead took to Twitter, posting Dan Bongino quotes from an episode of *Fox & Friends* he was watching. Then Trump and his Secret Service detail were off to his private golf club in Virginia.

Within Trumpworld, Bongino has other powerful allies as well. In January 2019, the president hosted a group of right-wing activists—led by Ginni Thomas, who's married to the Supreme Court justice Clarence Thomas—for an hour as the delegation ranted wildly about culture-war and LGBTQ-related grievances and also about some of the Trump White House's squishier hires.

One of the group's main gripes was their insistence that certain senior White House officials were not serving the president's best interests and were keeping Trump from hiring as many loyal supporters as they thought he deserved. During this confab, Thomas provided Trump with a list of potential hires for the White House and a title for which each name would be best suited.

On that list was Dan Bongino, listed next to a deputy chief of staff designation.

In the time since that meeting, Trump has yet to tap Bongino for any official assignment, though Bongino did get a signed contract with Fox News. It's a shame, because such a professional marriage would be (at least stylistically) a match made in MAGA heaven. Like Trump, Bongino is a loud, flamboyant product of New York City. "I'm a Queens kid; he's a Queens kid," Bongino told Lachlan in an interview in late 2018.

That was the last time Lachlan and Dan spoke on friendly terms. We published a story at *The Daily Beast* about Bongino leaving NRATV that resulted in a firestorm of tweets during the course of which Dan dubbed us "fake news specialists" who either "have the absolute worst sources in the 'journalism' business OR [are] complete BS artists." In a point of pride for Lachlan, he was dubbed an "alleged 'reporter,'" while Swin was just his "looney tune sidekick."

The numerous rage-tweets about us have since been deleted from Bongino's feed. Lost in the purge were tweets in which Bongino repeatedly suggested that Lachlan had slept with a married woman, and urged Swin to ask Lachlan about it. (Swin asked, and Lachlan sincerely pleaded ignorance.) Just as we go to press on this book, Bongino has sued *The Daily Beast* (which his complaint calls "a digital assassin and controlled by billionaire Clinton-devotees Barry Diller and Diane von Furstenberg") over that story.

Some of the other lower-tier members of the Fox ecosystem whom the president admires lean less on the decidedly rage-aholic end of the spectrum.

There's the frequent Fox guest Tom Fitton, the head of the conservative watchdog group Judicial Watch, whom Trump regularly quotes on Twitter and praises as a supposed authority on FBI, DOJ, and Obama-era "deep state" abuses. In the shadow of the "corrupt" Mueller investigation, Fitton thought he'd found the crime of the century, and the president was all about it. Further, Fitton has the distinct pleasure of having a flattering nickname, courtesy of President Trump himself: "muscle man." The president has recommended Fitton's Fox News hits to friends while in the same breath complimenting Fitton for his toned, gratuitously muscular shape and, in Trump's words, for "looking good."

And then there's Gregg Jarrett, legal analyst and author of *The Russia Hoax*, whom the president habitually watches and uses his quotable interviews to help sharpen his grievance-peddling talking points and whose book he has enthusiastically pimped. "**NEW BOOK—A MUST READ!** 'The Russia Hoax—The Illicit Scheme to Clear Hillary Clinton and Frame Donald Trump' by the brilliant Fox News Legal Analyst Gregg Jarrett. A sad chapter for law enforcement. A rigged system!" Trump tweeted in May 2018.

"Congratulations to Gregg Jarrett on his book, 'THE RUSSIA HOAX, THE ILLICIT SCHEME TO CLEAR HILLARY CLINTON AND FRAME DONALD TRUMP,' going to #1 on @nytimes and Amazon. It is indeed a HOAX and WITCH HUNT, illegally started by people who have already been disgraced. Great book!" he wrote in August 2018.

But all of them pale in comparison to the viral conservative-media sensation who managed to captivate the occupant of the Oval Office.

For the uninitiated, allow us to introduce you to Diamond and Silk.

SWIN had been following Diamond and Silk (Lynnette "Diamond" Hardaway and Rochelle "Silk" Richardson, formerly known as the "'Stump for Trump' girls") since at least early 2016, when they emerged seemingly out of nowhere as a female, African American, formerly Democratic-voting duo on YouTube. Their grift? They had seen the light, were now all aboard the Trump Train, and believed the modern Democratic Party to be an existential threat to black America.

Suddenly the pair were name checked by Trump on Twitter and invited to join him on the campaign trail.

Diamond and Silk's cable news appearances had a tendency to veer into some freakish spaces. In February 2016, CNN still thought it would be wise or productive to invite the North Carolina–based sisters on the air to comment on the news of the day. The duo ended up fanning the flames of the fringe theory that Trump's opponent Marco Rubio was a covert homosexual. Why? Because they read it somewhere on the internet.

"Marco Rubio told us to google Donald Trump, but I did one better— I googled *him*," Diamond (Hardaway) told the CNN host. "And when I googled him—you know, he owes America and the gay community an apology, because it sounds like that he may have had a gay lifestyle in his past . . . Google him . . . That's what's on Google. So you have to be cautious when you tell people to google people. Stuff will come up. Now, we don't know if it's true. So we are saying 'allegedly.'"

The following month, Diamond and Silk were stumping for Trump at a less savory venue, in an eighteen-minute "exclusive" interview with John Friend of *American Free Press*, talking about immigration and American workers.

"These people been in office for years and haven't done anything," Diamond told Friend. "They are okay with illegal people running in our country, and we don't even know these people."

Perhaps unbeknownst to Diamond or Silk, John Friend has been described by the Anti-Defamation League as a "virulent anti-Semite and Holocaust denier," and he's been fairly open in his writings and public statements about his feelings toward Nazism. "If you take an objective look at what [Adolf Hitler] did, what he was all about, the policies that he implemented and championed . . . you will recognize that this man and his movement were the greatest thing that's happened to Western civilization," Friend said on *The Brian Ruhe Show* in December 2015.

Associating with this Nazi hype man did nothing to slow Diamond and Silk's ascent within Trump's social and political circles. During the Trump presidency, the YouTube duo landed hosting duties at the Fox News online streaming service Fox Nation, brought down the house during their speech to the 2019 Conservative Political Action Conference, authored several songs such as the pro-Trump, anti-Eminem diss track "Trump's Yo President," and have been welcomed by President Trump at the White House on multiple special occasions. (They even got to go to Lara Trump's baby shower.)

To fully grasp the inextricable pop culture aspect of Trump's success and the Trump era itself, any self-respecting political observer or reporter must watch Diamond and Silk's video on a weekly basis, bare minimum. So we do.

Within the halls of 1600 Pennsylvania Avenue, Trump himself has many times commented to White House aides about how much he enjoys watching Diamond and Silk on Fox, going out of his way to reference and laugh over specific segments they've done on shows like *Hannity* and *Fox & Friends.* Those close to the president say that Trump has repeatedly said that he finds their style and humor "fantastic." One senior administration official joked to Swin that Diamond and Silk double as "senior economic advisers" to President Trump, citing a *Fox & Friends* segment in which the two women heralded the news that "black unemployment is low and home ownership is high" in the Trump years.

The president has also privately dubbed Diamond and Silk "my stars" and "my brilliant ladies" and has declared that "the internet loves them."

"Thank you to two great people!" Trump tweeted on April 6, 2019, linking to a tweet featuring a photo of the two ladies standing beside President Trump behind the Resolute Desk in the Oval Office. Curiously, the @DiamondandSilk tweet was from February 2019, and it's unclear why this specific post was on the president's mind.

For years, Swin has wanted to meet or at least jump on the phone with Diamond and Silk (particularly Diamond, clearly the front woman and primary voice of the outfit), but neither of them ever answered his emails seeking comment.

In late April 2018, Swin got his chance—all thanks to the bottomless cynicism of Republican congressmen. Conservatives on the House Judiciary Committee had called Diamond and Silk to testify at a hearing called "Filtering Practices of Social Media Platforms," during which the two Trump supporters hurled baseless allegation after baseless allegation that Facebook was targeting them for censorship due to their conservative viewpoints. (At the time, the sisters had 1.4 million followers on the social-media giant.)

Diamond and Silk potentially perjured themselves several times during the hearing, and it got so ridiculous that multiple Democratic lawmakers had to remind them that they were under oath and ask them if they knew lying under oath was, to say the least, ill advised.

At the conclusion of their madcap testimony, Swin approached the duo for a question. While talking to another journalist, Diamond saw Swin, furrowed her brow, and pointed.

"What's your name?" she inquired.

Asawin, he replied, though he added that they might know him as simply Swin, if at all.

Without another word, both Diamond and Silk gestured for Swin to step closer and closer to them, until he was in reach for the two to simultaneously embrace him in a big ol' group bear hug.

"We know who you are," Diamond said, mid-embrace.

"Then why don't you ever respond to my emails?" Swin asked.

"'Cuz we know how the media works!" one of them shot back as they were ushered out by their body man. On their way out the door, and when they weren't exclaiming, "Facebook is a liar!" to huddled reporters,

Swin asked if they were going to pay a visit to their good friend President Trump while they were in Washington, D.C., for the day.

Diamond replied they couldn't possibly comment and smiled.

Trump apparently never got to see his two "senior advisers" that day, however. But, according to Instagram, the duo did make it just a few blocks shy of the West Wing: to the lobby restaurant of Trump International Hotel for lunch, snapping a photo at a table shared with their pal Katrina Pierson, herself an actual senior adviser to the president's reelection campaign.

In more normal times, characters like Diamond, Silk, Bongino, and Jarrett would be at most tangential characters in the unfolding drama of an American presidency. The Trump era has turned them into something far more consequential: at best, informal advisers to a president who knows the power of media to shape events; at worst, literal policy makers whose pronouncements, tethered or not to the actual reality of events, directly inform the most consequential decisions of the nation's most powerful elected official.

We've often been asked during our time reporting on this White House why we focus such seemingly inordinate attention on the apparent sideshows playing out on the fringes of right-wing media. The answer is that it's not inordinate at all. These are the people who've captured President Trump's attention. And it's a direct and very short line from his attention to the official channels of communication and policy making at the West Wing. Enamor the president with a catchy sound bite, and a pundit could well end up shifting U.S. economic policy, or stoking a diplomatic conflict, or ousting a high-level government official or political appointee.

It would be an amazing level of influence were it handed to the wisest, most measured, even-handed, and responsible of pundits. Trump's favorite media personalities are . . . none of those things.

➡ "HE CAN'T HANDLE JAIL"

Unlike most members of President Trump's legal war council, the former New York City mayor Rudy Giuliani had a penchant for embedding a sense of gallows humor and excess into his day-to-day work.

Sometimes, he would get bored and kill time in a manner more closely befitting a crank caller than the lawyer and spokesman for the leader of the free world.

For all his fumbles and foibles, Giuliani was starting from a position of personal advantage and rapport with the forty-fifth president of the United States when he officially signed on to Trump's outside legal team in April 2018. "He's a cool guy," Giuliani had told us multiple times since that April, when citing their friendship and their shared style of controlled chaos and fame, if not infamy. "Control the agenda," Trump has told Giuliani on numerous occasions, while attaboy-ing him for his willingness to make copious media appearances, hurling himself on grenade after lobbed grenade, news cycle after news cycle, in the service of his client and pal Donald J. Trump.

The president trusted his outside counsel to keep his best interests at heart, or at least more so than he sometimes trusted his in-house White House attorney. Since the launching of the Mueller investigation, President Trump had asked those close to him if they thought it was possible or probable that Don McGahn, his first White House counsel, was helping the "corrupt" feds to nail the president by "wearing a wire."

When it came to people like Giuliani, Trump worried far more about unchecked flamboyance than pledged fealty.

And whatever else could be said of a Trumpist Giuliani, he had a way of speaking his mind, oftentimes unapologetically, bafflingly on the record, with a brazen no-fucks-left-to-give disposition. One Friday evening in early December 2018, he rang up Swin in response to a standard inquiry seeking comment on the most recent court documents made publicly available about Trump's estranged fixer Michael Cohen. On Giuliani's end, it sounded as if there were music and loud commotion in the background as Giuliani angrily vacillated between growling and slurring his sentences. Giuliani said the court docs had shown that they were "fucking angry with" Cohen and must want to lock him up "for four years" at least.

Then Trump's friend and personal attorney said something in a way that intimated the often grim and brutal realities of too many prisons in America: the violence, the retributions, the rape, the degradation, the deprivation.

"Believe me," Giuliani said, taking a suddenly more hushed tone. "He can't handle jail."

Then there was that time in the summer of 2019 when the Trump attorney called Lachlan to discuss a story the reporter was working on, only to interrupt the conversation to abruptly ask someone at his side, "You wanna go dancin'?"

"I'm having too much fun," Giuliani told Swin that year, around the time he was still working for Trump and also booking another new client—the authoritarian regime in Bahrain, where his firm landed a contract for training the police force. "One day, I'm gonna have to go back to boring lawyer work."

The guy was definitely having the time of his goddamn life as the world around him was razed and salted, often at the hands of his biggest client. But perhaps the weirdest back-and-forth that either of us had ever experienced with Rudy G. involved his emojis and typos.

During the late afternoon of December 18, 2018, Swin was sitting at the dinner table in the house of his Ohio-based in-laws, running out the clock on a slow workday. Then his phone started dinging with unsolicited text messages sent from Trump's "TV lawyer," as Michael Cohen would soon brand him in congressional testimony.

"On tarmac for almost one hour. I think Mueller knew I was on this plane and is delaying it so he gets me to say whatever he wants me to say. But I'm just incapable of lying 🐀 to save my own skin," Giuliani wrote.

Swin had no idea what in God's name was going on, but the bizarre messages kept coming:

"He wants me to say that 35 years ago DT didn't pay two parking tickets. You say so what's so important? Well they may have been right in front of then Soviet embassy. I WILL NOT BE BROKEN!"

Swin asked if this was supposed to be a (*Joke? Irony?*) tweet that Giuliani accidentally texted to a reporter. Giuliani clarified this was meant as a "Secret text."

"It shows you how far they will go but they can't brake me. I'm no rat 🐀 ," he assured Swin.

He added that he had "just landed and am seeing bail," to which he then corrected himself, texting, "Seeking bail. May be liberated by NYPD."

At this point, Swin wrote back, "Did someone steal your phone or are you just fucking with me, lol."

The former New York mayor replied, "Would I do that. I have now secured release of entire plane."

Swin was convinced that someone had stolen Giuliani's phone and decided to mess with some of the contacts in his cell, *or* that he had synced his messages on a computer he had left unattended. (*Maybe Giuliani's son, Andrew, who was also a staffer in the Trump White House, felt like playing some games*, was a thought that ran through Swin's befuddled mind.)

It didn't take long for Mr. Mayor to call Swin insisting that some plane, somewhere, that he had been stranded on by Robert Mueller had since been "liberated."

The ruse lasted for a few more seconds before Trump's media-friendly lawyer broke character and burst out laughing. Giuliani quickly revealed to Swin that he was, indeed, on a plane that was delayed on the tarmac and that he was feeling "bored." So, in an effort to cure his boredom, he decided to send the series of peculiar, outlandish texts to, according to him, roughly ten people—some were friends, some were fellow Trumpworld figures, some were political journalists he knew—to see what their reactions would be.

He said he wondered who would take the bait. He was curious about who would believe him or accuse him of going clinically insane. He wondered if any of the reporters he messaged would tweet out his claims at face value or as an emerging crisis. (Swin did not.)

Then he said goodbye and hung up.

This was a week before Christmas, and Donald Trump's attorney—brought on to shield the president in the face of a high-stakes Russia investigation—had just pranked Swin for no discernible reason beyond his mild episode of cabin fever and restlessness.

It took a few moments that evening for all of that to sink in. When it did, the only thing Swin could think to do was laugh hysterically (à la Sam Neill, at the conclusion of the film *In the Mouth of Madness*, staring paralyzed into the void).

We had done a lot of that over the first couple years of the Trump era, surrendering ourselves to a darkly comical nihilism that colored our interactions with the broader Trumpworld.

IT was late August 2018, a few months before Giuliani's call, and Donald Trump's legal team was getting impatient. Giuliani was hitting the TV news circuit to demand that Robert Mueller finish his investigation and publish a report on it by the following month. But the special counsel was either ignoring him or being obstinate. So Giuliani and his Trump legal team colleagues decided they weren't going to wait. Instead, they'd craft a "counter-report" that would, essentially, try to poison the tree of the investigation by attempting to preemptively discredit Mueller, his investigative team, and the federal law enforcement bureaucracy more generally.

We got wind of the workings of the report, of course, during our regular conversations with Giuliani, who routinely, and to our endless delight, made the usual plumbing of less senior leakers unnecessary. Swin asked him for information about the project, and Rudy was more than happy to dish details. It would be broken into two sections, he explained, one undercutting the rationale for and objectivity of Mueller's investigation and another responding to more substantive allegations stemming from the probe—or at least what the legal team anticipated those allegations would be. "Since we have to guess what it is, it is quite voluminous," Giuliani said of the report.

We wanted more details, so naturally we called up Giuliani's colleague on the legal team. But Jay Sekulow wasn't nearly as eager to talk. In fact, he outright denied aspects of what Giuliani told us. Of course they couldn't respond to Mueller's allegations, he said; they didn't know what those allegations would be. He conceded that the legal team was "preparing a comprehensive report that will include issues related to the commencement of this investigation through the legal issues of it." But he was incredulous at some of the details that Giuliani had, just minutes earlier and on the record, provided to us.

"Rudy said that?" Sekulow asked us, clearly exasperated and failing to muffle an audible sigh.

IT was a microcosm of the often amusing relationship between the two lawyers, or at least what their relationship looked like to those of us reporting on them. Both men are New Yorkers, but that's where the similarities end. In many respects, the two are polar opposites: Giuliani the moderate Republican, notorious divorcé, outgoing, and media savvy; Sekulow the devoted Christian, skeptical of the mainstream press, reserved, and intensely conservative. And while Giuliani seemed to revel in speaking with the press, even when doing so was at best a distraction and at worst an egregious legal or public relations misstep, Sekulow would almost never speak to the media without going off the record, and even then would hedge his language and tread carefully to avoid running afoul of a devised legal strategy. But while Giuliani was visible in pushing Trump's agenda, Sekulow wielded a far different, but no less effective, strategy that combined more targeted media advocacy with what amounted to a shadow legal team staffed with his own colleagues and loyalists. When Sekulow isn't orchestrating the president's Mueller strategy or running his own legal advocacy outfit, he's engaged in an activity far more typical for a middle-aged boomer: performing hokey classic rock covers. He's the drummer for an eponymous rock group, the Jay Sekulow Band, that somehow managed to lead with his name despite boasting members such as the former front man of the band Kansas, John Elefante, and the former lead singer and former producer, respectively, for the Grammy-winning Christian rock act Petra and the Grammy nominee Relient K. The Jay Sekulow Band's Facebook page bills it, excruciatingly, as a "unique alliance between law and music."

The band covers 1960s and 1970s classic rock standards, including tunes by the Beatles, Cream, and Boston. But it's also written some originals, particularly a ham-fisted song titled "Undemocratic," about the U.S. government's persecution of conservative Christians in contemporary America. "Democracy in motion means a right to take sides / Since when is one rewarded for the emails she hides?" ask a few lines of the song. It shares a title with, and was created to promote, Sekulow's 2015 book of the same name. The song's music video was published on the official YouTube channel of the American Center for Law and Justice, the nonprofit outfit that Sekulow leads and that employs a not insignificant portion of his immediate family.

Five of ACLJ's six board members are members of the Sekulow family, and over the last twenty years ACLJ has steered millions to Jay's sons, brother, and sister-in-law, among other family members. Some have even taken out six-figure loans from the nonprofit, only to have the bulk of those loans subsequently forgiven, with the difference classified as "compensation" from the organization.

ACLJ raises tens of millions each year, much of it in small-dollar increments courtesy of the group's incessant telemarketing fundraising pitches. They promise to defeat the liberals in court, to maintain traditional Christian conservative policies at the federal level, and, more recently, to expose the deep state saboteurs attempting to take down President Trump. One sample fund-raising call script filed in 2017 by the Donor Care Center, one of ACLJ's telemarketing contractors, instructed callers to continue pressing potential donors for money even if they said they were unemployed, were on a fixed income, or "have no money." For near-broke potential donors, the call script instructed telemarketers to appeal to people's religious faith, asking if they can "make a small sacrificial gift of even $20."

ACLJ's telemarketers were even instructed to pursue donations in the event they ended up on the phone with a bereaved relative. "I'm so sorry to hear that. I will update our records," callers were instructed to say in the event they tried to hit up a dead person for money and instead found themselves talking to a relative. "Let me ask," they were advised to follow up, "are you also a supporter of ACLJ, and if so, do you still want to receive updates?"

Trump brought Sekulow on board for the same reason he's hired so many staffers in the upper echelons of the modern American government: Sekulow was wary of speaking with reporters, but he was a great panelist on bomb-throwing Fox News shows, where he frequently attacked Hillary Clinton and other prominent Democrats and put up often facile legal defenses of the president's conduct.

But Sekulow brought far more to the table than legal expertise or knee-jerk support of the president. ACLJ raised more than $53 million in 2017, and the organization was where Sekulow's real value for the president's legal team resided. He was always ideologically aligned with the president, in spite of Trump's conspicuously impious lifestyle. He had a cadre of conservative lawyers at his disposal and a massive list of supporters around the country whom he could whip into a furor in the service of the Trump team's outrage-driven counterattacks against Mueller and any other law enforcement officer who deigned to investigate the president and his cronies. If things got really bad, Sekulow could even pen a rock ballad about the injustices of the would-be deep state coup against America's commander in chief.

FOR those on ACLJ's email marketing list, the warnings were frequent and dire. "We're on the brink of losing to the Deep State. We MUST take action now," one email pleaded. "I've been telling you the Deep State bureaucracy is willing to violate federal law to defeat the conservative agenda. But the Deep State corruption and lawlessness is deeper than you think . . . The only thing standing between politically corrupt lawlessness and the integrity of our constitutional republic is YOU."

"Our legal deadlines are looming," the email concluded. "But, TODAY, every Tax-Deductible gift you make to defeat the lawlessness in federal court will be doubled—dollar-for-dollar."

Donate now or the deep state will defeat the Trump agenda. It was a characteristic plea from ACLJ and one of dozens that showed how Sekulow's group was capitalizing financially on his official legal role on Trump's behalf. Supporting Trump independently would have juiced the group's fund-raising anyway. But Sekulow's actual representation of the president, as he derided the same deep state plots that pervaded ACLJ fund-raising pitches, added a tremendous amount of credibility to those pitches, even if Sekulow's role went largely unmentioned.

That role was public enough, certainly for ACLJ supporters who followed Sekulow's legal efforts. Less well known, and exposed only through *The Daily Beast*'s reporting at the time, was the extent to which ACLJ had become an unofficial extension of the Trump legal team. Sekulow insisted up and down that no such overlap existed, at least officially. But he admitted in interviews that a number of ACLJ attorneys were working behind the scenes on the president's behalf, fulfilling many of the more mundane legal tasks that befall any high-profile person engaged in legal wrangling with the federal government. But they've also waded into more weighty territory, crafting preemptive legal strategies that focus on constitutional challenges to any effort to, say, subpoena the president. Sekulow himself was deeply involved in negotiations between Trump and Mueller over the possibility of an in-person interview.

None of ACLJ's resources were going toward that activity, Sekulow repeatedly claimed. But that wasn't entirely true either. Trump's legal team frequently met in the conference room at the group's Capitol Hill offices, which sit less than a block from the U.S. Supreme Court. ACLJ didn't dispute that reporting. "Any non-ACLJ-related work that occurs at the ACLJ offices is reimbursed in compliance with all applicable tax laws," a spokesperson for the group told us at the time.

Nonetheless, it was common for sources to tell us that the president's lawyers—Giuliani, Ty Cobb, John Dowd—had popped into the ACLJ offices to discuss legal strategy.

It was in large measure a public relations strategy, so Giuliani's value was obvious. He was a fixture on cable news, where he tried, with varying degrees of success, to advance Trump's narrative of events in the face of spiraling legal controversy. Sekulow's role also complemented that strategy, but in far more subtle ways. He was quiet and more careful with the media but arguably did far more to advance a public narrative of Mueller corruption and a "deep state" conspiracy than Giuliani could in a thousand cable hits. And Sekulow did it entirely through an independent "educational" nonprofit with an eight-figure budget provided by anonymous donors who received hefty tax write-offs for their support.

▶ "OH, WE'LL FIND IT"

An entire generation of young Republican talent came up in the opposition. Eight years of President Obama, health-care fights, stimulus spending, Tea Party rallies, investigative hearings on Benghazi and Lois Lerner and Operation Fast and Furious, midterm drubbings, and a thoroughly botched 2012 campaign produced a field of up-and-coming GOP operatives and media voices and aspiring elected officials who had never known real federal political power. So when Republicans finally took the White House, a whole new crop of young Republicans were poised to finally put into action designs that for years they'd been reduced to simply shouting from a soapbox.

Many of these young professionals were not Trump fans. A bunch had worked for rival campaigns. Marco Rubio, Rand Paul, Chris Christie, and Ted Cruz were all products of the same Republican Party that had thrived in the opposition, and now they were working to get one of their own in the White House. Then Trump burst in and all that inevitability went right out the window. But at the very least there would be an R in the West Wing. And conservative stalwarts at flagship organizations like the Heritage Foundation and the Federalist Society would ensure that the detailed policy proposals conservatives had crafted as Obama-era alternatives would finally be something more than think tank white papers.

Lachlan too had come up during the Obama years, when he considered himself a Republican and worked, through media and reporting, to try to advance conservative policy and communications goals. He wasn't toeing a party line, but he believed that the GOP was advancing an objectively better vision for the country than its opposition. And he was moved by many of the issues considered quintessential Reagan-era conservative planks: reduced taxation, a smaller regulatory state, reduction of the national debt, a heavier reliance on the market, free trade, an energetic global U.S. military presence, and skepticism of what he considered progressive social engineering.

Trump seemed at best unconcerned with and at worst hostile to most of those positions. So when he won the Republican presidential primary in Indiana in May 2016, tallying the delegate count necessary to capture the Republican nomination, political reality set in. Not only was Trump a very different type of Republican than Lachlan was, but so too, it was suddenly clear, were the vast majority of Republican voters. It was obvious that there was not a significant constituency for the types of policies Lachlan favored. So be it. He literally burned his Republican voter registration card and figuratively washed his hands of the party. The GOP could go the way of Trump. Lachlan would go his own way. Everyone would be happier for it.

But there was a personal aspect to it as well. Lachlan worked with and befriended many of the Republican operatives who, in early 2017, found themselves looking for jobs in the new administration or in media gigs that would act as adjuncts of the Trump communications apparatus. And many of them were, like him, Trump skeptics—or outright opponents—before it became clear that Trump would be the GOP nominee. They shared a Reagan-esque antipathy to this new right-wing populism. But beyond the prospects for professional advancement, this new administration presented an opportunity to put into action many of the ideas they'd spent the last eight years musing about hypothetically. So they held their noses, deleted their social media histories, and shot off job applications.

Trump's potential talent pool, in other words, was large and fired up in spite of its collective misgivings. But Trump decided that few of them were good enough. Or, more important, loyal enough.

The early Trump administration was racked by staffing problems— namely, a catastrophic lack of it. The White House simply couldn't find enough people to fill the thousands of political appointments throughout the federal government. That problem was entirely of its own making. It's not that the administration's professional standards were too high; right off the bat, it would fill senior positions with people with as little experience as Lynne Patton and as much personal baggage as Rob Porter. Nor was there too small a talent pool to draw from. The problem was that Trump demanded absolute, retroactive loyalty. If you'd beaten an ex-wife, you could still land a senior White House post. But one negative tweet about Trump during the 2016 campaign—or, say, wondering aloud whether Trump should, in fact, "grab 'em by the pussy"—put your job application in jeopardy.

And if that tweet existed, Trump's team would find it. While the FBI conducted its own background checks, standard for political appointees in any administration, the White House personnel office scoured job applicants' social media pages for any hint of dissension.

In mid-2018, we ended up at a house party and in conversation with two sources, one of them a fairly senior White House aide and the other a House Republican staffer who was looking to land an administration post, ideally at State or Treasury, he said. Small talk quickly turned to what was, essentially, a preliminary job interview unfolding over cans of beer in a mutual friend's living room.

The White House official offered to do what he could to help out the Hill staffer in securing a job. He was friends with a senior guy in the personnel office who oversaw much of the internal vetting process. But first he had a few questions, and none of them had to do with ideology, policy ideas, or qualifications.

Instead, this White House aide wondered if the potential job applicant had publicly said anything negative about the president, either in the year and a half since he took office or in the two years prior during the presidential campaign. This Hill staffer had supported Rubio during the 2016 campaign, but he assured his potential administration patron that he'd purged his Twitter account early the following year, deleting every tweet including the few that expressed some mild criticism of Trump during the heat of the presidential race.

The White House official laughed.

"Oh, we'll find it," he said cryptically. "If you posted something on Facebook in 2007 and then deleted it, we'll find it."

As of our writing this, the Hill staffer had not been hired in any job in the Trump administration.

Trump loved to blame his early staffing difficulties on obstructionist Democrats in Congress. And it's true that they held up a huge number of his nominees to Senate-confirmed positions. But the vast majority of unfilled staff positions early in the administration were not ones that required a Senate vote. The personnel troubles that dogged the administration early were entirely a product of the president's pathological aversion to even the mildest criticism, from even the lowliest subordinate.

For much of the young crop of Republicans hoping to finally occupy the halls of federal power, that meant an even steeper climb into positions of influence in the new government. But for those with little media footprint and no moral compunctions with Trump; those who'd stayed silent, acquiesced to, or outright backed his presidential bid;

those who had no problem melding their private views and public personas to the toxic idiosyncrasies of the nation's new commander in chief, this new hiring strategy presented an amazing opportunity.

Trump was keeping some of the most talented political talent in the country out of the ranks of his administration. That left plenty of vacant positions for those with malleable ethical constitutions or who prized power and influence above such silly things as principles and ideas. Fortunately for Trump, D.C. still had quite a few of those, and there were a few more on the way.

LYNNE Patton showed up in Cleveland in the summer of 2016 ready for her coming-out party. The longtime Trump Organization employee, and right hand to Eric Trump, was determined to bring down the house. Virtually unknown in political circles at the time, Patton was in town for the Republican National Convention, and she had a prime speaking slot lined up on Wednesday evening, the third day of the convention, right between two Republican stars and onetime Trump rivals. Patton would come on right after Wisconsin's governor, Scott Walker, and right before Florida's senator Marco Rubio.

For Patton, it wasn't just a chance to make a first impression on the assembled crowd of prominent Republican officials, activists, and donors; she was determined to establish herself as the Trump campaign's— and, she was fully convinced, the Trump administration's—point person on all things pertaining to the African American community.

Patton arrived in Cleveland and immediately began making demands. She wanted the full VIP treatment. She wanted a private car service to shuttle her around during convention week. She wanted the full green-room treatment. Her handlers were a bit taken aback. Party conventions are generally staffed by political operatives and volunteers, many of them assigned to take care of the needs of the event's speakers and high-profile attendees. In 2016, they included senators, governors, billionaire businessmen, and household-name television personalities. Patton was demanding the treatment befitting the most prestigious convention attendees.

As she saw it, these other VIPs might have been powerful and important cogs in the American political machine. But this event wasn't about them, or even about the Republican Party. This was the Trump show, and she'd been a starring cast member for years. Patton intuitively understood a reality that only set in months later for her handlers and the rest of the Beltway convention staff that had flown out for the week: their party was now an extension of the Trump brand, and their old hierarchies were no longer operative. The Trump loyalists were now the VIPs. Oh, you govern a moderately sized midwestern state? You're one of a hundred legislators in Congress's upper chamber? Well, Patton was a vice president of the Eric Trump Foundation. If it wasn't yet clear to the party operatives in Cleveland how to order those positions in terms of importance, it certainly was to Patton.

Her speech went about as well as her handlers could've hoped. Patton surprised some observers when she threw a rhetorical bone to black America, assuring viewers that "as a minority, I personally pledge to you that Donald Trump knows that your life matters, he knows that my life matters." She went on to bemoan that, "historically, black lives have mattered less. My life mattered less. Whether we like it or not, there are people out there who still believe this to be true." It was a stark departure from a speech two days earlier by the Milwaukee sheriff, David Clarke, who blamed the Black Lives Matter movement for the recent deaths of police officers and led a round of applause for the recent acquittal of an officer who shot and killed an unarmed black man in Baltimore.

Clarke didn't get an administration gig; Patton did. But it wasn't because of her enlightened views on police brutality. It also wasn't due to her qualifications. The résumé she submitted to the Department of Housing and Urban Development listed an education at three schools: the University of Miami, Quinnipiac Law School, and Yale University. But it turned out she'd simply taken a couple summer classes at Yale. She studied law for two semesters at Quinnipiac but did not graduate. After the press took notice, she removed both from her LinkedIn page.

But Patton's chief qualification was not education, or pedigree, or experience, or breadth of policy knowledge. It was loyalty. The First Family adored her. She'd risen in the ranks of the Trump Organization to become an aide to Trump's three eldest children. Patton was a longtime servant of the Trump empire. That, it turned out, was the new chief determinant in federal employment.

And for Patton, Trump's election meant plenty of money and fame in her future. She planned to milk it for all it was worth.

Within six months of Trump's taking office, Patton landed a senior role at the Department of Housing and Urban Development, where she oversees all federal housing initiatives in New York and New Jersey and a multibillion-dollar public assistance budget. Her total lack of experience in any field of housing policy was naturally no hang-up for either the officials who appointed her or Patton herself; she jumped headfirst into the new gig and quickly began picking fights with the notoriously dysfunctional and scandal-plagued New York City Housing Authority and the city's mayor, the widely disliked Trump critic Bill de Blasio.

Like the Trump family itself, Patton has a gift for bombastic self-promotion and over-the-top political displays. Like the president himself, she maintained personal social media accounts in addition to the official government pages that came with her senior position in the administration. Those accounts are largely indistinguishable from the army of digital pro-Trump trolls that tend to pollute digital conversations on anything relating to the Trump administration. Full of memes and GIFs and emojis, Patton's personal social media pages promote Trump and his family with a juvenile vehemence more typical of a tween pop star fangirl than a high-ranking federal employee.

In late 2018, Patton pulled off her most impressive bit of political theater yet when she announced that she would move into an apartment in a Queens housing project in order to live among the people whom she was tapped to serve, and experience the housing conditions with which they're forced to live.

The move was clearly self-serving—Patton reveled in the press it earned her—but even critics had to admit that the thinking behind the move was laudable. NYCHA was in the midst of a massive lead paint scandal. It'd just been sued by the Department of Justice over allegedly routine negligence. Residents of the project where Patton moved in hoped that having a senior HUD official present might spur some needed action to get the place cleaned up.

But some of those residents also sensed that Patton was less eager to be living with them than she was to be *seen* living with them. She frequently had cameras in tow when she showed up to stay the night. The whole thing had a very reality-TV vibe to it.

That, it turned out, was no accident. As Patton was making a show of her stints in public housing, she was also in talks with a television producer to help create and star in a series about black Republicans in the Trump era. Devised by the creators of Bravo TV's *Real Housewives of Potomac*, the "docuseries" entailed trailing prominent African American Trump supporters including Patton, Trump's campaign hand Katrina Pierson, and Turning Point USA's communications director,

Candace Owens. Conspicuously not involved with the project was Omarosa Manigault, who, like Patton, had brought a reality-TV air to the Trump administration and angled to be its African American face. Patton, it seemed, was sliding nicely into both roles.

As Patton planned her NYCHA stunt, she was also pleading with HUD ethics officials for permission to retain her federal employment in some form even as she raked in TV income far exceeding the outside income limit for federal employees. Patton hoped to make in excess of $40,000 per episode, but federal rules allowed outside income of only $28,000 per year. Maybe she could take a leave of absence from her post for a couple months, she wondered, or even resign completely with the understanding that she'd be rehired when filming was completed? Ethics officials scoffed at the requests. But Patton seemed determined to carry on with the project in spite of the slight hiccup of her own agency's lawyers.

Patton's other starring TV role came in 2019, during one of the highest-profile congressional hearings of the Trump presidency. Michael Cohen, Trump's longtime lawyer and fixer, was testifying about all the dirty deeds he'd done at the president's behest, including arranging hush money payments to his mistresses just weeks before the 2016 election.

Cohen also flatly stated that his former boss is a racist. "In private, he's even worse," he told the House Oversight Committee.

Committee Republicans had a plan for countering this allegation against their president. And her name was Lynne Patton. Mark Meadows, the committee's ranking Republican, trotted Patton out as a testimonial to the success of a black executive in the president's orbit. "You made some very demeaning comments about the president that Ms. Patton doesn't agree with," Meadows complained. "In fact, it has to do with your claim of racism. She says that as a daughter of a man born in Birmingham, Alabama, that there is no way that she would work for an individual who was racist."

Patton stood behind Meadows, stone-faced. She had taken a day off from work to appear and stare down the former colleague now spilling the beans about the president. Whatever was happening at HUD that day, this was obviously more important. Patton didn't get where she was by being the smartest housing policy thinker in the room. She did so by staying loyal.

▶ "YOU'RE A PIECE
OF TRASH"

S cott Pruitt's ignominious downfall began in unlikely fashion for the time: it all started with a phone booth. The Environmental Protection Agency administrator oversaw the construction of a secure, soundproof cubicle in his office from which he could make calls without worrying about them being intercepted or about the career officials in the building—who he believed, rightly in some cases, were out to get him—overhearing him. It was initially planned, in mid-2017, as a simple secure phone line, with a price tag of under $14,000. By the end of the year, that cost had tripled as the EPA added more features, soundproof paneling, and silent ventilation systems. "It is a legal purchase," a career EPA official warned in an internal email, "but it will be scrutinized," according to copies of the exchange reported by Bloomberg News.

That official was only half right. The $43,000 phone booth was scrutinized. But it wasn't legal. Government investigators later concluded that the EPA had violated a law giving Congress control over federal agencies' purse strings. By that point, though, Pruitt had far bigger problems. The phone booth was just the first in a string of controversies that would dog Pruitt for over a year, subject him to intense congressional and media scrutiny, and eventually lead to his resignation.

Pruitt was arguably the most scandal-prone cabinet-level official of the early Trump presidency, and that was no small feat. But he had two things going for him that other senior federal officials did not, both of which prevented an early departure comparable to that of Secretary of Health and Human Services Tom Price or Secretary of Veterans Affairs David Shulkin. First, and most important, President Trump really liked him. Pruitt effectively discharged the president's environmental and energy agendas and managed to stay on his good side in spite of all the controversies. But he also had another, related asset: a staff of senior aides willing to go to the mat for him, play dirty, and pull out all the stops in an effort to protect their boss, insulate him from criticism, and discredit, or at least hamstring, those who came after him.

Trump, of course, came to office promising a new era of ethical government. He would drain the swamp, he insisted ad nauseam on the campaign trail, a facile pledge that often took the form of Trump's imposing new ethics regulations, only to waive them by presidential fiat every time they inconvenienced a policy or personnel decision.

More important to the administration than adherence to its own ethics rules was an official's ability to discharge the Trump agenda. So when Erik Baptist, a former oil industry lobbyist, signed on as a top EPA lawyer in mid-2017, he was quickly excused from the provisions of a White House ethics pledge that would bar him from working on issues affecting his former clients. The White House counsel, Don McGahn, explained that forcing him to adhere to those ethics rules would impede the administration's ability to carry out its regulatory agenda. "His deep understanding of . . . the regulated industry make[s] him the ideal person to assist the administrator and his senior leadership team to make EPA and its renewable fuel programs more efficient and effective," McGahn explained in a memo officially waiving provisions of the ethics pledge for Baptist's benefit.

This efficacy standard of ethics enforcement worked both ways. If you were important to the administration's agenda, its ethical considerations fell by the wayside too. But woe unto the federal official who is not able to rack up policy wins to outweigh the bad press of his or her unethical conduct. That's a lesson that Tom Price learned early.

Trump's first HHS secretary was tasked with what would be a crowning achievement for the new administration. Obamacare, a law that had bedeviled Republicans for years and that they had railed against since its inception, would be repealed. With majorities in both houses of Congress and an aggressive new White House, the GOP would finally roll back a signature Obama-era law, which of course had the added benefit for the president of sticking it to a man whom he despised and about whose presidential legitimacy he'd spread racist lies just a few years earlier.

Price was an ideal candidate to spearhead the Obamacare repeal effort. He was an orthopedic surgeon, a longtime Obamacare critic, and a former congressman who maintained extensive alliances in the House Republican caucus that would be crucial to shepherding a repeal bill through Congress. Trump appointed Price to the nation's top health-care regulatory post with Obamacare repeal at the front of his mind. Genteel, soft-spoken, a conservative very much of the Republican establishment, Price wasn't a typical Trump Republican, but for this singular task he seemed a perfect fit. Rolling back Obama's health law was the sole reason Price was in his post, a fact that the president didn't hesitate to publicly make clear.

"Hopefully he will get the votes tomorrow to start our path to killing this horrible thing known as Obamacare that is really hurting us," the president said in a speech to a gathering of Boy Scouts in mid-2017.

"He better get the votes," Trump joked. "Otherwise I will say, 'Tom, you're fired.'"

It turns out it wasn't a joke.

Things were looking up in May 2017, when Trump, Price, and dozens of House Republicans gathered in the White House Rose Garden for an event celebrating the lower chamber's passage of its Obamacare repeal bill. Price got a huge round of applause as Republicans jubilantly hailed the impending death of a law that they had worked for years to undo. Finally, with Price's help, Trump would get repeal done. And the HHS secretary would be feted as the man who was able to shepherd this controversial piece of legislation through a notoriously fractious Congress.

But it was not to be. Internally, Price quickly alienated much of the career staff at HHS. His efforts to sell Obamacare repeal were often hamfisted. In one instance, he made sweeping claims about repeal's cost-savings projections, only to be contradicted by the Congressional Budget Office days later. The White House quickly sidelined Price in the repeal effort, leaving Hill negotiations to Vice President Pence and the White House's budget and legislative affairs directors, Mick Mulvaney and Marc Short. In the end, they weren't able to get it done either. Obamacare repeal failed in the Senate, with Senator John McCain casting a deciding vote and flashing what instantly became an iconic thumbs-down sign to the Senate Republican majority leader, Mitch McConnell, as he dashed Trump's hopes of undoing his predecessor's signature legislative achievement.

Trump was not pleased with his HHS secretary. But Price stayed in his post for months after Obamacare repeal fizzled out. It wasn't until September 2017 that the deathblow landed. *Politico* reported that Price had been living large on the taxpayer dime, spending more than $1 million on private jet travel in less than a year on the job, a major break with the practice of prior cabinet officials. The negative press coverage that followed was swift and deadly. Ten days later, Price resigned.

In any other administration, that would be a fairly run-of-the-mill resolution to a major ethics scandal. Forced resignation is to be expected when a high-level official betrays the public trust in such a major way and embarrasses his boss in the press. But the subsequent year, full of other Trump administration scandals, would reveal that can't have been the full story. Price's resignation set off a wave of investigations into Trump cabinet secretaries and their travel and spending habits. Many of them engaged in conduct at least as objectionable as Price's, but none were cast aside with anything approaching the speed that Price was. What determined Price's fate wasn't his conduct itself; it was the personal displeasure that Trump had with his HHS secretary. Had Obamacare been repealed, Price would likely have weathered the storm. But he got on Trump's bad side. That, not any ethically problematic conduct on Price's part, determined his fate.

Pruitt was another story, and his ability to survive waves of scandal and media scrutiny neatly illustrated the standards of ethical conduct under Trump. The president loved him. Staying on Trump's good side kept him in office amid a rash of controversies that would've made Price blush. Pruitt's staff, unlike Price's, appeared to recognize that. And they set about determining their boss would not meet the same fate, unleashing a strategy of media aggression and presidential sycophancy that would insulate Pruitt from political pressure that would, in any other administration, have brought him down almost immediately. At the center of the strategy was a veteran Republican communications operative named Jahan Wilcox.

WILCOX could not have cared less what you thought about him or his boss. He joined Pruitt's team in early 2017 and quickly became one of the EPA chief's most trusted and relied-upon senior staffers. Pruitt, a devout Christian, was known to praise Wilcox in biblical terms, occasionally telling him during staff meetings that he believed Jesus Christ himself had sent his comms adviser to help them both carry out the Lord's work.

Wilcox had worked in the offices of Republican bigwigs such as Mitch McConnell and Senator Roger Wicker and built a reputation as a savvy and aggressive operator with a large Rolodex of top political reporters willing to take his calls. He served as a senior communications adviser to Senator Marco Rubio's 2016 presidential campaign and, when that fizzled out, decamped to North Dakota to work on the governor's race there.

When Wilcox joined the EPA in a senior communications post in March 2017, the agency was riding high. Pruitt was rolling back Obama-era environmental rules left and right, earning major plaudits from industry allies and conservative policy advocates. Obama, stymied by even Democrats in Congress who refused to go along with his ambitious environmental agenda, had instead opted for executive and regulatory actions to implement his agenda. The EPA was ground zero for those efforts, and because they were largely undertaken at the executive's behest, many could be undone with the flick of Pruitt's pen. He quickly moved to scrap Obama's Clean Power Plan, a major regulatory initiative to restrict greenhouse gas emissions from power plants, and to withdraw the United States from the Paris climate accords. Unlike Price's, Pruitt's fortunes didn't rely on securing congressional support. He could unilaterally enact much of the president's environmental agenda, and Pruitt handily earned the president's good favor by doing so.

For journalists covering the administration and its energy and environmental agendas in particular, Pruitt was a prime target from the get-go. The former attorney general for Oklahoma, Pruitt had spearheaded multistate lawsuits against Obama-era EPA regulations, and his industry-aligned agenda had earned him plenty of allies—and campaign donors—among the large companies he was tasked with overseeing, and occasionally prosecuting, in his perch as the nation's chief environmental regulator. As Pruitt's tenure kicked off, journalists dug into public records that illustrated how closely he'd worked with the oil and gas industry in Oklahoma and the influence that industry was slated to exert with Pruitt atop the EPA. And with officials like Baptist and Pruitt's deputy, Andrew Wheeler, a former coal industry lobbyist, filling the top ranks at the EPA, there was plenty of material for muckraking reporters looking to dig into the apparent regulatory capture unfolding at the agency.

Some reporters in particular quickly became regular antagonists for the EPA's press shop. They included Eric Lipton and Coral Davenport at *The New York Times*, Alex Kaufman at *The Huffington Post*, and Rebecca Leber and Russ Choma at *Mother Jones*. These reporters relentlessly covered conflicts of interest and regulatory capture at the EPA and the degree to which Pruitt's deregulatory agenda benefited private interests with which he'd collaborated for years and that had lavishly funded Trump's political efforts and supportive organizations.

Wilcox and his colleagues at the EPA's press office were, if not friendly, at least professional in their dealings with most of them. But for one news outlet in particular, it was a different story entirely. And it just so happened to be one of the most influential news outlets in the country. Starting early, and for the duration of his time at the EPA, Wilcox would wage a knock-down, drag-out war, both publicly and behind the scenes, against the Associated Press and its lead EPA reporter, Michael Biesecker.

Biesecker drew Wilcox's ire early with a story on Dow Chemical's apparent influence over EPA policy making on pesticides. The AP had obtained internal meeting schedules for Pruitt, which showed that the administrator had met for half an hour with Dow's chief executive before moving to scrap a study showing the harmful effects of the company's pesticides. Biesecker asked the EPA for comment. They denied that any such meeting had taken place. Biesecker, relying on internal documents rather than the word of an agency flack, reported the meeting anyway. But when both Dow and the EPA told the AP that the meeting had been canceled, it was forced to correct the story.

It was an understandable error given the conflicting information, and the AP issued its correction swiftly. But for Wilcox and his colleagues, it was a clear, early sign that Biesecker and his outlet were going to be their chief antagonists. And going forward, Wilcox went about his job treating the AP not as an adversarial news organization but as an enemy to be kneecapped. He considered Biesecker a "dishonest," "anti-Trump reporter," as he told him directly in a 2018 email. "It could be why the Associated Press moves you from beat to beat."

By September 2017, a few months after Biesecker first reported on the EPA's pesticide study, Wilcox wouldn't even respond to Biesecker's comment requests. But he wouldn't ignore them either. Instead, he would forward the reporter's emails to AP's Washington bureau chief, Julie Pace, and write his responses there. Pace would then forward Wilcox's responses to Biesecker, who would in turn reach out to Wilcox directly. It made for hilariously passive-aggressive exchanges between a reporter and a flack who clearly despised each other, and an editor forced to be something resembling the parent in the room.

If Wilcox came off as angry or upset during any of those exchanges, it certainly didn't reflect his internal mood about the AP spat. He loved every minute of it. He wasn't a policy guy, and certainly not an environmental policy one. He'd shopped around for other jobs in the administration before landing at the EPA, after all. At heart, Wilcox was a campaign operative, and on a political campaign your goal is victory for your principal. That was the mind-set he'd brought to the EPA. But victory requires an opponent that can be vanquished. For a policy aide at Pruitt's agency, that might be the Sierra Club or the Natural Resources Defense Council. For Wilcox, it was the AP. And he quickly turned his expertise as a campaign operative into a blunt instrument to wield against this perceived adversary.

If Wilcox's beef with the AP was rooted in objections about the tone of its coverage, it quickly became far more personal. He was less concerned with avoiding negative press coverage of the EPA than he was with ensuring that that coverage didn't come from the AP. If Pruitt was going to get beaten up in the press, he'd ensure that the AP's competitors were the ones doing the beating. When Biesecker or a colleague reached out about a scoop, Wilcox would occasionally feed that scoop to another news organization. If he got word that the AP had filed a Freedom of Information Act request with the agency, he would try to find newsworthy documents or communications that might turn up in that FOIA response and offer to provide them to another outlet before the AP got ahold of them.

And just as a political campaign might conduct opposition research on its opponents, Wilcox started digging into Biesecker's past in an attempt to sow doubts about his reporting and undercut his professional standing. In September 2017, he drafted a memo resembling the type of research document often produced by campaigns and political operatives. It laid out his case against Biesecker's coverage and what he considered the AP's professional duty to rein him in.

The memo, which was shared with at least one news organization that we know of, was headlined "Questions for the Associated Press" and included email addresses for Pace, the AP spokesperson Emily Leshner, and Sally Buzbee, the outlet's executive editor. It dredged up Biesecker's coverage of environmental issues in North Carolina during a 2014 stint as a beat reporter in the Tar Heel State. Biesecker, Wilcox wrote, "deliberately misled the public" and "invented facts to fit his narrative" in stories on a state environmental settlement with the company Duke Energy. The memo also brought up a 2013 scandal in which the AP's veteran Richmond politics reporter, Bob Lewis, was swiftly fired after erroneously reporting a story on possible criminal conduct by the then gubernatorial candidate Terry McAuliffe. (Wilcox had previously worked for McAuliffe's 2013 opponent, the Republican Ken Cuccinelli.)

The memo asked, "Does the Associated Press hold their reporters to different standards for mistakes against public officials associated with Hillary Clinton and the Democrat Party (Terry McAuliffe) than mistakes against individuals that serve in either President Trump's Administration or the Republican Party (EPA Administrator Scott Pruitt and former Governor Pat McCrory)?"

That openly hostile stance toward such a high-profile media organization drew plenty of hand-wringing from Washington's press corps, especially amid Trump's routine denunciations of the press as "the enemy of the people." But that was precisely the point. Wilcox and his colleagues were ecstatic when *The Washington Post*'s media reporter tut-tutted the EPA press shop with a headline featuring Wilcox's "anti-Trump reporter" accusation against Biesecker. Antipathy toward the press was just the sort of story that Pruitt's team wanted written.

They, and Wilcox in particular, understood a few key facts about life in the employ of Donald Trump. Foremost among them is that your job depends entirely on the boss's opinion of you at any given moment. For Pruitt and his team, that meant perpetually reminding the president that his EPA chief was doing things that Trump liked, namely rolling back Obama-era environmental regulations. Virtually every quote that Wilcox and his team gave to the press was crafted with a target audience of exactly one person and designed explicitly to remind him of the great job Pruitt was doing on the policy front.

But there's one thing that Trump likes even more than policy wins, and it's sticking it to his enemies. So even as Wilcox and his team took pains to inject EPA press coverage with appeals to its policy victories, they also picked every fight they could with reporters and reveled in every story about their conflicts with the press. Every breathless media report about the uncouth and aggressive EPA press operation was a win for Pruitt, a way to keep him on Trump's good side. And catering to the president's combative idiosyncrasies would soon be the only thing keeping Pruitt in his job.

LAYING out all the different overlapping scandals that eventually led to Scott Pruitt's downfall is difficult to do comprehensively and comprehensibly without some sort of three-dimensional, interactive chart. There was the aforementioned $43,000 phone booth; the expensive biometric locks on Pruitt's office door; the $3 million spent on an unprecedentedly large security detail; the use of that security detail's motorcade to travel to upscale D.C. restaurants; the University of Kentucky basketball tickets provided by a coal executive; Pruitt's tasking of staff to pick up his favorite brand of Greek yogurt; his efforts to use his position to land his wife a Chick-fil-A franchise; or the huge raises he secured for top aides in defiance of White House orders. As the scandals proliferated, so too did the congressional investigations into them. As those investigations progressed, they would turn up new, controversial details about Pruitt's conduct.

Even Pruitt's home life was embroiled in scandal. He had rented a room in a condo owned by the wife of a high-powered energy lobbyist, J. Steven Hart. Pruitt paid just $50 per night for a room in the

"Williams & Jensen house," as it was known among members of Congress, named for the firm that employed Hart. The sweetheart rate—no hotel in D.C. costs less than double what Pruitt was paying—raised persistent allegations of a conflict of interest.

Meanwhile, the same sort of controversy that dogged Tom Price was lingering around Pruitt. He was paying tens of thousands of dollars for private, charter, and first-class commercial jet travel and occasionally taking advantage of U.S. military aircraft for relatively short flights.

One EPA aide we spoke with compared the cascading series of controversies to the climactic battle scene at the end of *The Lord of the Rings: The Two Towers*. The heroes are attempting to repel a siege of orcs and find themselves forced to fight smaller skirmishes all over the walls of Helm's Deep. They beat back the invading horde in one corner of the battle, only to find themselves nearly overrun in another corner, where they must rush, swords drawn, to try to maintain their defenses. They're pulled in a million directions, but it seems as if they'll be able to hold off the enemy.

But then one giant orc, armed with a medieval explosive device, charges the wall, rests the bomb in a drainage passage at the base of the ramparts, and blows a giant hole in the heroes' defenses. The orcs come streaming through. This one disruptive blow turns the tide of the battle. The analogy wasn't perfect, of course; the orcs eventually lose when opposing reinforcements arrive. And by this point in Pruitt's tenure, reinforcements weren't looking likely.

The EPA aide compared that demolition of the wall to one Pruitt scandal in particular. The administrator had tasked one of his aides, his twenty-six-year-old scheduler Millan Hupp, with securing Pruitt a new mattress. Well, not new exactly. Pruitt actually wanted a used one. And he specifically wanted a used one from the Trump International

Hotel, which overlooks the EPA's headquarters. It was just one of a litany of controversies throughout 2018. What made the mattress dustup particularly damaging was not just the act in itself but how Pruitt handled it. His reaction crystallized what many who had passed through Pruitt's EPA in its first two years had come to realize: Like his boss, Pruitt demanded loyalty. But he would throw even his closest aides under the bus.

Hupp and her sister, Sydney, had both worked as servers at a Stillwater, Oklahoma, bar and grill called Eskimo Joe's before joining Pruitt's successful campaign for Oklahoma attorney general. They followed him to Washington, where they served as two of his closest and most trusted aides. But when Millan Hupp was dragged before a congressional committee in mid-2018 to testify about Pruitt's various spending controversies, she had no choice but to tell the truth about what she'd been ordered to do on her boss's behalf. Lying to Congress is itself a federal crime.

But Pruitt felt slighted. He considered the mattress anecdote particularly embarrassing. And he began lashing out at his scheduler in conversations with powerful allies in the conservative movement. Hupp had lied about his instructions, Pruitt alleged, or at least misunderstood them. Among the conservative luminaries he reached out to was Leonard Leo, the executive vice president of the powerful legal advocacy group the Federalist Society. Pruitt vented to Leo that Hupp had stabbed him in the back and wasn't to be trusted. The subtext of that conversation and similar ones around that time was obvious to Pruitt's allies: they were not to hire Hupp and supply her with a soft landing after her inevitable resignation from the EPA. Both Hupp sisters would eventually leave the agency and return to Oklahoma.

We still don't know why exactly Pruitt insisted on a Trump hotel mattress in particular—whether he'd stayed there once and simply liked the beds, or if it was some stranger attachment to things that bore the president's name. But we do know that the mattress saga represented the breaking of a dam that had held the EPA together during a tumultuous year. Current and former aides saw Pruitt growing paranoid and lashing out at staff, even those who considered themselves intensely loyal. His treatment of Hupp was particularly disturbing. And current and former aides who found themselves the targets of Pruitt-related investigations by Congress and agency watchdogs were struggling with massive legal bills. Pruitt, who'd created a legal defense fund to pay his own lawyers, wasn't even offering words of assurance, let alone financial assistance.

It was a cruel twist not just for Hupp but for the whole team of aides and advisers to a man who'd not just demanded loyalty from those around him but whose entire strategy for overcoming a year of bad press that would've taken down virtually any other administration official had revolved around unquestioning loyalty to his own boss.

From virtually the beginning of Pruitt's tenure, every public utterance by the agency, the administrator, or a member of his staff was calibrated to satisfy the tastes and sensibilities of precisely one guy—the only person who mattered. If those statements riled up the press, it wasn't just a necessary by-product; it was an added bonus. To the extent that Pruitt and his staff were seen as enemies of the fake news media, the thinking went, it would actually strengthen Pruitt's standing in the president's eyes.

But though Pruitt stayed in the president's good graces well into 2018 as additional scandals enveloped the EPA, Trump himself seemed to be the only person inside the White House standing by the embattled administrator. The agency's intense focus on pleasing the president meant, in many cases, either ignoring or working in active opposition to everyone else in the West Wing.

For Wilcox and his colleagues, trust of the White House eroded quickly. The EPA staff didn't feel that the midlevel West Wing staffers frequently assigned to assist Pruitt and other cabinet secretaries with public relations challenges were particularly adept at doing so. And worse, any discussions they had or material they shared with the West Wing seemed to inevitably leak to the press.

The breakdown in trust led to a breakdown in communication as the EPA staff resisted any effort by the White House to "help" Pruitt through the tumultuous first half of 2018. In April, the White House requested a complete list of the administrator's travel schedule and payments as controversy intensified over Pruitt's first-class air travel. The EPA completely ignored the request, even as it provided a steady stream of information to congressional investigators probing the matter. When Pruitt geared up for a pair of bruising congressional hearings in late April focusing on the various controversies dominating EPA headlines at the time, the White House reached out to the EPA and offered to help them prepare for the hearings. The EPA's response, in the words of one White House official, was "get lost." In the EPA's mind, they would at best provide poor advice on how to handle the hearings. At worst, Pruitt's strategy and talking points would end up in *The Washington Post* before the hearings even began.

As the EPA hunkered down and tried to weather the storm, many on Pruitt's staff considered senior White House officials just as hostile as adversarial journalists, congressional Democrats, or environmental groups determined to force Pruitt out. The White House chief of staff, John Kelly, was widely rumored to be angling for Pruitt's ouster. When the president called Pruitt in early April to offer some encouraging words—"keep your chin up," he told the administrator—Kelly followed up the next day with a far less amiable demand. These scandals had better stop, or your time in office will be coming to an end, he warned. A few weeks later, as Pruitt prepared for his pair of congressional interviews, senior White House staffers began reaching out to Republicans on the Hill and allies in the conservative movement cautioning them against defending Pruitt publicly. Better to cut bait, they intimated, than to further associate the Trump and Republican brands with an official who would soon be forced out under the weight of his escalating ethical troubles.

Tensions with the White House came to a head in May 2018. As Congress stepped up its Pruitt investigations, one name kept bubbling to the surface: Kevin Chmielewski, a Trump 2016 campaign advance staffer and Pruitt's former deputy chief of staff. He was well known to us; Pruitt aides had been pointing to him for months as the culprit behind a series of damaging press leaks that revealed much of the ethical conduct bedeviling Pruitt. Chmielewski had left the EPA in early 2018. He claimed to have resigned in protest of Pruitt's conduct. His former colleagues insisted he was fired for spotty attendance and lackluster time-card practices. In any case, Chmielewski had an ax to grind, and as Pruitt faced withering ethical scrutiny in mid-2018, his former senior aide went on the record in interviews with both congressional investigators and members of the press to hammer his former boss and allege widespread unethical, and perhaps illegal, conduct.

Here's where things get a bit complicated. It's a glimpse into how the sausage is often made in Washington, and it might make your head spin a bit. Here are the characters you need to know: Chmielewski, whom we've already met; the senior EPA press aide Michael Abboud; Secretary of the Interior Ryan Zinke; Alex Hinson, a top Zinke comms aide; Megyn Kelly, the former Fox News host who'd since landed at NBC; Michael Bastasch, a reporter at *The Daily Caller*; and Patrick Howley, then the editor in chief of the website Big League Politics.

In early May, Abboud was out at a party in Washington when he struck up a conversation with Hinson. Hinson hinted that Chmielewski had given an interview to Kelly for her new NBC show and that the interview would be extremely damaging to Pruitt. Abboud knew that Hinson and Chmielewski were friends and interpreted Hinson's comments as a signal that the two of them were collaborating to peddle dirt on Pruitt to the press.

The next day, Abboud called up Bastasch and Howley and told them that a top Zinke aide was collaborating with a disgruntled former Pruitt staffer who was trying to take down the EPA administrator. Word of that tip got back to Hinson, who informed the White House Office of Presidential Personnel, the West Wing office that oversees its cabinet agencies. And before the EPA knew what was happening, the story had been flipped on its ear: the emerging narrative wasn't that Hinson was helping Chmielewski peddle dirt on Pruitt; it was that Abboud was peddling dirt on Zinke in an effort to take the heat off his own boss. A story in *The Atlantic* on the dustup reported that the White House was livid not with Hinson or Chmielewski but with Abboud and the EPA.

The *Atlantic* story on the controversy was authored by Elaina Plott, a talented and well-sourced White House reporter who'd been doggedly chasing malfeasance and unrest at the EPA. "This did not happen, and it's categorically false," Wilcox told her for her story on the supposed Zinke-Pruitt feud. She'd already clashed with Wilcox over her reporting on the ouster of scheduling aide Millan Hupp. Once again she asked Wilcox for comment. "You have a great day," he told Plott. "You're a piece of trash."

The comment immediately reverberated around the Beltway, where Wilcox and the larger EPA press operation had already earned a reputation as the administration's most antagonistic press shop. Wilcox publicly apologized to Plott, and in our conversations with him he seemed genuinely remorseful that he'd allowed his emotions to get the best of him and crossed a line from antagonistic to hostile and insulting.

Privately, though, some Trump officials were giving Wilcox proverbial high fives. He'd said what many of them secretly wanted to say to the legions of perceived "enemies" in the political press corps. Indeed, the remark seemed like a natural—if perhaps extreme—extension of the press strategy that had kept Pruitt in office.

By that point, though, Wilcox and a number of his colleagues were burning out on the job. Pruitt seemed to have little concern for the aides who were going to the mat for him day in and day out. His compounding unforced errors, and the seeming blitheness of his increasingly problematic personal and ethical conduct, made defending him on a daily basis feel downright Sisyphean.

As it happened, Pruitt's days at the EPA were numbered anyway. Trump remained fond of his EPA chief in spite of all the controversies, and nearly as important Pruitt retained a key ally with the president's ear. In his corner was Harold Hamm, the billionaire oil and gas tycoon and high-dollar Republican fund-raiser who had thrown his full financial might behind the president's political and policy efforts, particularly in the areas of energy and environmental policy. Trump's reverence for Hamm, and the latter's backing of Pruitt, likely kept the EPA administrator in his post longer than anyone would've expected. But on July 4, 2018, during a meeting at the White House, Hamm finally gave his blessing to Pruitt's departure. We don't know what he told the president, but the weight of the scandals had simply become too much to bear. The next day, Pruitt announced his resignation.

MAKE AMERICA RAIN
AGAIN

Lachlan didn't write the headline, but the Trumpworld lobbyist extraordinaire David Urban will never let him live it down. "He Could Be Trump's 'Swampiest' Pick Yet" declared the headline of a June 2017 story about Urban, the principal at the K Street giant American Continental Group and then widely considered a contender to replace the outgoing White House chief of staff, Reince Priebus.

The story noted Urban's impressive list of high-dollar lobbying clients, which included Comcast, Monsanto, Walgreens, Raytheon, and Hewlett-Packard. ACG's nearly three dozen clients would present a real quagmire if Urban joined the White House, Lachlan wrote, given Trump's drain the swamp pledge and the ethics agreement he was requiring every administration appointee to sign, stipulating that they couldn't communicate with former clients while in government service or work on issues on which they'd lobbied for those clients. The ethics pledge would put wide swaths of policy work out of bounds for Urban absent a waiver to the pledge (waivers that Trump's White House has distributed liberally).

Urban didn't dispute anything in the story, but the headline clearly irked him. And it would continue to irk him for a long time. In

November 2018, Lachlan was on vacation in Europe when Urban texted, out of the blue, to see if there was any way we could change the headline more than eighteen months after the fact.

The headline remains as originally written, and Urban, though clearly bothered, has always been gracious about it. After the story ran, he invited Lachlan to his office to make introductions and put faces to names. It's a good way to inject some empathy into political reporting that, we're the first to admit, often glosses over the humanity of its subjects. Urban was friendly and affable, even after Lachlan showed up to the meeting late. Urban wore khaki shorts and a button-down, laughed about the *Daily Beast* story, and casually explained that while, yes, he was certainly a denizen of Washington's influence-brokering business, he took steps to disclose everything, to keep it all aboveboard, to avoid pushing any legal envelopes. The unspoken implication was that that set him apart from other Trumpworld figures plying their trade on K Street.

Urban helped spearhead Trump's political operation in Pennsylvania, which steered the state's electoral votes to the Republican presidential candidate for the first time since 1988. He was widely considered a candidate to chair the Republican National Committee but opted to stick with his thriving lobbying practice. And despite persistent whispers about a move into the White House, Urban seemed content to stay on K Street and continue plugging the president and his priorities through a steady stream of appearances on CNN, where he is a paid contributor.

Urban is the sort of political operative whom the cable networks simply can't resist in the Trump era. Those networks thrive on manufactured political antagonism, typified in the generic panel segment that pits a Republican against a Democrat, or a Trump supporter against a Trump opponent. But Trump's outsider status and the widespread distrust of or outright hostility to him among Beltway Republicans early in his political ascent meant that the crop of supporters from which the cable nets could draw was limited. If you were an out-and-proud Trump supporter in 2017, odds are you were already working in the administration or for one of the outside political groups supporting the president. But such overtly pro-Trump professions generally preclude a role as a regular pro-Trump cable commentator; the conflicts of interest are simply too apparent.

That meant that the networks increasingly turned to folks like Urban, Trump supporters who didn't have any official professional role in Trumpworld. But these aren't the sorts of people who are getting by on just the income provided by a cable news contract. Like Urban, they have day jobs and, more often than not, paying clients. The search for TV talent that would defend the president increasingly meant turning to people who work in Washington's sprawling political influence industry, whether as lobbyists, public relations executives, or "government affairs" advisers. Handed these powerful platforms, pro-Trump pundits have taken it upon themselves to go beyond simply defending the president and have actively gone to bat for the people and organizations that cut them huge checks to win favor and influence in Washington. In the Trump era, the influence business operates in greenrooms as much as boardrooms.

The cable networks didn't appear prepared for that dynamic. Fox, MSNBC, and CNN didn't have policies in place governing the appearance even of registered lobbyists on their networks, or whether their clients needed to be disclosed when discussing issues that might affect them. So when, for instance, Urban went on CNN in April 2019 to laud the proposed United States-Mexico-Canada free trade agreement, viewers had no idea that three days earlier he'd signed a lobbying deal for Trade Works for America, a dark money group working to ratify the deal.

The practice was by no means unique to Urban among cable news's pro-Trump pundits. The Republican consultant Scott Jennings routinely rails against clean energy and environmentalist policy proposals in his capacity as a CNN contributor. He's simultaneously working on behalf of some major coal, gas, and oil companies. The former campaign aide turned lobbyist Bryan Lanza even managed to exceed CNN's ad hoc restrictions on conflicts of interest among its on-air influence peddlers when he inveighed against the Mueller investigation while representing a Russian oligarch who was a person of interest in that investigation.

In their defense, Urban, Jennings, and Lanza were probably not doing anything that ran directly counter to their own political views. Jennings is a conservative; he's ideologically inclined to support a freer energy market that's naturally more beneficial to the fossil-fuel-dominated status quo. Lanza's former colleagues were caught up in what they all considered a sham investigation into Russia "collusion," and the oligarch he represented was collateral damage. And it was precisely the types of populist trade policies championed by the president that had put him over the edge in Urban's home state, so lobbying for a trade group supportive of those policies was a natural fit. But the fact remains that those conflicts of interest, undisclosed to cable news viewers watching them, ran afoul of basic standards of journalistic integrity.

Such conflicts aren't a new occurrence for cable news. What was new was the tremendous influence that such news programs wield over the attentions of the most powerful man in the American government. Urban-esque influence strategies, where a client gets a nice plug on the cable airwaves, were suddenly extremely potent tools for those in the lobbying game. And more broadly, people seeking influence and favor with the Trump administration were finding all sorts of new ways to ingratiate themselves with the president of the United States.

LARGE events are the lifeblood of Washington hotels, and few D.C. events are larger than trade association fly-ins. Industry lobbying groups bring their members to D.C., put them up in swanky suites, gather them in a hotel conference space, then send them over to Capitol Hill to hype their particular issue in the hope of getting some legislative carve-out or using the federal sledgehammer to keep a competitor at bay. Such events are by their nature political, so naturally, in the Trump era, the president's hotel has become a chosen destination. Simply by virtue of a hotel choice, part of a group's lobbying is already done!

So it was that the Seasonal Employment Alliance ended up at the Trump International Hotel in mid-2018. The group represents employers that rely on so-called H-2B visas, tens of thousands of which are given out each year to immigrant laborers who are granted temporary stay in the United States for nonagricultural jobs, typically in retail and hospitality. The industry has long been plagued by a stringent cap on the number of visas the Department of Homeland Security will give out each year. So politics is, for better or worse, integral to the business model, and its trade association is therefore essential.

On the board of the SEA is Veronica Birkenstock, the chief executive of the Texas-based H-2B agency Practical Employee Solutions. She is by most measures your average Trump-era red-meat conservative. She's pro-life and anti–gun control and favors lower tax rates. Even on the immigration issue, she's said she supports deporting illegal immigrants and building a wall on the southern border. But Birkenstock

also makes a living importing low-skilled laborers from foreign countries, an issue that repeatedly came up in 2018 as she challenged Representative Michael Burgess of Texas in an unsuccessful Republican
primary bid. Burgess's campaign even set up a website, dubbed the
Truth About Veronica Birkenstock, that called her "a political chame-
leon" whose "real business and actual political record prove she supports and lobbies Congress to give American jobs to foreigners over
Americans."

Birkenstock did her best to fend off the attacks, devoting significant
chunks of her own campaign website to attempts to debunk what she
called "myths" about the H-2B program. But the line of attack was a
potent one in a border-state Republican primary in the era of Donald
Trump. Which made it all the more ironic that Trump himself is one
of Birkenstock's clients.

Every year, the president uses the H-2B program to bring in scores
of temporary laborers to fill positions in his resorts as maids, servers,
dishwashers, bartenders, and landscapers. And for years, he's had
Birkenstock's company on contract to facilitate that immigrant labor
at his Trump International Beach Resort in Miami, for which Practical
Employment Solutions has secured more than a hundred temporary
foreign worker visas.

Birkenstock's company wasn't the only, or even the primary, H-2B
broker that the Trump Organization kept on retainer; it continues to take
full advantage of the program in its notorious and occasionally legally
questionable efforts to minimize labor costs at its various hotels, resorts,
and golf clubs. So when the Seasonal Employment Alliance visited
Trump's hotel in Washington, it was courting an obvious ally.

But the group wasn't going to take any chances. So in late 2018, it
brought on some more lobbying muscle from K Street—the heart of
lobbying in D.C. Its new representatives, Cove Strategies, would go

about attempting to secure more visas for low-skilled immigrants even as they proudly waved the banner of a president who, notwithstanding the hiring practices of his own company, insisted, at least publicly, on putting America first.

Few in Washington have so seamlessly made the transition from establishment swamp creatures to Trump devotees as the Cove Strategies principal Matt Schlapp and his wife, Mercedes, whom you might remember as the top White House comms aide turned Trump campaign bigwig who dubbed her colleague Kelly Sadler a "bitch" after Sadler ratted her out to the president. The Schlapps have carved out a niche for themselves as a Trump-era power couple, wielding influence in the president's inner circle and translating that influence into lucrative lobbying deals. And they do it all behind a veneer of authenticity and principle, putting on an air of indignation anytime someone—say, us—suggests that they're motivated by anything but an earnest desire for American greatness.

Trumpworld is full of hucksters who try to cloak their naked self-interest in the demagogic language of America First populism. But the Schlapps appear to effortlessly meld their political, ideological, and financial pursuits such that it's often difficult to figure out where one begins and another ends. And few in D.C. have shown themselves more adept at couching their private financial interests in language that appeals to Trump in particular. They're the ultimate Trump-era influence peddlers, simply because they know how—and are in a position—to influence the one man who matters in Washington today. And they have no compunctions about fully capitalizing on that ability.

MATT Schlapp's lucrative role as a for-hire Trump whisperer was on full display in mid-2019. He managed to turn the president's disdain for a top 2020 rival into a legislative force that nearly sank supposedly uncontroversial legislation opposed by a casino company that had hired Schlapp just months earlier.

The company was called the Twin River Management Group, and in early 2019 it hired a coterie of Trumpworld luminaries to oppose the Mashpee Wampanoag Indian tribe's efforts to obtain official federal recognition. The tribe wanted to build a casino in Taunton, Massachusetts, that threatened to compete with a Twin River casino in nearby Rhode Island. Twin River brought on Schlapp's Cove Strategies and the firm Black Diamond Strategies, which tasked the former Trump campaign aides Doug Davenport and Rick Wiley with the account. Twin River clearly needed to get in the president's good graces.

Schlapp, it turned out, was the man for the job. The House of Representatives and its new Democratic majority were considering legislation to recognize the Mashpee Wampanoag, and they considered the bill mundane enough to bring to the House floor under a process known as suspension. The suspension process requires a two-thirds vote to pass legislation and is generally reserved for uncontroversial legislation and designed to keep the chamber's legislative business moving along. Democrats expected that few would care or notice that its Mashpee Wampanoag legislation was receiving a vote.

But then Trump tweeted. "Republicans shouldn't vote for H.R. 312, a special interest casino Bill, backed by Elizabeth (Pocahontas) Warren," the president declared. "It is unfair and doesn't treat Native Americans equally!" This from a man who, in congressional testimony opposing Native American casino competitors to his Atlantic City resorts in the early 1990s, said, "They don't look like Indians to me."

There is exactly zero chance that Trump was aware that that legislation was coming to the floor before someone whispered in his ear. Who could that have been? Well, just an hour before Trump's tweet,

Schlapp had weighed in. And it just so happened that he'd invoked Warren's supposed support for the bill as well, with a not-too-subtle nod to controversy over her claimed Indian heritage that dogged her early presidential campaign. **"Soon full House will vote to reward Sen Elizabeth Warren with ... wait for it ... an INDIAN casino in Massachusetts,"** Schlapp jibed.

What happened was obvious: Schlapp saw that Democrats were bringing a bill to the floor that his client opposed, and he tailored a very Trumpian pitch in an effort to sink it—likely something to the effect of "'Pocahontas' Warren supports this bill; you should oppose it." The strategy worked, at least temporarily. House Democrats were caught off guard by the president's tweet. Knowing that it would marshal enough Republican opposition to an otherwise uncontroversial bill, and that it wouldn't be able to get the two-thirds vote required to pass it under suspension, they pulled the bill from the floor. It passed days later under normal House procedure.

The whole episode was instructive about what Trump-era lobbying by the president's K Street allies entails. We wrote a story to that effect. Schlapp responded with a pair of tweets. **"My wife and I follow the law, and she had no role in my advocacy,"** he wrote. **"The implication that this President marches to the beat of any drum other than his own is an absurd assertion."**

That last sentence gets to the heart of it. The suggestion that the president does his thing and can't be influenced by those around him is, to borrow Schlapp's phrase, absurd. It is of course true that Trump has his notorious idiosyncrasies and makes and comments on policy at the whim of his own addled psyche. But that is exactly why the Matt Schlapps of the world have been able to carve out such lucrative influence-peddling practices in the Trump era. Schlapp understands how the president ticks, and has the access and opportunity to act on that knowledge. Invoking "Pocahontas" to try to sink legislation that Trump wouldn't have been aware of otherwise was vintage Trump-era lobbying. Schlapp figured out the president's pressure point and then applied pressure. And true to form, he then tried to play off his advocacy as a principled position against cronyism, rather than a naked example of it.

It couldn't have been more obvious that Schlapp's lobbying on behalf of Twin River Management wasn't motivated by any real convictions or beliefs. Just a few months earlier, the conservative nonprofit that Schlapp runs on the side, the American Conservative Union, had put on its annual Conservative Political Action Conference. One panel at the event was titled "All Nations, One America: Why Conservatives Should Support Tribal Sovereignty."

CPAC, as the conference is known for short, quickly became a case study in the Trumpification of the conservative movement and the Republican Party. And that shift happened to coincide with Schlapp's transition from a generic, if swampy, Republican operative—he can be seen in a famous photo of the Brooks Brothers riot, among a group of Republican staffers who stormed a Miami-Dade polling location during the 2000 presidential recount—to one of the country's foremost Trump sycophants, and one who's cashing in on the role to boot.

The American Conservative Union's annual confab draws Republican politicians, activists, and voters from across the country and legions of journalists reporting on what was once a seminal annual event. The conference used to be a blast to cover. It was where elements of the conservative movement would gather to make their particular visions for the movement known or pitch their pet issues. When we first started covering the event in the early years of the second decade of the twenty-first century, CPAC was famously a place where the GOP's libertarian and social conservative wings would square off. Indeed, a flaxen-haired real estate developer of some note made waves in 2011 when, at the height of his Obama birther phase, he spoke at CPAC and derided the libertarian crank Ron Paul's 2012 election hopes, to cheers and jeers from the crowd.

The conflict made CPAC interesting. It made it entertaining. It made it a meaningful event. And it all but disappeared in February 2017. Overnight, the conference had become the Trump Show. When the conservative columnist Mona Charen was booed off the stage that year for criticizing Trump's predatory sexual proclivities, the then Breitbart editor Raheem Kassam stated, aptly, "Frankly [Never Trump conservatives] have no place at Trump-era CPACs anyway." For better or worse, he was entirely correct.

Schlapp was fully on the Trump Train at this point, so that was just fine by him ideologically. But it also presented exciting new opportunities to meld his roles as a lobbyist and an ostensible purveyor of conservative ideas. CPAC already had a reputation as a pay-to-play operation—pony up tens or hundreds of thousands of dollars to sponsor the conference, and you get lots of perks and access to its influential attendees—but even former ACU board members told us that Schlapp had taken access peddling at the conference to new heights, even giving sponsors the opportunity to shape the programming of the event.

So it was that CPAC 2018 featured a panel discussion on a totally obscure policy fight over foreign airlines' access to U.S. airports. The details of the policy fight are less relevant than how it was marketed at CPAC, where the conference's official social media channels hailed it as an imperative for the Trump agenda to crack down on unfair trade practices. It just so happened that Schlapp had been lobbying for Delta Air Lines on the precise issue, and on the precise side of the issue, that the conference was promoting. And a trade association representing Delta and two other U.S. airlines had written ACU a $125,000 check to underwrite that year's CPAC.

Schlapp is very sensitive to accusations that he uses his post at ACU, and its CPAC conference, to sell access and influence to special interests, including his own lobbying clients. Lachlan reported on the practice from CPAC 2018, and when the following year's conference rolled around, he once again inquired with ACU's spokesperson about a pair of top CPAC donors. Within minutes, Schlapp had personally called our editor to demand an explanation for those questions.

MERCEDES Schlapp nearly always kept her West Wing office door open, so it was odd in mid-2018 when, after inviting her colleague Cliff Sims to a meeting with a few people he'd never met before, Mercy (as colleagues know her) closed the door behind them. Even Sims's presence at the meeting was a bit odd, acquaintances of each remarked to us; he and Schlapp weren't out-and-proud internal enemies, but their relationship wasn't exactly warm either. But she said she wanted Sims's help with something, so he made the trek of a dozen or so feet from his office to hers.

Schlapp sat behind her desk as Sims took a chair against the wall. She made introductions. Sims was seated next to Van Hipp, a former chairman of the South Carolina GOP and one of D.C.'s premier Pentagon lobbyists. On a small couch in the office were two people one would normally be surprised to find in the Trump White House: Rick Harrison, co-owner of Las Vegas's World Famous Gold & Silver Pawn Shop, better known for his starring role in the History series *Pawn Stars*, and, sitting beside him, an employee of his production company.

"I wanted to bring everyone together because I think Van and

Rick have a wonderful idea that can help the president," Schlapp told the room.

Then it got weird.

She turned the meeting over to Hipp and Harrison, who proceeded to pitch Sims on their idea for what amounted to a reality-TV show starring the president of the United States while he was still the sitting president of the United States. They were working on a pitch for a new television series, with each episode focusing on a particular historical event. They wanted to enlist Trump for on-camera interviews once a week focusing on each episode's particular topic, according to several people with knowledge of their plans at the time.

Throughout the meeting, Schlapp kept talking up Sims. He's your guy, she told Hipp and Harrison. He does all the video work with the president. They see each other every morning. He can make this happen. He can go and pitch the president on the idea.

Sims was trying to be polite, but he explained that there was no way they could fit weekly on-camera interviews into the president's schedule like that. Hipp and Harrison anticipated the snag. Perhaps, they suggested, they could tail the president during his morning walk from the bottom of the residence elevator over to the Oval Office.

The meeting ended without any commitments, but Schlapp repeatedly followed up with Sims in the following weeks, pressing him on whether he'd pitched the president on the idea. The whole thing seemed very strange to Sims, who confided in multiple associates and friends about this strange occurrence, trying to figure out what on earth was going on. Why was Schlapp so big on this obscure idea? And why was she bringing it to him, rather than pitching the president herself, as her access to Trump would certainly allow?

Things really crystallized when Sims and others began asking around about Hipp. It turned out that he is a board member of Matt

Schlapp's American Conservative Union. And nestled among Hipp's high-profile defense and pharmaceutical lobbying clients was a conspicuous one signed in late 2017: Rick Harrison Productions. Hipp had been at the White House meeting plugging his client's latest project. Interestingly, Hipp didn't disclose lobbying the West Wing on Harrison's behalf until late 2018, after Sims left the White House.

The realization of all those connections also provided a clue about why Schlapp had come to Sims instead of pitching the president directly. She and her husband recoil at any suggestion that they're using their positions and influence with the president to advance their private interests. Having Sims propose the idea would provide a degree of separation: the Schlapps could claim it wasn't their idea; it was Sims's.

Harrison's history show never ended up happening. But in February of the following year, his fans could still find him addressing the main stage at the Conservative Political Action Conference.

When Swin approached Sims—who by that point did not want to punch the *Beast* reporter right in the jaw, for the record—about this story for our book in September 2019, Sims just chuckled and said, "No, thanks, I'm good. But I do love *Pawn Stars*."

➤ "I HAVE NO CLIENTS WHATSOEVER"

I f it seems that we're devoting an inordinate amount of space in this book to Corey Lewandowski, well, it is a lot of space, but it's not inordinate. The man who was canned from the Trump campaign after assaulting a Breitbart reporter, helped to take down a White House chief of staff, and has been eyeing a U.S. Senate run in New Hampshire (this book is scheduled to be released around the time of the New Hampshire primaries, so good luck, Corey!) is in so many ways a walking microcosm of the minions and misfits for whom we've titled this book.

We've followed Lewandowski's campaign to maintain his influence in the White House despite being widely reviled by virtually everyone in the West Wing not named Donald Trump. He was working so hard to maintain that influence for very tangible, financial reasons: from the first days of the Trump administration, Lewandowski had carved out for himself a very lucrative practice as what is commonly known in Washington as a shadow lobbyist.

Lewandowski is not a lobbyist as it's narrowly defined legally. But neither are the legions of influence industry professionals in Washington with titles like "public affairs consultant" and "vice president for government relations." Thousands of people ply their trade on K Street without ever officially crossing a very specific legal threshold into "lob-bying," which would require them to publicly disclose all sorts of infor-mation about their clients, how much those clients are paying, and what they're paying for. And Corey Lewandowski is the Trump era's quintessential shadow lobbyist.

He lost out on a Trump administration gig, due in large measure to the widespread distrust and antipathy he had drawn from elements of the president's inner circle. So he opted to ply his trade in the influence business. As the Trump administration kicked into gear, Lewandowski teamed up with his fellow 2016 campaign hand Barry Bennett to form Avenue Strategies, the first major Trumpworld lobbying shop. By mid-2017, Avenue had signed ten clients, including the Bank of Beirut, the U.S. arm of Venezuela's state-owned oil company, a division of the Puerto Rican government, and a leading payday lender called Com-munity Choice Financial.

Avenue's very first federal lobbying client was more obscure. About two weeks after Trump was inaugurated, it signed a deal with a com-pany called Flow Health, which had developed artificial intelligence technology that it said could help predict disease by synthesizing large amounts of genomic data. The company had just seen its five-year con-tract with the Department of Veterans Affairs canceled, due primarily to opposition from David Shulkin, the top health official at the VA at the time. Some of the concerns about the company's business model seemed reasonable: it planned to collect massive amounts of data from American veterans, but all of that data would be proprietary and used to build a database of information that would redound to Flow Health's financial benefit. But while privacy and data security were valid con-cerns, others raised just prior to the contract's cancellation were out-landish. One writer on the VA beat noted that Flow Health had a Russian sister company, and warned breathlessly, "Russian software programmers, possibly some of the same programs linked to the election scandal, were being recruited to work for Flow Health."

There was no evidence supporting that outlandish allegation. But if it wanted to ward off such claims, or more founded concerns about privacy and data security, the company needed a lobbying firm to help it get back in the VA's good graces.

"We were going to hire another traditional lobbying firm, and then when Corey announced, I said this makes perfect sense," Flow Health's CEO, Alex Meshkin, told us. "New White House, new games, let's go hook up with someone who can get us in the right door." He met with Bennett and Lewandowski, who assured him of their deep relationships with the president and their ability to bend VA policy in the right direction. Trump, they assured Meshkin, would be breaking from Obama-era VA policy in a big way. That was good news for Flow Health, and Meshkin was hopeful that his company would soon be back at work.

That hope dissipated a bit when Avenue sent over its lobbying contract for him to sign. The document was copied in large part from a sample contract on the website LawDepot.com. "Our in-house general counsel is like, 'Are we really going to do this deal?'" Meshkin remembers. Flow Health did end up doing the deal, or at least their part of it. They signed the LawDepot contract and sent it back to Avenue. But the firm's representatives never inked their end.

Despite the lack of a fully executed agreement, Avenue started doing some work for the company, if not quite at the high level they promised. Meshkin says Lewandowski arranged a meeting at the firm's offices, where he promised a sit-down with the VA's general counsel. Instead, Meshkin showed up to find a former Trump campaign aide who'd been put in charge of some VA issues during the transition. Meanwhile, Shulkin, Flow Health's prime enemy at the VA, had been unanimously confirmed by the Senate to continue to lead the agency. Bennett and Lewandowski assured Meshkin that "it's a good thing for us. He's just happy to have the position. He's gonna listen to everything Mr. Trump tells him to do." But he wasn't doing what Flow Health needed him to do—reinstate their VA contract.

Finally, one of Avenue's lobbyists, another former Trump campaign aide named Mike Rubino, informed Meshkin that Corey was going to "make the call"; at long last, he would exercise his supposed pull with the president on Flow Health's behalf. This is what Meshkin had hired Avenue for. He spoke to Lewandowski in late March. As far as he knows, "the call" never happened. Lewandowski stopped returning his calls. They didn't have a signed agreement, and eventually Meshkin just decided to walk away.

The whole episode left him wondering just how much pull Lewandowski and his ilk really had. "All these people attached to Trump that are peddling influence—how much of that information actually makes it into the White House?" Meshkin wondered aloud.

WHETHER Bennett, Lewandowski, and the rest really had the access they claimed depended on whom you asked. The internal jockeying for power and attention that dominated the early days of the White House was mirrored by those seeking to influence it from the outside. That meant for every person claiming intimate access to and sway over the president's thinking and decision making, there were just as many rushing to tell colleagues, reporters, and potential clients that that person was full of shit and that the president didn't even know his name, let alone seek his counsel.

But regardless of the level of actual influence wielded by Trumpworld's K Street contingent, they did indisputably have one very valuable commodity: an understanding of how the president thinks, operates, and comes to a decision. Trump is, to put it mildly, unlike his predecessors. An influence industry built around processes and modes of thinking designed with your standard postwar White House in mind was no longer operative in January 2017. Titans of the influence industry and their deep-pocketed clients all found themselves scrambling for someone who could at the very least tell them what the president was likely thinking on a given issue, how he'd go about making a decision, or the points to stress in trying to push him in one direction or another.

This new class of Trumpworld political influencers could market just that ability, and the financial upside was tremendous. Even without the ability to influence the president himself, a lobbyist's ability to predict which way the president would lean on a given issue could be tremendously valuable for a Fortune 500 company or a foreign government. And Trump's idiosyncrasies turned even mundane insights into his style of governance into K Street gold.

Few seeking influence in Trump's Washington knew how to deal, for instance, with this new president's caustic and chaotic Twitter presence. Never had a commander in chief so breezily issued official statements on any matter to cross his mind. Such statements moved markets, affected international diplomacy, and upended congressional negotiations. So when Lewandowski's Avenue Strategies opened up shop on December 21, 2016, it marketed an influence service that would have been laughable in any previous administration but was suddenly a very real financial concern for potential clients, and even had a new moniker.

"'Tweet risk' is now officially part of the Wall Street lexicon," declared a popular financial news site the day after Trump's inauguration. "The President of the United States is effectively commandeering entire companies via Twitter and forcing those companies to rethink their business models in the space of just a few hours . . . Worse, it's not clear that Trump's tweets are carefully considered—and that's putting it very, very kindly. More often than not, he seems to say whatever's on his mind irrespective of the impact 140 characters can have on corporate management teams that can't afford to wait and see if the new President really means it when he threatens punishing tariffs or whether he was just angry-tweeting (that's the Presidential equivalent of drunk-texting) at 3 in the morning."

For multinational corporations worth tens of billions of dollars, the uncertainty that came with tweet risk was untenable. But here were Trump's new cohort of aides turned lobbyists, and they promised to help insulate your company from the financial catastrophe that might ensue if the president decided to go after you by name on his kinetic Twitter account.

The first tweet risk occurred just a day after Avenue opened. On December 22, Trump opened fire on the defense contractor Lockheed Martin. **"Based on the tremendous cost and cost overruns of the Lockheed Martin F-35, I have asked Boeing to price-out a comparable F-18 Super Hornet!"** the president-elect declared. Losing out on the exorbitantly expensive F-35 contract would have been catastrophic for Lockheed. So the company turned to Avenue for advice on navigating this new administration. It retained Lewandowski and Bennett to shore up the company's relationship with the president.

"What people don't understand is how transactional he is," Bennett told us a couple years later. "He's perfectly willing to give you a win for a win for himself." And sure enough, Avenue was able to get Lockheed back in Trump's good graces in exchange for a talking point that the new president could trumpet as an early success for his administration. "I was able to get $600 million approximately off those planes," Trump said in an interview a few weeks later after a meeting with Lockheed's CEO, confirming that the F-35 project would move forward. It was a lie—those savings were announced long before the meeting—but Avenue had succeeded in preserving the company's relationship with the president by providing Trump with a fig leaf of self-promotion. Lockheed had tried to win Trump over with a mundane presentation on its improving financials and the importance of the F-35 project. But Trump doesn't care about the particulars; Avenue knew that all he wanted was a win for himself, never mind the actual substance of his objections. They gave him that, and business proceeded as usual. It was a thoroughly Trumpian bit of D.C. power brokering, and Avenue's understanding of Trump's approach to policy, and his unquenchable thirst for self-affirmation, might have saved Lockheed billions.

For policy wins like that, companies were willing to shell out a lot of money to these new K Street players. In D.C.'s influence industry, chaos and uncertainty mean a financial windfall. Businesses hate uncertainty, and anyone who can provide a measure of stability is a sought-after commodity. Firms with the ability to read or influence the president began raking in cash. It didn't even take much effort; the big clients were seeking them out. "I'll give you the secret of my marketing success: 'Hello,'" quipped Bennett. "They called. I never pitched. They just started calling . . . In our first week in business, we probably had 50 people who were trying to hire us . . . because they didn't know who else to go to."

It was a gold rush for Avenue. But as is often the case with Lewandowski, tension with colleagues soon proved untenable. He absolutely did not want to register as a lobbyist. Which is tough to do when you run a lobbying firm. And his characteristically caustic public persona was proving a liability for Avenue.

"Corey was a big name and a big target," Bennett told *The Washington Post* at the time. "The firm has been growing yet everything the firm did was associated with Corey, even though we have a lot of clients who Corey has not even met."

THE nice thing about being a shadow lobbyist is you can lie with impunity. There's no way to verify through public records that a shadow lobbyist represents a particular client or to see which issues he's working on or which officials he's contacting on clients' behalves. It's a black box of information, and that opacity served Lewandowski well as he continued peddling influence for special interests and flatly denying that's what he was doing.

Shortly after his departure from Avenue, Lewandowski was back on the TV news circuit. In mid-2017, he appeared on NBC's *Meet the Press*, where he launched into a soliloquy on the president's aggressive and hopeful legislative agenda, including tax reform, destroying Obamacare, and erecting a wall on the southern border. But then he mentioned a policy agenda item that was bizarre in its obscurity and randomness. "I think the general [John Kelly] should re-look at firing Richard Cordray," he remarked of the then director of the Consumer Financial Protection Bureau. "He is a person who is now all but running for governor in the state of Ohio and he's sitting in federal office right now."

The host, Chuck Todd, was taken aback. "I have to say, Corey, that was sort of a random thing you just introduced there. What's with the focus on Mr. Cordray? How is that at the top of the agenda there?" he asked. "Do you have any business interest here? Do you have a client that wants to see this happen?"

"No, no," Lewandowski insisted. "I have no clients whatsoever."

A month later, *The New York Times* reported that Community Choice Financial, a payday lender and former Avenue client that really wanted Cordray gone, had offered his new firm, Lewandowski Strategic Advisors, $20,000 per month to advocate on its behalf. Called on that reporting, Lewandowski tried to deny that he represented the company while leaving just enough wiggle room. The contract was never executed, he claimed. "They were a client under my previous firm. I left the firm in May." Asked whether he had consulted for Community Choice, even absent that contract, Lewandowski said, "I give advice—free advice—all the time. And when people call me, you know what I do? I answer their telephone calls."

About six weeks after the interview, Community Choice signed a new lobbying contract. The company began paying Turnberry Solutions, a new firm founded by the Avenue alums Mike Rubino and Jason Osborne and headquartered in the "Lewandowski Embassy." Corey denied up and down for months that he had anything to do with the lobbying shop based out of his house. Then, in early 2019, Turnberry officially hired him.

Lewandowski still clings to the fact that he is not, and has never been, a registered lobbyist. In fact, he's carved out a far more cushy position for himself as a K Street middleman. Rather than do the lobbying himself, he connects clients with firms that do the real legwork, and takes a percentage of the fees those clients pay. Sources familiar with his work have said those fees range from 10 to 25 percent. Community Choice alone has paid Turnberry $20,000 per month—incidentally the same fee it was reported the company had paid to Lewandowski's firm—which would net Lewandowski a nice fee for doing none of the actual advocacy work.

But on K Street, the real money lies in foreign government advocacy, and Lewandowski has thrown his very sharp elbows about in an effort to secure those high-dollar contracts for firms that can steer him some large finder's fees. And that role has put him at the center of a D.C. drama so bizarre that it could only ever have occurred in the era of President Donald Trump.

WHEN we reached out to a spokesperson for Jill Kelley, his chief complaint was that we referred to her as a Washington "socialite." The term was inherently sexist, he claimed. You wouldn't call a man a "socialite," would you? The gripe was fair as far as it went, but whether she likes it or not, Kelley is most famous for her role in a sex scandal that brought down one of the most celebrated military officers of the twenty-first century. Kelley was the target of a harassment and stalking campaign perpetrated by Paula Broadwell, a journalist and biographer of the disgraced former general David Petraeus. Broadwell viewed Kelley as a threat and pursued a harassment campaign against her that burst into public view when Petraeus was relieved of duty after it was revealed that he shared classified information with Broadwell, with whom he was having a romantic affair.

By the time that scandal exploded into public view in 2012, Kelley was a darling of high-profile military officers including the Marine general Jim Mattis, who would go on to serve as Trump's secretary of defense. She cultivated extensive connections at the Pentagon and even received honorary ambassador titles from U.S. Central Command, which Mattis then led, and the South Korean embassy in Washington. From Washington and her home in Tampa, Florida, Kelley served as an informal agent of U.S. foreign policy, connecting high-ranking military and diplomatic officials with their foreign counterparts in an informal, disarming setting. Senior officials in the United States and abroad reportedly adored her, and Kelley became something of a diplomatic power broker akin to famous past socialites such as Joanne Herring, of *Charlie Wilson's War* fame.

Whether "socialite" was a fair descriptor or not, Kelley cherished the role, and it proved both lucrative and fulfilling. When the Polish government sought U.S. assistance in beefing up its missile defense system in early 2017, the potential business opportunity for Kelley was a twofer: she could help advance Western geopolitical interests by facilitating Eastern European defenses against Russian encroachment and simultaneously get a piece of what was sure to be a high-dollar D.C. lobbying deal.

The client in that deal would be Poland's state-owned defense contractor conglomerate, Polska Grupa Zbrojeniowa, or the Polish Armaments Group in English. Made up of about sixty military, defense, and aerospace contractors, the group was looking for help enhancing the country's Wisla and Homar missile defense programs. Kelley had been tipped off to the opportunity by a contact in the Polish embassy who said PGZ was looking for new representation in Washington. Kelley didn't have the expertise to do that lobbying herself. What she did have was an uncanny ability to connect the right people, help them build relationships, and see that a deal was done.

She was savvy enough to know, during the first year of the Trump presidency, that arranging the right meetings would require bringing on board someone with high-level connections in the new administration. And it appears Kelley had already built a relationship with Lewandowski; in late 2017, they co-hosted a party at the Trump International Hotel to celebrate the first anniversary of Trump's election victory. Kelley began telling friends around D.C. that she and Lewandowski were teaming up to land PGZ a high-dollar lobbying deal that would help facilitate some major missile defense contracts.

Lewandowski, apparently, had other ideas.

At the time, he was still vehemently denying that he was doing any "foreign work," or any work on behalf of Turnberry Solutions. But in July 2017, he received an email from Ed Rogers, a veteran Republican lobbyist and principal at BGR Group, a powerhouse firm founded by the former Mississippi governor Haley Barbour. Rogers wanted an update on Lewandowski's contacts with the Azerbaijani ambassador to the United States, a BGR client. "Corey, we're [sic] you able to talk to the Azerbaijan ambassador?" he asked, according to a copy of the email that we reviewed. "Call and let's catch up for 15 minutes." Rogers cc'd Turnberry's Mike Rubino on the email. And Lewandowski, it turned out, was promising the Azerbaijani ambassador access to the Trump White House.

At the same time, Lewandowski was sitting in on Turnberry conference calls with clients and on one occasion traveled with Rubino and Osborne to Poland to court business there. That turned out to be the same business for which Kelley had brought Lewandowski aboard. But Lewandowski had already cut her out—or "fucked her over," as one source familiar with the arrangement described it to us. Instead of working with Kelley to facilitate a PGZ lobbying deal, Lewandowski did the connecting himself and landed BGR the contract independent of Kelley.

The contract, worth $70,000 per month, was officially signed on October 25, 2017. It's not clear what Lewandowski's cut of the PGZ-BGR deal was. But the lower end of his reported referral fees would've netted him $3,500 per month just for making introductions. And his jaunt to Poland with the Turnberry guys paid off as well. In January 2018, BGR signed Osborne as a subcontractor on its PGZ and Azerbaijan accounts. Three months later, it brought on Rubino too. When BGR signed the Polish Ministry of Defense in early 2019, it added Osborne to that account as well.

The PGZ contract was inked right before Kelley and Lewandowski co-hosted their Trump International Hotel election anniversary bash. But Kelley didn't know she'd been cut out until the contract showed up on the Justice Department's website, where all lobbyists and public relations professionals must disclose their relationships with foreign government clients. That didn't happen until November 20, about two weeks after the party.

Kelley had been partying at the Trump International Hotel with the very man who had just screwed her out of a lobbying deal that she herself had put together and brought to him. Lewandowski hadn't bothered to mention it.

▶ "THAT CHAPTER ISN'T CLOSED"

I n his years as an investigative reporter, Lachlan had spent an inordinate amount of time poring over financial records on file with the Federal Election Commission, the nation's elections and campaign finance regulator. Hundreds of hours spent scrolling through those documents meant he had a sense for what these records generally looked like and what is and is not a noteworthy bit of information. So in late 2018, as Lachlan sifted through a quarterly financial filing from the pro-Trump group America First Action, one particular line item, a $325,000 contribution from a company called Global Energy Producers LLC, practically leaped off the page.

He thought he'd just stumbled on a shady campaign donor. But a year of digging instead turned up a motley band of Trump-backing businessmen with some very shady associations, a cockamamie strategy to cash in on the Trump presidency, and an alliance with the president's personal lawyer that they'd try to use to kneecap political rivals from Hillary Clinton to Joe Biden to a career U.S. ambassador.

It turned out he'd also just stumbled on the fringes of a scheme by the president to solicit foreign government assistance with his reelection efforts, a scheme that would eventually result in a congressional impeachment investigation that once again engulfed the White House in a scandal very reminiscent of the Russia collusion inquiry that had dogged Trump's first two years in office.

The Mueller affair had its own quixotic, thoroughly Trumpian cast of characters at its center, replete with the typical idiocy and bombast that we—and hopefully, by this point in the book, you too—have come to expect from the president's team. But those characters were, by and large, known quantities at that point, people like Roger Stone, Paul Manafort, and Michael Flynn.

The Global Energy Producers fiasco offered a whole new casting call for the Trump show blooper reel. And these guys were on our radar before anyone else's. Initially, it wasn't because they'd attempted to assist Trump and Giuliani in their efforts to usurp a democratic contest. It was simply because the guys behind it, a repeated failure of a penny stock investor and a Ukrainian businessman with ties to the country's own corrupt political machine, had all of a sudden decided they too were going to be players in the vast expanse of amateurish graft that has defined the forty-fifth president's tenure.

America First is a notable node in the Trump graft network. It is the official super PAC of the Trump political operation. That's supposed to be an oxymoron; in theory, super PACs are wholly independent of the candidates they support. That's why they can accept and spend unlimited amounts of money, including contributions from corporations and labor unions. But that's mostly a legal fiction effectively circumvented by both political parties in ways that don't run afoul of rules barring campaigns from coordinating with super PACs. Barack Obama and Hillary Clinton both pioneered novel legal strategies for maximizing coordination with their supportive super PACs without crossing legal boundaries.

But Trump dispensed with the pretense altogether. In early 2019, he publicly endorsed America First as the official "independent" supporter of his reelection effort. Donating to America First, itself a landing ground for presidential loyalists hounded from more respectable corners of Trumpworld, was effectively the same as donating to Trump's reelection campaign. The contributions would just be routed through a different legal entity.

America First has received some massive financial contributions from big names in Republican fund-raising. The casino mogul Sheldon Adelson and his wife have each chipped in $5 million. The California real estate developer Geoff Palmer has donated $6 million. The group has counted no fewer than fourteen separate million-dollar donations since 2017.

Those were all noteworthy and impressive. But as Lachlan perused the group's financial records in late 2018, none of those donations stuck out like the six-figure contribution earlier that year from Global Energy Producers. What made it so noteworthy was that there was no record of this company's actually doing anything. There was barely a record of its existence. Incorporation documents on file in Delaware, a state renowned for the secrecy it affords companies headquartered there, showed that GEP had been formed just a month before its huge donation to America First. It had also written a $50,000 check to the Republican Ron DeSantis's successful Florida gubernatorial campaign.

The key to investigative reporting in the digital age is to find any unique bit of information—a name, a phone number, an address, a website—and plumb public records for every bit of insight you can glean on the people and organizations associated with it. Delaware makes it virtually impossible to find out anything about the companies incorporated there. But FEC records provided one bit of unique information: an address in Boca Raton, Florida. Small world, Lachlan thought; his parents had just moved to Boca a few years earlier.

Lachlan's first story on the GEP donation was a short blurb at the end of his weekly campaign finance newsletter, *Pay Dirt*. "Who's behind this six-figure donation to a leading Trump PAC?" the newsletter item asked. He kept digging on the address in Boca, and within a couple weeks he'd discovered two names. The people behind GEP were a pair of businessmen, the Soviet-born Lev Parnas and the Ukrainian-born Igor Fruman. Little did Lachlan know at the time that he'd just stumbled on a small cadre of Trump supporters who, with the aid of Trumpworld figures including Rudy Giuliani, would soon be front and center on the national political stage.

WHEN Michael Pues cut a $350,000 check to Lev Parnas in late 2010, he thought he'd be financing a cool new spy thriller starring Jack Nicholson. The movie, tentatively titled "Anatomy of an Assassin," was in its early stages, but Pues, a friend and client of Parnas's, was impressed by the star power. Parnas arranged for him to have dinner with Nicholson and the producer Rudy Durand at the Carlyle hotel in New York. Pues agreed to pony up the $350,000 investment, which he withdrew from his parents' retirement fund. Pues would later tell a federal judge that he trusted Parnas, who assured him he was a highly successful investment adviser who drove around in a Bentley and had never lost money for his clients.

The movie project fizzled. Pues lost his investment. He sued Parnas and won a breach of contract claim. The court ordered Parnas to repay Pues. Parnas still has not done so. And in the years since, the Pues lawsuit has provided some of the most interesting—and damning—information to come out about a major Trump donor during the first term of his presidency.

Parnas was not, in fact, a highly successful investor. By the time

GEP made its huge America First donation, his landlord was attempting to evict him over $11,000 in unpaid rent. Public records revealed a trail of business activity going back a decade and involving a host of investments gone bad, scrutiny from the Securities and Exchange Commission and the Financial Industry Regulatory Authority, and one joint business venture with a big-name music producer that could not have been more poorly timed. It came just months before the producer was criminally charged for orchestrating a multimillion-dollar Ponzi scheme that ripped off some of the biggest pop music acts of the last quarter century.

Parnas's early career in the financial services industry included a five-month stint in 1996 and 1997 at a penny stock brokerage called Euro-Atlantic Securities. A few years later, federal prosecutors would allege that Euro-Atlantic was a criminal front for the Colombo organized crime family. Parnas wasn't mentioned in indictments or accused of any wrongdoing, and indeed had moved on to other ventures long before those allegations became public. But he would remain in the penny stock game and take jobs with other legally dubious firms.

A couple years after he left Euro-Atlantic, Parnas took a position atop a firm called the Program Trading Corp. Parnas was its chief executive, and another one of his companies, Aaron Investment Group (remember that name), owned at least 75 percent of Program Trading, according to regulatory filings. About a year before Parnas took over the company, it had been fined more than $150,000 for fraudulently soliciting investment with fabricated claims of the firm's notable clients such as Shaquille O'Neal and George Foreman. Parnas signed on as CEO after those claims were settled, but according to regulators the firm kept failing to pay the fines. In 2005, FINRA expelled the firm over that failure. Parnas would nonetheless brag about his "nine years as CEO of Program Trading Corp." in future business pitches.

In 2009, Parnas took another position at a penny stock brokerage, registering with the firm Basis Financial LLC. He spent only three months at that firm, according to FINRA documentation. A few years later, the firm would be hit with allegations that it lured investors with fraudulent promises of impending IPOs for "highly suspect" penny stock companies. The activity had gone on for years, FINRA alleged, but Parnas wasn't named or implicated in the scheme.

Between his stints at Program Trading and Basis Financial, Parnas had started up his own business, which was itself listed on the "pink sheet" penny stock exchange. The firm was called Edgetech International, and it produced a PalmPilot-type device called the PC Edge, which it marketed as "the world's fastest hand-held Internet access device." Edgetech went in search of partners to help market and provide content for the device and in late 2006 found a major collaborator in Lou Pearlman, a big-time record producer who'd previously worked with some of the hottest acts in pop music, including the Backstreet Boys and 'N Sync.

By the time Parnas announced the partnership in a September 2006 press release, Pearlman was widely suspected of—and under investigation for—perpetrating fraud against his clients. Around that time, Justin Timberlake would compare 'N Sync's work with Pearlman years earlier to "being financially raped by a Svengali." Around the time that he signed up to work with Edgetech, Pearlman's business empire was being scrutinized by law enforcement in Florida. Just a few months after a Parnas press release announcing its collaboration with Pearlman, Florida's Office of Financial Regulation seized one of Pearlman's Orlando-based businesses. The following year, the Justice Department charged him with running a massive, $300 million Ponzi scheme. Pearlman died of a heart attack in federal prison almost exactly ten years after the Edgetech deal was announced.

Edgetech stuck around for another few years, but by 2014 the Securities and Exchange Commission wasn't convinced that the company was doing anything to merit its listing on the pink sheet exchange. The SEC suspended trading for the company, citing "a lack of current and accurate information concerning the securities of EdgeTech International, Inc. because questions have arisen as to its operating status, if any."

The year before, Parnas had launched a new company by the name of Fraud Guarantee. Its business model was more or less the opposite of its name, taken literally. Parnas claimed on its website that he had been the victim of financial fraud and was determined to prevent the same fate from befalling others. One of Parnas's co-founders was John Cardillo, a former NYPD detective who years later would go on to be a marginally popular pro-Trump radio host.

Another of Fraud Guarantee's co-founders was David Correia, a former professional golfer and longtime Parnas business associate. Correia also appears to share Parnas's pro-Trump sentiments, judging by a perusal of his Twitter account.

One tweet in particular caught our eye. Two days after Trump was inaugurated, Correia replied to a generic "thank you, it's been an honor"—type message from the outgoing vice president, Joe Biden. "[I] assume the day your son took his position in Ukraine was also a great moment?" Correia wrote. "I have a feeling that chapter isn't closed."

In the immortal words of the Boston front man Tom Scholz, it was more than a feeling.

ABOUT two weeks before Election Day 2016, Parnas began cutting big checks to Trump and the GOP. He gave $50,000 to a Trump campaign fund-raising committee and another $33,000 to a Republican political outfit aiming to win seats in the House of Representatives.

The giving subsided after Trump's election, then picked up in a big way in early 2018. Parnas starting writing more checks, and he was joined by Fruman, who runs a Ukrainian import-export business that deals in dairy, coffee, produce, and luxury goods, among other sectors.

Parnas and Fruman had a new business venture, and it would rely on courting extensive political favor with the Trump administration. Since the first year of his presidency, Trump had pledged to boost U.S. natural gas exports to Eastern European allies as a way of blunting Russian energy domination in the region. Ukraine was slated to be one of the major beneficiaries of the policy, and Parnas and Fruman had the connections in the latter's home country to capitalize. Now they needed connections in the United States as well. And dropping gobs of cash at the feet of the nation's most prominent elected officials seemed like a good way to go about it.

Political connections, and the donations used to secure them, were integral to Global Energy Producers' business model. When Parnas and Fruman approached the Russian American energy executive Felix Vulis in late 2018 to solicit an investment in the company, they bragged about their extensive relationships with top Trumpworld figures, Vulis later said in a lawsuit seeking to recoup that investment. They boasted specifically, Vulis said, of their ties to Rudy Giuliani; Mike Pence's then chief of staff, Nick Ayers; and the leading Trumpworld lobbyist and fund-raiser Brian Ballard.

Parnas and Fruman told Vulis, he recalled, that they "had made several large personal contributions to various political organizations, including America First Action, Inc. and Friends of Ron DeSantis, in excess of $400,000.00 in [Global Energy Producers'] name and that, as a result, [they] had garnered substantial good will with various power-ful political allies that would greatly assist the business." (A lawyer for GEP denied that they ever made such statements to Vulis.)

GEP was also staffing up in Trumpworld. By 2018, it had started enlisting multiple former White House communications hands to help manage its relationship with the press.

Global Energy Producers would leverage its Trumpworld relationships to win huge contracts to export energy products to Europe, Parnas and Fruman hoped. Their goal was nothing less, they told Vulis, than to become the single largest liquid natural gas exporter in the United States.

Just a few months later, Vulis was convinced he had been scammed. **"Your friends Lev and Igor have ripped me off for $100k,"** he texted David Correia in February 2019. **"All those stories I was told about them ripping off their 'friends' I could never imagined can apply to me. I sincerely offered them a partnership [where] I could bring them a lot of wealth. Instead they screwed me."**

Vulis filed a lawsuit in Florida in early 2019 seeking to recoup the $100,000 he had lent to Global Energy Producers, alleging that Parnas and Fruman had repeatedly ignored his requests for repayment despite an agreed deadline of December 1, 2018. His lawsuit also alleged that GEP was less a company for legal purposes than an alter ego for Parnas and Fruman. That would have major implications for other legal actions against the company.

More generally, Vulis's lawsuit, which was settled in August 2019 under undisclosed terms, also provided an unvarnished look at how these two businessmen were running a largely political operation reliant on paying money in exchange for political favor. Such an arrangement is hardly unique, of course, but the revelations in Vulis's lawsuit were striking for how nakedly transactional the whole operation was. In an era in Washington defined by such transactional relationships, Parnas and Fruman were simply playing the game.

But in true Trumpian fashion, they didn't seem to be playing it very well. Indeed, their apparent failure to repay Vulis on time resulted in stunning public revelations about an investment pitch and accompanying deliberations that they surely wished to remain private. And it wouldn't be the only time that the GEP executives' alleged deadbeat habits would expose incriminating details about the business for which they'd banked on the Trump administration's good graces.

PARNAS wasn't just making huge political contributions. With his Pues debt still outstanding, he and Fruman managed to find the resources to enlist the services of Rudy Giuliani, who would publicly describe the two men as his "clients," and who, it turns out, was on the Fraud Guarantee payroll. It began with a phone call in early 2018, CNN would later report. A mutual connection, whose identity remains unknown, arranged for a phone call between Giuliani and Parnas. As Parnas and Fruman worked to secure lucrative political deals with the Trump administration, they were also colluding with the president's personal attorney to dig up dirt on Trump's political opponents, upending a key U.S. diplomatic relationship in the process and eventually leading to a political and national security firestorm that would possibly even lead to the third impeachment vote in U.S. history.

Parnas and Giuliani had developed a relationship throughout 2018, when the former used his new Republican megadonor credentials to finagle meet and greets with powerful congressional committee chairmen, top GOP fund-raisers, and even the president of the United States himself. In late 2018, as Global Energy Producers sought Trump-facilitated energy export deals, Fruman got a call from a former prosecutor in Ukraine, Viktor Shokin, who wanted help exacting revenge for a political scandal in the country that had cost him his job a couple years earlier.

Shokin's target was an auspicious one: he wanted to go after Hunter Biden, the son of the former vice president and a businessman with extensive, and controversial, business ties in Ukraine.

Parnas and Fruman turned to Giuliani for help, according to extensive reporting on their efforts by *BuzzFeed News* and the Organized Crime and Corruption Reporting Project. Trump's attorney recognized a unique opportunity to advance the political interests of his highest-profile client. At the time, Joe Biden was widely seen as a likely 2020 challenger to Trump, and a formidable one. By assisting Parnas and Fruman in digging up dirt on his son's potentially shady activities there, Giuliani could get a head start on 2020 opposition research, with assists from people on the ground in Ukraine who knew where the bodies were buried.

At the same time, Giuliani could pursue a separate line of inquiry that might help undercut Special Counsel Robert Mueller's probe into 2016 election meddling, which was still very active at the time. It had been publicly reported that Democratic operatives had approached Ukrainian officials during the 2016 campaign to solicit damaging information about Trump's campaign chairman Paul Manafort's business dealings in the country (the same ones that eventually landed him in prison). If Giuliani could expose more information on that front, he could turn the Mueller narrative on its ear: it was the Democrats, not Trump, he could insist, who colluded with a foreign power.

Parnas and Fruman set up meetings with Shokin and other high-profile Ukrainian politicians. Shokin told Giuliani that he had been investigating a Hunter Biden consulting contract in the country when, in 2016, Joe Biden publicly called for Shokin's resignation over corruption allegations. Giuliani dutifully alleged a conflict of interest by the former vice president.

Not all of their meetings went so well. In April 2019, Parnas and

Fruman flew to Israel to meet with the billionaire Ukrainian oligarch Ihor Kolomoisky, who had gone into exile after Ukraine's government seized a bank he owned amid a criminal investigation. Kolomoisky had denied any wrongdoing, and with the election of Ukraine's new president, Volodymyr Zelensky, that April he was suddenly back in the good graces of the country's ruling administration.

But Kolomoisky didn't react well when Parnas and Fruman began pressing for a meeting with Zelensky. And he wasn't impressed with their name-dropping either. "They tried to say something like, 'Hey, we are serious people here,'" he later told *BuzzFeed*. "'Giuliani. Trump.' They started throwing names at me."

When Kolomoisky refused to cooperate, Giuliani and his clients went ballistic. Trump's attorney fired off a tweet accusing the Ukrainian of threatening to kill Parnas and Fruman. Lachlan called up Giuliani to get more information. He was cagey. "All I know is the allegations," Giuliani said. "When I looked online, there are questions about his having done violence in the past. That makes me very concerned."

Parnas and Fruman weren't just going after Ukrainian leaders; they also targeted the American ambassador to Kiev. In May 2018, Parnas and Correia, his longtime business associate, traveled to Washington for a meeting with Representative Pete Sessions, a Texas Republican who chaired the powerful House Rules Committee. Parnas, who posted photos from the meeting on his Facebook page, would later tell *BuzzFeed* that he used the meeting to bad-mouth the U.S. ambassador Marie Yovanovitch. And Parnas knew the precise buttons to press: Yovanovitch, he claimed, had been privately criticizing the president!

On the same day, Sessions penned a letter to Secretary of State Mike Pompeo. "I have received notice from close companions that Ambassador Yovanovitch has spoken privately and repeatedly about her disdain for the current administration," Sessions wrote. It took awhile, but in May 2019, Yovanovitch was recalled from her post.

IT was a couple months after Yovanovitch's departure from Kiev that the president held his now-infamous phone call with Volodymyr Zelensky, the newly inaugurated president of Ukraine. A former comedian who first burst into the public eye with a winning performance on Ukraine's *Dancing with the Stars* spin-off, Zelensky was a superficially Trumpian figure in his own right. Funny and affable, he parlayed television popularity into an insurgent presidential campaign that unseated an incumbent with a message focused on battling corruption. Zelensky told Trump in their phone call on July 25, 2019, that the American president's "drain the swamp" campaign mantra had been an inspiration for his own presidential bid. Zelensky was also sure to mention that he stayed at a Trump property the last time he was in New York.

Then Trump dropped the bomb. Or rather, threatened not to. Zelensky wanted the president to know that Ukraine was ready to get some more of those sweet American missiles—specifically some Javelins, the shoulder-fired anti-tank weapons manufactured by Lockheed Martin and Raytheon. Ukraine was still dependent on U.S. aid to maintain its territorial integrity against constant Russian-backed incursions and insurgencies in the country's east. Zelensky was still waiting on hundreds of millions of dollars in promised American military aid. Kiev was ready to receive more military support, he told Trump.

"I would like you to do us a favor, though," Trump replied. First off, he wanted Zelensky to look into the company CrowdStrike, which had conducted an internal investigation into Russia's hacking of the Democratic National Committee in 2016. Trump wanted Zelensky to help find the DNC email servers. Why he thought such a server existed, was in Ukraine, and could be obtained with Zelensky's help remains a train of thought indecipherable to those without direct insight into the president's conspiracy-theory-addled mind. The whole thing appears to have been born of the right-wing fringe, where cranks and kooks had insisted since 2016 that the DNC had covered up the real nature of the cybercrime against it, and might even have assassinated a staffer, Seth Rich, who had really provided internal emails to WikiLeaks. As it happens, this was central to Roger Stone's federal criminal defense at the time. It was also thorough, largely incomprehensible bullshit. Yet here was the president peddling it in his first official call with a key global counterpart.

If that had been all the president told Zelensky, it would've been just another minor national embarrassment in a string of cringeworthy presidential statements to other world leaders. But the president wanted more. He wanted Zelensky to look into the Hunter Biden allegations, and he even offered the assistance not just of his personal attorney, Giuliani, but of the attorney general of the United States. Trump was prepared to bring the full might of America's federal law enforcement apparatus to bear in investigating a political opponent.

All of this information emerged into public view thanks to a whistle-blower in the U.S. intelligence community who drew on secondhand accounts of the Zelensky call and other conversations with White House staffers to paint a damning portrait of the president's conduct. Naturally, the whistle-blower became the target of attacks from Trump and his allies, and the larger case against him fit nicely into Trump's larger narrative of victimization at the hands of malicious deep state bureaucrats. The strategy generally resembled that brought against Special Counsel Robert Mueller and FBI and congressional investigators probing Russian interference in the 2016 election.

There was a key difference this time, though. Rather than simply stonewall and obfuscate, the president agreed to release a transcript of his call with Zelensky. And the transcript basically confirmed the whistle-blower's central allegations. It remains utterly baffling to us that Trump, ahead of the transcript's release, apparently believed that it would exonerate him. Certainly that's what he and the Republican apparatus in Washington insisted up and down after the fact. But here was the precise text of exactly what was said, and what was said was very, very bad for the president.

It was, in other words, a totally unforced error on the president's part. He was behind the scenes employing the might of his official office for political ends. Knowing that congressional Democrats were chomping at the bit to bring down his administration, knowing that they would take any excuse to press for impeachment, and knowing exactly what he had said to Zelensky during that fateful phone call, he nonetheless agreed to put it all in public view.

As we write this, the outcome of this impeachment bonanza is very much up in the air. For all we know, by the time this is published, Mike Pence will be president, this whole scheme will have been plumbed in far more detail than is available now, and everything we're writing will be old hat. But for now, a truly striking theme throughout the scandal has been the emergence of crucial information about it through just those sorts of unforced errors.

At the top, it was the president freely volunteering details of his communications with Zelensky. He also mentioned on tape that he had sought a similar Hunter Biden investigation in China. He didn't need to say any of this, and each detail made his predicament worse.

And once again, Trump's minions and misfits mimicked some of his more destructive idiosyncrasies. Just as the president was publicly offering information that would damn him, we were getting big new details on the midlevel operatives working behind the scenes to advance his illicit crusade against the Bidens. And as with Trump, details about their activities were coming out due purely to their own ineptitude.

EVEN as Parnas and Fruman jet-set around the globe in their Giuliani-assisted influence campaign, and even as they and their company poured money into political campaigns, Parnas was ignoring demands from Pues, his former friend and client, to repay the money that Pues had invested in the "Anatomy of an Assassin" film project years earlier. A federal court awarded Pues $350,000 in damages in 2011, and with interest and legal fees the sum that Parnas owed had swelled to more than $500,000. So when Lachlan first reported that it was Parnas behind the huge GEP contribution to America First Action in the summer of 2018, Pues's attorney took note.

The attorney restarted legal proceedings in federal and state courts in an attempt to recoup the money owed to his client. And before long, those lawsuits started to produce more inside information about Global Energy Producers, its executives, and their political contributions. We found out, for instance, that Parnas had also been earning some money by referring clients to Ballard Partners, the lobbying firm run by Brian Ballard.

Of more immediate interest, though, were the detailed financial records emerging as part of the lawsuit.

When Lachlan first reported on the America First donation, it caught the eye of the Campaign Legal Center, a nonprofit watchdog group. The CLC filed a complaint with the Federal Election Commission alleging reason to believe that GEP was illegally masking the identity of the real donor behind its America First contribution. The company had been around for only a month, the group reasoned. It was unlikely that it had the capital to be making six-figure political donations.

Lachlan reported on that complaint and soon got a call from a Trumpworld communications operative. He said he knew Parnas personally and was livid at the story. He screamed that the CLC knew nothing about the company's finances and that its allegations were borderline libelous. He warned Lachlan not to lend credence to these fabulous allegations. GEP too vehemently denied the allegations. "The amount donated to America First PAC represents only a small fraction of the operating costs of GEP," the company said in a statement on CLC's complaint. "The implication that GEP is some sort of shell company, couldn't be further from the truth, as the company is committed to a longterm plan to export American LNG and is in the process of partnering with major industry leaders both domestically and internationally to achieve that end."

Months later, Pues's attorneys would submit records in federal court showing that the contribution did not, in fact, come from GEP. Wire transfer records showed that the actual donor was a Parnas-run company called Aaron Investments I LLC. The CLC had been even more correct than it knew, and the information had only emerged due to Parnas's years-old debts, which he still wouldn't—or couldn't—pay.

It was those records, released publicly and first reported by *The Daily Beast*, that made it clear that something was legally amiss with Parnas and Fruman's massive political spending spree. But the full depth of their alleged campaign finance chicanery emerged only on Wednesday, October 9, 2019. The duo had lunch with Giuliani at—where else?—the Trump International Hotel. That night, they traveled to Dulles International Airport, each holding a one-way ticket to Frankfurt. The FBI was waiting for them. Parnas and Fruman were arrested and charged with knowing and willful violations of federal campaign finance laws. At issue were contributions not just to America First, but to Representative Sessions, House Republican leader Kevin McCarthy, and a handful of state-level officials whom Parnas and Fruman had allegedly plotted to bribe with campaign donations in exchange for assistance in securing permits for a recreational cannabis business they were starting up with a Russian émigré in Sacramento. Correia, Parnas's longtime business partner, allegedly even drafted a spreadsheet detailing each politician they needed to pay off, then circulated it to Parnas, Fruman, and an unnamed Russian businessman who allegedly provided them with at least $1 million with which to make those contributions.

As we write this, we still don't know what the outcome of that case will be. Parnas and Fruman have pleaded not guilty to the criminal charges against them. But the indictment alone largely vindicated the reporting we'd been doing for more than a year. It also underscored a common theme throughout the Parnas and Fruman fiasco: these guys are really, really bad at graft. First off, they had violated a rule of criminal conduct spelled out by fictional kingpin Stringer Bell in the HBO series *The Wire* when he asks a subordinate incredulously, "Is you takin' notes on a criminal fuckin' conspiracy?" If allegations are accurate, Giuliani's team of misfit henchmen were literally writing down the names of people they planned to bribe and the sums each would receive, then going out and trying to bribe them. They even wrote to each other about the need to ensure—illegally, prosecutors say—that their identities remained hidden. "This is what happens when you become visible . . . the buzzards descend," a Parnas associate told him when media coverage of GEP's America First donation began to swirl. "That's why we need to stay under the radar," Parnas replied.

As we write this, Pues's lawsuit against Parnas, Fruman, and GEP is still ongoing. To the extent that it alleges anything illegal in the manner in which they've financed the president's political operation, the parties involved all flatly deny any wrongdoing. But every day that lawsuit goes on is a day when more incriminating information might emerge—the type of information that led the FBI to this case in the first place. It's rare that reporters and the public get such an unvarnished view into the inner workings of an international political and business operation the way we have in this saga. The fact that we have is a testament to just how ham-fisted Parnas and Fruman have been throughout this ordeal—in undertaking the venture with hundreds of thousands of dollars in unpaid bills, in blaring their meetings with high-profile Trumpworld figures across public social media pages, and in issuing blanket denials of credible legal allegations, only for elements of those allegations to be confirmed by records released in the course of the very legal disputes they didn't bother to resolve before embarking on this new business venture.

That's been a godsend for us. Just as the chaotic and amateurish operations of much of the Trump administration have provided us with internal details that would've stayed well out of the limelight in any prior administration, the bumbling business practices of Global Energy Producers and its executives have served, unintentionally, to give us a rare, unvarnished view of how they've gone about monetizing their political connections.

Such efforts are of course present in any administration. Indeed, political corruption is as old as government itself. Trump's plan to export more natural gas to Europe is just the sort of policy that, in any era in Washington, would attract pigs to the trough as companies recognize lucrative business opportunities in the offing.

What sets the Trump era apart is the rank incompetence of the people looking to cash in on such opportunities. The simple process of googling an address in some FEC forms set off a series of investigative stories that would expose incredible details about people looking to get rich off Trump. And it wouldn't have been possible if they hadn't been so sloppy about it. That's great for us reporters. But it doesn't inspire confidence in the administrative abilities of our present leaders that Trumpworld can't even seem to do corruption right.

► "AN AVERAGE NOBODY"

The United Talent Agency's after-party at the 2019 White House Correspondents' Dinner had a fairly impressive guest list. The ranking Democrats on the Senate Intelligence and Judiciary committees stopped by. Their former colleague Al Franken was there too. The *Daily Show* comedian Aasif Mandvi made the rounds, as did the actress Danielle Panabaker. The media industry heavyweights Wolf Blitzer, Dana Bash, Jake Tapper, and Ali Velshi were all spotted. Even Sir Kim Darroch, the United Kingdom's ambassador to the United States, dropped in for high-end cocktails and hors d'oeuvres.

Also in the crowd was the former White House press secretary Sean Spicer. But he didn't appear to be doing much partying. Instead, he was sticking a microphone in the faces of other high-profile partygoers as he jostled for on-camera interviews in his capacity as a correspondent for the syndicated television newsmagazine *Extra*. The place was packed, and pretty soon Spicer's interviews were getting in the way. The hosts of the party told Spicer that if he wanted to interview guests, he'd have to step out on the sidewalk. "He was getting in the way of guests trying to move around the party and basically just killing the vibe," one of the party hosts later told us. "It was so sad and just the perfect microcosm of his career falloff."

We can't say whether Spicer was sufficiently humiliated. But we were humiliated for him. It was painful to watch. It wasn't Spicer's first cringe-worthy *Extra* assignment either. A couple months earlier, he interviewed Secretary of State Mike Pompeo on the latter's lawn. Spicer asked Pompeo about his musical tastes and which film should win Best Picture at the Oscars.

Spicer's predecessors in previous White Houses went on to be the top communications executives for Fortune 500 companies, to run highly successful public relations firms, or to host their own cable news programs. And here was Spicer, groveling for thirty seconds of camera time with people who, after a stint in any prior administration, would've been his peers in the eyes of D.C. society and the city's political industry.

It was a dramatic fall from grace for the man who, while running communications for the pre-Trump Republican National Committee as a "chief strategist," was widely liked and respected by the reporters he worked with on a daily basis. His seven-month stint as White House spokesman, starting right at the beginning with his bald-faced lies about Trump's inauguration crowd size and his later bizarre assertions about Syria and Hitler's "Holocaust centers," shattered all of that goodwill and turned Spicer into a national laughingstock.

To his credit, Spicer was a good sport about it. So when he got the opportunity to be a contestant on the wildly popular game show *Dancing with the Stars*, he fully embraced it. He remained a laughingstock, but at times it was tough to tell whether his former colleagues and professional acquaintances were laughing at him or with him. In his opening night appearance on the show, Spicer burst onstage in white pants and an absurd, frilly lime-green top that looked like an outfit for a belly dancer in a science fiction movie. He nonetheless grinned from ear to ear as he made his reappearance on national television, seeming to revel in finally being able to strut for the camera without a cable news host or a roomful of angry reporters berating him.

Washington heaved a collective groan when Spicer's first *DWTS* episode aired. And it only got sadder when he took it upon himself to take the skills he honed during a lifetime in the political trenches and put them to work in an effort to win a whole new, and wholly absurd, democratic contest. Spicer was going to win this thing, and he was going to do it with thoroughly Trumpian tactics and with the support, literally, of Trump's political operation. When, after the first episode aired, Mike Huckabee suggested that a Spicer win would "create an emotional meltdown in Hollyweird," Spicer went full culture war in an effort to secure his advancement on a television game show. "Clearly the judges aren't going to be with me," he complained in a since-deleted retweet of Huckabee. "Let's send a message to #Hollywood that those of us who stand for #Christ won't be discounted." Over the next few weeks, Spicer's "candidacy" turned into a minor cause célèbre for the Trump political operation. He even received an official endorsement from America First Action, the Trump campaign's official super PAC. That's right, a political group with an eight-figure budget was, right as election season heated up, throwing its weight behind a *Dancing with the Stars* candidate. As we write this, Spicer has just been eliminated from the season's competition—though he did receive a pat-on-the-back tweet from Trump, one stating that he was "proud" of Sean's stint, on his way out the *DWTS* door.

Spicer is perhaps the best illustration, though certainly not the only one, of the inevitable consequences of service to Trump by those who volunteer for such duty. High-profile people who have served in the highest echelons of his administration have been stuck with post-government work in the various political arms of Trumpworld— the campaign, the super PACs, the dark money groups. Aside from organizations that are explicitly pro-Trump, there is little professional upside to having served in the Trump administration—unless of course your career plan includes a stint on a celebrity dancing show. And that's assuming you can make it out without landing under indictment or in federal prison—no sure thing when serving this president.

In prior administrations, senior White House positions were springboards to extremely lucrative jobs in corporate America. With very few exceptions, almost no Trump White House officials have managed to secure C-suite private sector gigs after leaving the president's employ. Their boss's stink has rubbed off on them.

And despite demanding unquestioning loyalty from those he employs, Trump is very stingy about reciprocating. "We're all on our own, man," as Michael Caputo, a 2016 Trump campaign adviser, told us in late March 2019.

In the years since Trump's election, Caputo had become a peripheral figure in the Trump-Russia investigations and had been interviewed by Special Counsel Robert Mueller's team. Because he had ended up on the wrong end of negative publicity, Caputo's legal costs had ballooned to upwards of $200,000, his business had closed two of its offices, he laid off half of his workforce, and his company said farewell to about three-quarters of its client base. If Trump hadn't won, there'd be no Mueller probe, and Caputo would have dodged the otherwise inevitable federal crosshairs. "Why did my family, my children, myself, my company, my employees, my clients, why did they all get trashed?" Caputo asked rhetorically.

In early 2018, Trump set up a legal defense fund to cover just those sorts of costs for his White House subordinates and other allies caught up in the Mueller probe. The Patriot Legal Expense Fund Trust, as the group was officially dubbed, brought in hundreds of thousands of dollars from high-figure Republican donors such as the casino mogul Sheldon Adelson.

Whom that money actually supported remains more or less a mystery. Transparency requirements are lax for legal defense funds, so the group never had to say whose legal bills it actually paid. But we do know that Caputo was not among its beneficiaries, even though he stayed loyal to the president to the end and consistently maintained that the whole Mueller probe was a sham.

Caputo at least made it out alive and a free man, with a salvageable reputation and without any sort of excommunication from Trumpland. Indeed, shortly after the Mueller report was finally sent to the Justice Department, Trump invited Caputo and his family members over for a private meet and greet in the Oval Office. Others weren't so lucky.

Paul Manafort, Michael Cohen, Michael Flynn, Rob Porter, Roger Stone, George Papadopoulos, Rex Tillerson, John Kelly, Steve Bannon, Kirstjen Nielsen, Tom Price, Scott Pruitt, John Bolton, Kelly Sadler, David Shulkin, Anthony Scaramucci, and legions of others who've toiled away in the service of the president but didn't make it into this book—they've all been taken down a peg or humiliated one way or another, all because they opted to associate with DJT. President Trump, a man who prizes loyalty and genuflection as if it were a rare form of oxygen, has already sicced legal threats on several former "loyalists" since his presidency began.

For all the bodies piled up on the street, some Trump alums did manage to level up into prominent and lucrative post-administration gigs. Hope Hicks landed a gig as Fox Corporation's top communications executive. Josh Raffel, a former consigliere to Jared Kushner and Ivanka Trump, is running comms for the e-cig giant Juul. Other senior officials managed to earn back spots at the companies they'd left to join the White House. Reince Priebus is back at his white-shoe Milwaukee law firm. The former chief White House economist Gary Cohn landed a plum gig at Harvard University's Institute of Politics. And some mid-level Trumpworld operatives secured gigs in various arms of D.C.'s political economy.

But by and large, those leaving Trump's administration are shunned by the commanding heights of American business and culture to a far greater degree than officials in any prior White House. Many of them can't even get a meal in public without being hounded by angry citizens.

But it's not, we suspect, just the baggage that comes with serving such a gleefully divisive figure that lands these folks in their unfortunate employment (and dining) predicaments. It's the general sense, among both those who follow political events as closely as we do and the American public more generally, that something in Trump's Washington is broken.

During the hectic months of mid-2017, unquestionably the most exhausting and excruciating time to be covering White House politics, we co-opted a term to describe the unending shitshow that surrounded us and in which we were forced to immerse ourselves daily. We called it "omnishambles," a convergence of complete chaos, ineptitude, and scandal in which few really know what's going on and fewer still what will come next. In the omnishambles presidency, no one is really steering the ship. The captain is shit-faced, and we're all just hoping that the wind blows us past that next looming iceberg.

If, like us, you feel overwhelmed by political events these days, it's a product of that constant, mind-numbing dysfunction. Trump himself is of course to blame for the state of things in Washington. But just as important to comprehending the depths of this national moment of insanity is the ridiculous crew of minions and misfits he's brought along for the ride. If he's at the tiller, they're manning the oars. And they're rushing us full speed ahead to some unknown but almost assuredly disastrous destination.

For us, the Trump era has made for a weird mix of emotions. There's a perversely proportional relationship between the horrors and dysfunction of daily life in Washington and the professional and financial benefits accorded to the town's press corp. The worse things get, the more people want to hear us describe how bad they are. *BuzzFeed*'s editor in chief, Ben Smith, once relayed an anecdote from a friend in Brazilian political journalism. "You could tell his country was in political crisis because everyone was talking about politics all the time," Smith wrote. "In a normal country, nobody cares about politics."

It follows that in a normal country there's much less demand for political journalism—for folks like us. As reporters, we sometimes crave dysfunction because it gives us something to write about, entertaining and compelling stories about the people and institutions degrading political life in this country. As Americans and normal, non-sociopathic everyday people, we sometimes wish we were unemployed, or at the very least bored.

And as much as the man at the top has set the tone for this ridiculous moment in American history, it's all the people below him who have really sustained our bylines over the past few years. You can write only so many stories about the president of the United States. Below him lies a seemingly unending trail of political toxic waste dumped by those ostensibly brought to Washington to drain the swamp they're now poisoning.

As a plurality of these minions, misfits, and co-conspirators can attest, Donald J. Trump has spent a lifetime chewing people up and hacking them out with some bile to boot. They're not the victims you should feel sorry for, of course. Still, if there's any pathos to the denizens of Trumpworld, it's that—in keeping with the inspiration for the book you're now done reading—most every bagman and water carrier for this president ends up a Henry Hill.

"We ran everything," Hill, played by Ray Liotta, says at the very end of Martin Scorsese's *Goodfellas*. "Everybody had their hands out. Everything was for the taking. And now it's all over. And that's the hardest part. Today, everything is different. There's no action. I have to wait around like everyone else . . . I'm an average nobody. I get to live the rest of my life like a schnook."

ACKNOWLEDGMENTS

LACH

I've been blessed to work under some amazing bosses and editors during my decade-plus in Washington, including Matt Sheffield, Rob Bluey, Mike Gonzalez, Matt Continetti, Mike Goldfarb, Aaron Harison, John Avlon, Noah Shachtman, Jackie Kucinich, and Sam Stein. I owe a tremendous debt to each of them for their mentorship and guidance, and for constantly helping to improve my work.

I wouldn't have made it to Washington but for the patience and empathy of Oxford Academy's Leon Palmieri, Zack Hayden, Phil Cocchiola, Phil Davis, and Mike Susi. And I owe the joy I get in being a professional gadfly to Hamilton College's Ted Eismeier. Keith Urbahn, Matt Latimer, and their team of consummate professionals at Javelin were instrumental in getting this book across the finish line, and we could not have done it without them.

Thank you to Anna and Lou for putting up with long hours of writing and the numerous bouts of exasperation and exhaustion. And to Griff for always giving me the perspective of a smart person who's not steeped in this daily insanity.

And the most eternal, undying, inexpressible gratitude to Mom and Dad, to whom I owe everything and whom I will never be able to sufficiently thank or repay. I love you guys.

SWIN

Firstly, I'd like to thank the Deep State. Keep up the good work, especially you, "Derek." (Derek knows why.)

I'd also like to thank my bosses over the years—such as but certainly not limited to Noah Shachtman, John Avlon, Jackie Kucinich, Sam Stein (in spite of his numerous dad jokes), David Corn, Nick Baumann, Dan Schulman, Monika Bauerlein, and Clara Jeffery—for not firing me when they had the chance(s).

To my mom, Parita; my dad, Apinya; my sister, "Tammy"; my second mom and childhood babysitter, Uam; and the rest of my sprawling, overachieving family—from Boston to Bangkok—for somehow never making me feel like the idiot son (even though I am 150 percent the dumbest, least impressive one in the family.)

I owe you guys—and Alisa and Chris!—the world, and then some. I am what I am because of your sacrifices and your support. I hope I'll earn it someday.

On an unusually earnest note, I would like to extend the warmest of thanks to my lovely wife, Elizabeth Nolan Brown, for being a better person than I am, a superior writer and thinker, and the person who makes this all worth it. Also, thank you, babe, for bringing ragdoll cats into my life. (I know they can't read this, but Esme and Gemini, you guys get shout-outs, too. Gemini, stop stealing your sister's food, I'm serious.) And shout-out to the Ohio contingent—see you at Christmas, Keith, Diane, Becca, Geoff, Baby Oliver, and the whole crew!

I would like to thank my closest of friends; there are too many of you to count and list, and you know who the hell you are, but I'm going to at least start by thanking Timothy K. Mak, because he was best man at my wedding, and he said he would be mad if he didn't get an acknowledgment. Dear friends such as Julius Taranto, Wesley Lowery, Dave Weigel, Sahil Kapur, Byron Tau, Jonathan Swan, Robbie Suavey, Carrie Soave, Justin Webster, Sam Ruchlewicz, John Hudson, and *all you other idiots who are gonna text me like "What the hell, man" for not putting your name in here* will be in my heart forever as well, for all your love and carousing.

Raising a shot glass to my wonderful reporting partners in crime, such as Betsy Woodruff, Erin Banco, Max Tani, and so forth, whose ideas I've all stolen for this book, leaving them bitter, forever alone, and penniless. (Don't sue, please.)

And I'd like to tip my hat to people in this godless, depraved business of ours who were gracious and warm to me back when I was a brat and less than nothing, such as Jason Fagone, Tara McKelvey, Adam Serwer, Ron Rosenbaum, Maggie Haberman, Bill Press, the *Bangkok Post* crew (hope you're seeing this one, fellas!), Marc Cooper, and Peter Suderman, among other stand-up folks. Furthermore, this book is un-dedicated to all the high-school-cafeteria-clique, overfed, undersourced, backbiting, supremely unimpressive members of an effete media class. (You know who you are.)

To Dan Spinelli, our intrepid fact checker for *Sinking in the Swamp*— Lachlan and I owe you about twelve rounds of thank-you drinks. Cash that in sometime this decade, okay?

And to our agents (Keith and Matt), book editors (Wendy and Terezia), mentors, teachers, and professors who made this all possible, I truly hope we were only minor-to-moderate pains in the ass.